SOCIOLOGY

An Introduction

The Dryden Press
A division of Holt,
Rinehart and Winston
Hinsdale, Illinois

SOCIOLOGY

An Introduction

Reece McGee and Others

The author wishes to thank all sources for the
use of their material. The credit lines for
copyrighted materials appearing in this work
are placed in the Acknowledgments section at
the end of the book. These pages are to be
considered an extension of the copyright page.

Design by Stephen Rapley
Photo research and production
services by Jo-Anne Naples
Copyediting by Nancy Clemente

Sociology

An Introduction

by Reece McGee (Editor)
and
Contributing Authors
in chapter order

Robert M. Pankin (1)
The Chinese University of Hong Kong

S. Dale McLemore (2)
The University of Texas, Austin

O. Michael Watson (3)
Purdue University

Patricia Comstock-Shaver (4)
West Los Angeles College

J. Kenneth Benson (5)
The University of Missouri, Columbia

Helen Rose Fuchs Ebaugh (6)
The University of Houston

J. Kenneth Benson (7)
The University of Missouri, Columbia

Charlene Thacker (8)
The University of Winnipeg

Patrick S. Mazzeo (9)
Central Oregon Community College

and

David T. Wellman (9)
The University of Oregon

Sharon McPherron (10)
St. Louis Community College at Florissant Valley

Michael Micklin (11)
Battelle Human Affairs Research Centers

Joseph E. Ribal (12)
El Camino College

Michael N. Ryan (13)
Niagara County Community College

William R. Garrett (14)
St. Michael's College

Kathleen V. Friedman (15)
The University of North Carolina, Chapel Hill

Thomas J. Yacovone (16)
Los Angeles Valley College

Abraham Levine (17)
El Camino College

R. Kelly Hancock (18)
Portland State University

William T. Feigelman (19)
Nassau Community College

EDITOR'S ACKNOWLEDGEMENT

As anyone who has ever written or edited a textbook knows, it is impossible to acknowledge by name every individual who has played some part in the work. Most of those who influenced an author during his or her formative professional period cannot even be identified and, further, many who labor in the publishing house are unknown to him. In a work with multiple authors such as this one, the problem is insurmountable. I must, nonetheless, name what names I can in poor payment of the great debt owed to the many others who made this work possible. Sincere thanks go to Betty, my wife, who lost me to the work for great chunks of time and who, additionally, listened to me talk of it endlessly, copyedited early manuscript, wrote transitional material, gave sound advice on illustration, and put up with the tantrums and complaints which editing tends to produce. Great debts are owed to Ray Ashton, Managing Editor, who conceived the project and stood godfather and midwife to it and to me throughout every step of the endeavor. Without his good humor, diplomacy, generosity and acumen, the work would have collapsed. Nancy Clemente, Manuscript Editor, made invaluable contributions to organization, clarity, style, and force of presentation; the literary quality of the book owes as much to her as it does to me and its authors. Mary Ellen Stocker, Developmental Editor, rode herd on "the monster," as it came to be called, from the first, and never lost a page, misfiled a reference, or forgot an inquiry. That something so complicated proceeded as smoothly as this did was largely due to her devotion. Paulette Shenck, whose only formal title was "Secretary," labored valiantly and with good humor for multiple bosses who frequently gave her contradictory instructions. Stephen Rapley designed the book and did much of the graphic illustration that lends so much to it. Jo-Anne Naples did copyediting, permissions, and invaluable photo research—hidden chores that most readers are unaware of but have much to do with the success of a text as an instrument of communication. And finally, of course, the Editor and Publisher are completely in debt to the authors of the various chapters who not only produced the work in the first place, but then had to endure the agony of seeing it reworked, and sometimes cut drastically, by others. To these people and all of the unnamed others who assisted, my sincere and abiding gratitude.

RMc

A LETTER TO THE INSTRUCTOR

If you have read the letter to the student reader, you know what I hope he or she will obtain from studying this book. It may be important for *your* use of it, however, to know something of what its authors, publisher, and I attempted to do in it to assist you in your classroom task of teaching with it. I think I can best describe that attempt by explaining it under three topical headings: (1) what the book is intended to be; (2) how it was written; and, (3) what you can do for all of us in response to it.

What This Book Is Intended To Be

More than anything else, our over-riding aim in producing the book was to make it a *teaching tool,* an instrument you can use effectively in the first course in sociology. To that end, it is not by any means the product of one person. Rather it is the result of the collective effort of a large number of people with the single aim of producing the best introductory text possible: best in intellectual quality, reader appeal, substantive coverage of the field of sociology, layout and illustration for teaching purposes, utility for various kinds of institutions and course approaches, and so forth. The product you now hold in your hands was thus a collaborative effort among sociologists, editors, artists, publisher, printer, reviewers, and even student contributors, who did some reviewing and wrote much of the end-of-chapter study material.

The authors Every chapter author represented here is an experienced undergraduate classroom teacher of the subject matter about which he or she has written. While some have national, or even international, reputations as research specialists, none was selected for that reason. All, except Professor Watson, who is an anthropologist, are professional sociologists. Many, as you will see from the "Contributing Author" page, are teachers in community or state colleges, people perhaps properly described as "the infantry" in the sociological battle for student learning and understanding. But regardless of institutional affiliation, all are experienced teachers of undergraduates in the subject matters they represent. (One or two have gone on to other kinds of positions since they accepted the commission to do this work.) Some of the authors were friends or acquaintances of mine at the time I agreed to undertake the editorship of this volume, people whom I knew of my own experience to be outstanding teachers of undergraduate students. The others, unknown to me at that time, were recommended to me by friends as fitting the qualification I demanded: "teachers with a rage to teach." I believe that, as you read this volume, you will agree the selection procedure was successful. I believe, in other words, that you will agree with me that this is a *teaching* book, a text produced *by* sociologists *for* beginning students with the single aim of adequately introducing them to our field.

I, too, am pleased to call myself an undergraduate teacher. I have been one for twenty years; for the last ten of them a specialist in the teaching of nothing but introductory sociology at Purdue University. I am proud to own the title that university has generously granted me, "Master Teacher," but I do not claim it. If you are satisfied that all of us have done, or even approached doing, what this book is meant to do, that will be quite adequate for me.

The Nature of the Book

The description of the authors of the book given above suggests what kind of a work it is. It is, we think, determinedly eclectic and thoroughly comprehensive. That seems to us to be the overwhelming consensus in the field concerning what a good introduction to sociology should be. We have tried to explain and exemplify every major concept normally treated in the first course in sociology, to describe and explain the dominant theoretical positions in the field—and the quarrels associated with them—the classical researches, and to begin, at least, to indicate the kinds of qualifications, hesitations, objections and uncertainties associated with *any* statement that claims to say "this is what sociology is."

Additionally we think we have offered you and the student reader the kind of information and assistance you might like in the instructor's manual, student study guide, and end-of-chapter materials concerning discussion questions, test items, suggested research projects, research paper topics, audio-visual aids and other adjuncts to basic classroom activities. Many of these, incidentally, were generated from undergraduate student input, and

Ms. L. Ann Geise, author of the study guide, worked for me for two years as an undergraduate teaching assistant in my massive introductory course.

How the Book Was Written

It is unusual for an introductory text in sociology to have multiple authorship of the kind represented here. Eighteen different sociologists and an anthropologist authored the chapters of this volume under my editorship. The book is hardly a random collection of opinions, however; this is how it was produced: I began by content-analyzing the fifteen introductory textbooks which had been the best sellers over the preceding ten years to determine what topics were universally or commonly treated. My rationale for this procedure was that since these books had met wide public acceptance among our colleagues, they must in some way have been doing what sociologists expected of them. Then, taking common coverage as mandatory, and what in my judgement was useful or outstanding treatment as exemplary, I developed a chapter-by-chapter topical outline of what I judged to be a comprehensive introduction to our field. Introductory sociology, unfortunately, turns out to be a very wide subject indeed, and there are many topics that could have been included but were not, simply for reasons of space limitation. Science as a social institution, perhaps along with sport and medicine, and radical sociology, are only examples. For the same reasons, I decided not to devote a separate chapter to the status of women and sex roles in society, but to try to present those topics adequately within other treatments. With this outline in hand, I proceeded with the search for authors already described. In negotiating with each author I explained what kind of book I envisioned and how the suggested outline for his or her chapter had been derived. Since each was a subject-matter specialist, of course, my outline had to be acceptable to the individual writer or altered as each saw fit.

As first drafts of chapters came in, the Dryden Press junior college advisory editor, Professor Thomas J. Yacovone, and I reviewed each, responding—sometimes in lengthy detail—to the author. *Each first draft was also read by a minimum of two other sociologists:* an undergraduate teacher of the subject matter of the chapter and a research specialist in it. Some first drafts received as many as five or six reviews. All of these comments were then referred back to the author who would revise the work as he or she saw fit in the light of reviewing. *Second drafts were subjected to the same reviewing process with different professional reviewers.* In a few cases, such as the chapters on economics and politics, reviewers from other disciplines were also called upon for comment.

In all, more than 120 professional reviewers read the entire manuscript, or chapters thereof, before publication. We believe we may correctly claim that this is the most widely prepublication-peer reviewed sociology text ever published. Because reviewers either approved of what they read, or because we responded to their comments seriously, we are confident that the book has an excellent chance of meeting your approval.

After the second, or, in some cases, third, drafts of chapters were reviewed and responded to by the authors, I took over. As Editor of the volume, I performed three basic functions: editing, rewriting, and reorganization. In the case of some chapters whose authors had a flair for the written language and logical organization, little was required beyond routine editing and reference-linkage with other chapters. In others, minor rewriting (sentence rearrangement, insertion of transitional, introductory or summary sentences, and so forth), and reorganization was required. In a few instances individual authors, while masters of their subject matter, were not as fluent as desireable in written expression, and I rewrote portions of their work in my own style, keeping to their ideas and wording as much as possible. When I was finished, the manuscript went to a professional manuscript editor—the first non-sociologist to be involved in the process—for final stylistic polishing. I wrote most of the chapter summaries and wrote the captions for and fixed the placement of each illustration after selecting it from the thousands available in the libraries of collections and researchers. (Illustrations, incidentally, had to meet a strict criterion of teaching relevance: whether so captioned or not, every illustration, including cartoons, had to be *capable* of being captioned by some significant sentence in the manuscript itself. Each, in other words, was selected to illustrate an instructional point.) The book, thus, has been designed throughout *by* sociologists *for* students. I had veto power over every element, including even some design features. If you find you have complaints about the book, they should be directed at me, not the publisher.

What You Can Do For Us

The preceding pages have indicated how much, and in what ways, this book is the product of a collaborative effort. As indicated, the collaboration had its goal in the desire to produce the best possible introductory text. That goal cannot be attained, however, until one more set of collaborators has been enlisted in the project: you, and the rest of its users. The book is now as finished (and as good) as we can make it until it has been extensively tried out in the classroom; the proof of a textbook is its utility in teaching. We expect the book to be popular enough to eventually warrant producing a second edition and we expect the second edition to be better than the first because, by that time, if you will help us, we will have the benefit of your experience with it to show us how it can be improved. We urge you to let us know about that experience, to comment as freely and critically as you would like, and to make suggestions for improvement. We think we have done a good job, but have no illusions concerning perfection. Until we know how the book has worked for you, the teacher in the classroom, however, we cannot be certain what alterations are required. We would appreciate hearing from you and will take your responses seriously.

If, when you have used the book, you find you have something you would like to say to us about it, please contact us. We will welcome your comments.

February 1977
Reece McGee
Department of Sociology-Anthropology
Purdue University
West Lafayette, Indiana 47907

A LETTER TO THE STUDENT

If you are like most students, before you want to take a course or read a particular textbook, you want to have some idea of its utility for you, some belief that it will "do you some good" in some way. Looking at this book and the course it accompanies, you might well ask: What is the value of sociology? What can it—especially if you take only one introductory course, perhaps reading only this one book—do for you? Why should you bother with it and why, if it is required in your college or university, should you be forced to spend a quarter or a semester on it? (Or even two?)

There are many ways in which these perfectly reasonable questions could be answered, but the one that seems to make the most sense to my own students is that a general understanding of sociological principles can enable them better to understand and control their own lives. To see why this is so, however, requires you to understand something else first, which you may have to take on faith until you've gotten into the book a bit. And that is that social phenomena truly are "real" and do influence each of us a great deal. This may be a little difficult to grasp, or even seem misguided, because our society has a strongly individualistic flavor. We are all brought up in many ways to believe that the answers to questions about human behavior are best found by examining the characteristics of the individuals involved. To put this another way, our culture (see Chapter 3) is strongly *psychologistic;* it looks to individuals for explanations of behavior. (What is the explanation for murder? Study murderers, obviously.)

But a great deal of human behavior *cannot* be adequately explained by reference to the individual characteristics of particular social actors. We may understand why Byron Witsqueak Cadwallader committed suicide by examining the poor fellow's biography and psychology. (He was the runt of his family, was improperly toilet-trained, had athlete's foot and dandruff; his children hated him, his wife ran off with an itinerant balloonist, and the day he killed himself, his own dog bit him.) But facts like this cannot explain variations in suicide rates between different cities or neighborhoods or between different racial, ethnic, religious, and occupational groups (psychiatrists kill themselves much more frequently than chiropodists). And they cannot explain such matters as the influence of the calendar, economic conditions, or social mobility on suicide. (More people kill themselves on holidays than on workdays, in a booming economy than in normal economic periods; and those who have "made it" kill themselves more frequently than the perpetually poor.) Further, it is simply impossible to explain or interpret the characteristics and behavior of human *groups* on an individualistic-psychologistic basis. (Why do all modern armies organize their combat forces into units of approximately similar size?) It is to analyze such group behavior and differences between groups that sociology exists. So one reason for studying sociology is simply that it is an attempt to organize our understanding of the whole world of phenomena "out there," which is very real and has an impact on us, but with which most of us are unfamiliar except through personal rather than analytic experience.

And the reason that doing *that* is useful is that until we understand some aspect of our world (such as how germs transmit disease), we are at the mercy of it. Ignorance usually is not bliss, and learning something about social behavior and its impact on our own very personal selves gives us the opportunity to react with or against it. Thus, knowing something about sociology offers the possibility of greater control over our own lives. Knowledge in this sense contributes to personal freedom, and that seems to me a good reason for pursuing it.

The Theme of This Book

This brings us to the organizing theme of this book, which, crudely stated, could be called "how to live with the system." What I mean by this is that you live, and will continue to live, in a complex, highly organized, bureaucratized, "massified" society. And unless you know something about it and how it works, you will be as much at the mercy of your ignorance as the "savage" who has no knowledge of the existence of "germs." (If you are of European extraction, your ancestors once believed they could avoid the plague by saying the rosary and breathing through a nosegay of fresh flowers—and they died by the millions.) In each of the chapters that follow, we will examine an important aspect of how human social systems work, how to understand them, and how individuals behave in them. This is knowledge that, while abstract and analytical, is highly *useful* in your own life, if properly understood.

The object of the book is to tell you some things about the ways in which the social world works. Knowing them, you may then deal with it—and your own existence in it—more effectively. One need not always be at the mercy of bureaucracy or racism or a political machine any more than one need be at the mercy of "germs." But in order to deal with them effectively and *freely,* you must understand what they are and how they function. The biblical injunction "You shall know the truth and the truth shall make you free" (John 8:32) is no less true today than when it was written. Only by *understanding* society and how it seems to operate can we free ourselves from bondage *to* society. That, it seems to me and your authors, is a goal worth striving for.

The Organization of the Book

We begin the book with two chapters about the field of sociology itself, why it sees things the way it does and how it goes about exploring them. Understanding these is necessary to understanding the rest of the book, to seeing how and why the sociologists come to the conclusions they do when studying a particular subject matter. Part two consists of five chapters describing the fundamental ideas with which sociologists work and which they use to organize the subject matter. These concern the human individual and the human group and how they are related and the basic organization of society itself. In one sense, the entire field of sociology is "about" these things; no matter what sociologists study, they use these ideas as tools of analysis.

Part three consists of four chapters about important *structural elements* of any society—elements of the ways in which societies are put together and operate and which occur in any complex society anywhere on the globe. Part four devotes one chapter to each of the five basic social institutions that appear in some form in every society, no matter how simple. These are the family, education, religion, politics and government, and economics. A social institution may be thought of as the way in which a society organizes the human activity necessary to getting done what must be done if the society is to survive. Part five concerns social control and deviation, collective behavior, and social change.

This is not the only possible way in which the book could have been organized. Sociology is not a highly unified field crystallized in a tight logical structure. Different sociologists do not always agree on what the field is or does, much less on what it ought to be and be doing. Thus the particular order and organization of this book is not the same as you might find in another text.

The field is also beset by paradoxes, which you will find reflected in our chapters. For example, do ethnic subcultures such as those possessed by American blacks or French Canadians form *in response to* oppression by some dominant majority, or is the repression a response to the existence of a competing subculture? Evidence can be found to argue the matter either way, which may mean that in some cases the former explanation is correct and in some the latter. And again, even given the same evidence, different sociologists may disagree.

The book and the course for which it is required, then, should not be looked to for final answers about the truth of things. Their purpose for *your* purposes, rather, is to give you a perspective, a way of looking at and understanding the complexities, ambiguities, inconsistencies, and paradoxes of the world about you, and to offer you ways of dealing with it and living in it more successfully than you otherwise might. If, before you read this book, you hold some opinion that sociology is "all a crock," remember that the notion that there are tiny invisible animals in the water he drinks ("germs") might seem "all a crock" to an illiterate "savage" too—but they could kill him nonetheless. Just because something seems to "go against common sense," that is, contradict the popular understanding of things, does not prove it is incorrect. Much "common sense" is called that because that is exactly what it is—common. Not necessarily correct; just popular.

Finally, a word about how to *approach* the book: every author represented here—the people who wrote the chapters—is or was at the time of the writing an undergraduate teacher of the subject he or she wrote about. I selected many of them because they had the reputation of being "teachers with a rage to teach." Your authors and I have enjoyed working on the book and we hope you will enjoy reading it. Beyond that, we hope you will find you profit from it. We do not expect you will agree with everything we say here, but when you don't, at least stop to think about the matter. In the long run, that is what a first book in sociology is for: to give you the chance to think about your life and your society in a new way rather than just taking them both for granted in the ways you have been taught to accept them. Good luck and best wishes.

Reece McGee, Editor
Purdue University
Spring 1977

CONTENTS

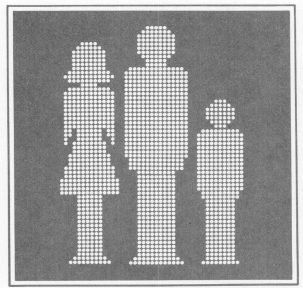

**PART ONE
THE FIELD
OF SOCIOLOGY**

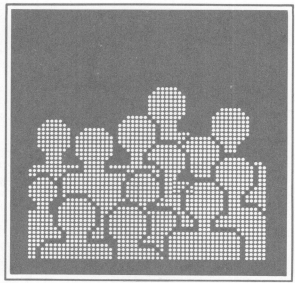

PART TWO
THE ORGANIZING CONCEPTS OF SOCIOLOGICAL ANALYSIS

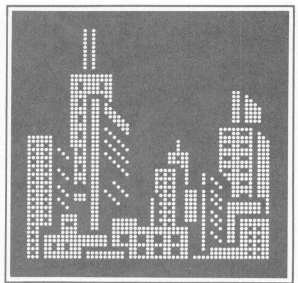

PART THREE
ELEMENTS OF
SOCIAL
STRUCTURE

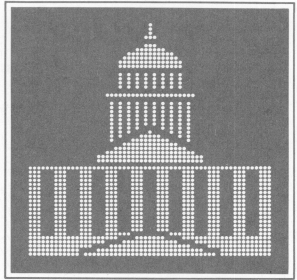

PART FOUR
SOCIAL
INSTITUTIONS

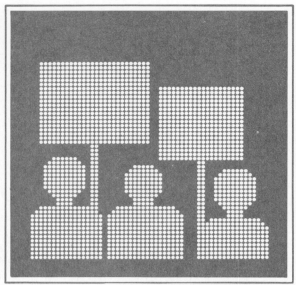

PART FIVE COLLECTIVE BEHAVIOR AND SOCIAL CHANGE

PART ONE
THE FIELD OF SOCIOLOGY

As indicated in the letter to the student, this book is subdivided into five major parts. This first part consists of two chapters on the field of sociology itself. Later parts explore its contents and conclusions.

Chapter 1 is about the *nature* of sociology: what kind of a discipline it is, how it differs from the other social sciences and from its great bugaboo, common sense, the ways in which it can claim to be called "scientific," and what that means in the sociological context. Most of the chapter focuses on the ways in which sociologists, both classic and modern, have viewed the world, the "views of social reality" that typify the discipline. This is important because one's view of reality determines what reality one sees. The questions you ask determine the answers you get.

Chapter 2 is about how the *scientific method* is used in sociological research. The subject is important because of the point made above about the nature of the questions you ask determining your answers. This is true of any question of any kind, of course, but it is especially important with questions about human behavior, because the *meaning* of human behavior is always interpretive. You do things because of motives (meanings) of your own, but other people may interpret what you're doing differently because they have motives of *their* own and do not share yours. Thus, when sociologists try to explain the world, they pay very close attention to the *kinds* of questions asked about it, and the *way* in which they are asked, because the question is an essential part of the meaning of the answer. The moral of Chapter 2 could be, "If you really want to *know* about the world, you'd better be very self-conscious about how you go about finding out."

CHAPTER 1
THE NATURE OF SOCIOLOGICAL INQUIRY

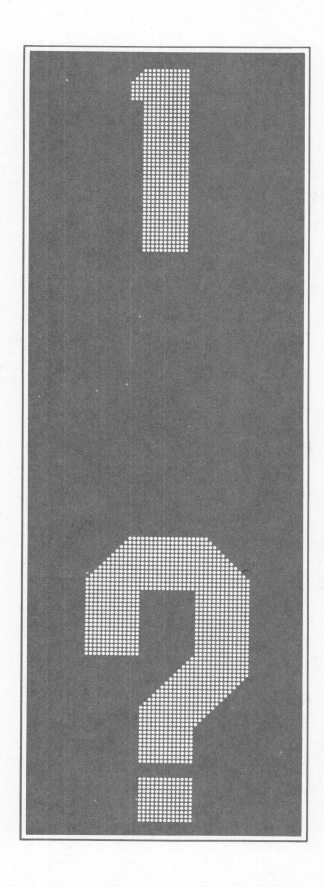

The different people shown in these pictures, and the different things they are doing, have something in common. That common element is the subject matter of sociology. All the individuals in the illustration, to put it very simply, are doing what is expected of them in the situation in which they find themselves. People are following directions, going in the same way at the same time, and so forth. They are, in other words, behaving in an orderly manner. And that is the great and fundamental subject matter of the field called **sociology**.

Introduction: What Is Sociology?

Sociology is largely the study of *social order*. Social order means the regularity or pattern we see in human affairs all about us. It includes such simple things as a stranger at a lunch counter handing you the ketchup when you ask for it, drivers stopping when the light turns red, and being able to count on the fact that when you go to the drug store, the druggist will not shoot you. It also includes such complicated things as people of one place speaking the same language and following the same political procedures for generations or even centuries.

Social order is not just a matter of people doing what they are *told* to do. No one forces the people in the photograph to follow the rules they are obviously following. In many instances, such "rules" are not orders or laws or regulations at all. They are simply the ways people have learned that things are done, and *that* is why they follow them. (What law requires men to wear trousers as the standard garment for covering the lower body?) Social order means the immense regularity, the repeated patterns, found in human behavior everywhere. That regularity—and the forms it takes and how and why it occurs and changes over time—is what sociology is all about. That is the basic subject matter of the field: what, in one way or another, most sociologists study.

In order to carry out that study, and in the process of doing it for the century in which the field has been in existence as a distinct discipline, sociologists have developed a set of *concepts* (ideas, intellectual tools) and *theoretical perspectives* (specific ways of looking at and comprehending their subject). This chapter will introduce you to these perspectives, and Chapters 3–7 and 12–16 will explore the major dimensions and meanings of the principal sociological concepts. These are *culture, socialization* (learning and internalizing the rules and values of a group), and the cluster of ideas associated with the notion of *social organization.* Chapters 8–10 and 17–19 explore others. Such concepts and perspectives together are the way of understanding human society that is the field called sociology. Regard them as a set of rules for analyzing things or as a lens of a particular shape that shows what the world looks like viewed from a particular perspective. If you choose to understand human behavior in terms of ideas like culture, socialization, social role, social group and institution, and so forth, then you are using the tools of sociology and your understanding will be a sociological one. Sociology is the field that uses these ideas to explain the world or, put another way, that shakes the world down into these categories.

This is not, of course, the only possible way of looking at the world. There are also the natural sciences, which use an almost entirely different set of intellectual tools and study an almost entirely different subject matter. And, still within the general "way of knowing" called "science," there are the other social sciences. Many of these have more or less the same *subject matter* as sociology, but they study it from different perspectives and with very different conceptual tools.

Sociology and the Other Social Sciences

There are five academic fields that commonly classify themselves, or are generally classified, as social sciences: economics, political science, anthropology, psychology, and sociology. Three of these are general or broad studies of human behavior, while two limit themselves to the more specific aspects of it associated with economics and politics. Anthropology, psychology, and sociology also concern themselves with economic and political behavior, but that is not their central concern. Their central concern is human behavior in general and in its entirety.

Because they share a central concern, these three fields often study overlapping or even identical

> **sociology:** the study of human social and group behavior, concentrating on the social interaction between people, the social organization of people, and social order and social change.

subject matter. All, for example, are interested in aggression, marriage, and what is called "mental illness." What distinguish the three are the perspectives from which they approach the subject matter and the conceptual apparatus with which they define and classify and explain it. Traditionally, for example, psychology has been interested in the individual. Thus, its perspectives and concepts often deal with people at the individual level: attitude, motivation, perception, and so on. When a behavior has been explained in these terms, the *psychology* of that behavior is said to be understood. Sociology traditionally has been interested in *groups,* in *collective* rather than individual human behavior. Thus, its perspectives and concepts largely focus on the collective level: status and role, group and institution, organizations and collective behavior such as that seen in crowds, wars, strikes, and religious rituals—things people do or produce *together.* (The concepts, such as "role" and "status," will be specifically explained in later chapters.) Anthropology has a tradition rooted in the study of what were once called "primitive" peoples. (The common usage now is "preliterate," meaning without possession of writing.) Because of this historical focus, the major anthropological thrust is *cultural;* and the total life-ways of non-Western peoples, with concepts and perspectives appropriate for dealing with them, are the principal subject matter of anthropologists.

As noted, however, there is a great deal of overlap between the three, and in some areas subfields have developed that bridge them, social psychology, for example. Further, all of the disciplines have subareas of interest other than those traditional ones mentioned here. In addition to its traditional academic study of the individual, for instance, psychology has also had for many years a "clinical" branch mostly concerned with the study and treatment of mental illness. Anthropology, in addition to its traditional cultural interests, also includes archeology, linguistics, and physical anthropology, the study of physical form and change. For these reasons, the descriptions of the three general social sciences given above should be understood merely as suggestions of major interests and perspectives. The division of intellectual labor described is the general way in which the study of human behavior has been undertaken, and sociology's place in it is clear. It is not by any means the only social science, or the oldest, but it has developed interests and perspectives that, in general, the others do not share, and that is its claim to existence as a discipline.

Sociology and Common Sense

The legitimacy of the sociological claim is persistently challenged, however, by the claim of "common sense." From the newspaper, the political rostrum, and even sometimes the pulpit comes the critique that sociology is "merely an elaboration of the obvious"; that its sometimes pretentious language "just says in complicated ways what everyone already knows"; and that sociological research is largely devoted to proving expensively "what anyone with any sense already knows." (Members of Congress with an interest in budget cutting love to find federally funded research projects with elaborate titles and then explain that what the research is "really" about is something very simple and intuitively obvious—at least to sensible people like their constituents.)

There are probably a number of reasons why the challenge of common sense is directed at sociology so much more frequently (or so it appears to sociologists) than it is at other academic disciplines. One is that sociologists, unlike anthropologists, historically have tended to study their own societies more than they have those of other peoples. Thus because sociologists study phenomena that other members of their own society have some, if not scientific, familiarity with, their findings often *appear* "obvious," although they might not have been before the fact.

We read with relish anthropological descriptions of weird practices in the daily life of the Cannibal Islanders, but do not stop to think that if such reports were read to the natives reported upon, the conclusions would often be "just common sense" to *them.* Similarly, psychology is popularly understood to be about "the unconscious" and "why we *really* do things even if we don't know it," and is not expected to be as familiar as the home, workplace, and church, which are the subjects of sociology. People do not expect to have special knowledge of a subject like physics because they consider it esoteric, although they have lived with and by it every day of their lives. But because they are familiar with the objects the sociologist studies, they feel they already have a special knowledge of them and resent any sociological claim that they do not. (In the same way, students who are members of racial or ethnic minorities sometimes regard themselves as experts on race or ethnic relations. It would be more accurate to say that they may be expert in the experience of minority group membership.)

Another reason sociology experiences the critique of common sense is that people often fail to distinguish between the things they have a general awareness of and the things they know and understand *precisely.* But knowing that something is so and knowing *why* it is so and to what exact degree and in what exact ways it is so are not the same things. Establishing such precise knowledge about "what everybody knows" is one of the tasks of sociology.

Finally, there is the fact that common sense is frequently wrong. Consider the following propositions, which many Americans, at least, might consider "just common sense":

1. Since people tend to avoid unpleasant experiences, one way to deter them from particular actions is to punish them when they commit them. The greater the punishment, the greater the deterrent effect.

2. When black people move into a formerly all-white residential neighborhood, property values decline.

3. Most American Roman Catholic priests support the Church's ban on contraception.

4. Reading or seeing pornographic materials increases the likelihood of committing sex offenses.

5. Suicide rates go up in times of stress, such as wartime.

6. The welfare rosters are filled with able-bodied people who would rather loaf than work.

Each of these statements would undoubtedly be perceived as true by many Americans. Each might also be regarded by many as obvious or "just common sense." According to the sociological evidence, however, all of them are false. In each case, in fact, the evidence *contradicts* the statements: not only are the statements untrue, the truth is just the opposite of what is claimed.

This is not to dispute that the critique of common sense is sometimes valid. Sociologists, like other people, occasionally make fools of themselves by saying things in public that they would have been wiser to keep to themselves or check out more thoroughly. Like other people, sociologists sometimes dress up simple thought in complicated language, and the professional jargon of the field is sometimes so exotic as to be unintelligible even to other sociologists. And one of the jobs of the discipline is to explore conventional wisdom, some of which, unlike the examples above, turns out to be correct. In such cases, the sociologist has examined the obvious; but one cannot know, as we have seen, until one tries. If you are dubious about the legitimacy of the field, you will do well to withhold a decision until you have finished this book. It is not written in jargon, so you will be able to make up your own mind whether what you find in it is just common sense or not. We suspect that when you are finished you will know a great deal about human society (and your own society, and perhaps yourself) that you did not know before.

Sociology and Science

We have indicated that sociology is one of the social sciences. There is, however, some argument about whether the fields called social sciences are "really" sciences at all. And within sociology itself, there is argument whether sociology is, can be, or even *ought* to be scientific in its work. All of this revolves around what we mean by "science," of course.

Clearly, none of the social sciences has the immense body of rigidly verified information that we associate with the physical sciences. Similarly, none of them possesses a carefully constructed body of logically interrelated propositions, like the **scientific theory** found in physics. Nor can any of

> **scientific theory:** a coherent group of established or verified propositions accepted as explaining or accounting for a class of phenomena.
>
> **empirical:** that which is knowable through observation; the truth as shown by observing the facts of the world rather than through divine revelation, for example, or imperial edict.

them claim a body of generalizations called "scientific laws," like the laws of thermodynamics, although psychology, at least, may have some approximations of such laws. So if we define "science" as referring to a body of knowledge of a particular kind, then few people would claim that the social sciences are "really" sciences.

But science is not usually defined by scientists as a body of information. That's a popular understanding, not a scientific one. Rather, most scientists would more or less agree that science is a means of gathering or constructing a certain kind of knowledge. *The purpose of science is the creation of reliable knowledge about the empirical world.*

There are two words in the last sentence that merit special attention: *reliable* and *empirical*. The first, *reliable,* means pretty much in science what it does in ordinary language: something you can count or rely on. That means something that holds still, that does not change its nature when your back is turned. Reliable knowledge is consistent; it stays the same from time to time and from knower to knower.

Empirical means observable, and implies observable or knowable through the human senses. Empirical knowledge, then, is knowledge gained through observation rather than intuition or divine revelation or the emperor's edict. It is knowledge gained when you or someone else looked, smelled, heard, felt, or tasted or used some instrument to extend the reach of those senses. The empirical world is the world as it may be known in such ways. We can know about the moon empirically, and knew a lot about it even before men actually went there, through telescopes, spectroscopic analysis of its reflected light, and so on. But if there is a "place" called heaven, we cannot find out about it in the same ways because it is not part of the empirical universe; it cannot be known through physical (sense) observation. That is why you do not read scientific studies of the geography of heaven, the biology of evil spirits, or the chemistry of love. (A chemist might perform a chemical analysis of a substance alleged to be a love potion, or a biologist a study of the body in the state of sexual arousal, but neither would say he was studying "love." Love is not susceptible to empirical observation.)

Characteristics of Science and the Scientific Method

Science, then, as scientists understand it, is the pursuit of a particular kind of knowledge about some aspects of the universe in which we live. It goes about this pursuit by using what is called *the scientific method.* Scientific method is the means through which empirical knowledge is discovered or created. It is a disciplined, systematic way of observing those aspects of the world that are observable, or knowable, or discoverable through the human senses.

The scientific method is the most powerful tool that people have yet invented for pursuing empirical knowledge. The reason for this is that the method, as it has historically developed, has certain characteristics that, taken together, produce better results for the creation of empirical knowledge than any other means we have. These characteristics (which may also be called the characteristics of science itself) are (1) intersubjective reliability, (2) objectivity, (3) quantifiability, and (4) theoretical orientation. They are explained below.

Intersubjective reliability   This multisyllabic name is more complicated than its meaning, which is simply that several observers, making the same observation in the same ways, would have similar results. A piece of information is intersubjectively reliable when people can agree on it. If your sociology professor tells you there is another person in front of the classroom with him, everyone in the room can check to see if that is so, and (presumably) everyone would either agree or disagree that it was. The statement may or may not be *true,* but its truth or falsity is *testable* by independent observation by multiple observers.

If, however, your professor announced that he had an invisible blue kangaroo with him up there and that, furthermore, the kangaroo was weightless, without substance, and so forth, there would be no way for anyone to test the truth of his assertion. It would not be an intersubjectively reliable statement, although it might be logically possible for such a creature to exist. Thus the notion of intersubjective reliability is not a question of *truth.* A statement could be both true and intersubjectively *un*reliable—for example, anything you told me about what you were thinking this instant. Intersubjective reliability has to do with the possibility of verification, of *testing* for truth.

Objectivity   When we accept science as a particular way of knowing things, we accept a framework that permits and demands *objectivity.* This means making knowledge statements or truth claims in terms of some recognized or public standard, rather than our subjective feelings or value biases. Objectivity means describing the world as it is observed to be, whether we like or approve of what we observe or not. An anthropologist, for example, might be horrified to observe a society in which every other infant born was burned alive as an offering to the gods, but simultaneously be forced to recognize that the practice had the effect of keeping the population stabilized in relation to its food supply. If he were properly objective, his report of the practice would simply describe what occurred and its apparent consequences. He would not qualify his observations with adjectives such as "horrifying, bloody, terrible," and so forth.

Objectivity is probably more difficult in the social than in the natural sciences for two reasons. First, many natural scientists do not, as a rule, *care about* their findings. They are curious to find out what happens in a given case, but do not care *what* they find out. They are only rarely emotionally involved in the facts. Social scientists, because they are involved in the facts they study, may want to believe that certain things are true, which creates the danger of seeing what they want to see. A second problem that makes objectivity easier in the natural sciences is that the presence of the observer, or the act of observing, does not normally affect the thing observed. In the social sciences it may. A chemical subjected to certain conditions will always respond in the same way, whether someone is watching it or not. Human beings under observation, however, frequently alter their "normal" response to take account of the observer, so that the very presence of the observer changes the nature of what is being observed.

Quantifiability   A third characteristic of science is that propositions or truth statements must be *quantifiable,* or potentially quantifiable. That means expressible in numerical terms, capable of being *counted.* This, in turn, implies that the phenomenon being described must in some way be *measurable.* The measurement may be very precise (.000675 milligrams) or relative (faster, larger, less). In order to measure and quantify, most disciplines that call themselves sciences use some version of the technique called the **experimental method.**

The experimental method   Perhaps an example of the experimental method from an everyday experience will help clarify the discussion. You buy eight new batteries for your portable tape recorder. You put four of them in the recorder, and after checking to see that they are in correctly, try to operate the machine. It does not work. After rechecking, you decide that one or more of the new batteries must be bad. This **hypothesis**—this proposition you are going to test—is verified when the recorder operates with another set of batteries in it. The next problem is to determine which battery is bad. You take one of the good batteries from the second set out of the machine, and replace it with one of the questionable batteries, eventually finding one battery that will not operate the machine. You have been able to discover via an experimental technique which battery was defective.

Let's examine the elements in the example. The first element was an hypothesis: that a battery was bad. The next step was the attempt to verify that hypothesis. You established a **control group,** a group not subjected to experiment: the second set of batteries, which you knew was good. The first set of batteries was the **experimental group.** In systematically trying each battery in the experimental group, you applied a stimulus to the group to see what change would occur. That is, each time you tried a different battery, you applied a new

intersubjective reliability: the characteristic a piece of information or statement of events or relationships is said to have when multiple observers, using similar methods of test, can agree upon it.

objectivity: the characteristic information possesses when it is described in terms of some public standard rather than a private or subjective one. The statement that an object has certain dimensions, for example, is an objective one, whether true or false, because the standards involved (feet, inches, meters, etc.) are publicly known. The statement that it is beautiful, however, is not objective because there are no public standards of beauty.

quantifiability: the possibility of description in numerical terms; countability or measurability.

experimental method: precise observation and testing carried out under carefully controlled conditions. Typically, the experiment is performed with sets of identical units, groups, or materials; conditions in one (the control) are held constant, while those in the other or others (the experimental) are allowed to vary in known ways.

hypothesis: the precise statement of something only believed or guessed at, but not yet proven, for the purpose of testing its truth.

control group: the unit for which conditions are held constant in the experimental method.

experimental group: the unit for which conditions are permitted to vary in the experimental method.

stimulus. Finally, on discovering the bad battery, you were able to conclude it *was* bad, because all the other batteries you tried would, in fact, operate the tape recorder.

The experimental method, in its classical form, contains the following elements: an experimental group and a control group with the composition or membership in each randomly assigned, and a stimulus that is applied only to the experimental group. Both groups are observed before the stimulus is applied and then afterward. If the experimental group changes, it is possible to conclude that it is the stimulus that produces the change. Of course, there may be other confounding elements that affect the operation of experiments. These will be discussed further in Chapter 2. As you can see from even the simple example of the tape recorder, however, the experimental method permits and encourages precise measurement because of the possibilities of *control* in the experimental situation. If all elements in the situation can be controlled, the experimenter can then permit one to vary by a known or measurable degree, and observe any reaction that occurs, measuring it with precision as well.

The reason that quantification and measurement are so important in science is that they permit us to know *with precision.* Quantification—counting—is significant scientifically for the simple reason that mathematics is the most precise form of statement, the most precise language, people have. It may be adequate for your own purposes to inquire if the water is hot enough to bathe and to be told that it is still "only lukewarm." But the information is far more accurately conveyed by the report that the water is 82° Fahrenheit. The more precisely something is known, the better it is known.

Theoretical orientation   Finally, science as a way of knowing things is characterized by an *orientation to the theoretical.* We mean by this that the object of science is to produce a body of propositions, or truth statements, that are logically and systematically interrelated in order to *explain* some broad category of phenomena. Merely producing a catalogue of careful descriptive or observational statements is not enough; that is only the beginning. From observations of what is, scientific knowledge moves to an "if-then" stage describing how the world appears to operate. And from that level it moves again to a category of much broader generalizations ("laws") that try to explain the principles that underlie the operation. This whole structure of interrelated propositions of different kinds is called *scientific theory,* and the production and enlargement of theory is the purpose of science. Theory gives *coherence* and *scope* (range or breadth or depth) to what would otherwise be a more or less random assortment of empirical statements about the world. (The scope of the laws of thermodynamics is far greater than any number of precise descriptions of the ways in which particular bodies fell, came to rest, and so forth.)

Sociology as a Scientific Perspective

Earlier in this discussion we noted that sociology is one of the fields commonly called a "social sci-

ence." This label implies that it utilizes the scientific method in its work and that the knowledge produced by that work has, at least to some degree, the four characteristics listed above—that is, that it is in some way intersubjectively reliable, objective, quantifiable, and theoretically oriented. We also noted, however, that sociologists themselves are in disagreement concerning whether the field *is now* a science, whether, if it is not, it *can ever become one,* and, if it has such potential, whether it *should.*

Probably few sociologists would quarrel with the conclusion that to some degree sociological knowledge could be called "scientific." Although its concepts do not have either the precision of expression or the degree of agreement among practitioners that, say, the concepts of physics have, most sociologists agree in general on what the basic ideas mean and would concur in their presence or absence in a given observation. ("Social interaction," for example, may be variously defined, but a group of sociologists viewing the same event would probably pretty much agree on whether interaction had occurred.) Intersubjective reliability, then, is to some useful degree established. Equally, few sociologists would quarrel with the notion that observations of human behavior *are* quantifiable. Again, there might be hot dispute on the best way to quantify in a given instance, or whether a particular measure "really" expressed the thing measured, but that quantification is possible is beyond much doubt.

The criteria of objectivity and theoretical orientation are the subject of great debate in the field. One question raised is: How can one apply scientific method to the study of the social world? The *naturalistic position,* at one extreme, is that there should be no difference in the methods used to study the physical, or natural, world and those used to study the social world. Opposed to that position is one called *humanism.* Humanists hold that the human social world is quite different from the natural world, and must be studied with different methods.

There is an underlying theme in this discussion of experimental method and the attack on it. Those who practice sociology via the scientific method argue that they can be objective, unbiased, and value-free, although no one believes that the pure experimentalism of, say, chemistry is possible in sociology. People who attack that position argue that methods are, in fact, expressions of a point of view and that therefore they cannot be unbiased and value-free. This is the core of the dispute. The humanists argue that real objectivity is impossible, because the researcher is a part of the research situation and therefore involved in it, at least reactively (the situation will react to *him*). In short, to study the social world is to alter it in some way. Further, to attempt to treat people or social situations in an objective or value-free manner, as the horticulturalist treats a plant experiment, is to diminish their freedom and individuality and deny one's responsibility for any consequences. The naturalist might reply, however, that in fact in many instances value-free objectivity *is* possible, at least to a useful degree, and that many kinds of observation or study do not particularly affect the subjects.

These quarrels about objectivity have important theoretical implications. The scientific method was invented and matured in the natural sciences, where, as a rule, investigators did not have to concern themselves with the effects of their research on its subjects and where studying the world would not alter it. Under these conditions, the search for abstract theory is a sensible one. The natural world does not, presumably, change its nature, so that once that nature is known, it is known for good and may be theoretically explained. But if the social scientist, in studying the social world, alters it, then a search for scientific theory of the kind associated with the natural sciences is meaningless and, perhaps, even immoral. (For even the theoretical statement that a given social phenomenon was or was not true could cause people to react against it, as voters will sometimes switch their votes in order to confound pollsters whom they perceive as claiming to know how the voter will behave.)

We cannot resolve such questions here, and indeed they may be unresolvable. Most contemporary American sociologists are probably more or less in the naturalistic or scientific position, although humanists are gaining a greater voice. There is more than one way to view the world sociologically, and it is to the assumptions underlying competing views of the nature of social reality that we now turn.

Basic Assumptions in Sociology

Before we can explore the great classical and contemporary views of social reality, it is necessary to discuss briefly the kinds of *assumptions* that form the basis for all sociological theories. Understanding the nature of these assumptions provides a starting point for understanding any theoretical position. We may classify such assumptions into three categories. The sociologist must adopt at least one from each class to develop his view of social reality.

The first category involves an assumption concerning *the nature of human nature*. What is it assumed to be like? Are we good, bad, rational, irrational, etc.?

The second category involves *the nature of society* and how it is possible. This is a most important assumption. Typical in this category are assumptions that the whole of society is different from the sum of its parts, or that the sum of the parts of society (individuals) is equal to the whole of the society, or group. Another possible assumption is that societies are composed of the relations and interrelations among and between people as they associate in their groups. Still others assume that societies are composed of *institutional* interrelationships, such as "the military-industrial complex."

The third category concerns an assumption about *how society works*. In other words, what is the basic mechanism that provides the moving force for the phenomenon we call society? For purposes of analysis in the rest of this chapter, we will focus on four such mechanisms: the processes of *conflict, accommodation, cooperation,* and *assimilation*. This list is not exhaustive, and is only used here as a convenient way to help identify theoretical positions in the discipline.

Classical Views of Social Reality

Theoretical perspectives in sociology are usually examined in terms of "classical" and "contemporary" periods, which might usefully be thought of as meaning nineteenth and twentieth century. The classical thinkers of the nineteenth century were all Europeans who established the basis and defined the interests of the discipline by making certain kinds of assumptions, and asking certain kinds of questions, about the nature of human nature and society. So significant were their assumptions and questions, and so profoundly influential on the thought of their time, that they continue to dominate theoretical work in the field today. Contemporary theoretical perspectives, most of which are American, have to a great degree expanded and elaborated upon the work of the classical thinkers.

The classical theorists (at least one of whom, Marx, would not have called himself a sociologist) were all, in one way or another, reacting in their work to three great historical trends that shaped their times. These were (1) the political revolutions of the late eighteenth to mid-nineteenth centuries, with their effects on the decline of absolute monarchy and the rise of democratic political and social ideals; (2) the new ideals of humanism, rationalism, and the nobility of human nature, associated with the historical period called the Enlightenment, which was the culmination of the Renaissance and the Reformation, ending the medieval view of the world forever; and (3) the Industrial Revolution, which, along with its many other profound effects, created the new paradox of affluence for many along with grinding poverty for others. (The significance of this paradox is that previously great affluence had always been limited to a very, very few, while most people lived on the margin of survival. When the Industrial Revolution generated relatively great wealth for many, those who remained poor were confronted for the first time in history with the fact that poverty might not be a natural condition.) *Progress,* one of the dominating ideas of the nineteenth century, had clearly occurred. But the various paradoxes created by political and economic turmoil and the forces of industrialization and urbanization, secularism and rationalism, confronted the theorists with questions concerning its price and process.

Emile Durkheim (1858–1917)

Durkheim, a Frenchman, has probably had greater effect on American sociology, at least, than any other individual. He might be called the inventor of the contemporary perspective called functionalism (discussed below), which dominated American sociology for fifty years and still remains a major force. In a series of works, *On the Division of Labor in Society* (1893), *The Rules of Sociological Method* (1895), *Suicide* (1897), and *The Elementary Forms of the Religious Life* (1912), Durkheim either implied or spelled out his position on the three assumptions that define a view of social reality.[1] His views are developed in his discussions of social facts, social order, and the division of labor.

Social facts Durkheim discusses the nature of human nature by raising the question: What is a social fact? *Social facts* are ways of acting, thinking, and feeling that are external to the individual and culturally created, such as customs. Social facts have coercive power; they can control an individual's behavior in spite of resistance to them. It is not that one chooses to go along with the prevailing social mode, it is simply that one does not realize there *is* a choice.

People learn ways of doing things in specific educational settings and from socializing agents such as the family and peer groups. We learn them so well that to do them differently does not occur to us. For example, when we meet a friend on the street and ask, "How are you?" we would be amazed and disconcerted if he replied by giving us a description of the state of his health. The *social fact* is that such an inquiry is defined as a greeting or acknowledgement of recognition, not as a question. And when the friend replies by saying, "Fine, thank you," we do not take it as a statement of physical or mental condition. Rather, he is accepting our acknowledgement of the relationship between us and reciprocating the acknowledgement. Given that we *are* acquainted, the expectation that we will behave this way is socially coercive; to fail to do so is to breach the relationship. Human nature, then, is essentially passive. We are the products of our society, and much, if not all, of our behavior is either in accord with its coercion of us or reactive to it. Society creates the individual; the individual does not create society.

Social facts are found "within" society or social groups. It is the group that exerts pressure on the

Emile Durkheim, 1858–1917

Durkheim was born in France to middle-class Jewish parents. He spent most of his life as an academic and is considered by many to be the father of modern scientific sociology as well as the originator of the functionalist school or position in that field (it had other forerunners in anthropology). He is probably best known in the United States for *Suicide* (1897), which is a model of empirical research and statistical/probabilistic reasoning. Durkheim's other major works include his doctoral dissertation *On the Division of Labor in Society* (1893), *The Rules of Sociological Method* (1895), and *The Elementary Forms of the Religious Life* (1912). One of Durkheim's major goals in life was to establish sociology as a scientific discipline in his country. While he did not succeed during his lifetime (though he held the first professorship in sociology ever to be established in France), his influence on modern American sociology remains overwhelming.

> **division of labor:** the way in which the work and other activities and functions of a society are allocated to its members for performance, typically according to social categories. The simplest and most universal division of labor is by age and sex; the more complicated forms are represented by the social occupational structures of the industrial societies. Note that the term includes *social* function or performance as well as occupation. In Britain, for example, some pursuits or activities are associated exclusively with the aristocracy. An American contrast is the ugly phrase "nigger work."

that people are morally and psychologically dependent on society. We survive only through interaction with others. Without the assistance of adults, no infant could live. Without the cooperation of others, no adult could continue to live. The social group or community is essential to the individual and predates him in time; he is born into it. But in any group or community, there *must be* order; people cannot live in anarchy. (Adults *must* care for infants, for instance, for the group to survive.) Social order, then, is the precondition for individual life. Order exists because it is fundamentally necessary; it precedes all else.

For *behavioral* order to exist, there must be *moral* order, a code of right and wrong, requirement and prohibition. The moral order is the source of social facts, the constraints on behavior that make society possible. Religion is the ultimate moral authority and is, in a sense, produced *by* society for the purpose of perpetuating itself.

The division of labor The way society works, Durkheim believed, is through *the division of labor.* This is the way the essential tasks in a society are divided and assigned to people. The assignment is usually on the basis of social categories and always includes a division by age and sex (men's work, women's work, children's work). In complex societies it may become very intricate.

Although society is ultimately rooted in its moral order, individuals must have some reason beyond coercion to cooperate with each other, and most of us, after all, are rarely conscious of the coercive power of social facts. (It does not occur to us that we have a choice about passing the ketchup.) This

individual who attempts to resist the coercion of social facts. Social facts are independent of individuals.

Social order To explain the existence and perpetuation of social facts, Durkheim addressed the question: Why is there social order? His answer is

Societies characterized by *organic solidarity* are based on difference; those characterized by *mechanical solidarity* are based on sameness.

is a simple way of saying that Durkheim believed society was impossible without some kind of *integrative device,* a social glue that would bond people together and to the moral order itself. The condition where such bonding was absent he called **anomie**: a state in which social facts had lost their coercive power. Durkheim found the glue, or social cohesion, in the ways in which the fundamental work of a society was accomplished, the things, such as food production, that have to be attended to if the members of a group are to survive. On the basis of anthropological information and his own views of Europe, Durkheim defined two types of social cohesion that he thought represented "primitive" and industrial societies. These are, respectively, **mechanical solidarity** and **organic solidarity**.

The contrasts between the two types of social solidarity, and the characteristics of societies manifesting them, are shown in Table 1-1. The essential distinction Durkheim drew was between solidarity based on *sameness* and solidarity based on *difference*. In simple societies, characterized by mechanical solidarity, people are bonded together and to the group because all are essentially alike. Each individual in a given category (man, woman, child) has the same tasks as every other, shares the same values, and holds the same expectations. Tradition is the guiding force. In complex societies, characterized by organic solidarity, integration is accomplished through *difference,* people being bonded by their dependence on each other for essential services. (The doctor needs the mechanic and the mechanic needs the doctor.) Rationality is the guiding force.

Having worked out the mechanical-organic model for social bonding, Durkheim next analyzed the nature of moral order (the basis of society) in the two types of society. He concluded that each type of society has a different kind of moral order based on different types of law. The society bonded by mechanical solidarity in the division of labor is characterized by *repressive law,* a legal code that punishes the transgressor for violating the moral code shared by all. In the more complex society bonded by organic solidarity, however, mere punishment would not repair a breach in social relations created by transgression. The social need would not be to uphold and reaffirm a moral code shared by all, but to reknit a social fabric torn by moral violation. Thus societies based on organic solidarity are characterized by *restitutive* law, a legal code aimed at restoring a social balance. The purpose of repressive law is to maintain a simple order by punishing any deviation; the purpose of restitutive law is to maintain a complex order by repairing damage to social interrelations.

Summary Durkheim's perception of human nature was that it is essentially passive and morally neutral. The person is the creation of the society and will do and be whatever is required for society to endure. The nature of society is that it has an existence independent of individuals and is coercive over them. The mechanism through which it works, however, is individual *cooperation* expressed in the division of labor.

In all of these concerns, Durkheim was responding to what he perceived as a dominating problem of modern history, the decline in social cohesion caused by industrialization and secularization. This, he concluded, was due not to any inherent imperfections in the division of labor or to the specialization of institutions in and of itself. Rather the transition from a European society based on mechanical solidarity to one based on organic solidarity was not yet complete. Moral codes appropriate to the mechanical state still endured, although they had become obsolete. The society of the future would be based on spontaneous interaction developed from an occupational base.

Karl Marx (1818–1883)

Marx, a German Jew, was trained in law but switched to philosophy. Although his influence on contemporary sociology has not been quite so great as Durkheim's, his impact on our century has probably been greater than that of any other single individual, with the exception of Jesus of Nazareth. His best-known works are *The Communist Manifesto* (1848, with Friedrich Engels) and *Das Kapital* (1867–1894).[2] The latter contains the subjects of principal interest to sociologists: Marx's ideas on the nature of (Western) society, social structure, and social change. The three assumptions that constitute a view of social reality emerge from the discussions in these books of the relation between

anomie: a condition of normlessness, being without values, that results in the weakening or dissolution of the social ties between people.

mechanical and organic solidarity: Durkheim's terms for the two varieties of social organization he believed were polar opposites in human society. Mechanical solidarity is social organization based on "sameness" or similarity of persons, values, activities; it characterizes tribal societies. It is "mechanical" in that the members of such societies are alike, like mass-produced machine parts, and the basis of the social order of the society is their similarity. Organic solidarity is social organization based on reciprocal, interdependent differences, like those between the organs of the body; it characterizes industrial societies. It is "organic" in that the members of such societies, although very different in values and activities, are dependent on each other for the smooth functioning of society.

Table 1-1 Characteristics of Durkheim's types of social solidarity

Mechanical

Found in simple, preliterate societies
Moral and social similarity
Great conformity to tradition
Individual difference and variation restricted
Most property communally owned
Religion in the form of cult and daily ritual
Individual thought and conduct controlled by community opinion
Widely extended kinship network
Interpersonal relations based on loyalty and trust
"Sacred" orientation: life ordered by religious values
Sentiment or feeling as a major value
Repressive, or punitive, law

Organic

Found in complex, industrial societies
Moral and social diversity
Essentially traditionless
Individual difference and variation encouraged
Most property privately owned
Religion formally institutionalized, as in churches
Little community control over individual thought and conduct
Nuclear family (parents and children as principal kin)
Interpersonal relations based on contracts
"Secular" orientation: life ordered by worldly values
Rationalism as a major value
Restitutive, or restorative, law

individuals and social systems, the dominant social institutions, and the productive system and social class. Marx called himself a philosopher, however, so remember that our discussion of him here imposes a sociological framework on his ideas. He is also a figure of immense importance in economics and political science.

One idea may be said to have dominated Marx's thinking beyond all others, the notion of **dialectical change.** Essentially, dialectical change is change arising from the conflict of opposing elements. In any system, such as a society, the existence of one element (called the *thesis*) tends to produce a counterforce (called the *antithesis*) to oppose it. The conflict between the thesis and antithesis produces yet another element that resolves the original contradiction—the *synthesis* (see Figure 1-1). In Marx's theory of social class, for instance (discussed in detail later), the capitalist and worker classes are clashing elements, and the new element that resolves their conflict is a workers' revolution resulting in the communist workers' state. For Marx, dialectical change was the process through which history operated, and it was likely to require social revolution. Conflict, thus, is inevitable in history because it is the normal means through which change takes place. Contemporary sociological conflict theory (examined later) is an outgrowth of Marxian ideas.

The individual and the social system   Human nature, Marx thought, is essentially good. People as individuals are not evil, but conditions of life may become so, or even make people act in evil ways. European industrial civilization of Marx's time presented, he thought, a terrible paradox, a terrible contradiction: the paradox of poverty and injustice existing within the framework of a society in which justice and plenty were possible for all. Poverty and injustice are impossible relationships for human beings to live in. But since human nature is essentially good, and Western civilization is a social system committed, in essence, to honesty and decency, how can poverty and injustice exist?

Marx's reasoning toward resolution of the paradox is interesting. He has two pieces of data. First, poverty and injustice exist. Second, all people in the system claim they are honest and decent. After examining the actions of individuals, Marx con-

Karl Marx, 1818–1883

Born and educated in Germany, Marx went to England after the failure of the socialist revolution of 1848 and spent the remainder of his life there (much of it pursuing his studies in the British Museum). He collaborated with Friedrich Engels in writing *The Communist Manifesto* in 1848. The writing of his major work, *Das Kapital (Capital)* occurred during the years 1867 to 1894; Engels edited and completed the last two volumes after Marx's death. With V. I. Lenin, Marx is generally considered the father of modern Communism.

cludes that for the most part this claim is factual. It is through this reasoning process that Marx finds the crucial distinction between individual behavior and the nature of social relations. It is this distinction he uses to resolve the paradox. Individuals are generally honest and decent. It is the system, or the social structure, that produces poverty and injustice. Therefore, the solutions to social problems are to be found in the social environment, rather than in individual faults. Scientific analysis of the social environment is a logical necessity for the analysis of social problems.

The dominant social institution   Marx addresses the nature of society by asking how an exploitive system can operate when people are basically good. The answer must be found within the structure and normal operation of society's major institutions. In the Western world the analysis must focus on the economic institution because it is, in his opinion, dominant.

Thus Marx gives us a major sociological postulate: the dominant institution theme. No society can be analyzed without understanding the structure and organization of the basic relationships of its central institution. The structures and relations of that institution are bound to penetrate the rest of the society in question. The central institution could conceivably be any in the society: the family, the political order, education, the military, the economy, religion.

Marx, however, had no doubt that the economic institution—capitalism—was dominant in Western society. He argued that an unnatural social relationship totally penetrated that institution and thus dominated the whole society. That unnatural social relationship is the contract. The contract is a short-term specific relationship based on the exchange of one promise for another. It is legalistic, formalized, segmentalized (in dealing only with one aspect of a personality or one particular performance), and brings rationalism, secularity, and instrumentality into human relations. That is, a contract treats the parties to it as instruments for dealing with one another. Marx found this distressing because he believed that the natural relation between human beings was one of spontaneous cooperativeness based on good will.

The productive system and social class   For Marx, "the way society works" is through its economic productive system. Under the Western capitalist system, there are two types of production: production for use and production for exchange. Each of these has different implications. Things can be *used* for human purposes, or they can be exchanged to create *wealth*.

Those who control the exchange process through ownership are in an economically dominant position. Those who do not control the process are "out of the mainstream" and become dependent upon those who do. Ownership of or access to the means of production determines social standing and social power.

Marx argues that exchange, in and of itself, is not

dialectical change: the idea that change occurs as a consequence of the opposition of inconsistent or conflicting elements. The existence of one element, the thesis, tends to produce an opposing element, a counterforce called the antithesis. The conflict between them is resolved through the creation of a third, unifying element, the synthesis. An example may be seen in American race relations in the past generation. The black protest cry "Freedom Now!" was responded to by segregationists with the cry, "Never!" Out of that clash came the civil rights program of gradual integration.

Figure 1-1
The process of dialectical change

The general model

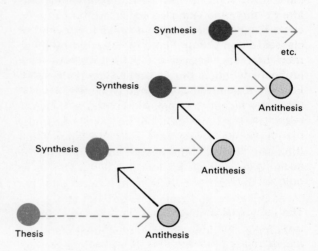

Marx's example

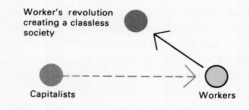

productive. But reward accrues to those who participate in exchange relationships, not to those who participate in the productive process. Out of this system of production for exchange grows a social structure that supports the system of capitalist economics. This leads Marx to his classic analysis of **social class**.

According to Marx, there are two social classes. There are the property-owning capitalists, the **bourgeoisie,** on the one hand, and the propertyless, the **proletariat,** on the other. There is a natural conflict of interest between the two, because it is to the interest of the capitalist to exploit the labor of the worker to the greatest degree possible. The worker actually *creates* value through his labor, for example in farming, through the planting, care, and harvest of crops that would not exist without his effort. The landowning capitalist, to the contrary, creates nothing of value, but reaps the reward of his ownership through land rentals paid by those who do create. Because the capitalist has invested nothing of value in the system, he is free to exploit it as much as possible. A farmer who owns his own land may be able to increase his income by working a sixteen-hour day, but to do so he must sacrifice some of his free time. The landowning capitalist, on the other hand, loses nothing by raising the rents on his land in such a way as to require sixteen-hour days from his tenants, because it is they who work the land, not him.

The capitalists came to the contest with an unfair advantage, for they inherited the feudal mantle of power. Because of their previous positions of power, they took over the institutions of the newly developing industrial society, and molded them to fit the economic system. This capitalist economic system is characterized by contract relationships. As a result people are alienated from their work, their community, and themselves.

Alienation is a very important concept in Marx's thought. For him, it was a condition in which things that have a natural relationship come to have an unnatural one.[3] There is a natural relationship between workers and the product of their labor. It is that product which represents the natural payment to workers for their labor. Under a capitalist system, however, workers do not get the full amount of what they produce. They are alienated from their production because of the absence of reciprocity.

With this analysis, Marx suggests that there is a closed, tightly integrated Western industrial social system that exists in spite of considerable conflict. The system is so closed and so tightly integrated that piecemeal change cannot occur. Thus, Marx concludes, there is a need to change the entire system, that is, to eliminate private property and contractual social relations. The change will have to be revolutionary, because the bourgeoisie will not willingly give up their position of exploitive advantage. The revolution will occur when the members of the proletariat, recognizing their common interests, band together to throw off the "yoke of oppression" and create a worker's state. This will be organized along communistic lines. The greatest good for the greatest number will dictate policy and every person will contribute what he can to the society and in return receive from it what he needs. In time even the worker's state will "wither away" (because *any* state is by definition coercive), and the revolution will end in a classless society.

Summary Marx believed that human nature is essentially good. Western society was exploitive in nature as a consequence of its economic system, but this was a historical accident that could be remedied. The way that society worked was through the *conflict* of opposing interests, but a "natural" society would be harmonious and work through spontaneous cooperation among its members.

Max Weber (1864–1920)

Weber was a German academic. Unlike Durkheim, whose primary concern was always the nature of social order, or Marx, who could be said to have been a theorist of social structure and social change, Weber paid much more attention to the individual and the relations between the individual and society. One of his strongest and most consistent emphases is on *meaningful social action,* the meanings that specific acts have for the persons exhibiting them. Thus his theories tend to focus on the significance of *ideas* in social life, reasoning in the direction that ideas precede and lead to behavior. We can see the three basic assumptions that underlie Weber's theoretical position in his discus-

Max Weber, 1864–1920

Weber was a German academic who, though he suffered from ill health throughout most of his life, nevertheless exercised a profound influence on European and American sociology as a consequence of the work he accomplished during productive periods. Often said to have been engaged in a lifelong dialogue with Marx, Weber directed the thrust of many of his major works to the criticism or elaboration of what he regarded as simplistic elements in Marxian thought. He is probably best known in the United States for his classic *The Protestant Ethic and the Spirit of Capitalism* (translated 1930); but the thesis of this book—the influence of ideology on social structure—is also carried forward in *Ancient Judaism* (translated 1952), *The Religion of China* (translated 1951), and *The Religion of India* (translated 1958). His major work, still incompletely translated into English, is *Wirtschaft und Gesellschaft* (*Economy and Society*, 1922).

social class: a category of persons sharing similar economic positions or relatively similar amounts of property, income, or wealth, with resulting similarity in life-style. In Marxian thought, a social class consists of those persons with a similar "relation to the means of production," those connected to the economic structure of society in similar ways, for example, industrial workers.

bourgeoisie: Marx's term for property owners.

proletariat: Marx's term for the propertyless.

alienation: the condition of being estranged, separated, disunited, unreconciled. The concept of alienation is important in much sociological theory. It was originally introduced by Marx, who saw industrial workers as "alienated from" their work by the separation of labor and product. It is now often used in five different, although related ways to refer to a sense or condition of powerlessness, meaninglessness, normlessness, isolation, or self-estrangement.

sions of the nature of social action, the types of social action, and the concepts of social relation and authority, as well as in his view of the increasing importance of rationality in Western life.

The nature of social action   Weber's ideas about human nature emerge from his discussion of social action. Weber, like Marx, set out to analyze West-

ern society, and looked for a feature that distinguished it from others. He found it in the *extent of rationality* present in the West as a consequence of the Industrial Revolution. This is an important theoretical principle for Weber, and his theory may be best understood by focusing on it. Human beings, for Weber, are rational creatures.

For Weber, *rational* has a very precise meaning: action specifically calculated to attain particular ends, or goals. If behavior is directed toward a goal, it is said to be rational action in Weberian terms.

Consideration of rationality leads Weber to the definition of certain theoretical concepts. The first of these is *social action*. Social action is action with subjective meaning attached. That is, the behaving person takes others into account when he acts. Social action is behavior undertaken with reference to or in the light of one's understanding of the other. There is a cultural and emotional context to all social action.

Two other important terms are *meaning* and *motive*. *Meaning* refers to both subjective intentions and conscious purposes. Meaning is defined in terms of the person who is behaving. For example, if your instructor, while grading a pile of term papers, decides that he is out of cigarettes and must go out to the store to buy some, his true *intention* may be to get away for a while from the awful grind of reading the papers. But the *meaning* of his departure should be understood and interpreted on both levels. He *is* going for the cigarettes; he is also giving himself a break. The meaning of the act is on both levels.

Motive is a cultural device by which we direct action. The concept of motive adds legitimate meaning to, or justifies, the social act for the individual actor. It is *why* one acts. In the given example, your instructor might have felt guilty about leaving the work he had to do. By finding a culturally permissible motive to do so, he was able to take the break he needed. For Weber, human beings are rational but they act in terms of subjective meaning and motive. These lead toward the goals or ends desired.

The types of social action   To this point, we have described only Weber's views on individual behavior, or social action. His notions on the nature of *society* can be found in the conception of *types of social action*. Social action, he believed, is best understood within a means-ends scheme, on the basis of whether rationality is present or absent, and to what it is directed. Different types of societies are typified by different applications of rationality in their conventional means-end schemes of social action. There are four types of social action: *rational action, evaluative action, affective action,* and *neutral traditional action.*

Rational action   In rational action the person chooses a goal rationally or deliberately and selects the most efficient manner of achieving it. To do this he must consider the consequences of all of the behavior he will engage in, including whether it is worthwhile to pursue a goal whose achievement would involve too many undesirable results. A society typified by decision making of this kind is a rational or rationalistic society.

Evaluative action   In evaluative action, the goal is not chosen through systematic consideration, but is an absolute cultural value desired for its own sake. The means for achieving it may be subject to rational calculation, however. In medieval Europe, for example, the attainment of personal religious salvation was a universally shared goal, accepted without question as good, but there were alterna-

tive means for its achievement (penance, pilgrimage, giving alms, taking religious orders, and so on).

Affective action   In affective action, goals are not specifically "chosen" at all. The end desired is simply emotional satisfaction. The way to achieve it is through spontaneous reaction in a given situation, in other words, by following one's emotional "instincts." The popular press view of the "hippie" phenomenon of the late 1960s with its emphasis on "letting it all hang out" while "doing one's own thing" on all occasions would be an example.

Traditional action   Traditional behavior means acting in ways that are habitual to the social surroundings in which one is found, so that *decision* is unnecessary. Rationality does not enter into the action at all. One behaves as tradition dictates, without question. We can see traditional social action in the behavior of the men described below, the neighbors of a Mexican farmer named Jesus Reyes. Reyes has adopted modern agricultural techniques and has quadrupled his corn crop as a result. His neighbors, however, retain their traditional farming practices and get very poor yields of inferior quality.

Why do they cling to the old ways? They can see. They can reach out and touch Reyes's towering corn. But they do not change. Even men who work on Reyes's farm follow the old ways on small plots of their own. Why? "Asi es!—that's the way it is." It is said with a shrug that answers everything and nothing.[4]

The concepts of social relation and authority   The way society works can be found in Weber's concepts of *social relation* and *authority*. A social relation is defined as the behavior of several people in which the action of each takes into account and is oriented to the behavior or action of the others. Social relation is social action multiplied. That is, people gathered together behave by taking into account each other's actions and orienting their own behavior toward those actions. Social structure in this situation is added through authority, and the idea of authority has a major role in Weber's theory.

There are three types of authority: charismatic, traditional, and rational-legal. *Charismatic authori-*

ty has to do with almost magical qualities possessed by or attributed to an individual. We often call this kind of authority personal magnetism, but the crucial factor is that people possessing **charisma** have the ability to attract groups of people and sway them to their will. Jesus, Hitler, John F. Kennedy, and the Beatles are all examples.

Traditional authority is the authority that is perceived as *always* having been held or wielded. Thus the reigning monarchs of some European countries may be obeyed so long as they follow the traditions of their thrones. The tradition both gives them authority and insures obedience so long as its user does not violate it. If the monarch violates the traditional duties and rights he is seen as possessing, however, the people may decide he holds power illegitimately and may overthrow him.

Rational-legal authority is conferred by and in organizations by their *rules.* Organizations are goal-directed, and the rules are the means through which goals are achieved. Some of the rules define offices and authority for the incumbents of offices, who will be obeyed so long as they themselves follow the rules. Such organizations are seen as rational, and the rules are viewed as a sort of legal code. We know them today as bureaucracies (see Chapter 7). Weber's theory of bureaucracy remains the basis of much contemporary study and research.

In Weber's view, society works through cooperation and accommodation—people take the behavior of others into consideration and adjust their own behavior to take account of it. This view emphasizes his concern with the role of rationality in human affairs. His observations of the role of rationality in Western society combined with his studies of several Eastern social systems (ancient China, India, and Judaism) led him to formulate a theory of the historical development or evolution of society. He believed that increasing rationalism was the key to social change. As a society grows more rational, it evolves from a society dominated by traditional authority through one led by charismatic authority to one characterized by rational-legal authority.

Summary As you can see, the assumptions that define Weber's views of social reality are somewhat more complex than those of Marx and Durk-

> **charisma**: the power of personality, "personal magnetism."
>
> **functionalism (structural functionalism)**: the theoretical position that sees activities as being defined by their effects or consequences for the social system within which they occur. The function of a traffic light, for example, is to control the flow of traffic at an intersection.

heim. Human nature, the nature of society, and the way it works (its mechanism) are not one thing, but consist of possibilities. Human nature is not *inherently* rational, but has that possibility and tends in that direction. And it *is* rational in the sense that social behavior consists of choice making, even though (as in the case of traditional social action) individuals may not be aware of choosing. The nature of society, too, is various, as determined by the variety of social action that becomes typical in a given society as a result of historical accident. But, Weber believed, there is here, too, some tendency toward increasing rationality, at least in the West. The mechanism through which society works is social action, action taking account of other people, which implies *cooperation* and *accommodation*.

Contemporary Views of Social Reality

Contemporary views of social reality are for the most part extensions and elaborations of the classical positions outlined above. Structural functionalism can be viewed largely as an outgrowth and elaboration of Durkheim's ideas, conflict theory as rooted in Marx, and symbolic interaction as stemming from Weber. Exchange theory has elements of both Marx and Weber. As we did with the classical theorists, we will describe the major elements of each so as to expose the three basic assumptions that constitute a theoretical position.

Structural Functionalism

Structural functional theory, often called **functionalism,** has tended to dominate the explanatory reasoning of sociology (and other social sciences) for the past fifty years. It is the logical extension of Durkheim's thinking. Just as Durkheim saw individuals as acting out the necessary requirements for collective survival, so the functionalists see people as fulfilling the requirements that the society has for its own perpetuation. Functionalism's views on the nature of human nature, the nature of society, and the way it works can be found in its conception of the relation between the individual and the society and its concepts of social system and function.

The individual and society Functional theorists see people responding to the requirements of their societies. They find their place within the social order and tend to stay in that place. People *can* change, but they do it in the manner prescribed by the society in which they live. Thus to the functionalists, society is the active agent in history, and human beings are basically passive responders. To a large degree, individuals are "overwhelmed by" the pressures their societies place on them to conform to social expectations, and they reflect such pressures most of the time. If they assert their own wills to act differently, even the individuality of the act is likely to conform to societal definitions of what is possible and permitted. American social protestors, for example, are far more likely to burn property than themselves, although Buddhist monks in Vietnam a few years ago took the opposite course. A functionalist might say that Americans burn property in protest because in the United States property is more important than people. Individuals are almost seen as "tools" or properties of society.

The concept of social system One of the crucial concepts of functionalism is that society is a *system*. System is defined by three characteristics: *balance, boundaries,* and *interrelationships.* First, a system is balanced, or tends to be balanced. Any destabilizing forces present tend to be subject to the inertia of other parts of the system. This "balance model" is an important element in functionalist thought and may be likened to a simple physical process. If one pushes down one end of a playground teeter-totter, the other end must rise, but its weight (inertia) will resist the push. Or, for another example, pressing on one side of a rubber balloon results in a bulge outward elsewhere, which reduces itself as soon as the initial pressure is re-

American social protesters are likely to burn property; Buddhists burned themselves. Watts in 1965; Vietnam in 1963.

leased. The balloon (system) thus restabilizes; it regains its "balance" or former state.

Second, a system has boundaries. You can describe the items that are in the system and those that are outside it. Part of keeping the system balanced has to do with maintaining or slowly altering the boundaries of that system.

Third, all the parts or elements in a system are related to each other. That is, if one element in the system changes, all the other parts of the system will also have to change their state in response. Each part is interrelated with and dependent on every other part.

The functional notion of system is clearly based on what is called the *organic model* in social science. This means the idea or conception of society as "like" a living organism or, at least, having some similarities to an organism. Although it is easy to carry such parallels too far—and they are often misleading—it probably does clarify the idea of system to use such language. Thus society, like the human organism, is composed of elements and subsystems, like the digestive and respiratory subsystems of the body, that are each balanced, boundaried, and internally interrelated. Each element in turn is related to the others as a whole, performing functions for the others and the body as a whole.

The concept of function   The way society works, in the functionalist perspective, can be seen in the concept of function within a system. All parts of every system are either *functional* or *dysfunctional.* Most parts are functional: they perform a positive service by helping to maintain the system or its balanced state. Dysfunctional elements are either useless (in which case they tend to be discarded or disappear) or have negative effects. The human heart, for example, is clearly functional for the body and all of the subsystems within it. But a heart defect is dysfunctional; its performance or existence not only does not contribute, it detracts or even endangers.

This kind of reasoning seems clear enough when applied to a living organism, as when we look at the organs and systems of the body. It may become somewhat more murky when applied to society, however. For example, many commentators on social problems regard crime as dysfunctional for the society, dangerous and damaging at the least, threatening collapse at the worst. Durkheim, however (who, you remember, might be called the first functionalist), saw crime as having *positive functions* for society. It strengthens the moral order, he argued, by calling attention to the importance of the laws violated, and sometimes by forcing us to define them more precisely as well.

Functionalists also draw a distinction between *latent* and *manifest functions,* because the social utilities that things have are not always apparent. An element's manifest function is overt and obvious, that purpose or end for which it is explicitly intended. Its latent function, if any, is the social purpose served "unconsciously," unknown and unintended by those who perform the act in question. Most Americans, for example, are familiar with the flag-raising ceremony that precedes many public sports events. If asked what the purpose of the ceremony is, those who conduct it or the spectators might well reply that it has patriotic meaning and is intended to remind participants of the rewards of living in the United States and, perhaps, to fuel their patriotic sentiments. A sociologist of religion, however, might view it as a latently religious ceremonial in the "unacknowledged, common (social) religion" that many Americans share regardless of their church membership (see Chapter 13).

The way society works, then, is that all of its various elements are in constant interaction with their own environments, and, in ways both latent and manifest, react to environmental stimuli to support the general welfare of the social system as a whole. Things that serve no such useful purpose tend to be discarded or to find new, positive, functions. The minority of elements that are actually disadvantageous and act to endanger the system or throw it out of balance are actively resisted. The system may also shift its structure so that a new balance is struck, thus removing the threat of a dysfunctional element. For example, when a new invention disrupts the established way of doing things, the system will either reject it or adjust to it, incorporating it into the culture.

Table 1-2 shows some ways in which functionalists have traditionally applied these ideas to understanding what are called *social institutions.* As we will see in Chapters 5 and 7, a social institution is a conventional way of getting something important done in a society, for example, bearing and rearing children. When customary means for accomplishing such things become so conventional that they are regarded as "the only way," they are said to be social institutions, or to have become institutionalized.

Summary   The functionalists view human nature as plastic, readily molded by the society into any form useful to the society. The nature of society is similar to that of an organism; it is a system of action and interaction among its members that is

Table 1-2 Some social institutions and their functions

Social institution	Function performed
The economic system	Production and distribution of necessary goods and services
The educational system	Socialization of the young to cultural values, transmission of basic information and skills, "keeping the kids off the streets"
The family	Procreation and rearing of children, basic socialization, sexual regulation and satisfaction, transmission of social status
The law	Maintenance of internal order in the society, formal enactment of the moral order, control of deviants
The military establishment	Protection from external threat, exploitive aggression
The political system	Organization of power, legitimation of authority, routinization of collective decision making for the general welfare

In the functionalist view, social institutions perform social functions—have utility—for the perpetuation of the society itself and are developed *by* the society to accomplish that purpose.

balanced, boundaried, and interrelated. The mechanism through which society works is the *cooperation* or coordination created by systemic interdependence.

Conflict Theory

The idea that conflict is at the base of all social arrangements is the pure model for **conflict theory**. At the present time, however, there are no pure conflict theorists. In the history of sociology, there have been only two or three people who have taken conflict as the basis for their thinking about human social life. The two most influential modern conflict theorists are Ralf Dahrendorf and Lewis Coser. Their work has helped redirect the attention of sociologists to the nature and functions of conflict in modern life.[5] Paradoxically, these two thinkers have focused on the *integrative* nature of conflict. They raise the question of how conflict holds society together, but do not assume it is the basis of social life. The conflict perspective's assumptions about human nature, the nature of society, and how it works are found in its views on power and authority, the role of associations, and the role of conflict in society.

Power and authority *Power* is a crucial concept for conflict theorists. Power is defined as the probability that an actor can carry out his will despite resistance. *Authority* is also crucial. Authority is the probability that a command will be obeyed. Authority is *legitimate power,* and is always associated with social roles. Legitimate power is assumed to be a common and necessary feature of social life, and therefore needs to be studied. By saying that power and authority are necessary, conflict theory assumes that in some sense people must either be in dominating positions or be dominated by others, or, at minimum, that direction and leadership are necessary in social affairs. The nature of most human beings is to follow; only a few lead.

The role of associations According to Dahrendorf, conflict and authority are primarily embedded in associations; conflict between individuals is socially unimportant. An association is any social organization where authority exists. It is composed of two quasi-groups, holders and nonholders of authority. When these quasi-groups recognize their separate interests, they become interest groups, or classes, and the probability of conflict in the society becomes higher. Conflict tends to produce a movement toward stable change, or balance in the system. In effect, a balance of forces will occur, and over time stability will be established. Change takes place through change in the authority system. Coser and Dahrendorf reason: if we have conflict in society, but society remains relatively ordered, and even stable, conflict must contribute to order and stability.

The role of conflict in society The basic mechanism that makes society work is social conflict. By social conflict sociologists normally mean a struggle over values and claims to scarce resources—that is, status, power, and things. Conflict takes the form of attempting to neutralize, injure, or eliminate rivals. It is usually seen as a conscious and personal social process, taking place between organized groups.

Some of the outcomes of social conflict are described by Coser's theory, and have been expressed in a series of formal and abstract propositions as follows:

1. The more unlimited the goals of the opposing parties in a conflict, the more prolonged the conflict will be. This is true because when goals are global, or relatively unlimited, each participant will feel more threatened. It is harder to secure "unconditional surrender" from an enemy than a negotiated armistice.

2. The more that people think *total* attainment of goals will involve a cost greater than that required for victory, the less prolonged the conflict will be. The reason for this is that when a victory is at hand, the temptation to "settle for" what one has won appears overwhelming when compared with the cost of further sacrifices for ends that may not be attainable.

3. The more intense the conflict, the more clear-cut will be the boundaries of the respective parties. The reason is that under the pressure of severe conflict, "fence straddling" will not be permitted; the "with us or against us" mentality will take over. There will also be strong efforts to draw away from and distinguish oneself from the enemy, as when the teaching of German was forbidden in some American schools during World War I.

4. The more intense the conflict, the greater the solidarity within conflicting groups. This is in part a function of the "with us or against us" mentality and in part a result of the ideological simplification that occurs under pressure; fine points and qualifications become obscure. As people withdraw from any identification with the enemy, they draw more closely together and identify more closely with each other, seeing themselves as "all in the same boat" and therefore sharing common interests.[6]

Summary For the conflict theorists, the nature of society is usually some kind of balance of forces between opposed or conflicting groups or associations. Human nature is largely passive in that most people are followers, dominated by a few. But

---

conflict theory: the theoretical position that views social conflict as a principal means through which human groups interact and as the basis for social structure; the notion that structure is the negotiated outcome of conflict.

symbolic interactionism: the theoretical position that views social interaction between individuals, ordered by their symbolically defined, reciprocal expectations for each other's behavior, as the basis of all social life.

gesture: a motion or sound that becomes associated with some meaning through repeated experience of the association, as when we learn that it is proper to say "ouch!" (a meaningless sound), or that a hand is waved in greeting or farewell.

---

because rewards and resources are scarce, the effect is to make human nature competitive. The mechanism that keeps society going is *conflict* between organized groups over the rewards available within the social system. Because it is rarely possible for one group to dominate another permanently, a kind of dynamic stability is created by the continuing contest.

Symbolic Interactionism

Symbolic interaction theory was introduced to American sociology through the lectures of George Herbert Mead at the University of Chicago in the 1930s.[7] **Symbolic interactionism** (or interactionism for short) is usually regarded as a microtheory (small-scale theory) designed to explain socialization, and will be covered more extensively in Chapter 4. Some interactionists do treat it as a total theory of society, however. What it looks like in this regard is sketched below. The theoretical assumptions implicit in interactionism are found in its views of symbols and meaning, expectations and behavior, and roles and interaction.

Symbols and meaning Mead begins his reasoning with the assumption that human beings, like other animals, are incessantly active. They constantly make **gestures**—movements or sounds—that are reacted to by others. But only human

beings quickly turn gestures into **symbols,** sounds or acts that come to stand for something else, to have a *meaning.* Symbols become *significant* when they have the same meaning for the person receiving them as they do for the person making them. Meaning, thus, is *shared* and is social. It is learned through *interaction* with others. Being human means possessing the capacity for thought, which is a consequence of *language* (a system of significant symbols). Humanness is a social phenomenon. People are thus entirely social beings, and their very humanity is the product of symbolic social interaction with others. Human nature is entirely *social.*

Expectations and behavior Society is the total sum of the interactions its members have with one another. It is composed of groups within which people relate to one another and the relationships between such groups. Behavior within groups and intergroup relations are ordered, or structured, by expectations created by both significant (individual

The meaning of a symbol is shared and social. It is something people put into the symbol, not a quality of the symbol itself. Consider the quite different meanings associated with the cross in these photos; yet the people in each would commonly claim that their use of it was Christian.

or personal) and generalized others. Through interaction, people learn to reflect on their own behavior, and come to have certain expectations about it and the behavior of others. That is, they observe behavior and learn to expect that similar patterns will occur as new situations are created. They also learn that others have similar expectations for themselves. The patterns of relations between people and their groups constitute the structure of society. The nature of society is that it is a collection of reciprocal expectations and expectation-fulfilling behavior.

Roles and interaction Society works because human beings are capable of symbol-using behavior, as a consequence of the possession of language. The most important product of this fact is self-consciousness. The human infant becomes self-conscious as a result of exposure to language. As his own language skills develop, the child learns first the meanings of words and the attitudes associated with them by those who use the words, and later the expectations these people have for his behavior. In time, he comes to have similar expectations for others. Sets of these expectations that are associated with the behavior of particular other persons are called *roles,* and roles are functions or reflections of group membership. Thus through his interaction with "Mommy" and "Daddy," the child learns both how he may expect them to behave and how they expect him to behave. Mommy and Daddy, in turn, behave the way they do because they are acting out a social role, a "part" in a "play" called "the family" (which they, in turn, learned themselves while growing up).

The generalized "parts" that people learn to play (father, mother, Catholic, plumber, and so forth) exist in the culture of any given society at a particular time and define "how one ought to act" in particular roles. These are called role expectations and also include how one behaves toward members of other groups and what the relations between groups should be or how they should take place. For example, in growing up in a family the child will learn not only how he or she is expected to act toward other family members, but also how the family and its members relate to other groups such as the church, the government, and so forth. Mommy and Daddy may grumble as they prepare their tax forms, but they acknowledge that they ought to pay taxes, and the child learns that aspect of the relation of the citizen to the state.

Summary In the interactionist view, human beings are active and communicative. Society is an extremely complex network of actions and interactions between individuals, all of them organized and "powered," or motivated, by group membership, with its resulting roles and role expectations. Society continues to function because people are socialized to meet role expectations from the time of birth and because the interdependency of individuals makes them rely on each other for necessary services and rewards. Further, the internalization of the requirements of various roles motivates

symbol: a sound or written notation with an invented relation to something else that makes it *stand for* the latter in meaning. The relation between the two is entirely arbitrary, not given in nature, and is invented by some person. Symbols become *significant* when we learn their meaning.

Role playing: We learn our behavior and our expectations from others.

Recent sex scandals in Washington exemplify exchange theory.

the person *to wish* to fulfill them; thus society works through *cooperation* in fulfilling expectations. Punishment or withdrawal of rewards for inadequate role performance provides additional motivation. These ideas are spelled out in more detail in Chapter 4.

Exchange Theory

Another modern view of social reality is **exchange theory**. This is neither so well developed nor so widespread as the other theories we have discussed, but it is becoming more popular among sociologists. Because it is based on only a few works by two or three individuals, it is not yet a fully elaborated theory, and so is only briefly summarized here.

The nature of human nature   People act rationally. Each person sets goals and finds the most appropriate means within the society to achieve those goals. Since goals are sought in the presence of and from others, those others must be taken into consideration, because they will often influence, or even control, one's access to goals. This situation produces the basic exchange relationship. Behavior, in this sense, becomes social. Behavior often takes the form of exchange because social and psychological resources are in short supply and must often be obtained from others. Thus we exchange money for goods, labor for money, submission to legal or bureaucratic authority for employment or safety, emotional "strokes" (rewards) for reciprocal reinforcement or support from others, and so forth.

The nature of society   Reality is to be found in the individual, and not in the abstract entity called society. The sum of the individuals and exchanges adds up to and is equivalent to society. From time to time, these exchanges may result in complex organizations, such as armies, universities, or corporations. Exchange theorists tend to concentrate their research on complex organizations.

The way society works   The process of exchange is a process of accommodation, a sharing of values and meanings. According to this view, people must get what they can from others in given relationships by giving the others what they require. People are able to reward and punish each other, actually or potentially, and to accommodate themselves to the social situations they find themselves in by exchange of goods, services, and psychological rewards.

Summary   For exchange theorists, people are rational and dependent on others to achieve their goals. Society is merely an exchange network. Society works through the exchange process, the mechanism of *accommodation*.

Summary

Sociology is the study of social life, in particular its orderliness or regularity. It is also a particular way of thinking about social reality or, more precisely, a set of such ways of thinking, all of which use a common set of ideas and categories. Along with economics, political science, anthropology, and psychology, sociology is one of the social sciences.

Sociology has conventionally understood itself as standing within the scientific tradition, and although there is now some disagreement about this, most of its practitioners would still put it there. Science may be understood most broadly as a framework, or model, for a particular kind of analysis and as a method. This model and method are applicable in many subject areas, but to be called a science, a discipline must also demonstrate the four characteristics of the scientific method: (1) intersubjective reliability, (2) objectivity, (3) quantifiability, and (4) theoretical orientation. Science, then, is a particular way of knowing certain kinds of things, those that can be observed and quantitatively expressed. To the degree that sociology follows or fits into the scientific tradition, it, too, is a way of knowing such things, and to some degree it meets the four criteria enumerated above. It does have a subject matter, social order and change, that is largely its own. It uses the scientific method to some degree, although not all sociologists agree that this is possible in the study of social life. It has a body of theories, some of which are quantifiable to some degree.

All sociological theories are based on assumptions concerning (1) the nature of human nature, (2) the nature of society, and (3) the way society works. In general, the differences between the classical and contemporary views of social reality flow out of divergences in these assumptions (see Table 1-3).

The three great classical theorists in sociology were all Europeans of the last century, Emile Durkheim, Karl Marx, and Max Weber. For Emile Durkheim, human beings are morally neutral and are coerced by *social facts* (rules and customs). Society is to be understood primarily in terms of its *moral order,* which is the source of social facts. Society works through individual *cooperation* through the division of labor, which, in turn, produces *social cohesion* or solidarity, the force that binds individuals to each other and the society. There are two kinds of social solidarity: *mechanical solidarity,* as represented in simple or preliterate societies, and

> **exchange theory:** the theoretical position that sees the exchange of mutually valued and necessary tokens or activities, and the interdependence between persons thus created, as the basis of social life.

organic solidarity, as seen in industrial societies. These produce two different forms of the division of labor and different legal-moral systems. Mechanical solidarity is found in social systems based on similarity, where the moral order is universally shared by everyone and forces all members of the society to behave in very similar ways. Organic solidarity produces societies based on differences among individuals, where social order is based on mutual interdependence.

For Karl Marx, people are basically good, and poverty and social injustice are the products of society and the way it is organized. In the Western world, the economic institution is dominant, and, hence, the root of social evils is capitalism, the principal Western economic system. Capitalistic society is based on production, of which there are two kinds: production for human use and production for exchange. The former is natural, but production for exchange is unnatural and thus exploitive. Production for exchange has produced the two basic social classes, the *proletariat,* or propertyless workers, and the *bourgeoisie,* or capitalist property owners. There is a natural *conflict* between them, and because of the dominating position of the propertied, the propertyless are *alienated* from the products of their labors and from themselves, and are exploited for profit by the propertied. When the proletariat recognize their common condition, they will revolt, destroy the capitalist system, and create a communist workers' state.

Max Weber found the distinguishing characteristic of Western society to be the extent to which *rationality* was its guiding mentality. This consideration led Weber to concentrate on *social action* as behavior understood in terms of its meaning to the participants. For Weber, people are rational beings who act in order to accomplish their ends. But while the individual is rational and his behavior always has meaning for him, it need not always

Table 1-3 Assumptions of classical and contemporary views of social reality

Theorist or theory	Nature of human nature	Nature of society	How society works
Classical theorists			
Durkheim	Passive, morally neutral, controlled by "social facts"	Preeminent, an active agent, controlling individual behavior	Through individual cooperation in the division of labor
Marx	Good, cooperative, decent	Determined by the nature of the dominant institution; in capitalism, the economic system	In Western capitalism, through exploitation and conflict of interest groups
Weber	Rational, choice-making	Varying; determined by the type of social action that is historically typical	Through collective taking account of others and accommodating to them
Contemporary theories			
Functionalism	Reactive, responsive to social requirements	A balanced, bounded system with all parts interrelated	Through cooperation and interdependence based on the need to survive
Conflict theory	Mostly subordinate, subject to domination by leaders	A dynamic balance of competing or conflicting groups or associations attempting to secure their own ends	Through group conflict resulting in some kind of more or less stable equilibrium
Symbolic interactionism	Social, active, communicative	Interaction networks of groups and individuals	Through cooperation in the fulfillment of reciprocal expectations
Exchange theory	Rational, interdependent	A resource-exchange network	Through accommodation: bargaining and trade-offs

take place within the framework of a logical relation between means and ends. Thus societies may be essentially rational or nonrational in character, depending on the kinds of social actions that predominate in them. There are four possible types of social action and thus four possible types of society: (1) rational, (2) evaluative, (3) affective, and (4) traditional. Society works through these kinds of social action, in which people *accommodate* their own behavior to their understanding of the behavior of others.

Contemporary sociological perspectives are, in significant part, extensions and elaborations of these classical views. There are four major "schools," or positions, in today's sociology: (1) structural functionalism, (2) conflict theory, (3) symbolic interactionism, and (4) exchange theory. In *functionalism,* human beings are essentially *re-*active, responsive to the requirements their societies impose upon them. Society is a *system,* or is composed of various systems, whose purpose is self-perpetuation. Social systems have three basic characteristics: (1) balance, (2) boundaries, (3) interrelationship and interdependence. Society works through *cooperation* resulting from interdependence and the requirement of balance. Thus whatever is *functional* (useful, purposeful) for the perpetuation of any given social system is likely to endure. Whatever is *dysfunctional* (useless or disadvantageous) is likely to be extinguished or disappear.

Conflict theory is similar to exchange theory in that society is seen as a series of trade-offs and people as essentially rational in the sense of knowing what they want or need. The basic difference between the two is that, while exchange theory assumes an essentially rational and ordered system of exchange, conflict theory assumes that people are unwilling to give up values through exchange and must be forced to do so by threat or violence. Thus, *conflict* is the way in which society works. Social structure is a reflection of *power,* so society is a kind of dynamic equilibrium among competing groups. The normal relation of person to person, then, is one of *dominance* and *subordination.* But since individual conflict is rarely productive, people form associations to secure their interests. Society works through the *conflict* of various types of associations (group with group, nation with nation). Instead of being pathological, conflict serves the positive function of maintaining a balance between competing groups.

Symbolic interactionism is most applicable to microanalysis of individual interactions, but has been extended by some to the level of a macro theory of society. In this view, human beings are social, active, and communicative. Abstract thought, which is the peculiar characteristic of human beings, as opposed to other animals, is made possible only by *symbols.* Society consists of the interactions that take place between people as individuals and between people in groups. Group life creates sets of expectations for other people's behavior, and the fulfillment of such expectations (role requirements) is what makes social life possible. Society works because people *cooperate* in acting out role expectations that are learned through infant socialization to the general culture and, later, through socialization to specific group rules, customs, and expectations.

Exchange theory presumes that human beings are rational and resources are limited, so that people must engage in trade-offs to get what they want or need. Society consists of people in relation to each other engaged in such exchanges; the exchange relationship *is* what composes "society." Society "works" because everyone needs some things from others, and must obtain them through more or less calculated interaction with others.

You will be meeting these various theoretical views, summarized in Table 1-3, throughout the book. Remember that none of these is "right" and the others "wrong." They are views, *perspectives,* ways of looking at things. Any of them provides a reasonable explanation of the way the social world works, but each calls our attention to different aspects of it, emphasizing some things and ignoring others. That is the purpose of theory.

Review Questions

1. Explain some of the basic concerns of most sociologists. Upon what fundamental assumptions does the discipline operate? What general type of questions does the sociologist ask?

2. Contrast how Durkheim, Marx and Weber aproached man, society and sociology. Which of the four modern theories discussed in this chapter best relates to each man? Explain.

3. What is science? List and describe the four basic characteristics of science. How well does sociology meet each of the criteria?

4. Discuss the controversy between the naturalists and the humanists as to the nature of sociology. Which perspective appears most reasonable to you? Why?

5. In what ways is sociology similar to and different from other sciences? Specifically other social sciences such as psychology and anthropology?

Suggestions for Research

1. Examine the mass media for applications of sociology, with particular emphasis on newspapers and magazines. Many newspapers have fairly recently developed "lifestyle" sections which often reflect a sociological perspective. Clip out several examples to indicate the scope of the discipline and present to your class, explaining how these articles relate to sociology. Most articles will be presented in a much more popular style than found in professional journals, but the sociological connections should still be obvious.

2. Acquaint yourself with the professional literature in sociology, probably available in your departmental library. Familiarize yourself with some of the larger and general ones such as *American Sociological Review, American Journal of Sociology, Social Forces,* and *Social Problems.* Also give attention to more specialized journals, such as *Journal of Marriage and the Family* or *Social Work.* Note content, format, style. You will want to read at least a few entire articles to get a deeper look at these elements.

3. Academia is probably one of the most obvious vocations for the sociologist; in addition, there are numerous

other alternatives for a person with such a background. To get a better idea of the role of the sociologist, interview an administrator or counselor within your sociology department in regard to this topic. What are the various alternatives open to the graduating student in sociology, at both undergraduate and higher levels?

4. Devote a term paper to studying the sociological perspective which has enjoyed the most popularity in your lifetime: structural functionalism. You will want to refer to the works of Talcott Parsons among others. How does this particular perspective view man? society? What methodology does it support—a naturalistic or a more humanistic approach? How do structural functionalists explain such things as social class inequities?

5. Conduct a small sample survey, using at least two different groups. Draw one group from students in sociology or the social sciences. Select the other from a science or engineering field. Discuss the role of sociology in today's world with students in both groups and be alert to any differences between the two that seem significant. In comparison to science or engineering, how do they view sociology as legitimate? What are their views toward the "soft" sciences in general? Toward the more theoretically-oriented fields? How meaningful or necessary do they consider the role of sociologist in contemporary society? In what areas is he needed, if at all?

CHAPTER 2
SCIENTIFIC METHOD IN SOCIAL RESEARCH

MIAMI BEACH, DEC. 6—PROFESSOR T.B. MURRAY ANNOUNCED TODAY THAT AFTER YEARS OF TESTS WITH MICE HE HAS PROVED CONCLUSIVELY THAT WAR DOES NOT CAUSE CANCER. THE TESTS INCLUDED SHOOTING AT THE MICE WITH A WATER PISTOL FILLED WITH CARROT JUICE EVERY DAY FOR 25 YEARS. PROF. MURRAY SAID THAT ALTHOUGH THE MICE BECAME QUITE TESTY AND TURNED ON HIM SEVERAL TIMES, NONE WAS A VICTIM OF CANCER. THE PROFESSOR DEDICATED HIS REPORT TO HIS 836 LAB ASSISTANTS WHO HAVE MYSTERIOUSLY DISAPPEARED OVER THE PAST 25 YEARS.

Your first reaction to this cartoon should have been to smile or chuckle; if it wasn't, the artist missed his aim. But let's hold it there for a moment: Why is the cartoon funny? The drawing is clearly nonsense. But is that *why* it's funny? Reflection will show that it is not. The thing is funny because it's satirical. It pokes fun at the hundreds of newspaper reports of scientific research we have all read by adopting their solemn tone while reporting a ridiculous content.

But no matter how absurd the content, the method of experimentation is not ridiculous. In fact, the humor of the cartoon depends on the contrast between the silly content and the sensible method. That method is the scientific method in research, and it is the subject of this chapter.

Let's go back a moment and see what the drawing actually says. A professor announces an important conclusion based on years of research: war does not cause cancer. The tests used to reach the conclusion are briefly described along with their unforeseen side effect. Those few sentences of text in the cartoon contain or imply the five major steps in the scientific method.

1. We can presume that since the fictitious Professor Murray carried on his work with the juice-soaked mice for twenty-five years he had some *plan* in it. It is unlikely that a quarter century would be devoted to so unusual a project without a great deal of forethought.

2. We may infer from the report of the tests that the professor was operating from a *research design;* his operations were planned in such a way as to permit him to draw a conclusion from them. Shooting at mice with a juice-filled water pistol *is* some kind of model of war, however ridiculous.

3. The report does not describe the method, but *data gathering,* collecting of information, did take place. Observations of various tests and their apparent results were recorded in some fashion for twenty-five years.

4. We also have to infer that there was some kind of *data analysis.*

5. And finally, the results of the research are *interpreted* for us: war does not cause cancer.

What has been described here in this light-hearted way are *the five steps in the research process.* These steps and this process are what apply the methods of science described in Chapter

1 to the process of making observations of a scientific character.

You will recall from the preceding chapter that science is a way of gathering evidence of an observational kind. The kind of knowledge that is called "scientific" is knowledge based on observation of the world. You will also remember that science is one way of thinking or knowing, that it involves a special logic of its own. This logic includes the ability to examine the evidence on both, or several, sides of a particular issue and the ability to think about that evidence clearly and carefully. Thus, to understand the way scientific methods are applied in a particular field, we have to understand that the "scientific method" refers not only to *ways* of doing things (such as the proper way to conduct an experiment), but also to the ideas behind what is done, the reasons that they are done that way. To put it another way, mechanically following a certain pattern for conducting an experiment will not guarantee its success. The pattern is adopted for a reason, and the reason has to do with the logic of what you are trying to discover. The experiment will not work if the pattern is right and the logic of its application is wrong.

What this chapter is about, then, is the ways that sociologists apply the scientific method in their research work and the reasons why they adopt the particular techniques they do. The five steps in the research process outlined above are the same in any field that uses the scientific method, but what one does in order to accomplish each of the steps varies from field to field. The object remains the same in every case: to produce sound observational data (evidence) with which our knowledge of the world may be first tested and then expanded.

The research methods described in the following pages are those that have been used to produce the information on which the rest of this book is based. In most cases, the authors of the chapters do not describe in any detail the actual research that led to the conclusions—the facts and ideas—they tell you about. To get at them, you will have to go to the works cited in the notes. The purpose of this book is to tell you what sociology is about and what it knows about what it is about, not how it knows that it knows it. But behind the conclusions and generalizations and facts you will be reading lies investigation of the types described in this chapter.

Planning for Research

As we have seen, the research process consists of five steps: (1) planning, (2) research design, (3) data gathering, (4) data analysis, and (5) interpretation of results. The last four all flow from the initial stage, planning the research.

The Role of Planning

Seasoned social researchers are often asked to help "make sense" out of some information another person has collected. Typically, the investigator, let us call him Morris, says something like this: "I have just completed interviewing 112 people to determine their attitudes toward income equality between the sexes, and now I need help to figure out what all of these facts mean. What do I do next?" The standard reply to that question is, "Probably you will have to start over." Even though in some cases such a judgment may be flippant or harsh, often it is all too appropriate. The justification for assuming that the investigator probably has made a mess of it rests on a lesson confirmed repeatedly in the experience of social researchers. Useful, meaningful, and defensible social research should be *planned* carefully in every respect, including what to do with the information after it has been gathered. If a person fails to think ahead in detail and does not know until the information is in hand what to do with it, the chances are very good that he has made uncorrectable errors. Such errors frequently stem from the way the information was gathered in the first place.

The Hypothesis and Preliminary Planning

How does the researcher begin to plan? Recall our fictitious amateur investigator Morris and his decision to study attitudes toward income equality between the sexes. Had he observed that some of the young (or old) people he knows favor (or oppose) income equality? Did he believe a study of attitudes might assist (or retard) movement toward income equality? Did he wish to test an *hypothesis,* an idea he believes or guesses to be true but that is not yet proven, about why some people favor or oppose income equality? These and many similar questions may have led to the decision to study income equality between the sexes. It is such initial questions that pose the *problems* to be solved through research and provide the basis for the development of a research plan.

Let us suppose that Morris has started with an idea or "hunch"—an hypothesis—that there is a connection between a person's income and the probability that that person will favor income equality between the sexes. Perhaps Morris has noticed, for example, that people with higher incomes seem generally to be in favor of income equality, while those with lower incomes seem generally to oppose such equality. He may have reasoned as follows: the higher one's income, the more likely it is one will believe that women are physically and mentally capable of performing any job a man can perform and that women, therefore, should receive equal pay for equal work. Whether this is true he can discover by interviewing people.

At some point near this stage in the process, the investigator will usually consult the research literature on his topic to see what others have done and found out. He may find in the course of this research that the question he is interested in has already been answered to his satisfaction. But even if that is not the case, he will need to know what *is* already known, and how it was discovered, in order to avoid duplication of effort and errors that others may have made in *their* investigations. He may also acquire some ideas for his own research strategy in this way.

The Role of Theory

It is at this point that *theory* plays an important role in the research process. Ideally, an experimenter does not set out simply to find how certain things are interconnected. He begins with an hypothesis about *how* and *why* some specific factors relate to some other specific factors. The hypothesis may have originated as the experimenter's own hunch or idea, as in the case of Morris, or it may have arisen as a product of previous research or theorizing by the experimenter or other scholars. In either case, it is here that the reasoning of the sociologist (or anyone working within the framework of science) departs conspicuously from common sense.

In commonsense thought, "theory" is often regarded as inferior, or even opposed, to "fact." At the least, it is commonly believed that theories merely fall down before or are corrected by fact; at the best, that they are vague statements of possible truth. But among scientists generally, theory is considered to be an essential guide to the discovery of meaningful facts. Whether one wishes to manipulate a factor, control it, leave it free to vary, or exclude it from the study depends completely on the theory of the investigator.

Theory is a body of linked generalizations based on tested observations (facts) that, taken together, explain or account for some major chunk of reality. Theories are usually too abstract or too general to be tested directly. Rather, one works on an "if-then" sequence of deductive logic: If energy is matter, as implied by Einstein's theory of relativity, then light should be affected by gravity like any other energy/matter. Thus we could test this idea by seeing what happens to a particular beam of light when it passes through a particular gravitational field.

In the sociological case described earlier, our investigator Morris, who already has a hypothesis about the way in which the world works, might sift the theoretical literature in order to find possible explanations for the association he thinks he has found. There may well be more than one. A given fact might have a number of possible explanations. Particularly in such a case, the experimenter would have to design his research to determine not only what the facts about his hunch are, but the reasons they are that way—that is, which of the possible explanations for them is the proper one. In this process, theory precedes, assists in the discovery of, and gives meaning to facts. Hence, while theories must be submitted to the test of facts and modified by them, it is pointless to gather various pieces of information without having a theory to organize and direct the search for them. As an old scientific saying has it, theory without fact is meaningless; fact without theory is mute.

Operational Definitions

Let us now imagine that, knowing what he wants to know and why he wants to know it (that is, what it will mean if he finds it out), Morris conducts the interviews. He gathers data from the study participants on both their annual incomes and their attitudes toward sexual equality by using the following written questions: Please indicate your approximate annual income by placing a check mark in the appropriate blank: under $2,000 _____; $2,000–$4,000 _____; $4,000–$8,000 _____; $8,000–$12,000 _____; $12,000–$18,000 _____; $18,000–$24,000 _____; $24,000 and over _____. Do you favor sexual equality? Definitely yes _____; yes _____; uncertain _____; no _____; definitely no _____.

After each participant in the study has provided the requested information, Morris is ready to test the hypothesis that incomes and favorable attitudes toward income equality are related. Or is he? You may have noticed already some of the difficulties that could be encountered. For instance, if a person places a check mark to indicate an income between $4,000 and $8,000, this could mean his income is exactly $8,000. But if a person places a check mark to indicate the income range labeled $8,000–$12,000, his income also could be exactly $8,000! In other words, a person having an annual income of $8,000 could *correctly* check either of the two blanks in question. This problem arises because the categories $4,000–$8,000 and $8,000–$12,000 overlap. It may be solved by changing the limits of either category. For example, the first category may be restated as $4,000–$7,999. All of the other categories in the series could be changed similarly so that no category would overlap with another. All categories would then be *mutually exclusive*.

Also troublesome is the fact that the income ranges shown are of different sizes. The range $2,000–$4,000 is half as large as the range $4,000–$8,000. If a person marked the former category, we probably would assume his income to be near the middle of the range (approximately $3,000) since we would not know his exact income; and if a person marked the latter category, we probably would assume an income of approximately $6,000. In the first case, our assumption could not be in error by more than $1,000, but in the second case we could be wrong by as much as $2,000. Finally, in regard to income, the highest range indicated—

> **operational definition:** a definition constructed in terms of the specific operations to be used in measuring or otherwise categorizing that which is defined. For example, "Temperature is what a thermometer measures." An operational definition of a chocolate cake would be the recipe for it.

$24,000 and over—does not even permit a plausible assumption concerning the midpoint of the range.

If we turn our attention to the question concerning sexual equality, we find an important flaw there too. Our investigator's interest is in *income* equality between the sexes, but the question as written refers only to sexual equality. Although many people no doubt would assume correctly that income equality was at issue, others might have in mind equality before the law or equality in performing household duties. For these reasons, many people who favor or oppose income equality might mark "uncertain."

We see then that the basic information needed to test the idea behind the study may be seriously questioned from a purely technical standpoint. Fortunately, mistakes of this kind may easily be avoided in the planning stage of a study. But, usually, once such mistakes have been made, the study is beyond repair.

Each of the mistakes described above shows the importance of stating a general idea in terms of the *specific operations* to be undertaken in the analysis stage of a study. These specific operations give a particular meaning to terms such as income and equality. Such particular meanings are referred to as **operational definitions**.

Alternative Explanations

What if Morris has avoided the errors mentioned above and possesses reasonably accurate information on incomes and opinions of income equality? Suppose further that the evidence strongly supports his hypothesis of a connection between income levels and opinions concerning income equality: that those with high incomes in general favor income equality between the sexes, while those with low incomes in general oppose income equality. May we now assume that Morris's reasoning is correct and that those who have high incomes are more likely to agree that women are capable of performing any job a man can perform? No, we may not. Why? Because, among other things, Morris may have reached the right conclusion for the wrong reason. The idea that income levels and opinions concerning income equality are "linked" through the belief that women can perform any job has, to this point, not been demonstrated and may be untrue.

We now want to know whether Morris has gathered information bearing on this essential point. If not, even accurate income and opinion information would be insufficient to support the suggested line of reasoning. The findings as they stand would show only that the argument *may* be correct.

But let us press the matter one step further. If Morris has foreseen the importance of having information showing directly the views the study participants hold on women workers, and if this "linking" or explanatory information also shows—as expected—that those with high incomes agree that women are as capable as men and that there should be income equality between the sexes, the argument would be strengthened but not concluded. To achieve a satisfactory argument, Morris also would need to rule out some of the most important *alternative explanations* that might be offered to account for the income-opinion connection.

You may already have considered some alternative possibilities. To suggest only one plausible example, may it not be true that those possessing high incomes also have gained more years of formal schooling and are *for that reason* more likely to favor income equality? Morris almost certainly would need to consider this possibility *in advance of the study* and be prepared to examine the study results in terms of this line of reasoning. Both the "equal-capability hypothesis," as we may now refer to Morris's original idea, and the "formal-schooling hypothesis," as we may label the idea just suggested, may "explain" or "account for" the fact that incomes are directly related to opinions concerning income equality between the sexes. Each of these two explanations (as well as

some others you may think of) serve to link incomes and opinions. Each attempts to explain *why* the observed relation or connection exists.

Causal Inference and Elaboration

To see clearly how either explanation could work, we have to make **causal inferences,** that is, we must determine the cause-and-effect relationship between the different factors we have observed. A moment's reflection will reveal that the two proposed explanations almost certainly serve in different ways to connect incomes and opinions. It is plausible to argue that as people's incomes go up, they have more opportunities to observe capable women at work and that these experiences lead to or "cause" the belief that women are as capable as men, and thus also the opinion that they are entitled to receive equal pay for the same work. This argument is depicted in Figure 2-1.

The arrows in Figure 2-1 show the direction of causal influence. Each square represents a **variable,** a condition or characteristic that can exist in different states or amounts. In this case, the explanatory factor (the belief) is an **intervening variable,** a variable that interferes between other variables to alter their relationship. The belief that women are as capable as men has come between the **independent variable** (the factor "causing" the differing beliefs about the capability of women) and the **dependent variable** (the opinion concerning equal pay). The independent variable is the factor manipulated in an experiment to see how it influences other factors; the dependent variable is the factor allowed to vary. The assumption is that variation in the dependent factor is *dependent on* the independent factor.

The investigator in this example is engaged in a process of thinking called **elaboration**. Through this process, we may consider the relationship of any two variables (such as income and opinion) in the light of some third variable (such as a belief in equal capability). As we shall see, a careful elaboration is of critical importance in the effort to understand the causes of social behavior.

The particular sequence outlined in Figure 2-1 is not as plausible in regard to years of schooling—at least not when we consider only a single genera-

New Yorker, January 28, 1974. Drawing by Dedini; © 1974 The New Yorker Magazine, Inc.

Elaboration.

causal inference: the logical operation of assigning a cause-and-effect relationship to an observed set of events.

variable: a quality, condition, or value that may vary, or exist in different states or amounts. Examples are age, income, height, gender, and so forth. Variables are of concern in science because different degrees or qualities in one phenomenon are often associated with variations in others. Human males, for instance are usually taller and heavier than human females; or, to take a social example, sales of ice cream by street vendors are likely to vary with the temperature.

intervening variable: a variable that intervenes between (interferes with) the independent and the dependent variables and alters their relationship. For example, there is a correlation between gender and weight (males tend to be heavier than females), but age represents an intervening variable—adult females are heavier than infant males.

independent variable: the variable manipulated in order to determine its influence on other (dependent) variables.

dependent variable: the variable permitted to vary (not manipulated) in order to determine whether it is influenced by another (independent) variable.

elaboration: the process of testing the effect upon a relationship between two variables of the introduction of a third.

tion. Within a given generation, an increase in a person's years of formal schooling presumably leads to *both* an increase in income and various changes in the way one views social issues. Our elaboration in this case places the explanatory or "antecedent" variable (education) *before* both the variable we have treated as independent (income) and the variable we have treated as dependent (opinion). It also excludes entirely the intervening variable (belief). An analysis along these lines might show that we do not need to know a person's income level or the extent to which he believes women are as capable as men in order to understand differing opinions of income equality between the sexes.

The main point to be stressed here is that one must think ahead during the planning stage of a particular study and consider the specific elaborations to be tested. Certain information will be needed to establish whether connections exist between particular variables. Additional information will be needed to examine some of the main competing explanations of the connections that are discovered.

Figure 2-1
The logic of causal inference

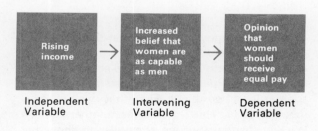

Rising income	Increased belief that women are as capable as men	Opinion that women should receive equal pay
Independent Variable	Intervening Variable	Dependent Variable

Research Design

The term *research design* refers to the process of planning an entire study so that specific elaborations may be tested. It requires that you know what you wish to know in advance, gather the proper data to find it out, and get the data *in the form* that will permit specific critical tests. You must, in other words, foresee the elaborations that will be required before gathering the data in order to insure that the data are obtained in the proper form to permit the tests to be conducted. In the case we have been considering, Morris's research design should have permitted him to foresee that there might be a relation between high income and years of schooling that would lead people with those characteristics to favor income equality between the sexes; and consequently, he should have prepared some test to tease out that relationship if it existed.

The logically most powerful research design known to science is the classical experiment, and many investigations, particularly in the physical sciences, are constructed along its lines. Other types are laboratory social experiments and experiments done outside the laboratory. Any of these may raise issues of ethics in sociology, because social research is conducted with human beings, and we will address this issue in the course of our discussion.

The Classical Experiment

The most stringent model of clear thinking is the *classical laboratory experiment* of the physical or biological scientist. By studying a subject through the classical experiment, scientists try to accomplish at least two things. First, they wish to show that as one variable (X) changes, another variable (Y) also changes. Second, they wish to show that only changes in X bring about changes in Y. These points are illustrated in Figure 2-2. By using the classical experiment, scientists can *manipulate* the presumed "causal" factor X to see what effect, if any, is produced in Y. They also are able to *control* all of the other factors they believe may influence Y and, therefore, to rule out certain alternative expla-

nations of any changes that occur in Y.

The reason for the great logical power of the classical experiment is the possibilities it offers for *control* of experimental variables. This rigid control also permits *precise measurement,* another very important feature in research. Consider a simple example from the field of botany. Suppose that we wish to determine the effect of a certain chemical on plant growth. We could begin with sterile soil samples of known, identical mineral content and plant in two such samples seeds selected at random from the same parent plant. We could then add to the soil in one sample a measured amount of the chemical in question, withholding it from the other, and subject the two to identical growing conditions of light, water, and so forth. Under these conditions, it would be fair to conclude that any marked variation in growth between the two samples was due to the presence or absence of the chemical, and the plants' growth could be precisely measured. Various elaborations are also possible; we could test many paired samples under varying growth conditions and with varying amounts of the chemical. Conclusions based on classical experiments of this kind have logically convincing results.

Obviously, there are many obstacles to direct use of classical experiments in the social sciences. Some of these obstacles are essentially technical in nature. It is often very difficult, if not impossible, for the social researcher actually to alter a social condition to see what effect the alteration would have. Even if such alteration is possible, it may be impossible to *prove* that the subsequent effect is the consequence of the alteration made rather than the consequence of something else that also occurred. In short, the degree of control over experimental variables demanded by the classical experiment is usually impossible in social research. Very precise measurement is also a problem.

Some of the control and measurement problems may to some degree be solved through the use of laboratory social experiments (described later), but these raise the often unanswerable problem of how we can be sure that changes occurring in the laboratory—in artificial social situations—would also occur in real social life. More important, however, is the problem of the ethics of manipulating human subjects in the ways required by the classical experiment.

The Ethics of Social Research

As indicated above, the great power of the classical experiment is its high degree of control over its variables and experimental conditions. But to exercise such control over human beings, while sometimes possible in social research, would often be dangerous, frightening, or in other ways harmful to the subjects. We could imagine, for example, an experiment concerning political opinions where a group of people might be isolated for a long time and subjected to massive doses of propaganda in order to influence their opinions. But the isolation would constitute unlawful imprisonment, and the influences might well be permanent. It would cleary be immoral to do such a thing. Such an experiment did in fact take place in 1950–1953, but it was not conducted by social scientists. It was performed on American prisoners of war by the Chinese Communist forces in Korea and was called brainwashing by the press. It was in violation of international conventions on the treatment of POWs, and some prisoners died as an indirect consequence of their treatment.

The general ethical issues of social research may be posed by such questions as the following: When the social scientist is able to manipulate human beings so as to produce known effects, how may the rights of the individuals affected be protected? If a planned social experiment seems likely to produce effects that some people might consider undesirable, who shall decide whether the experiment shall be conducted, and how shall the decision be made? In short, even if it were possible for social scientists to conduct classical experiments or something approximating them, under what conditions, if any, should such experiments be permitted?

Social scientists have come up with two kinds of answers to this last question, and the universities working together with the federal government have constructed another. In social science in general, the ethical issues posed by the degree of control demanded by the classical experiment have been solved by controlling or manipulating *data* rather than people. This was seen in the description of elaboration above. If you have data adequate in both kind and quantity, it is possible to exert statistical controls over it that approximate the

Figure 2-2
The logic of the classical experiment

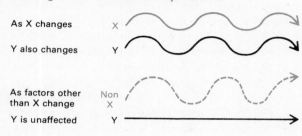

As X changes

Y also changes

As factors other than X change

Y is unaffected

Therefore, changes in X lead to or cause changes in Y

To a degree, the Chinese laboratory social experiment in political persuasion worked. Some of these American POWs in Korea stayed behind after the war, opting to go to China. (All but one have since returned to the U.S.)

controls of the laboratory. (If you suspect that race is a variable influencing public opinion on some matter, for example, you could control for race by separating your subjects' responses into those made by blacks and those made by whites and then inspect the results for each to see if they differed.)

A second social science response to the ethical issue has been to create within the professional associations, such as the American Sociological and Psychological Associations, codes of and committees on ethics. The codes tell investigators how they must conduct their research in order to safeguard the rights of subjects. The committees act as referees for questions about ethical practice.

Finally, in response to the federal government, universities now have, as a part of their institutional government, committees on the use of human subjects. All proposals for research that use human beings as subjects in any way must be referred to these committees for approval before the research may be conducted.

For both ethical and technical reasons, then, classical experiments are rarely, if ever, performed in the social sciences. But in designing their research, sociologists attempt to come as close as possible to the standards of the classical experiment. As a rule, the closest approximation to them is the laboratory social experiment.

The Laboratory Social Experiment

The *laboratory social experiment* is a modification of the classical experiment. In it, the social researcher applies as much of the logic and rigor of the classical experiment as possible given the difficulties and ethical problems involved in studying human behavior. The best way to see how this logic can be adapted for social research is to consider a specific example. Suppose we wish to study what influences people's opinions concerning the proposed construction of a nuclear power plant in their community. Specifically, we wish to determine whether a given advertising campaign will lead people to favor or oppose the construction of the plant.

Hypothesis We may imagine the following research steps: First, we list every factor that reasonably may be supposed to affect people's beliefs about the construction of the plant. This step im-

mediately requires us to hypothesize, to decide which factors are likely to be significant and why. This task, in turn, requires us to be familiar with existing theories and research findings that bear on the problem of opinion change. We may discover a hypothesis that people are most likely to be persuaded by arguments that appear to be unbiased. Or we may think that change in opinion depends on a "hard sell" based on people's fears about a possible nuclear accident. Or we may hypothesize that people are mainly influenced by information received from others whom they admire or respect. Some such hypothesis, and there are many possibilities, would form the basis of the study.

Sample Second, we select a **sample** of people to be studied. If the community where the nuclear power plant is to be built is small, the sample might include every adult in the community. At this point, we must carefully estimate just how much our actual research design will depart from the classical experiment and in what respects. For example, to approximate the classical experiment closely, we would need to enlist people for the study who are identical in all of the things important to the research (which is obviously impossible), and then to "expose" them to the advertising campaign while not allowing any other important factor to change (which is also impossible, of course). Since these things cannot be done, we must find *some practical substitutes for achieving experimental manipulation and control.*

A logical, though by no means simple, technique for approximating the control found in the classical experiment is to select two groups of people who have been "matched" for the presence of the indicated factors—perhaps such things as sex, age, level of education, income, type of occupation, depth of religious belief, and degree of faith in science. This matching may be achieved in two ways: One method is to find pairs of individuals who are similar or identical to each other in the ways that are important for the study; this is called **pair matching.** The other, and easier, way is to assure that as far as possible the important traits are represented equally in each of the two study groups; this is called **frequency distribution matching.**

In our example, we will use frequency distribution matching because pair matching is very difficult. Besides having equal representation of the factors listed above, our two groups should be equal in the extent to which they initially favor or oppose the construction of the plant. The more nearly the two groups are matched, of course, the greater the experimental control in the study.

Exposure In the third step of our procedure, we expose only one of the two matched groups—the *experimental group*—to the advertising campaign, while leaving the other group—the *control group*—entirely alone. This exposure, which approximates the experimental manipulation of the classical experiment, may be done in a laboratory to assure that no other influence is acting on the group at the time. We should also take steps to prevent members of the control group from receiving any information that might alter their opinions during the study period. Finally, we determine whether the opinions of those in the experimental group and the control group have changed after the exposure of the experimental group to the advertising campaign.

Suppose we find that the opinions of those in the experimental group have become, on the average, more or less favorable toward the construction of the power plant, while the control group has remained, on the average, at the same opinion level. This would be evidence that the advertising campaign had some effect on people's opinions about the power plant. We still might wonder exactly which aspects of the advertising campaign were influential. We also might wonder how deep or lasting the changes in opinion would turn out to be. For answers to these questions, other specific studies would be required.

Social Research outside the Laboratory

Most social research is conducted outside the laboratory. In nonlaboratory studies the gap between the design called for by the classical experiment and the design actually adopted is, understandably, much greater than in laboratory studies. For this reason, it is much more difficult to approximate the features of the classical design in nonlaboratory studies than in laboratory research. In most nonlaboratory situations, the main methods are two kinds of statistical control: **selection control** and **control by internal comparisons**. Selection

sample: in the statistical sense, some portion of what is being studied (usually a population) representative of the whole considered. A geological test boring is a sample, and so is the frosting you get by drawing your finger across the surface of a cake.

pair matching: the construction of control and experimental groups for study purposes by selecting pairs of units (such as people) matched on all qualities relevant to the question under study. One of each pair is then assigned to the experimental group and one to the control group.

frequency distribution matching: the construction of control and experimental groups for study purposes by insuring that the frequency with which any relevant variable appears in one group is matched in the other.

selection control: careful selection of the units to be studied to insure the best possible approximation of what is to be investigated; finding the purest possible examples of the phenomenon under investigation.

control by internal comparison: a form of elaboration that controls the *kinds* of comparisons made of data to insure comparability.

"Four years of research, and now you tell me you forgot which is the control group!"

G. Spitzer, APA Monitor, August 1971. Reprinted by permission.

control is control of the way people, organizations, communities, or other units of analysis are selected for study. Control by internal comparison is simply control of the kinds of comparisons that are made between types of data once the information has been gathered (for example, the comparison of data by race, mentioned earlier.)

Social researchers use each of these methods to compensate for the fact that they cannot directly control the different factors involved in their studies. Obviously, both types of control provide a weaker logical foundation for drawing conclusions than does the direct control of the classical experiment or the fairly precise control of the laboratory social experiment. Here we will consider how control is exercised in three basic types of nonlaboratory research: the natural experiment, the comparative historical study, and survey research.

The natural experiment A *natural experiment* involves studying an existing situation, something going on in the real world, that constitutes a test of some kind. To conduct a natural experiment, a sociologist might seek an existing situation in which two or more groups of people are similar in important respects but have undergone, or are about to undergo, different experiences. For example, suppose we hypothesize that exposing children to television raises the level of their feelings of anxiety. To test our idea, we might locate two similar communities that did not have television, one of which was soon to receive it. We could then compare the children in them both before and after television was introduced. Suppose that after one year elapses, we find that the children in the community *with* television have increased feelings of anxiety, while those in the other community do not.

Can we conclude that the introduction of television caused this difference? No, because other factors may have affected the change. The reason is that our selection control was not perfect: our communities were similar but not identical. Of course, the more similar our two communities, the more effective our selection control. But almost never can we find a natural study situation that exactly fits our requirements. Thus, we must rely also on the second method of control, internal comparisons of the information we have gathered.

There are probably several possible explanations for the difference in children's anxiety feelings and a number of internal comparisons of data we could undertake. To consider just one example, suppose we find that the community with television has a higher number of factory workers and that, during the study period, unemployment increased in an equal proportion among the factory workers within the two communities (an intervening variable). We might then decide to compare only the children of factory workers in the two communities to see whether feelings of anxiety have increased among those in the families of unemployed workers.

To do this, we would have to make an internal comparison of the data based on the employment status of the adults. Suppose we discovered that in *both* communities anxiety had increased among 70 percent of the children of the unemployed, while it had not increased at all among the children of the employed in either town? Such findings would argue that the introduction of television was not the cause of the increase in feelings of anxiety among the children. They would, however, support an alternative explanation. Since unemployment has increased in equal proportion among the factory workers in the two communities, and since there are more factory workers in the community with television, the overall increase in feelings of anxiety among the children in the community with television may be due to the larger *number* of families and children who are affected by unemployment in that community.

This explanation, however, leaves many questions unanswered. To suggest only a few: How *large* was the increase in feelings of anxiety among the children whose fathers were unemployed in the two communities? How many employed fathers in the community with television actually purchased television sets? Did anxiety increase more among the children of fathers who had been unemployed for longer periods of time? These and other questions could lead us to attempt to exert still more statistical control over our data by the method of internal comparison. Also, a detailed examination of the cases that did not fit a given explanation (called a deviant case analysis) could be an important source of new explanatory ideas.

The comparative historical study Some of the most influential sociological studies are *comparative historical studies,* studies using historical material as research data. These studies are far removed from the laboratory and from any possibility of direct control over the study materials. Nevertheless, the researcher attempts to exert as much control over the data as possible. Let us examine briefly how some of the ideas we have been discussing were used by Emile Durkheim in his classic work *Suicide* at the turn of the century.[1]

Durkheim examined information on suicides from several different countries, different regions of different countries, different periods of history, different religious groups, different times of the day and year, and so on. By focusing on differences in *rates* of suicides (such as the number of suicides per 100,000 people in a given group per year), he was able to investigate the factors related to variations in the occurrence of suicide among the different groups.

For example, many believe that people who commit suicide are mentally unbalanced. To examine this possibility, Durkheim reasoned as follows: if different groups of people—say, men and women or Protestants, Catholics, and Jews—show different *rates* of insanity, and if insanity is an important cause of suicide, then those groups having the higher rates of insanity also should have correspondingly higher rates of suicide. Even in this brief form of the argument, you will notice some of the elements of the logic we have been discussing. The researcher wishes to see whether the presence of one thing, such as maleness or Protestant belief, is regularly connected to another thing, in this case insanity. In this particular study, of course, he cannot alter experimentally the sex of different individuals or their religious beliefs in order to see whether such changes lead to suicide. Nor can he control experimentally all of the many other factors that might enter into and affect such a relationship. He can, though, compare different groups that are similar or different in theoretically important ways. If satisfactory information is available, the researcher can reach back into history or across national borders to discover groups that may be matched or may serve as experimental or control groups.

By proceeding in this way, Durkheim found that although mental illness was almost equally common among men and women, men were much more likely to commit suicide than women. He also found that although Jews were more likely to suffer mental illness than were Protestants and Catholics, they were less likely to commit suicide. From evidence of this type, Durkheim concluded that group differences in rates of mental illness could not adequately explain group differences in rates of suicide. In a similar fashion, Durkheim argued against the role of alcoholism, nationality, climate, and so on as causes of suicide.

If these and other nonsocial factors could not account for the group differences in suicide rates that are known to exist, then what could? Durkheim's answer, in greatly simplified form, is that different social environments exert different amounts and kinds of pressure on individuals within them. Protestants, for example, are freer of the control of the church than are Catholics; but one of the prices of the Protestants' increased freedom from group control is an increased probability of suicide. Similarly, when political or economic crises decrease the unity or cohesion of a society, individuals are under less pressure to conform to society's rules and are more likely to commit suicide. In short, in the Western world, the greater the degree to which an individual is integrated into intimate social groups, the lower the probability that he will commit suicide. Thus, the married commit suicide less frequently than the unmarried, and people kill themselves more frequently in peacetime than in wartime.

Survey research The most common type of sociological research is the *survey.* Surveys probably are already familiar to you in some form. The results of public opinion polls concerning the degree to which people favor or oppose some course of action taken by the President, or approve or disapprove of a particular policy, are reported frequently in newspapers and magazines. Business firms employ poll takers to discover how consumers are reacting to types of packaging or television commercials. Candidates for political office often commission polls to discover how well they are known or which issues are uppermost in the minds of the voters.

Three essential elements distinguish the survey from other forms of research. First, *paper-and-pencil instruments* of some kind are used, such as questionnaires, interviews, and **attitude scales** (checklists on which people's feelings about an issue may be indicated). Second, these are administered *in the field,* that is, in natural situations—homes, offices, street corners, and so forth. Third, *samples* of the population are questioned in order to obtain an estimate of the characteristics of the entire population concerned. The researcher goes to the people he wishes to study, selecting a sample of them in some way, and asks questions. The answers he obtains are assumed to be representative of the whole population his sample is drawn from. How he goes about this and how he may be sure that his assumption is correct are discussed in the following section on data gathering.

Although most political and business surveys are not undertaken by sociologists, the methods employed by different kinds of survey researchers have many points in common. An outstanding difference between the sociological survey and the types with which you may be more familiar is that the sociologist begins with an hypothesis and proceeds according to a theory. This means that the research must be able to accomplish more than simply to describe a situation, for instance, that among males over twenty-one, 37 percent prefer a blue soap wrapper, 24 percent prefer a green wrapper, and the remainder don't care. The sociologist studies the interrelationships among factors and chooses plausibly among competing explanations.

To see how the sociologist exerts control in survey research, consider briefly some research on health care behavior. Several studies have shown that mothers of high **socioeconomic status** are more likely to use preventive health care services for themselves and for their children than are mothers of low socioeconomic status.[2] To explore further the relationship between status and health care behavior, Bonnie Bullough reasoned as follows.[3] Since we know already that people of high socioeconomic status are more likely to use preventive health care services than people of low

socioeconomic status, it should be useful to study only those at one level or another to see whether people of the same level differ very much in the use of such services. If so, then some factor or factors besides the socioeconomic one must be involved. On the basis of this reasoning, Bullough decided to survey a sample of people living in three poverty neighborhoods in Los Angeles. By limiting the study to people of low socioeconomic status, Bullough attempted to exert selection control. By selecting only people who were likely to be similar in socioeconomic status, she hoped largely to eliminate socioeconomic status as an explanatory factor.

Sometimes, of course, a researcher may wish to be sure that the members of a survey sample will resemble one another in more than one way and will extend selection control at this point to include some additional factors. Bullough did exactly this. She restricted her sample further to include only mothers who had recently given birth to a baby. Thus she assured that the people in her sample not only were similar in socioeconomic status but also were of the same sex and would recently have needed to use certain preventive health care services.

So far we have concentrated on how Bullough designed her survey to locate influences other than socioeconomic status on preventive health care behavior. But what about socioeconomic status itself? Does restriction of the sample to poverty neighborhoods assure sufficient similarity of income? It narrows income differences, but rather large gaps in income remain. Some sample participants had monthly incomes greater than $900, while others had monthly incomes lower than $200. Are these remaining differences in socioeconomic status large enough to be a possible explanation of whatever differences may exist in preventive health care behavior?

The answer to this question in Bullough's study was yes. In other words, not only does the broad range of socioeconomic statuses to be found in most communities appear to influence preventive health care behavior, the much narrower range to be found within poverty neighborhoods also seems to have an effect. Whenever selection control has been only partially successful in removing the influence of a particular factor, the researcher may attempt to control the remaining influence of the factor by the method of internal comparison. Bullough accomplished this by dividing her sample into two groups, one above the poverty line established by the Social Security Administration and one below this line. She was then able to compare the health practices of the two different groups.

In these and similar ways, Bullough was able to select and continue to refine her sample population. By doing this, she was able to establish that poverty and lack of education did contribute to neglect of preventive care, but that the effects of these factors were reinforced by "the culture of poverty," which includes feelings of powerlessness, hopelessness, and social isolation—what sociologists often call alienation, following Marx's usage. Bullough also found that identification as a black or Chicano contributed to alienation. The form of preventive health care most affected by alienation was family planning activity, although all others except dental care (which was largely related to income) were also affected.

Data Gathering

Once a social researcher has clearly formulated his research design, he must decide how to gather the information called for by that design. In fact, the researcher needs to give some attention in the planning process itself to the different ways of gathering data. Whether it is possible to gather some information at all and whether certain information can be gathered more readily in one way than in another will have some influence on the development of the research plan. Some artificiality in our distinction between research design and data gathering now becomes apparent. But it is nevertheless true that the researcher ideally considers first what information he needs and then alternative ways of obtaining it. If only certain methods of data gathering are feasible, the researcher may have to modify his design to accommodate them. But he will attempt to choose the method that alters it least.

The primary methods of data gathering are direct observation, participant observation, surveys, and secondary sources. Secondary sources are existing records, such as vital statistics or the U.S. Census,

attitude scale: a device used in questionnaires and interviews to measure the degree to which a respondent holds a given attitude toward something. Attitude scales commonly state an attitude or preference, such as "I think we ought to bomb Sardinia back to the Stone Age," and then ask the respondent to indicate the degree to which he agrees or disagrees with the stated opinion.

socioeconomic status: one's "social standing" or position in society as related to wealth, income, and social class, the last of which tends to be determined by family lineage, education, religion, place of residence, and occupation. The term is often used in preference to *class* alone because many of the contributing factors listed above are interrelated.

Street corner surveying.

originally collected by someone else for different purposes. Methods that *create* the data to be studied in the course of gathering it, such as observation or surveys, are said to utilize primary sources. Each of these methods confronts general and sometimes special problems concerning the **validity, reliability,** and **representativeness** of the data that it may gather, and so we will consider these before describing specific data-gathering methods further.

Fundamental Problems: Validity, Reliability, and Representativeness

As just indicated, while any particular sociological data-gathering method may have special problems of its own, three are fundamental: *validity, reliability,* and *representativeness.* They represent problems in the nature of knowledge itself and thus span all methods of gathering information.

Validity The problem of *validity* is a matter of *truth.* If data are valid, they are true measures or statements; if they are invalid they are not. Empirical truth is known through comparison; we check the truth of one statement or measure by comparing it with the results of others already accepted as true. Validity, then, is a matter of agreement with already accepted knowledge. A commonsense validity-checking technique that all of us practice is that of comparing the reading of a measuring instrument, perhaps a bathroom scale, against a known quantity of the phenomenon to be measured, say a twenty-five-pound bag of dog food. If they agree, we conclude that the new scale gives a valid measure of weight, that it does, in fact, measure what it is supposed to be measuring. If it read "85 degrees Fahrenheit," we would conclude it was not a valid measure of weight.

Reliability The problem of reliability is a matter of *consistency.* If a measure or instrument gives consistent readings, it is said to be reliable; if its readings are inconsistent, it is not. Thus in the example just given above, a bathroom scale that did not give consistent readings would be considered worthless for the purpose for which it was intended. If you stepped on your scale fives times

in a row and got five different weight readings, you would not think much of the scale.

These matters are somewhat complicated by the fact that a given instrument, observation, or data set can be valid although unreliable, or reliable although invalid. Keeping to the example of the bathroom scale, you might weigh yourself five times in a row and get five identical readings, all of which were wrong—as measured by your doctor's office scale—by three and a half pounds. Your scale, then, would be reliable (it gives consistent results), but invalid. But a bathroom scale has built-in validity as a true measure of *weight.* It may be both wildly inaccurate and completely unreliable, but, no matter how badly it does it, it *does* measure weight.

If, however, you chose to weigh yourself by standing five times in a row on an unbreakable fever thermometer, you would get results which were reliable, but invalid. The five readings might be identical, but they would not be true measures of weight. Obviously for it to be of utility, a body of knowledge must have both qualities, validity and reliability, to a useful degree. (A bathroom scale need not be as accurate as a chemical balance for it to serve the purpose for which it is intended.)

Representativeness The problem of representativeness is a matter of *typicality.* If the data gathered by a particular method are typical of the larger population from which they were drawn, then the data are representative of that population. This makes it possible to generalize from the data you have to the whole reality from which it came. If the data are unrepresentative, or atypical, then all you can know is what you have in hand.

To return to our familiar bathroom scale: If you have established that *your* scale is both valid and reliable in its measurement of weight, this would not necessarily lead you to conclude that all bathroom scales were valid and reliable, or even that all scales of the same brand could be trusted. Bathroom scales are notoriously inaccurate. If a friend asked for a recommendation, you might well preface your praise by the reminder that you had experience only with this one example. You do not know, then, whether the scale you have is typical, whether it is representative of similar products.

Representativeness is an important criterion of knowledge because it permits generalization. If you know that your scale is typical of its particular brand, this permits you to say, "Brand X scales are accurate," which has greater logical scope than merely the statement that your own particular scale is accurate. Representativeness permits us to know more on the basis of less. We will return to this problem in some detail in the discussion of surveys.

Data-Gathering Techniques

As indicated earlier, there are four major methods with which sociological data are most commonly gathered: direct observation, participant observation, surveys, and the use of secondary sources. Each of the four methods creates unique problems of validity, reliability, and representativeness as a consequence of its own nature, and these will be noted in the following discussion.

Direct observation   The advantage of the trained sociological observer over any other person usually does not lie in the keenness of the sociologist's observations. Very few sociologists are trained—as was Sherlock Holmes—to reach nearly miraculous conclusions concerning the background, occupation, and hobbies of a person merely by glancing at his clothes, his posture, the signs of wear on his shoes, and the stain on his left forefinger. If we may presume that the great Holmes was trained to notice *everything,* we may say in contrast that the sociologist is trained to notice primarily those things that are indicated to be important by the hypothesis he is testing. He is trained to exclude from his vision many things that may be of interest to another observer. He is deliberately *selective* in his observation.

The first thing the sociologist who wants to gather data by direct observation must do is decide what to observe. Suppose a sociologist has the opportunity to observe, for purposes of his research study, a work group in a factory or a crowd of people who have assembled to protest a government action. Which group he chooses will depend on the question guiding the study. If the question is "Why do some groups have high morale and work

validity: a quality attributed to propositions or measures to the degree to which they conform to established knowledge or truth. An attitude scale is considered valid, for example, to the degree to which its results conform to other measures of possession of the attitude.

reliability: a quality attributed to propositions or measures to the degree to which they produce consistent results. An attitude scale is considered reliable, for example, to the degree to which the same respondents, or very similar respondents, receive the same or very similar scores upon repeated testing.

representativeness: a quality attributed to sample data when it is typical of the larger population from which it was drawn.

Direct observation is the traditional research method of the cultural anthropologist. Margaret Mead is shown among a group of the natives she is studying.

together cooperatively?'' the observer will probably prefer the factory work group to the crowd. But if the question is ''Why are some approaches to social change more effective than others?'' observing the crowd of protesters will probably be more instructive.

The process of selective observation does not end with deciding which group to observe. The next question is what specifically *about* a given group should be observed. The sociologist observing the factory group would have little interest in the relative strengths of two different building materials the workers were using. But he would be interested in observing matters that bear on his guiding question, such as the social positions (or *statuses*) represented in the group, the differences in honor (or *prestige*) accorded to various individuals, and the amount of control (or *authority*) exerted by different members of the group. While paying attention to these and related features of the situation, the observer would ''screen out'' many things of possible importance for some other purpose. (For example, the sociologist might not notice at all a number of physical conditions that would ''leap to the attention'' of an observing physician.)

Problems   In all cases of direct observation, the problems of validity, reliability, and representativeness are bound to crop up. To see how these problems present themselves, consider further our study of the factory work group. Suppose the observer has decided to count the number of times each worker gives an instruction or direction to any other worker during an eight-hour period. Suppose, too, that during the period of observation Worker A gives more instructions to Worker B, who, in turn, gives more instructions to Worker C. From such findings, the observer may conclude that Worker A has greater authority than Worker B, and that Worker B has greater authority than Worker C.

If it is true that the authority ranking of the three workers corresponds to the observer's conclusions, he may claim to have some evidence of the *validity* of his method. But this claim raises another question. How are we to establish that the observed authority ranking is in fact true? Occasionally an argument for the validity of a method may be

established in a direct way, but frequently such an argument must rest on indirect evidence. In the case of the work group, the answer is deceptively simple. Authority in any human organization is delegated to the people who occupy certain statuses—people with titles such as supervisor, technician, and mechanic. If the three titles just listed signify decreasing amounts of authority, and if the holders of these titles are, respectively, Worker A, Worker B, and Worker C, then there is a correspondence between the two authority rankings. Note that we have not yet *proven* that the method of counting the number of instructions is a valid measure of authority, but we do have some evidence in its favor.

For the sake of argument, assume that the counting method described above is valid. If the method is valid, then a proper application of it will lead one to discover the ''pecking order'' in a work group. But what happens if a valid method is hard to learn and can only be used correctly by a highly trained person? In a very active work group in which there is much moving about and in which many instructions are given, a poorly trained observer may have trouble recording the activities of the group and may make mistakes. If so, the counting method, though valid, might not be *reliable;* that is, it would not yield consistent results.

Social scientists have evolved several approaches to make methods more valid and reliable, both by cutting down the problems for the observer and by reducing the impact of the observer on those observed. To suggest only one, a researcher might observe a work group for a period of several weeks before beginning to record the observations as data in a study. At first, the workers would probably be quite conscious of the observer's presence and would behave in a number of artificial ways. But after awhile, they would probably begin to relax and pay less attention to the observer. At some point, the workers might begin to do certain things that were, strictly speaking, against the rules of the company—things they might not do if they were very concerned about the observer's presence. Finally, the observer might get to know some of the people in the group well enough to ask them if things changed when he left the room. If after several weeks the group seemed largely to ignore the observer, the observer might with some confidence begin to accept the information he was gathering as valid. Undoubtedly, though, many possible sources of bias still exist in this situation. The researcher must maintain a critical attitude toward the information being gathered.

Finally, there may be the problem of representativeness. Of course, if the researcher's only purpose is to find out about the particular work group he is observing, this problem would not arise. If, however, he hopes to generalize from his observations of this group to other similar groups, he will have to try to ascertain how his study group is, in fact, similar to others and how it is different. The differences will then have to be taken into account in any attempt at generalization.

The problem of representativeness is one that dogs many direct observation studies. In a strict sense, no phenomenon or event is ever *exactly* like another, and so any attempt to generalize from observation of only one event is dangerous. A common way of at least partially solving this problem is to observe and compare more than one example of the phenomenon under study. For instance, our researcher might study several different groups in the same plant, or similar groups in different plants, in order to find commonalities among them from which he could more safely generalize.

Participant observation   We cannot leave the subject of direct observation without mentioning projects in which the researcher becomes an active member of the group under study, simultaneously participating and observing. Studies conducted through such *participant observation* have the advantage of giving an "inside" view of the workings of a group. They usually are rich in character portrayal and show in a dynamic, detailed way the human side of group life. They have the disadvantage, however, of bringing into sharp focus problems of validity, reliability, and representativeness.

Problems   The role of participant observer involves many problems of method and ethics. To what extent should the researcher explain to those being studied the details of the research? If people know what the researcher is doing, will they alter their behavior or deliberately mislead him? When should the researcher actively question people and

Which person is the observer?

when should he simply wait for the questions to be answered in a natural way? If the researcher publishes his results, will the people who have trusted him be harmed?

Implied in these questions are important issues of reliability and validity. If the participating observer is known to *be* an observer by other group members, they may behave differently when he is present than they would do otherwise. Thus the validity of his findings may be compromised. And since he can never be certain that he is not being either deliberately or unconsciously misled, ascertaining validity is very difficult. Furthermore, the meaning of what he observes must necessarily be filtered through his own understanding of his experience in the situation, an understanding that might not be shared with a different observer. Thus, the reliability of his information is necessarily suspect. He may try to overcome some of these problems through such devices as secret tape recordings or photographs, but such practices raise ethical issues that cannot be ignored. And finally, of course, there are problems of representativeness similar to those posed in direct observation—how typical the group is of other, similar, groups.

Surveys   Like direct and participant observation, *survey research* gathers information directly from the individuals whose behavior it describes. But unlike them, survey research *asks people about* their attitudes or behavior instead of observing them directly. Going to the study population directly, at home, in the office or workplace, or approaching them through the mail, the survey researcher asks questions, and the answers he receives become his data.

The standard and most common techniques used for asking questions in survey research are interviews, questionnaires, and attitude scales. An interview is a prepared list of questions that an interviewer asks a subject in a face-to-face encounter, either remembering the answers or recording them in some way (see Figure 2-3). A questionnaire is also a prepared list of questions, but it is administered by giving the list to the respondent and asking him to fill it out in written form himself (see Figure 2-4). An attitude scale consists of a list of statements with several possible responses to each; the respondent is asked to reply by checking the answer that most closely indicates the strength of his agreement or disagreement with the statements. A good example of an attitude scale is the one Bullough used in her study of health care behavior to measure feelings of powerlessness; see Figure 2-5.

Both the face-to-face interview and the questionnaire often use attitude scales. They do so because scaling procedures offer several advantages. First, researchers have learned that many people are more willing and better able to respond to a particular subject if it is presented to them in several specific statements than if they are asked one very general question. The attitude scale breaks a complicated question into several more nearly definite parts. Another obvious advantage is that the researcher can assign numbers to different levels of intensity of attitudes. Using these numbers, the researcher can estimate the intensity of a given attitude held by a particular person in comparison to others who have responded to the same statements. Even though the numbers are not exact representations, they nonetheless facilitate the task of estimating the strength or weakness of a respondent's attitude.

Sample representativeness Like other data-gathering methods, the survey must confront the problems of validity, reliability, and representativeness. Representativeness, however, looms larger in survey research than in other methodological approaches, and so we give it special attention here.

Figure 2-3
Survey conducted through interviews by National Opinion Research Center

-2-   BEGIN DECK 01

We are faced with many problems in this country, none of which can be solved easily or inexpensively. I'm going to name some of these problems, and for each one I'd like you to tell me whether you think we're spending too much money on it, too little money, or about the right amount. First (READ ITEM A) . . . are we spending too much, too little, or about the right amount on (ITEM)? READ EACH ITEM; CODE ONE FOR EACH.

		Too much	Too little	About right	Don't know	
A.	Space exploration program	3	1	2	8	06/9
B.	Improving and protecting the environment	3	1	2	8	07/9
C.	Improving and protecting the nation's health	3	1	2	8	08/9
D.	Solving the problems of the big cities	3	1	2	8	09/9
E.	Halting the rising crime rate	3	1	2	8	10/9
F.	Dealing with drug addiction	3	1	2	8	11/9
G.	Improving the nation's education system	3	1	2	8	12/9
H.	Improving the conditions of Blacks	3	1	2	8	13/9
I.	The military, armaments and defense	3	1	2	8	14/9
J.	Foreign aid	3	1	2	8	15/9
K.	Welfare	3	1	2	8	16/9

The reason that representativeness is especially troublesome in surveys is that surveys study only *samples* of larger populations. But usually the purpose of survey research is to answer questions not just about the sample, but about the larger population from which it is drawn. The researcher wants to be able to *generalize* from his results. (Direct and participant observation studies usually focus on a complete unit of some kind, although they may be undertaken in the hope of generalization to larger populations.)

When trying to generalize from the results of a study of a sample, we have to deal with many problems of *sample representativeness*. If we assume that the data gathered are valid and reliable for the *sample* of people who were studied, how can we be sure that the conclusions reached are also correct for similar people who were not studied? If the sample studied does not properly represent some larger definable group, then any generalization based on the sample may be wrong or misleading.

Figure 2-4
Self-administered survey conducted by a U.S. Congressman

CONGRESSMAN TIM HALL'S 1976 QUESTIONNAIRE

	CONSTITUENT 1 YES NO	CONSTITUENT 2 YES NO
THE ECONOMY		
1. Do you consider unemployment a more serious economic problem than inflation?	☐ ☐	☐ ☐
2. Do you support Congressional efforts to reduce unemployment by providing public service jobs?	☐ ☐	☐ ☐
3. Should revenue sharing, a program which returns some $6 billion a year in federal taxes back to local and state government, be continued?	☐ ☐	☐ ☐
4. Do you support my efforts to increase the federal estate tax exemption from $60,000 to $200,000 in order to assist family farms and small business owners?	☐ ☐	☐ ☐
5. During the past year, has your family's standard of living . . .		
improved?	☐	☐
remained about the same?	☐	☐
declined?	☐	☐
FOREIGN POLICY		
6. Do you generally agree with the foreign policy being conducted by President Ford and Secretary Kissinger?	☐ ☐	☐ ☐
7. Do you think the U.S. should restore economic relations with Cuba?	☐ ☐	☐ ☐
8. Should the U.S. renegotiate our treaty with Panama?	☐ ☐	☐ ☐
9. Do you favor the resumption of military aid to Turkey?	☐ ☐	☐ ☐
10. Do you favor a larger Congressional role in foreign policy?	☐ ☐	☐ ☐
ENERGY AND ENVIRONMENT		
11. Which of the following action or actions do you favor to help reduce U.S. dependence on foreign oil?		
a) do you favor the construction of nuclear power plants?	☐ ☐	☐ ☐
b) do you support additional federal research in solar energy?	☐ ☐	☐ ☐
c) do you support deregulation of oil and gas prices?	☐ ☐	☐ ☐
12. Do you think the criticism leveled at the major oil companies has been justified?	☐ ☐	☐ ☐
13. Do you favor the break-up of the major oil companies?	☐ ☐	☐ ☐
CRIME		
14. Should persons convicted of crimes involving firearms receive mandatory prison sentences? ..	☐ ☐	☐ ☐
15. Do you support the reimposition of the death penalty for certain crimes?	☐ ☐	☐ ☐
16. Do you favor the decriminalization of the use of marijuana?	☐ ☐	☐ ☐
17. Do you favor the banning of cheap, small firearms, commonly called Saturday night specials? .	☐ ☐	☐ ☐
MISCELLANEOUS		
18. Do you support my efforts to keep the Postal Service from closing small rural post offices? ...	☐ ☐	☐ ☐
19. Do you support subsidizing the Postal Service from additional money from the general treasury?	☐ ☐	☐ ☐
20. Which of the following actions do you support in order to maintain the soundness of the social security system?		
a) increase social security taxes	☐ ☐	☐ ☐
b) provide funds from the general treasury	☐ ☐	☐ ☐
c) do not provide cost-of-living benefit increases	☐ ☐	☐ ☐
21. Do you support a national catastrophic health insurance system to cover extraordinary medical expenses?	☐ ☐	☐ ☐
22. Do you favor a Constitutional amendment restricting the Supreme Court's ruling on abortion? .	☐ ☐	☐ ☐
23. Do you approve of a federal/state grain inspection system in order to eliminate present abuses and fraud?	☐ ☐	☐ ☐

Other comments _____

_____

(please print) NAME _____ ADDRESS _____ CITY _____ ZIP _____

Figure 2-5
Bullough's hopelessness scale

1. Sometimes I feel that life is not worth living.
2. It is possible to get ahead if a person tries hard enough.
3. I have always been optimistic about my own future.
4. I think that education pays off in the long run.
5. I feel hopeful.
6. I do not think I will ever really be successful.
7. In spite of what some people say, the lot of the average man is getting worse.
8. It's hardly fair to bring children into the world with the way things look for the future.

strongly agree
agree
uncertain
disagree
strongly disagree

The respondent is asked to pick one of the five possible answers to each question, from strongly agree to strongly disagree. The responses are assigned numbers, five for strongly agree down to one for strongly disagree. Note that not all of the items are in the same direction—some are optimistic, some pessimistic in tone. If a respondent consistently indicated strong agreement with pessimistic items and strong disagreement with optimistic items, we would probably be quite safe in assuming that he truly did have hopeless feelings about life.

By way of example, consider some of the problems faced by a public opinion researcher who wishes to predict the outcome of a presidential election. The researcher knows on the basis of prior experience and the research literature that a person's stated preference for a presidential candidate depends on many factors, including age, sex, region of residence, race, ethnic group membership, religious affiliation, income, party membership, occupation, and education. It also depends to some extent on the way the question is asked and even on who asks it. The researcher's basic problem, then, is to select a sample of people that is small enough to make the study feasible and large enough to include people who will reflect accurately the impact of all of the different factors that affect an eligible voter's presidential preference.

One often impractical solution to this problem is to estimate as nearly as possible the total number of eligible voters in the nation who exhibit each of the essential traits, and then to select a sample so that each group is proportionately represented in it. In other words, if 51 percent of the eligible voters are females, then 51 percent of the sample would consist of females who are eligible voters; if 11 percent of the eligible voters are black, then 11 percent of the sample would consist of eligible voters who are black, and so on. In this manner the researcher would attempt to construct a sample that is a small replica of the population of eligible voters in the entire country. If he is successful, what is true of the sample will be true also of the population it represents.

The problem of representativeness cannot always be solved so neatly, however, because a researcher usually cannot find out readily which factors must be represented in a sample or in what

If a sample is not representative, erroneous conclusions may be drawn.

proportion each factor should appear. The main method social researchers use to obtain a representative sample when they are "flying blind," so to speak, is the **probability sample,** a sample drawn so that each individual in the population has the same statistical chance of being included.

The most widely known and used (but frequently misunderstood) type of probability sample is the **random sample.** News sources commonly report the results of small surveys of a supposedly "random" sample of people. In the vast majority of such surveys, the reporters select as participants people presumed to have some knowledge relating to the news event in question, or simply stand on a street corner and question whoever walks by. Usually, of course, reporters try to interview a "cross section" of the population—they question men as well as women, old people as well as young, upper class as well as lower.

But samples of those with special knowledge, those who happen to be walking by, or those who in commonsense terms seem to represent a cross section of the population, are not random samples. This confusion often occurs through failure to distinguish between "chance" (lack of deliberate selection) and statistical randomization. A sidewalk sample selected by chance by our hypothetical reporter might well be chosen without deliberate bias *on his part,* yet still be highly unrepresentative of the community as a whole. If he stands on Courthouse Square at 10:45 on Tuesday morning, his sample is likely to overrepresent lawyers and county government workers, the retired and, perhaps, the unemployed, while underrepresenting school-children, factory workers, and people like school-teachers. If he happens to choose a street leading from a factory at 5:15 in the afternoon, he would be likely to draw a very different group.

To draw a random sample or some other probability sample one must (1) define exactly which people constitute the population to be sampled—for instance, all of the people listed in a particular city directory; and (2) select people for inclusion in the sample by a procedure that gives each person an equal or known chance to be included. One way to approximate the condition that every person in the list will have an equal opportunity to be selected is (1) to number in order the names in the list, (2) to decide how large the final sample is to be, and (3) to use a table of random numbers or some other *mechanical* procedure to select the desired number of individuals. The third step is especially significant because ideally it eliminates the researcher's preferences or biases. You can easily see from an inspection of this suggested set of steps some of the reasons why most samples that are selected are "convenience" samples, rather than random or other probability samples. To achieve simple randomness is not always a simple matter.

Why attempt to achieve randomness in the first place if it is so difficult? When the news reporter claims to have interviewed a random sample of people, he is, in effect, attempting to persuade the audience that his report is "fair," not "stacked" to represent any particular viewpoint. As we have seen already, a sample is random when every person in the defined population has had an equal chance to enter. Such a sample is "fair" in the sense that the researcher has not deliberately excluded any opinion (or other relevant characteristic).

But even if a sample is fair in this sense, what assurance have we that it also is representative? Would it not be possible to draw a random sample that *by chance* gives a disproportionately heavy weighting to a particular viewpoint? The answer is yes. But, happily, the *probability* of drawing an unrepresentative sample by random means is known and, therefore, can act as a guide to the researcher's effort to determine what his results mean. The chance is comparatively small that one will randomly draw a highly unrepresentative sample.

Validity and reliability In surveys as in other data-gathering methods, it is important to assure validity and reliability. In the case of attitude scales, such as the powerlessness scale Bullough used, tests of validity might include inspection of the content of the statements used (face validity) and comparisons of a person's powerlessness score with some theoretically related item of behavior (criterion validity), for example, whether he is active politically.

The attempt to establish **face validity** is really a commonsense procedure. A statement such as

probability sample: a sample drawn in such a way that every unit in the population being sampled has the same statistical chance (probability) of being drawn.

random sample: a probability sample that insures each member of the population sampled an equal chance of being drawn through some essentially mechanical procedure: blind drawing, use of a table of random numbers, etc. The random sample is the simplest and most common form of probability sample.

face validity: an essentially commonsense test of validity; the assertion that "it makes sense" to believe that a given measure is valid for some specific reason.

"I'm taking an opinion poll on the Equal Rights Amendment. . . . Is the man of the house in?"

"Dunagin's People" by Ralph Dunagin. Courtesy of Field Newspaper Syndicate.

"When I make plans, I am almost certain I can make them work" appears to most people, "on its face," to refer to how confident or powerful a person feels. But if a person feels powerful, we may reason, then he should engage in some kinds of behavior that reflect that feeling. He might, for example, vote in all public elections and be active in an organization that attempts to influence public policy. Consequently, if most of those who appear to feel powerless on the basis of their agreement with the powerlessness statements act in ways that are consistent with those expressions of feeling, and if most of those who appear to feel powerful also act in ways that are consistent with *their* stated feelings, then we have some evidence—**criterion validity**—beyond face validity that the answers given are true and refer to real differences in the respondents' attitudes.

Similar kinds of reasoning are involved in discussions regarding reliability. To illustrate, consider a situation in which many of those who feel comparatively powerless, as judged by their answers to seven of the eight items in a scale, have tended to give answers to the eighth item indicating feelings of power. This contradiction may lead the researcher to reject the eighth item as being unreliable. Or he might measure feelings of powerlessness in a particular group at one time and then repeat the measurement at a later time to see whether his results are similar. If they are not, and if there is no compelling reason to believe an actual change has occurred in the attitudes of the study participants, then he might dismiss the scale as being unreliable.

This discussion has focused on the validity and reliability of attitude scales because such scales are often used in survey research and because validity and reliability problems arise most strongly with them, since they represent indirect measures of otherwise unobservable phenomena. The kinds of questions raised concerning scales, however, may also be raised with regard to interviews and questionnaires that do not use scaling. In all cases, these questions should be carefully considered in the planning process, so as to eliminate as many problems as possible. Knowing exactly what you wish to know, and the form in which you wish to know it, and what you will do with it when you have it, can avoid many errors.

Secondary sources In addition to gathering data by observational and survey techniques, social researchers often get their information from secondary sources, collections of information amassed by other people. These sources of information are often extremely important to sociologists. The U.S. Bureau of the Census, for instance, gathers enormous amounts of information that may constitute part or all of the data used in a social research project. Many other federal agencies such as the Bureau of Labor Statistics, the National Center for Health Statistics, and the Federal Bureau of Investigation, to name only three, gather and publish various kinds of valuable reports. The list of official sources may be extended to include the publications of numerous agencies of the United Nations, state and local agencies within the United States, and national agencies throughout the world. Many social research questions can be answered more easily by drawing on the resources of a library than by undertaking special field research.[4]

Problems In addition to the problems of validity, reliability, and representativeness that you may by now regard as normal, the use of secondary sources for data poses special dilemmas. A major one is that, while it is very convenient to have someone else gather your data for you—perhaps particularly when that "someone else" has resources like those of the United Nations or U.S. government to do the job—the data gathered may not be *exactly* what you would have collected for the problem you had in mind or may not be in the form your hypothesis requires. In such cases it is necessary to make do with what is available, sometimes even to the point of the presumption that the data represent what you wish they did.

A similar problem is that the researcher may not know the degree of reliability or validity of secondary source information. The U.S. Census, for example, is highly reliable, and its degrees and areas of unreliability are known. But the census of the USSR is much less accurate, and is sometimes altered by the Soviet government for political purposes. And some countries do not have a census at all or enumerate only urban areas, or their figures are so inaccurate as to be essentially worthless.

Representativeness may also be a problem. The uniform crime reports published by the FBI, for example, are the best general crime statistics available for the United States. But they emphasize the crimes of the lower class and underreport middle- and upper-class crime and are subject to local variability in reporting units.

Data Analysis

We can now turn to what one *does* with social research information after it has been collected. In a properly conducted study, the researcher will have planned much of this phase of the study before he prepares questionnaires or other data-gathering devices, and before he selects a sample and spends the time, energy, and money to get in touch with each person in the sample. Once the data have been gathered, many different techniques of analysis may be used. Some of the most useful are very simple and easily learned. One of these is the frequency count.

Frequency Counts

Suppose that a researcher is interested in people's opinions on elective (voluntary) abortion and that he has gathered some data on a small sample of people. Suppose also that a person who is most favorable toward elective abortion is given a score of 5, while one who is least favorable is given a score of 0. All those who are in between, of course, are scored 1, 2, 3, or 4, depending on how favorable they are. Now, the first question the researcher must try to answer is this: "How many people in the sample received opinion scores of 0, 1, 2, 3, 4, 5?" And all the researcher needs to do to answer this question is count the number of times each score was received. A convenient way to do this is to write down the six score numbers (0–5) and place tally marks beside them as he goes through his data. The total number of tally marks beside each score number is the **frequency count.** As we shall see, this simple procedure (which you probably already know) is an extremely useful tool of sociological analysis.

Grouping the data We seldom are satisfied to know how strongly a number of people hold a particular opinion. We usually wish, also, to know

---

criterion validity: the establishment of the validity of a measure by checking its results against those of another measure of the same phenomenon.

frequency count: a tabulation of the frequency with which an event or phenomenon appears.

range: statistically, the "spread" of scores or values in a distribution from lowest to highest; for example, "The range of ages in my family is from six months to thirty-eight years."

---

how different groups of people compare in regard to their views. For instance, suppose we wondered whether men or women are more favorable toward elective abortion. To learn this, we would first divide the sample into men and women. Then we would construct a separate frequency count for each sex, place the two counts side by side, and compare them. Since in our example there are six categories of opinion (0–5), this comparison may not show immediately whether men and women agree or disagree on elective abortion. For example, more men than women may have scores of 5, while more women than men may have scores of 4, and so on. And in many actual studies, the **range,** or spread, of the scores may be much greater than six. So it may not be easy to answer a research question merely by inspecting the frequency counts.

Under these circumstances, we may wish to *group the data* in more than one way. In addition to grouping the data according to sex, as suggested above, we may group it by opinion scores. To illustrate, we may consider scores of 0, 1, and 2 together to stand for an "unfavorable" opinion on elective abortion. In the same way, scores of 3, 4, and 5 may be grouped together as "favorable." By using these simple methods, we can construct a table like Table 2-1, labeling the rectangles with letters for convenience in referring to them. Note that Table 2-1, as it stands, shows no frequency counts. There are, instead, the four rectangles, called *cells,* waiting to be filled. How do we fill them?

Cross tabulation To put tally marks into the appropriate cells of the table, we first examine the information for each person in our sample, noting *both* the person's sex and the opinion score. These two characteristics may be represented by a *single* tally mark in one cell. If a woman has an opinion score of 3, we put one tally mark in cell b; a man with a score of 2 gets a mark in cell c. This procedure, called *cross tabulation,* is continued until each person's score has been examined.

We are now almost ready to answer the question "Do men and women agree concerning elective abortion?" Only two small steps remain. First, we count the tally marks in the cells of our table. Second, we express the resulting frequency counts as percents. If roughly the same percent of men and women are found in cells a and b (that is, are favorable), then the sexes agree on elective abortion. If there is a substantially higher (or lower) percent of the men in cell a than women in cell b, they disagree. In this case we may state the result by saying that there *is* an association, or **correlation,** between a person's sex and his opinion of elective abortion. That is, the two things are related in some way.

Elaboration   The discussion thus far has tried to show how one may combine the simple procedures of grouping data, cross tabulating, and counting frequencies to determine whether two variables are correlated. It is important to recognize that these same methods can be used to elaborate the analysis. For instance, suppose we find that women are more favorable toward elective abortion then men. Suppose, too, that we are uncertain about this finding. Could it not be true that the women in our sample are on the average younger than the men and that younger people are more favorable toward elective abortion? If so, our finding is perhaps a reflection of the fact that the men and women in our sample differ in age. To test this idea, we need only to construct two tables similar to Table 2-1—one for the men and one for the women. In each of these two tables, we would cross tabulate by noting simultaneously a person's age and opinion score (as before). If there is no difference between the opinions of older and younger people shown in the two tables, then we may assume age has little to do with the opinions on elective abortion.

The examples presented here are intended to

Table 2-1   Men's and women's opinions about elective abortion

Opinion	Men	Women	
Favorable (3, 4, 5)	a	b	
Unfavorable (0, 1, 2)	c	d	

show you how to use simple techniques to continue an analysis from one question to another and, thereby, to test a tentative conclusion. It is true, of course, that many methods of analyzing data are far more complex than those we have described. But the basic ideas underlying more sophisticated forms of data analysis are similar to those outlined here.

Unstructured Data and Content Analysis

We have emphasized thus far the kind of information that easily lends itself to counting and tabulation. These same tools may be used to assist in the analysis of data to which the usual numerical procedures are not easily applied. For instance, some researchers do not use highly structured interview or questionnaire forms, preferring instead simply to talk to people about different problems and to record the conversations in shorthand, in note form, or afterward from memory. Or sometimes a researcher may request permission to tape-record an entire conversation and then use the tape as a basis for an analysis.

These approaches have the obvious advantage of providing a more nearly complete record than the standard interview or questionnaire. They also sometimes create a greater sense of freedom and congeniality between the researcher and the study participants and, therefore, lead to richer and perhaps more candid study results. Some of the disadvantages of these approaches include longer and more expensive interviews, problems in gathering strictly comparable information from each study participant, and the sheer volume of information accumulated.

In any event, the processes of analysis suggested above can be adapted to help analyze the content of unstructured data. For example, the researcher may examine the notes or tape recordings for each participant to determine whether certain traits or characteristics are present or absent. Perhaps he is interested in whether people are concerned about the industrial pollution of a particular lake and has asked them to tell about some of the main problems of their community. If a person spontaneously mentions as a problem the fact that the Scrappo Corporation is dumping its wastes in Lake Lovely, then the researcher may tabulate this point. If a large number of people mention the same problem, the researcher may then attempt to decide which of the study participants feel strongly about this issue. Or he may wish to determine which participants who feel strongly are in favor of the existing practices and which oppose it. In this way the researcher may develop tabulations and cross tabulations by analyzing the content of the data.

Content analysis may also be applied to written materials other than those developed by the researcher himself, especially published materials.[5] The themes of popular novels, science fiction, and comic strips have all been subjected to content analysis by sociologists to determine what "messages" they carry in addition to their apparent content. One analysis found that the "Little Orphan Annie" comic strip had a bias against the poor and the nonwhite, reflected principally in the negative ways in which such people were portrayed.[6] According to another study, science fiction has a promilitary, pro-action, anti-intellectual bias.[7]

Interpretation

In our consideration of planning, design, data gathering, and data analysis and the relations between them (summarized in Table 2-2), we have mentioned certain critical problems relating to the interpretation of the results of a social study. We have noted several times the importance of considering more than a single explanation of any correlation that may be discovered and of determining, or at least of assessing plausibly, the sequence in which different factors affect one another. We have also implied that an interpretation may accept or question the validity of some information that has been gathered—a choice that may determine whether a conclusion is supported or overthrown. And we

> **correlation:** a numerical expression of the measured degree of association between two variables; specifically, the degree to which variation in one is associated with variation in the other. Correlation is expressed as varying between +1.00 and −1.00 and may be either *positive* (direct) or *negative* (inverse). For example, in almost any human population, there will be a positive, or direct, correlation between measured height and weight; as one goes up, so will the other. Similarly, after the age of, say, sixty, there is likely to be a negative, or inverse, correlation between age and amount of strenuous physical activity; as age goes up, the amount of strenuous activity goes down.

have touched upon the very important problem of estimating whether the findings of a particular study may apply to the larger population that is assumed to be represented by the sample chosen for study. We now amplify these points through a brief consideration of some common errors of interpretation.

Connections and Causes

Throughout this chapter, we have seen that the idea of a connection or correlation between events is basic to any analysis that aims to explain why or how things happen the way they do. We have raised several such questions in the course of the chapter. Why are some people more favorable toward equal income for men and women than others? How does television viewing affect children? Why do rates of suicide differ among groups? You will encounter many more questions of this type as you proceed through the remainder of this book.

The discovery of a correlation affords the starting point for an answer to our questions. But we must guard against the easy assumption that the existence of a correlation means that one of the factors is a *cause* of the other. To argue that a correlation represents a cause-and-effect relation, certain minimum standards must be met. For example, it is generally held that the "cause" must appear at an earlier time than the "effect." If a window is suddenly shattered, we try to find the cause in certain events that occurred before the window was broken. Similarly, if race "riots" occur in a city, we

Table 2-2   Some relations between research design and research methods in sociology

| Method | Type of Research Design | | | |
	Laboratory experiment	Natural experiment	Comparative historical study	Survey
How data are collected	Direct observation, interview, questionnaire, attitude scale	(1) Interview, questionnaire, attitude scales; (2) secondary sources; (3) participant observation; (4) content analysis	(1) Secondary sources; (2) interview, questionnaire, attitude scales; (3) participant observation; (4) content analysis	Interview, questionnaire, attitude scale
Where data are collected	Laboratory	On site	(1) Library (2) on site	On site
How data are selected	By a precise design	By closest possible approximation to precise design; sampling	By closest possible approximation to precise design; sampling	By sampling
Typical problems addressed	Individual and small group behavior, attitudes, attitude change	Social change, group behavior, disaster studies, community studies	Social change, social institutions (family, industry), modernization, revolution	Attitude and attitude change, politics, consumption, mass behavior
Level of possible control over variables	High	Low	Moderate to low	High to moderate
Means of control over variables	Selection and exclusion, control group(s)	Site selection, statistical case comparison	Case selection and comparison	Statistical comparison

search for causes in the events preceding the outburst. Mistakes made in the time ordering of events may result in errors of interpretation.

Suppose a person unfamiliar with the United States noticed that divorces occur very frequently among couples who recently have moved to the state of Nevada. He might conclude from this that moving to Nevada is a cause of marital discord and divorce. Anyone familiar with this situation would be able to explain that this correlation arises because people who wish divorces frequently move to Nevada (at least temporarily) to take advantage of that state's lenient divorce laws. In a case of this type, we would dismiss the argument that moving to Nevada causes divorces because it confuses the independent and dependent variables—the "cause" and the "effect." Clearly, in such an instance we cannot correctly interpret the correlation until we discover the true time sequence.

The classical experiment is omitted here, because it is virtually impossible in social research. However, whatever research methods sociologists choose, they attempt the closest possible approximation to the rigor and control of the classical experiment.

Once we are assured that the time sequence between correlated factors has been established, we still may wonder whether the earlier factor has any causal significance for the later one. For instance, roosters crow and *then* the sun rises; the leaves begin to fall and *then* winter comes. In order to show that an earlier factor is *genuinely* connected to a later factor, we must construct an explanation of the connection that outlines in detail how the first factor gives rise to the second. We would not, for example, be able to construct a satisfactory explanation to show that the crowing of the roosters causes the sun to rise. In the first place, we would not be able to trace the way in which the crowing leads to the sun's rising. In the second place, we would be able to show that the sun rises whether or not the roosters crow.

It is easy to see in the examples just given that the first of the two events probably is not causally connected to the second event. But in most of the questions of interest to sociologists, the matter is much more complicated. Does an increase in marital instability lead to increases in juvenile delinquency? Does an influx of black people lead to increased racial tension? Do economic depressions lead to an increase in alcoholism? The complex issues raised by such questions require the sociologist to exercise great caution in interpreting correlations, even when the time sequence has been reasonably well established. One of the most useful tools available in this effort is the method of elaboration discussed earlier.[8]

Types of Group Differences

Another error of interpretation arises because people often do not recognize the base of comparison on which a generalization rests. Consider the following statement: "Working-class people contract tuberculosis more frequently than do middle-class people." When confronted by such a generalization, we must wonder not only "Is it true?" but also "If it is true, in what sense is it true?" Suppose a person assumes the statement to mean nearly all working-class people contract tuberculosis and almost no middle-class people do. This is an extreme interpretation, to be sure, but it does not contradict the generalization. Another, more plausible, interpretation might be that although tuberculosis is no longer a common disease, it occurs somewhat more frequently among the working class than the middle class.

Obviously, interpretation would be easier if the generalization had been more specific in the first place. Regrettably, we are frequently faced with such unspecific generalizations and are left to wonder whether they rest on one type of *group comparison* (such as very large versus very small) or some other type (such as small versus smaller).

Some generalizations involve another type of group differences, *overlapping distributions*. An example is: "Women are shorter than men." In this particular case, we immediately recognize that the generalization refers to averages, not to all women and all men. We know that in large populations many women will be taller than the average man and many men will be shorter than the average woman. But many other kinds of group differences that tend to occur as overlapping distributions are not so easily understood, especially if the comparisons involve a possible implication of group superiority or inferiority. For example, such qualities as "intelligence" and "honesty" are of this form, but people sometimes do not interpret them in this way. Whether you are interpreting the findings of others concerning group differences or are presenting conclusions of your own, it is crucial to determine the type of group differences involved.

Lying with Statistics

One final problem of interpretation is that statistical presentations may inadvertently (if not deliberately) create false impressions. This, presumably, is what prompted Disraeli's famous statement: "There are three kinds of lies: lies, damned lies, and statistics." No doubt you already are familiar with many questionable statistical techniques used by some advertisers, political campaign managers, newspapers, and others who wish to persuade. For example, claims about percentage increases may be made in which no basis for comparison is given: "our product cleans 18 percent faster"; "save 30 percent." Or a reference may be made to a "U.S. government report" or a study by "an independent laboratory" that is intended to "prove" that Perfumo deodorant is superior to all other deodorants tested. But what if the report says that although there were small differences among the products, none of them was very good?

These and many other abuses of statistical data have been discussed in an instructive and entertaining book by Darrell Huff entitled *How to Lie with Statistics*.[9] Huff explains how newspapers may create the impression that there is a crime wave, how samples may be selected with particular biases, how graphs may be constructed to emphasize or deemphasize certain trends, how irrelevant information can be presented as if it were relevant, and so on.

Scholars, of course, are trained to do everything

How to Lie with Statistics

In the summer of 1976 a large American oil company published widely an advertisement illustrated by two pies. The uncut one was labeled *a monopoly*, and the other, cut into many pieces of various sizes, was labeled *not a monopoly*. The advertisement was a response to proposed federal legislation intended to prevent control by any single firm over the entire petroleum production process, from oil well to gasoline pump. This kind of control is common in the industry today.

The thrust of the ad was, "We're not a monopoly." Why not? Because, the reader was told, more than sixteen thousand companies in fact share a piece of the pie, and that could not be monopolistic.

But did the ad in fact tell us everything we need to know in order to understand the situation? Probably not. First, it referred only to U.S. oil companies. That leaves out of consideration several of the largest companies in the world, which do a large amount of business here but are owned elsewhere. Then it claimed that "not one *American* oil company accounts for more than 8½ percent of the oil *produced in this country*" (italics added) and concluded that no monopoly was possible. What about all the oil produced abroad but owned by these same firms? The volume that accounts for is a significant share of all of the oil consumed in the United States in 1976.

Finally, the ad leads us to believe that it is depicting more than sixteen thousand separate, independent firms. Is that true? Or are some of them, in fact, owned and controlled by others while being depicted as independent? We cannot answer that question from anything in the ad, and it might prove extremely difficult to answer at all. (It is sometimes a problem to both the Federal Trade Commission and the Internal Revenue Service as well.) We do, however, have one clue. Turn over any gasoline company credit card and see what other companies also honor the card. Some such arrangements are undoubtedly genuine trade-offs of service between independent firms for the sake of customer convenience. But are they all?

Do you think statistics like these tell the truth?

within their power to avoid presenting their findings in ways that intentionally invite misinterpretations, especially misinterpretations that are favorable to the argument they support. They are trained instead to interpret their findings with as little bias as is humanly possible. Nevertheless, even accurate and conscientious displays of numbers may be misinterpreted. A good example of this point is what Huff refers to as "The Well-Chosen Average."[10]

Practically everyone is familiar with some concept of an average. Frequent references are made to the "average person" or the "average family." Yet it is not always completely clear what is meant by such references. Perhaps we may safely assume that most of the time people have in mind the average that results when a series of numbers is added and the resulting sum is then divided by the total number of units in the series. This kind of average is called the **arithmetic mean** or, simply, the mean.

Suppose we wish to know the average income of families in the United States. The mean may be calculated by listing all of the pertinent incomes and dividing by the number of incomes. Now in a real sense no statistical "lie" has been told in this instance; but the resulting calculation, though perfectly correct, would include a number of extremely high incomes that would cause the average to be much higher than most of us might expect. To understand how extreme numbers, either high or low, may seem to "exaggerate" an arithmetic mean, consider the following simple example: (1) add the numbers 8, 8, 10, 14, and 40; (2) divide the resulting sum of 80 by 5; (3) notice that the average of 16 is larger than four of the five numbers on which it is based. In this way an arithmetic mean of incomes, though absolutely correct, may create the impression that more people earn the "average" amount than actually is the case.

A different kind of average, the **median,** is more serviceable in this particular respect. The median is the number that divides a series of numbers into two equal parts; half the numbers lie above the median and half below it. In our simple example above, the number 10 is the median because two numbers lie above it and two lie below it. Notice that the number 10, though no more "correct" an "average" than the number 16, may for the purpose of assessing incomes be more nearly representative of the series of numbers than the mean.

A third type of average refers to whatever is most frequent, common, or typical. A person might say in regard to incomes that "the average person earns less than $10,000 per year." Even if the mean and the median are above $10,000, the income that occurs most frequently—and therefore the one that many people will consider the "average"—may be lower than $10,000. The number that occurs most frequently in a series is called the **mode**. In the example above, the number 8 is the mode, because it occurs twice and the other numbers occur once each.

Thus, a person may select the mean, the median, or the mode—each a correct average—to represent a series of numbers. Whether one or another of these averages is to be preferred depends upon the researcher's purposes. Anybody who wishes to interpret correctly the resulting findings must be aware of the different emphases contained within these averages. Although the statistics may not lie, the interpreter may convert them into lies by "reading into" them a meaning that is unwarranted. In order to overcome this problem, researchers will often report more than one of the averages discussed here.

Summary

Sociology is an empirical field, which means it concerns the perceivable world and has as its subject matter phenomena derivable from observation rather than intuition, "common sense," or artistic inspiration. Because it is concerned with empirical matters, sociology has generally adopted the scientific method as its most powerful tool for investigation and has based its research process on scientific techniques. Thus the research methods sociologists use are extremely important in determining what they find out. And because of this critical influence of research methods (the questions you ask determine the answers you receive), the planning and design of a research study are as important as the way in which it is actually carried out.

Planning involves knowing beforehand not only exactly what you are going to do and how you are

going to do it, but also what you expect to find out and possible *alternative explanations* of the results. This includes consideration of how the data might be explained through the *logic of causal inference* and the process of *elaboration*. Only after completing this basic planning is the sociologist ready to construct the *research design* according to which the actual study will be conducted.

Research design is usually dictated by *theory;* that is, theory is appealed to for the purpose of defining problems to be studied and what would constitute appropriate answers for them. Then specific techniques of going about securing such answers can be developed. The most powerful of such techniques is the *classical experiment,* because it permits the investigator to know with high certainty whether or not his hypothesis is correct. But because of the ethical and technical problems involved in studying human behavior, it is rarely possible for sociologists to perform classical experiments. Instead, they must often resort to techniques that are logically less powerful (that is, less convincing), but that may still approximate some features of the classical experiment. These techniques include *laboratory social experiments, natural experiments, comparative historical studies,* and *survey research.*

Once the research has been planned and designed, the data called for by the design must be gathered. There are two basic types of *data gathering.* Data can be gathered from primary sources: such techniques include *participant* and *direct observation* and *survey* techniques such as *interviews, questionnaires, attitude scales.* Or data can be drawn from *secondary sources.* No matter how collected, however, data must be *valid, reliable,* and *representative* if sound conclusions are to be based on them. Wherever possible, statistical tests to determine the data's dependability in this regard should be conducted. When these are not possible, a convincing logical case for the data's validity, reliability, and representativeness must be made.

Once the data have been gathered, they will be subjected to *data analysis.* This process may involve very complicated statistical manipulation and the use of punched cards or computers. But at bottom, it is almost always a matter of *counting:* tabulation and cross tabulation through which different *variables* are organized and compared. For data derived from *unstructured interviews*—documents, diaries, and other published materials—a *content analysis* may be performed in order to turn such materials into quantifiable (countable) form.

It is only at this point, after the data of the study have been quantified and ordered through analysis, that the investigator is ready to make an *interpretation of the results. Connections* between different variables that have been established through cross tabulation must then be tested for causal relations to insure that every apparent link or connection is indeed the product of a *genuine correlation.* In addition, the interpreter must be wary of *improper comparison of group differences* and, even unintentionally, of *lying with statistics* by selecting those most favorable to the support of the research hypothesis.

Review Questions

1. What conditions in the classical experiment must be met in order to establish causality?

2. Does the natural experiment afford the researcher more or less control than that feasible in the classical experiment? Why?

3. List and explain different situations where a respondent might not choose to be truthful in answering an interviewer's questions or completing a questionnaire.

4. You are studying a particular behavior pattern and are interested in every resident in a given city as the population from which to draw your random sample. Would that city's telephone directory provide an adequate pool from which to draw? Why?

5. Discuss the advantages and disadvantages of the unstructured interview. When is this type of interview preferable over the highly structured setting? When is it less preferable?

Suggestions for Research

1. Explore the various types of classical experiments, with attention to different levels of control and types of conditioning—classical, instrumental, intermittent, etc. Show how the different types vary, indicating when each type is preferable. Include examples of well-known experiments, such as the Pavlov models. A good starting place for references is introductory psychology texts.

2. Using introductory texts and other material in statistics, learn to use a table of random numbers. Devise several problems for yourself making use of such a table. Draw your conclusions. Are you totally satisfied with the randomness of this procedure? Why? Show your classmates how to make use of these tables. You may want to consult with an instructor in statistics, possibly within your department of sociology.

3. Obtain an attitude scale(s) from an instructor of methodology in the department of sociology. Complete the questionnaire, and with the help of the instructor, interpret your responses. How well do you think the scale reflects your feelings or attitudes measured by the scale? How could it be better?

4. Your local newspapers are probably filled with articles based on sample surveys. Investigate several such articles in terms of the types of samples drawn. Are they true random samples? Why or why not? What measures, if any, have been taken to prevent bias? How effective do these measures appear to you? How could the methodology be improved? How valuable is the man-on-the-street sample survey? Do some types of samples appear to be appropriate only in certain situations?

5. The sociologist makes use of a variety of measures to study group differences. Some of those most familiar to you are the arithmetic mean, the median, and the mode. What different functions are served by these three measures of average? When is each particular measure most appropriate? Cite examples in your paper.

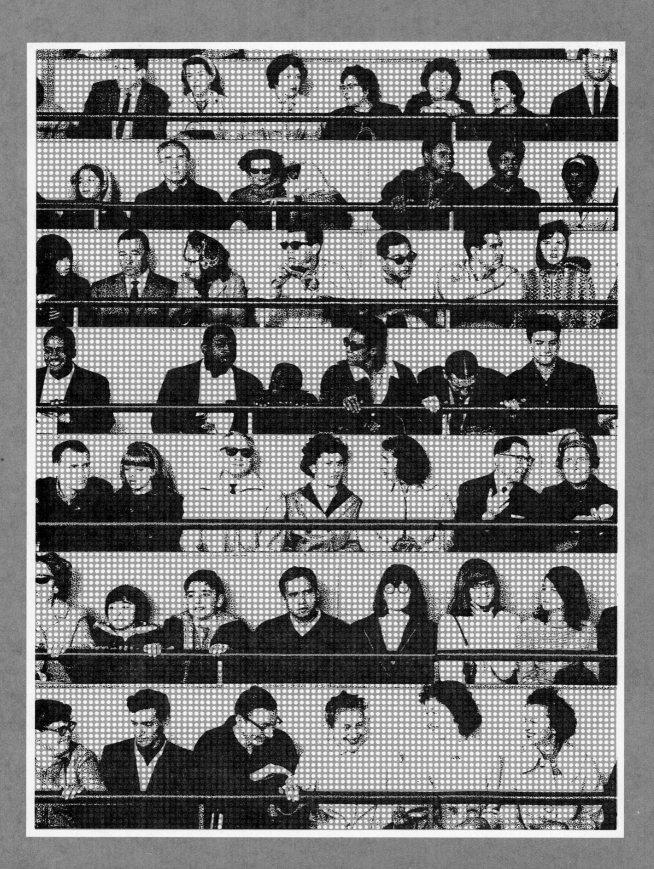

PART TWO
THE ORGANIZING CONCEPTS OF SOCIOLOGICAL ANALYSIS

In the following five chapters, we take up eleven fundamental sociological concepts, the basic mental tools with which sociologists perceive the world *sociologically*. The use of these ideas, in the ways in which the chapters explain, is what makes a given description or explanation of something *sociological* instead of psychological or economic or chemical. And any sociologist, doing any kind of sociological work, will find these tools required again and again, in the same way that any carpenter, no matter how sophisticated his collection of power tools, still reaches again and again for hammer, screwdriver, and ruler.

Chapter 3 discusses the concepts of *culture* and *society*, perhaps the most basic and irreducible of all sociological ideas. Chapter 4 deals with *socialization*, the social interaction process that produces the human *personality* and makes us what we are instead of something and someone else. You will find here that, although we think of ourselves as unique individuals, born the way we are now, in fact we are products—constructions—of social interaction between ourselves and other people; and when the interactions change, so do we.

Chapter 5 summarizes and previews another fundamental conception: *social organization*. This is the idea that people are *people,* instead of some kind of weak and hairless ape, because they are socially organized. Being organized, in fact, is a basic survival requirement, and is what leads to everything else: language, group behavior, society. It is the foundation upon which all *human* behavior rests.

Chapters 6 and 7 explore the various levels or categories of social organization, and how they interlink: *social roles* and *situations, groups* and *organizations, institutions* and *society.* These three chapters, 5-7, will be referred to again and again throughout the remainder of the book.

CHAPTER 3
CULTURE AND SOCIETY

There were 117 psychoanalysts on the Pan Am flight to Vienna and I'd been treated by at least six of them. And married a seventh. God knows it was a tribute either to the shrinks' ineptitude or my own glorious unanalyzability that I was now, if anything, more scared of flying than when I began my analytical adventures some thirteen years earlier.

Erica Jong, *Fear of Flying*

We finally got off the ground and, to my surprise, Paul turned to me and said, "You know, I've sat next to and closely watched many people while planes were taking off, and I've found that every single one of them was more or less nervous. Either they said they were, or they were visably tensed up, sweating, making unnecessary motions with their hands, or doing something else to reveal their anxiety. You're the very first person I've watched—and I've been observing you closely for the last few minutes—who has shown no signs of fear whatever. I can hardly believe it!"

Dr. Albert Ellis,
How to Master Your Fear of Flying

Strangely enough, there have been virtually no extensive surveys made on the subject of fear of flying. In all the traveling by air I do, however (about forty flights a year), I have yet to meet a passenger who would not admit to some nervousness, and I have talked to many who confess they are afraid even though they fly as often as I do. It is safe to say that all the comforting statistics in the world are not capable of reducing the element of fear to any appreciable extent. In other words, most people fly even though they are afraid.

Robert J. Serling,
Loud and Clear: The Book for People Who Are Afraid of Flying

Why does Erica Jong fly when doing so frightens her? Clearly she feels that she should be able to fly without fear—that there is something wrong with her for fearing flying. And the author of *How to Master Your Fear of Flying* agrees with her, for he has written a book that is mainly concerned with overcoming what he considers an irrational fear.

Does it seem sensible to you that so many people use a form of public transportation that is uncomfortable for them and for which there is no good alternative if they don't? For, in fact, Erica Jong has very few other choices that will serve her purpose, even if she is willing to take the time. What's going on? What values are so important that the personal comfort of millions of people is sacrificed?

"Time is money," "time is of the essence," "time flies," and we fly along with it. We tolerate many frustrations in order to "save time." So we "make time" in order to do what? To produce, to accomplish, to succeed. It doesn't matter much what we produce as long as we don't "waste" time. We even produce time-saving machines in order to do more producing, and the airplane is one of them.

People from other countries may view our activities with astonishment. To them a leisurely noonday meal or a conversation with a friend may be more important than getting the job done quickly. They may take pride in their work and do a good job, but they may not hurry at it. They have a different scale of values.

If you want to be a winner in the United States, you are expected to work hard and play hard. "Goofing off" is not rewarded unless you *work* at it. You will "climb the ladder of success," have "get up and go," be "well motivated"; but you most certainly won't "let time slip through your fingers." You will also fly if that is necessary to get you from Chicago to Los Angeles and back in three days in order to return to work on time.

So what are you going to do? Fly. Even if you can find a good train, you probably won't take the time to ride it, because over the years a lot of people have decided what you must do to be a winner. And all of us must follow along to some extent. Failing to do so can result in anything from discomfort to imprisonment. So if you want to do something rather innocent like take off for three hours every day at noon in order to relax, be prepared for an uneasy time. Most people around you will think your behavior self-indulgent, if not odd, and you may come to agree. After all, is it right to waste that much time when you could be doing something useful or kind? You'll never amount to anything that way. You could at least answer your phone.

But let's suppose you decide to run away to Mexico, where the pace of life is less hectic than in the United States. Well, it's a long drive from New York or Chicago, especially at fifty-five miles an hour, the train connections and accommodations are poor, and the ships are few. Anyone for a plane?

Introduction

The quotations above pose questions of interest on both a social and a psychological level. The answers to them, however, are likely to be framed in terms of the subject matter of this chapter, culture. True, a psychologist might explain why a *particular individual* chose to fly even though flying terrified him by talking about his individual needs for achievement or fears of rejection. But such psychological explanations can hardly account for the fact that *thousands* of people choose to fly, even when they prefer other forms of transportation.

Why do most people who prefer trains or boats not travel on them even when they are available? Usually not for psychological reasons, but because these forms of transportation "take too much time." And the use of the airplane and the accent on time saving it has permitted and encouraged have also meant that other forms of long-distance transportation (except the private car) are increasingly unavailable. Thus, we find that even if we have the time to take the train one way to San Francisco to attend the sociological convention, the Santa Fe no longer carries passengers. (And of course we could not take it back home, even if that were possible, because by then classes will have started and we could not afford the leisure of the three-day trip.)

What all of this points out, of course, is the interrelatedness, and the compelling quality, of human cultures. Because our industry and commerce operate most efficiently on a round-the-clock, mass-production basis, "time is (becomes) money." As a result, any procedure that "saves" time is likely to be adopted. Procedures judged to be "inefficient"—not time-saving—are likely to fall into disuse. And whether the individuals involved "like" that state of affairs or not, they are stuck with it because that is the way their world has come to work. Other alternatives are gradually closed off to them.

A culture is an integrated whole in which, in general, all major elements are more or less synchronized with all the others and all are more or less logically consistent with one another. Individual members of a society are in one sense prisoners of their culture—they have learned it as they grew up. Like the sociologist who wants to take the train, even if they would prefer to alter it, they are likely to find they can't. This chapter explores the concepts of culture and society as social scientists in general, and sociologists and anthropologists in particular, understand and use them.

Culture and *society* are words common to everyday English, and you have doubtless used them yourself. "She's certainly a very *cultured* woman," "the people of that country have very little *culture*," "I read it on the *society* page of my newspaper," and "she belongs to a very exclusive *society*" are sentences in which we can easily understand the usage of the terms *culture* and *society*. You might think that your familiarity with these words would help you understand their sociological meanings, but in fact your familiarity poses problems, because these words are used differently in sociology than they are in everyday English. Sociology, like the other social sciences, takes ordinary words, like *culture* and *society*, defines them precisely, and applies them to concepts that are basic to the discipline. You have your own commonsense understanding of the two terms, but since they are used differently in sociology, it is crucial to distinguish the technical from the popular usages.

The Meaning of Culture

Definitions

Culture is an important concept in all the social sciences, but it is a basic concept in sociology (and

the fundamental concept in anthropology). As the term is popularly used, *culture* refers to the "finer things of life": good taste, a refined manner, and achievement in and appreciation of fine arts, music, and literature. Thus, in everyday English we speak of a person who eats the proper foods at the proper places with the proper utensils and using the proper manners as being a "cultured" individual. Similarly, this cultured individual reads the proper kinds of books, sees the proper kinds of plays, listens to the proper kinds of music, and enjoys the proper kinds of art. In these examples, *culture* is applied to individuals, but the popular usage of the term is also extended to refer to groups of individuals—peoples, nations. In this sense, we refer to a nation that has achieved refinement and distinction in its arts as being a nation of "high culture."

In sociological usage, the term *culture* is much more inclusive than in the examples given above. The simplest way to define culture in its sociological sense is to say that it refers to anything that human beings do that does not have a biological basis. By defining culture in this simple and general way, we can see that the concept includes *all* human phenomena that are not the products of biological inheritance. Thus, the sociological concept of culture includes not only what is learned as refined and proper behavior, but *all* learned behavior; it includes not only learning to place a high value on a beautiful painting, but learning to place *any* value on *anything*; not only learning to use the correct eating utensils, but learning to use *any* tools (and how, and when, and why).

In the sociological sense, then, **culture** *includes any piece or pattern of behavior, any attitude, value, or belief, any skill that human beings learn as a member of a human group, plus the use or manufacture of any material item that is derived from these human abilities*. In the sociological sense, a hot dog with mustard, a T-shirt, saying "howdy" with a sexy wink, calling your father "the old man," and dancing the polka are as much a part of culture as are eggs Benedict, a tuxedo, kissing a woman's hand, referring to "my father," and the minuet. Further, the songs of a preliterate tribesman are no less traits of culture than the sonnets of Shakespeare, nor are the designs scratched on a piece of wood by an Australian **aborigine** any less an example of culture than the paintings of Leonardo da Vinci. These are simple, but important and elusive, points. The sociological interpretation of the concept of· culture treats all learned human products and abilities equally. No distinctions are made between them on the basis of taste and refinement, nor are judgments made about their quality. Sociology places all such phenomena in the same general category, the category of culture.

Uses of the Term *Culture*

In sociology the term *culture* is used in several slightly different ways. First, it is used to refer to that general and universal human phenomenon discussed above, common to all humankind, at all times and in all places.

Second, the term is used to refer to culture as it is manifested by a certain human group having a particular pattern of ideas, behavior, and material **artifacts** (manufactured things) that characterize that group and distinguish it from other groups. This sense of the term refers to *a* culture, as in the phrases "American culture" and "the culture of the Yir Yoront of Australia."

Third, *culture* is used in compound terms to denote subunits of a particular culture. All members of a complex culture share the same life-style to a large extent, but within that large culture are smaller groups that have interests and outlooks somewhat different from those of the other members of the culture at large. These small groups, called **subcultures**, derive their distinctive differences from such bases as occupation, ethnic affiliation, geographic region, socioeconomic status, age, and sex. Thus, within American culture, we can speak of a physicians' or truckdrivers' subculture, Afro-American or Irish-American subculture, Southern California or Appalachian subculture, teenage or retired people's subculture, men's or women's subculture, and so on.

When the ideas and behavior patterns of a subculture conflict with those of the majority of the members of a culture, the subculture is called a **counterculture**. The term **culture conflict** is used to refer to the clash between the subculture and the larger culture. Probably the best-known example of a counterculture is the "hippies": the group of young people in the United States in the late 1960s

culture: the attitudes, beliefs, behavior patterns, skills, all the conventionally accepted ways of doing things, that characterize humankind or a specific human group. Culture includes rules of behavior, both those recognized as rules and those implicit in "the way things are done." The term can be used on a variety of levels, for example: human culture in the Neolithic period, Imperial Egyptian culture, black culture, upper-class culture.

aborigine: an original, indigenous inhabitant. The term is often used to refer to the natives of Australia.

artifact: a manufactured or human-produced *thing;* tool, weapon, toy, etc. Any item of material culture.

subculture: the behaviors and interests of a subunit of a larger group that are peculiar to the subgroup and not shared with others in the larger group. In the United States, for example, there are racial, regional, ethnic, occupational, and age subcultures, among others.

counterculture: subcultural behavior patterns that contradict or conflict with those of the larger culture in which the subculture exists.

culture conflict: the condition in which subcultural norms are in conflict or violent disagreement with those of the larger culture.

whose modes of dress, behavior patterns, and political ideologies ran counter to those accepted by Americans as a whole.

Characteristics of Culture

So far we have defined culture as everything that human beings learn to do, think, use, and make. But simply to define culture so broadly and let it go at that would be a disservice to your understanding of the nature of culture, its content, and its powerful influence on human thought and behavior. So, in the pages that follow, we will play with the concept of culture, take it apart and rearrange its pieces, so that you can better understand its essence.

Sir Edward B. Tylor, an English scholar of the last century, is considered by anthropologists to be the founder of their discipline; and sociologists view Tylor, if not with quite the same reverence as anthropologists, as an influential figure in the development of their discipline. In his book *Primitive Culture*, published in 1871, Tylor defined culture as "that complex whole which includes knowledge, belief, art, morals, law, custom, and any other capabilities and habits acquired by man as a member of society."[1] Tylor's definition is considered to be the first view of the concept of culture in its modern, social scientific sense; and it is still generally accepted and used in the social sciences as a base from which elaborations can be built. In his definition, Tylor sees culture as an entity composed of parts ("complex whole"), lists some of the parts ("knowledge, belief," and so forth), and leaves an opening in the definition for the inclusion of unlisted parts ("any other capabilities and habits").

That Tylor viewed culture as learned is reflected in the segment of the definition that reads "acquired by man." That man—by which Tylor meant all human beings—learns culture in the context of a human group is indicated by the phrase "as a member of society." Thus, Tylor saw culture as a totality, composed of various parts, that is learned through the agency of society. Other, later, definitions of culture, though built on the foundation laid by Tylor, emphasize other aspects of culture. One such definition frequently cited is that offered by Clyde Kluckhohn and William Kelly, who see culture as all "historically created designs for living, explicit and implicit, rational, irrational, and nonrational, which may exist at any given time as potential guides for the behavior of men."[2] This view of culture stresses that the culture human beings learn comes to them from the past and provides a set of rules ("designs for living") as guides for behaving.

Kluckhohn and Kelly also make the point that some of these cultural guidelines are consciously stated ("explicit") and some are more hidden ("implicit"); that some are obviously useful ("rational") but some are not ("irrational"); and that for some rationality is not a consideration ("nonrational"). We could go on listing definitions of culture for page after page and note that each definition emphasizes a different aspect of the concept. In fact, such a compilation was made in 1963 by Alfred Kroeber and Clyde Kluckhohn, who listed and dissected over 150 definitions of culture as the term is used in the social sciences. On the basis of this analysis, Kroeber and Kluckhohn offered their own definition of culture. Although more specific and detailed than Tylor's, it carries the flavor of his classic version: "Culture consists of patterns, explicit and implicit, of and for behavior acquired and transmitted by symbols, constituting the distinctive achievements of human groups, including their embodiments in artifacts."[3]

Keeping these definitions of culture in mind, and recognizing the fruitlessness of trying to duplicate Kroeber and Kluckhohn's compilation of definitions, let's examine the many characteristics of culture.

Culture Is a System

Culture is an entity composed of numerous different parts—a "complex whole." These parts are integrated, put together in such a way that each part is related to the other parts. Thus, culture is a *system*, an entity made up of interrelated parts in which the functioning of the whole is dependent on the integration of the parts. A change in one part of the system will alter the relationships between parts and cause reverberations in the system as a whole. Consequently, viewing only one, or some, of the parts of a cultural system in isolation will not lead us to an understanding of the system as a whole.

What are the "parts" of a cultural system? The rings on your fingers and the shoes on your feet are parts of a cultural system. So are the Empire State Building and jet aircraft. Thus *things*—material things—are parts of a cultural system. Other parts of a cultural system are **norms**, those guidelines for regulating interaction discussed later in this chapter. Rules for greeting and leave-taking, business transactions and baseball games, marriage and running for mayor, are all parts of a cultural system. Ideas, attitudes, values, and beliefs are also parts of a cultural system. Using the color red to represent courage and the color white for purity, viewing time, space, matter, and the nature of reality in particular ways, and considering tulips beautiful and dandelions a nuisance are no less parts of a cultural system than anything else. Before we put some order into this overwhelming complexity, let's consider another facet of the parts of cultural systems.

The parts of a cultural system may be classified in categories. One approach to classification is *analytic*. It takes an entire cultural system, an integrated and patterned whole, and attempts to break it down into smaller constituent units. The smallest meaningful unit of culture is called a **trait**, an example of which would be the ring on your finger. A ring is obviously a small unit, but consider the ways in which this single item fits into a larger pattern. To fully understand a ring, we would be interested in knowing more about the technology used in making it; and to fully understand that technology we would have to know more about the economic patterns of the culture in which the ring was produced, and so on. Further, we could reach a more complete understanding of the significance of the ring only after we knew the relative values of the various materials from which the ring is made and what determines these values. We would also have to find out more about the various relationships symbolized by particular rings. Some rings symbolize marriage; others indicate graduation from a particular university or membership in a certain organization. But then we would have to know more about marriage, universities, and organizations. Where do we draw the line?

Although breaking culture down into its traits is useful, most sociologists are more interested in looking at components of culture larger than traits. This approach, called *synthetic*, is more concerned with investigating how traits are built up into broad patterns than in tearing culture down into tiny bits. Related traits can be put together at a higher level to form **trait complexes**. Using this approach, we can view a ring as an item of jewelry related to bracelets, necklaces, earrings, and other items of personal adornment. Such trait complexes can be put together to form still broader categories, called configurations, which form the overall patterns, the distinctive flavor, of a particular culture. A common practice in sociology is to view culture as made up of three large and interrelated configurations, or components: material culture, normative culture, and cognitive culture, each of which will be discussed in turn (see Figure 3-1).

Material culture That component of culture to which objects—physical traits—belong is *material culture*. This category includes anything that

norms: social rules and customs either requiring or prohibiting, permitting or discouraging, behavior.

trait: the smallest meaningful unit of culture. A trait can be material, cognitive, or normative: for example, a cigarette, the knowledge of how to smoke it, and the belief that smoking cigarettes is bad for the health.

trait complex: a system of related traits making up some kind of cultural whole; for example, "tobacco smoking," including manufacture, use, and disposal of tobacco products and smoking accessories, the knowledge of all related processes, and all of the attitudes, norms, and values associated with the entire system.

material culture: physical things with cultural value or use, whether manufactured or used or valued in the natural state.

Figure 3-1
The three major components of culture

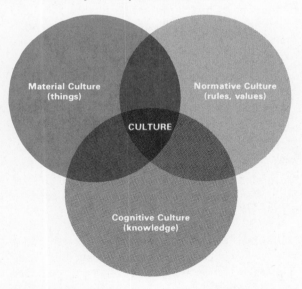

Culture as a whole is made up of three major components. In practice, these overlap. For example, you have knowledge (cognitive culture) about how you ought to use (normative culture) specific things (material culture), such as firearms or automobiles.

Material culture. Things like rocks exist independent of culture, but the *use* of them makes them a part of it.

human beings use or make. The inventory of these material traits is quite large in any culture, and in contemporary industrial cultures, it is enormous. No one has ever bothered to compile an exhaustive inventory of the material traits of a culture, but such an inventory is not necessary, for we can derive these traits from their definition. A ring is quite obviously a material trait, because its existence is dependent on culture. Less obviously, perhaps, a bunch of flowers presented on St. Valentine's Day is also a material trait of culture. True, flowers have an existence independent of culture, but it is the *use* of the flowers that identifies them as part of culture.

Normative culture More elusive is the major component of culture that sociologists identify as *normative*. Norms are rules for behaving, standard ways of doing things, blueprints for expectations about behavior. Norms are both prescriptive and proscriptive; that is, they tell us the things that we should do as well as the things that we shouldn't. There are norms in any society that cover all areas of behavior, except the unique or the very trivial, and sociologists recognize different varieties of norms.

Folkways, mores, and taboos William G. Sumner, an early American sociologist, identified two such varieties of norms, which he called *folkways* and *mores*, in his book *Folkways*, published in 1906.[4] The difference between these two types of norms is not in their content. They both apply to many of the same areas of behavior, and both types are largely survivals from an earlier time. The important distinction between them lies in the degree to which a member of a society feels compelled to conform to them, the intensity of feeling associated with adherence to them, and the strength of the reaction to their violation.

Folkways, synonymous with customs, are the norms that simply specify the way that things are usually done. Adherence to folkways leaves some room for eccentric, but harmless, behavior, and violations of folkways usually provoke only mild feelings and raised eyebrows. Most folkways have been handed down to us from the past, and their beginnings and original functions have been blurred by time. For example, the custom that when a gentleman walks with a lady, he keeps between her and the street (takes the outside position) seems to have originated in medieval Europe, where it was the habit to empty chamberpots into the streets from overhanging second-story windows. As a culture changes, folkways change with it, old ones being discarded and new ones being added.

Codes of dress and rules of etiquette are common examples of folkways. To take a more specific example from our own society, imagine a semiformal, "sit-down" dinner party. There are certain expectations about how a guest at such a gathering is supposed to act. Let's say that a male guest slurps his soup and mashes up his peas with his fork in order to eat them with his knife. He would certainly be violating folkways regarding table manners. As a result, he might be considered impolite or crude, but there would probably not be a strong reaction to his violation of these norms, although others might feel embarrassment for him. Nor is it likely that the guest would be punished for his indiscretions, although the host might not invite him to another dinner party.

But consider behavior of a more serious nature on the part of the guest at our hypothetical dinner party. Suppose he began to use foul and abusive language in speaking to the host during dinner, or even went so far as to fondle the breasts of the hostess. In engaging in these outrageous behaviors, he would be violating norms more serious than those classified as folkways. He would be guilty of breaching **mores**, norms embedded in what members of a society consider to be morality. Mores, like folkways, come to us from the past and change with time. But unlike folkways, mores involve rather clear-cut distinctions between right and wrong, and are associated with values that a society holds dear.

Adherence to these norms is considered essential to the smooth functioning of the society. Violations of mores provoke relatively intense feelings and strong reactions. Punishment, ranging from avoidance and ridicule to death, is often meted out for the violation of mores. The dinner guest in the example above would no doubt be told to leave and never come back, and it is even possible that he would be struck by the host, or one of the other guests, and thrown bodily from the house. Such are the reactions violations of mores provoke.

A type of norm that evokes even more intense feelings and greater compulsion to comply than mores is the **taboo**, a word that comes to us from Polynesia through anthropology. The culture of any society contains within its normative component some norms that are considered so basic that to violate them would be to weaken the moral integrity of the society. Special norms of this kind are called taboos, and to violate them generates feelings of the utmost intensity, from dumbfounded shock to rage. Examples of taboos in our culture are having sexual relations with close, "blood" relatives or with corpses. It is even sometimes the case that the violation of a taboo is so abhorrent, so unthinkable, that no specific punishment exists. Thus, although cannibalism is a tabooed act in our culture, some states do not have laws that specify it as a crime. Or, from another culture, consider the case of the Sioux father who discovered that his son and daughter had been having sexual relations. So strong was the taboo in Sioux culture against sexual activity between brother and sister that the stunned and disbelieving father could

> **normative culture:**   all norms and expectations for behavior; social rules and customs.
>
> **folkways:**   customs; norms with only mild demands or requirements for conformity.
>
> **mores:**   almost equivalent to morals; norms with strong requirements for conformity and severe sanctions or punishments for violation.
>
> **taboo:**   a special variety of norm for which conformity is deemed socially essential. Tabooed behavior is considered terrible and loathsome, and taboo violators are likely to be considered crazy.
>
> **law:**   a special variety of norm characterized by specific enactment, attachment of specific punishment, and enforcement by special agencies of the society.

bring himself to say only, "Now I am the father of dogs!"[5]

Laws   The mention of the lack of legal sanctions for the violation of certain taboos leads us to a discussion of **laws**, another type of norm. Laws are like the other types of norms discussed above in that they regulate social behavior, but they are unlike other norms in some important respects. First of all, typically we know where laws come from. They are norms that are formally enacted by legislative bodies, for specific purposes, to regulate particular forms of behavior. Second, punishment for the violation of various laws is clearly stated and is conceived as fitting the offense. And third, punishment is carried out by a branch of society (a judicial system) that has authority over individual members of the society.

The intensity of feeling connected to laws varies with the nature of the law. Thus, overtime parking and an ax murder, while both violations of laws, are poles apart in the responses they provoke. All contemporary industrial societies have laws, of course, consisting of an elaborate written code of statutes administered by large numbers of specialists (police officers, attorneys, judges, and so on). But laws do not necessarily have to be written down. In some preliterate societies, norms that are recognizable as laws exist, specific norms for which specific punishments are meted out. The laws are not written, obviously, in societies that

The Car Is All Right, But Your Crabgrass Is Illegally Parked

It is unlawful for a child to solicit money on the street for any purpose whatever. It is therefore unlawful for children to solicit donations for UNICEF. (190-10)

It is unlawful to let your homing pigeons loose in the 7th Ward, but not in any other ward.

In the city of Chicago it is an offense punishable by a $50 fine for a person to ride in an elevator and wear a hatpin the point of which protrudes more than one-half inch "beyond the crown of the hat in, upon, or through which such pin is worn."

It is unlawful for a sidewalk newspaper stand to sell any publication "except daily newspapers printed and published in the city."

It is unlawful to "utter lewd or filthy words, sing any song the words of which are suggestive of indecency or immorality, or to make any obscene gesture in the presence of other persons." Remember that.

It is unlawful to wash windows in such a way that you get water on the sidewalk between 7 am and 7 pm during the months from May 1 to October 1.

It is unlawful to play hopscotch or skip rope on the sidewalk without a permit.

It is unlawful to skate in the street.

It is unlawful to sell fruit of different sizes in the same container. The Board of Health is required to inspect every fruit, vegetable, or berry sold within the city of Chicago.

It is unlawful to tell fortunes in the park.

It is unlawful to take a cigaret butt out of a public ashtray with intent to resell it.

It is unlawful to play a musical instrument on the beach, or to display a flag there, without a permit.

It is unlawful to "indecently exhibit" a stud horse. Horses and cows are required to mate only "in some enclosed place out of public view."

It is unlawful to build a car showroom within two hundred feet of a church.

It is unlawful for a liquor licensee to give away popcorn or pretzels.

It is unlawful to give away a cigaret within one hundred feet of a school building.

In a section labeled "promotion of marriage", the ordinances of the city of Chicago deem it unlawful for anyone to take money for arranging a marriage.

According to city ordinance 99, subsection 9, "All weeds . . . are hereby declared to be a public nuisance."

Excerpted from Ron Berler, "The Car Is All Right, But Your Crabgrass is Illegally Parked," Chicago, August 1975. Reprinted with permission of the author.

have no writing systems, but they are nonetheless present in oral form.

There is no difficulty in seeing the differences between laws and other types of norms, but it should be pointed out that these other types of norms are sometimes codified into laws. Thus, the outrageous behavior of our dinner guest toward his hostess could constitute the violation not only of some of society's mores, but of its laws as well. His actions might constitute assault, and the host might feel compelled to call the police to arrest his unruly guest and to press legal charges against him. Figure 3-2 illustrates certain relationships between various types of norms and the adherence to them. Note that the boundaries between folkways, mores, and taboos are not always definite, that they fade into each other. These hazy boundaries may vary among different subgroups within a society.

Popular norms and pressure group interests (and the idiosyncrasies of legislators) are sometimes enacted into law.

Explicit and implicit norms   Some norms within a culture are *explicit*, out in the open; and everyone in the culture is able to formulate the rule. We all know that to murder someone is a crime, a violation of a legal norm, and we all know that it is considered immoral to walk around in public with no clothes on. Explicit norms are learned through formal means, as when parents tell their children, "Don't talk with your mouth full," or "Nice boys and girls don't hit each other."

Other norms are *implicit*; they lie hidden beneath the surface and are not easily stated. Who has ever told us explicitly to cover the body of a dead person, yet who would doubt that this is proper behavior in the treatment of a corpse? Other examples of implicit norms include the rules governing how we use our bodies in face-to-face interaction. A recent study demonstrated that people from different cultures use their bodies differently when conversing with each other and, furthermore, that there is almost no formal and explicit way of transmitting these rules. They are just "picked up," probably through imitation of others. When Arab men converse with each other, for example, they typically do so at closer distances, in louder voices, with more direct facing toward each other, using more touching and direct eye contact, than do American men.[6] Implicit norms are less subject to conscious control and verbal statement than the explicit ones. They are, in short, rules that you know, but you don't know that you know them.

Real and ideal norm behavior Finally, a distinction must be made between *real* and *ideal* behavior in relation to norms. A norm is a rule, explicit or implicit, a statement about the ways in which people in a particular culture should or should not behave. Following a norm rigidly is *ideal behavior*, absolute conformity to norms. But, as we all know, norms are constantly being violated, and the degree to which norms are followed in *fact* is *real behavior*.

Every society has some slippage, some leeway, between real and ideal behavior, and no norm is always followed "to the letter" by everyone. These small deviations from norms are tolerated, even expected, but there are limits to the deviation. Perhaps we all secretly admire the adventuresome and independent person who believes that "rules are made to be broken," but every society, although tolerating some eccentricity, has limits of toleration for nonadherence to norms. Too great a gap between ideal and real behavior is considered disruptive in any society.

Cognitive culture Ideas, attitudes, values, and beliefs constitute the *cognitive culture* of a cultural system. These cognitive elements of culture provide members of a society with a framework for viewing the world, a means of constructing and understanding reality, and consist of the thoughts that shape their existence. (This is, in part, what

cognitive culture: knowledge, ideas, attitudes, values, and beliefs; the *mental* component of culture, with the exception of expectations for behavior, which are a part of normative culture.

Implicit norms. This young man is carrying a *borsette*, a small clutch bag or pocketbook. The custom is common in Italy, but few American men would be caught dead with one. Why? Because in our culture there is an implicit norm that equates male use of purses with homosexuality. (It is acceptable, however, for a man to sling an old army musette bag over his shoulder—that's macho.)

Figure 3-2
Types of norms

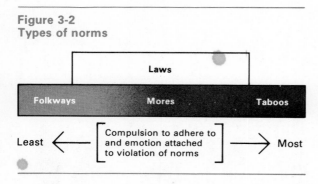

Chapter 1 is about.) Normative culture consists of the rules for behaving, but it is cognitive culture that is the *source* of these rules, the matrix in which they are embedded. The cognitive elements of culture cover all aspects of human life and can be as simple as an opinion about what pair of socks look best with what shirt, as day-in and day-out as the attitudes one sex has about the other, or as complex and crucial as a set of beliefs concerning the fate of the human soul after death.

If, as suggested earlier, it would be fruitless to attempt an inventory of all the material elements of a culture, it would be impossible to list all of the cognitive elements, so pervasive are they and so difficult to tap. We can, however, isolate certain major themes that reflect the basic values that permeate every culture. The major cultural values of American society have been identified by the sociologist Robin Williams and are recognizable to all of us.[7] They include, for example, the values placed on hard work as an end in itself, the achievement of success, and practicality and efficiency in all matters. These values are reflected in themes that appear in the popular media (films, novels, television programs) and in everyday conversation; and they mirror the world view of American culture, the assumptions we have about the nature of the real world, and the ways in which we live out our lives.

Other cultures, however, have different assumptions about reality, as Carlos Castaneda has brilliantly pointed out in his series of books about Don Juan, a Yaqui Indian sorcerer who conveyed to Castaneda a view of time, space, matter, and causality—a "separate reality"—quite different from the dominant Western one.[8] Those who comment on Castaneda's accounts of Don Juan by saying, "Did he really *believe* all those things?" or "Are those things that Don Juan does really *real?*" have missed the whole point of the books (and, incidentally, of much of anthropology as well). Castaneda vividly "translated" one cognitive culture (Don Juan's) in terms understandable, if not acceptable, to another (ours).

Systems of symbols, of which language is the most obvious, play a prominent role in cognitive culture, but a discussion of the human capacity to manipulate symbols will be delayed for a later section in this chapter and for Chapter 4.

Culture Is Diverse

There are some recognizable universals that apply to all cultures. All cultures have norms that regulate sexual relations between their members. All cultures assign economic activities to individuals on the basis of age, sex, skill, and other basic criteria. All cultures have norms that govern the exchange of goods and services, and all cultures have some sort of technology with which their members exploit the resources of the physical environment. But what is more striking than these and the many other common characteristics across all cultures is the diversity—the flustering range of differences—between them.

While culture is common to all human societies, every society has a unique culture, a "design for living" that, when viewed as a total pattern, is different from all other cultures. Some cultures forbid marriage between certain kinds of cousins; other cultures insist on it. Some cultures assign important economic activities to men; other cultures assign these roles to women. In some cultures, individuals who display bizarre behavior are considered to be mentally ill; in others, such individuals are thought to be specially gifted. Members of some cultures share goods equally. Members of other cultures buy cheap and sell dear. Members of some cultures make their living with bows and arrows, members of other cultures with internal combustion engines. And on and on, in a bewildering and almost endless series of differences.

Cultural relativity The documentation of the diversity of culture has given rise to a very important point of view within the social sciences, that of **cultural relativity**. This notion sees each culture as being a unique adjustment to a particular set of circumstances and puts forward the idea that to understand and appreciate the structure and content of a particular culture, you must understand its particular circumstances. To take a simple example, you cannot compare and evaluate the use of a clay pot to hold water in one culture and the use of a metal pitcher to hold water in another merely by assessing the differences between these utensils. You must also consider their ''goodness of fit'' within their total cultural context.

The concept of cultural relativity is particularly important when we are considering activities in another society that violate the moral standards of our own. For example, nineteenth century American missionaries in Polynesia were shocked by the female inhabitants' custom of going bare-breasted and insisted that these women cover themselves in Mother Hubbard dresses. This caused endless confusion among the natives, who did not share the American fascination with the female mammary organ. It also appalled the missionaries that young people were permitted, even encouraged, to engage in sexual relations before marriage. The Americans did not understand that Polynesian marriage rules were the reverse of our own: in the United States, marriage is the appropriate occasion for pregnancy; among the Polynesians, pregnancy was the appropriate occasion for marriage.

Ethnocentrism The principle of cultural relativity can be stated as a caution: ''Don't judge one culture on the basis of the norms of another culture.'' Failure to adhere to this principle results in **ethnocentrism**, which is the viewing of all other cultures from the point of view of one's own. For the lay person, ethnocentrism can lead to faulty conclusions about other cultures; for the social scientist, to be ethnocentric leads to disaster.

Ethnocentrism is common around the world and could be, in fact, one of the cultural universals. Probably it serves some useful purposes. In small preliterate societies, for example, ethnocentrism promotes solidarity and cohesion within the socie-

cultural relativity: the idea that the culture of a people may be understood properly only in and on its own terms. For example, the polar Eskimos traditionally put their elderly on ice floes to die when they became economic liabilities, but this practice cannot be properly understood as murder in the conventional American sense.

ethnocentrism: viewing other cultures from the point of view and value perspective of one's own. Calling the traditional Eskimo practice of setting the elderly adrift murder would be ethnocentric.

''Nobody likes to fall, Rocco—but this is ruining our image.''

Sidney Harris/Saturday Evening Post.

Cultural relativity: Would a Japanese person understand this cartoon?

ty, a feeling of "us" against "them." But as the technology of industrial societies has shrunk the world through faster means of communication and transportation, more cultures have come in contact with each other than ever before, and the positive value of ethnocentrism has sharply diminished. With cultural diversity more obvious now than it has ever been, tolerance for this diversity is increasingly necessary.

Culture Is Shared

Although cultural diversity is great, all "normal" human beings, in one sense, share culture. That is, everyone is a participant in that uniquely human phenomenon called culture. But, of course, not everyone in the world shares the *same* culture. Culture is shared at the level of particular cultures. Of course, all members of a particular society do not know everything everybody else knows, for no single individual ever embodies all the intricate details of his culture. But all members of a particular society, having a particular culture, share a "core" culture, a basic set of common expectations toward social life. Even in a complex, **heterogeneous** society such as our own, with its numerous subgroups and regional differences, there are a large number of commonly shared beliefs. Included in the core of American culture, for example, are emphases on the freedom of the individual and on achievement through hard work. There are even more commonly shared beliefs in the simpler, smaller, and more **homogeneous** societies of the world.

But we should not conclude that everyone, even in small societies, sees the world in exactly the same way or holds exactly the same convictions. An incident that occurred among the Gururumba, a small, preliterate society in the highlands of New Guinea, should make the point sufficiently clear. Philip L. Newman describes a Gururumba belief concerning "lightning balls," stones having great magical power. When lightning strikes a tree and disappears into the ground, the Gururumba dig deep holes near the tree in search of the "lightning balls" formed by the electrical discharge. One day when Newman was watching some men dig for lightning balls, a man named DaBore told him

there were no such things as lightning balls. Newman commented:

> As far as could be discovered, this was the only part of the supernatural belief system [DaBore] did not believe in. He had no rationale for his disbelief, nor did it stem from trying one out and finding it did not work. Like other men he had a spirit house in his garden, and attributed his various illnesses and misfortunes to ghosts, sorcerers, and witches. There was nothing in his life history or his position in society that would help explain it; he just did not believe in them.[9]

The cumulative nature of culture Social heritage is a phrase applied to culture to emphasize its cumulative nature. Kluckhohn and Kelly referred to the cumulative aspects of culture when they termed it "historically created designs for living." The point is that the culture shared by an individual with other individuals in the same society is the product of centuries—or millennia—of gradual accumulation and transmission of knowledge and techniques. In a way, then, every culture is a repository for everything that ever went before it. Of course, not all the objects ever invented or all the ideas ever formulated are present or are used in a culture, but the knowledge of them is there.

Thus, the Egyptians don't build pyramids anymore, but they *know* about them (and could probably construct one if they had a good reason to do so). Industrial societies don't use the stone and bone tools of their distant ancestors, but museum cases full of these implements show our awareness of them, and few people would be unable to make a serviceable—if not expert—stone spear point. Very few things are ever lost from the "memory" of a culture; they are just replaced by new things. But even in spite of replacement of most elements, a surprising number of cultural traits have a remarkable persistence. Most Boy Scouts know how to produce fire with a bow-drill, a very old invention.

Culture as an adaptive mechanism The cumulative nature of culture provides us with ready-made solutions to universal human problems. The use of fire, for example, doesn't have to be rediscovered by each new generation but is already there—as part of culture—waiting to be used. The discovery and invention of countless solutions to human problems of survival raise the point that culture is an *adaptive mechanism*. Human beings, in contrast to other animal species, are almost totally dependent on culture to adapt to their physical environments. Culture makes extensions of ourselves possible that enable us to keep warm without fur or thick blubber; to hunt gazelles (which are far swifter than we are) and elephants (by far our physical superiors); and to outfly even the most inspired of sea gulls without the aid of wings on our bodies. Culture helps us come to terms with our physical—and social—environment so that we may pursue our basic needs in a relatively efficient manner.

Culture Is Learned

Culture is a phenomenon that is over and above biology and is not transmitted genetically. This means that human beings acquire culture through learning. All "normal" babies everywhere are born, in regard to culture, as blank sheets of paper. What gets written on this blank paper depends on where and when the baby is born. It depends, in other words, on what *culture* the baby is born into. Of course, this blank paper does have some biological underpinnings: every newborn baby is the product of millions of years of biological evolution, during which time human beings became human, that is to say, developed the *ability* to be bearers of culture. This ability, this capacity for culture is, to be sure, genetically transmitted as part of the organism, but *culture itself must be learned*.

This means that an Eskimo child is not born with a natural inclination to speak the Eskimo language or an urge to hunt seals and chew animal skins into the suppleness necessary to make clothing. Eskimos do these things simply because they learn to be Eskimo. If we put an Eskimo baby in the care of an American family living in Los Angeles, the child would grow up speaking English, playing baseball, eating hamburgers, and doing all the other things that Americans do because those things are part of American culture, which is different from Eskimo culture. And both of these cultures, in turn, are different from all others. To repeat, human beings are born with a capacity for culture, but what culture they learn is dependent on what culture they grow up in.

heterogeneous: the condition whereby members of a given population or category do not share many characteristics. For example, the population of a very small town in northern Utah is likely to be quite homogeneous: most or all will be white; most or all Protestant (perhaps even Mormon); etc. The population of San Francisco, to the contrary, will contain every race, religion, occupation, and so forth, and thus will be heterogeneous.

homogeneous: the condition whereby members of a given population or category share many characteristics.

social heritage: a term emphasizing the cumulative nature of culture, the fact that "nothing is forgotten" in cultural history.

Culture is learned.

Human beings owe their humanness, and their capacity for culture, to their enormous abilities to learn. Think of it: Children are born knowing nothing of culture, but by the time they reach maturity they have learned to manipulate a complex system of symbols—language—with remarkable facility. They have learned to appreciate the past and ponder the future. They have learned where souls go when the body dies, how to drive automobiles or ride horses, how to make love, how the world came into being, how to differentiate mother's brother from father's brother, what to cherish, and what to fear. For all cultures contain such elements and pass them along to their new members.

What is remarkable about learning a culture is not that it takes so long—and childhood constitutes a relatively long period of time in any culture—but that such a complex system gets learned at all. Look into your own mind for evidence of these complexities. If you are familiar with the game of baseball, pause for a moment and consider the complicated set of rules that governs the game. An appreciation of its complex rules, which you carry around inside your head, can be obtained by explaining the game to an Englishman who has never seen it played. While you're at it, have your English friend explain cricket to *you*.

Culture is learned behavior, but is there no behavior that is *non*cultural, that is, genetically transmitted? Yes, there is. There are certain reflexes, such as sneezing, that are involuntary responses to certain stimuli, such as dust in the air. Some convincing research demonstrates that all human beings share ways of expressing the basic emotions (fear, sorrow, and so on).[10] Human beings also have some biological needs, or "drives." The need for food and drink (the drives of hunger and thirst) and the need for reproduction (the sexual drive) are basic prerequisites for life. (Drives and reflexes are discussed in more detail in Chapter 4).

But culture is a mediator for these universal biological traits, a filter for their expression. Culture tells you that a sneeze is an expulsion of demons from the body (as in medieval Europe) or a sign of virility (as in Japan). Culture tells us when we should feel sorrow or fear. It is culture from which we learn to eat with chopsticks, forks, or our hands. It is also culture from which we learn when and where to eat, with whom, and, to a surprisingly

large extent, *what* (some cultures don't share our disdain for dogs or insects as food). Sexual drives are biological, but with whom we can have sexual relations, and with whom we cannot, and under what circumstances, are culturally mediated.

Learning in nonhuman species Human beings possess culture, and culture is learned. Other animals do not have culture (a point discussed later). Does that mean that other animals don't learn? Of course not, as any trainer of dogs and horses will be quick to point out. But dogs and horses are trained by human beings, not by other dogs and horses, while people learn culture from other people. But wait, you urge, are there not animals that learn from members of their own species? Yes: the songs of some species of birds are learned, as is the hunting behavior of some predators. But there are even more striking examples, more relevant to our discussion of culture and learning.

Consider the example of a group of monkeys on a small island in Japan. In the early 1950s researchers started leaving food—sweet potatoes—on the beach near the water. At first, the monkeys rubbed the sand off the sweet potatoes before they ate them, until one day a young female dipped her potato in the water to clean it. Within a few years, about 90 percent of the monkey population were cleaning their potatoes by dipping them into the water.[11] This was clearly an example of a new idea that spread throughout the group, but could it be considered an example of culture? Keep that question in mind until we come to the section on symbols, which will be concerned with the learning skills of other nonhuman primates.

Feral or "wild" people For the moment, let's refer to that part of Tylor's definition of culture that said it was acquired by a person as "a member of society." This is an obvious, but extremely important point. The reciprocal of learning a culture is having a culture taught, and a culture is taught by the members of the society into which a child is born. Children, thus, grow up learning the behavior and values that their culture teaches them are correct.

But what would happen if, for some reason or other, a child grew up in the absence of human company? Cases of children who were raised by animals run through the folklore of the world, dating at least from the time of Romulus and Remus (the legendary founders of Rome), who, as the story has it, were suckled by a she-wolf. Such stories make fascinating reading, but the documentation of their authenticity is scanty at best. We do, however, have ample documentation of one such case, from France in the last century. It involves Victor, the "Wild Boy of Aveyron" (with whom you may be familiar from François Truffaut's film *The Wild Child*).

Victor was found in the forest—naked, dirty, and covered with scars—and was taken in by Itard, a French physician. Dr. Itard worked with the boy in an effort to teach him language, but all such attempts failed. It appeared that Victor was incapable of learning. Finally, the boy ran away, never to be seen again.[12]

Dr. Itard's failure to teach Victor the rudiments of culture may have had two causes: First, Victor may have been mentally deficient. It was once a common practice in some parts of the world to abandon a retarded child in the wilderness. The few who survived may have been the sources of stories about children "running with animals," and Victor may have been such a child. Second, there may be a "critical period" in human development beyond which learning a culture is impossible. Victor may have been beyond this stage and thus have had a greatly diminished capacity for acquiring culture. Whatever the case, the point remains that there must be someone there to teach a culture; it cannot simply be picked out of the air.

We will close this section with the suggestion that the essential questions to ask in seeking to understand the nature of humanity and culture are not questions regarding culture *or* biology. It's not as simple as that, for it is probably true that what people *are*, the essential nature of humanity, is the result of the interaction of culture *and* biology.

The anthropologist Clifford Geertz maintains that we are not creatures who were biological beings first and only later had a cultural layer superimposed over our "basic" nature. The cultural, social, and psychological aspects of humanity are not contained in neat layers, to be stripped off, one by one, to reveal the "real" self. Geertz argues persuasively that our true nature lies in the fact that all human beings are products of their unique and

feral: wild or existing in a state of nature, or having reverted to such a condition after domesticity.

Learning a culture is a complex process. If you were British, you'd know what is going on here. Cricket is really not at all like baseball.

various cultures, and that these unique and various cultures cannot be torn away without tearing away the meaning of humanity itself, leaving totally unworkable brutes. Thus, Geertz concludes that "one of the most significant facts about us may finally be that we all begin with the natural equipment to live a thousand kinds of life but end in the end having lived only one."[13] We human beings have, in other words, only one crack at culture.

Culture Is Based on Symbols

What makes us so different from other animals is that we have culture. And culture is not based so much on quantitative differences between human beings and animals, on the fact that we learn so much more than the other animals, as it is on qualitative differences, on the fact that culture is something different in *kind*. Descartes, the famous seventeenth century French philosopher, put these differences this way in his *Discourse on Method*: "Not only that the brutes have less reason than man, but that they have none at all." What makes us different from all other animals is the ability to use *symbols*, and symbols are the basis of culture.

The meaning of symbols A symbol, as we saw in Chapter 1, is something that represents ("stands for") something else. Thus, in our culture, the noun *table* stands for an object on which we eat our meals; the color white stands for purity; a flashing red light at an intersection stands for "stop"; and a wave of the hand stands for "hello" or "goodbye." The anthropologist Leslie White defines the ability to symbolize as being able "freely and arbitrarily to orginate, determine, and bestow meaning upon things and events in the external world, and the ability to comprehend such meanings."[14] Further, White maintains that the meanings of symbols cannot be perceived with the senses.

Let's examine White's notion of the symbol by using language, the most conspicuous example of the human ability to symbolize. First, symbols are arbitrary. That is, we invent them or designate them at our convenience; they do not exist in the nature of the object referred to. Thus, when we call an object a table, there is nothing about the qualities displayed by the object to tell us that it should be called *table*. There is no "tableness"

connected to the object. This is shown by the fact that in Spanish the object is called *mesa,* and in other languages it has other names. The relationship, then, between a referent (in this case a table) and what we call it is arbitrary, and it is we human beings who bestow the meaning on the symbol.

Second, you can't interpret symbols through your senses. For instance, there's nothing in the word *table* that would enable Spanish speakers to interpret its meaning with their senses. We call the object *table* only because that is what English speakers have "agreed" to call it. If you wanted to call the object *watunga,* you certainly would be free to do so, but to have *watunga* become accepted you must have everyone in your speech community agree on that as a choice. This might be difficult, because, after all, the word *table* seems to have caught on. To use a less concrete example, there is nothing in the color white to tell us that it should be a symbol for purity, as it is in our culture. In other cultures white is symbolic of other things, mourning, for example, in China.

Symboling in animals When a dog responds to the command "roll over," it is not, as a careful look at White's definition will reveal, engaging in symboling behavior, but is acting in accordance with what White calls a *sign*. The dog has attached a "meaning" to the combination of sounds that make up the command "roll over," but it has not bestowed the meaning on the combination of sounds. But do animals have *no* capacities to engage in symboling behavior? A look at some attempts to teach animals such behavior will shed some light on this question.

In the 1930s W. N. and L. Kellogg, husband and wife psychologists, "adopted" an infant chimpanzee the same age as their own child and raised the two babies together. The Kelloggs were careful to give the two infants the same stimuli. They developed at about the same rate and in the same ways until the Kellogg child began to acquire language, at which time the cognitive development of the human child greatly outstripped that of the chimp. Long and careful attention was devoted to teaching the chimp to speak, but the results were disappointing. The chimp was finally able to retain the use of a very few simple English words, but the experiment was deemed a failure.[15]

In the 1940s a similar experiment was undertaken by K. J. and C. Hayes, another husband-wife team of psychologists. The results were about the same, and it appeared that the gap between chimpanzees, one of the most intelligent of subhuman animals, and human beings was enormous and unbridgeable.[16] But two very important considerations were overlooked in these two experiments: first, that chimpanzees differ from people in important anatomical ways, ways that make it nearly impossible for a chimp to duplicate human speech sounds; and second, that language is not the only human symbol system.

In the late 1960s, in one of the most creative and exciting experiments of its type, Alan and Beatrice Gardner took a young chimp named Washoe and attempted to teach her a system of symbols based on gestures. This system, called American Sign Language (ASL), is one widely used in this country by deaf-mutes. In teaching this system to Washoe, care was taken not to use spoken language in any way, but to rely entirely on ASL for communication. At the end of the experiment, Washoe was able to use about 150 ASL gestures. She was able to put these gestures together spontaneously to generate crude "sentences." When, for example, an experimenter put a doll in Washoe's drinking cup, Washoe responded by signing "baby in my drink." On another occasion, Washoe was on a small island and noticed that her human companions on shore were drinking iced tea. She then began excitedly and repeatedly to sign, "Roger ride come gimme sweet eat please hurry hurry you come please gimme sweet you hurry you come ride Washoe fruit drink hurry hurry fruit drink please." Not the most literary arrangement of words, you'll agree, but the point could not be mistaken.[17]

In another, similar, experiment David Premack taught a chimp named Sarah to communicate by arranging differently shaped pieces of plastic in different orders.[18] The results were that Sarah showed the same capabilities as Washoe. But could these capabilities be interpreted as symboling behavior? Not really, because the accomplishments of Washoe and Sarah (and other chimps in experiments stimulated by these two) lack the crucial elements in White's notion of symboling behavior, the ability to bestow meaning arbitrarily. These chimps learned something that they would

Chimpanzee Washoe using American sign language to name objects: in this case, the word "sweet" for a lollipop.

not have learned without the intervention of human beings.

If Washoe and Sarah started teaching the symbol systems they learned to other chimps (and as a matter of fact Washoe is being watched now to monitor any such attempts), we would have to grant them another step on the road to culture. And why not? Would it be threatening to our concept of ourselves as unique creatures, alone capable of culture? It probably would, but for now all we can say about animals other than ourselves is that they are capable of more "culturelike" behavior than was earlier thought possible. Thus, our concept of ourselves is not yet seriously threatened.

Cultural Processes

Cultural systems are not stable. Some cultures change at faster rates than others, but cultural change is a universal phenomenon. In this section we will look briefly at some of the processes through which cultures change.

Innovation

One process of cultural change arises from sources *within* culture. This source of cultural change is called invention, or **innovation**. Innovations can come about through the discovery of new materials in the environment for which a use already exists. Thus, if a preliterate society that uses stone tools discovers a new type of stone, more easily worked and more durable than the old, this new and better material will probably replace the old stone. This type of discovery is much more likely to occur in simpler societies than in more complex ones, because as a society's culture gets more sophisticated, more things are known and less remains to be discovered in the environment.

Another type of innovation comes about from putting already known materials to new uses. Gunpowder, for example, was an amusement in Chinese culture a long time before it was put to use as part of a weapons system. This example is no rarity, either, for it often happens that things that have been "just lying around" are put to new uses that have a radical impact on cultural change. Innovations are also made by recombining elements into new complexes, or by inventing new processes, new ways of doing things. Given the existence of the boat and the steam engine, the invention of the steamboat was almost inevitable.

The saying that "necessity is the mother of invention" does not hold up well under the weight of empirical evidence, for most innovations come about by accident, rather than by discovery through conscious effort. Even in our own complex society, which has a class of specialists called "inventors," the discovery of some of our most useful items has been accidental. The antibiotic properties of penicillin were accidentally discovered by Alexander Fleming, and Charles Goodyear hit upon the process of vulcanization (which prevents the deterioration of rubber) by accident.

Polygenesis: independent innovation An interesting aspect of innovation is that important discoveries are made, more often than you might expect, in different cultures independently, or in the same culture by different, and independent, sources. This phenomenon, called **polygenesis**, is illustrated by the invention of several important items, ideas, and processes independently in the Old and New Worlds. A calendar for computing the passage of time, the mathematical concept of zero, and the domestication of plants for food resources

are some examples. An example of independent invention within the same culture is the idea of the biological evolution of animal species, "discovered" independently in the last century by Alfred Wallace and Charles Darwin (who gets most of the credit). This example, by the way, serves to point out that innovations are not limited to materials; new ways of looking at things are just as important as material inventions.

Other striking examples of polygenesis include: the invention of calculus by Newton in 1671 and by Leibnitz in 1676; the invention of photography in 1839 by Daguerre, Niepce, and Talbot; the discovery that disturbances in the earth are correlated with sunspots by Gauthier, Sabine, and Wolfe in 1852; the discovery of the periodic law of chemical elements in 1869 by both Mendeleev and Meyer.

The cumulative nature of innovation One last point concerning innovations: There are certain inventions that are primary, so basic that they persist and remain unchanged. But further secondary inventions arise from new applications of the primary inventions. The discovery of the use of fire is one of the most basic achievements of humankind. No one knows exactly how this discovery came about, but it was doubtless by accident. Fire was probably first used by human beings for cooking, for protection from animals, and for warmth. Indeed, fire retains all of these functions today, but it is used for such a wide variety of other things, from making steel to making crystal, that it would be difficult to list them all. The wheel and the lever, based on physical principles whose application virtually surrounds us in industrial society, are other examples of primary inventions. If a cure for cancer is discovered in the near future, it will probably be based on the application of a primary concept already in existence: the germ theory of disease.

Diffusion

Changes in cultural systems do not arise entirely from sources internal to them. Inventions and discoveries that occur in one culture are often borrowed by another culture. This is so often the case, in fact, that borrowing, or **diffusion**, is the major source of change in any culture. Ralph Linton, a distinguished American anthropologist, estimated that about 90 percent of the elements in any culture are based on diffusion. This is true even in our complex and rapidly changing industrial society. In his famous "100 percent American" passage, Linton followed a typical American through his day and pointed out that almost everything an American does, uses, and thinks was developed elsewhere and comes to us through diffusion.[19]

Some important elements of culture were invented only once and spread throughout the world. A striking example is the alphabet, the idea of representing sounds with written symbols, which originated somewhere on the Sinai Peninsula around 2000 B.C. From that beginning, the alphabet diffused, over time and through space, to many different cultures. Today, every language that has an alphabetic writing system owes this fact to an invention that took place 4,000 years ago.

The use of tobacco is another interesting example of diffusion. Tobacco, which is a product of the New World, was taken from the Indian tribes of eastern North America, in the form of pipe smoking, to England. From England, the practice of pipe smoking diffused to Holland. Dutch and English sailors spread the habit throughout the Baltic area, and from there it spread through Russia and Siberia, across the Bering Strait and back into the New World! The Spanish found tobacco used, in the form of cigars and cigarettes, by the Indians of the Caribbean and took the practice back to Spain, from where it spread throughout the Mediterranean area into the Middle East.

In the examples above, the evidence for diffusion is clear. In some other cases, we have very little documentation of diffusion. Nevertheless, certain complex combinations of elements that occur in several different cultures are considered too complicated to have been invented independently. Thus, the occurrence of the folktale that we know as "The Musicians of Bremen" (involving a group of traveling animals), which is found in essentially the same form all over the world, is assumed to be the product of diffusion.[20] All this talk of diffusion makes one curious about what Italian cuisine was like before Marco Polo brought macaroni from China and tomatoes came to Europe from the New World.

It should not be assumed that diffusion implies

> **innovation:** a discovery or invention, or the process of discovering or inventing.
>
> **polygenesis:** multiple, independent innovation; innovation by more than one person or people independently of one another.
>
> **diffusion:** the transmission of traits from one culture to another.
>
> **acculturation:** diffusion between adjacent cultures.
>
> **assimilation:** the fusion of two or more different cultures into a new one unlike the originals. Analogous to the compound in chemistry.

that once a new item or idea arises in one culture it rapidly spreads, unresisted, to other cultures. Sometimes sets of ideas and objects in a particular culture are not structured in a way that would make certain elements easily acceptable. In the last century, American Indians created new ideologies in response to oppression by the dominant Anglo-American culture. These religious beliefs held that by performing certain rituals and casting off all articles of European origin, the dead ancestors would reappear and the whites, who were destroying the tribes' way of life, would disappear. This "Ghost Dance" religion won eager acceptance among many tribes, most notably those on the Great Plains, but was rejected by the Navajo.[21] Why? Because the Navajo greatly fear the spirits of the dead and wanted no part in a movement that had at its core the return of the dead. These new ideas simply did not fit well into the existing Navajo culture and so were rejected.

Acculturation   There is a certain special case of diffusion called **acculturation**. It involves the diffusion of cultural elements by direct contact of two (or more) cultures. Acculturation is, in many instances, forced borrowing, as when one society conquers another and seeks the alteration or destruction of the culture of the subordinate society. Some societies resist acculturation, others accept it eagerly.

Assimilation   Acculturation is often only part of a process that finally results in **assimilation**. This is

The 100 Percent American

Our solid American citizen awakens in a bed built on a pattern which originated in the Near East but which was modified in Northern Europe before it was transmitted to America. He throws back covers made from cotton, domesticated in India, or linen, domesticated in the Near East, or wool from sheep, also domesticated in the Near East, or silk, the use of which was discovered in China. All of these materials have been spun and woven by processes invented in the Near East. He slips into his moccasins, invented by the Indians of the Eastern woodlands, and goes to the bathroom, whose fixtures are a mixture of European and American inventions, both of recent date. He takes off his pajamas, a garment invented in India, and washes with soap invented by the ancient Gauls. He then shaves, a masochistic rite which seems to have been derived from either Sumer or ancient Egypt.

Returning to the bedroom, he removes his clothes from a chair of southern European type and proceeds to dress. He puts on garments whose form originally derived from the skin clothing of the nomads of the Asiatic steppes, puts on shoes made from skins tanned by a process invented in ancient Egypt and cut to a pattern derived from the classical civilizations of the Mediterranean, and ties around his neck a strip of bright-colored cloth which is a vestigial survival of the shoulder shawls worn by the seventeenth-century Croatians. Before going out for breakfast he glances through the window, made of glass invented in Egypt, and if it is raining puts on overshoes made of rubber discovered by the Central American Indians and takes an umbrella, invented in southeastern Asia. Upon his head he puts a hat made of felt, a material invented in the Asiatic steppes.

On his way to breakfast he stops to buy a paper, paying for it with coins, an ancient Lydian invention. At the restaurant a whole new series of borrowed elements confronts him. His plate is made of a form of pottery invented in China. His knife is of steel, an alloy first made in southern India, his fork a medieval Italian invention, and his spoon a derivative of a Roman original. He begins breakfast with an orange, from the eastern Mediterranean, a canteloupe from Persia, or perhaps a piece of African watermelon. With this he has coffee, an Abyssinian plant, with cream and sugar. Both the domestication of cows and the idea of milking them originated in the Near East, while sugar was first made in India. After his fruit and first coffee he goes on to waffles, cakes made by a Scandinavian technique from wheat domesticated in Asia Minor. Over these he pours maple syrup, invented by the Indians of the Eastern woodlands. As a side dish he may have the egg of a species of bird domesticated in Indo-China, or thin strips of the flesh of an animal domesticated in Eastern Asia which have been salted and smoked by a process developed in northern Europe.

When our friend has finished eating he settles back to smoke, an American Indian habit, consuming a plant domesticated in Brazil in either a pipe, derived from the Indians of Virginia, or a cigarette, derived from Mexico. If he is hardy enough he may even attempt a cigar, transmitted to us from the Antilles by way of Spain. While smoking he reads the news of the day, imprinted in characters invented by the ancient Semites upon a material invented in China by a process invented in Germany. As he absorbs the accounts of foreign troubles he will, if he is a good conservative citizen, thank a Hebrew deity in an Indo-European language that he is 100 per cent American.

From Ralph Linton, *The Study of Man*, © 1936, pp. 326–327. Reproduced by permission of Prentice-Hall, Inc., Englewood Cliffs, New Jersey. Originally published by Appleton-Century-Crofts.

the fusion of two or more different cultures into a new "compound" that is essentially unlike the originals. Thus we can speak of American Indian acculturation where we see that tribes have borrowed cultural elements from one another or from the dominant Anglo-European culture. But the general American culture is an example of assimilation because it is a new culture based on the intermingling of older European cultures. (Some of you may not know, for example, that the popular "American" food pizza was virtually unknown in the United States, outside of Italian-American communities, before World War II. It may also surprise some to learn that pizza, as we now know it here, is also virtually unknown in Italy, although the Italians enjoy a somewhat similar dish of the same name.)

Cultural Lag

One final but important point about processes of cultural change is that components in a cultural system change at different rates. Furthermore, a change in one sector of a culture stimulates changes in other sectors: all sectors move toward integration of the whole. When one component of a cultural system lags behind another component to a degree approaching malfunction, the term **cultural lag** is applied. W. F. Ogburn, an American sociologist, coined the phrase *cultural lag* and used it to describe the condition that results when material culture changes so rapidly that cognitive and normative cultural elements do not keep up.[22] Examples abound in our own culture. An important one is the fact that our technology is on the verge of being able to create human life in a test tube, but our attitudes, values, and beliefs about life are integrated into a less advanced technology and have not advanced rapidly enough to keep pace with technological change. That is, we don't yet have the ideologies to deal with such advances.

Another case in point in American society is the possible relationships between "the pill," the moral code of the United States, and the role of women in the social system. Although reasonably cheap and efficient contraception has been available since the invention of vulcanized rubber, neither of the most prevalent forms of contraceptive, the condom and the diaphragm, really gave *women* control over conception. The condom, of course, is a male contraceptive, and the use of the diaphragm could be confirmed or forbidden by the male. With "the pill," however, women can for the first time in history control whether or not they become pregnant, and there is nothing that their male partners can do about it. "The pill" also offers possibilities for female sexual freedom that earlier contraceptives did not. It is entirely possible that both what is called "the new morality" and the sudden decline of the American birthrate may be results of this innovation in contraceptive technology. Moreover, Women's Liberation and what some regard as the current war between the sexes can be viewed as elements of cultural lag resulting from the failure of American cognitive culture to "catch up with" the technological change.

The Meaning of Society

Like culture, society is one of the most basic concepts in sociological thinking. And like the term

cultural lag: a condition in which one component of culture changes more rapidly than another, resulting in some period of maladjustment between them. Often used to describe the case where material culture changes faster than cognitive or normative culture.

Cultural diffusion.

culture, the term *society* is defined more precisely in sociological usage than in popular usage. You probably have the idea that *society* refers to a group of people, and, indeed, the term retains that sense in sociology, but with many more implications than the mere physical existence of a group of people. In defining society in sociological terms, two aspects of the group are especially important: (1) the social organization that regulates interaction between group members and (2) the size of the group.

To constitute a society, the members of a group must be interrelated by a pattern of social organization (see Chapter 5) through which interaction is regulated. In this regard, society can be defined simply as a number of individuals connected by interaction. But this aspect of society, although necessary, is not sufficient in itself to distinguish society from, say, community, which is also a group of people bound together by social organizational patterns.

The other important dimension of a definition of society is the *size* of this group of interacting people. In regard to size, then, sociologists define society as the largest socially organized group distinguishable from other such groups. Combining both aspects of the term, we can define **society** as the *largest distinguishable unit of interacting individuals who share a pattern of social organization that regulates the interactions between them.*

We should also note here that the term *society,* like the term *culture,* is used in two ways in sociology. First, it is used in an abstract, general sense to refer to the concept, as in references to "the study of society." Second, sociologists use the term to refer to a *particular* society, a specific group of interacting people with a specific set of organizational patterns for regulating interaction, as when they refer to contemporary Japanese society. The first usage refers to the *concept* of society, while the second designates a particular example of the concept.

Before we continue our investigation of the definition of society, let us pause and consider the differences between the terms *culture* and *society.* The two are sometimes used synonymously in the sociological literature to refer to roughly the same things. This is confusing, and sloppy besides, because the concepts to which the terms refer have

distinctive, even obvious, differences. Culture is the *totality* of human learned phenomena, while society refers to only a part of that totality. Culture concerns *all* the ways in which human beings learn to view the world, to behave, and to make and do things. Society concerns only those ways of thinking, doing, and acting relating to the organizational patterns that constitute a specific set of rules for interaction.

The same distinctions apply when we refer to *a* culture or *a* society. To call a human group a culture implies that we are referring to the total and distinctive way of life of that group. Calling the same group of people a society implies reference to the social organizational patterns of that group of people, which are only a *part* of their culture.

The Size of Society

Just how large is a society? In sociological usage, the size of a society is not specified by the *number* of people who belong to such a group. A society may have many members or very few. Instead, it is specified by the level of organizational inclusiveness and distinctiveness involved. A society is an autonomous (independent) unit of individuals sharing a pattern of social organization.

Frequently, the autonomy involved is political, and in such cases the term *society* may be used synonymously with *nation-state.* But some societies are culturally autonomous and transcend national political borders, as do the Polar Eskimos, who migrate between Canada and Soviet Siberia. And a few nation-states are composed of more than one culturally autonomous society, as is the Soviet Union.

Societies, then, may be quite small or very large. But they are always characterized by distinctiveness from other groups and the presence of social organizational patterns among their members that other groups do not share.

Interaction and Societal Organization

Sociologists are primarily interested not so much in society's size as in how the interaction between people in society is regulated. Interaction can be defined as a human action that is directed to or takes account of another person or persons. An interaction, then, is an event or, more precisely, a *process*, that takes place *between* individuals. Through interaction, individuals exchange information, come into conflict or cooperate, and in general *deal* with each other. An interaction can be an exchange of pleasantries or a threat. It can be as trivial as asking the attendant at the service station to "fill it up" or as important as national leaders conferring to resolve the problems of the national economy. In brief, interactions involve the ways in which people relate to each other.

Every society has a pattern of organization that regulates the interactions between people in the society. This complex societal organization involves a set of rules (the norms discussed earlier in this chapter) that provide expectations for individuals who enter into interactions with others and act as guidelines that serve to insure that interactions proceed smoothly. This pattern of organization is essential in any society to prevent chaos, to insure the integration of the individuals who are members of that society, to maintain the "social order."

Societies can be quite large. The United States is a society with over 200 million individual members, and the chances that everyone in it will interact with everyone else are nil. But the point is that there are *rules*, more or less shared by everyone in the society, that provide guidelines for the interaction of one member of the society with any other member. Thus you may never order an ice cream cone in Cleveland, but if you ever have the opportunity, you'll know how to do it. A businessman who has never left his native San Francisco will know what to expect should he ever have to transact business in New York. But if the same businessman went to Mexico (or any society other than his own) to close a deal, he would be unwise to make any assumptions about members of other societies sharing his set of rules for interaction. Latin Americans, as Edward T. Hall has pointed out in his book *The Silent Language*, share expectations about business transactions quite different from those shared by Americans.[23]

The sharing of such rules among the members of a society is an important criterion in the definition of society. And the fact that each society's rules vary to a greater or lesser degree from the rules of other societies is an important criterion for distinguishing one society from another.

society: the largest distinguishable unit of individuals who share a pattern of social organization that regulates the interactions between them. Roughly equivalent to the largest group of people who share a common culture, although political boundaries will sometimes split a population of the latter description.

Some people regard the Amish rejection of automobiles and tractors as an example of cultural lag.

Summary

This chapter has introduced you to culture and society, two of the most basic and important concepts in contemporary sociology. We have defined *culture* in two senses: First, we have said it is that universal and uniquely human phenomenon consisting of patterns of thinking and believing, doing and behaving, making and using that all human beings learn in growing up as members of a human society. Second, we have discussed culture in the sense of *a* culture, the distinctive life-style that characterizes a particular society and that serves as a basis for the social-organizational patterns that distinguish one society from another.

In discussing culture, we noted that it has five basic characteristics. First, culture is a *system*, a whole made up of interrelated parts. The three major components of culture are *material, normative*, and *cognitive* culture. Material culture is composed of things: tools, weapons, toys, and so forth. Cognitive culture is composed of *knowledge*, for example, the way in which a particular tool is used to produce an artifact. And normative culture is composed of *rules, values*, and *attitudes* and the like, the do-and-don't judgments we impose on ideas and things. Important elements of normative culture are: *folkways*, or customs; *mores* (important norms that can be thought of as almost the same as morals); and *taboos*, a special kind of norm whose violation is considered unthinkable, obscene, or reprehensible in the extreme. *Laws* are another kind of norm. They are primarily distinguishable from the others by the fact that they are formally enacted, that punishments for violations are clearly stated, and that they are enforced by special agencies of the society. Norms may also be *explicit* or *implicit*, "real" or "ideal."

A second major element of culture is its *diversity*. So various are human cultures that, in order to understand them, we must practice *cultural relativity*, the habit of viewing them on their own terms rather than ours. Failure to do this creates the familiar, and sometimes terrible, phenomenon called *ethnocentrism*, the habit of judging others from the perspective of our own normative system.

Third, culture is *shared*, both among different societies and among generations. Thus culture is *cumulative*, and it can act as an *adaptive mechanism*, enabling the people of one time or place to adjust to their problems by using solutions worked out at other times and in other places.

Fourth, culture is *learned*. Human beings are born with a genetic capacity for culture, but the culture itself—its content—must be learned by each individual. In general, only human beings seem to be capable of doing this. Other animals can learn, of course, but only human beings seem to be capable of spontaneously generating cultural elements themselves. Certain quite intelligent non-human species, chimpanzees in particular, have been taught elements of human culture (specific symbol systems, for example), but they do not seem capable either of generating them themselves or of transmitting them to others.

Finally, culture is based on *symbols*, and it is only through the use of symbols that human beings can learn it. According to recent research, chimpanzees are capable of greater symbol-using capacity than previously believed and thus capable of more "culturelike" behavior. But no animal species has ever developed a culture of its own, and none seems capable of transmitting culturally acquired learning.

Cultural processes—the ways in which culture is generated, distributed, and changed—include innovation, diffusion, acculturation, assimilation, and cultural lag. *Innovation* means invention, which, while probably more rare than we usually believe, is not unique either. Most cultural innovations have probably occurred only once, but a surprising amount of *polygenesis* (multiple independent invention of the same thing) also exists. An important aspect of innovation is that it is *cumulative*. One invention springs from or utilizes another, as we see when we observe that the first automobiles were often motorized carriages.

Diffusion refers to the spread of culture through borrowing by one society from another. In the process, a cultural item, or its use, is often somewhat modified to fit the needs of the borrowing society, and various phenomena influence the rate and degree of diffusion of given items. *Acculturation* is a special case of diffusion between geographically adjacent societies. *Assimilation* refers to the process of fusion of cultural elements from two or more cultures that produces a new compound unlike the parent cultural elements. The melting pot metaphor often used to describe American culture is a familiar example.

Finally, *cultural lag* refers to the situation where one component of culture changes more rapidly than another can "keep up," producing a period of adjustment often believed to produce social problems of one kind or another. In most cases, cognitive or normative culture lags behind material culture.

In discussing society, we noted that, like *culture* the term *society* is used in two senses: In an abstract, general sense, society refers to the organizational patterns that regulate interaction in the largest distinguishable unit of interacting people, as in "the study of society." In a specific sense, the term refers to the organizational patterns that characterize *a* society, a specific group of people sharing a particular set of organizational patterns.

Finally, keep in mind that culture and society are *concepts*—constructs of the human mind. They are abstractions, not things having a physical existence. No sociologist has ever seen (or felt, touched, heard, or smelled) culture or society, any more than a physicist has ever seen energy or a psychologist has seen thought. Culture and society serve as principles for the pursuit of sociological knowledge, conceptual frameworks that guide sociologists in their research.

Review Questions

1. Describe and contrast the different types of norms discussed in this chapter: folkways, mores, laws, and taboos. Which type is most important? Why?

2. Explain the relationship between culture, subculture, and counter culture. What is culture conflict?

3. Discuss the difference between explicit and implicit norms; between ideal and real behavior. What is meant by tolerance limits in regard to norms?

4. Do humans share any noncultural behavior? If so, provide a few examples. Define *reflex* and *drive*.

5. Explain why you think this chapter opened with readings on the fear of flying. What relation does this topic have to a discussion of culture?

Suggestions for Research

1. Study social class as subculture. You may want to make a broad study, touching on the different groups; or you may prefer to focus on one specific group: the upper class, the middle class, the working class, or the lower class. (Sociologists have created many different classifications, but these are some basic ones). What types of behavior patterns and values—if any—do you find peculiar to a specific social class? Do you believe this stratum is significantly different from others? In other words, does the group appear to be self-conscious? You might team up with a few of your classmates and each of you choose one class, then pool your research.

2. Time is one of many bases for subcultures. Select a period in the history of the U.S. to study as a subculture; most historical periods are characterized by trends that mark their culture off from other periods in time. A few examples would include: the turn-of-the-century years, the period during a major war such as World War II, the nationalist, or the Victorian periods. In what ways were these times unique? Do their peculiar characteristics appear to be something that was only limited to that time? Why or why not? These historical subcultures constitute the social climate of the day, which includes values, outlooks and behavior patterns—and sometimes personality types.

3. Interview a foreign student attending your college or university. Discuss his or her perceptions and reactions to American culture. Compare aspects of life-styles which appear to differ greatly between the U.S. and the student's homeland. Remembering the discussion in this chapter on ethnocentrism, can you apply it to your reactions as the student describes another culture? To his or her reactions to the U.S.? Or is the attitude more relativistic?

4. Study a series of television programs dealing with minority subcultures, racial or ethnic or a specific social class. Is the program's portrayal of this group objective or slanted? How are members of the larger culture portrayed? The interaction between the latter and the minority group? Evaluate the series from your own perspective. How do your friends and classmates react to the series?

5. Examine changes in the American ethos during your lifetime. You will undoubtedly have many ideas based on your own experience and observations; you can fortify these ideas by library research. Take a number of traditional American values such as hard work, practicality and/or anti-intellectualism, family life, and others. Study how these values have changed, if at all, or possibly collapsed, in the past two decades. You might want to read about the "pendulum" theories of social change which postulate that drastic and upsetting changes in values are followed by a return to a more balanced social ethos.

CHAPTER 4
PERSONALITY AND SOCIALIZATION

The Things upon Which a Child's Mind Should Be Built

We must take great care that the child sees beautiful things, and if things of ugly shape and ugly color are shown to it, it must be taught to see that they are ugly. If we provide it with pictures, plain or colored, they must be simple and beautiful. There is no more reason why we should expose a child to ugly sights than to ugly smells. We must do the same as regards the child's ears; it must learn to know the difference between a beautiful voice and an ugly one, both in speaking and singing.

The Book of Knowledge, 1919

The Passion to Explore

He's a demon explorer. He pokes into every nook and cranny, fingers the carving in the furniture, shakes a table or anything else that isn't nailed down, wants to take every single book out of the bookcase, climbs onto anything he can reach, fits little things into big things and then tries to fit big things into little things. A tired-out mother calls this "getting into everything" and her tone of voice says that he's a nuisance. She probably doesn't realize what a vital period this is for him. A baby *has* to find out about the size and shape and moveableness of everything in his world and test out his own skill before he can advance to the next stage . . . That he "gets into everything" is a sign that he's bright in mind and spirit.

Dr. Benjamin Spock,
Baby and Child Care, 1975

The two quotations above, from two authoritative sources of advice about child rearing, show some interesting contrasts that we may attribute to the fifty-year gap between them. The first, from the era of World War I, is clearly of what might be called the "bent twig" persuasion—"Just as the twig is bent the tree's inclined." It implies that children are impressionable and will be molded by what they experience. Thus, they should be shielded from the ugly or the distasteful in order to develop beauty and good taste in their own lives. The second quotation, from the famous Dr. Benjamin Spock, seems to indicate that children are somewhat more hardy. They should therefore be allowed to explore and experience the world as it is because a wide range of experience is good for their development.

Different as the implications of these two quotations are, they do agree on one point: how children are treated has something to do with what kind of adults they will become. They are not born with futures whole and fixed; what they become is a function of how they are reared. That rearing process is a large part of what sociologists call *socialization,* and the product of the process is **personality**. These are the subjects of this chapter, and its principal point is that personality is a social product, the outcome of the interactions between the individual and those around him.

This may sound strange to us, despite some earlier agreement with the notion that children can be influenced by the ways in which they are treated by others. The suggestion that personality—our most intimate possession—is somehow a social phenomenon, rather than an individual and subjective one, sounds almost bizarre. It seems so because we have also been reared to think of personality, or "the individual," as a separate unit, something uniquely different from all others and acting independently of them. Western society, and perhaps American society in particular, has strong strains of individualism. Most of us have been brought up to think of ourselves as unique, independent, and responsible for our own behavior. But this idea is a myth. Our personalities, our very "selves," are *social* products. Society is not only "out there," *around* us, it is *in* us, a part of our very nature, sometimes causing us to behave in ways we do not wish or like.

Chapter 3 suggested that the culture in which we grow up has a great deal to do with what kind of people we become in a general way (Americans do not act like Japanese). It also influences deeply most of our behavior through setting general limits on the possible—even the conceivable—and setting out rather clear, if not always entirely precise, rules about what is demanded, permitted, and prohibited. In this chapter, we turn from this macro-level approach to human behavior and focus on the individual. *Within* the limits offered by our particular culture, how do we learn to be what we are? What is the human personality? How does it develop? What are the effects on it of such things as instinct, aptitude, sex, race? Is our biology our destiny or not? And, once we have some understanding of what personality is, where does it come from? How is it formed? How can it occur that some people in a given culture "turn out" one way and some another, and that some follow the social rules and others break them? Culture is not a straitjacket, as is shown by the variation among the members of a particular culture. In the following pages, we will explore some of the sources of that variation.

Information about what human personality is and how it operates can be valuable to you in thinking about yourself and in assessing the behavior of others. If biology really *were* destiny, for example, then it would be foolish to hope or expect that people would ever change their behavior. But since behavior is learned, and since even personality is largely learned, then change is possible, because what has been learned can be unlearned. And if people behave the way they do not because of their chromosomes or skin color or gender, but because they have been subjected to specific social stimuli and taught to respond to them in particular ways, then our ability to understand and deal with them is greatly enlarged. Indeed, as we will see, to an amazing extent, people behave *as they are expected to* by others, and the expectations are not of their own making. This knowledge is a very important key to freedom for ourselves and improved ability to get along

> **personality:** that portion of a person's behavior that is consistent over time and in different situations; the way in which one typically relates to life situations.

with other people and secure what we need from them.

The Meaning of Personality

Personality is that part of a person's behavior that is consistent over time and from one situation to another, the way in which one typically relates to life situations. Thus, when we say that "Tim is a conformist," we mean that Tim is likely to agree with those he is with in most situations. When we speak of Mary as achievement-motivated, we are implying that Mary will try hard to succeed at whatever she encounters in life. Both of these characteristics are aspects of personality.

Much recent work in social psychology has been concerned with how social situations affect behavior. Mary may not be achievement-motivated in *every* situation after all. For example, if she fails several times at what she is trying to achieve (or is told she has failed), her motivation to try her best at this task may disappear. A skillful social psychologist can arrange situations in which people are more likely to conform or less likely to do so, regardless of their individual personalities. (If the other members of Jerry's group put great pressure on him to agree with them—although he thinks they are wrong, and despite the fact that everyone knows how independent-minded he usually is—he may very well "give in.")

In no situation yet studied has any person's behavior been exactly the same on all occasions. Knowledge of personality alone—at least so far as we have been able to learn about it—is not all we need to know to understand why people act the way they do. Nevertheless, the persistence of differences among people in their typical ways of behaving means that personality remains an important concept. How then do people "get" a personality—are they just born with it?

The Biological Bases of Personality

Biological Determinism

In the latter part of the nineteenth century, many people believed in *biological determinism:* The idea that human beings are what they are and behave as they do because of their biological inheritance alone. Charles Darwin's important work in evolution was interpreted by many as demonstrating this. Darwin found evidence that those members of a species who are best suited biologically to survive in their environment are most likely to reproduce. Their chances of living long enough to produce offspring are better. Over many generations, those characteristics best adapted to the way a particular species fits into its ecological niche become more common, and those characteristics less suited to survival tend to disappear.

Darwin's ideas about evolution and survival were widely misinterpreted as applying to many other things besides living organisms, including human society. It was easy for the wealthy and powerful to assume that their success was due to a natural, biological superiority. Thus they developed a belief, called **Social Darwinism,** that human societies evolve in the same manner as living species, with the rich and powerful possessing superiority in the struggle for existence. In the powerful industrial countries, the upper classes used Social Darwinism to justify the low wages of their own working classes and the colonization of less developed parts of the world.

But biological superiority alone cannot be the explanation. For one thing, societies are not living organisms and therefore do not evolve in a biological sense. For another, the differences in wealth and power between members of the human species are so great that they cannot be a result of genetic differences. Indeed, one might speculate that the very poor who survive might be biologically tougher than their more affluent neighbors. There are many reasons for human inequality, and

that topic will be discussed in Chapter 9. However, even in the late nineteenth century it was obvious to some—Karl Marx and Emile Durkheim, to name two—that variation in human conditions of life and behavior could not be explained solely as a result of biological differences.

Instinct theory   The doctrine of biological determinism has not died easily. It is still alive and well in some areas of criminology and medicine today. In the early part of this century, many students of human behavior pursued biological explanations in the form of instinct theory. An **instinct,** as the term is used biologically, is an unchangeable, complex behavior that is transmitted from parent to offspring genetically (in the same way, for instance, as human eye color is transmitted). Instinctive behavior cannot be learned, neither can it be unlearned. It is behavior that is biologically programed into the physical makeup of the creature, which has no choice about exhibiting it. A bird builds a nest or cares for its young because it is programed to do so. In the proper environment and at the appropriate stage of maturity, it mates, constructs a nest, and cares for its hatchlings. Human beings, however, have no instincts for building cribs or taking care of children (or anything else); they must *learn* to be parents.

Instinct explanations for human behavior were popular until the 1920s, but their inadequacy for scientific explanation soon became apparent. Few who believed in them could agree on the list of what instincts people did or did not have. (One psychologist of the 1920s proposed an instinct for playing baseball.) Further, the lists were often inconsistent; how could people instinctively be both competitive and cooperative?

But perhaps the ultimate stumbling block for those who wished to believe in instincts was the problem of the negative case. By definition, behavior that is instinctive is essentially invariant; it cannot be altered by an act of will. An organism behaving instinctively has no choice about the matter, and all organisms of the same species behave pretty much the same way in response to instinct. There are no exceptions. But invariant behavior in human beings has been impossible to find. If there were an instinct for self-preservation, suicide—and perhaps even recklessness—would be impossible. So would maternal infanticide if there were an instinct for mothering. Social science today recognizes no human behavior that can properly be called instinctive.

Drives and reflexes   Today we recognize that although human beings do not have instincts there are biological *elements* in human behavior in the form of drives and reflexes. A **drive** is an internal, biologically based stimulation that the organism feels impelled by its own biological state to reduce. Hunger, thirst, and sexual arousal are the foremost examples. Depriving us of food, water, or sex creates a kind of organic tension within us, and the discomfort of that tension motivates, or drives, us to seek its satisfaction. But what exactly people will *do* about the discomfort cannot be predicted on the basis of knowing that they are experiencing it. In this way, drives are quite different from instincts. The discomfort we experience as a result of not being able to satisfy our drives *is* a part of our biological makeup, as is the comfortable feeling experienced as a result of satisfaction. Neither are complex *behaviors,* however, and the ways in which a drive may be responded to are highly variable. Thus, neither sexual behavior nor eating, for example, may be called instinctive.

The behaviors known as **reflexes** are also biologically based. Reflexes are simply involuntary muscular responses to the stimulation of certain nerve receptors. They include such familiar phenomena as the knee jerk (the patellar reflex) when the doctor taps you just below the kneecap with his rubber hammer and the contraction of the pupil when a bright light is shined in your eye (the pupillary reflex). But while reflexes do represent unchangeable responses to specific stimuli, they are not complex behaviors. (Neurologically, they are quite simple.) Thus, they, too, should not be confused with what is called instinctive behavior in other life forms.

The Nature-Nurture Controversy

In reaction to the errors of the biological determinists, early sociologists argued that environment determines the differences among human

---

Social Darwinism: the belief, popular about 1865–1920, that human societies *evolve* in the same manner as living species and that the rich and powerful have biological superiority in the struggle for existence. Popularized by Herbert Spencer, an early British sociologist-philosopher (1820–1903), this view saw history and social change as resulting from the "struggle for existence" and "survival of the fittest." (Darwin used neither term.) When applied to social affairs, it is likely to result in reactionary defense of the existing social order, because that order is viewed as having "survived," thereby demonstrating its superiority or "fitness." Social Darwinism is still found occasionally among political columnists and members of Congress, but it is so defective as social theory that it was abandoned in social science long ago.

instinct: a complex, unchangeable, genetically transmitted behavior. Among lower animals, nest building and direction finding are common examples. No instinctive behavior among human beings has ever been demonstrated to exist, although the belief that people have instincts (for example, for self-preservation) remains popular.

drive: an internal, biologically based stimulation, such as hunger or thirst, creating discomfort that an organism is impelled to reduce through behaving in such a way as to satisfy it.

reflex: an involuntary muscular response to the stimulation of certain nerve receptors. The knee jerk is a familiar example.

© 1964 United Feature Syndicate, Inc.

beings. The social environment—other people—was viewed as especially important. Those who argued for "nurture" (environment) in place of "nature" (biology) felt that individuals are what they are because of the way others have behaved toward them and because of the opportunities they have had to develop themselves. In their view, biology is unimportant. This, also, is too simple a view. We are beginning to learn that we are not as different from other species as we had thought. For example, other primates also communicate, learn, and make and use tools, as we saw in Chapter 3. And studies of dolphins indicate that they are highly intelligent—just how intelligent we do not know.

Human beings cannot be understood apart from their bodies. The physical capabilities of the human species are relevant to behavior. The human ability to walk erect, to grasp and manipulate objects, and to perceive depth, as well as the size and complexity of the human brain, are among the advantages common to the species. Moreover, physical differences between people, including hereditary differences, are related to how their personalities develop and what they achieve. For example, although standards of beauty vary markedly from one culture to another, within a culture those people thought to be physically attractive are responded to differently from those thought to be ugly. Differences in intelligence, health, aptitudes, and temperament, like variations in "appearance," have advantages or disadvantages.

Today, social scientists no longer argue about nature *versus* nurture. Instead, they try to discover how biological factors interact with environment to help shape personality. There are good reasons for thinking that, while people are not just born with whatever personality they develop, what they are

Drives do not determine behavior.

born with plays a part in affecting what they become.

"Human Nature"

If human beings are neither programed at birth through instincts nor totally pliable—a sort of blank tablet on which others may freely write—what are they? How do we differ from other species? Besides the characteristics common to the human species mentioned above, human beings share with only a few aquatic creatures like dolphins and whales the ability to vocalize *voluntarily*. Other animals can use sound to communicate—when hungry, or frightened, or hurt, for example. But they cannot use *particular sounds when they choose to communicate particular ideas*. As we saw in Chapter 3, researchers recently have begun to communicate with chimpanzees through gestures and other symbols. But we cannot teach them to speak. And although complex symbolic systems can be developed without speech, speech is a great advantage.

The popular belief in "human nature" in the sense of behaviors that are common to all human beings because they are human has no basis in fact. The things that *are* common to all normal members of the human species are some biological capabilities, drives, and reflexes. Human *behaviors* are overwhelmingly responses to *present situations* based on *past learning,* not the result of some characteristic common to all human beings. Consider the likelihood that a person will cheat on an exam. Depending upon past experience, some of us are more likely to cheat than others. We have *learned* to be relatively honest or dishonest. In addition, however, the *present* situation itself can affect what is likely to occur. To illustrate this, we can compare two extreme situations. In one, a man sitting on a park bench is asked if he will answer a few questions. In the other, a woman responds to the same questions, but in this case her entire academic future depends on her answers. Moreover, she is left alone with books and notes when the examiner is unexpectedly called out of the room.

Are people equally likely to cheat in each of these situations? No, because people do *not* always behave the same way. When people say about a behavior, "Well, that's just human nature," the behavior they are referring to is usually a matter of *cultural convention or norms.* Whether we are lazy, ambitious, selfish, or competitive, is not due to "human nature," but to how we have *learned* to behave and react to specific situations.

Inherited Elements of Personality

As indicated earlier, the physical and mental capabilities and potentials transmitted genetically through inheritance do have relevance for human behavior and personality. Although inherited characteristics do not *determine* either personality or behavior, they may set limits on what is possible for an individual, or open doors for some that are closed to others. Whether one *uses* such potentials, and to what degree and how—whether one walks through the doorway—is likely to be greatly affected by social influences. Five kinds of inherited phenomena have been of particular interest to sociologists, either because they appear to influence personality or because they have been given considerable social significance in Western culture. These are aptitudes, intelligence, race, temperament, and sex differences.

Aptitudes An aptitude is a basic biological capacity for some specific skill or behavior. The degree of aptitude for various activities varies among people. Some people have a greater aptitude than others for playing a musical instrument. No matter how many lessons they receive, people without aptitude for the game never become very good tennis

> **aptitude**: a talent or capacity for some specific ability, skill, or behavior.
>
> **intelligence**: the capacity for certain mental achievements.

players. An aptitude is a talent. It is not something you can learn. Even with the greatest opportunity and motivation, without some aptitude a person will never become a superior athlete, musician, artist, scholar, or leader.

However, what becomes of aptitudes depends on people's opportunities to develop them. Sometimes barriers to development are cultural. An aptitude for playing stringed instruments cannot be shown in a culture that does not use them. Other obstacles are social. Without time, materials, and social approval, abilities may never be developed. Thus middle-class children generally are more likely to develop and express whatever artistic, intellectual, or social aptitudes they have than are lower-class children.

Intelligence One element of personality of special interest to social scientists is the capacity for certain mental achievements—what is more loosely called intelligence or IQ (intelligence quotient). Intelligence has been defined by some as "what the IQ tests measure," but most social scientists are not happy with that definition. They make a distinction between differences in individual intellectual capacity and the *measures* of this capacity. The techniques for measuring intellect all reflect learning and motivation as well as biologically determined potential. But that is not the only problem. More fundamental is the uncertainty about what we mean by intelligence. One dictionary defines it as the capacity for understanding, and psychology texts are likely to speak of it in terms of problem-solving ability. But what kinds of problems? Does the same capacity, whatever it is, have the same effects on the ability to do mathematics that it does on the ability to diagnose the trouble in your carburetor or to balance the family budget? Is skill at cooking or taste in decorating a living room attributable to the same capacity as the ability to perceive the meaning of a poem?

One reason that our understanding of intelligence is so vague and uncertain is that, by and large, the standard intelligence tests tend to measure only a very limited range of skills. Most are paper-and-pencil tests, which have nothing to do with manual dexterity, for example, another kind of problem-solving skill. And most are deeply influenced by verbal ability: a child who reads well is likely to perform better on them than one who does not. Thus, the tests are distinctly weighted toward people whose backgrounds have emphasized these traits. Further, the scoring of the intelligence tests is capricious, not based on a clear standard. Why, for instance, is the ability to properly sum three four-digit numbers a measure of the same amount and kind of intelligence as the ability to figure out what a two-dimensional figure would look like if folded up into three dimensions?

Despite these and other problems, researchers in this field generally agree that (1) there are biologically based differences in intelligence among people; (2) these differences are heritable—that is, the parents' genetic qualities affect those of the child; and (3) IQ test scores reflect these genetic differences to some degree. We also know that IQ scores are related to how well children do in school and to the occupational prestige they are likely to achieve as adults. But those factors, in turn, are related to a host of social phenomena and are hardly the consequence of intelligence alone.

There is considerable disagreement among researchers about *how much* of what an IQ test measures is inborn and how much is the result of learning and motivation, and also about *how much* of the difference between individual scores is due to heredity. Because we have no valid way to measure purely biological intellectual capacity, the controversy will continue. However, comparisons of performances of unrelated persons, of parents and their children, and of **siblings,** including twins, provide some information. These data support the belief that IQ tests do measure *something,* and that they measure it fairly reliably. That is, repeated testing of the same person usually results in similar scores. Moreover, this something is at least partly biologically determined, and it is a heritable char-

acteristic. There is still plenty of room for disagreement. One researcher estimates that perhaps as little as 50 percent of individual differences in IQ scores is the result of heredity. Another places the estimate at 80 percent.[1] In any case, it is clear that the test scores reflect much that is *not* due to inherited ability.

We should not overestimate the importance of genetically determined characteristics. These do set the limits on the range of things a person can do in a particular physical and social environment. But the behavior that actually occurs is never determined by biological endowment alone. Past and present environmental factors and the immediate state of the person always contribute to determining the behavior that results. Even the same person in the same situation will behave one way when he is sick and exhausted and another when he is healthy and alert.

There is a growing concern among some social scientists and parents about the negative effects on schoolchildren of being labeled according to their IQ test scores. This labeling can adversely affect children's learning, since children who are labeled low in intelligence may not make the effort to achieve more than the label implies is expected of them. Besides the harm done individual children, cultural and social-class bias in the tests acts to perpetuate social-class and ethnic-racial differences from one generation to the next. Whatever their real abilities, middle-class children have advantages over lower-class children in obtaining "good" scores and so being moved through the school system toward middle-class careers.

Race   *Race,* biologically defined, refers to inherited differences that can be used to distinguish various categories of people. There is some question whether or not these differences are related to personality and human behavior. So far, despite the efforts of many to prove the contrary, there is no accepted scientific evidence that any of the biological differences on which racial classifications are based are responsible in themselves for observable differences in other characteristics. Moreover, we can question the importance of race as a determinant of behavior by noting enormous variations in personality and behavior *within* any race. The most likely sources of any systematic differences associated with race are cultural and social-class differences, and those are generally due to racism and the expectations it helps to bring into being. This subject is discussed in detail in Chapter 9.

In the United States, the greatest controversy and the most research have concerned possible differences between blacks and whites. One of the problems in trying to determine what is inborn and what is learned, however, is that in this country a number of people labeled black are more similar genetically to white people than they are to other blacks.

Race and IQ Historically, the question concerning racial differences that has probably aroused the most interest is that concerning race and intelligence. English-speaking whites, at least, appear to have believed for centuries that white people were the intellectual superiors of nonwhites, perhaps blacks in particular. This contention was called into question scientifically after World War I, which saw the first application on a wide scale of adult IQ testing on more or less normal populations (American draftees of all races). Although the results at first appeared to validate the long-held belief in white superiority in intelligence, since white draftees, on the average, scored higher on the army IQ test than black soldiers did, more refined analysis of the results soon proved that the differences could be accounted for by social background. Indeed, statistical elaboration of the data showed that, on the average, black soldiers from the northeastern states had *higher* IQ scores than white soldiers from the deep South.[2] Differences in scores by race, then, could not be racial in origin, but were probably accounted for by social-class, educational, and other social differences between the races. Almost all further research along these lines produced similar results, and most social scientists have concluded that purely racial differences in intelligence do not exist.

The controversy was recently revived, however, by a psychologist, Arthur Jensen, and an engineer, William Shockley. They argue that, on the average, whites consistently score fifteen points higher on standardized intelligence tests than blacks, and that this must be due to genetic differences. If social

siblings: children of the same parents.

Taking the Chitling Test

1. A "handkerchief head" is: (a) a cool cat, (b) a porter, (c) an Uncle Tom, (d) a hoddi, (e) a preacher.
2. Which word is most out of place here? (a) splib, (b) blood, (c) gray, (d) spook, (e) black.
3. A "gas head" is a person who has a: (a) fast-moving car, (b) stable of "lace," (c) "process," (d) habit of stealing cars, (e) long jail record for arson.
4. "Down-home" (the South) today, for the average "soul brother" who is picking cotton from sunup until sundown, what is the average earning (take home) for one full day? (a) $.75, (b) $1.65, (c) $3.50, (d) $5, (3) $12.
5. "Bo Diddley" is a: (a) game for children, (b) down-home cheap wine, (c) down-home singer, (d) new dance, (e) Moejoe call.
6. If a pimp is up tight with a woman who gets state aid, what does he mean when he talks about "Mother's Day?" (a) second Sunday in May, (b) third Sunday in June, (c) first of every month, (d) none of these, (e) first and fifteenth of every month.
7. "Hully Gully" came from: (a) East Oakland, (b) Fillmore, (c) Watts, (d) Harlem, (e) Motor City.
8. If a man is called a "blood," then he is a (a) fighter, (b) Mexican-American, (c) Negro, (d) hungry hemophile, (e) Redman or Indian.*

*Those who are not "culturally deprived" will recognize the correct answers are 1. (c), 2. (c), 3. (c), 4. (d), 5. (c), 6. (e), 7. (c), 8. (c).

The Dove Counterbalance General Intelligence Test. One of the principal problems with the conventional IQ test is that it is culturally biased, favoring middle-class values and experiences. To demonstrate that different cultures produce different skills and knowledge bases, sociologist Adrian Dove invented the "Chitling Test." A few questions from this test are here. It is, of course, a test of familiarity with some aspects of the southern black culture of poverty, not of actual intelligence, but Dove's point is that standard IQ tests are culture tests too. Few white Americans will pass this exam.

factors accounted for the observed differences, Jensen and Shockley maintain, they would not remain consistent over time, as many studies have shown they do.[3]

It is true that such differences do exist. Jensen and Shockley cannot explain, however, the fact that the range of scores within the two populations is the same. That is, while the median scores for whites is typically about 100 and that for blacks about 85, some blacks score as high as any whites, and some whites score as low as any blacks. This suggests that something beside genetic makeup is contributing to the average difference. And the results of almost every competent study made of the matter for forty years suggest that this something is social experience.

The most important point about the race-IQ controversy is that there is no way to verify the hypothesis that racially based differences exist. If all children grew up in an identical environment, we could attribute to heredity whatever IQ differences appeared. A fair test would require that everyone share equally in the good things in a society and that racism be eliminated. Since the attainment of such a goal is impossible—no one, not even an identical twin, receives *exactly* the same treatment as anyone else—the controversy concerning racial differences in intelligence is scientifically meaningless. The problems in measuring intelligence make it even more futile. We can conclude this section by noting that the weight of scientific opinion holds that differences in intelligence do not exist as a consequence of racial-biological heredity. Such differences as are observed can be attributed to social and cultural differentials in upbringing and experience.

Temperament   *Temperament* refers to basic, persistent, and diffuse personality characteristics. Presumably, temperamental differences between people are based on biological variations. However, as with aptitudes, the biological basis alone does not determine behavior. Initial biological differences interact with experiences to shape what we call temperament. For example, some infants are spontaneously more active than others. These initial variations are probably not learned. But different responses to a baby's activity (or passivity) can have different consequences. If parents are accepting of an active child, and respond actively and playfully, the child may well develop a more cheerful personality than if the baby's behavior is seen as troublesome or bad and is punished.

In adult personality, variations in expressed temperament occur along such dimensions as warm—cold; strong—weak; happy—unhappy; introverted—extroverted; trusting—suspicious; cooperative—competitive; aggressive—passive. Although a precise, scientific meaning is difficult to assign to such terms, any parent has probably observed that babies can be classified as to the degree to which they exhibit such characteristics. It seems likely, then, that some such general tendencies toward behaving or reacting in these ways may be inborn and more or less characterize people throughout their lives. Clearly, however, even if such tendencies do exist, they are greatly modifiable by social experience.

Sex differences   Until just a few hundred years ago, there were often good reasons for significant differences in what men and women did and what characteristics it was useful for them to develop. Because death rates in most societies were very high, if the group was to survive, women had to spend their adult lives bearing and nursing children. This, combined with the importance of physical strength for certain vital tasks performed by men, meant that apart from whatever other biological differences there might be, men and women would typically behave differently. These differences in what men and women could do continued to be of critical importance until the combination of low infant mortality, lengthened life expectancy, and industrialization transformed some human societies.

This transformation began about three hundred years ago. Yet in modern societies most people continue to expect somewhat different things from men and women, and the belief persists that there are personality differences that are due to sex. Perhaps the greatest sexual equality exists in societies in which techniques for obtaining food, clothing, and shelter are so simple that there is not much basis for a division of labor. But such societies are very rare.

Historically, the first criteria used as a basis for assigning different tasks to different people have been sex and age. In virtually all societies, this has meant that the jobs of greatest power and prestige are dominated by men. In industrial societies, this continues to be the case. Since it is obvious that on the average males are stronger than females, one would expect that jobs such as longshoreman would be held mostly by males—as the job title suggests. But the chairman of the board of almost any large (or small) corporation is also a man—as the title suggests. Is this a consequence of biological differences, or does it result from a combination of discrimination and the different ways in which boys and girls are raised? The traditional demands of motherhood can no longer be held primarily responsible, because women in highly industrialized countries can now expect to have about two children during their twenties and to live into their seventies.

In modern societies, it has so far been impossible to determine exactly how much of the typical difference between the sexes is inborn, because we begin to teach children their sex roles at birth. Children come to think of themselves as male or female at a very early age (usually before three). Their early sex identification will be reinforced repeatedly as other people think of them and behave differently toward them because of their sex. How often do brothers and sisters receive the same toys at Christmas? To predict a parent's response to a child who gets a black eye from winning a fight with the school bully, or to a child who is crying, it is helpful to know the child's sex. Little girls are encouraged to be "sweet"; little boys are pushed toward assertiveness. If boys and girls have different inborn characteristics, it is also true that they get a great deal of help from adults in developing their inclinations.

Those who argue for the importance of learning rather than biology in determining personality differences between males and females often cite the pioneering work of anthropologist Margaret Mead.[4] During the 1930s, she studied three separate cultures in New Guinea. In one culture, the Arapesh, both sexes showed characteristics we usually think of as female. Both men and women were gentle and unaggressive. Parents cooperated in caring for their children, with the emphasis on affection rather than discipline. In contrast, the Mundugumor, whether male or female, were com-

"Are you the opposite sex or am I?"

Look Magazine, April 9, 1963. Reprinted by permission of Chon Day.

Many sex differences are learned.

petitive and aggressive. Neither parent was especially affectionate with the children. Both sexes were harsh, suspicious of others, and aggressive. Finally, the Tchambuli reverse our traditional ideas as to what is normal for males and females. Women do most of the work related to the physical survival of the group. The men spend much of their time performing ceremonies. The women are the more practical, while the men are inclined to gossip and to fuss over their appearance. In this culture, it is the women who are believed to be stronger emotionally and more highly sexed.

Recently, Eleanor Maccoby and Carol Jacklin reviewed over 2,000 books and articles concerning sex differences in motivation, abilities, and behavior.[5] They found convincing evidence for only four sex-related differences. One of these—that boys are typically more aggressive than girls—appears very early, usually before the age of three. But for the other three—that girls have greater verbal ability than boys while boys excel in visual-spatial ability and in mathematical ability—the differences do not appear until eleven years or older. This does not prove that they are learned rather than inborn. It could be that certain levels of maturation are required for basic biological differences to show themselves. But the question of learned versus inborn differences remains.

With regard to other important characteristics, there is no persuasive evidence for or against the existence of sex-determined differences. Are girls, just because they are treated like girls, typically more fearful and timid, more passive, compliant, and "maternal"? Are boys usually more competitive and dominant? We do not know. But it does appear that biological differences between the sexes are probably not nearly as important as culturally learned differences—apart from the obvious differences in reproductive function and average physical strength.

Social Theories of Personality Development

We have learned from the preceding discussion that, although it is important for social science to recognize the biological *basis* of much human behavior, biology can rarely be said to *explain* it. The pure biological determinism of the last century crumbled in the face of the immense differences in human personality and behavior. If behavior were completely determined by genetics, it could not be as variable as it is. Instinct theory suffered even more from the same contradiction. Some human behavior does take place in response to drives, but again, human behavior shows a bewildering variety of responses to the inborn drives. Reflexive behavior, while much more specific, is simple, and no explanation for human personality or behavior can be built on so narrow a base. There *do* seem to be genetically transmitted differences between human beings with regard to intelligence, aptitudes, and temperament, but personality is too complex a phenomenon to be accounted for by them, and, further, their effects are greatly qualified by social experience and cultural opportunity. Similarly, some differences in behavior or personality may be associated with race or sex, but they cannot be proved to be biological in origin and may well be learned. Biology, then, cannot be said to explain human behavior. For explanation, we must look instead to social, group, and individual influences on human personality and activity.

There are six main approaches to the study of these questions in modern social science: *behaviorism,* the *psychoanalytic approach, psychological*

humanism, the *developmental theories, cultural determinism,* and *symbolic interactionism.* The first four of these are associated mainly with the field of psychology, have little influence in modern sociology, and will be discussed only briefly here. Of the two purely sociological approaches, symbolic interactionism so completely dominates the sociological understanding of personality that it is virtually the only true personality theory most sociologists even consider, and so it will be treated at considerably greater length. All six approaches, however, have one thing in common that differentiates them from the biological explanations described previously. Although each begins with somewhat different assumptions about the development of the adult person, all see personality as something that one largely acquires or develops through interaction with other people.

Behaviorism

Behaviorism is based on the assumption that people are the results of their experiences and that one is what one does. The key concepts in behaviorism involve two kinds of *conditioning:* classical and operant.

Conditioning   Some of the earliest work in behaviorism—the first and famous experiments on **classical conditioning**—was done by the Russian physiologist Ivan Pavlov (1849–1936). *Classical conditioning* means training an organism to exhibit an involuntary response when presented with a stimulus that would not normally evoke the response. In Pavlov's best-known experiments, he conditioned dogs to salivate at the ring of a bell. A hungry dog (or person) will salivate involuntarily when food (a "natural" stimulus) is placed before it. This is an *unconditioned response.* Pavlov rang a bell (another stimulus) when he gave food to the dog. This "conditioned" the dog to associate the sound of the bell with the presence of food. After being conditioned this way many times, the dog would salivate at the sound of the bell alone, even in the absence of food. This is a *conditioned response.* It is psychologically significant because salivation is an involuntary action, a reflex over which an organism has no conscious control.

Pavlov's work enables us to understand some

behavior that seems to be irrational. For example, a *possible* explanation for why *some* people overeat is that they were fed whenever they cried when they were infants. Babies cry when they are uncomfortable or want attention, not just when they are hungry. If parents not only correct what is bothering the crying babies but feed them as well, the babies could make an association between feeling better and eating.

The second major form of behavioral conditioning is **operant conditioning,** a form of learning in which reinforcers change the frequency of a behavior. Operant conditioning occurs when a creature does something and almost immediately experiences **reinforcement** in the form of pleasure or pain. The pleasure is a *positive reinforcer,* the pain a *negative* one. As the process is repeated, a positively reinforced behavior becomes more frequent, and a negatively reinforced behavior becomes less frequent. Operant conditioning may be most familiar in connection with learning experiments utilizing rats. In maze learning, for example, the rat is often given an electric shock when it makes an incorrect turn in the maze and a food pellet when it finds its way to the end of the maze.

Criticism   A major criticism of behaviorism is that it does not take into account what a person thinks. Most of the behaviorists' findings have been based on experiments with animals (rats, chimpanzees, pigeons). Explanations of the behavior of these creatures cannot include what they are thinking, because we have no way of knowing this. Behaviorists, however, believe that knowing what people think cannot increase our understanding of human behavior.

Social learning theory   Some sociologists, called *social learning* theorists, have been influenced by the behaviorists. George C. Homans is the best known of these. Homans points out that people communicate symbolic rewards and punishments to each other whenever they are together, and thus affect each other's behavior. A smile can be as important a positive reinforcer as a gift; a frown can be as negative as a slap. Much depends on who is involved. Some people's smiles and frowns are very important to us; others' reactions are not. Social learning theory is concerned with how the

> **classical conditioning:** training an organism to exhibit an involuntary response when presented with a stimulus that would not normally evoke it.
>
> **operant conditioning:** encouraging or discouraging the exhibition of specific behaviors through the application of positive or negative reinforcement.
>
> **reinforcement:** an event that affects the frequency of a learned behavior. A *positive* reinforcement increases the frequency with which a behavior will be exhibited by rewarding it through following it with a pleasurable experience, for example, being fed or praised. A *negative* reinforcement decreases the frequency with which a behavior is exhibited by following it with the infliction of pain or some other unpleasant experience.

Males are, typically, more aggressive than females, but most *behavior* is learned.

Unresolved Oedipal crisis.

rewards and punishments we communicate to each other affect how we act.

Social learning theory is criticized for not being able to specify the conditions under which something will be a positive or negative reinforcer. This problem is not serious if one wishes to explain rat behavior. But it is serious if the goal is to explain human behavior. As Homans admits, "People find the damndest things rewarding."[6] Why do some people spend years with someone who is constantly hurting them? Why did Joan of Arc prefer death at the stake to denying her "voices"? Why did Peter deny he knew Christ and later die for his belief that Christ is God? Social learning theorists cannot tell us.

The Psychoanalytic Approach

Sigmund Freud The psychoanalytic approach originated with Sigmund Freud (1856–1939). Although his work is open to a number of serious criticisms, it is probably impossible to overstate Freud's impact on modern social science.

Freud began publishing in a Western world in which accepted beliefs included the idea that people are born with a "still small voice"—their conscience—that serves as an infallible guide to behavior. If people behaved badly, then they deserved to be punished because their behavior was a matter of choice. Punishment was not a way to change behavior, but a just retribution for a wrong. People were believed to behave rationally. Freud contradicted all these beliefs with his revolu-

tionary idea that behavior and personality are affected by mental states of which the individual is unaware.

Freud saw personality developing as the child passes through a series of stages. These stages are marked by biological factors, but their outcome reflects social experience. Depending on what parents—especially mothers—do, children may become fixated—stuck—at a certain stage. The various forms of **neurotic** behavior are the result of fixation. The Freudian stages are:

1. *The oral stage* (birth to about one year): The child's major source of pleasure is being fed. Fixation can occur if the child is either frustrated or overindulged. As adults, "oral" personalities include alcoholics and people who overeat.

2. *The anal stage* (one to three years): Here the crucial factor is when and how the child is toilet-trained. Fixation at this stage results in "anal" personalities, such as people who are grasping and stingy.

3. *The phallic stage* (three to six years): The child begins to experience pleasure from his sex organs. Here Freud introduces his concepts of the **Oedipus complex,** for boys, and the Electra complex, for girls. Allegedly, the child sexually desires the parent of the opposite sex, and consequently is jealous of the parent of the same sex. Boys are jealous and resentful of their fathers, girls of their mothers. But normally the child is denied these desires for the opposite-sex parent and is fearful of his adult rival.

Conflict with someone you depend on for survival is dangerous. If all goes well, an Oedipus or Electra complex is avoided as the child represses hostility, becoming no longer aware of it, and *identifies* with—admires and tries to imitate—the parent of the same sex. This is the Freudian explanation for why most boys imitate their fathers and girls their mothers.

4. *The latency period* (six years to adolescence): The child begins to be concerned with people outside the family—other children and adults (such as teachers). This is a time in which erotic impulses are latent.

5. *The genital stage* (adolescence and beyond): With the coming of physical maturity, the sexuality that was repressed during latency reappears, and the person must prepare for marriage and adult responsibilities.

Today, most social scientists agree with Freud that childhood is normally an especially important period in shaping adult personality. His concept of identification is often used to explain why children (and adults) imitate others. We recognize the existence and importance of the unconscious mind, and we acknowledge the sensual nature of children. It is with general principles such as these that Freud made his greatest contribution. But many of his specific hypotheses have not stood up well to the evidence. For example, there is no convincing evidence that the psychosexual stages Freud hypothesized explain adult personality. But there *is* evidence that differences in feeding, weaning, and toilet training have no effect on adult personality, contrary to what one would expect if the Freudian ideas were correct.[7]

Erik Erikson In recent years, the psychoanalytical perspective has broadened to include a concern not only with "sick" people, but also with degrees of self-development. The work of Erik Erikson is a good example of this new humanism in psychology. Erikson, like Freud, believes that there are stages of personality development, each of which poses a kind of crisis for people on their way to maturity. Successful coping at each stage is necessary if the individual is to have a chance for full personal development. But, unlike Freud, Erikson sees these challenges as primarily social in nature

neurotic: of or pertaining to *neurosis,* a relatively mild, learned, emotional disorder that handicaps or distresses a person without preventing him from carrying on his life. Common classic neuroses are *anxiety* (groundless fear of things or situations that are not feared by others) and *psychosomaisis* (imaginary illness or excessive fear of becoming ill).

Oedipus complex: the Freudian concept that a male child will sexually desire his mother and be jealous of his father. It is named for the Greek legend in which Oedipus, who was separated from his parents as a child and did not know them, meets and kills his father, then king of Thebes, and later meets, falls in love with, and marries his mother. (As you would expect, he comes to a bad end.) Freud believed that an inevitable stage in the development of the male child was one in which he relives this drama through developing sexual desire for his mother and consequent jealousy of his father. This Freud called the "Oedipal crisis." If unsatisfactorily resolved in normal maturation, Freud believed, it led to a "complex," a continuing neurotic hangover from the earlier state that would cause the individual to engage in irrational or phobic behavior. Not one to discriminate against males, Freud discovered a corresponding problem for women, the *Electra complex,* named for another figure from Greek mythology.

and is concerned with development that goes beyond simply not being neurotic (see Table 4-1).

Erikson sees as basic to all positive personality development the general tendency to trust people, including oneself. This does not mean blind gullibility, but rather, unless there is evidence to the contrary, a tendency *not* to expect the *worst* from people. If basic trust is adequately established, the child can develop a healthy autonomy and self-respect. Erikson's work constitutes a bridge between the psychoanalytic and humanist views of personality.

Psychological Humanism

Psychological humanism is concerned with the question: What is a "fully functioning," "self-actualizing," or completely healthy personality? How is such a personality developed? Most people in this field are clinical psychologists, and they are concerned with helping people to lead happier, fuller lives.

Carl Rogers and Abraham Maslow   Two major figures among the humanistic psychologists are Carl Rogers and Abraham Maslow. Rogers believes that everyone has a tendency toward "self-actualization," the realization of one's potentials, and stresses that the human need for acceptance and approval is essential if self-actualization is to occur. Mental health depends on a correspondence between the person's self-concept and his behavior.

Maslow, like Rogers, believes that there are degrees of development of personality, and he shares Rogers's interest in people who approximate the ideal of being fully functioning or self-actualizing. Maslow studied a number of individuals he believed were much nearer to self-actualization than most of us are. He concluded that such people perceive reality particularly well. They accept people (including themselves) and nature as they are. Although they generally conform to the norms of their society, their behavior tends to be more spontaneous than that of most people. They are concerned with basic issues rather than details. They like having a certain amount of privacy, but they do like other people. They want to be helpful

when they can, but prefer a few close friends to many superficial ones. They are not racially prejudiced, and they are creative. They have faults, too. A really perfect person (if one were to exist) would probably be a pain to everyone else.

Humanistic psychologists share a belief that people can become happy, creative, and helpful. This requires effort on their part and help from others. For example, to return to Erikson, it is difficult for a child to develop basic trust if his parents hate him. In common with all the personality theorists, humanists begin with the assumption that personality is not something fixed at birth. It develops through interaction with other people.

Groups   In recent years, there has been a growing awareness of how groups can act to help members solve their problems and generally become happier, more productive people. The Human Potential movement, which is a part of this larger movement, is based on the humanistic approach. Sometimes the groups are called sensitivity training or encounter groups. Whatever minor differences exist between the different approaches, they share the assumptions of humanistic psychology that people can change, and that what is important is the present, not the past. They also believe that what is significant to a person is how *he* perceives his experience, not how someone else might. The goal of such groups is to increase understanding of others and of one's self and to achieve self-acceptance.

Developmental Theories

Unlike the other major approaches to personality, the developmental approach focuses on the physical maturation of the child. It does not deny the importance of experience and social interaction, but it reminds us that people are biological as well as social. The researcher best known for this approach is Jean Piaget, a Swiss psychologist. After many years observing children, he has accumulated evidence that cognitive and moral development can only proceed in stages determined by the child's intellectual capacity, which, in turn, can develop no faster than his physical maturation.

Piaget's four developmental stages are shown in

Table 4-1   The stages of human development as conceived by Freud and Erikson

Freud		Erikson	
Developmental stage	Characteristics	Developmental stage	Crisis
1. Oral (birth to 1 year)	Feeding as principal stimulation and source of pleasure; attention centered on oral gratification	1. Oral-sensory (birth to 1½ years)	Basic trust versus mistrust: learning to develop trust in one's parents, oneself, and the world
2. Anal (1-3 years)	Attention focused on bowel and bladder function as a result of toilet training; first independence discovered through ability to control elimination	2. Muscular-anal (1½ to 4 years)	Autonomy versus doubt and shame: developing a sense of self-control without loss of self-esteem
3. Phallic (3-6 years)	Discovery of the sex organs and that they may be manipulated for pleasure; first awareness of sexuality; jealousy of same-sex parent in competition for affection of opposite-sex parent (the Oedipal crisis)	3. Locomotor genital (4 to 6 years)	Initiative versus guilt: developing a conscience, sex role, and learning to undertake a task for the sake of being active and creative
4. Latency (6 to adolescence)	The Oedipal crisis is resolved or suppressed; erotic impulses become latent and concern centers on others outside the family	4. Latency (6 to 11 years)	Industry versus inferiority: receiving systematic instruction, developing determination to master whatever one is doing
5. Genital (adolescence and beyond)	Sexuality reappears with physical maturity; heterosexual interests focused on nonfamily members dominate; assumption of adult roles and interests	5. Adolescence	Identity versus role confusion: not "Who am I?" but "Which way can I be?"
		6. Young adulthood	Intimacy versus isolation: study and work toward a specific career, selection of a partner for an extended intimate relationship
		7. Adulthood	Generativity versus stagnation: parental preparation for the next generation and support of cultural values
		8. Maturity	Ego integrity versus despair: development of wisdom and a philosophy of life

Note that while Freud and Erikson differ on the number of stages in development and their specific content, there is general agreement on the progress of development and its emotional-sexual content. Freud chooses a specifically sexual metaphor to describe the stages of maturation, while Erikson focuses on emotional crises that must be resolved. One of the principal differences between the two schemes is that Erikson sees development as continuing after physical maturity.

Table 4-2. Very small children, those in the *sensory-motor stage* (birth to two years), cannot understand their society's rules, no matter how diligently they are taught. In the *preoperational stage* (two to seven years), they can learn the rules, but they perceive them merely as something not to be questioned—though not always obeyed. Finally, in the *concrete-* and *formal-operational stages,* they develop the full capacity to reason. They understand the spirit as well as the letter of the law. They can learn the meaning—or lack of meaning—of rules, and that they can be modified.

One of Piaget's principal contributions is to point out that moral judgments, as well as intellectual abilities, require a certain level of maturation. A five-year-old asked, "Who did the worse thing, a child who deliberately smashed a glass or a child who, in trying to help his mother, accidently broke a whole tray of glasses?" will usually answer, "The child who broke the most glasses." A ten-year-old will typically hold that the deliberate destruction of one glass is the more serious offense.

Like those beginning from a psychoanalytical or a humanistic approach, Piaget and his students recognize that human development proceeds in stages. But they remind us that the child's capacities are determined by his physical as well as his social development.

Cultural Determinism

Cultural determinists view personality as almost entirely the result of culture. All significant differences in personality are learned, and what is learned is determined by the culture. Cultural determinism became popular as anthropology grew and studies appeared showing the wide variations in behavior considered ideal by different cultures.

Cultural determinism reached the height of its influence during the 1940s. The concepts of basic personality, social character, national character, and modal (typical) personality were developed to express the idea that within a culture a particular personality type would be most common and considered normal. With some notable exceptions (for instance, Margaret Mead), students of national character ignored differences in behavior typical of

"Well, I'm 26. I guess I'm through with all my stages."

Chronicle Features Syndicate.

males and females, old and young, and so forth. Most of their conclusions were based on observations of small, isolated, and technologically simple societies. In such societies, we should expect considerably more homogeneity in beliefs and behaviors than in large, complex societies characterized by considerable racial and ethnic, regional, religious, and (probably most important) social-class differences.

David Riesman The major attempt to apply this approach to a large, complex society is David Riesman's *The Lonely Crowd.*[8] Riesman was concerned with the problem of social control. How is it that society gets at least the minimal conformity to norms necessary for its survival? He suggested that this is accomplished through three distinct types of "social character."

The first of these is the *tradition-directed* character. People with such a character accept the legitimacy of norms because, to their knowledge, these are the only norms that have ever existed. In societies where the tradition-directed character is pervasive, there should be few pressures on a person to change, since most people share the traditional beliefs. Little social change occurs, and conformity to conventional ways is usually unquestioned. Tradition-directed personalities are typical of small, isolated societies with simple technologies.

According to Riesman, during the period of early industrialization, a new character type emerged: the _inner-directed_. This person learns certain norms and values early in life and tries to follow them no matter what others may say or do. Because an industrializing society is characterized by instability and rapid social change, the consistency in norms characteristic of tradition-directed societies disappears, and people facing challenges from others as to the rightness of their ways and beliefs require strong inner direction to guide them.

Finally, in an economically developed country, the _other-directed_ character becomes the dominant type. Social change accelerates. Most people learn to adapt and go through life changing their beliefs and behavior in response to the changing expectations of those around them.

How close is the relationship between culture and personality? To understand why and when people are apt to behave in certain ways—and what meaning this behavior has—one must know the culture. Yet even in small, traditional societies, behavior is less uniform than foreign observers first thought. One recent review of the culture and personality literature concludes that generally there appears to be greater variation in personalities _within_ cultures than between them.[9]

Symbolic Interactionism: The Development of Self

Symbolic interactionism, or simply interactionism, is more closely identified with sociology than with psychology. Indeed, it is _the_ dominating sociological understanding of personality, cultural determinism being too unspecific for scientific purposes, and the psychological theories too individualistic and inadequately social in nature. Interactionism, as we saw in Chapter 1, is always associated with the name of George Herbert Mead, who founded it. Like the other views of personality discussed above, it assumes that interaction between individuals is a necessary component of personality development. But interaction largely takes place between people in terms of _symbols,_ in particular, language; and so detailed attention is

Table 4-2 Piaget's stages of child development

Developmental stage	Characteristics
Sensory-motor (birth to 2 years)	Learning to observe and "reconstruct"; e.g., an attractive object held before the child and then dropped will not be "tracked" at 8 months, but by 19 months a coin shown in the hand and then hidden will first be sought in the hand and then in the hiding place
Preoperational (2–7 years)	Acquisition of language, beginning of dreaming while asleep, first attempts at symbolic play (letting one object "stand for" another), first attempts at graphic representation (drawing), confusion of words and symbols with the things symbolized; by age 7, symbols are clearly understood and manipulated
Concrete-operational (7–11 years)	Performing imaginatively or mentally what previously would have been acted out; distinguishing among logical classes of things
Formal-operational (12–15 years)	Advanced symboling; use of metaphor; reasoning contrary to fact (if—contrary to fact—such and such were true, then . . .)

paid to the nature of language and symbolizing and their influence on the process that results in human personality.

Using language (and its learning and employment) as his framework of analysis, Mead described three stages of development through which the human personality passes in the course of maturation. Mead called them the stage of developing self-consciousness, the play stage, and the game stage. After briefly describing the initial socialization of the child, we will elaborate on these three stages of personality development. Then we will consider what Charles Horton Cooley called "self-concept"—the image we have of ourselves—how we acquire it, and its importance in the development and maintenance of the self, or personality.

Socialization and language   The process through which human infants learn to become social beings and members of their societies is called **socialization**. A useful synonym is enculturation of the individual, since what happens is that the culture is impressed upon a young human being who initially has none. In the course of this socialization process, the personality is developed. The vehicle through which socialization takes place is language. In the process of interacting with others through the use of language symbols, we develop our personality.

Mead's three stages[10]   Of course, an infant does not learn language all at once. Indeed, the constant talk directed at the child almost from birth is at first not understood as symbolic. If children perceive the verbal noises about them at all, they must appear first as *signs,* merely as sounds attached to certain events or objects, in the same way that dark clouds are attached to rain. Later, children begin to acquire the *meaning* of words and, just as important, the norms and values that society attaches to the events for which they stand. As children mature, they begin to talk to themselves. In so doing, they acquire the same meanings and values that others have been unconsciously teaching them. In short, they learn to use and understand symbols.

The stage of developing self-consciousness   The *stage of developing self-consciousness,* the first of

Mead's three stages, is apparent in most children by the age of two. It is the product of language learning and the social interactions that necessarily accompany it. Consider the following. The child approaches the television or hi-fi and reaches out a hand to twirl the dial (as he has done many times in the past). Suddenly, he slaps himself on the wrist with his other hand and says, "No-no, bad boy, mustn't touch!" The act of reaching for the dial has stimulated in him the same response that his action had previously elicited from someone else. In reacting to himself as he has learned others will react to him, the child has *internalized* the role of someone else; he has made the other a part of himself and has become conscious of himself in the same way that others are conscious of him. He has become *self-conscious,* an action that is possible only through the use of language. Language is the medium that allows us to see ourselves as others see us and to consider ourselves as objects as well as subjects.

The metaphor of the theater is commonly used to make this point. The self can be viewed as consisting of two parts, subject and object (or actor and role). The subjective aspect of self is the actor, the "I" that initiates, plans, and experiences. The objective aspect of self is the part played by the actor, the "me" that others observe acting out the initiatives of the actor. The "me" consists of a number of roles (for example, student, son or daughter, sister or brother, Catholic or Methodist), while the "I" thinks about these roles and acts them out.

The play stage   The *play stage* is the second major growth stage of the human personality. The types of play engaged in and the mentality that makes them possible continue to illuminate the functions of language and society in forming the human personality. As the child grows up, verbal ability increases and play takes on increasingly organized form. At the age of three, a little girl having the traditional tea party with her dolls and teddy bear may vary her voice range from high squeaks to low growls in order to play all the roles her task requires. She may also move to stand behind each "actor" as she plays the part. A year later, she will probably conduct the entire enterprise from one spot and in one voice. At the age of three, she needs the physical differentiation in order to remain clear in her own mind what role she is playing at any instant; by the age of four, she can maintain the differentiation mentally without difficulty. She has reached a level of verbal organization where she can manipulate the various roles without physical action.

It is useful at this point to define more precisely the concept of role. In any society, there will be certain groupings whose social organization is standardized, for example, the family and the war band. The social organization of each of these standard groups will consist in part of conventionalized behaviors for the individuals who make them up. These standardized behaviors may be thought of as positions (such as mother, little boy, or chief). The way in which given individuals actually enact their positions is called a **role.** And people know how to play roles because norms attached to the various positions inform us how to act them out, how we are "supposed to" behave as a mother, little boy, or chief. During the course of language learning just described, children learn the norms that are relevant to the roles they play in interaction with the members of society with whom they come in contact. And that learning defines their positions at a particular time.

The norm that makes the television a no-no is a part of the role description of small boy family member; a girl might be treated somewhat differently. In the tea party example, the little girl having the solitary party with her dolls is likely to enact the role of mother to the dolls. She behaves "as a mother is supposed to," that is, according to the norms she has learned for mother behavior. Acting out the mother role, she treats her dolls as children—who had better behave as she has been made to!

The significance of play, once it becomes organized by a degree of sophisticated verbal ability, is that it is likely to involve the child in a great deal of role playing. Children from four to eight years of age spend large proportions of their free time in imaginative role playing of one kind or another. Cowboys and Indians, mothers and fathers, fairy princesses, soldiers, and teachers are all common roles assumed by children in play. Children learn two things through this kind of activity. They learn to play the adult roles around them, and they learn who they are by "being" who they are not. They try

socialization: the process through which the human young acquire the culture of their societies and their own personalities, largely through interaction with others and the acquisition and utilization of language.

role: any regularly recurring cluster of activity enacted by individuals occupying a particular position; for example, the activities conventionally associated with occupying the positions "mother," "doctor," or "elderly person."

Role-learning: A worried father counts his paper money, a stack of bills before him. His son shows the same concentration counting coins.

out different roles, seeing how it might be to play a specific role or to feel a particular emotion. In every case, the role chosen is organized by norms as the child has learned them. In this sense, play is a significant preparation for later life.

All the roles in children's play are those of *particular others*—a firefighter, mother, fairy princess, and so on. Models for these roles come from television, storybooks, and daily life. They are always concrete, in the sense that the child is imaginatively imitating some person, character, or occupational role as seen from his own viewpoint. Role playing is fluid, subject only to the limitations of the child's own understanding of the role or position. While children may play in the company of others cooperatively, the others do not determine the character of the role played. That is, a child can define his own role as a cowboy, for example, without reference to the way another child acts out her role as an Indian. Behavior is adjusted to that of the other child's in order to keep the play going, but the *character* of the roles played is independent. The play requires only transitory agreements between the children as to the general outlines of their behavior.

The game stage When the child reaches about eight years of age, a new level of personality development appears. This level, which Mead called the *game stage,* is the third and final stage of personality development. It is manifested by the child's ability to demonstrate the mental and verbal organization demanded by and incorporated in games.

In play, roles are free, fluid, and independent of each other; games, however, are organized by and constituted of rules (explicit norms). That is, in play children can do and be what they wish, and other players can adjust their behavior accordingly. But in games, the roles are related to each other by rules that define what those roles are and how they are to be played. The rules also define the object of the game, the limits placed on the players, the "ground" on which the game is to be played, and so on. In free play, the action *is* the play; in a very profound sense, however, games *are* rules. In play, the meaning of the role is what one does with it. In games, however, the meaning of the role is defined

by the rules of the game. In perhaps the most simple and universal of all games, hide-and-seek, there are only two roles—hider and seeker—although more than one person can take either role and any number can play the game. But there is no meaning in hiding if no one seeks, or in seeking if no one hides. Thus, in games *the meaning of one role lies solely in its relation to the other roles; it has no meaning outside that relation.* A sociological definition might put it that play is characterized by role playing, while games are characterized by position-enactment, since the rules are, in effect, the social norms of the game.

The reason game playing symbolizes a new stage of personality development is that the player, in order to do his part, must know the roles of all the other players and adjust his behavior generally to theirs (while in the play stage one needed to know only one role and could vary it as one chose). The game of football illustrates the need to know others' roles in order to play the game properly.

When a quarterback is deciding what play to call, he must take into consideration not only what might work but also how every person on the field has been performing, the ground position, score, time, down, weather, and so on. In addition, he must act within the limits permitted by the rules. A pass-defense problem cannot be solved by shooting the defender to be eliminated. In order to make the decision, then, the quarterback must know the role not of *particular others* but of a *general other:* he must assess his expectations for all other players within the possibilities dictated by the rules. He must know the roles of all other players *simultaneously,* as a response to the total situation. The significance of games for the social development of the human personality lies in their duplication of the individual's experiences in the social community. Most people organize their behavior around their expectations of a generalized other, which is to say around their understanding of norms and positions and how the society expects them to behave.

Society becomes a part of us because of our learned understanding of its expectations (norms), which we internalize in our personality structure. We learn this understanding through language, and we integrate it into our personality through the use of language and role playing. Thus, language makes us social through an involved learning process in which we internalize the values and expectations that constitute the normative system and social structure of our society.

Self-concept   Charles Horton Cooley (1864–1929) is often regarded as the cofounder, with Mead, of symbolic interactionism. His principal contribution was examination of the *self-concept*—how one sees and evaluates one's self. The notion of self-concept is sociologically important because it calls attention to the fact that what we think of ourselves often determines how we behave; people who do not believe that they can swim do not often go off the high board.

The looking-glass self   Cooley coined the phrase **looking-glass self** to refer to the origins and nature of self-concepts. The looking-glass self, he asserted, has three elements: (1) our imagination or image of how we appear or present ourselves to another; (2) an imagination or image of the other's judgment of that appearance or presentation; and (3) some self-feeling about that judgment, such as pride or shame that another sees us in that way. Thus, we accumulate a set of beliefs and evaluations about ourselves—who and what we are and what that means in our society. This is the **self-concept.**

Self-concept is learned   Cooley's understanding of how the looking-glass self operates is still widely accepted today. It implies, of course, that we learn our self-concepts from and in interaction with others. In the same way that we find out literally "what we look like" by inspecting our reflections in a mirror, we find out figuratively "how we appear to others" by inspecting their reactions to us. How do we know that we are tall or short, good-looking or plain, or even male or female? Only because all of our lives and in one way or another others have told us so. Or, to put it within the looking-glass self framework, because we have interpreted their reactions to us as telling us so. (Not all people are equally important to us, of course; once a self-concept is formed, the reactions of what are called "significant others" become most important to us,

> **looking-glass self:**   a term coined by Charles Horton Cooley to describe the process through which the *self-concept* is formed. It has three stages: (1) an idea of how we "appear" to another, (2) an idea of the other's judgment of that "appearance," and (3) some self-feeling, such as pride or shame, about the imagined judgment.
>
> **self-concept:**   how one sees and evaluates one's self; one's self-image.
>
> **self-fulfilling prophecy:**   a forecast or expectation whose existence creates the conditions for its own fulfillment.
>
> **Pygmalion effect:**   a special type of self-fulfilling prophecy in which people conform to the expectations that others hold for them regardless of their true characters or abilities; as when school children believed by their teachers to be dull act dull.

and we may feel free to reject some reactions and adopt others. But every person's self-image begins with and remains influenced by the responses of some other people.)

An essential quality of the self-concept is that it is subjective. It goes on in our heads and is based on our interpretation of the reactions of others, which are frequently ambiguous. But this means that the self-concept is peculiarly vulnerable to error. First, we may misinterpret the reactions of the other, assigning them meanings the other did not intend. Second, the responses of all others to us is not entirely consistent, so we receive mixed messages about ourselves in the course of interacting with a number of people. Finally, of course, our own behavior is not entirely consistent either, so that varying responses from others are sometimes an accurate reflection of varying behavior on our own part, although we may not be aware of it.

The Pygmalion effect   These facts about the nature of self-concept make possible two different kinds of **self-fulfilling prophecies**—forecasts that create the conditions for their own fulfillment. The first kind we bring on ourselves, and the second others impose on us. The first is a commonplace to psychiatrists (because it is often deeply involved in neurosis), while the second has become familiar to sociologists and educators under the name **Pygmalion effect.**

© Jules Feiffer.

The looking-glass self in action.

In the first instance, it often happens, since we *are* social creatures, constantly interacting with each other, that the things we expect to happen do occur, brought about by our expectation of them. If you really do believe that other people are unfriendly and manipulative, ready to "do you in" or "take you" at any opportunity, you are likely to find many who will treat you that way. Your own expectations of them will create the response that you receive.

The Pygmalion effect works in a similar way: the expectations that others hold of you may produce confirming behavior. You may already be familiar with the basic Pygmalion concept (so called after a George Bernard Shaw play of that name) from the musical or movie *My Fair Lady.* In that fiction, a young Cockney girl, Eliza Doolittle, ignorant, prejudiced, and speaking an atrocious dialect, is remade into an English society lady by a gentleman with high expectations for her. The point is that, despite her background, she alters her behavior to conform to his expectations for her, becoming something quite different from anything anyone, herself included, would have believed.

The Pygmalion effect also works in the other direction: people may learn to be (or "play") stupid, crazy, or "bad" to conform to others' expectations for them. Children considered "dull" by their teacher often act so as to confirm the teacher's expectations. This, of course, permits the others to continue to treat them in the ways they expect them to behave, and so the process is circular, or self-confirming.

The Socialization Process

We saw earlier how socialization *works,* how children, through interaction with others, acquire symbols and meanings, begin to apply them to themselves and play roles, develop a self-concept, and so forth. But socialization does not happen just once, in childhood, and then result in a finished and thenceforth unchanging product: the personality. It is a lifelong phenomenon that never ends; personality formation is never completed, although the major dimensions probably are set in childhood.

As you have seen already, the principal *vehicle* of the socialization process is social interaction utilizing language. It is primarily through interaction with others that we acquire a personality, or a "self." Although any interaction with anyone may have some effects on us, some people and some situations are likely to be much more important than others. Certain *agents of socialization* usually dominate the process: the family, the peer group, the school, and the mass media. The socialization process is also tied closely to the *life-cycle.* Different socialization agents have differing values and importance and influence at different stages of life. Further, the process does not always work the same way, or as well, for everyone. Three standard kinds of *problems of socialization* are discussed below. In addition, the absence or withdrawal of interaction can have profound effects on socialization, and we devote a section to what is known about that. Finally, socialization is also deeply interrelated with the phenomenon of *social control,* the various ways in which a society secures conformity to its norms.

Primary Agents of Socialization

In most societies, the *family* is the most important socialization agent. In some societies this means that a number of people will be involved in this process in important ways. The "family" in highly industrialized societies often includes only one or both parents and their dependent children. Parents, or people playing the parent role, are most important to the children's socialization. Most of the child's early interaction is with these people, and his dependency makes him especially likely to take them as models to be imitated. There is evidence that children tend to imitate most those who have power or control over things they want.[11] Who fits this description better than the adults who are caring for the child? Siblings also have a part in socialization. Younger children are especially likely to imitate older ones, which is what we would expect if the less powerful tend to imitate the more powerful.[12]

Outside of the family, probably the major influences on the child are the school and the **peer group,** a group whose members are of the same sex and similar ages. Much of the socialization gained in school comes from peers, as well as teachers.

The most powerful socializing agents are those on whom the child is most dependent, emotionally as well as physically, and those with whom he or she has the greatest amount of face-to-face interaction. Cooley called such interaction "primary" because it is crucial in the individual's personal and social development. Typically it occurs in **primary groups**.

peer group: a primary group composed of members of like age and sex. It is typically formed in work and play situations and is probably the most important socializing agent aside from the family.

primary group: a small group, such as a family or play group, where relations between members are characterized by emotional intimacy, face-to-face interaction, and revelation of total personality.

Parents are the most important agents of socialization, and children learn by imitating them.

Copyright, 1971, G. B. Trudeau. Distributed by Universal Press Syndicate.

Pygmalion effect.

Along with the notion of self-concept, the concept of the primary group is probably Cooley's best-known contribution to sociology. A *primary group* is a small group, like the family or children's play group, where interactions between members are frequent, emotionally close, and based on the interplay of members' total personalities, rather than only one aspect of personality. (In your classroom, for example, your instructor is likely to observe only one, or a very few, aspects of your total personality. Your family or your roommate, however, knows many sides of it.) Primary groups are sociologically important because so much of individual socialization takes place within them. They are psychologically important to individuals because most of our emotional needs, like needs for affection and approval, are met within their bounds.

In modern societies, however, socialization also occurs through exposure to the *mass media*—books, magazines, newspapers, radio, films, and television. In our society, the most important mass medium is television. At least 95 percent of homes in the United States have televisions, and in the typical home, a set is on about six hours a day. Numerous studies have been done in an effort to determine the effects of television on children. In 1971, the U.S. Surgeon General's Scientific Advisory Committee on Television and Social Behavior concluded that there is evidence that television has an impact.[13] Although the nature of that impact remains controversial, the committee concluded that both aggressive and "pro-social" behavior is to some degree related to the kinds of programs children watch. Most of the studies the committee

cited concerned aggression, and the committee concluded that violent programs encourage aggressive behavior in at least some children. We do not know the extent to which television influences children's ideas of what is and what ought to be. But given the time the average child spends watching television, it would be surprising if it had no effect.

Socialization and the Life-Cycle

All societies expect somewhat different kinds of behavior from people of different ages. In addition to the distinctions made in traditional societies between children, mature adults, and the aged, modern societies often include the stage of adolescence. Adolescents are physically mature and are expected to behave more maturely than children. Yet they are not extended the privileges (and obligations) of an adult.

Each transition from one age group to another poses certain challenges by demanding somewhat changed behavior, and societies vary in the difficulty of adjustments required at such times. For example, although old age everywhere brings physical decline, it is far more pleasant in some societies than in others. In many traditional societies, the old are honored for their wisdom. But in rapidly changing societies, old people are often regarded as out-of-date rather than wise. Their economic usefulness is deliberately reduced through retirement, and they are segregated from the rest of society in retirement communities or "homes." It is little wonder that many of the elderly resist socialization to the role society has defined for them: useless, old-fashioned, and meddlesome people. However, most old people are powerless to do anything about their fate and face the task of adjusting more or less gracefully.

Socialization into the adolescent role is difficult partly because there is so much confusion about what the role is or should be. This being the case, many adolescents push for maximum freedom and minimum responsibility, while their elders hope for the reverse. Particularly in a society in which adult roles are to some degree open to choice for many people, adolescence can be a trying period. The questions "Who am I?" and "What do I want?" that trouble so many teenagers in modern societies would never have occurred to their ancestors, who moved from childhood to adulthood immediately with few choices to make.

The mature adult role is difficult to learn in American society: how to be a successful participant in the economy, the community, and in marriage and child rearing. Obligations and responsibilities are heaviest during this period of life. Yet in most societies these disadvantages are more than offset by the power and prestige of adult status. Adult roles in societies with simple economies and technologies are often physically difficult, but usually not otherwise demanding. In complex, industrial societies, many adult roles require skill and complex decision making. Socialization to adult roles *within* a culture also varies in difficulty. The socialization in becoming a priest or military officer, for example, is more intensive and demanding than is socialization for most roles in our society. For roles that require a marked break with past behavior, specialized institutions are set up to accomplish the needed change. For the priest there is the seminary; for the officer, the training camp.

Some occupations, while not requiring such extensive changes, do involve a certain amount of specialization beyond simply learning job skills. Especially in the professions—for example, law, medicine, teaching—there is an effort to turn out new members who have not only certain knowledge and skills, but also certain values, attitudes, and beliefs. "Fudging the data," for example, should be unthinkable for the research scientist.

"Aw, Mom . . . If the guys ever saw me on that thing they'd run me outa town."

"Dennis the Menace," © 1974 Field Newspaper Syndicate T.M.®

The peer group is a primary agent of socialization.

Socialization to old age is difficult—and sometimes painful—in American society.

Copyright, 1971, G. B. Trudeau. Distributed by Universal Press Syndicate.

And not becoming emotionally involved with patients often becomes automatic with physicians and nurses; the pleasing bedside manner may conceal the basic noninvolvement.

Effective socialization requires knowing not only what is expected of one at each stage in life, but also when one has arrived at that stage. Again, modern societies are less helpful than traditional ones. Typically, traditional societies mark important transitions in the life-cycle with **rites of passage.** There is a public ceremony, following which the person views himself, and is viewed by other members of the community, as having passed into a new status. In modern societies, confirmations and bar mitzvahs, marriages, and funerals remain as relatively weak vestiges of the old definitive rites.

The age at which one becomes an adult is especially flexible. Some people successfully assume an adult status by their late teens, while others have not done so (often from choice) by their late twenties. This means that confidence that one is doing "the right thing" is weakened. It also means that recognition of the person as an adult is inconsistent. Sometimes a young person is treated as an adolescent, sometimes as an adult.

Problems of Socialization

By the time that most people reach adult status, the socialization process—while never over—has been satisfactorily accomplished to a large degree (at least to the point that most of us do what is expected enough of the time that things do not completely fall apart). But three kinds of problems can occur that have profound effects not only for

People are sometimes socialized to subcultural values.

the individuals concerned, but for the whole society. These problems may be more common in complex, industrialized societies, but they are probably never entirely absent anywhere. The problems are (1) faulty or inadequate socialization, (2) socialization to deviance, and (3) socialization to social disadvantage.

Faulty or inadequate socialization This type of socialization results from a failure of proper *parenting*—the failure of parents to "bring their kids up right." Such failures may result from lack of positive parental emotional support and control, and they have the consequence of producing children who are, in a sense, uncivilized, who have never internalized reasonable norms for their own conduct. (The parental failure is probably the result of similar problems in the parents themselves.) Faulty socialization results in neurosis; the child, usually because of a combination of lack of loving support and excessive parental criticism, comes to think badly of himself or herself and has a poor or distorted self-concept. Inadequate socialization can even produce psychopaths, individuals so completely centered on meeting their own emotional needs that other people do not exist for them except as objects to be manipulated.

Socialization to deviance This type of socialization is usually the result of upbringing in a subculture whose norms are defined as deviant by the larger society. Thus the child may be perfectly adapted to that subculture, adequately socialized to its values and behaviors, but be what people outside that subculture regard as the wrong kind of person. Most criminals learn their behavior from other criminals, and the street gangs and juvenile authority lockups of major cities are frequently breeding grounds for further antisocial behavior.

Socialization to social disadvantage   This type of socialization occurs among the very poor and among disadvantaged racial and ethnic minorities. Here, again, the child may be adequately and satisfactorily socialized to the life around him, but in learning his subculture, he learns all of the mechanisms that it has generated to accommodate its location in the social order. These, in turn, become the bars of the prison that keep him there in later life. Common among the very poor, for example, are attitudes of disdain for education, irregular work habits, poor economic patterns, and excessive drinking. While there may be nothing deviant or morally wrong about these, they form a pattern that, if followed, is almost certain to socially disadvantage their possessor.

Effects of Isolation on Socialization

Isolation can have devastating effects on socialization. Studies of human beings and other primates confirm the necessity of social interaction for normal development. The best-known of the primate studies are those of the psychologist Harry Harlow. In one classic study, Harlow separated infant rhesus monkeys from their mothers and all other monkeys. The infants were given a "wire mother"—a dummy made of wire—equipped with a bottle for feeding. Some also had a terry cloth mother—a dummy covered with terry cloth. All the monkeys who had a choice chose to cling to the cloth mother, even though they got food only from the wire mother. Although the monkeys who had a cloth mother got some degree of comfort that the other monkeys lacked, none matured normally. When put with other monkeys as adults, they were unsocial, behaved bizarrely, and were not able to mate. The few female monkeys impregnated by normal males did not mother their offspring, and their rejection sometimes took the form of physical attacks on their infants.[14]

The evidence for human beings comes from

> **rites of passage:**   social ceremonies or conventions marking and celebrating the transition from one stage in the life-cycle to another. The customs surrounding birth, marriage, retirement, and death are examples.

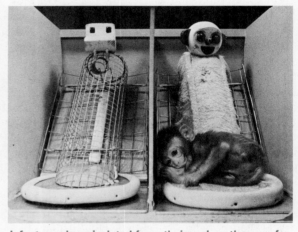

Infant monkeys isolated from their real mothers prefer a soft surrogate mother.

several sources, for example the discovery and study of children kept in isolation. One such child is a girl named Anna, who had been largely deprived of human interaction until she was about six years old. Discovered by authorities at that age, Anna lacked the characteristics we consider human. She could not talk or walk properly and was almost entirely helpless. Anna was afraid of people and reacted wildly. She never fully recovered, despite efforts to help her.[15]

Feral children, such as the boy Victor discussed in Chapter 3, are probably also the result of severe social deprivation. At one time it was thought that these children, who were found with wild animals, were wild and animallike because they had been reared by animals. But it seems more likely that, as the psychologist Bruno Bettelheim suggests, it is adult human beings, rather than animals, who are responsible for the feral child's behavior. It is very likely that such children, found living apart from other people in the countryside, were abandoned by their guardians. They show similarities to isolated children found in urban places who have not had contact with wild animals.

Moreover, feral children are also similar to children called *autistic*. The autistic child usually has not been severely isolated physically, but like the isolated and the feral children, autistic children suffer severe impairments in communication with other people. The problems of some of these children, particularly those labeled autistic, may stem from a biological deficiency, although at least for some autistic children it is clear that the problem is not lack of intelligence. Thus, the evidence is substantial that if extreme rejection or isolation of a child occurs, that child will not develop properly.

Socialization and Social Control

We do not need to assume that people are basically antisocial and aggressive to conclude that if everyone acted on impulse at all times, the social order would collapse, and the species itself could not survive. How then, is society made possible? Through what sociologists call **social control,** the imposition of norms and sanctions on individuals' behavior to produce normative conformity.

The most important element in social control is socialization. Fear of punishment also plays a role,

but no society can rely entirely on force or punishment to secure acquiescence to its norms. Self-control, which is learned through socialization, is vastly more efficient and effective. If the only reason the child stays away from the cookie jar is fear of punishment, it is likely that quite a few cookies will be eaten; parents cannot watch children twenty-four hours a day. Nor can governments watch their citizens every minute. And most of us probably prefer a system in which little watching is done. Clearly, the most effective form of social control is that which has been internalized so that people come to *want* to do what they are *supposed* to do. I want the cookie, but the guilt I would feel at disobeying my mother is worse than going without it.

People who have learned all the norms and so deeply internalized them that they rarely commit a deviant act are probably very uncommon. It seems unreasonable to define as socialized only saints. It also seems unreasonable to equate humanity or "humanness" with conformity. However, unless children are socialized to feel guilt at the violation of the rules, society would be impossible, since many major rules concern how one behaves toward other people. Yet societies—especially complex, rapidly changing ones—do change *some* rules. For example, a campaign contribution that once was legitimate is no longer legal. What appears to be crucial, not only to the functioning of society but also to the well-being of the person, is internalizing a moral philosophy to guide behavior in ways that minimize damage to one's self and others.

Summary

This chapter examined two major topics, the nature of *personality* and the development of the self through the process called *socialization*. Under the first topic, we considered the biological bases of personality and some of the debates about their influence. We explored the idea of *biological determinism* and found that the evidence does not support the notion that human behavior is fixed; biology is not destiny. This led to consideration of the *nature-nurture controversy*, where review of the available information indicates that neither heredity alone nor environment alone can account for the observed behavior of human beings. Nor is there any reason to suppose that some kind of basic or fundamental quality of *"human nature"* goes very far toward an explanation. Human nature turns out to be whatever we have been taught is right, proper, and just in our particular society.

Biological explanations do appear to have something to say concerning aptitudes, intelligence, race, sex, and temperament. Some capacities called *aptitudes are* differentially distributed in the human population and *are* matters of genetic endowment. But possession of an aptitude for some behavior or activity does not mean that we *will* exhibit it. Both social and cultural factors must support the exhibition or it will not take place. The Trobriand Islander who has the capacity to be a genius on the harpsichord will never know that such a thing exists.

Intelligence is to some extent an inherited capacity, but all consideration of it, especially with regard to race, is muddled by our lack of any clear definition of the concept and the apparent impossibility of measuring it in any general way. Concerning the controversy over *race and IQ,* the overwhelming weight of the scientific evidence is that the two are unrelated. Such things as *temperament* and *sex differences* were also reviewed, and we concluded that while there may be some inherited variations in them, their effects in adult life are largely the result of social learning and conditioning.

From this consideration of the biological bases of personality, we turned to various *social theories of personality* and how it develops (see Table 4-3). *Behaviorism* generally argues that behavior (and, hence, what we call personality) is a matter of conditioning, *classical* or *operant.*

Psychoanalytic theory, associated with the great Sigmund Freud and his followers, sees both behavior and personality as the consequence of very early experience overlying basic patterns or tendencies, such as the Oedipal crisis. Like the psychoanalysts, the *psychological humanists* and *developmental theorists* discern stages of development through which the normal personality passes on the road to maturation. This perception implies that success or failure in one stage affects what can occur in later stages. Underlying all these schools of thought also is the idea that personality is learned through social experience, with the nature of the experience determining, at least in part, the

> **social control:** the imposition of norms and sanctions, including socialization and the law, to produce conformity to societal norms. Such sanctions and norms include ideas of right and wrong, honors and dishonors, rewards and punishments.

nature of the result.

Cultural determinists, by contrast, view at least the personality type that seems to be most prevalent in a society as a response to the needs the society itself has for a particular kind of people at a particular period in its history.

The latter half of the chapter was devoted to the process through which the human *self* develops— *socialization.* Whereas most of our theories of personality were drawn from psychology, consideration here is largely sociological. *Symbolic interactionism,* associated with the names of George Herbert Mead and Charles Horton Cooley, is the dominant sociological view on the development of self. Mead's work was concerned with language as the vehicle through which socialization takes place and which enables the child first to comprehend meaning and later to adopt social roles. This process is seen as occurring in three stages: the *stage of self-consciousness,* the *play stage,* and the *game stage.* The key to it all, in Mead's view, is the acquisition of symbol-using behavior through using language. By learning to talk, the child is able to take and internalize the roles of others, thus introducing society into his own personality structure.

Cooley is primarily important for his ideas about *self-concept* that center on the notion of the *looking-glass self.* This can be summarized very simply by saying that we do, indeed, see ourselves as others see us. That fact, in turn, makes possible the *Pygmalion effect* and one kind of self-fulfilling prophecy: people, including ourselves, act as they are expected to by others, "living up (or down) to" the expectations others have for them or are perceived as having.

The final portion of the chapter was devoted to various aspects of the socialization process itself, the *primary agents* through which it takes place (most notably the family and peer group) and the effects on it of the *life-cycle.* (New statuses require

Table 4-3   Social theories of personality development

Theory	Principal concepts	Central ideas, propositions	People
Behaviorism	Classical conditioning Operant conditioning	Conditioned response Positive and negative reinforcement for learning	Pavlov In sociology, Homans
Psychoanalytic	Developmental stages Neurosis Oedipus and Electra complexes	Behavior or personality in adults as a consequence of responses learned as a child and/or frustration of psychosexual development	Freud, Erikson
Psychological humanism	Developmental stages in emotional maturation Autonomy Self-actualization Creativity Trust	Personality stages as a series of crises to be surmounted on the way to self-realization, autonomy	Rogers, Maslow
Developmental	Physical maturation Moral and cognitive development	Intellectual and personality development as a correlate of physical development	Piaget
Cultural determinism	Culture creates personality Tradition-, inner-, and other-directed types of national character	Personality type as a product of cultural requirements for its own survival	M. Mead, Riesman

Symbolic interactionism	Interaction
	Significant symbol
	Self-consciousness
	Role playing
	Play stage and game stage
	Self-concept
	  Looking-glass self
	  Pygmalion effect
	Socialization
		Self-concept learned from interaction with others
		Interaction takes places through symbols, particularly language
		Meaning is social
		Personality is learned
		Roles as the product of socialization
			G. H. Mead
			
			Cooley

new behaviors, which must be learned.) *Problems of socialization* were discussed: how the process may go wrong through *inadequate socialization,* or socializing people to *deviant norms* or *norms that handicap* their life performance. Finally, we considered the catastrophic effects of isolation on socialization and the relation of socialization to *social control,* the way in which a society maintains order and stability among its members. Socialization, we concluded, is the most effective of all agents of social control. Rules that we do not wish to violate are enforced more surely than those that require the police, no matter how effective police enforcement may be.

Review Questions

1.   Contrast the six approaches to studying personality development: behaviorism, social learning, psychoanalysis, psychological humanism, developmentalism, and symbolic interactionism. What major theorists are associated with each?

2.   Describe the three societies in Riesman's scheme: tradition-directed, inner-directed, and other-directed. Connect each with its corresponding stage of technological growth in a society. What type of person exemplifies the social character of each of these societies?

3.   Both Freud and Erikson view human development in terms of successive stages, yet they differ on some very important points. Discuss how their theories differ. How similar are their schemes of developmental stages?

4. You have just read about George Herbert Mead's three stages—developing self-consciousness, the play stage, and the game stage. Explain the child's growth and development in each stage. What roles are played by these concepts: the looking-glass self, the particularized other, and the generalized other?

5. Discuss Margaret Mead's studies in New Guinea. Describe sex role differentiation among the Arapesh, the Mundugumor and the Tchambuli. What do her findings suggest about American sex role stereotypes?

5. Discuss class bias in testing with an academic counselor or other appropriate personnel, perhaps in your department of education. What changes have been made in IQ tests since you were a child? What do educators predict to be the role of the standardized test in the future? What are the alternatives to standardized testing? How do the tests which are presently available differ? What appear to be recent trends in testing?

Suggestions for Research

1. Investigate how traditional sex roles function to shape the personality. Provide a background of historical reasons for differences in personality according to sex. Which aspects of traditional male and female behavior seem most resistant to change? Least resistant? You may want to refer to Judith Bardwick's *Readings on the Psychology of Women.*

2. Imitation plays an important role in the child's development, as he is constantly exposed to a variety of models. In the last two decades, the media have provided a variety of models—at times causing controversies over the impact of the media upon developing children. Select at random twenty television programs and watch them closely, taking notes on your observations. What kinds of models are provided by men, women, and children? What types of personalities are rewarded or reinforced in the programs? What kind of an impact would you expect these shows to have upon the child? What proportion of these models diverge from traditional, middle-class roles?

3. Use twenty magazines selected at random rather than television shows and analyze models as in number 2 above. Here you will be relying on visual elements without the audio elements and will want to be especially aware of the subtle messages behind the picture. Advertisements will provide models to study, too. You may want to clip out interesting examples and include them with a written report.

4. Investigate the various avenues provided in your community for persons wanting or needing counseling who cannot financially afford a professional psychologist. Is there a crisis center? How does it operate? Does your school's department of psychology or counseling provide any services, perhaps as training for graduate students? What types of counseling are provided by the local clergy? How do the various counseling alternatives compare, in your judgment, with professional, paid psychological assistance? Approximately how many people are using these alternative services?

CHAPTER 5
SOCIAL ORGANIZATION AND ITS COMPONENTS

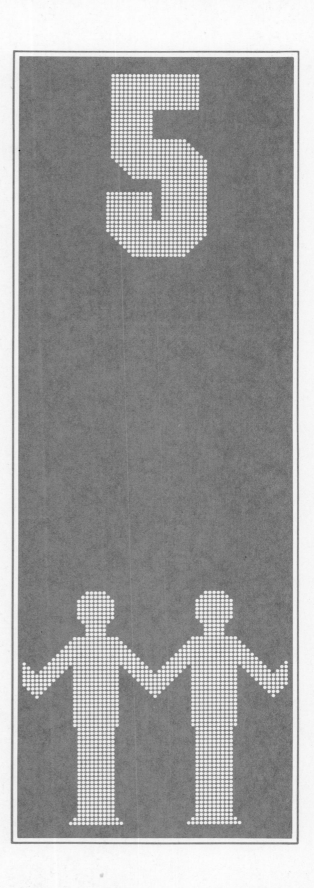

The complicated structure in the picture is, obviously, a metropolitan freeway interchange. We use it to symbolize the subject of this chapter because that subject is in fact invisible, although it is *in* the photo. The subject, of course, is **social organization,** which the sociologist understands as *the process through which social life becomes recurrent, patterned, and orderly.* It is readily visible in social life around us, and we can find it in immense variety once we know what to look for. Indeed, once we know what to look for, it is difficult to find behavior that is *not* socially organized.

To how many male readers has it ever occurred to wear their wife's or girl friend's clothing to class, or, to female readers, to come dressed in a swimsuit or formal gown? How many of us call our sisters "Mom" or behave in traffic court as we do at a football game or New Year's Eve party? Treat our classmates as we do our parents or consider manufacturing our own automobiles? How many of us share the Japanese attitude toward suicide or the Latin American attitude toward time? How many of us could even function among the Sioux, whose language has no words for "time," "late," or "waiting"? All of these questions seem unusual, or even bizarre, because they suggest violations of the social organizational forms that are familiar to us. Although we could engage in any of the suggested behaviors, doing so would violate the order and regularity of life as we have learned to live it and as we expect others to live it as well. So deeply are such expectations ingrained in us, in fact, that some of the suggestions may seem a bit "unreal."

To see just how ingrained our expectations about social behavior are, consider a homely example. You go to a lunch counter, order a hot dog, and, when you are served, ask the man next to you to pass the mustard. What would you bet that he will *not* do so? If you are any sort of a gambler at all, you would only take the bet for small stakes and at astronomical odds, because you know that it is extremely unlikely that the person next to you will refuse. But *why* is it so unlikely? And how do you know it's unlikely? Nothing forces the individual to respond to your request; no law requires him to cooperate with you. But he will and you know that he will. If someone bet you enough money, you might be willing to bet your life on it, because the odds of losing would be so small. (And, in fact, we *do* bet our lives on such matters all the time: that the cars coming at us on the highway will stay in their own lanes; that a maniac will not shoot us on the street if we go out; and so forth.) And the reasons that we are able to make, and usually win, such bets, lie in the process of social organization. We know we will get the mustard, be safe in our own traffic lanes most of the time, not have to worry about being murdered for no reason by strangers, because social life is recurrent, patterned, and orderly, and we have learned the patterns and the order in which they recur.

The process of social organization, which we will be exploring in detail in this and the next two chapters, can be understood as the product of six phenomena that this chapter introduces and describes briefly. These are (1) *social roles,* (2) *social situations,* (3) *social groups,* (4) *organizations* (sometimes called large-scale organizations or associations), (5) *social institutions,* and (6) *society.* While you are undoubtedly familiar with each of these names, each has special sociological meanings within the framework of the concept of social organization, and these will be explained as we come to them. The two following chapters take up the sociological study of the six phenomena in greater detail. Chapter 6 deals with social roles, situations, and groups; and Chapter 7 explores organizations, social institutions, and society.

The Concept of Social Organization

Social organization originates or is brought forth in social *interaction* between individuals. It is the product of people dealing with one another in normal life. It may be identified, or its presence may be known, through certain *key characteristics:* connections between activities, control of some people by others, differentiation, and repetition. Social organization has both *normative* and *behavioral* dimensions; norms define patterns of organized behavior, and the behavior itself manifests them. It also has both *subjective* and *objective* components as a consequence. From the normative perspective, social organization is "in our heads." From the behavioral perspective, it is "out there," available for inspection in the world. Each

> **social organization:** the process through which social relationships become recurrent, patterned, and orderly. The components of social organization are social roles and situations, social groups and organizations, and social institutions and society. All social organization is based in and originates from interaction.

of these aspects of what we mean by social organization is examined in the following pages.

Origins in Interaction

When a number of people interact with each other over a period of time, their ways of relating tend to become patterned, to fall into predictable routines. One person in a group may take the lead in choosing courses of action, while another may develop or propose new ideas for the others to react to. Some may contribute to the work of the group primarily by assisting and supporting the activities of others. These patterns in the behavior of group members might become relatively stable over time so that whenever the group is together we could expect them to be reenacted. We could say, then, that social organization, a regularly recurring pattern of relationships, has emerged from their interactions.

Family travel routines may provide a familiar example. Any of you who have ever taken a lengthy automobile trip with your own or another family have probably observed that a set of work assignments is likely to form itself quite spontaneously among the travelers. Perhaps mom is the principal driver, spelled occasionally by dad and the oldest child, while dad acts as navigator and map reader and the kids more or less select the quarters for the night. Upon arrival, different people take on different unloading chores, and if the group is cranky after a hot day on the road, one individual may play therapist/clown to relieve the tension.

Two important ingredients of social organization are present in this situation. A pattern of leadership is present: one person tends to guide the group in sorting out courses of action. A division of labor is present: the members have begun to make distinct contributions to the life of the group.

Social organization has origins in elementary interactions of this type. This is easy to forget because so much of social life appears to be fixed and permanent. As children, we encounter a world already worked out, a set of social patterns already in place. Patterns of family life, ways of making a living, procedures for handling disputes, and many other aspects of life *appear* to us to be a permanent and natural order of things. (Remember why the Three Bears got upset? "Someone's been sitting in *my* chair": The natural order of things had been disturbed.) Only as we get older, and sometimes not even then, do we realize that our social world has been created through interaction and that it can be modified. We realize, that is, that the world as we experience it is a response to a particular set of rules. A different set of rules would produce a different world; what constitutes "my chair" can be altered or redefined.

Identifying Characteristics

The social patterns that we call social organization can be quite varied. It is therefore useful to have some guideposts for identifying them. Here we will discuss four basic guideposts, or identifying characteristics.

A recurrent connection One indication of the presence of social organization is a recurrent connection between sets of activities. This means a repeated tendency for one type of social activity to follow regularly after another or for two types of social activities to be regularly found together. One researcher found, for example, that activity dealing with tensions between group members regularly followed periods of task activity.[1] We see this pattern when, after a day on the road, mom jokes with the kids to overcome their irritability.

Control Another mark of social organization is *control* by some persons over the behavior of others in a distinguishable group of people. If we observe the activities of a series of youth gangs and find that there is a regular tendency for members to follow the lead of one or two persons, then we can conclude that this is a feature of social organization in such groups. We might then try to find out why such a pattern regularly occurs. Or we

might try to discover what determines who becomes the navigator on the family trip.

Differentiation Still another identifying mark is *differentiation* among the activities of different types or categories of people. If people of different nationalities behave differently or if there are differences between sexes in the types of activities carried out, we suspect that social organization is present. Among our family of tourists, it may always be the youngest child who fetches the motel ice cubes, and, in most American homes, it is a male task to take out the trash.

Repeated activities and behaviors The *repeated* appearance of similar activities or behaviors in similar social situations also indicates the presence of social organization. When we observe, for instance, that many live-in organizations such as armies, prisons, and fraternities subject new members to periods of intense indoctrination, often accompanied by hazing, we may suspect that the practice is aimed at accomplishing the same goals for the different organizations in question. The basic training or pledgeship period in this case has the goals of forcing the recruit to drop old statuses and adopt a new one: member of the organization. More simply, when you drive into a gas station and pull up to the pumps, pretty standard events are likely to follow.

Although some regularities of the kinds listed above might possibly be attributed to nonsocial factors such as biology, social organization implies social causation or, at least, the accomplishment of social goals. A baboon troop, for example, shows all four characteristics listed above, presumably appearing among individuals on a biological basis. But the behavior has social purposes and effects. That is why it persists; the troop could not survive as a unit without it.

Normative and Behavioral Dimensions

Social organization has both normative and behavioral dimensions. The *normative dimension* derives from the *norms* that define proper and improper, approved and disapproved, preferred and discouraged behavior in a society. The norms may, for instance, define a preferred family form, certain other family forms that are tolerated but not preferred, and still other forms that are wholly unacceptable. In our society, for example, legal marriage between one male and one female is preferred. Common-law marriages between one male and one female are permitted, but clearly not preferred. "Marriages" between members of the same sex have an unclear legal status at this time; that is, partners in such arrangements do not have the same legal rights (such as filing joint tax returns) that apply to heterosexual marriages. However, such marriages are at least tolerated to the extent that people are not usually prosecuted for such living patterns. Polygamous (multiple-spouse) marriages are prohibited, and people contracting such marriages have been legally prosecuted and imprisoned.

The *behavioral dimension* of social organization is the *usual* or *typical* as opposed to the normative. It is based on observation, on *actual* behavior, as opposed to preferred or ideal behavior. Participants in social life generally have some sense of what is to be expected or anticipated, based on their experience in particular situations. We have seen certain kinds of behaviors on a regular basis before, so we expect to see them and are not surprised when they occur. On a normative basis, we may continue to disapprove of some behaviors that we see every day. In fact, on a normative level we may disapprove of some actions that we regularly carry out ourselves. For example, many of us disapprove in principle of breaking the law, while doing so habitually with regard to the speed limits. But whether we approve or not, we come to *expect* the behavior in question simply because it is common.

Recent changes in marriage and family living patterns in our society bring these dimensions into sharp relief. It seems clear that we are in a transitional period in which norms regarding marriage and sexual relations are being redefined. In general, the normative standard is still the one-man-one-woman legally contracted marriage. Sexual experimentation prior to or outside of the marriage bond is still disapproved. Joint living arrangements in the absence of a legal marriage are still discouraged. Despite this, there appears to be widespread experimentation, perhaps especially among young people, with a variety of joint living arrangements

outside of marriage. Included here are patterns ranging from common-law marriage to communal living arrangements approximating (in some cases) group marriage.

Such alternative living arrangements have become so frequent as to cause little surprise, at least within college and university communities. Informal norms are even developing to govern how to address and interact with couples who are living together but not married. (No small matter; how *does* one introduce the person with whom one is living? "Lover" has European connotations foreign to us; "common-law spouse" is legalistic, difficult to say, and often inaccurate for the situation under discussion; "boyfriend" or "girlfriend" seems adolescent and also inaccurate.) In this area of social life, then, there is a significant difference between normative and behavioral expectations. Most people continue to adhere to the old standards, but they are not surprised to encounter alternative arrangements.

Much of social life is characterized by such mixtures of normative and behavioral standards. The current situation in marriage norms is by no means unique. Economic behavior has long displayed similar differences. Norms defining proper, approved economic action with respect to honesty, fairness, competitive pricing, and so on, are widely violated. People enter financial transactions with a "let the buyer beware" attitude because they have so frequently experienced violations of the norms. During the 1960 presidential campaign, the Democrats circulated an extremely effective campaign poster with a picture of Richard Nixon and the legend "Would You Buy a Used Car from This Man?" The poster was effective because people know that used car salesmen are notoriously untrustworthy in their claims. Now it even seems prophetic.

Subjective and Objective Realities

Social organization is, from one standpoint, a very *subjective* phenomenon. It exists largely in the minds of participants. People organize their world by creating shared categories and interpretive frameworks. All people with similar cultural backgrounds have the same general conceptions of and make the same general distinctions among differ-

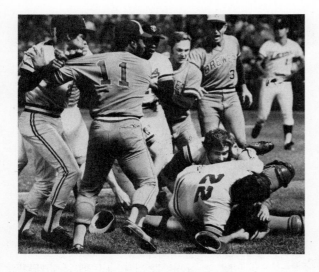

Despite the overwhelming power of social organizations, behavior is not always entirely predictable.

ent types of people, things, and situations. And in their interactions with each other, they rely on these shared beliefs and attitudes. They interpret the actions of others on the basis of commonly held assumptions about life and typical reasons for action.

Such sharing of subjective frameworks is never perfect; there is almost always some inconsistency between people's perspectives. But a fairly extensive sharing is necessary if social life is to be sustained. To return to two examples used earlier: we expect to get the mustard when we ask for it at the lunch counter, and we expect other cars to stay on their own side of the road. And in almost every case we are right. Otherwise, society would not work at all. If the actions of others were largely unpredictable, we could not live.

But behavior is not always *entirely* predictable, despite the overpowering effect of social organization. Once in awhile, somebody will ignore our request for mustard or grumpily tell us to get it ourselves. And once in awhile, we may encounter an oncoming car in our lane. Of course, the consequences of the latter situation are potentially more serious than the results if we have to procure our own mustard, but the point is basically the same. It is risky to rely on the subjective definitions of

participants in a society as our *only* guide to their social organization and activity.

There are also difficulties with a thoroughgoing *objectivism* toward social organization. We may misinterpret the behavior of people by failing to consider *their* subjective frameworks. On the basis of a purely external, objective analysis, we may form combinations of activities that are ridiculous from the standpoint of participants. Events associated with each other from an external view may have no meaningful connections in the minds of those who are participating in them. For example, the sociologist would expect to find the use of plastic religious figurines on car dashboards associated with lower-class social position. But people who buy a magnetic Jesus for their car would be unaware of any class component in their behavior.

Another problem with objectivism is that even seemingly objective analysis by the external observer often rests on subjective distinctions. Terms describing race or occupation, for example, are grounded in a set of subjective definitions shared by some groups of people. What, exactly, is a truck driver? An objective observer might use U.S. Census Bureau categories of occupations to define truck driver. In this case, the definition would be based on the Census Bureau's practice of processing individuals into categories and relying on certain broad occupational distinctions. But would the census definition adequately distinguish the cross-country teamster driving a "big rig" from the boy who delivers night orders for pizza? Whether or not the distinction was important would depend on what the observer wished to do with it, that is, *his* subjective intention in asking the question in the first place. The point is that, no matter how objective the definitions we use, someone makes subjective decisions about who is or is not included in the category.

The Components of Social Organization

As we noted in the Introduction, social organization can be viewed as having six basic components: (1) social roles, (2) social groups, (3) social situations, (4) organizations, (5) social institutions, and (6) societies. As is obvious from this list, social organization occurs at every level of social behavior, from

Figure 5-1
The components of social organization

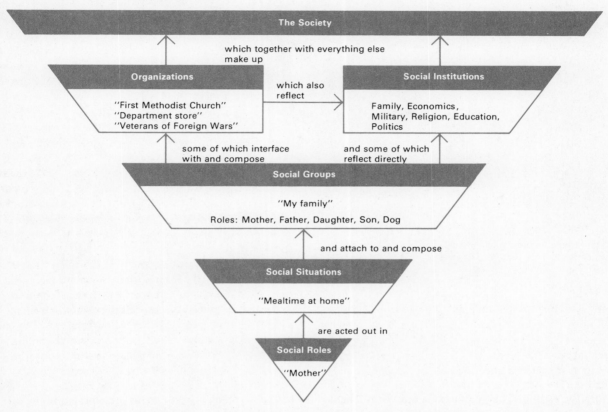

micro to macro, from the very small-scale to the very large-scale. A role is merely one aspect of individual behavior; a society is the largest theater in which an individual plays his part. Furthermore, each of the six components is a building block for the next listed: that is, *roles* are played in *social situations,* which define *group behavior;* groups are components of *organizations,* which, in turn, often reflect *social institutions,* which are the fundamental components of a *society.* These relationships between the various components of the process of social organization are shown schematically in Figure 5-1.

Each of these components has been the focal point for a distinctive kind of analysis: role analysis, situational analysis, group analysis, organiza-

tional analysis, institutional analysis, and societal analysis. These distinctive types of analysis will be considered in Chapters 6 and 7. Here we will define and describe the components themselves, beginning with roles and proceeding in the direction of increasing complexity and inclusiveness.

Social Roles

Social activities are organized around the roles played by individuals occupying positions. As we saw in Chapter 4, a *role* is any regularly recurring cluster of activity enacted by individuals occupying a particular position. One familiar example of a role is the occupational role. Workers on a construction

Figure 5-2
The distinction between role repertoires and role sets

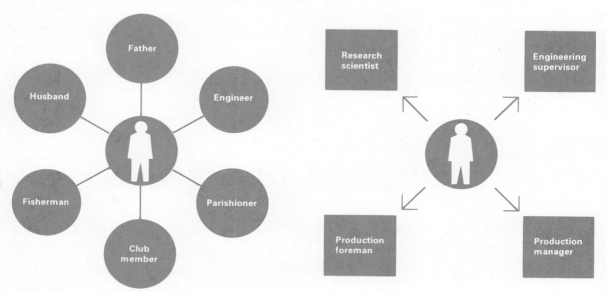

Role repertoire of an individual: the individual plays all of the roles

A role set in an industrial organization: the engineer regularly interacts with the occupants of the other roles

job, for example, carry out quite specialized activities and resist any changes in the pattern. If we watch them closely, we can distinguish many separate occupational roles, such as carpenter, bricklayer, plumber, electrician, hod-carrier, and so on. We might also discover that violations of a role boundary, such as a carpenter doing electrical work, are met with resistance. And we might find that each worker is a member of a labor union that establishes standards for entry into the trade and defends against incursions on its activities by unqualified workers or members of other unions.

Occupation, of course, is only one role that people enact. People also enact sex roles (male, female), family roles (father, mother, sister, brother), political roles (voter, politician, bureaucrat), religious roles (priest, parishioner), medical roles (doctor, patient), educational roles (teacher, student), and so on. But in every case, we identify the role by recognizing a position (mother, priest, doc-

tor) and linking it to an associated complex of activities that are appropriate to or typical of its occupants.

Roles do not exist in isolation. Rather, they are linked together in orderly ways. We will discuss two types of linkage between roles here: role repertoires and role sets.

Role repertoires   A person typically plays a number of different roles simultaneously. A man may be a father, husband, carpenter, voter, parishioner, and fisherman. A woman may be a mother, wife, lawyer, voter, parishioner, and tennis player. The term *role repertoire* refers to the total catalogue of social roles played by an individual. The roles in the repertoire are held together by being enacted by the same person.

Individuals may maintain a degree of consistency between their roles by playing each role in a way that makes it compatible with other roles in the repertoire. A considerate mother is also apt to be a considerate wife, and a mean father is likely to be a mean husband. But in modern societies, a great deal of inconsistency and conflict usually develops between the roles played by an individual. Consequently, people must constantly readjust their behavior to suit the role they are playing at a given moment. Some actors become quite skillful at shifting roles and using role diversity to their advantage. Others, however, get caught in dilemmas and find one role difficult to reconcile with another. A woman, for instance, might have difficulty reconciling the roles of wife, mother, and research scientist. Such a situation is called **role conflict**: the tension created by inconsistency or contradiction in expectations among various roles in an individual's repertoire.

Role sets The second type of linkage between roles is *role sets:* clusters of roles that are reciprocal; that is, roles that are tied together in such a way that one must be played in interaction with another. For example, the role of father is played in relation to a series of other roles played out by related actors. It usually involves interaction with a mother, a child, an employer, and so on, but at a minimum demands that someone play the role of child. To be a father, one must have a child. Roles in a cluster of this kind are reciprocal in the sense that the *obligations* for one role are *rights* for the other. Further, they are reciprocal in the sense that a degree of coordination in time is required. One must carry out the duties of fatherhood in relation to a child who responds to the father's actions. The distinction between role sets, which involve reciprocal roles, and the individual's role repertoire is shown in Figure 5-2.

Role sets are an important social phenomenon because linkage between the parts of society occurs through them. The different sectors of the society—economic, political, familial, religious, educational—are geared into each other through the adjustment of role sets. In this way, the role demands on a person occupying positions in different sectors are adjusted to each other. Work and recreational roles, for instance, must be at least minimally compatible with family roles if both are to be maintained.

> **role repertoire:** the total catalogue of social roles played by an individual.
>
> **role conflict:** the tension created by inconsistency or contradiction in expectations between various roles in an individual's repertoire.
>
> **role set:** a pair or cluster of roles that are reciprocal, so that each may be played only in interaction with the other(s), e.g., teacher/student, parent/child.

Roles are linked in orderly ways; they do not exist in isolation.

Figure 5-3
Role sets linking the family to other parts of society

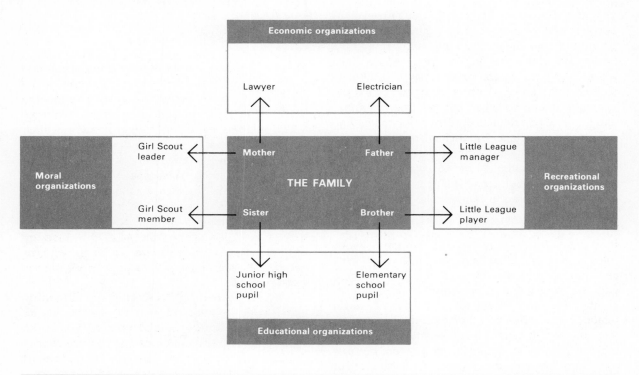

In the situation shown in Figure 5-3, we might guess that the mother's occupational role as an attorney (which involves her in the social institution of law) could sometimes carry over into her activities as a Girl Scout leader. She might, for example, advise the local Scout Council about legal liabilities connected with a proposed bus trip for the girls. In that instance, two different social institutions are linked to each other through the person of the mother-attorney-Scout leader. The father, for his part, must reconcile the time requirements of his job with those of the Little League, for which he acts as a manager. In his role as father to a Little League player, he may have to mediate between the time requirements perceived by his son as stemming from *his* roles as a Little League ballplayer and as a student.

Many role sets involve antagonistic combinations of perspectives and expectations, and by studying such sets we can gain an understanding of the tensions in the society. For example, the landlord-tenant relation in American society is filled with tensions growing out of conflicts of interests between them, as is the car dealer–customer relationship. It is probably not an accident that folklore conventionally depicts landlords as hardhearted skinflints and auto dealers as thieves. In each case, the economic and general well-being of the consumer is inversely related to the economic interests of the provider of services. What is good for the customer-tenant is bad for the dealer-landlord.

Behind both of these tensions, of course, is the problem of investment capitalism. If funds can be invested, say, at 12 percent interest in Treasury notes, while the car dealer or landlord interacting fairly with customer or tenant will receive only an 8 percent return on his money, inevitably there will be pressure on the car dealer and the landlord to generate the higher return. Such pressures show up in shoddy business practices on the car lot or inadequate maintenance of rental property. The problem in the relationship is that each party's economic interest in it is his or her *only* interest.

Roles and larger social systems   This brings us to a very important and interesting feature of roles, specifically, their grounding in social situations and larger social systems. Up to now, we have treated role as if it existed in isolation and have spoken of moving our analysis upward (in terms of organizational complexity) from role at the base. In fact, of course, the roles we play are not isolated entities sealed off from the larger social world. They are intricately linked to one another, in repertoires and sets, and the repertoires and sets are joined together to form larger complexes. For example, the role of teacher is played not only in relation to the role of student but also in relation to a larger situation (the classroom), an organization (the school organization in a state or city), and an institutional complex (the American educational system). (See Figure 5-1 again.)

In playing their roles, teachers respond to norms and expectancies stemming from all of these sources. They typically behave in accordance with normal classroom procedure as understood by all concerned. They conform to rules established in the school organization and carry out generalized expectations that are, in a sense, part of the culture—understood throughout the educational institutions of the society. In carrying out their duties, then, teachers affirm the standards, norms, and expectations of the larger social complexes.

Beyond this, situations, organizations, and institutions are linked to other features of the social order. These may be conceived as linkages between distinct but related spheres of social life, as in Figure 5-3. The classroom situation, for example, is tied to the family situations of the various pupils. The pupils play roles both in the classroom and in their families. The two situations are linked through the *role repertoires* of the participants. These linkages can have important consequences. The student performing poorly in school may be belligerent at home, and a child who is abused at home

> **social situation:**   a complex social setting involving multiple actors playing different roles.

may not perform well in the classroom. Note that such consequences would occur because of the inevitable linkage of the two roles through the person enacting them. Individuals subject to pressures or anxieties in one role often act out their problems in other roles. Thus, some aspects of an individual's role behavior may be explained by examining his other roles and inferring a *social-psychological connection* between the two. For example, the anxiety and feelings of inferiority stemming from poor school performance on the part of our Little League player might cause the child to be aggressive toward his father, who, as coach, was exerting pressure on him to practice more.

The connections between situations, organizations, and institutions are not always social-psychological. They may also be *structural* in the sense that role requirements in two or more social contexts may be geared into each other quite apart from the subjective reactions of the occupants. Here the concept *role set* is useful. The role of teacher, for example, is geared into the role of parent in several ways. The expectations of parents regarding the performance of their children are part of the teacher's role. In a similar way, the teacher's expectations regarding behavior and study effort are part of the parents' role.

In summary, both role repertoires and role sets are important in knitting together the different strands of social life.

Social Situations

The concept of situation entered prominently into the preceding discussion of roles. Here we will examine it in more detail. Defined precisely, a **social situation** is a complex social setting involving multiple actors playing different roles. In the social situation, both the role sets and the role repertoires of the actors come into play. Each actor brings to the situation some preconceptions about the interaction that will take place, including antici-

A social situation.

pated actions and reactions on the part of other participants. The course of action each actor anticipates is based to a large degree on the roles typically played by others in the situation.

Also important in the situation are some general patterns of interaction, recurrent sequences of action that have come to be normal or expected. Over time, actors in situations develop certain regular norms and routines concerning how the interaction is to take place. The actors, then, not only enact their separate roles, but also do so in accordance with established rules or routines.

Some frequently encountered situations are the classroom, the religious ceremony, the committee meeting, the athletic event, the assembly line, the concert, and so on. For example, before you came to your sociology class for the first time, you probably had a pretty good idea what you could expect from the instructor and other students, even if you had never met any of them. If you had been asked on the first day of class to write down a list of predictions about how both would behave, it would probably have proven to be highly accurate.

Definition of the situation   Obviously, then, the subjective perspective of participants is an important feature of the situation. The term *definition of the situation* has been applied to this subjective outlook.[2] Each participant brings a subjective definition to the situation, and this definition determines to a considerable degree his actions in the situation. Consequently, an important problem for

actors in a situation is anticipating correctly the definitions under which others are operating. Actors may also try to control the situational definitions of others, through persuasion, indoctrination, establishment of rules, manipulation of incentives, and so on.

Situational control   Actors often differ considerably in their power to define the situation for others. The teacher, for example, has control of incentives and formal rules in the classroom that permit him to define the situation for students. They defy his definitions at their own peril. To do so on a regular basis, they must be willing to forego the considerable rewards dispensed by the educational system in which the teacher's role is grounded and legitimated. They must also risk the negative labels (dunce, delinquent, retardate) that the teacher can apply.

Situational control by one or a few parties is seldom complete. Actors typically develop devious ways of conforming to expectations minimally while maintaining certain limited spheres of autonomy into which the dominant actor cannot reach. For example, in school situations youth subcultures develop. These provide some minimal degree of protection and encouragement for nonconformity to school demands. Of course, the subculture does this because it provides an alternative situational definition with attendant penalties and rewards.

Such alternative subcultures or countercultures are an important feature of most organizations, especially those in which clients or inmates of some kinds are processed by a professional staff, such as mental hospitals.[3] Alternative subcultures have long been a feature of prison life.[4] In recent years these have sometimes become politicized and militant, leading to a series of prison rebellions like the one at Attica.

Situational control may also be limited by role reciprocity. In role-reciprocal situations, the ability of one actor successfully to perform his role is limited by the cooperation of the other actor or actors in performing their roles. To return to the classroom example, if your sociology instructor were to assign the class 5,000 pages of reading a week, they would refuse to perform that much work. And if, in retaliation, he gave failing grades to the entire class, it is extremely unlikely that the grades would be permitted to stand. Students are unaware, as a rule, of the degree to which their cooperation with an instructor is essential for the successful performance of the instructor's role, although they may be very well aware indeed of the reverse.

Any social situation to some degree may be likened to a playground teeter-totter; what one actor does inevitably influences the performance of another because they are bound together through mutual interaction. If we are to play on the contraption at all, I must go up when you go down, and both of us must cooperate for the thing to work.

Variations in situations   Situations differ considerably. Some are not regulated and routinized, like the classroom, but are continuously constructed and improvised, like small friendship groups. But even in such small, informal groups, certain regular patterns of interaction and dominance frequently develop. In children's play groups, for example, there is often a single ringleader who incites the others to naughty acts, while another child typically acts as the voice of conscience for the group.

At another extreme, we see highly routinized situations extensively regulated by rules of **hierarchical** authority patterns. College class registration is a tediously familiar example. The type of organization called a bureaucracy, discussed in detail later, is a structure intended by its creators to regulate situations through rules, specialization of tasks, and hierarchical authority. We are all familiar, for instance, with the routine that governs obtaining driver's licenses from the state bureaucracy empowered to dispense them.

Social Groups and Other Social Categories

Social groups   Two or more individuals whose interaction is characterized by patterned roles and role relationships make up a *social group.* The individuals relate to each other in relatively predictable, recurrent ways, based on their roles. Group life consists, in large part, of a network of roles linked to one another in patterned ways.

Patterned interactions of this kind generally must be built up over time. After the participants have

definition of the situation (or situational definition):   the individual's subjective understandings, expectations, and perceptions of a given social situation; the mental basis on which one acts or makes decisions.

hierarchical: of or pertaining to hierarchy, the ordering or stratification of relationships into upper and lower, superior or inferior. When applied to human social relations, a hierarchy almost always implies some complex organization of relationships, as in the hierarchy of the Roman Catholic Church or the hierarchy of rank in the military officer corps.

social group: two or more individuals whose interaction is characterized by patterned roles and role relationships.

Countercultures provide a means of avoiding conformity to the dominant culture's requirements.

interacted with each other for awhile, their interaction gradually assumes a predictable, role-oriented pattern. Once the pattern has developed, we can even speak of the behavior of the individuals as controlled or guided by the pattern. The roles imbedded in the life of the group assume a regulative capacity, guiding and controlling the behavior of the individuals. The children's play groups mentioned above are again an example. Once the pattern is established, it may be sustained over time even though the individuals change. Some individuals may leave the group without disrupting the pattern, because they are replaced by others who take up their roles. (There is almost always someone to invite others to naughtiness in the play group.) In this sense, the pattern assumes a degree of independence from the particular individuals carrying it out at any specific time.

All of us are members of numerous social groups. The family, of course, is a social group involving linkages not only to immediate relatives but also to a network of extended kin. Although in our mobile urban society we may not interact directly with all our kin, certain stable relationships are maintained through correspondence and long-distance phone calls and reinforced on special occasions such as holidays, weddings, funerals, and family reunions. In addition, there are friendship groups, extending from those we see frequently to those we correspond with once a year at Christmastime. There are groups we become associated with through various activities, people with whom we work or study, play tennis and backgammon, participate in political campaigns, and so on.

Many of these groups are part of larger organizations. An informal golf or bowling group may develop among workers in a department of General Motors. Many sociologists have stressed the importance of such affiliations for linking the individual to the impersonal purposes of large organizations. Studies of military organizations in World War II, for instance, indicate that such informal ties can be important in sustaining individual morale.

Other social categories It is important to distinguish social groups from other social categories that sociologists frequently use, such as populations, publics, and crowds. These are distinguished from groups by the absence of *sustained interac-*

tions between individual members. The people in these categories share certain characteristics but are not linked together by recurrent interaction patterns.

Populations and publics A **population** is a category of individuals who share one or more characteristics but do not necessarily interact with each other. For example, all U.S. citizens share a legal status insofar as they are members of the same nation. This characteristic distinguishes them from citizens of Mexico or Afghanistan. Within the general category of U.S. citizens, there are numerous other populations of people who share some characteristics, such as male, female, married, single, divorced, employed, unemployed, incomes over $30,000 a year, age over sixty-five, enrollment in college, residence in New York City, red hair and left-handedness. These, too, are populations.

Although populations are not socially organized, because their members do not interact and do not share common norms or role expectations, they do frequently constitute a base out of which social groups form. The Black Power movement, for instance, grew out of mutual concerns shared by black people. When a sufficient number of blacks realized their common problems and began to organize in an attempt to meet them, a distinct social group grew out of what was previously only an unorganized category of individuals sharing a skin color. Most social movements have their origins in social categories of people who share one or more characteristics. Awareness of common plights or similar interests among individuals in a given population is the first step toward creating organized groups with the visibility and power to achieve common goals.

A special type of population is the **public:** a population in which the characteristic individuals share is interest in some specific aspect of social life, such as a particular television show, an athletic event, a political candidate, a commercial product, or the services of a particular professional person. Publics, therefore, are popularly known as markets, fans, clientele, political constituencies, or "users." A public place is a geographical area that is open to anyone who may be interested in being there (any public that wishes to use it). All those who enjoy the city park on a given Sunday afternoon are known as the public in the park. Likewise, the people who subscribe to *Playboy* magazine constitute a public, as do all those who use Avon products.

Publics may have some *very limited* form of social organization: there is usually some order in the behavior of people in public places in terms of appearance and behavior. But norms and role definitions are minimal, and there is little or no social interaction. However, like populations in general, publics may provide a basis for the formation of social groups.

Crowds A set of people temporarily *collected* in time and space, without the *sustained* interaction pattern of a social group is a **crowd**. Publics and populations, by contrast, need never be collected in order to exist, and rarely are. In terms of degree of social organization—that is, formalized norms, roles, and interaction patterns—crowds are more organized than populations and publics, but they are not as permanent or stable as social groups. They stand midway between populations and publics, which are basically unorganized, and social groups with their high degree of organization. Like populations and publics, however, crowds have the potential for becoming organized groups—whenever interaction among participants is sustained over a long enough period of time for discernible patterns to develop.

Crowds differ from publics in that some minimal degree of interaction occurs among members, even though this interaction is usually temporary and loosely structured. If, for example, the people in the park on a Sunday afternoon gather to protest a nudist group that arrives to picnic in the park, the unorganized public can rapidly be transformed into a crowd that has a common stimulus. In most crowd situations, a leader emerges who provides direction and sustained impetus for the crowd to rally around some cause, in this case, assuring that the nudist group feels unwanted in the public park. While the crowd is interacting to get rid of the nudists, some minimal rules exist to control behavior. For example, except in rare lynching situations, participants are not allowed to murder or seriously mutilate other people that they consider undesirable or wicked.

Usually crowds disperse after a short period, and

population: a category of individuals who share one or more characteristics, such as place of residence or left-handedness, but do not necessarily interact.

public: a type of population in which the characteristic the individuals share is an interest in some aspect of social life, such as a product, event, or political candidate.

crowd: a set of people temporarily collected in time and space without the sustained interaction pattern of a social group.

A social group is two or more individuals whose interaction is patterned by roles which enable them to interact in recurrent, predictable ways.

Figure 5-4
A typical organization chart

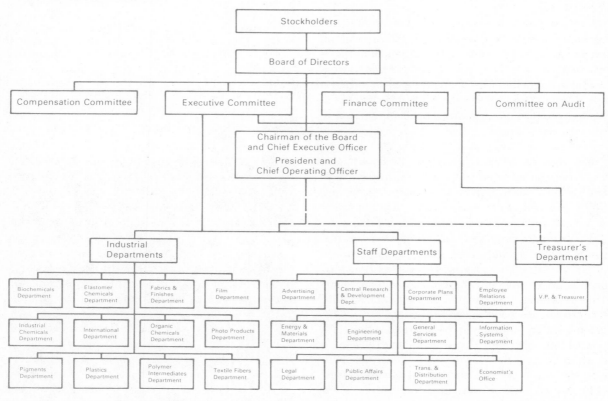

the minimal amount of social organization they have generated disappears. But in some instances, crowds can provide the basis for social groups, as when some members of the crowd decide to join together on a more enduring basis and organize to achieve some specific goal, such as putting pressure on the city government to prohibit nudist groups from exposing themselves in public places. (Various types of crowds, such as audiences and mobs, will be discussed in detail in Chapter 18.)

Organizations

The modern world is filled with **organizations**. We spend a good part of our lives in them and find ourselves continuously dependent on them. Examples include schools, factories, businesses, church-

es, government agencies, political parties, labor unions, and civic clubs—everything from the George Washington Carver grade school to the Teamster's Union and the Knights of Columbus. Here we will briefly discuss the major characteristics of organizations and the linkages between them.

Characteristics of organizations *Organizations* are complex clusters of interrelated roles and role sets established or operating to fulfill some purpose or set of purposes: making war, producing items for sale, extracting natural resources, providing public entertainment or clean drinking water.

Interconnection of roles The roles within organizations are highly *interdependent,* in the sense that occupancy of one role connects the individual to a large number of other roles. For example, occupying the position of supervisor in the payroll department of a large industrial concern links a person to subordinates in the payroll department, immediate superiors in the chain of command, the higher authorities in the division, such as the comptroller, and peers supervising related departments.

Such connections between roles are not random, but orderly and predictable. The individual will interact differently with persons occupying different positions. The payroll supervisor will interact differently with subordinates than with superiors. Furthermore, the *likelihood* of interacting with any particular person in the organization will vary with one's position. The payroll supervisor is most likely to interact with those in positions directly geared into his—supervisors, subordinates, coworkers. Chances are, he will have little interaction with the public relations staff or the assembly-line worker. These differences in frequency or likelihood of interaction will be accompanied by differences in style or type of interaction. Some interactions will express relationships of superiority; others will be carried out on a more egalitarian basis.

Much of this could be said of any cluster of related social roles. In organizations, however, the patterning of role interrelationships is much more systematic than in most other circumstances. The reciprocal obligations and interactive sequences are quite explicit and are often formally stated. The performance of any one role is highly dependent on a series of finely articulated role performances by others occupying related positions. Thus, organizations may be said to have relatively complex divisions of labor or differentiation of roles. This involves both specialization of roles and their coordination.

Specialization and coordination of roles   The link between *specialization* and *coordination* can easily be seen by examining a typical organization chart, such as the one shown in Figure 5-4. Looking across the chart horizontally at its base, we see a number of distinct departments. Each is specialized to carry out a specific, limited part of the organization's overall task. These distinct tasks must be coordinated in some way if they are to fit together and contribute to desired objectives. The task of

> **organization:** a complex cluster of interrelated roles and role sets established or operating to fulfill some purpose or set of purposes.
>
> **organization set:** a group of organizations of the same general type with some interaction among them. The set is likely to act as a standard-setting and norm-defining agency for member units.

coordination is handled by offices or divisions at higher levels. Thus, as we move up the chart from bottom to top, we see several different levels. Each succeeding level is typically responsible for controlling the work of components below it.

The type of control exercised by higher authorities can vary widely. The supervisory lines in the chart may in some organizations stand for rather strict, tight control that leaves the lower units little or no autonomy. In other cases, the lines may stand for loose supervision in which the lower units are allowed to set their own objectives and procedures within broad limits.

The horizontal relationships between separate units on the same level may likewise vary widely. In some instances there may be almost total isolation between such units. Each may carry out its work without significant contact with other units on the same level. By contrast, in other organizations rather extensive, consultative relationships between lateral divisions may be important.

Linkages between organizations   Organizations, like roles, are engaged in intricate ways with one another. Few exist in isolation. Furthermore, linkages between organizations appear to be an increasingly important feature of social organization in industrial societies. Linkages between organizations are of many different types, but two concepts are of particular value in understanding such connections: organization set and interorganizational network.

Organization sets   An **organization set** is a population of organizations of the same general type, with some interaction between them, such as religious organizations and universities (see Figure 5-5).[5] Organizations in the set may carry out similar

Figure 5-5
The organization set of sociology departments at major American universities

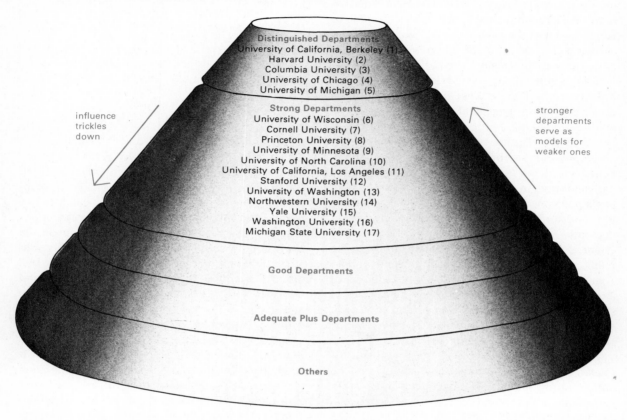

influence
trickles
down

stronger
departments
serve as
models for
weaker ones

Distinguished Departments
University of California, Berkeley (1)
Harvard University (2)
Columbia University (3)
University of Chicago (4)
University of Michigan (5)

Strong Departments
University of Wisconsin (6)
Cornell University (7)
Princeton University (8)
University of Minnesota (9)
University of North Carolina (10)
University of California, Los Angeles (11)
Stanford University (12)
University of Washington (13)
Northwestern University (14)
Yale University (15)
Washington University (16)
Michigan State University (17)

Good Departments

Adequate Plus Departments

Others

activities, produce similar products, or perform similar services. And they are connected in similar ways to other types of organizations. Universities, for example, have similar relationships to federal government agencies.

Furthermore, a set tends to develop a normative character. Each organization tends to look to others in the set as models. For example, university departments of physics may form a set in this sense. Certain departments in the set may enjoy greater prestige and display higher performance levels than others in the set. In fact, a fairly intricate "pecking order" ranging from the most-respected to the least-respected departments tends to develop. Departments ranking relatively low tend to mimic the behavior of the higher-ranking ones, often several years after the fact. Individual physi-

Within the set, probably all university sociology departments look to those of "distinguished" rank as models. Work roles and professional styles of persons in those departments may be perceived as "what one ought to do and be" as a successful sociologist, and the work of faculty members in these departments will be very influential in defining what sociology *is*. The set can also be conceived as a set of sets, however, with distinguished departments looking only to each other as models (if anywhere at all), strong departments looking to the distinguished, good departments looking to the strong, and so forth. From this vantage point, work styles, curricula, etc. may be seen to "trickle down" from the best departments to those below them in the prestige hierarchy.

cists may chart their personal success and mark the stages of their careers by their mobility (or lack of it) through the organization set.

The organization set is useful in explaining organizational behavior because it is a standard-setting, norm-defining unit. Members of specific organizations judge the adequacy of performance of their organization against the standards maintained in the set and exemplified by its high-ranking organizations. If required, they expend resources in an effort to bring their organization up to standard. This is a pervasive pattern.

Religious congregations, for instance, move toward standards in this way. One congregation within a denomination becomes a reference point in defining the standard. A number of congregations consider it a model of a good church program, and try to imitate its standards for weekly services, choirs, auxiliary youth groups, and so on. As each congregation grows in size and financial capacity, it moves closer and closer to realization of the model.[6]

Interorganizational networks More complex than the set, the **interorganizational network** is a web of multiple organizations engaged in a substantial amount of interaction with each other as a consequence of mutual interdependence (see Figure 5-6). The organizations carry out different types of activities yet are dependent on each other because each provides services or goods necessary to the others. Thus, as the members of each organization pursue their objectives, they are drawn into interactions with other organizations controlling needed resources.

Organizations may be drawn into interaction by this resource dependence even though their activities seem opposed. For example, welfare agencies and employment agencies sometimes develop an interlocking dependence. The welfare agency may depend on the employment agency to provide job training and job placement for its recipients. The two organizations are drawn into cooperative agreements because of this mutual dependence. Their relationship may become highly developed, even though the two agencies differ considerably on broad issues of social policy toward the poor and unemployed.

The interorganizational network appears to be an

> **interorganizational network:** a multiple-membership web of organizations engaged in interaction with one another as a consequence of mutual interdependence. A common example is the producer-distributor-retailer web.
>
> **social institution:** a persistent, normative pattern of ways of carrying out common activities characteristic of an entire society; patterns of custom concerning a set of activities, such as family or education, that have become so normative as to be mandatory.

increasingly prominent feature of social organization in industrial societies. In order to produce this book and put it into your hands, for instance, its publisher (one organization) is dependent on the services of a number of other organizations with which the publisher is linked: a printing company, suppliers of paper and ink, photograph archives, trucking firms, the postal service, bookstores, and so forth.

As the number of organizations devoted to specialized tasks has grown, the relations between them have become more crucial. Some observers think that some networks have become so powerful as to gain a virtual stranglehold on the society. The well-known military-industrial complex is a large, loosely integrated coalition of organizations including defense industries and federal agencies dealing in military and foreign policy. Some have argued that in recent decades this complex has become all-powerful within its spheres of operation and has become a major force in the setting of both domestic and foreign policy.

Social Institutions

The activities of people in a society are characterized by many broad regularities and continuities over time. When such patterns of behavior become so customary among a people that they are completely taken for granted not only as the way things are done, but also as the way they should be done, they are said to have been institutionalized.

We recognize, for example, that family organization in a given society is quite similar in a large number of families. There are differences, of

Figure 5-6
An interorganizational network

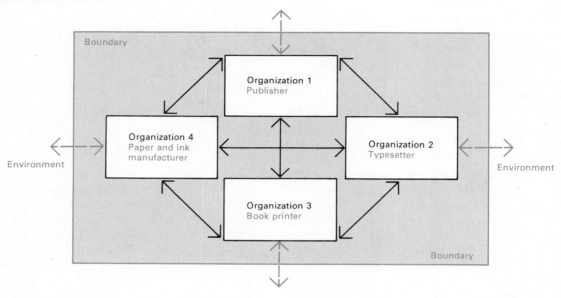

This network shows four organizations performing distinct but related tasks. Solid arrows indicate the flow of resources within the network. Dashed arrows indicate the flow of resources between the network and other units beyond its boundaries. A variety of interorganizational networks could be represented in this way, including employment agencies, health agencies, and manufacturers of related products.

course, but these can generally be seen as variations of a basic pattern. Thus, we can speak of the American family or the Russian family and refer by such terms to certain broad, stylized regularities in the organization of sexual and kinship relations. Included in such a pattern would be such considerations as the form of marriage (monogamous, polygamous), authority relations in the family (relative dominance of father, mother, grandparents, or children), typical task organization in the family (the usual duties of each family member), patterns of sexual relations (the sexual rights and obligations of each family member), child-rearing practices, and so on. Such broad, patterned regularities tend to persist over time. Gradual change occurs, but thoroughgoing transformations in short time periods are quite rare.

The term **social institution** is used to refer to these broad, persistent regularities in behavior. More precisely, a *social institution* is a persistent, normative pattern of ways of carrying out common activities characteristic of an entire society. The activities may be specified in different ways. The usual practice is to think of several distinct spheres of human activity that seem to hang together in

people's experience. The patterns characterizing each distinct sphere then compose an institution. In dealing with industrial societies, it is common practice to recognize many distinct institutions—economic, political, religious, educational, familial. Within each of these institutional spheres, there is a recurrent and persistent pattern of social relationships. These relationships and the growing specialization and differentiation of institutions will be discussed in detail in Chapters 12–16.

Societies

As we saw in Chapter 3, a society is the largest distinguishable unit composed of individuals who share a pattern of social organization that regulates the interaction between them. Clearly, then, a society is a more encompassing unit than all those previously discussed. It consists of a complete complex of social relationships: the roles, groups, situations, organizations, and institutions prevalent among the people in the society. These elements of social organization are woven together in distinctive patterns.

Students of societies try to describe and to explain the patterned ways in which the components of social organization are linked together. For example, we may be interested in how family structure and economic structure are linked to each other. Thus, we might discover in some countries a fine line separating economic from family activities. The linkage between the two institutions would then be accomplished through the roles of specific family members. A woman might play a family role as mother and an economic role as wage-earner. These roles involve her in distinct but related spheres of activity. In this kind of society, then, economic roles are geared into family roles and vice versa.

It is convenient to think of societies as synonymous with nation-states, because data are generally available for nation-states but not for smaller or larger units, and many researchers who study societies do use nation-states as units. However, as we saw in Chapter 3, societies are not always the same as nation-states, although they often are. In some nation-states there are multiple, separate patterns of social organization that are only nominally linked together by a political center. This appears to be the case in many areas of Africa, where centralized nation-states have been formed without regard for cultural and societal boundaries. The central governments face the task of bringing together diverse ethnic and tribal groups with distinct patterns of social organization.

In some other cases, societal boundaries are broader than nation-state boundaries. For example, in some respects the United States and Canada appear to be developing similar patterns of social organization. Occupational structures and the structure of economic organizations overlap to a degree worrisome to many Canadians. The trend seems to be toward convergence of the social organization of the two societies. Thus, at some future time the political boundary between the two

School as a social institution—that is, a persistent, normative pattern of carrying out common activities which characterizes an entire society.

The Tall Ships on a Bicentennial visit. A society is a complete complex of social relationships: roles, groups, situations, organizations, and institutions.

countries may be the principal difference between them.

The difficulties cited above lead to an important point about societies as we encounter them in the modern world. Most of the national populations on the modern scene are not characterized by fully integrated, cohesive patterns of social organization. The boundaries of distinct social patterns do not neatly coincide with one another. A particular pattern of political organization may encompass a larger population than do the patterns of family organization. An economic structure may extend beyond particular political boundaries. These inconsistencies produce a great deal of tension and conflict within populations. Each group committed to different institutional patterns may struggle for control over a central political apparatus. The winning group may use its political dominance to impose its pattern on the other groups. This appears to be a common pattern of conflict in much of Africa today. Even the relatively well-established countries of Europe and North America have in

recent years experienced a resurgence of such conflicts.

Connections between the Components of Social Organization

There are intricate connections between the major components of social organization. When we look at some of the broader categories, like societies or institutions, we do not sever their connection to roles, situations, groups, and organizations. Instead, we may see institutional and societal arrangements as abstract patterns drawn from the investigation of constellations of roles, situations, groups, and organizations. The economic institution in American society, for example, is composed of some generalized roles and role sets (occupational roles, consumer roles, and so on); some patterned situations confronted again and again by members of a population (situations in which purchases are made, contracts are negotiated, resources are allocated, and so on); and some organizations and organization sets (the industrial organization, the labor union, the manufacturer's association, the regulating agency, and others). Thus, we cannot grasp societal institutions without understanding the roles, situations, groups, and organizations through which people carry on their activities.

By the same token, the analysis of smaller units—roles, situations, groups, and organizations—requires an understanding of institutional and societal patterns. It is impossible to explain adequately the behavior of a specific organization like General Foods without a general investigation of the larger complex in which it is grounded, such as the patterns of economic exchange and contractual agreements characteristic of the society. In Chapters 6 and 7, we will analyze in more detail the interconnections between the components of social organization.

Summary

In this chapter, we have described the concept of social organization and its various components. We defined *social organization* as the process through which social relations become recurrent, patterned, and orderly. It originates in the interactions of people within social groups and is identifiable by (1) recurrent connections between sets of activities; (2) control by some persons over the behavior of others; (3) differentiation between the activities of different types or categories of people, and (4) the repeated appearance of similar activities in similar situations.

There are two distinctly different—although sometimes related—dimensions of social organization, the *normative* and the *behavioral*. The normative dimension is the regularity produced by the existence of social rules, the "oughts" and "ought nots" of a society. The behavioral dimension is the regularity produced simply by what is typical or customary in behavior, whether or not it is produced by response to social rules. The normative dimension of social organization produces a great deal of social regularity because people do obey many rules, such as marrying only one person at a time. The behavioral dimension also produces much regularity, because people often act in typical ways; men, for example, almost universally wear trousers. A great deal of social life is characterized by some mixture of these two dimensions.

Social organization also has both *subjective* and *objective* aspects. From one perspective, it is largely a subjective phenomenon, existing in the minds of the participants. This is so because people organize their "realities" around shared definitions and categories. But social organization also has an objective component in that certain behaviors or events may be observed to cluster together in fact. The objective and subjective dimensions of social organization can never be completely separated, because events merely associated with one another objectively may have no meaningful relation in the minds of the participants.

The major components of social organization are *social roles, social situations, social groups, organizations, social institutions,* and *societies. Social roles* are patterns of activity organized around specific social positions, such as mother or police officer. *Role* is the behavior recognized as typical in a given society for the occupant of a given position. Roles do not exist in isolation; they tend to be linked together in orderly ways, two of which are the role repertoire and the role set. A *role repertoire* is the total catalogue of roles played by a particular individual at any point in his life. There tends to be a degree of *consistency* among the various roles in the repertoire because the individual plays them in similar ways or with a similar style. But role consistency is never complete, and *role conflict* may result when one role is hard for the individual to reconcile with another. *Role sets* involve roles that are *reciprocal,* where the performance of one requires interaction with another, as in the set parent/child. Role is an especially important concept in social organization because it is through roles that individuals are linked to social groups and the larger society and various social components, such as groups, organizations, and institutions, are linked to one another.

A *social situation* is a complex social setting

involving multiple actors playing different roles. This implies that the situation, or others like it, exists over time, so that actors bring to it some expectations of what will take place in it. Thus, they have a *definition of the situation* that guides their expectations for their own behavior and that of others. Anyone growing up in a given culture shares thousands of situations with others from the same culture. Consequently, definitions of such situations will also be widely shared, a fact that gives normal social life its marked regularity.

A *social group* consists of two or more people whose interactions with each other are characterized by roles and patterned role relationships, enabling them to interact in predictable ways. Such patterns must be constructed over time, and, consequently, groups are distinguished from other collections of individuals by their persistence. The group is among the most important features of social organization, if not the primary one, because it is the means through which individuals are linked to larger categories such as organizations, social institutions, and the society. People participate in all levels of social organization through the medium of the group. Students are *members of* the organization called the university, for example, and with it the institution of education, but their *participation in* the university takes place in groups called classes, fraternities, athletic teams, dormitory residents, and so forth.

Groups must be distinguished from other kinds of social categories such as *populations, publics,* and *crowds.* The principal distinction to be made is that these are not characterized by *sustained* interaction among their members. A *population* is simply a set of individuals perceived as sharing some characteristic, like left-handedness. A *public* is a form of population in which the characteristic the individuals share is an interest in some aspect of social life, such as a product or entertainer. There need not be interaction in publics and populations, although there may be some on a very limited level. *Crowds* have some minimal social organization; their members are collected in place and time and do interact somewhat on a temporary basis. They are, however, transitory.

Organizations are complex clusters of highly interrelated roles and role sets operating to fulfill some purpose or set of purposes, such as produc-

ing and selling milk. They are primarily distinguished from other social organizational units by the deliberate and systematic patterning of role relationships within them. Organizations have complex divisions of labor (differentiation of roles) involving both role *specialization* and *coordination* of a deliberate nature. Few organizations exist in isolation; most are intricately linked with others through organization sets and interorganizational networks. An *organization set* is composed of organizations of the same general type, such as universities or manufacturing plants producing similar products, and the members of such sets tend to look to each other as models. An *interorganizational network* is composed of different organizations that are related through mutual dependence and the provision of services to each other. Such networks are increasingly prominent features of life in industrial societies.

Social institutions are the broad, stylized regularities that characterize whole societies and operate to organize spheres of activity such as the family, education, law, politics, religion, and economics. They are not organizations, but societal behavior patterns that have become the norms for the ways in which things should be accomplished in a particular society. The American family, for example, may be said to be monogamous, neolocal (married couple deciding own residence), patrinomial (children taking husband's last name), and somewhat patriarchal (husband as principal authority in decision making). The American family has these characteristics because such behaviors are stylized in American society and typify the actual interactions in most families.

A *society* consists of a complete complex of social organizational relationships characterizing a population in which rules regulating their interaction are shared. In this century, societies are often coextensive with nation-states, but they need not be. Some societies can overlap national boundaries, and some nations, such as India and the Soviet Union, include more than one society.

Review Questions

1. Describe your own role set, listing your various roles and their reciprocal roles.

2.   Explain a few hypothetical situations in which different roles seem incompatible. Is role conflict inevitable in each situation? Why?

3.   Define a social group, population and public. How do they differ? What do they have in common? Where do crowds fit in?

4.   List several examples showing how social organization pervades social life. Then note some exceptions where social organization is less typical.

5.   Explain the normative and behavioral dimensions of social organization in your own community.

Suggestions for Research

1.   Some sociologists contend that many roles may become so stereotyped as to obstruct individual creativity and psychological well-being. This has been argued particularly strongly in regard to sex roles. Read Warren Farrell's *The Liberated Man* to gain a clearer understanding of the male role in American society. What is it about this role that Farrell finds harmful or undesirable? How does he propose to resolve the problem?

2.   Make a study of adolescence and how it is often a time of intense role conflict and role incompatibility. Why does this conflict seem to arise for so many teenagers in this society? What part is played by the peer group? By parents? By the school? How do most adolescents deal with the problem?

3.   Select one social institution for an in-depth study: religion, family, education, economy, politics, for example. What need does the institution fulfill? How does this institution relate to other institutions? Is there overlapping? If so, is it desirable? Why? You may want to focus on changes over time in this institution or the major problems faced as it attempts to meet its goals.

4.   Role behavior is of much interest to the psychologist as to the sociologist. Explore the former's perspective through reading appropriate sections in psychology texts. For a more focused reading, you may want to use Sidney Jourard's *The Transparent Self*. How does the psychological perspective differ, if at all, from what you know of the sociological one?

CHAPTER 6
SOCIAL ROLES, SOCIAL SITUATIONS, AND SOCIAL GROUPS

Ship's Company

The first man sailing on a hollowed out tree trunk was a sailor. The first man who had a boy with him was a captain. . . . Only if the young sailor keeps this elementary state of affairs in mind will he be able to see his captain clearly. . . . In practice, every captain looks like an old fool and never is. . . . He is the best argument against atheism that I can think of, for every quarrel, every tension, even the grimmest conflict among members of the crew is entered into with the underlying knowledge that if worst comes to worst, there is always somebody to give the final verdict.

Mates are basically the unhappiest people at sea because they are busy becoming captains. As everyone who has been an adolescent knows, not to be something yet is a depressing situation. What's more, every mate is convinced that he is better than his captain, for his captain only tells him what to do, rarely does it himself. The happy mate, quite satisfied with his situation, is for some reason unsatisfactory. A man who wants to remain a mate is a bad mate, and a man who is a mate and wants to become a captain is frustrated, so one can easily see that a mate's lot is a hard one. . . .

[Engineers] are the happiest addition to the ship's staff since the advent of steam. The officers of the glorious age of sail may never have felt there was something lacking; who sails on a windjammer now, after having traveled on steam, misses not the engine but the engineers. . . . Engineers have one idiosyncrasy: they think about everything in terms of engines. They know that the ship is sailed by the deck officers and that sailors and a captain are necessary but they consider them as people who profit by the engines. . . .

The bos'n is the petty officer in charge of the foc'sle and his personality determines the mood of the seamen. . . . The best bos'ns are firmly and sincerely convinced that the ship would sink like a stone but for their benevolent vigilance over the fox-hunters on the bridge. The bos'n is the one man who really knows how to handle the ship, and if he comes across a captain who handles her as well as he does, he will not be impressed but saddened. He'll mutter, "A body can want to know too much," and ask for a transfer at the end of the trip.

Jan DeHartog, *"Ship's Company"*

This tongue-in-cheek description of some of the ship's company of a merchantman contains a lot of informal sociology relevant to the subject of this chapter. Social roles and situations are highlighted. People are perceived by the writer as possessing certain characteristics—even psychological ones—as consequences of the occupational roles they fulfill aboard ship. Further, anyone who occupies a particular role is apt, as a result, to behave pretty much like anyone else in the same job, because the expectations that others hold for him will be the same. To describe this as a sociologist would: Social situations produce regularities in human behavior because of the similarities in social roles that occur in like situations, and few situations are unique. Thus the order and pattern we find in social life.

The quotation does not specifically mention social groups, but their presence is implied and may be taken for granted, as any reader at all familiar with ships will realize. The Engine Gang (sailors who work the ship's engines and below-deck machinery) will be a coherent group among the ship's company, and the Deck Gang (those who handle cargo, sail and maintain the ship) will be another. Informal groups not created by the fact of work assignment may form around the galley or the radio shack, and the officers will be a group separated by rank and function from the crew.

In this chapter, we will discuss in detail these three social organizational concepts: social role, social situation, and social group. All three have become fields of study in their own right, and each has produced its own distinctive type of analysis. Each type of analysis emphasizes features of social reality that are especially important to the concept in question and develops some distinctive research questions or problems. We will consider these types of analysis individually and try to capture the basic questions that lie at the core of each of them.

Role Analysis

Many sociologists focus their work on social roles. This type of work is called "role analysis" or "role theory." Role analysis is directed at understanding social interaction through the exploration of interconnections between roles and the adjustment of

> **role expectation:** the individual's subjective understanding of how he is expected to behave in a particular role, or a similar expectation concerning another person and that person's expectations for himself. Role expectations may be *behavioral* or *normative*.

individuals to roles. Most role analyses focus on the subjective processes accompanying the enactment of social roles. In this kind of analysis, it is not sufficient to describe clusters of activity from a purely objective standpoint. Rather, the analyst must seek to understand the actors' perceptions of their activities, how the participants arrange and interpret their activities.

To get at the subjective dimension, role analysts have used the concept of **role expectations**: the subjective understanding that participants share of appropriate behaviors in particular roles. The behavior of participants is governed to an important degree by these shared expectations. Thus, people act, as a rule, in accordance with what they understand to be appropriate behavior for persons occupying their role. Their perceptions of what is appropriate are in turn based on what *others* expect of persons carrying out that role.

In the reading on the ship's company, the author commented that the bos'n will not like it if the captain handles (cons or pilots) the ship too well. Put sociologically, this is an expectation for the bos'n's role that *he* will be the master ship-handler; and if the captain shows too great an expertise in that area, the bos'n sees it as an infringement on his own prerogatives. And we may presume that if the captain values his bos'n, he will keep his own ship-handling abilities well hidden so as not to offend him. Thus, both the bos'n and the captain, and also the rest of the ship's company, have a *shared* expectation of what constitutes appropriate behavior. Social life has a modicum of order because people tend to share certain role expectations, and these expectations are complementary and reciprocal. That is, the roles are adjusted to each other. The expectations of one role are linked to the expectations of other related roles. The expectations for bos'ns are geared into the expectations for their captains and vice versa.

The Term Paper Mills Grind Again

In the early 1970s, students at Harvard and the University of Michigan were discovered turning in identical papers purchased from the term paper mills. The resulting publicity drove the mills underground, but not out. . . .

The firms usually do business through the mail, making contact with potential customers by advertising in campus newspapers and on student union bulletin boards and by passing out business cards as exam time approaches. Their ads also appear in National Lampoon and other magazines popular with students. . . .

Many of the companies conspicuously stamp FOR RESEARCH ONLY on their papers, or have students sign a declaration on the order form stating that the paper "will be used for research purposes only." Educational Research in Chicago has gone so far as to copyright its material. Insists Archie Jaudon of College Research Services in Austin, Texas: "A student buys a copy of a paper for research purposes. He knows he is not supposed to use it verbatim. We expect the student to read and redo the paper. Time is so much a factor at a university—students have to wait weeks for a book at the library. We can help them avoid that."

College officials are unimpressed with this argument. . . . Students caught turning in purchased papers are typically put on probation or expelled, say college administrators. . . .

Condensed from Candace E. Trunzo, "The Term Paper Mills Grind Again," MONEY Magazine, February 1976, by special permission; © 1976, Time Inc. All rights reserved. Drawing by Edward Sorel.

We turn now to a series of problems concerning roles. These constitute the major analytical questions of role analysis, questions concerning (1) behavioral and normative expectations, (2) conformity to role expectations, (3) the relation between role and self, (4) role consistency, and (5) role consensus.

Behavioral and Normative Expectations

The concept of role expectation itself has some ambiguities. One of the principal difficulties, as we saw in Chapter 5, is distinguishing between **behavioral** and **normative expectations**. Some of our expectations about how others will behave are behavioral, based on past experience, on what we have known others to do under the same circumstances. In following these expectations, we orient our behavior according to a set of conceptions about how others *typically* behave, rather than on the basis of any normative principle.

We also have *normative* expectations, those

Normative and behavioral expectations do not always coincide.

based on the sense of the proper, the good, the preferred patterns of behavior. Normative expectations are statements of "ought." Fathers ought to (are expected to) support their families. Mothers ought to care for their children. Children ought to obey their parents. Normative expectations, then, place obligations of various kinds on role players. They must conform to these moral demands if they are to gain the approval of other participants.

Most behavior is guided by a combination of normative and behavioral expectations. When we contemplate a course of action, we respond both to conceptions of what we *will* do (based on what we and others in similar roles have done in the past), and what we *ought* to do. Sometimes these two different dimensions may be so intertwined in our experience that we are unable to distinguish between them. Does a father support his family because of the norm that says this is proper behavior or simply because it is customary for fathers to support families? Probably both.

In other circumstances, we may experience a painful separation between the two dimensions. For example, it is a clear violation of norms governing schoolwork for the student to turn in pages prepared by someone else. Nevertheless, in recent years firms selling term papers have flourished on a number of college and university campuses. Under these circumstances, a student could experience inconsistency between normative and behavioral expectations. The norms clearly prohibit the use of bought papers, but the student may know of many fellow students who use them and get away with it.

Role analysis often focuses on the reactions and choices of people experiencing such conflict between normative and behavioral expectations. In the case of the students, the analyst might explore such questions as: Will students feel anxious or tense because of the disparity between what they ought to do and what other students are doing? Will they have difficulty deciding to prepare their own papers? Will they resent those who use the bought papers? Will they become cynical toward the whole educational system?

Conformity to Role Expectations

Another set of questions centers on the problem of conformity to role expectations. *Why* do we behave as we are expected to? Two broad answers to this question have been important in role analysis. One emphasizes processes of socialization; the other stresses social control. Through socialization, as we saw in Chapter 4, we learn what is expected and internalize these expectations. Then we conform to role expectations by doing what we consider right or appropriate.

The *socialization process* is partly explicit and focused, as in grade school or a medical school. But socialization also occurs in more subtle ways. Just by existing in any setting, we tend to absorb the perspectives and assumptions shared by others. These form a taken-for-granted background to all of our actions. Such generally understood expectations need not be taught explicitly. In fact, in

> **behavioral expectation:**   a role expectation developed on the basis of prior experience in a particular social situation.
>
> **normative expectation:**   a role expectation based on the norms or rules of how people *should* behave in a particular situation.

many cases efforts to teach them in a formal way would probably be ineffective. Yet these generalized expectations play an important part in controlling behavior.

The role of physician, for example, has many explicitly specified obligations that are taught in medical school. But it also involves a variety of informal understandings without which the role could not be played. These include expectations about how physicians should interact with their patients, the way they view their patients, the issues on which the doctor consults the patient, and so on. These expectations are understood by physicians and patients alike. They are part of the culture of medical care; physicians and patients have learned them as a consequence of growing up and living within a distinct social group.

Role behavior is also governed by the ongoing processes of *social control.* Involved here are a variety of sanctions that others may invoke. Sanctions may reward behavior that conforms with role expectations and punish behavior that violates them. A great deal of research on roles concerns the effects of different kinds of sanctions. For example: Are monetary incentives more effective than symbolic ones—prestige, honor, affection? Or, among symbols, which are most effective, and for whom? Consider recruiting practices in different branches of the U.S. armed forces. In recent years, the army, navy, and air force have emphasized education and vocational training to attract volunteers. But the Marine Corps, by contrast, has used subtle combat and masculinity themes, with the low-key admission that the Corps is "looking for a few good men." The sociologist might wonder whether the two different "pitches" produced different kinds of recruits for the various organizations. (And whether the reduced stress on "toughness" in Marine training, resulting from some fatalities among recruits, will have a similar effect.)

The Relation between Role and Self

Adjusting self-concept to the roles we play is not always easy, but it reduces tension.

The conformity problem is closely linked to a third set of questions centering on the role-self relation: the degree of compatibility of fit between the individual and the role (or roles) he plays. Each of us builds up certain more or less stable characteristics, including as a prominent feature a self-concept or sense of identity. That is, we all have certain relatively stable images and ideas about ourselves. These self-concepts will either conflict or harmonize with the roles we are expected to fulfill.

If harmony prevails, there is of course no problem. But if conflict prevails, we must either adjust our self-concept to our roles (or vice versa), or experience a disturbing amount of tension between them. If we adjust our conception of self to the roles we play, we will minimize tension and feel that carrying out the expectations is compatible with our own wishes. Role behavior then will be relatively spontaneous and easy.

But if we are unable to resolve the conflict between role and self, role behavior becomes difficult. It involves a feeling of tension between what we want to do or feel comfortable doing and what we are expected to do. In extreme instances, such conflict leads to a sense of alienation from roles, a feeling of being coerced into carrying out activities against our wishes.

A recent phenomenon of academic life presents an excellent example. During the latter stages of the war in Vietnam, the U.S. government resorted to widespread conscription to fill its needs for manpower in the military services. But the Selective Service Act permitted educational exemptions, and the war was extremely unpopular among many college and university students and faculty members. This situation created a very serious tension in the role-self relation for many faculty members. In their role as teachers, they were expected to examine and grade students, and the academic ethics in which most had been trained required them to maintain strict performance standards as a condition for granting passing grades. But failing a student for poor academic performance might result in his being dropped from school, drafted, and sent to risk his life in Vietnam, surely a desperate penalty for schoolroom laziness or incompetence. Many faculty, responding to self-needs and self-expectations, chose to violate the teacher role, and accept work as passing that they would not otherwise have done. This practice may well have contributed to the general "grade-inflation" phenomenon that came to public attention in 1976.

The socialization–social control problem is also related to the issue of consistency between role and self. At one extreme, socialization might produce a thorough fit between role and self. Individuals would then fully accept the expectations associated with their roles and would conform to those expectations spontaneously. Social control in the form of sanctions, rewards, and punishments would be unnecessary. (Americans really do not need laws prohibiting cannibalism in order to prevent it.)

If matters were this simple, there would be no problem. But in the vast majority of cases, socialization does not produce a perfect fit between role and self. Individuals only partly internalize roles, or they internalize some roles but not others. In a given situation, they may experience a sense of uncertainty or even internal conflict regarding roles, partly wanting to conform and partly wanting to rebel. They may respond to a mixture of internal desires and external constraints. They may have difficulty sorting out for themselves why they are taking an action and be unable to separate in their own experience the spontaneous from the coerced. Their actions may be controlled largely by sanctions—rewards for conformity, penalties for deviance.

Many people a good part of the time are like the creative artist who takes a commercial art job in order to eat, hating the fact that he has to take it while recognizing that he must; despising the work

Too Many A's

College grades, along with almost everything else, have been going up lately. Stanford University undergraduates were astonished recently to read in the student paper that their grade point average had spiraled to 3.5+ (or just under an A). "I've worked hard to get good grades here, and I thought they would help when I was ready for grad school," said Patricia Fels, a senior. "Now I find out everybody has good grades."

Indeed, in the past few years, the grade glut has been spreading across academe. At Yale, 42% of all undergraduate spring-term grades were A's, and 46% of the senior class graduated with honors. "It's ridiculous," says Eva Balogh, dean of Yale's Morse College. "They get a B and they bawl. It takes a man or woman of real integrity to give a B." At American University, 75% of all grades last spring were A's and B's, leading an undergraduate dean to ask for a faculty inquiry. At the University of Pittsburgh, the average grade was C five years ago; now it is B.

Why? Many students are using pass/fail options in difficult courses, thus reducing the percentage of low letter grades. For their part, many professors started giving higher grades in the late '60s to help students escape the draft, and some have wanted to avoid what they regard as the "punitive" effects of grading. . . .

From "Too Many A's," *Time*, November 11, 1974, p. 106. Reprinted by permission from TIME, The Weekly Newsmagazine; Copyright Time Inc. Drawing by Jack Davis.

Grade inflation may have resulted in part from teachers' self-role tensions produced by the Vietnam war.

© Jules Feiffer.

the job requires, while wishing from professional pride to do the best possible job at it, and so forth.

Role inconsistency. Who is the better man by conventional social standards?

Role Consistency

Another problem in role analysis is *consistency* or *inconsistency* among roles. Where multiple roles are played by the same individual, he may find some of the expectations incompatible with each other. To satisfactorily meet the expectations of one role may require that he violate the expectations of another, as in the case of the hungry artist. This kind of conflict occurs within the role repertoire of the individual.

Analyses of this problem have generally recognized that such conflict is more characteristic of urban-industrial than of traditional societies. The differentiation of roles and of institutional complexes in urban-industrial societies creates a separation of role expectations. The expectations associated with work become separated from those associated with religion or family. Thus, the same individual playing roles in several distinct social contexts may find the expectations conflicting, or at least uncoordinated with each other, as when, for instance, an office develops the informal expectation that junior executives will work late, while their wives expect them home for dinner. We will

pursue this problem of differentiation again in dealing with institutions in Chapters 12–16.

Studies of conflict between roles have focused on two interesting issues: First, what are the consequences for the individual experiencing conflict between roles? It may be argued, for example, that individuals exposed to such conflict are more likely than others to suffer anxiety or mental illness. A review of research studies on mental disorders by Robert Kleiner and Seymour Parker provides confirming evidence of a kind. They found that an abnormally large proportion of those people suffering anxiety or mental illness had role inconsistency problems.[1]

A second issue is: How does the individual manage inconsistent roles? Perhaps individuals vary in the capacity to manage multiple, partially conflicting sets of expectations. Some individuals may be quite adept at moving between roles, at playing first one role and then another, and at playing one role off against another. Others may be unable to carry out such agile maneuvers. Career women and working mothers offer excellent examples of both. Some women seem perfectly capable of handling the often conflicting demands of a role in an occupation or career and the roles of wife and mother without apparent damage either to themselves or to their husbands or families. Others, like some male counterparts, appear incapable of doing both without incurring severe stress themselves and/or imposing strains on their families.

Another kind of inconsistency is incompatibility between roles contained in a role set, roles that must be played in relation to each other by *different* actors. Inconsistency occurs when the expectations of one role are opposed to those of the other. If both actors in such a case conform to their *own* role expectations, they will conflict with each other. This problem occurs whenever you enter into a relationship where the other party's expectations conflict with different expectations that are part of your own role. The captain who was required by the ship's owners to steer the vessel himself when coming into port would be set up for such conflict not only with the bos'n but with the local pilots as well.

The individual caught in such conflict cannot meet one set of expectations without violating another set. The supervisor in industry, for another example, is subject to incompatible expectations, some coming from higher management and others from subordinate employees. This type of role conflict is quite common in urban-industrial societies. Many roles in these societies are linking roles serving a "go-between" function, like that of the supervisor. It seems clear that societies characterized by totally integrated, perfectly meshing role sets are not common in the modern world, and models based on such role sets are generally considered utopian.[2]

Role Consensus

A final problem in role analysis is consensus (agreement) or disagreement regarding roles. Here we encounter the problem of disagreement about expectations. Individuals engaged in interaction can go forward with it only if there is some minimal degree of understanding between them about the expectations of *each* role. Where such common understanding or consensus is lacking, interaction may be confused or conflicting. Such relationships may finally break down completely. Where, for

example, a husband and wife hold sharply opposed views about their roles, marital difficulties frequently result. A common contemporary example is disagreement concerning household division of labor in family situations where the wives work outside the home. Husband and wife often disagree about how much domestic responsibility she should retain and how much he should assume.

Situational Analysis

The social situation in which role behavior is played out can be grasped as a whole, worthy of analysis in its own right. Situational analysis is less clearly identified as a distinctive mode of analysis than is role analysis. But it is frequently employed by many social scientists, and there are some for whom situational analysis is the most fundamental of all sociological approaches.

We are all familiar with certain regularly recurring situations in which two or more persons join in carrying out an event of some kind. The events in question are infinite. Workers on an assembly line, family members at the dinner table, students and teachers in a classroom, players and spectators at a football game, parishioners at a religious ceremony, buyer and seller at a market—all are participants in situations. The events carried out have sufficient regularity and predictable order to permit us to think about them as distinctive occasions. The events that occur at a football game are highly patterned and predictable. We can go to games in hundreds of different locations and yet anticipate with fair accuracy the kinds of things that will take place. And we generally have no difficulty in distinguishing football games from religious ceremonies or other events.

In part, what is involved here is a set of cultural definitions and expectations for specific situations. We anticipate the correct behavior for each situation because we have been exposed to a common culture. Observers not sharing our expectations would have considerable difficulty arriving at classifications of events that seem natural to us. They might, for example, confuse football games with religious rituals, a preposterous error from our standpoint, but an understandable confusion for one not sharing our cultural definitions, especially since many football games are opened with a religious invocation and a quasi-religious flag ceremony.

Sociologists engaged in situational analysis closely examine such generally understood events. They try to explain how situations are enacted, how they shape the behavior of individuals, how they acquire recurrent features, and how they fit into larger structural and institutional contexts. In analyzing situations, they do not lose sight of roles but try to understand how multiple roles are played out in situational contexts. Two topics are of particular importance in situational analysis: situational definitions and situational contingencies.

Situational Definitions

As we have already seen, situations are not purely objective sets of events. Occurrences that seem similar to an initiated observer often have subjective meanings that make them quite different. (The flag ceremony before a football game *looks* very much like a religious ritual, but few Americans would perceive it as such.) Situational analysts generally insist that these subjective features, the *situational definition* discussed in Chapter 5, are absolutely essential to understanding the events.

Actors bring to an event certain expectations. They *expect* certain things to happen. They also think certain things *should* happen. Thus, just as with role behavior, we encounter here both a *behavioral* and a *normative* dimension. Few situations fully conform to our definitions, but in most instances we have a framework within which to interpret even an unanticipated event. Thus, unexpected developments typically do not destroy our sense of order. Indeed, our expectations may allow for a degree of randomness, or unpredictability.

Situational definitions consist in part of roles. We anticipate in a general way the roles to be played by participants in a given situation and prepare ourselves subjectively to respond to the roles others will play. We also anticipate that others will respond to us in a certain way because of the role they have assigned to us. In coming to a classroom, we anticipate the behavior of others partly in terms of role assignments. The teacher will lecture; the students will ask questions; the teacher will an-

swer. We fit ourselves into a place in this interchange and act accordingly.

Such subjective definitions also include generalized expectations that go beyond the roles of participants. These expectations apply to the situation as a whole. Norms concerning decorum, mood, and demeanor are involved. A religious ritual is a solemn occasion. All participants approach it with that understanding.

Furthermore, situational definitions include anticipated courses of action, that is, sequences in which we expect a given situation to develop. We expect roles to be carried through in a predictable sequence and to be geared into each other in a predictable way. The sequencing or sequential ordering of the interaction is anticipated.

In many situations, the subjective definitions incorporate certain well-understood rules specifying the appropriate course of events. Some rules are formalized, the rules of procedure in a court of law, for example. The socialization process for lawyers involves the internalization of these rules and the development of expertise in their use. But these rules too are flexible and contingent to some degree, not absolutely rigid. Thus, both lawyer and judge must keep in mind a wide range of alternatives and responses defined as legitimate within the rules of the court.

Rules governing interaction sequences are not always formalized. Even small, informal friendship groups appear to develop some generally understood rules. These may specify both general norms and particular courses of action. "Doing the dozens," for example, refers to a patterned interaction sequence common to informal groups of young black males in urban ghettos. This is a relatively standardized pattern in which insults are exchanged in an escalating pattern until one youth breaks the sequence by "losing his cool" or by failing to come up with an adequate response. The rules of this game are not written down, but they are so widely understood that the skills are transferable from one informal group to another.

Situational Contingencies

Situational analysis involves an effort to grasp the larger context in which action takes place. The situation imposes limits on the participating actors, presenting them with opportunities and providing channels for action. Responses are *contingent,* or dependent on, the limits, opportunities, and channels present in the situation. These features of the situation can be called **situational contingencies**.

Situational contingencies frequently enter into explanations of action. For example, it has been argued that criminal behavior depends partly on the inclination of the individual, but also partly on the opportunities available. If a man wants money and legitimate work is not available, then he may turn to illegal activities. The desire for money combines with the situational contingency (the unavailability of work) to produce an illegal act. In other situations, where legitimate work is available, the intention to get money may produce social and financial success. Some analysts have developed a theory of delinquency by extending this type of reasoning (see Chapter 17).[3]

Consider another example. In a study of a French manufacturing plant, Michel Crozier found that the maintenance department, which was responsible for repair of machinery, was unusually powerful in the affairs of the plant. Its power was situationally based. The rules of the plant had become so restrictive and elaborate that no department could take any action that would seriously affect other departments. Even superior officials in the plant could have little influence on lower-ranking department heads because the rules were so restrictive. There was, then, little "uncertainty" in the organization. The rules spelled everything out and left nothing to chance. Nothing except mechanical breakdowns. When the machinery failed, everything stopped until repairs were made by the maintenance workers.[4]

This contingency—the unexpected mechanical breakdown—gave the maintenance department a special power over other departments. Because the maintenance workers could carry out repairs speedily or slowly, whichever suited them, they had the power to delay or expedite the work of other departments when breakdowns occurred. Theirs became the one department with the power to exercise control over the one uncertainty in the system, and they were able to use this power to defend themselves and extract benefits from oth-

situational contingencies: the limitations and opportunities present in a given situation that determine what may, although not what will, occur.

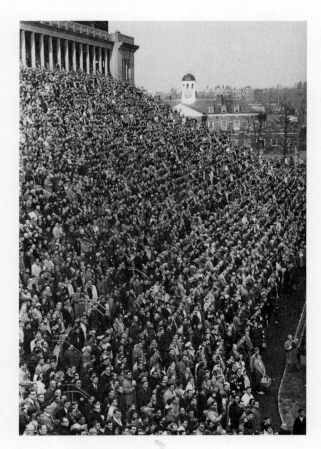

Pledging allegiance at a football game. What are these people *really* doing?

ers. The restaurant headwaiter who accepts tips from customers who wish to be served first is in a similar position: he controls *access* to desired rewards as a contingency of his position in the situation.

Any situation may be analyzed partly as a set of contingencies similar to those described above. The sociologist looks for the contingencies affecting the choices of people and the outcomes of their choices. In describing a situation, the analyst may try to sort out the many contingencies and to show how they might combine. A typical course of events may be explained partly by reference to the total set of contingencies affecting actions and their outcomes.

Social Group Analysis

You will recall that Chapter 5 defined a group as two or more people whose interactions are characterized by patterned roles and role relationships, and noted that such patterning could only develop as a consequence of interaction over time. It was also remarked that groups are at the very heart of social organization, because they are the linkages between different individuals and between individuals and larger social units like organizations and social institutions. For these reasons, the social group has been a focus of sociological attention for a long time. There are three general areas of concentration, three types of research problems, that have organized much of the effort in the study of groups. These are (1) the development of social systems, (2) the formalization of group structure, and (3) group influence on the individual.

The Development of Social Systems

One persistent puzzle for students of social groups is the formation of *social systems*. Analysis of these systems involves an effort to isolate the basic components of group life and to discover how they are related to each other. This effort is similar to those of other scientists to discover systematically patterned relationships among a series of physical components. Chemists, for example, analyze molecules and atoms as systems of chemical compounds, and biologists study the anatomy and physiology of the frog as elements of an organic, living system. In every case, the researcher is interested in the *system,* the interrelationship between the individual elements involved.

In the effort to discover the basic elements of social systems, a number of analysts have concentrated on relatively *small groups,* such as work groups, friendship groups, and committees. These groups have been studied both in natural settings and under contrived experimental conditions. Here we will concentrate on the major elements that have been identified in small-group studies.

Social interaction   As noted in Chapter 5, the origins of social organization lie in social interaction. As people interact over time, they begin to develop relatively stable, patterned ways of relating to each other. Interaction may begin with only the barest guidelines for appropriate behavior. For example, you may know that others expect you to keep a certain physical distance from them, in our culture normally somewhere between two to three feet. You realize the expected form of greeting is a handshake, a nod of the head, a "hi," or some facial expression recognizing the other person's presence. But aside from these general behavioral expectations, you may well be unsure of just what to talk about, what kind of language to use, or what type of behavior is most appropriate when you first begin to interact with strangers.

This uncertainty is what causes us to feel awkward when we first enter strange groups. We come to be more comfortable as we get to know people better through interacting with them and accumulating specific information about their expectations. Thus, interaction is a basic element in social systems, the process that permits groups to cohere and persist.

Norms   As individuals interact with each other over a period of time, interests and behavioral expectations begin to emerge and to crystallize, and the group develops norms that serve as guidelines for what is acceptable behavior and what is not. In a curious paradox, as normative patterns develop in this way, group interaction becomes both more spontaneous and more predictable; more spontaneous because, until people "know the ropes," they behave tentatively, and more

The American social situation now makes possible contingencies for young women which were not available in the past.

predictable because knowing the ropes means knowing what to expect.

A good example of how a social system evolves on the group level is William F. Whyte's study of *Street Corner Society.*[5] Whyte studied the Nortons, a gang of young Italian-American men who centered their social activities on particular street corners and the adjoining barbershops, lunchrooms, poolrooms, and clubrooms. Few of the gang members had completed high school, and most of them were unemployed or had only irregular employment. The group was brought together and built around Doc, who was respected both within the gang and by other groups in the area.

Over the course of several months the Nortons developed norms and customs that were never written down or even formally decided upon, but that every member of the group understood. For example, a corner boy was not expected to be

chaste, but it was considered beneath him to marry a girl who was "no good." It was also taboo for anyone to "mess around" with somebody else's girl. Most of the time, no one in the group had much spending money. However, if someone was lucky "at the tables" or got overtime pay at a job, he was expected to treat the rest of the gang. Selfishness and reluctance to share were frowned upon.

Roles   Some norms hold true for all members of the group, but specific expectations also develop that are associated with various social positions in it. Regardless of which member assumes the leadership position, for example, certain things will be expected of him. Thus, specific roles tend to develop within the group and to become part of its social organization. Just as society defines many categorical roles that individuals internalize, such as father, politician, student, and female, every group develops special roles for its own members. The way one group expects a leader to behave, for example, may be very different from the way another group defines leadership. Different role expectations make each group unique.

In the Nortons, Doc was boss. When he suggested an activity, it was understood that everyone would go along with him. Since he had good connections with other gangs, as well as with the racketeers and politicians in the area, he was expected to see that diplomatic relations were maintained. If any boy got into trouble, it was Doc who interceded for him. In return, the boys were expected to look up to Doc and respect his position.

Figure 6-1 shows the social organization of the Nortons. The position of the boxes indicates the relative status of each corner boy. The lines between the boxes show how communications were apt to occur and who was most likely to influence whom in the group. Since bowling was a favorite pastime for the Nortons, there was a close connection between a boy's bowling skill and his position in the group. If a boy wanted to increase his prestige, the best way to do it was to excel in the Saturday night bowling matches. Each boy in the group knew his place and what he could and could not get away with. Ridicule and social ostracism were leveled at anyone who was "uppity" and didn't "know his place." In a fascinating aside, Whyte even suggests that bowling scores reflected knowledge of "place" in the gang: Alec was a better bowler than Doc and consistently registered higher scores when Doc was not present; but when Alec bowled *against* Doc, he rarely managed to win.

Leadership   Leadership in a group is related to its goals and the values held by group members. In the Nortons, Doc was recognized as the only leader and given prestige for his position. In many groups, however, several leaders, each responsible for various tasks, may emerge. Robert F. Bales, a sociologist at Harvard University, conducted a series of

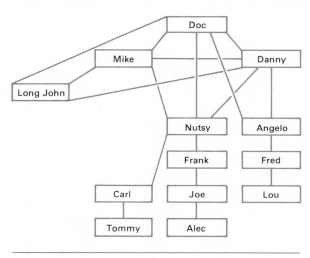

Figure 6-1
The social organization of the Norton street gang

laboratory experiments in the 1940s that focused on leadership in small groups, and developed a system of categories for recording the process of group interaction.[6]

One of the principal findings of Bales's research is that when a group solves a common problem, two types of leaders usually emerge: (1) a task leader, who focuses on getting the job done, and (2) a social-emotional leader, who supports group members and reduces tensions that arise in the course of meeting task goals. Given the fact that different talents are involved in the two leadership roles, Bales hypothesized that the roles would be likely to be performed by different persons. His research verified his initial prediction and led to the realization that leadership in a group is not one-dimensional. One individual may assume a leadership role when it comes to mobilizing a group for a task, and another individual may emerge as a leader when problems or conflicts arise among group members.

The network of interrelated roles within a group that influence the ways in which actors relate to each other constitutes the social structure of the group. This structure is independent of any one person; it defines role behavior regardless of who plays a given role at any time. Thus, a certain degree of predictability is possible. Although each individual may add personal dimensions to the enactment of the roles, certain standard expectations remain a part of each role regardless of who plays it at a particular time. It is on the basis of such recurrent, predictable patterns of behavior that we speak of groups as social systems. In social systems, group elements remain relatively stable, are interconnected with each other, and are defined in terms of social structure, such as roles and role relationships, rather than on the basis of individual personalities.

Formalization in Group Structure

A second body of analytical problems coming out of group analysis concerns the *formalization of relationships*: the process by which the interactions of group members become explicitly regularized, rather than just understood. This routinization has been found to be related to: (1) the degree to which group behavior is explicitly codified through rules or regulations, (2) whether a group is primary or secondary in nature, (3) size, (4) the presence or absence of factionalism within the group, and (5) the influence on the group of larger social units, such as organizations. These phenomena are discussed below.

Formal and informal groups Some groups operate with few explicit rules or regulations governing their interaction. In such groups, people relate to each other on the basis of unstated, but well-understood norms and role expectations. These understandings may be based on frequent interaction extending over a long period. In groups like Doc's gang, members simply proceed on the basis of such unstated rules. Likewise, family relationships tend to be governed by such understandings. Groups of this kind are called *informal groups.*

By contrast, *formal groups* are those in which relationships are governed by explicit rules and where the rights, obligations, and relations among group members are precisely specified, often in writing. It is more than a coincidence that most of the formal groups we can think of are part of organizations. In organizations, explicit attention is paid to the specification of appropriate relationships. Elaborately detailed rules and job descrip-

Groups differ by degree of formalization in relationships.

tions characterize the organization, and groups of people within the organization relate to each other at least partly on the basis of these specifications.

In modern societies, there is a tendency for informal understandings to give way to formally prescribed relationships. In recent years, for example, there have been proposals that husband-wife relationships be formalized by precisely specifying the obligations of each partner in a marriage contract, and some persons follow that practice now.

Primary and secondary groups   In addition to his work on self-concept, discussed in Chapter 4, Charles Horton Cooley produced an enduring distinction between two types of groups, primary and secondary.[7] The difference between them is in the type of relationships that exist among their members. In *primary groups,* you will recall from Chapter 4, individuals know each other personally, interact face to face, communicate in many nonverbal ways, and experience the "we-feeling" that characterizes a close-knit human community. Group members are bound together by a sense of close identification and emotional involvement with each other and the group itself. They not only share certain interests or personality traits but are intensively and extensively bound to the group. It is clear who belongs and who does not. Frequently, the group develops a name or symbol to identify itself to outsiders and to increase the sense of identity among members, like the Jets in *West Side Story.*

Cooley developed many of his ideas by observing the play groups of his own children. He was intrigued with the ways groups form and the interplay of self-identity with group identity. A family, play groups, friendship cliques, and gangs are examples of primary groups; such groups are, as we saw in Chapter 4, important socializing agents. Primary groups are informal because members understand the implied structure without elaborate formal codes.

Cooley defined **secondary groups** less precisely, characterizing them as having features more or less opposite those of the primary group. Interaction in secondary groups thus is less intimate than in primary groups, and communication is frequently not face to face but through mediators and formal means. A secondary group is held together by the fact that individuals need the group and its resources for their own purposes, rather than by members' devotion to the value of the group itself. People are thus involved in secondary groups only segmentally, rather than as total personalities. Goals, membership requirements, and sanctions for deviance may be formalized in written statements. Most voluntary associations, such as the Civil Liberties Union and the American Sociological Association, are secondary groups.

Both primary and secondary groups are *organized* in the sense that predictable interaction patterns develop in them. Primary groups, however, are characterized by informal organization, whereas secondary groups are based on formal organization. In the former, roles are understood and require little specification; in the latter roles are more specifically defined. Differences in the degree of role specification between the two types of groups are evident when we compare what is expected of a student in a university (a member of a secondary group) with what is expected of a friend (a member of a primary group). In the student role, degree requirements and "passing" grades are clearly specified by university rules. But any attempt to "go by the book" or carefully weigh costs and rewards when it comes to assisting a friend threatens the bonds that exist in friendship.

Group size   The formalization process appears to result in part from increase in the size of groups. As groups increase in membership, rules and roles tend to become more formalized. With increasing size, it becomes more difficult to maintain face-to-face contacts and personal relationships. Impersonal mechanisms of communication and coordination of group activity then become more likely. Although it would be a mistake to describe this as an inevitable pattern, it does appear difficult for large groups to avoid the encroachment of formalized rules and role expectations.

Georg Simmel was one of the first sociologists to suggest that the number of members in a group radically transforms its properties.[8] He began with an analysis of what happens when a **dyad,** a two-member group, becomes a **triad,** a three-member group. First of all, the number of possible relationships changes. Members A and B of the dyad (the original relationship) begin relating to member C. As a result, a relationship is established between A and C as well as B and C. In addition to a simple increase in the number of relationships, there is a potential for new types of relationships to evolve. Coalitions and confrontations are now possible because two members can gang up against the third.

Theodore Caplow's book *Two against One* depicts the types of coalitions a triad can muster that are impossible in a simple dyad. The triangle tragedy, popular in American romance stories, where one spouse or lover falls in love or has an affair with a third party, exemplifies how coalitions with a third party can threaten dyadic relationships. So does Cold War politics, where relations between the two superpowers are often threatened by their ties to client states.[9]

In addition to the alliances and coalitions possible in a triad, the level of intimacy and dependency changes when a third member enters a dyad. The popular saying "three's a crowd" expresses the reduced sense of intimacy that frequently occurs in a triad. Most basically, if one member of a dyad dies or departs, the group is broken up and ceases to exist. However, a triad can survive the loss of one person either by continuing to exist as a dyad or by replacing the lost member. The precariousness and the intimacy of monogamy as an institutionalized form of marriage lie in the dependency each marriage partner has on the other.

As groups increase in size, there are predictable consequences. As long as a group numbers fewer than twenty or so, informal organization is still possible, although the patterns of social relationships become more complex and subgroups tend to form within the larger group. Instead of two-member coalitions, *subgroup* coalitions can easily evolve and lead to internal conflict.

When group size increases to the point where face-to-face interaction is no longer possible, there is a tendency toward formal organization in which roles and responsibilities are explicitly delineated. Subgroup conflict, in this case, is regulated by formal procedures, such as grievance committees and supervisors whose job is to hear complaints and reduce tensions.

Another interesting aspect of group size is that similar groups tend to organize themselves in units of similar size, perhaps as a result of the phenome-

secondary group: in essence, any group other than a primary group, but particularly one characterized by absence of interpersonal intimacy, indirect communication, formalization, and segmental personality disclosure.

dyad: a two-member group.

triad: a three-member group.

Voluntary associations like this choir are common features on the American scene. Most are secondary rather than primary groups.

A triadic relationship is always inherently unstable because coalition formation causes one party to be left out.

non called **span of control.** Span of control means the range and degree of control that it is possible for one person to have over a number of others. Thus, a narrow or limited span of control means that, while only a few people may be supervised, the degree or detail of the supervision may be great. Contrarily, a large span of control permits supervision of a large number of people, but not in great detail. It is on this principle that every army in the world is organized into overlapping units of size approximating those of the American army fireteam, squad, platoon, company, battalion, and so on. These would seem to represent the maximum number of persons (about 3, 9, 40, 250, and 1,000, respectively) who may be effectively supervised by one individual in differing degrees of detail.

Factionalism Another internal factor that produces formalization is *factionalism.* When a group is divided into opposing **factions,** small groups with interests of their own, there is frequently a tendency for each side to impose specific obligations on the other. The membership must resort to

explicit rules and regulations where the basis for mutual trust has been eroded. Neither side trusts the other to fulfill its obligations spontaneously, so rules are imposed, and each may threaten to punish the other in some way if obligations are not fulfilled. Union-management relations are a classic example of this pattern. The obligations of each party are precisely specified in a contract, and violations of formalized expectations are met with penalties or punishments of various kinds, such as strikes and lockouts.

Influence of larger social units Social groups are also subject to pressures toward formalization stemming from outside their own boundaries, from the larger social units to which they are linked. In fact, many sociologists have looked for master trends in societies that would account for increasing formalization.

You may recall from Chapter 1 that Max Weber argued that the industrial-urban societies of Western Europe were becoming *rationalized,* meaning that social relationships were increasingly being evaluated by criteria of efficiency in the pursuit of specific goals. This tendency, he thought, was developed to a high degree within the capitalist firm and then extended to other social contexts. The rationalization process involves the specification and enforcement of rules and roles with a view toward efficient, predictable goal achievement. In the face of this tendency, informal and merely customary understandings give way to formal, contractual relationships. Down this road lies bureaucracy, an organizational apparatus that Weber both admired and feared. We will return to this problem in the discussion of organizations in Chapter 7.

span of control: the range and degree of control it is possible for one person to have over a number of others. In general, as the number of people controlled increases, the degree of control decreases.

faction: a small group with interests of its own within a larger group or organization. The usual implication is that certain interests of the faction are contrary or disadvantageous to those of the larger unit.

in-group: persons who identify with each other in some way and would thus mutually refer to themselves as "we."

out-group: persons whom members of an in-group identify as not belonging to their group and would thus refer to as "they."

reference group: a group taken by an individual as a frame of reference for self-evaluation and attitude formation. A reference group may be *normative* or *comparative;* that is, a group from which one adopts values or behavior or a group against which one measures oneself.

Group Influence on the Individual

A third category of problems in group analysis concerns the *influence of the group on the behavior of the individual.* Much of the research on this topic focuses on three phenomena: (1) in-groups and out-groups, (2) reference groups, and (3) susceptibility to group pressure.

In-groups and out-groups   In the 1940s and 1950s, many American sociologists and social psychologists turned their attention to the internal structures and dynamics of small groups, especially to problems of group identification and social pressures toward individual conformity to group norms. Muzafer Sherif, for example, conducted group experiments with boys in a summer camp to determine how gangs formed and how intergroup conflict occurred as the boys became identified with and committed to a particular gang.[10] Group boundaries became very rigid and clear-cut as conflict arose and the gang rallied its forces to fight another gang. The *in-group,* that is, members who identified with each other and showed a sense of we-ness, were clearly differentiated from the *out-group,* people who were not part of the group.

In one experiment, Sherif created a situation where two gangs were very hostile to each other and engaged in continual intergroup warfare. He then simulated a crisis, a rupture in the waterline that provided the only source of water for the camp. Interestingly enough, the gangs were able to work together, side by side, to repair the leak. An overriding goal can cause rival groups to forget their differences and work together for their common interests.

Street Corner Society also documents the tendency of small groups to designate who is "in" and who is "out."[11] The Nortons identified themselves as distinct from the College Boys, a category of people who had gone to college and were perceived as considering themselves "better than us." Constant rivalry existed between the groups. Warfare broke out when a College Boy dared to date a Norton's girl or was seen in an area defined as Norton territory.

Frequently, a strong in-group sense leads to defining things in terms of ownership: "our territory," "our girls," "our basketball court," or "our duds." Infringement on in-group territory or symbols by a rival gang is taken as a dare and has often been the cause of gang warfare, as depicted in *West Side Story.*

Reference groups   An individual's orientation to a group can have different consequences, depending on the importance of the group to the individual. A

reference group is a group that an individual takes as a frame of reference for self-evaluation and attitude formation. Reference groups can be either groups we belong to or groups we don't belong to. As Robert K. Merton has pointed out, sociology has traditionally recognized the influence of membership groups on the values and attitudes of group members.[12] But the distinctive concern of reference group theory is those groups that influence us even though we don't belong to them, nonmembership groups.

For example, a classic study of the American soldier conducted during and immediately after World War II showed that the married soldier was more likely than the single soldier to come into the army with reluctance and a sense of injustice. Either the married soldier compared himself with his unmarried army associates, who he felt did not have to sacrifice a wife and family; or he compared himself with his married civilian friends, who he felt had escaped altogether the sacrifices he was making. In comparing himself to either of these two reference groups—single soldiers and married civilians—the married soldier felt deprived.[13]

Merton distinguished two functions that reference groups have for the individual, and differentiated types of reference groups on that basis. *Normative reference groups* are a source of values and norms assimilated by the individual. *Comparative reference groups* serve as a context and measuring rod for evaluating oneself and others.[14] In some

Solomon Asch conducting a laboratory experiment in perception and susceptibility to group pressure.

instances, the same group can serve both functions for the individual.

In other cases, a particular group serves one or the other function. In *Street Corner Society,* for example, Doc decided at one point to run for a local political office. He rallied his gang into campaigning for him by presenting them with strategies that politicians use to win votes. None of the boys had campaigned before or knew much about the political process, so Doc tried to orient them by showing them what other campaigners did and how they had to evaluate themselves if the campaigns were to be successful. The comparative reference groups he presented were previous campaign groups that had been successful in getting their candidates elected.

Susceptibility to group pressure   Reference groups exert influence and social pressure on the individual to conform to certain norms. A number of experiments in social psychology during the past thirty years have demonstrated how susceptible to influence by group pressures many people are.

Solomon Asch conducted a famous series of laboratory experiments that provided a model for studying group pressures on the individual.[15] A group of people, usually numbering between four and ten, were gathered in a room. All but one were confederates of the experimenter; that is, the experimenter told them what responses to give during the experiment. The one "naive subject" was unaware that the others knew what to expect. The subjects were asked to judge the length of a set of lines. First, they were shown a card on which appeared a standard line. Then they were shown a second card having three lines, one equal in length to the standard line, the second longer, and the third shorter. The subjects were then asked to state aloud which of the three lines on the second card was equal to the standard line.

The experimenter had arranged for all the confederates to give their responses before the naive subject gave his. The confederates would give an incorrect answer. Invariably, the naive subject would experience a growing anxiety as he realized that his original judgment (as yet unstated aloud) was different from that of all the other subjects. When his turn came, the naive subject would often get up so as to view the lines from the same angle as the confederates, come back to his seat, hesitate before making a choice, and, in 32 percent of the cases, give the response that the rest of the subjects gave, even though the factual information before him indicated that their response was incorrect.

This experiment was repeated many times with amazingly similar results. The disturbing fact about it is the frequency with which naive subjects gave incorrect responses despite the physical evidence before them. These experiments demonstrate the tremendous effect a reference group can have on us. Not only is it difficult emotionally to take a stand against majority opinion, but group norms and opinions can influence us to question our own judgment. The naive subjects actually questioned the validity of their original opinion when faced with a unanimous judgment that differed from theirs.

In an attempt to determine whether it was the *number* of other people that made social influence so powerful or whether it was *agreement* among other group members, Asch conducted other experiments in which he varied the size of the group that participated.[16] He found that group influence

Table 6-1 Number of trials in which naive subjects yielded or did not yield.

	Trials in which naive subject yielded	Trials in which naive subject did not yield
Unanimous majority	76 (80.9%)	68 (35.1%)
Nonunanimous majority	18 (19.1%)	126 (64.9%)
Total	94	194

remained unchanged if the majority was three or more. What is crucial, therefore, in determining group pressure on the individual is not the *number* of others who agree on a response but their *unanimity*.

The importance of unanimity of response over group size was further tested by an experiment conducted by J. S. Mouton, R. N. Blake, and J. A. Olmstead in 1956.[17] The subjects were seated in separate cubicles and asked to estimate the number of metronome clicks they heard at a designated time. Each set of three trials consisted of fourteen, thirty-two, or forty-nine clicks. Through his earphones, the naive subject heard the responses given by four other confederate subjects before giving his own. In each trial, the confederates underestimated or overestimated the number of clicks. In some trials, all the confederates agreed with each other. In others, they did not give a unanimous opinion even though all responses were incorrect.

The results of this study, given in Table 6-1, show that naive subjects tended to give in to group influence principally when faced with a unanimous majority. When even one other subject dissented, unanimity was disrupted, and the naive subject felt freer to make an independent judgment. This fact held true whether the other dissenting subject gave a correct or an incorrect response. Thus, social support for a given response is not the critical factor. Rather, what is critical is the absence of a *unanimous* set of group responses. It is difficult for people to dissent from group unanimity.

These experiments on the effect of group pressure on individuals were conducted under controlled laboratory conditions, but it is probable that the same processes operate in real-life social situations. We are constantly influenced by the judgments and opinions made by people with whom we identify. Just how much the judgments of others affect us depends on how important they are to us. If they constitute a reference group, we are more likely to be influenced by their opinions than if we do not identify with them normatively or use them as a point of self-comparison.

Market researchers and political pollsters have long been aware of the pressure of group influence. The most powerful strategy a political candidate has in the last days before an election is to convince the public that a majority of voters like themselves are going to vote for him. Television and magazine advertisers go to great lengths to show that intelligent, hard-working, fellow citizens just like us know a good product. The underlying, often unspoken questions behind commercials are: What's the matter with you? Why haven't you wised up and realized that Greasy-Off Oven Cleaner is superior? Thousands of people like you have been using the product and enjoying the hours of leisure afforded by reduced oven-cleaning time.

Groups have a pervading influence on our lives. We do not live in isolation. During most of our lives, we are either directly involved in group interactions or are being influenced by group norms. In addition to the informal groups that are such an important part of our lives, we are involved in formal organizations that set standards for us as well as help us meet basic needs.

Summary

Because social organization is so broad a concept and field of study, individual sociologists have tended to concentrate on only one of its aspects at a time—roles or groups or organizations, and so on. This concentration on only single "slices" of social reality has produced distinct *modes of analysis* geared to the nature of the "slice" selected.

Role analysis, or role theory (as it is more commonly known), has tended to focus on the subjective aspects of role behavior, to seek ways of understanding the meanings and interpretations that guide people in role enactment. The principal concept of role analysis is *role expectation,* which calls attention to how people perceive their own roles and the expectations they have for others, including their perceptions of what others expect of them. This leads to a stress on the nature of *shared expectation* as the basis for social organization. This, in turn, produces certain major research problems, such as the problem of distinguishing between *normative* and *behavioral expectations, role conflict* and ambiguity, the problem of why people *conform* to role expectations, the whole issue of social control, and the problem of the relation between *role* and *self* and role *consistency* and *inconsistency.*

Situational analysis moves the focus from the individual to the social situation and the cultural understandings and values that produce situational regularities, such as the similarities between all football games. The attempt here is to understand how situations are enacted, how they shape individual behavior, and how they fit into larger societal and cultural contexts. The major questions in this mode of analysis involve *situational definitions* (how people define and classify situations and what cues they use to do so) and *situational contingencies,* which affect opportunities and limits for behavior within specific situations.

Analysis of social groups has focused on three major concerns: (1) the development of social systems; (2) formalization in group structure, and (3) the influence of the group on the individual.

Attempts to answer the question of *how social systems develop* in the first place lead to consideration of the basic components of group formation and behavior. These are *social interaction, norms, roles,* and *leadership. Interaction* enables groups to cohere and persist and involves learning and responding to behavioral expectations. Experience interacting with one another in a group leads people to develop *norms* concerning what may and may not be expected and acceptable behavior. But norms are only *general* expectations for any group member; in addition to norms, all groups sooner or later develop expectations concerning how *individuals* may be expected to behave and what part they play in the group. These individualized expectations are *roles,* and every group has roles that its members play in it.

All groups also develop *leadership* roles. These may be either informal or formal and explicitly defined in positions such as president of the company. Two basic types of leaders are *task leaders,* who take charge of accomplishment, and *social-emotional* leaders, who support other group members and act to smooth out tensions arising from the problems of interaction and meeting group goals. The network of interrelated roles within a group is its social structure. This tends to persist over time, even though individual members of the group may come and go. It is this feature that turns specific groups from something unique into *social systems.*

Degree of *formalization* is also an important aspect of social group structure. Formalization is the process through which interaction among group members becomes explicitly regularized. The tendency for informal organization to be superseded by formal organization seems to be common in modern industrial societies.

The distinction between informal and formal groups is closely akin to that drawn by Charles Horton Cooley between *primary* and *secondary groups,* a differentiation based on the *kinds of relationships* existing among members. In primary groups, individuals know each other as total personalities, interact on a face-to-face basis, communicate in many ways including the nonverbal, and experience the group as a "we-feeling. ' The family and the child's play group are the outstanding examples. *Secondary groups* are characterized by segmental (rather than total personality) involvement of members, more indirect communication—some of it mediated by formal means—goal orientation, and formal organization.

Formalization tends to increase with increasing group *size* and appears unavoidable once a certain size has been reached. Two other phenomena that produce increasing formalization in groups are *factionalism,* where formalism is resorted to as a means of negotiating tension or conflict, and *pressures from outside* the group's own boundaries, from the larger social units to which they may be linked.

The subject of *group influence on the individual* was discussed under three topics: in-groups and out-groups, reference groups, and individual susceptibility to group pressure. The "we/they" distinction is the hallmark of the *in-group* versus the *out-group.* It is perhaps most marked in conflict situations and may be a product of conflict itself. Its effect on the individual is to induce conformity to group norms.

A *reference group* is a group the individual uses as a model for his own behavior and self-evaluation. The norms and values of the group, as perceived, become the standard by which the person judges himself. A reference group may be *normative* for an individual (a source of values and norms to be assimilated) or *comparative* (a standard against which to measure himself), or both.

The reference phenomenon may be what creates the degree of *susceptibility to group pressure* demonstrated by Asch and others in laboratory small-group experiments. The general conclusion to be drawn from these studies is that even artificially created groups of which we are only temporary members may have great influence over our behavior, particularly when group opinion appears unanimous.

Review Questions

1. Explain how specialization affects and is reflected in your own life-style. What role is then played by coordination?

2. Compare the social interaction in a dyad with that in a triad. In what ways are they similar? different? In what way does the triad serve as a model for larger social groups?

3. Using your own life experiences as a framework, list examples of some of the different groups discussed in this chapter: dyad, triad, primary group, secondary group, in-group, out-group, reference group.

4. Explain trends characteristic of the last few decades in the U.S. in regard to human interaction. What roles are played by primary groups? secondary groups?

Suggestions for Research

1.   Usually, social groups are regarded as an integral part of society. Sometimes, however, a small group takes on certain characteristics that enable it to function as a small society or subculture. Study this phenomenon by reading and reporting on William F. Whyte's *Street Corner Society.* Explain the concept of social group as it is portrayed in Whyte's account.

2.   Role incompatibility or conflict grows more likely as one takes on more roles. Probe this topic in relation to the women's movement. Is it possible for a woman to multiply the important roles in her life without serious conflict? What types of things can ease role accumulation? One helpful source may be *Sex, Career and Family* by Fogarty, Rapoport and Rapoport.

3.   Read and write a report on Alvin Toffler's *Future Shock.* What does Toffler see as the future for primary group relations in our society? Why are primary groups necessary, if at all? How would Toffler like to deal with rapid social change? If you have seen the film, compare it with his book. The film may be available for viewing in your school audio-visual center.

4.   In discussing the dyad as a social group, the author of this chapter explained how divorce rates in our society and marital unhappiness may reflect the tremendous expectations spouses place in an important but fragile dyad, monogamous marriage. Explore the marriage dyad as a social group, giving particular consideration to its strengths and weaknesses. You may want to read literature supporting alternatives to traditional monogamy such as *Open Marriage* by Nena O'Neill and George O'Neill.

5.   Explore the family as a primary group. Most sociologists acknowledge that the functions filled by the family have changed over time; has this altered the importance of this primary group? Why or why not? What makes the family such an important primary group in the U.S.? What detracts from its success in fulfilling basic needs? You may want to include William Goode and William Kephart among your references.

CHAPTER 7
ORGANIZATIONS, SOCIAL INSTITUTIONS, AND SOCIETY

Most of you will recognize the accompanying photograph as representing a legislative or deliberative body. Some with greater memory for detail may recognize exactly what body it is and, perhaps, even what it is doing. The photo is of the Committee on the Judiciary of the U.S. House of Representatives. What the committee is doing in the picture is preparing to debate the articles of impeachment to be charged against Richard M. Nixon.

This picture captures a historical moment neatly representative of the chapter's subject matter. The Committee on the Judiciary is an organization in its own right as well as a subunit of a larger organization, the United States Congress. Both organizations are part of the social organizational pattern reflecting the social institution called the polity, the institution of politics and government. And in the specific instant of time captured in this photo, those organizations and that institution were acting for the society in which they existed.

This chapter continues and concludes the description begun in Chapter 5 of social organization and the ways in which sociologists analyze and study it. Here we consider the more complex levels of the social organizational scale: organizations, social institutions, and society. All are studied as subject matters in their own right in sociology, and certain specialized modes of analysis have been developed for the investigation of each. This chapter describes the principal ones in some detail.

Organizational Analysis

Organizations are a familiar feature of modern societies. Every sphere of social life is increasingly characterized by organizational structures. **Voluntary associations** take on functions as diverse as religious activity (the Baptists), political expression (Common Cause), community betterment (local organizations to stop littering), and physical self-improvement (the World of Health spas). Economic activities are carried on increasingly by large-scale organizations of considerable structural complexity like General Motors, U.S. Steel, American Telephone and Telegraph (AT&T), and International Business Machines (IBM). Government agencies, characterized by bureaucratic structure, grow in size and extend their influence into wider and more diverse spheres of social life.

In the large, complex organization, the components of social organization examined in Chapter 6—roles, situations, and groups—are brought together. Indeed, an organization is a formal group. Many different roles are carried out in an organization, and they are complexly interrelated. The various departments of an organization become situations for the participants. There are official definitions for most of these situations, such as the rules that regulate the operation of the assembly line, and almost always these definitions are accompanied by informal understandings between participants that further define the situation.

Organizational analysis focuses on how roles and situations are arranged within large-scale, complex units like universities, hospitals, retail stores, manufacturing plants, research laboratories, and so on. The key issue in such arrangements is *structure,* the very essence of formal organization. Considerable variation exists among organizations in the form and nature of their structure, and questions concerning what purposes they serve, and how efficiently, have not yet been fully answered. For this reason, the following discussion focuses on the concept of **organizational structure**.

We will examine first some of the ideas, such as specialization, centralization, and formalization, that are used to describe aspects of structure. Then we will consider two common types of organizational structure: bureaucratic and professional. Finally, we will turn to the problem of structure *formation* and examine four common ways in which sociologists have tried to explain it.

The Concept of Organizational Structure

Organizational structure is the patterning of social relationships within an organization, the way in which roles and situations are pieced together to form distinctive overall patterns. Sociologists have identified a number of different dimensions of organizational structure. Each dimension may be seen as a continuum, a continuous series stretching from one extreme to its opposite. Individual organizations will occupy different positions on a continuum. By observing the structure of an organization, we can assign it to a position along the

voluntary association: an organization in which membership is maintained by choice rather than compulsion or ascription. Examples are bridge or bowling clubs, the Kidney Foundation, political parties, and so forth.

organizational structure: the pattern of social relationships within an organization; the way in which social roles and situations link to form distinctive, permanent patterns.

continuum, that is, say that it has a high or a low degree of a given characteristic. Three of the most important dimensions of organizational structure are specialization, centralization, and formalization.

Specialization is the degree to which tasks are divided and assigned to distinct roles or departments. At one extreme lie organizations in which a large number of distinct tasks can be identified. At the other are organizations in which there are few distinctions of this kind. A barber shop, for example, typically has few, if any, task divisions. All of the barbers in the shop do the same things. By contrast, a university department is often highly specialized, with each member offering courses about areas of knowledge not shared by other members.

Centralization is the degree to which decision making is concentrated in certain roles. At one extreme would be an organization in which all issues of any importance are decided by one person. At the opposite extreme would be those in which everyone shares equally in the decisions.

Formalization is the degree to which the roles and role interactions are precisely specified. Some organizations have highly specific rules and procedures governing the behavior of participants. Sometimes these are stated in written form, as in a rule book. Work in welfare agencies where public aid is dispensed to the poor is typically governed by highly specific rules regarding eligibility for benefits. By contrast, social workers in a private agency (supported by philanthropy or by user fees) may have less extensive rules and more flexibility to make judgments on the basis of their professional training.

If we were to look for these dimensions in a series of organizations, we could proceed in a

Formalization.

number of ways. We might look at an organizational chart showing the various positions and departments and the linkages between them. Counting the number of separate departments in such a chart would give us a rough indication of the extent of specialization. Counting the number of levels from top to bottom would suggest how centralized the organization is. To get an estimate of formalization, we could obtain a rule book and count the number of separate rules. None of these procedures would be adequate by itself, but each gives some idea of how research could proceed.

Notice how these dimensions are linked to roles and situations. The presence in an organization of a large number of distinct roles for which expectations vary widely amounts to specialization. Likewise, the separation of an organization into a number of distinct departments (purchasing, manufacturing, shipping, sales, and so on) creates a series of different situations. Formalization refers to the manner in which role performances are controlled.

In looking at organizational structure, we are taking a distinctive point of view. Rather than seeing the social world as a set of contingencies confronting the individual, we are looking for a pattern in the contingencies themselves. We seek labels—formalization, centralization, specialization, and others—that will help describe the differences we see between organizations. Then we seek ex-

planations for such differences. At this point we have crossed a boundary of considerable importance. Here *organizational structure* becomes a focus of attention in its own right, not merely a setting affecting individual actions. We set out to explain structural patterns, not simply to use them as explanations for individual choices and their outcomes.

Organizational Types: Bureaucratic and Professional

The analysis of organizational structure is sometimes advanced by constructing *types.* This involves bringing together a number of separate characteristics in order to grasp the organization as a whole. By this device, we try to see a general pattern in a series of separate observations.

The concept of **bureaucracy** is a device of this kind. A bureaucracy is an organization having high degrees of specialization, centralization, and formalization. Bureaucracies have four major organizational characteristics. First, *work is specialized* through the establishment of multiple departments and roles with unique assignments. Second, *control* is exercised *through a chain of command* originating at the top of a hierarchy of graded positions. The progression of authority downward through military ranks from general to private is an example. Third, *authority* in the bureaucracy *is attached to positions* rather than to individuals. That is, people exercise authority by virtue of their occupancy of positions, and the authority is transferable from one occupant to the next, as in the transfer of control from one manager to the next in a business firm. Fourth, *rules* in a bureaucracy *precisely define the obligations of participants.* In extreme cases, this precision may lead to complete routinization: the reduction of tasks to simple routines. Routinization tends to be maximized at the lowest levels of the hierarchy.

The **professional organization,** such as the American Bar Association, is another major type of organization. It contrasts sharply with bureaucracy in several ways (see Figure 7-1). Chief among these is the lack of centralized authority and the diminished importance of rules or formalization. Because of these features, the professional practitioner retains some autonomy to apply his expert knowledge as his judgment dictates. Where bureaucracy tends to produce rule-bound routines, the professional organization promotes the flexible application of knowledge.

These two types—bureaucratic and professional organizations—are useful in helping to clarify our thoughts. Actual organizations, however, often combine features of both types. An industrial concern may have a highly bureaucratic production component and a professionally organized research component. Patterns are even more complex in many large hospitals, where bureaucratically and professionally organized components are in constant contact. In fact, in the hospital the overlapping of these components is so intricate that some roles involve a mixture of bureaucratic and professional regulation. The nurse, for example, is both a functionary of the hospital bureaucracy and a skilled member of a professional team.

These two types, of course, merely *describe* organizational structure. To *explain* structural patterns, we have to ask other kinds of questions and try to answer them. *Why* are welfare agencies more bureaucratic than research laboratories? What are the origins of observed structural patterns? By what mechanisms are they maintained? In asking these questions, we plunge more deeply into the problem of *structure formation.*

A number of different answers to the problem have been offered. The four major explanations have to do with *goals, needs, power,* and *environment.* In the following pages, we will consider these explanations and the complications associated with each.

Organizational Goals

It has frequently been argued that the explanation of structural patterns in organizations is to be found in goals. It is assumed that every organization is directed toward the accomplishment of a purpose. Indeed, many have argued that the commitment to a specific goal is what distinguishes organizations from other social forms. Included as goals are very broad and abstract purposes, such as to heal the sick, to end poverty, and to make a profit, as well as rather specific objectives stated in a more concrete form. Such objectives include producing Cadillacs for a selected clientele, developing job opportunities for unemployed fathers, and helping former mental patients readjust to

bureaucracy: an organization with high degrees of specialization, centralization, and formalization; or a process or behavior with those characteristics.

professional organization: a formal organization of persons possessing expert knowledge, usually operating with less formalization and greater flexibility than a bureaucracy in deference to the independence and expertise of its members. The American Medical Association is an example.

Kaufman in The Christian Science Monitor, © 1958 TCSPC.

Specialization.

Figure 7-1
Bureaucratic and professional organizations

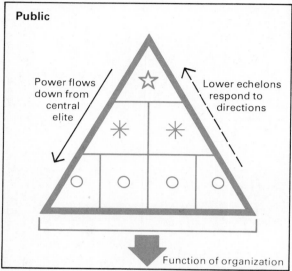

Bureaucratic organizations: Members (☆ ✳ ○) work for the organization (△) so that it can serve a public (☐). Power (↓) flows down from a central elite (☆) to lower echelons (✳ ○) who respond by complying with directions (↑), thus accomplishing the organization's function (⬇).

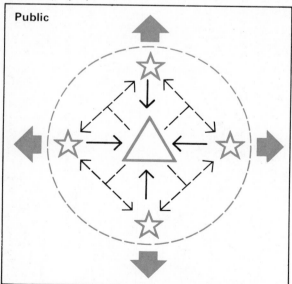

Professional organizations: An organization of paid specialists (△) responds to the needs of individual elite practitioners (☆) who control it (→). The organization is established by the elite for the purpose of assisting (⇢) their own activities (➡) vis à vis the public (☐).

home life. The more specific objectives translate the abstract goals into a workable program.

Goal beneficiaries   Organizations may be distinguished from one another partly on the basis of goals. The sociologists Peter Blau and W. Richard Scott, for instance, proposed four kinds of beneficiaries and classified organizations according to the type that best characterized them.[1] *Mutual-benefit associations* aim to promote the interests of their own members; examples are labor unions, professional associations, and burial societies. *Business associations* operate to provide a profit for their owners; IBM, Exxon, grocery stores, and department stores would fall into this category. *Service associations* exist for the purpose of serving a "clientele" requiring special assistance; hospitals, schools, and welfare agencies are examples. *Commonwealth associations* provide service to the general public; examples are the federal government, the military, and the postal service.

There are, of course, other schemes for defining beneficiaries. One common distinction is simply between the organization's clients—whether patients, customers, or consumers—and its own membership, who perform a certain amount of their activities in service of their own rather than the client's ends. The degree to which the organization's normal routines are directed toward one or the other of these beneficiary groups is often used to describe the organization. A typical complaint of college students, for example, is that the student health service is run primarily for the benefit of its own staff and their convenience.

Goals and structure   Now, with the concept of goals and goal beneficiaries in mind, let us return to the problem of structure formation. If, as proponents of the goal explanation maintain, organizations tend to move toward the achievement of goals, then the parts of the organization may be assumed to *be formed* in ways that contribute to goal achievement. In other words, an organization will develop structural forms that support its pursuit of goals. Likewise, the argument runs, structural forms that block or inhibit goal pursuit tend to be rejected.

Take as an example a business firm with two alternative structural arrangements to consider. It can operate in a centralized, bureaucratic way with top executives exercising tight control over all units. Or it can grant a semi-autonomous position to its operating units and achieve coordination through negotiations between units. Which of the structures—centralized or decentralized—will the firm choose? The answer from the goal argument is that the structure selected will be the one leading to the most effective goal pursuit. Thus, if the goal is profit making and if a centralized structure is most profitable, then the organization will become centralized.

Following from this reasoning is an explanation for the structural differences between organizations. If we see differences in structural arrangements, we can suspect that there are also differences in goals. By finding the differences in goals, we can then account for the structural variation.

Broad classes of organizations   You can see how this method works by comparing broad classes of organizations. For example, since the goals of schools differ from the goals of businesses, we would expect to find, and do find, that their organizational structures differ too. This kind of reasoning was used by Amitai Etzioni to explain the varying bases of *compliance* in organizations, that is, the ways of gaining and maintaining conformity among members.[2] Etzioni classified organizations on the basis of means of compliance, distinguishing three basic organizational types: coercive, utilitarian, and normative. **Coercive organizations** use force, usually physical force, to achieve their goals. Prisons and concentration camps use fences, iron gates, cells, and armed guards to assure that inhabitants "stay in line"—and inside. Coercive means usually result in alienation of the members from the organization.

Utilitarian organizations rely on money and other material rewards to motivate members to comply with the goals of the organization. Business firms and corporations offer salaries, wage incentives, bonuses, and fringe benefits to encourage members to work for the organization. Members of utilitarian organizations have a calculative orientation; that is, they calculate they will receive personal benefits for complying with organizational goals.

Normative organizations gain and maintain membership commitment by convincing members

coercive organization: one that secures compliance from members through force; for example, a prison.

utilitarian organization: one that secures compliance from members through money or other material rewards; for example, a business corporation.

normative organization: one that secures compliance from members through appeal to value commitment; for example, a church or the Heart Association.

Coercive organizations use force to achieve their goals.

The Joy of Work

At first gulp, the weekly revel in Michigan City, Ind., resembles any other Thank-God-It's-Friday affair. Tired workers slump over the piano in their favorite bar, draining their beer mugs and slogging through a few stanzas of song. But the 350 employees of Sullair Corp.'s headquarters can do their unwinding in the company's own "gourmet" cafeteria or at its lavish picnic grounds. The pizza, barbecue and beer are on Sullair. And often as not the song is Sullair's own: "Pump that air, pump that air, pump that air for old Sullair, as those compressors go rolling along," warbled to the tune of the old field artillery song.

Sullair, a producer of air compressors for industrial drills and other tools, may well be the nation's foremost practitioner of corporate paternalism. A Christmas turkey for each employee is only the beginning. There are four tennis courts—two indoor and two outdoor—with free lessons by a full-time pro, and a shop that sells tennis gear at wholesale prices. Those who tire of the free athletics—including squash, basketball and swimming in an Olympic-size pool—can study anything from auto repair to guitar at company expense. They can sustain themselves on Cornish hen, frogs' legs and homemade pastries at the "Cafe La Bastille," the atmospheric cafeteria whose prices start at 75 cents for a hot, three-course meal. There are clubs, dances, theater parties and excursions to baseball games, all at company expense. And on special occasions, Sullair workers celebrate in grand style: the Christmas party starts at 8 a.m., with the accounting department blending Bloody Marys and shucking oysters for everyone.

All this largesse is the work of Donald C. Hoodes, 49, the president of Sullair, who founded the firm ten years ago. "I always hated every boss I ever worked for, so I decided things would be different here," says Hoodes, who was fired for insubordination at his previous job. "All work is hard, so we have to have some fun." And thus far at least, Hoodes isn't facing any insurrection from his 1,267 stockholders. Sales and profits both rose by more than 40 per cent in 1974, giving Sullair a 30 per cent share of its U.S. market, and operations for the first three quarters of 1975 were running comfortably ahead of the 1974 pace.

The benefits don't stop at amusements. Sullair pays the whole cost of standard employee benefits, including insurance, bonuses and free drug prescriptions, and has a new stock-ownership plan for employees. The company goes on to ease much of the pain of modern economic life. Two supermarkets give Sullair folks 10 per cent discounts, with the company picking up half the tab. Gasoline from the company pump costs workers 35 cents a gallon, a bargain that costs the company an estimated $3,000 a month. Even the snacks are subsidized: the office vending machines dispense coffee and candy bars at only a nickel each. . . .

of the *value* of the organization's goals. For example, a church gets committed members by convincing people that belonging will help them live a good life and achieve eternal salvation. The Cancer Society gains members by showing them how worthwhile and necessary it is to work for the elimination of cancer.

Etzioni argued that variations in the compliance structure result from the efforts of organizations to be effective in reaching their goals. An organization will tend to adopt a compliance structure suited to its goals. Thus, a prison is driven toward coercive control because its major goal is to protect society by maintaining custody of criminals. It would be ineffective in reaching this objective if it relied on normative persuasion.

Similar organizations The goal argument should also hold for organizations of the same general type. For example, if we see that some elementary schools are organized in an authoritarian way,

Utilitarian organizations rely on money and other material rewards to secure member compliance.

giving students and teachers little independence and flexibility, while others are democratic and equalitarian, then we are led to suspect goal differences as well. Even though the two types of schools share the broad goal of educating students, there may be important differences between them in more concrete objectives. The authoritarian school may concentrate exclusively on developing the academic abilities of students, promoting maximum learning in math, language, science, and so on.

The equalitarian school, by contrast, may have a broader conception of educational goals. The development of social skills and capacities for creativity may be prominent objectives. Discovering these differences in objectives, then, we might say that the structures vary because the goals vary. The first school has an authoritarian structure to drill students in fundamental skills, while the second seeks to promote the kind of free and open exchange in which creativity and social skills are developed.

Problems with goal explanations The goal explanation, despite its obvious strength in the cases cited above, poses some serious problems. The difficulty is that the concept of organizational goals raises another interconnected cluster of questions. Let us consider some of these briefly.

Disagreement about goals There are often disagreements within an organization about what its goals should be, especially at the level of concrete objectives. For example, professors and administrators in universities often disagree about how much emphasis to place on research and how much on teaching. These differences of policy reflect basically different conceptions of the goals of the university.

Change of goals Goals often change over time. Many organizations appear to drift away from their original goals. Partly this drifting is due to the necessity of converting abstract goals into concrete objectives. We must, therefore, distinguish between **official goals,** which are publicized "company policy," and **operative goals,** which affect and determine the ongoing functioning of the organization on a day-by-day basis. One way to discover an organization's operative goals is to study actual decisions of top decision makers in the organization, especially decisions about how allocation of resources (money, personnel, time) are made. It is not unusual for decision makers, by their priority allocations, to betray the fact that operative goals do not always accord with official goals. In a study of correctional institutions for delinquents, for example, it was found that resources were consistently allocated to custodial aspects of the institutions rather than to professional treatment personnel, even though the official goal of the institutions was rehabilitation.[3]

Changes in official organizational goals frequently result from differences between operative and official goals. Although organizations can survive for a time with different official and operative goals, there is a tendency for pressures to build up,

> **official goals:** an organization's formally stated objectives.
>
> **operative goals:** an organization's objectives as determined or demonstrated by its day-to-day operation; frequently different from official goals.
>
> **goal displacement:** deflection from original objectives through the accretion of inconsistent day-to-day commitments as operative goals.

whether internally or externally, for the organization to "be what it professes." In some instances, the organization makes a deliberate effort to restate its goals more realistically. In other instances, the leaders of the organization gradually come to realize that its goals have, in fact, changed without deliberate planning.

David Sills's study of The National Foundation for Infantile Paralysis shows how an organization can explicitly restate its goals as a result of operative goals evolved by its members. The foundation was set up after the depression to assist polio victims by soliciting small amounts of money from many people through the March of Dimes. The new concepts of fund raising, patient care, and community responsibility that the foundation promoted rallied highly committed people who were organized on a local level. When the Salk vaccine was discovered, some twenty years later, organizational members were reluctant to disband. They had developed operative goals that included a sense of accomplishment and fellowship along with the official goal of fighting polio. As a result of internal pressures, the leadership of the foundation broadened and redefined the official goal of the organization to include "concern for general public health." A succession of goals resulted in which the foundation took on new goals rather than disband once its original official goals were achieved.[4]

In the example above, the organization changed its goal when the original goal was accomplished. Official goals can also change through the process of **goal displacement.** Goal displacement occurs when an organization is deflected from its original goals through a series of day-to-day commitments that define the "character" of the organization. An example is the Tennessee Valley Authority (TVA),

Normative organizations gain compliance by persuading members of the moral value of their goals.

which has been extensively studied by Philip Selznick.[5] The TVA was set up by Congress to build dams and generate electrical power in the Tennessee Valley through grass-roots strategies of getting local people involved in planning and constructing the projects. Because of its commitment to grassroots ideology, TVA brought into its leadership people from the local community, including members of local power groups who resisted official TVA goals. By absorbing resistant elements into its policy-determining structure, a process called **cooptation,** the TVA hoped to avert threats to its stability or existence.

However, the organization did not anticipate the extent to which the coopted members of its policy board would influence day-to-day decisions on immediate and pressing problems. As a result of this influence, a series of commitments was made that ultimately led to the displacement of official goals by operative ones. To cite just one example, coopted local community leaders exerted influence to reverse the original official policy of providing a protective strip of publicly owned land around public reservoirs. Local farmers resented public

ownership of prime farm acreage around the reservoirs, and the coopted board members supported them and forced TVA officials to allow private purchase of the land.

Multiple goals   Many organizations have multiple goals, some of which may be incompatible with others. That is, the structural arrangements required to realize one goal may be inconsistent with those required to realize another goal. The organization may, nevertheless, be committed to both goals. The prison, for example, is supposed to incarcerate criminals in order to protect the society, but it is also supposed to rehabilitate prisoners. These two objectives appear to require incompatible structures. The authoritarian control and rigid rules designed to maintain security generate so much hostility and resentment on the part of inmates that rehabilitation becomes more difficult. Similarly, the open, less restrictive structure needed for rehabilitation may undermine security.

Inaccurate goal statements Members of an organization may use goal statements to divert attention from their actual purposes. The acknowledged goal may serve only to manipulate public opinion or divert attention. while the actual goals remain unstated. For example, the Central Intelligence Agency apparently disguised its effort to recover a lost Russian submarine by presenting the operation as a mining venture, and Richard Nixon defended Watergate crimes on the grounds of "national security." Such deception about goals is widespread and is not restricted to the intelligence field. This makes it very difficult to discover goals and to use them in explanations.

Organization Needs

An alternative to the explanation of structure on the basis of goals is an explanation grounded in the concept of needs. Organizations have needs in the sense of requirements for survival and for adequate functioning. If the organization is to be maintained as an operating enterprise in reasonably good order, some requirements or needs must be met. For example, some colleges have closed in recent years because their enrollments were not large enough to generate sufficient income to keep up with rapidly increasing costs. Students were needed by these colleges in larger numbers. We could say that students were a resource essential to the survival and well-being of these schools.

Assuming that all organizations have needs of various kinds, we can try to explain structural patterns on the basis of needs. Suppose, for example, we discovered that a large number of small, financially weak colleges were changing their rules to give more autonomy and flexibility to students in their selection of courses and in their private lives. Suppose we found, too, that colleges that made such changes experienced an increase in enrollment leading to financial stability. We might argue then that the structural changes (increased autonomy and flexibility) were responses to the need for increased enrollments. In this case, the need of the organization for increased enrollment explains the structural change.

> **cooptation:** appointing people to a group for the purpose of securing their cooperation and allegiance, particularly when the persons involved are known to be hostile to the group's values or goals.

The needs of an organization may conflict with its goals. That is, the effort to meet the survival and maintenance needs of the organization may be incompatible with goal pursuit. Resources may be diverted from objectives to satisfy needs. In universities in recent years, the increased costs of fuel have forced some cutbacks in teaching programs. The instructional goals of the university then suffer so that basic maintenance of the physical plant can be continued.

Once an organization is established, decision makers may, in fact, become almost exclusively committed to meeting the organization's needs. Its goals may recede into the background and be used only to justify decisions to the public.

Selznick's study of the formative years of the TVA shows how this pattern can develop. The TVA began in the 1930s with wide-ranging objectives, including social reform as well as economic development in the Tennessee Valley region. Some of its objectives were threatening to local and regional interest groups (state and municipal officials, farm organizations, and so on), and these groups opposed the TVA. The opposition, Selznick contended, threatened the existence of the agency. Gradually, the TVA leadership adjusted its goals and reorganized its programs in order to reduce the opposition. The leaders of opposing groups and organizations were drawn into the administration of TVA programs. This process of cooptation reduced their opposition at the cost of removing the critical edge from the programs. Thus, ultimately, TVA modified its goals and made compromises with its opponents in order to survive. Goals were modified so that needs could be met.

Extending this line of thought, some observers have argued that in modern organizations of considerable size stated goals are less important than control over resources. Goals may change or be modified to increase resource control. A marketing firm, for example, may completely alter its product

PERSONNEL DEPT.

NOW HIRING

ON THE CONTRARY!.. OUR COMPANY'S ATTITUDE TOWARD ITS FEMALE EMPLOYEES IS TOTALLY NON-SEXIST ...A CHICK WITH LEGS LIKE YOURS COULD REALLY GO PLACES WITH US!

© 1976 by NEA, Inc. T.M. Reg. U.S. Pat. Off.

Reprinted by permission of Newspaper Enterprise Association.

lines. Likewise, profit making for investors may become a matter of secondary importance. The crucial consideration is that the organization maintain and/or extend its control over resources—capital, labor supply, land, machinery, markets—so that it can adapt to changing circumstances. From this point of view, then, structural patterns will be formed or modified on the basis of calculations of resource control.

Problems with explanations based on need The concept of organizational need is itself beset with problems. Indeed, the concept is the focal point of another set of issues. First, the definition of needs may vary from one group to another. Opposing groups in an organization may advance incompatible formulations of needs, making it difficult to arrive at a definitive statement. Second, organizational needs may in fact be incompatible with one another. Consequently, painful choices must often be made between compelling needs. An explanation based on needs, then, may have to be supplanted by one focused on the process through which participants assess and define needs. Third, needs, like goals, may change over time. Explanations based on fixed conceptions of needs are then undone by the changes. Furthermore, such changes suggest the importance of a different kind of explanation, one accounting for changes in need definitions.

Organizational Power

Still another way of explaining the problem of structure formation involves the concept of power.

An organization's operative goals often differ somewhat from its official goals.

Stated generally, the argument is that the structure of an organization is accounted for by the power of various groups to control the organization's development. Thus, the structure of the organization depends to a large degree on which group is in control. That group can determine what structural forms will develop and adopt those that work to the group's advantage in gaining benefits from the organization.

Eliot Freidson has recently developed this kind of argument in regard to hospitals and the medical profession.[6] The social structure of the hospital gives autonomy to the physician in that no other occupational group can control the work of the physicians. It also gives dominance to physicians in that they can to a large degree direct the work of people in other occupations. The medical profession uses its power in the society and in the ruling bodies of hospitals to maintain its dominance over other occupations in the day-to-day work of the hospital. To put it another way, an organizational structure—the division of work between occupations in hospitals—that works to the advantage of one occupation (physicians) and to the disadvantage of others (for instance, nurses) is maintained by the power of the advantaged occupation.

The kind of argument advanced by Freidson for hospitals can be extended to all organizations. In looking for the groups that hold power in an organization, we find that power can be derived from a variety of sources, three of which are especially important. First, the power source can be *formal* and *legitimate*, for example, executive posts or memberships on governing boards. In this sense, the president of a company and the chairman of the board hold power. Second, power can be lodged in *informal, illegitimate* sources. Some occupational groups may gain power from the central importance of their tasks in the work of the organization. Recall the case of the maintenance department, mentioned in Chapter 6, that exercised power based on its control over the speed of equipment repair. A third source of power is *linkage to influential or strategic groups* outside the organization itself. Freidson pointed out in his argument that physicians in any particular hospital enjoy dominance because their profession is powerful in the larger society, while professors may enjoy status on campus as a result of familiarity with federal fund-granting agencies.

Power explanations have an obvious appeal and have gained a wide following in recent years. Arguments emphasizing power can be readily used to deflate other kinds of explanations, especially those of the goal or need variety. When we recognize that goals or needs must ultimately be defined by social groups, we are driven to look at power differences between groups. Whose goals will be implemented? Whose conception of the needs will prevail? These questions push us inevitably toward power explanations.

Problems with power explanations Despite the recent popularity of power analyses, we must recognize once again that we are looking at a puzzle rather than a definitive answer. Like goals and needs, power in organizations is a complex phenomenon that we have only begun to untangle. In the first place, many situations involve combinations of several power sources. Second, few organizations involve a totally one-sided power structure. Rather, most appear to have pluralistic structures in which many groups exercise some degree of control. Further, a group may be quite powerful in some matters but relatively weak in others. Finally, power relations, like other organizational features, tend to change over time. We do not as yet fully understand the processes through which

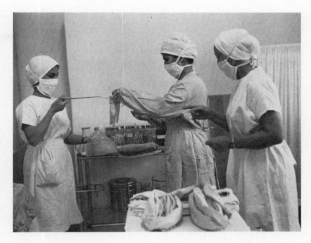

The division of labor in hospitals is a rigid and thoroughly conventionalized one. Its principal latent function is the maintenance of the physician's authority over other hospital functionaries. Here, surgical nurses serve the operating physician.

power structures develop, change, and relate to each other.

Organizational Environment

The fourth major way of explaining structure formation involves the environment of the organization, the other parts of society to which it is linked. All components of the larger society that affect the organization or that are affected by it are included in the environment.

The relationship between the internal structure of the organization and its external linkages has been an important topic of research in recent years. Two distinct approaches to the problem have emerged. First, many argue that the organization adjusts to its environment. They stress the dependence of the organization on its environment. The second, opposing, view emphasizes the organization's influence on its environment. Certain structural features of the organization are said to permit its domination of the environment. The organization may become extremely bureaucratic or it may develop a multinational structure in order to dominate the environment. Here we will concentrate on the influence of environment on internal structure.

An organization facing a changing environment

may be driven toward a flexible, adaptable structure. When conditions and job demands are constantly changing and fresh problems demand frequent decision making, it is necessary to have a structure in which people are challenged to contribute ideas and solutions, rather than simply physical skills.

Extending this type of reasoning, one can argue that organizations are dependent on their environments for resources. A manufacturer, for example, is dependent on a market for products. Instability or unpredictability in the market poses a problem. Can the organization expect a continuing supply of resources? Should it expand its production capacity to meet increased demand or close existing facilities because of declining demand? When such uncertainty exists, the organization may respond by altering its structure, perhaps by establishing a new division to study the environment—a market research division. Thus, increased specialization and a more complex division of labor result from uncertainty in the environment. Internal structures change because of changes in the external environment.

Problems with environmental explanations Like the explanations based on goals, needs, and power, environmental explanations constitute a cluster of questions in their own right. First, how much of the society is relevant to any particular organization? The boundaries are difficult to draw. Second, to complicate matters further, different environments may be relevant to different parts of the same organization. The environment crucial to a sales department may have little resemblance to that important for a manufacturing department. Finally, it is difficult to use the environment as an explanation because we do not understand how specific environmental sectors may act to elicit an organizational response. Just attributing changes to the environment is no explanation.

Social Institutional Analysis

Chapter 5 defined a social institution as a broad, persistent pattern of carrying out common activities that characterizes an entire society. It is, in other words, a way of doing things that has be-

come so conventionalized in a society that it is normative, *the* way in which those particular things are carried on. Institutions, then, are rooted in a society's norms as well as in its social organization. They operate through the patterned linkage of roles, situations, groups, and organizations described earlier.

Social institutions have fascinated sociologists for years both because their exact origins are often impossible to pin down and because, despite their bewildering variety around the world, some appear to be universal. Thus, every society ever known exhibits some form of the five institutions we will examine in Part 4 of this book: family, education, religion, economics, and polity (politics and government). Many others, such as military, charitable, and legal institutions, seem to be almost universal.

In previous discussions, and those following, we have tended to focus on problems of structure. We cannot do this with social institutions because, in effect, they have none. Being patterns, ways of doing things, social institutions themselves are without structure, although the groups and organizations that enact them (families, schools, churches, courts, and so forth) of course have social structures of their own and links to each other that may be studied. Rather, the focus of institutional analysis tends to be on their origins and functions, the purposes they perform for a society and its members.

The Origins of Social Institutions

As indicated above, in one sense no one can say exactly how a particular social institution gets started in a specific society. A way of doing something is invented or borrowed from another society, becomes so popular it is eventually perceived as conventional, and finally becomes embedded in the norms as *the* appropriate way to carry out that particular activity. In some instances, institutional forms become so firmly fixed that they are adopted as normative by law or religion as well as by popular custom. In this very loose and general sense, then, we can say we "know" about the origins of social institutions.

But in any more specific sense, we cannot say so. It might be possible, for example, to trace the custom of monogamous marriage in Western society back to the facts that Christianity has always prescribed it and that Christianity has its origins in Judaism, which also demanded **monogamy** at the time of Jesus. But the ancient Hebrews were polygynous (consider David and Solomon), and Islam, which also sprang from Judaism—several centuries later than Christianity—in some places still permits **polygyny** today. How then, did monogamy become institutionalized throughout the Western world? How did it become the form of marriage so conventional that, in many Americans' eyes, at least, any variety of **polygamy** appears not only exotic but even immoral? (The Mormons in the United States were bitterly persecuted in the nineteenth century for practicing polygyny.) So far as the sociologist knows, the only answer to such questions is: historical accident. It simply happened that way.

Using the functionalist analytic approach, however, both sociology and anthropology have developed another kind of general answer to the question of the origins of social institutions. Like the historical approach, functionalism cannot give us answers to specific questions such as that posed in the paragraph above, but it does offer a perspective on the nature of social institutions themselves that has been widely adopted as useful. This uses the concept of **functional requisites or imperatives** for societal survival.

Social Institutions as Responses to Functional Requisites

A functional requisite or imperative (the words are used interchangeably) can be defined as *a fundamental societal survival problem*; a problem that must be satisfactorily resolved by every society in some way if the society is to endure. Different analysts have offered differing lists of what these problems are, but all would include such things as food production and distribution, mating and child rearing, defense against other societies, and the maintenance of internal order. You can easily see that if *some* means of satisfactorily accomplishing each of these things were not adopted, no society would survive for long. (It can be argued, for example, that one of the reasons for the breakdown of the Roman Empire was a failure to maintain internal order in the transfer of political power from

> **monogamy:** marriage of one man to one woman.
>
> **polygyny:** marriage of one man to two or more women.
>
> **polygamy:** marriage of three or more persons of both sexes; polygyny is a form of polygamy, as is polyandry, the marriage of one woman to two or more men.
>
> **functional requisite or imperative:** one of the fundamental problems all societies must solve in order to survive. These include but are not limited to food production and distribution, mating and child rearing, defense against other societies, and the maintenance of internal order. Some imperatives stem from the psychobiological needs of human nature and some from the requirements of social organization.

one individual or faction to another, a problem that haunts many dictatorships.)

Whatever the exact number and nature of functional requisites, that some *do exist* is uncontestable. These fall into two categories. The first type provides for the biological, and perhaps psychological, maintenance of *individual* human beings—the provision of food and water, for example. The second type provides for the maintenance of *social* organization, which is also a requirement for individual survival. Defense against other societies is an example.

The functionalist understanding of the imperatives is that, because they *are* imperative, they *must* be solved. A society either finds solutions for them or faces extinction. Once some satisfactory solution to the problem, whatever it is, is discovered in a particular society, it is apt to become conventionalized. The way of doing something that "worked" historically becomes the way the problem in question "ought to" be responded to. And the behavior and forms of the social groups involved in the problem solving may become normative as well. That is, it is accepted as proper that certain social groupings should perform certain activities. And the ways in which they perform them are allotted to roles within the groups as the proper functions for the persons who fulfill the roles. The conventional expectations for family roles in American society are an example: Dad is supposed to be the "breadwinner," while Mom keeps house, cooks, takes most of the responsibility for child rearing, and so forth. It is, obviously, not the only possible division of role responsibility in the family, but it is one that works and it is the one that became conventionalized in American society. Social institutions, thus, are the prescribed patterns of social organization that a society develops for meeting the functional imperatives.

Because the imperatives are essentially the same for any society, certain institutions will, as we noted earlier, appear in *some form* in every society. But different societies have solved the same problems in differing ways, and the "political" activity of, say, Australian aborigines, may not at all appear to resemble American political practices. What "worked" in one cultural-historical situation may not have worked in another, or social conditions were very different, or other solutions offered themselves first and were adopted instead. (The structure of American government, for example, is an obvious adaptation of British practice, modified for American conditions.) Hence the immense variety of institutional forms among human societies around the world.

Clearly, it would be impossible to attempt a description of each social institution in every society in the world, or even major variations among them. We cannot even devote a separate chapter to each of the institutions of American society without doubling the length of this book. In addition to the five covered in Part 4, we would have to add science, law, medicine, charity, military institutions, and perhaps sport, communication, and so on. But to see how the functional interpretation of institutions works, let us consider briefly the military institution.

The Military Institution: A Functional Analysis

The military institution is both ancient and widespread. In the modern world, military functions are usually carried out by government agencies. That is, the military institution is subordinate to the institution of politics and government, and as we shall see in Chapter 15, the functions of the military outlined here can be considered functions of the modern polity. But the military institution was not always subordinate to government. In preindustrial

societies, such as those of feudal Europe, the military institution was autonomous. And historically it probably arose before the institution of politics and government.

The origins of the military institution are lost in prehistory. In the simplest sense, the male hunting band may have been the first "warrior" group, and among hunters and gatherers even today, it is not uncommon for all adult males to assume responsibility for what is probably the most fundamental military function: the defense of the community against external marauders. The fundamental social function served by the military institution, then, is probably *defensive*: the *maintenance of societal integrity* in the face of external threat.

Once the military is organized for this purpose, however, it is probably but an easy step to a second very common function of the military organization, the *maintenance of internal order*. Many modern armies perform police duties (or may be called upon to perform them when normal police forces are inadequate for the maintenance of order, as in riot situations). Indeed, in some developing countries, where the army may be the only national-scale, well-organized, disciplined agency there is, it frequently performs tasks normally associated with civil government: road and bridge construction, irrigation and public sanitation, and even education. The significance of bureaucratic social organization, so long associated with the military, is apparent here.

Warfare as we know it today, however, probably did not originate among people at the hunting and gathering stage, and few, if any, contemporary hunters and gatherers practice it in our sense of "war." It is likely that strictly "military" activities did not begin until human groups had passed beyond the hunting and gathering stage to the gardening stage, where they could amass some surplus food and other goods.[7] Only then would raiding for plunder become profitable. Hunters and gatherers own little property worth stealing, do not keep livestock, and have no use for human slaves. With the beginning of stable village life and the practices of cultivation and animal domestication, however, surpluses accumulated that made raiding economically profitable and slavery useful. It may well be, then, that another major function of the military institution, *societal aggrandizement at the expense of neighbors*, began in this way. To some extent, it continues to the present day. Germany and Japan in World War II are examples.

But modern wars are not really fought for the purpose of plunder or, as a rule, even to acquire territory in any literal or permanent sense. The great Prussian theorist of war Karl von Clausewitz defined war as an "extension of diplomacy," by which he meant that warfare in the modern world is a political instrument and is always aimed at political ends.[8] This means, as a rule, that the military institution is an agent of the nation-state (or some group attempting either to establish or take control of a state) and that it has as one of its functions the forwarding of the policies of the state. In any modern society, then, as we noted earlier, the military must be seen as *an instrument of the government* in power or of the groups that control the state if they are not directly represented in the government.

As well as performing certain general functions common to all societies, the military institution in any specific society, like any other social institution, will be a reflection of that society and of its history and culture. One familiar example from American experience illustrates the point nicely. In many ways, the Japanese forces in World War II were organized and equipped in ways very similar to the American, and basic battle tactics were also similar. But you have only to read first-hand accounts by American fighting men to learn how alien to our mind was the psychology of the individual Japanese soldier, sailor, or airman. Americans who faced them had great respect for Japanese fighting capacity and courage, but regarded much of their behavior as "crazy." The Japanese Kamikaze (suicide plane) forces would have found few volunteers among American airmen, and the practice of blowing oneself up with a hand grenade in preference to fighting to the death or capture seemed utterly incomprehensible to Americans.

Even in the most developed countries the military may be called on to perform civilian functions in unusual circumstances.

Kamikaze (suicide) plane in center is shot at by battleship gunners protecting a U.S. aircraft carrier, June 1945. American cultural norms and psychology make it unlikely that American troops would engage in suicide missions.

Societal Analysis

The *society* is even more encompassing and complex a form of social organization than the institution. A society includes people, a set of institutions and the patterned linkages between them, and,

Figure 7-2
Colonialism as an intersocietal system: the nineteenth-century British Empire

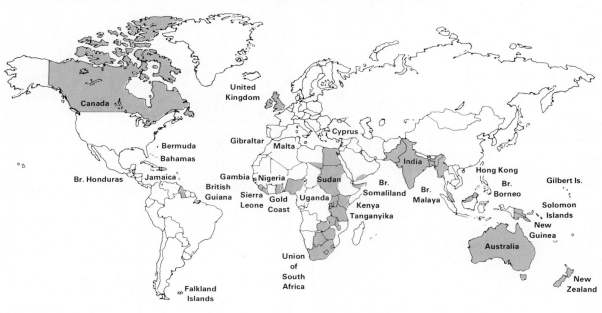

usually, a culture. Thus, it includes peoples in roles, situations, groups, and organizations, acting out norms. Societal analysis focuses on how these components are tied together. We will look first at different approaches to societal analysis and then at some of the major perspectives developed by social scientists.

Approaches to Societal Analysis

The principal approaches sociologists have used in studying society are the case study, the comparative study, and the study of intersocietal systems or complexes. Each method is suited for handling different kinds of questions.

Case study   The purpose of the intensive analysis of a single society that is termed a *case study* is to discover the linkages between all of the components of social organization within a particular society. It may focus on the prominence of organizations, the patterning of situations, the precision of role expectations, the articulation of institutions,

or many other questions. Both the integration of the parts of the society and the tensions and contradictions would be studied. Such studies are intended to produce an understanding of the specific society as a complete unit. Many come from the discipline of anthropology.

Comparative study   The second approach is the *comparative study:* an analysis of the similarities and differences between two or more societies. The usual purpose of such studies is to explain or account for the differences between societies. In some cases, the comparative study amounts to the contrast of two case studies. In other cases, however, the study compares a large number of societies.

In studies of several societies it is usually necessary to limit the number of societal components that are examined. Reinhard Bendix, for example, concentrated on the relationship between political and economic institutions in his study of four industrial societies, the Soviet Union, East Germany, Great Britain, and the United States.[9] He found that the techniques of social control within industrial organizations (an aspect of economic institutions) depended on the political system. In the Soviet Union and East Germany, there was more reliance on direct, close supervision over production processes. In the U.S. and Great Britain, by contrast, there was more reliance on training and internalization of norms. In these societies, workers are not closely supervised, but rather are expected to meet the standards for good performance that they have been taught. These differences Bendix attributed to the greater importance of centralized political control in the Communist societies.

Intersocietal systems or complexes The third approach is the study of *intersocietal systems or complexes:* the examination of a set or network of societies that are linked to each other in significant ways. Analysis focuses on the relationships between the societies, the social organization of their linkages. In this type of analysis, each society is viewed as an actor in a larger system, just as an organization can be viewed as an actor within an interorganizational network. Within such intersocietal systems, we may discover relationships of dominance and subordination, as when superpowers dominate client states. Or we may find relationships of mutual dependence, as in a network where each society produces goods needed by others in the network. Some important analytic concepts involve intersocietal systems. For example, the concept of colonialism implies a relationship of economic and political subordination between advanced and underdeveloped countries (see Figure 7-2).

In recent decades, an important development on the world scene has been the increasing influence of formal organizations that represent the interests of multisocietal systems. Examples include the European Economic Community (Common Market), the Organization of Petroleum Exporting Countries (OPEC), the North Atlantic Treaty Organization (NATO), and others. It seems likely that multinational complexes of these kinds will become more important objects of sociological attention in the future.

The study of multisocietal systems involves an important break with comparative analysis because it recognizes that each society is influenced by others in the network. The explanation of patterns on the basis of societal *processes* is supplanted by a focus on societal *influence.* Consider, for example, theories of economic development. Theories developed from a comparative standpoint treat each society as a separate unit within which certain processes take place, such as accumulation of capital and political centralization. Theories derived from analysis of multisocietal systems stress that the economic development of societies depends heavily on their linkage to larger systems, for instance, the links in a colonial system. From this point of view, it is wrong to consider each developing society simply as a separate unit within which certain casual relationships are merely repeated.

Perspectives in Societal Analysis

As in the analysis of organizations, we will focus our discussion of societal analysis on the core issue of *structure formation.* The key question here is how and why social structures differ among different societies. There is, of course, considerable variation among societies in the way social relationships are developed and maintained. For example, in some societies social life is carried out largely in relatively small groups (families, communities) and governed by long-established traditions or customs. In such societies, formal organizations are relatively rare and unimportant, at least in affecting the daily round of life. Deliberate, precise calculations of the efficiency of actions for reaching certain goals are also rare in these societies. By contrast, other societies (more familiar to us) place much importance on the precise calculation of the consequences of actions. In these societies large, complex organizations are a prominent feature.

Urban-industrial societies, like the United States and Canada, are of this type—more rationalized and formally organized. But even in these societies, there is a complicated mixture of the informal and the formal, the customary and the rational. These differences are sometimes linked to geography, with some regions more traditional and others more formal and rational, and sometimes linked to whether a location is rural or urbanized, with cities being more formal and rational than rural areas.

In their efforts to explain the structural features of urban-industrial societies, social scientists have

Gemeinschaft and Gesellschaft: Medieval food production and a modern, mass-production chicken processing factory.

formulated a number of influential perspectives. Each includes both a conception of the structural features of importance and an explanatory argument. Each perspective should be seen not as a finished theory, but as a set of interrelated questions that guide investigators. In some respects, the several perspectives have become competitive, partially contradictory to one another, and each has attracted proponents and critics. In other respects, they overlap in significant ways. In the following pages, we will examine four perspectives that have been important in recent sociology: the great dichotomy perspective, intrasocietal differentiation, institutional dominance, and rationalization.

The great dichotomy   The first of these perspectives is what some sociological thinkers have called *great dichotomy* hypotheses. There are a number of these, all based on the dichotomy, or split, between two polar opposites. All share in common the thesis that the social history of most of the societies of the world can be perceived as changing along a continuum from simple to complex, rural to urban, homogeneous to heterogeneous, undifferentiated to specialized. Examination of societies at either end of such a continuum, then, can show us the social structural possibilities and serve as a useful theoretical model for social change.

The intellectual "father" of the great dichotomy theorists was the German thinker Ferdinand Tönnies. He named the two opposite types of social structure the **Gemeinschaft** and the **Gesellschaft**, usually translated into English simply as "community" and "society."[10] The *Gemeinschaft* is based on what Tönnies called the "natural will" of human beings, and people relate to one another as total personalities within a communal context. Each person is bound strongly to the community and does not pursue private interest at its expense.

Social life is governed by tradition and custom, which go unchallenged. People's positions, based on family and community ties, are stable and secure, although not equal. The preliterate tribe and the medieval European agricultural village would be classic examples of the *Gemeinschaft*.

The *Gemeinschaft*, Tönnies says, is shattered by the emerging urban-industrial-capitalist order. At the core of this new social structure is the "rational will" of human beings. The rational will is calculative and examines all practices with a view toward efficiency in pursuing goals. The unreflective life of the *Gemeinschaft*, based on custom and community, comes under rational scrutiny. Individuals begin to pursue private interests at the expense of others and of the community's general interest; relations among people are increasingly based on calculation of private advantage. Social relations narrow in scope and become more specific and purposeful. These tendencies give rise eventually to a new form of society, the *Gesellschaft*, a type approximating urban-industrial society.

Although the work of Tönnies himself is little used today, the perception of societies moving along a continuum of social change, with similar structural beginnings and terminal points, has informed a large number of theoretical and empirical studies of communities, social change, and social organization. We will meet it again in later chapters.

Intrasocietal differentiation Another perspective on society, reminiscent of Tönnies's ideas, involves the degree of differentiation of institutional structures. *Intrasocietal differentiation* means the development in a society of distinct sets of activities. Thus, differentiation means *specialization* in the sense that different types of activities come increasingly to be carried out in structurally separate and distinctive settings.

For example, as differentiation progresses in a society, economic activity may be sheared off from family relations and controls. The family may cease to be a significant social unit for the production of goods and services. And at the same time, new organizational forms governing such production may emerge. At this point, specialization has occurred; the family has lost control over certain activities that have become centered in a new

> **Gemeinschaft** and **Gesellschaft**: the terms used by Tönnies to describe two polar-opposite types of social organization, or societies characterized by such organization. The *Gemeinschaft*, which could be translated as "community," "rural," "folk," or "simple," is tradition-based; and the individual is bound to the group by strong, stable ties of family and community. Social relations are broad and encompassing. The *Gemeinschaft* parallels Durkheim's social organization based on mechanical solidarity. The *Gesellschaft*, which could be translated as "urban-industrial society," is based on rationality; and the individual is bound to others mainly by calculations of personal advantage. Social relations are narrow and limited. The *Gesellschaft* parallels Durkheim's social organization based on organic solidarity.
>
> **intrasocietal differentiation**: increasing specialization or separation of functions and activities once unified within a society. In a simple society, for example, the family may be the only important social group and include within its sphere religious, economic, legal, political, medical, and educational activities. As differentiation progresses, these functions are increasingly split off and become performed by other, specialized, groups and organizations.

institutional location, the economy. Over time, gradual change may move more and more activities from the control of the family and community into more specialized units, such as manufacturing concerns, political parties, and religious organizations. In this regard, consider the difference between the modern American family and the frontier family of the nineteenth century, in which all members contributed something to the economy— Father farmed or raised livestock; Mother gardened and made clothes, soap, candles; the children all helped by doing chores; and members of the community helped each other harvest crops, build barns, and make quilts.

Many sociologists see increasing specialization as the main thrust of societal modernization.[11] As they see it, the major features distinguishing a modern from a traditional society (a *Gesellschaft* from a *Gemeinschaft*) is the modern society's more precisely specialized set of institutions—political, economic, military, religious, educational, familial, and so on. In the traditional society, these functions are not so clearly distinguished. Social life is more thoroughly integrated within family and communi-

Differentiation and specialization: A century ago most artifacts for daily use were produced in the home, as depicted in this woodcut of a quilting party. Today almost everything we use is produced and distributed by highly specialized suppliers, as are these imported blouses in a department store.

ty. Religious, economic, and political activities are all carried out within the same social settings and with a minimum of specialization of roles. And in some instances, it may be difficult to see distinctions at all. A single act or set of acts may have religious, political, economic, and familial functions. Among the Yir Yorount, an aboriginal Australian tribe, for example, virtually the entire social organization of the society centered on the stone ax, which could be made and owned only by males, although much of its actual *use* was performed by women and children. Highly tradition-oriented, the Yir Yorount had a religious rationalization for almost every daily act. Thus, in their lives, even the simple act of lending or borrowing an ax incorporated economic, familial, and religious functions.[12]

Through the differentiation process, the many spheres of social life gradually gain some measure of autonomy. Sets of rules or norms governing economic activity, for instance, grow up in the context of religious, communal, and familial expectations but gradually become separate and independent. This involves the removal of various traditional restraints on economic action, a shearing away of restrictive norms that have limited the production and distribution of goods and services. Increasingly, the economy operates according to its own rules.

This transition can be seen in the roles, situations, and organizations through which economic activity is conducted. Economic roles become separated from familial and communal roles. The **entrepreneur**, the worker, the banker, and others govern their activity by norms specific to their

economic functions. Similarly, as economic actors, people regularly encounter situations of a purely economic character, where each is expected to calculate a rational course of action without regard for the expectations to which he responds in other settings, such as the church or family. In addition, economic organizations—manufacturing concerns, marketing companies, banks, and so on—increasingly develop according to purely economic criteria, calculations of advantage and disadvantage in the marketplace. Thus, a set of distinctively economic actions are gradually wrenched free of the hold of traditional and customary restraints. Through this process, an autonomous economic institution emerges.

A similar process occurs with respect to other institutional arrangements. Political organizations, educational systems, legal institutions, science, and technology are gradually freed of traditional and customary restraints. Each sphere develops somewhat separate norms and expectations. Science, for example, progresses according to principles of discovery and verification and in relation to established bodies of knowledge distinctive to the scientific sphere. To contribute to the development of science, scientists subordinate their other social roles to the expectations governing scientific research. Religious, familial, even nationalistic restraints are irrelevant to their performance. As the differentiation process intensifies, science is split into numerous, distinct disciplines—biology, chemistry, physics—each with somewhat autonomous principles of research and bodies of knowledge.

The transition to a highly differentiated structure poses significant problems for a society. Indeed, the process may entail a substantial degree of disruption and disorder. The bases of social action adequate at one point in time are ill-suited to the emerging order. Traditional and customary restraints are often relaxed unevenly, affecting some institutional spheres but not others. Some population segments are left behind as a society advances, while others are at the forefront of the process. Thus, the possibility of the breakdown of social order haunts the differentiating society.

The Yir Yorount, for example, perished entirely as a society, in part because well-intentioned missionaries gave steel axes to women and children. Since a major foundation of their social organization had been the *ownership* of the ax by males and its *lending* to females and children, actual possession of axes of their own by women and children disrupted the division of labor, the age-grade structure, gender differentiation, and even the tribe's theology. Similarly, in the contemporary United States, the independence of science mentioned above has created distinct tensions in some religious belief structures, and certain of the more fundamentalistic sects are fighting back with propaganda, political action, and, in some cases, litigation. Although probably no American scientist today would be tried by a theological court for holding that the earth revolved around the sun, as Galileo was, there would certainly be some danger for evolutionists if church courts existed in modern society.

Emile Durkheim Understanding the differentiation process has been a major preoccupation of sociologists. Indeed, many classic theoretical positions were formulated in response to this problem. As we saw in Chapter 1, for example, Emile Durkheim analyzed the problem in terms of a transition from mechanical solidarity to organic solidarity.[13] In a society characterized by mechanical solidarity,

---

entrepreneur: one who undertakes to carry out an enterprise, an employer of labor; in the more popular sense, a risk-taking businessman. The self-made "captain of industry" of the last century is an excellent example.

Schism in the Synod

The question of whether or not Jonah actually spent three days in the belly of a whale has long been a point of angry controversy for the 2.8 million members of the Lutheran Church-Missouri Synod. To Synod conservatives, the Biblical story of Jonah—like the accounts of Adam and Eve in Eden, Moses' parting of the Red Sea and Daniel in the lion's den—is literally true; moderates interpret them symbolically.

Within the last two years, this fundamental disagreement has led to the moderates' establishing a separate organization called Evangelical Lutherans in Mission (ELIM) and a separate Concordia Seminary-in-Exile (Seminex). Last month, at the Synod's biennial convention in Anaheim, Calif., the conservatives, led by Synod president Rev. Jacob A.O. Preus, closed ranks to virtually expel the moderate opposition. The final break came two weeks ago at an ELIM national assembly in Chicago when the moderates voted unanimously to form a separate synod, formally splitting with the Missouri Synod, the second largest—and most conservative—Lutheran group in the United States. "Anaheim said conclusively that whatever we might have chosen, the choice is not ours," said the moderates' Rev. C. Thomas Spitz. "We are out!"

The Chicago dissidents—who have taken "Christ Alive, Church Alive" as their slogan—plan to organize a transitional synod of "clusters" of congregations, groups and individuals. These, in turn, may eventually join up with the other two major Lutheran groups, the Lutheran Church in America and the American Lutheran Church. Moderate dissenters who elect to stay within the Missouri Synod will continue to get ELIM support, and even the new, liberal Lutheran Church in Mission, incorporated last February, is recognized by ELIM leaders as a possible haven for moderates. . . .

The increasing differentiation and separation of institutional spheres in modern society is not without cost. The independence of science has raised grave questions for literal religious interpretations and has sometimes created problems within churches.

the division of labor (specialization of tasks) is minimal. The society is held together by the homogeneity of tasks and by a sense of collective identity rooted in common experience and shared views. This mechanical solidarity breaks down as people of diverse origins are brought together in urban areas and forced to compete with one another for a livelihood.

One hope for reestablishing solidarity, Durkheim argued, is through the development of a precisely calibrated division of labor in which distinct tasks mesh nicely. Such a society would be characterized by a high degree of specialization. Yet people would gain a sense of solidarity—organic solidarity—based on their contributions to common tasks.

Durkheim was not sure how to achieve organic solidarity. At times, he seemed to assume that it would be a natural, inevitable outgrowth of the differentiation process. At other times, however, he clearly regarded it as something that would have to be engineered by enlightened leaders and managers. Finally, he expressed hope that occupational associations organized along industrial lines—incorporating workers in a given industry regardless of their rank—might give people a sense of involvement in and regulation by a social group that would, in turn, be linked to the other groups composing the society. Durkheim seems never to have been satisfied with his "solutions" to these problems and always to have feared that social order would disintegrate, leaving individuals without social ties and normative regulation.

Structural functionalists   Durkheim's interest in institutional differentiation has been continued by contemporary structural functionalists. A prominent member of this group, Talcott Parsons, has argued that the differentiation of institutions is the key process in the modernization of societies.[14] He identifies certain major steps in that process which are essential to moving a society forward. These steps, which Parsons calls evolutionary universals, are arranged in sequential order so that each one builds on prior steps. Every society, he argues, must take these steps or fail to develop into a modern nation-state. In general terms, the evolutionary universals describe a society that is breaking out of communal restraints and segmentation and developing broadly based but specialized insti-

tutions at the national level. Two of the evolutionary universals are: the development of an administrative apparatus capable of drawing the society together around a national center; and social stratification, the development of a ranking system based largely on occupational achievement and free of ties to family, community, and bureaucracy (stratification is discussed in detail in Chapter 8).

One of the interesting features of Parsons's work is his effort to analyze the modern, differentiated society as a value-integrated system. Many writers have despaired of the breakdown of normative order and the erosion of common values accompanying modernization. In part, as we have seen, this was Durkheim's problem. Yet Parsons argues that the modernized, differentiated society *is* an expression of common values. In his view, it is a rational society in which commitments to the values of universalism and achievement prevail. These values commit the society to rational action, that is, to the application of general standards to all, regardless of race, family, or community of origin (universalism), and to the evaluation of people on the basis of performance (achievement). They are essential, he argues, for subduing and exploiting the environment—developing natural resources, manufacturing products, and so on.

Thus, according to Parsons, societies with such values are more successful than others in accomplishing economic development. The gradual but unrelenting application of these values brings about a rational organization of the whole society. Traditional restraints fall away. Specialized, rationally organized institutions develop. Segmentation of the population based on region, race, and social class is eroded. The whole population is drawn into full and free participation in the political process. Thus, Parsons finds normative-value integration in the modern industrial society. He views the democratic-capitalist societies of North America and Western Europe as the most modernized societies in the world.

"Critical" sociologists   Many other students of societal differentiation are less optimistic than Parsons and the structural functionalists. "Critical" analysts, such as Herbert Marcuse and Jurgen Habermas, also see differentiation and the accom-

panying rationalization of social life as crucial features of modern societies.[15] Unlike Parsons, however, they see a narrowing of perspectives, a closing in of viewpoints around a narrow, technical rationalism.

Modern institutions are excessively specialized in their functions. Although each deals with a set of specialized functions, all do so in a technically rational, not a broadly humane way. All institutions are incomplete and one-sided in the sense that they stress the technical and efficient manipulation of means. They have lost the capacity for raising questions about ends and for posing alternatives to the present order. People, likewise, become as narrow and one-dimensional as their institutions. They occupy technical positions and acquire high levels of specialized knowledge. But in the process they lose the capacity for criticism, for considering alternatives. Fixed in this mode, then, the advanced industrial societies go forward manipulating people and exploiting nature. They lack the capacity to analyze and alter their course.

Summary The differentiation of institutions involves the division of activities into more and more specialized units. This is accompanied by the development of new control centers coordinating and articulating the diversified segments of the society. The whole process is beset with tensions and conflicts and with periods of severe discontinuity. The total breakdown of order is threatened at times. Emerging at the end of the process is a modernized, differentiated nation-state with specialized institutions incorporating the whole population. Some degree of centralized control in the form of a state apparatus and bureaucracy appears to be a necessary outcome. Observers differ substantially in their assessment of the implications of the differentiation process.

Institutional dominance A third perspective on society that has preoccupied analysts concerns the control exercised by institutional spheres within a given society. Broadly stated, the problem is to discover and to explain the dominance of some institutions over others. Dominance in this case refers to determination, the capacity of one institution to determine the form of others. Much of the debate on the issue of **institutional dominance** has

> **institutional dominance:** the idea that a single social institution, such as economics or religion, dominates the social organization of a given society in the sense that all other institutions are colored or shaped by it.

developed in response to the work of Karl Marx and to later formulations of the Marxist position.

Karl Marx As we saw in Chapter 1, the relationship between the economic institution and other institutional spheres was the focal concern in Marx's work. In the economic sphere Marx placed *productive forces*—tools, machinery, raw materials, technical know-how—and *economic relations*—the established system of ownership and control over the productive forces and the norms governing the production and exchange of goods. There is tension between these two elements. Certain kinds of economic relations permit the advance of productive forces, while other patterns obstruct such advance.

For example, the capitalist system of economic relations is said to be far more productive than feudalism. Under capitalism, resources can be freed from various communal and traditional restraints and utilized more freely. Laborers can be hired and fired according to the dictates of the market without regard to social or moral obligations toward them. Restrictions on the use of money, trade, and so on fall away in the face of the emerging capitalist order.

Under these circumstances, the productive forces—factories, business organizations, technology—undergo an extraordinary development. Vast amounts of money are accumulated and invested in new tools, machinery, techniques, and resources. The result is a great outpouring of goods, converting the society into a mass market whose purchases continue to fuel the expansion of the productive forces. These developments are possible because of the shifting economic relations.

Here we encounter the problem of institutional dominance. According to this perspective, developments in the material substructure of the society—economic relations and productive

How Much Does a Baby Cost?
Claire Williams

In 1969 when we asked the question "How Much Does It Cost to Have a Baby?" we concluded that despite growing inflation, with a little common sense and a lot of will power a young couple could have a baby and their bank balance too. It would be difficult to make as confident a claim in 1976. We don't have to tell you that inflation is still with us, but a true index of how much it is, is the serious dent it has made in the pocketbook marked "Family Planning." Seven years ago our estimate of expenses to bear a baby and to feed, clothe and shelter him or her through the first year of life was $1,651. That figure has increased by over 60 per cent today—so when baby is about to make three, balancing your budget may require a new kind of family arithmetic.
The Editors

. . . To help you know what you can expect, we have compiled an estimate of what a couple having a moderate income will spend on a baby from conception to first birthday. These figures were arrived at by researching Government and industry statistics, going on make-believe shopping sprees through baby boutiques, poring through mail-order catalogues and finally talking with new mothers about what they actually spent.

Baby's First Year

Mother's Medical Expenses $965
(Includes obstetrician's fee of $350 and hospital bill of $615 for a four-day stay in a semiprivate room, as well as fees for the delivery room, anesthetist, nursery, routine nursing and medication, and so on.)
Baby's Doctor. $165
(Includes newborn care in the hospital [$35], nine routine office visits and one emergency visit at $10 each, plus $30 for inoculations.)
Mother's Maternity
   Wardrobe $255
Diapers. $200
(A year's supply of disposables.)
Baby's Clothing $225
Baby's Food $370
(For bottle-fed infants.)

Nursery Furniture and
   Equipment. $340
Baby-Care Needs $65
(Includes bottles, sterilizer, toiletries and health needs.)
Baby Sitters $60
Baby Pictures. $60
   Total. $2,705

Excerpted from Redbook Magazine, April 1976, p. 96. Reprinted by permission of Redbook Publishing Company. Photo by Ken Heyman.

Rationality and institutional dominance. This cost-accounting approach to having a baby would have been regarded as absurd in medieval times and as peculiar, at the very least, in the U.S. only a century or so ago. Feature stories of this kind, however, are a familiar phenomenon on the contemporary landscape.

forces—"determine" developments in the superstructure—polity, religion, education, science, the arts, and so on. However, it should be stressed that this is by no means a one-way process. Rather, the relation is one of interaction. Developments of the substructure "kick off" certain changes in polity, in consciousness, in artistic expression. Ultimately, these changes create a self-conscious revolutionary class that takes control of the political apparatus and uses the state as a tool for modifying the economic arrangements. Thus, crucial changes in the economic sector depend finally on transformations of consciousness, of cultural expression, of politics. Tensions and contradictions in the substructure initiate and provide a continuing impetus for change at other levels. In this sense, Marx's theory is materialist, or economic, in its location of the sources of change. But the overall argument stresses interaction rather than a simple cause-and-effect relationship.

The Marxian analysis of institutional dominance has been highly influential. It has provided a benchmark formulation with which later analysts have been obliged to grapple. Both Marxists and anti-Marxists have found in the formulation a complex of interrelated problems.

Max Weber As you will recall from Chapter 1, Max Weber was preoccupied with Marx's arguments, but believed them faulty. Rather than accepting Marx's ideas about the dominance of the economic institution, Weber tried to test them by conducting a series of comparative-historical studies of different societies. The work for which he is best known is *The Protestant Ethic and the Spirit of Capitalism*, an attempt to explain the rise of capitalism in Western Europe.[16]

In this work Weber argues that the *material* preconditions for capitalism were present in many parts of the world at the end of the European feudal period. Only in Europe, however, were those conditions combined with a set of beliefs, an *ideology*, in a way that brought about a sustained drive toward capitalistic organization. That ideology, Weber says, was provided by the ethical principles of Protestantism, in particular, Calvinism. The ethics of hard work, thrift, and self-denial meshed nicely with the requirements of early capitalism for capital accumulation, rational calculation of investment

Protestant ideology and capitalism. Weber argued that certain values especially prominent in Protestant morality, such as hard work and thrift, linked easily with the practical requirements of early capitalism. To some extent they still do. The accent on thrift in this savings and loan company's advertisement is aimed at the customer, but borrowing money to buy a house also provides profit for the company.

and operation, and so forth. Thus, Marxian economic determinism was not an adequate explanation for the development of Western social structures, and the dominating institution, if there was one, was religion.

Followers of Weber and Marx Following Weber, Talcott Parsons, mentioned earlier, S. M. Lipset, and others have argued that a society is guided in its development by certain widely shared values.[17] These constitute standards for the evaluation of activities, people, and objects and have the effect of bringing specific kinds of activities to the fore. Thus if, in a given society, military values appear to determine other features of institutional life, it is because the values of that society give priority to military functions. Nazi Germany would be a good example.

Summary   The dominant institution perspective has provided an important theme for societal analysts. Marx "invented" the idea, and many later analysts have attempted either to refute or to modify his theories. This perspective has proved to be a useful device with which to think about societies, as is indicated by the fact that the major works of Weber, and some modern commentators such as Parsons, have been in this tradition.

Rationalization   The *rationalization* process was a major concern of Max Weber, as we saw in Chapter 1, and his work on rationalization has provided the basis for much modern societal analysis.

Max Weber   In modern societies, Weber argued, traditional and emotional bases of action decline and are replaced increasingly by rational-calculative action. Calculations of monetary costs and returns are at the core of this process. Once the process is under way, however, there is a tendency to extend the principle of rational calculation to wider and wider spheres of social life. Through this process of rational calculation, planning, scientific analysis, and the like penetrate all spheres of society.

The organizational expression of rationalization is bureaucracy. Weber anticipated the growth of bureaucratic organizations both in size and in importance. As we saw in the discussion of organizations in Chapter 6, bureaucracies develop centralized control and planning based on expert knowledge. Subordinate units are rigidly controlled by elaborate rules. Specialized divisions are formed to provide for the application of expert knowledge. Tasks of lower participants are reduced to simple, repetitive routines to assure accurate, dependable performance.

Weber argued that rationalization in this sense arose in the economic sector first and then spread to other societal spheres. Criticizing Marxism, he argued that socialism would not liberate society from these rationalizing tendencies of capitalism. Rather, socialism would provide for the extension of rationalization to other spheres with accompanying bureaucratization. Thus rationalization, once unleashed, would tend to become all-pervasive.

Modern theorists   In recent years Weber's argument has gained new credibility as pervasive rationalization and bureaucratization have become obvious and undeniable features of social life. A number of aspects of the present situation in the industrial societies have stimulated new interest in the issues Weber raised. These include the growth in size, complexity, and influence of bureaucracies; the development of new, more sophisticated methods of production based on scientific technologies; the increased importance of science, scientists, and scientific establishments in the determination of decisions in both the private and the public sectors; the enhanced capacity of large, rational organizations to control the public through sophisticated marketing and advertising; and the increasing intervention in the market by large-scale government bureaucracies to bring the whole economy under rational control.[18]

Developments of these kinds have a bearing on all of the levels of analysis discussed in Chapters 6 and 7. Occupational roles tend to become more highly specialized, with divisions based on degrees and types of expertise. Calculativeness pervades role relationships, even in the family. Individuals find their lives to be more regulated, less autonomous. A general smoothing out of social differences takes place. People increasingly encounter situations that are predetermined, centrally regulated, or manipulated by bureaucratic organizations. In effect, organizations become the dominating features of social life. Roles are brought in line with organizational requirements. Situations are regulated by organizational manipulation. Institutional constraints based on tradition and history are overridden by the drive toward organizational rationality.

Assessments of this modern situation vary from buoyant optimism through a guarded hopefulness to grim pessimism. Among the more optimistic is Etzioni's book *The Active Society* (1968).[19] Etzioni argues that the current situation permits the development of a genuinely rational society, in conscious control of its own destiny. He contends that the diverse components of the society may be integrated rationally, on the basis of scientific study and expertise. Traditional and ideological limits to rational reorganization can be broken through. Yet this need not involve subordination or manipulation of the component parts of the society. Each component, indeed each individual, may have a significant input in determining the society's direction. Thus, Etzioni views rational control and direction as compatible with wider and more significant participation.

A less optimistic stance is taken in recent work by Daniel Bell. In *The Coming of Post-Industrial Society* (1973), Bell contends that contradictions will appear in industrial societies as the increasingly bureaucratic-technocratic social structure develops.[20] For one thing, this structure will come into conflict with the strain toward wider participation in the political system. The tendency toward rational planning and control by scientific-technical experts located in large bureaucracies runs counter to the principle of democratic participation in significant decisions. Bell does not offer a prediction regarding the resolution of these tensions. Rather, he envisions a series of conflicts of uncertain outcome.

The "critical" sociologists have produced more pessimistic assessments. As noted, Marcuse has characterized the advanced industrial societies as one-dimensional. By this he means that a narrow technical rationalism has spread throughout the society. People have been drawn into the support of the existing system by narrow calculations of their immediate economic interests. As a result, the massive machinery of production, which dominates people and nations and which exploits nature, goes unchallenged. People have lost the ability to envision alternative forms of society and to criticize the present form.

As we saw earlier, this type of analysis has been extended by Habermas. In particular, Habermas contends that the rationalizations of science and technology have become legitimating ideologies of the advanced industrial societies. Decisions are made and justified on the basis of scientific study or technological efficiency. The populace has been led to accept scientific-technical analyses as bases of action. Thus, reliance on these analyses is a way of maintaining support for the present order. Consequently, the underlying pattern of class dominance and the fundamental irrationality of advanced industrial society escape attention and criticism. The domination of people, the exploitation of nature, and the manufacture of weapons of total destruction, then, will continue unchecked and largely unchallenged. Thus, in Habermas's view, narrow, technical rationalization, exemplified by science and technology, prevents the emergence of a genuinely rational society.

Summary   The hypothesis that rationality is a dimension on which social structure and change may be properly understood was first introduced into sociology, like so much else, by Weber. His work on bureaucracy used it as the central principle. Today Weber appears to have been amazingly foresighted, as we see what Tönnies might have called "rational will" pervading almost every aspect of modern societies. This development has been greeted with both acclaim and alarm by various sociological writers, but in either case, the attention paid to the matter shows that it is a phenomenon of central importance in understanding the nature of society in the modern world.

Summary

This chapter has explored some of what sociologists know about large-scale social organizational phenomena: *organizations, social institutions*, and *society* itself. Each has been extensively studied in its own right. A variety of analytic approaches have been developed for each area, no one of which, by itself, may be adequate for complete understanding. You should, therefore, regard what has been presented here as a set of alternative perspectives on the subject matter of social organization. In the cases of organizations and society, analysts have tended to focus on problems of structure and structure formation as theoretically central. In the case of social institutions, the focus has tended to be on their origins and functions.

In its concentration on structure and structure formation, organizational analysis has often focused on three structural elements: *specialization*, the degree to which tasks and roles are differentiated; *centralization,* the degree to which decision making is concentrated in a limited number of roles; and *formalization,* the degree to which roles and interactions are specified. These three structural elements are often prominent in analytic work utilizing *organizational types* in which different varieties of organization, such as the *bureaucratic* and the *professional,* may be contrasted along these dimensions. The characteristics of a bureaucracy, for example, are a specialized division of labor, a chain of command or hierarchy of control, the attachment of authority to positions rather than people, and a marked development of rules for specifying behavior. A professional association, in contrast, is chiefly marked by lack of central authority and lack of formalization.

The question of why particular organizational structures originate has been answered in a variety of ways, probably none of which is alone adequate to serve as an explanation. Principal among these answers have been explanations related to *organizational goals* (that what an organization is created to do determines its structure). Studies in this framework have categorized organizations according to their *goal beneficiaries* and according to the *types of goal attainment* or membership affiliation (*coercive, utilitarian,* or *normative*). They have also pointed up the distinction between *official* and *operative* goals, which is important because the latter sometimes have a tendency to undermine the former. This sometimes results in *goal displacement,* as exemplified by the effects of cooptation in the TVA.

An alternative explanation for organizational structure involves *organizational needs.* This argument sees a particular structural form as an adaptation to needs or requirements for survival.

The argument that *power* determines organizational structure has also been advanced, and it has much to recommend it because it seems to subsume the goal and need explanations—*someone* must determine what an organization's goals and needs are, and there is frequently competition to do so. Thus, the groups with the power to control decision making may determine the organization structure.

Finally, *environment* has been appealed to for the explanation of structure, the idea here being that organizations are to some degree linked to external environments, both affecting and being affected by them, and that organizational structure will reflect these relationships. An organization operating in an extremely uncertain environment (say, with regard to securing necessary resources) may have to develop a flexible, decentralized structure. One that dominates its environment may choose a rigid hierarchy as more appropriate.

The analysis of *social institutions* has tended to center on their origins and functions because, as *patterns* for behavior and social organization, they have no structure as such. In a historical sense, it is often impossible to determine the origins of specific social institutions, and they must frequently be viewed simply as historical accidents. The functionalist perspective suggests a kind of general answer to the question of origins, however, by hypothesizing that social institutions form in response to the demands of *functional imperatives* or *requisites:* the fundamental problems that a society must solve if it is to endure. These are of two kinds: those relating to the satisfaction of basic human biological and psychological needs and those required by the necessity for social organization itself.

Although different institutional theorists have somewhat differing views on exactly what the imperatives are, probably all would agree that among them are food production and distribution, mating and child rearing, defense against other societies, and the maintenance of internal order. Because such problems are universal—every society must confront them—certain institutions such as the family are also universal, although the forms that even these universal institutions may take vary widely (because the same general problem may be approached in an almost infinite number of ways).

A brief description of a functional analysis of the military institution was given to illustrate this perspective and the kinds of things that can be done with it. The military institution serves at least four social functions: (1) the defense of society in the face of external threat, (2) the maintenance of internal order, (3) societal aggrandizement at the expense of other societies, and (4) the furtherance of the policies of the nation-state. Moreover, the development of the military in any particular society is influenced by the history and culture of that society.

Societal analysis tends to take the form of *case studies, comparative studies,* or the study of *intersocietal systems.* Regardless of which approach is utilized, analysts of society typically center their attention on the problem of societal structure and how it is formed.

This problem has been so central to societal analysis for so long, in fact, that four great traditions have developed in the form of perspectives on it, ways of approaching and analyzing the subject matter. These are the traditions or perspectives we called: (1) the *great dichotomy hypothesis,* associated in sociology with the name of Ferdinand Tönnies; (2) the problem of *intersocietal differentiation,* which we associated with Durkheim, the functionalists, and certain "critical" sociologists, but which in some ways relates to Tönnies's interests as well; (3) the perspective of *institutional dominance,* associated primarily with Marx's ideas and with Weber's work in religion; and (4) the *rationalization hypothesis,* associated with Weber's work on bureaucracy and certain modern proponents and critics.

Review Questions

1. Describe the form of social organization known as bureaucracy, focusing on the advantages and problems inherent in this particular type of organization.

2. Contrast the different goals held by various organizations discussed in this chapter: mutual-benefit, business, service, and commonwealth.

3. Compare Ferdinand Tönnies's Gemeinschaft and Gesellschaft societies. How do these ideal types relate to Emile Durkheim's mechanical and organic solidarity? What is the nature of social interaction in each?

4. Max Weber contended that certain values found in Protestantism were supportive of modern capitalism. Which values were these? How did Weber believe them to be related to capitalism?

5. Contrast the three modes of studying societies discussed in this chapter: the case study, the comparative study, and the intersocietal systems or complexes approach. What is the focus of each method?

Suggestions for Research

1. Many stereotypes, often unfavorable, have been perpetuated about bureaucracy. Investigate these stereotypes, with an open mind to both the strong and the weak points in a bureaucracy. Two works which may be of help to you are *Bureaucracy in Modern Society,* by Peter Blau and Marshall Meyer, and *Formal Organizations,* by Blau and W. Richard Scott. You may also want to refer to some of Max Weber's works.

2. The label *bureaucracy* has typically been given to big business and government. In many senses, it is similarly applicable to the university. Study the university as a bureaucracy. You may want to make some comparisons between the larger, more bureaucratic schools and smaller ones. How are students and faculty alike affected by a bureaucratic structure? Do the advantages such as efficiency outweigh the disadvantages? You might want to talk with personnel in the counseling divisions about the growth of bureaucratic practices in the university.

3. Compare the two types of societies known as *Gemeinschaft* and *Gesellschaft.* Although these specific terms arise out of the theories of Ferdinand Tönnies, other sociologists and anthropologists have made similar dichotomies, such as Robert Redfield with his folk and urban societies. Although the two extremes are simply ideal types, their characteristics may be studied in terms of a continuum.

4. Study interinstitutional activity by selecting any two of the major social institutions to examine. Note how one affects and is affected by the other. Does one appear to dominate the other? If so, why? You might want to explore the relationship between these two institutions in previous times in addition to the present.

5. Make a comparison of the three approaches to societal analysis described in this chapter: the case study, the comparative study, and the intersocietal systems or complexes approach. Give examples of each in sociological literature. Which sociologists have used which approach? Why? How are they similar? different? You may want to begin your study by referring to books on methodology in sociology.

PART THREE
ELEMENTS OF SOCIAL STRUCTURE

The four chapters that follow explore some aspects of social *structure*. Social structure is what results when some sets of broad social organizational relationships become so "frozen" by custom that they form a social reality of "the way things are" in a society. (The "freezing" process is called *institutionalization*.) In these chapters we will concentrate on American society, but we will occasionally contrast American social structure with others elsewhere.

Chapter 8 is about social differentiation and mobility. *Differentiation* means the process through which people invent or recognize socially significant differences between them and then fix those differences into social *categories*. Age and sex differences, for example, are perceived as significant in every culture in the world. Differentiation is socially important because we attribute different behavior characteristics categorically to people recognized as different; children, for instance, are perceived as being less socially competent than adults. *Social mobility* means movement through social space. It is virtually absent in some societies, but is pronounced in the United States.

Chapter 9 is about minority groups and relations in heterogeneous societies, again a major feature of the American social scene. The role of minorities in a society and the effects of minority status on a group's members have great significance for the people involved and the society that enfolds them.

Chapter 10 describes one of the dominating features of the modern world, the city, and the processes and life-styles that go with it, which we call urbanism. Chapter 11 sketches the biosocial phenomena that represent the stage on which all human social life is played out: population and its effects.

CHAPTER 8
SOCIAL DIFFERENTIATION AND MOBILITY

We hold these truths to be self-evident, that all men are created equal, that they are endowed by their Creator with certain unalienable Rights, that among these are Life, Liberty and the pursuit of Happiness . . .

The Declaration of Independence of the United States of America, July 4, 1776.

These ringing words, undoubtedly familiar to all of you, are among the most famous in the American language, and may be almost as well-known to English speakers outside the United States as to Americans. But, apart from their political context in the American colonies' break from British rule, what do they *mean*?

It does not take a sociologist to inform us that, in fact, all people are *not* created equal and that while we may all enjoy God-given *rights* to life, liberty, and the pursuit of happiness, not all of us attain those goals in equal degrees. Even now, 200 years after those words were written to announce the formation of a new nation, the citizens of that nation are markedly distinguished from one another in a variety of ways, and inequality among them is pronounced in many areas of life.

Some inequalities among human beings, of course, are the result of inherited physical and mental characteristics. Some people are bright and some are mentally dull; some are tall and some are short; some are physically stronger than others, and so forth. But it is doubtful that such biological differences have much to do with the *social* differences and opportunities visible among the population of any modern industrial state.

It is possible that a few occupations, such as commercial airline pilot, Supreme Court justice, or surgeon, may require special skills, intelligence, or aptitudes, and thus be able to command greater social reward. And there may be some activities, perhaps pro football or hockey, that would be difficult or impossible for the mentally dull or physically weak. But on the whole, most people are biologically able to accomplish most normal activities, and differences in reward for some activities, or differences in opportunity for some individuals, cannot be shown to be closely related to biological capabilities.

Reward and opportunity are not distributed equally among the population. The poor outnumber the rich by large proportions. Access to high-prestige occupations, education, health care, and many other things are not equally available to all. Even birth and death rates and the frequency of certain diseases vary widely among subgroups and, in some cases, between the sexes.

What all of this reflects—the Declaration of Independence notwithstanding—is **social differentia-**

tion: the fact that all societies everywhere (with the possible exception of a few very small preliterate groups) make distinctions among their members that are socially rather than biologically based. All societies differentiate among their members on the basis of criteria that are *assigned* social significance. And on the basis of such social distinctions, rewards and opportunities—**life chances**—are differentially distributed. (A life chance is the probability of any given social outcome: dying before you are thirty, receiving a college degree, possessing an automobile, contracting tuberculosis, being hit by a truck tomorrow, making $50,000 a year.)

Social differentiation might be called the sociological variable par excellence, because it touches almost every facet of life. Religion and tastes in food, occupation and recreational preferences, length of life and causes of death, sexual practices and residential location, reading habits or lack of them, family size, and hundreds of other matters are all related in various ways to social differentiation. For this reason, the study of differentiation is very important to you. *What happens to you in life is greatly influenced—sometimes determined—by the social differentiation practices of your society.*

To a significant degree, social differentiation in all industrial societies follows the same general rules. But specific historical and cultural differences do affect practice in individual nations. (Many European customs, for example, reflect former feudal social structures, the monarchical system, and so forth.) This chapter focuses on social differentiation in the United States, but the principles operating there are frequently applicable elsewhere with appropriate modification. For example, to some extent the social position of black Americans is paralleled by that of Indians in many Latin American countries. With this chapter, then, we approach what sociologists call the **social structure** of society rather than its general forms of *social organization,* discussed previously.

Major Forms of Social Differentiation: Stratification and Sexual and Ethnic-Racial Differentiation

Three types of differentiation are generally acknowledged to be socially significant, *stratification,*

> **social differentiation:** the process of distinguishing among people according to socially assigned criteria, for example, wealth, birth, or occupation.
>
> **life chances:** the probability of experiencing any given outcome in life, such as becoming a physician, marrying a movie star, or dying of tuberculosis.
>
> **social structure:** the total pattern produced by the social organization of a given cultural group or society, especially in its institutionalized form; those patterns of interaction that have become customary to the point that they are culturally *normative.* The concept of social structure includes the patterns of relations between and among social groups and institutions. For example, all American states have compulsory education laws that require *families* to keep some of their members in school until some minimum age or else be subjected to *legal* sanctions, which might include imprisonment or fines. Such laws thus involve, at minimum, the legal, educational, economic, and familial institutions of the society, plus certain roles and organizations in each.
>
> **stratification:** the ways in which given societies rank their members as superior or inferior to one another along the three dimensions of class (income and property), status (prestige), and power.

sexual differentiation, and *ethnic-racial* differentiation. **Stratification** variables include income and property (class), prestige (status), and power differences. As we will see in detail in Chapter 9, *ethnicity* refers to national, religious, and/or other cultural characteristics considered to be socially significant in a particular society; *race* is a similar concept, but is based on *inherited* characteristics considered socially significant. In everyday usage, the term *ethnicity* is often considered to include racial characteristics. As we consider the extent and significance of stratification and sexual and ethnic-racial differentiation in this chapter, we will discuss ethnic and racial differentiation together.

Social Differentiation and the Division of Labor

The three major forms of social differentiation are all related to the division of labor. In a complex society, roles in the division of labor become quite specialized. For example, you leave your shelter in the morning, a house put together by a team of carpenters, electricians, plumbers, and other occupational specialists; you go to work or school via a public transportation system operated and assembled by another group of persons, or you travel in a car not of your own making. You may drop your children off at a day-care center or a school where they are taught by still others. You do not grow your own grain, make your own clothing, or maybe even clean your own house. In turn, you yourself are now or will be performing a specialized task such as food preparation, shelter construction, or defense.

How are the three forms of differentiation related to the role taken in the division of labor? Stratification, sexual, and ethnic-racial differences determine to some extent which role you take. For example, being female has traditionally prevented persons from bearing arms in war or from seeking construction jobs. In American history, being black or Jewish or Irish Catholic has prevented individuals from obtaining high-paying and high-status occupations.

Social differentiation has also been related to which roles in the division of labor are *available*. For example, a family's economic and social circumstances often determine the occupations of their children. Wealthy parents can afford to finance their children's higher education and thus provide them with qualifications for high-status occupations. The contacts and influence of a powerful and prestigious parent may give the offspring a competitive edge in a tight job market. Some studies also suggest that more subtle factors, such as exposure to parents' attitudes toward occupational achievement, are related to the kind of occupation the children attain.

Social differentiation is related to the division of labor in yet another way. The part taken in the division of labor is an important determinant of an individual's economic standing, status, and power. Occupations are neither equally rewarded nor equally regarded, nor do they carry equal amounts of power over others. The bank manager makes more money than the clerk; the surgeon has higher status in the community than nurses; and the chairperson of the board influences more people's lives through decisions than does the assembly-line worker. Which role you assume in the division of labor does make a difference, then, in just where

you will be ranked on the class, status, and power continuums of a community. And that, in turn, strongly affects your life chances.

The relations of the three major types of social differentiation to role in the division of labor are diagramed in Figure 8-1. You can see that the three forms of social differentiation may determine what kind of role is assumed in the division of labor. Role in the division of labor, in turn, may determine class, status, and power. As we shall see later, these relationships are important in transmitting social position from one generation to the next.

Social Differentiation in Preindustrial and Industrial Societies

Characteristics considered to be socially significant vary from one type of society to another. Age, strength, or physical skills may be important differentiating factors in some societies, but not in others. Likewise, the amount of inequality in regard to economic goods and services, prestige, and power (the stratification variables) varies, as do the factors governing their distribution. Let us briefly examine preindustrial and industrial societies to determine important forms of social differentiation in each.[1]

In preindustrial societies, production is primarily dependent on animal and human sources of energy. In contrast, industrial societies depend on nonhuman and nonanimal sources, such as hydroelectricity, petroleum, and nuclear power. One of the chief characteristics of those preindustrial societies that exist by *hunting and gathering* is lack of economic surplus, which leads to relative economic equality among the society's members. In the case of prestige or social status, however, there may be great inequalities based on advanced age, powers thought to be supernatural, and personal qualities such as generosity or hunting skills. The exercise of power in these simple societies is dependent on personal respect and persuasion, because political development is limited and no one has an economic surplus with which to reward followers. Valued personal qualities, then, are important forms of social differentiation in simple societies, because they determine to a great extent the distribution of prestige and power.

Unlike hunting and gathering societies, preindustrial groups that practice *horticulture*—garden-

Figure 8-1
Relations of the three types of social differentiation to role in the division of labor

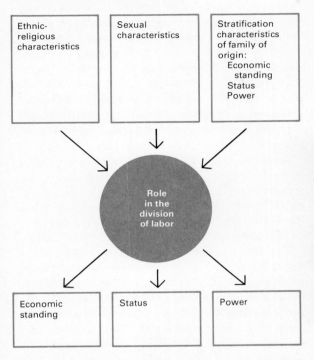

Ethnic-religious characteristics	Sexual characteristics	Stratification characteristics of family of origin: Economic standing Status Power

Role in the division of labor

Economic standing	Status	Power

horticultural society: a society in which *gardening,* the working of the earth with digging stick or hoe, is the basic form of food production.

agrarian society: a society that uses the plow to engage in *farming.* The plow, of course, is more efficient than the hoe and permits both better utilization of a given plot as well as the planting of larger areas.

A Ngatatjara man of western Australia shapes a spear shaft. Hunters and gatherers usually accumulate no economic surplus, and their material goods and technologies are likely to be simple. Nomadism does not lend itself to the accumulation of possessions.

ing—to meet their food needs are able to accumulate some limited economic surplus. This enables them to spend time in pursuits other than meeting subsistence needs, for example, making ceremonial objects, like masks and special buildings, and waging war on surrounding groups. Because **horticultural societies** need not move as frequently as hunting and gathering groups (since the food supply is more stable), individuals are able to accumulate possessions, like military spoils and ceremonial objects. The possibilities for economic inequality are greatly increased in horticultural societies because members can accumulate economic surpluses and live in one place for a relatively long time.

Agrarian societies (those using the plow) differ from horticultural societies in that their advanced technology makes possible greater farming production and thus greater economic surpluses. These foster even more extensive economic differentiation among the population. The invention of money is particularly important, because it allows people to accumulate extensive economic surplus in a reusable, easily stored form. The advanced technology of agrarian societies is also applied to military production, making those who control such technology capable of exploiting others in the society.

Industrial societies, with their reliance on highly advanced technology and new forms of energy for production, create much greater economic surpluses than agrarian societies. People in industrial societies are more occupationally specialized, and the chief determinant of economic standing, prestige, and power is occupation. Specialization occurs not only among individuals, but also on the community level, so that some communities are noted for auto production (Detroit), some for steel (Pittsburgh), some for leisure activities (Palm Springs), and so on. Power tends to be less centralized in industrialized than in agrarian societies. Political parties and voting rights lead to more widespread political participation, and the state takes over many economic and social functions that were previously beyond its domain. The latter is especially true in modern socialist states.

Stratification

The Components of a Stratification System

Ranking of persons   As indicated previously, stratification refers to differences in income and property (class), prestige (status), and power. Theoretically, we can rank individuals on each of these dimensions. Consider your own community. If you could determine the wealth of each person or household, you could then list them in order from low to high on the basis of how much wealth they possess. It should also be possible to rank persons on the basis of their prestige in the community and their power, although these are more difficult tasks. Prestige is subjective rather than objective. It cannot be counted, like money, but must be determined from social evaluations made by others in the community.

Likewise, power is difficult to measure. Social power can be defined as the ability to impose one's will on others in the community. The bases of power vary; for example, the possession of secret religious knowledge or control over scarce economic resources may each be sources of power. Determining the basis of power and exactly who is wielding it is difficult. We shall discuss it in some detail later on. For now, it is sufficient to point out that there are differences in degree of wealth, power, and prestige among persons in a community, and it is possible to rank persons from low to high on each of these variables. *Ranking* is the essence of any system of social stratification.

A category of individuals ranking relatively close to one another in economic standing, status, and power is called a **social stratum**. We usually distinguish three main social strata, often called social classes or just classes: lower, middle, and upper. Social scientists tend to make even finer distinctions, for example, lower-lower, middle-lower, upper-lower, and so on. The term *working class,* referring to manual workers, is often used synonomously with the term *lower social class,* although some sociologists prefer to reserve *lower class* for those manual laborers who are not stably employed. Strictly speaking, *class* should refer only to the economic situation of persons, but it is often used to indicate both economic and status ranking, in which case it is likely to be rendered *socioeconomic status*.

Ranking of occupational positions   Not only may we rank individuals in a community on the class, status, and power dimensions, but we may also rank their occupational positions. The division of labor in itself does not constitute a stratification system. To have a stratification system, tasks and roles must be not only *different* but also *unequal in rank.* Some of the bases for ranking are that some occupations are more highly rewarded than others, some require or attract persons with more education, and some involve more decision making than others.

Positions also differ in the prestige accorded them by the community. The occupations of U.S. Supreme Court justice and physician, for instance, are generally regarded as higher than those of shoe shiner and street sweeper.[2] Several inequalities associated with occupations may account for such differences in prestige ranking. Positions that are highly rewarded tend to be highly regarded as well. Positions demanding scarce skills and lengthy training, like that of physician or lawyer, command more respect than positions requiring little training or skills. Judges, doctors, corporate executives, and others who, because of their positions, can make decisions that influence the fate of others also command high social evaluation. Some positions may be considered more important than others for the functioning of society, for example, heads of government. In addition, the **white-collar–blue-collar** prestige distinction represents a more positive evaluation of mental labor than of physical labor.

Social inheritance In addition to ranking of persons and occupational positions, another vital element in stratification is *social inheritance:* the transmission of social position from one generation to the next. **Social position** is one's place in the stratification system, how one ranks in the stratification variables of class (economic standing), prestige (status), and power. If social inheritance is operating, children whose families rank relatively high in the class, status, and power dimensions are likely to rank relatively high in these dimensions when they become adults. They will tend to occupy a social position similar to that of their parents. Likewise, children coming from families of relatively low social position will tend to occupy relatively low social positions as adults. Although obviously, in most industrial societies, some people of humble origins do rise to occupy high social position, in general, social standing can be said to be inherited in the sense indicated here. Most of us will occupy positions in life similar to those of our parents; and where differences do occur, they are not likely to be vast.

The Necessity of Stratification: A Functional Interpretation

From the discussion of differentiation and stratification in preindustrial and industrial societies, you can see that stratification is a *pervasive* fact of social life. Historical records show that class, sta-

---

social stratum: a category of individuals ranking relatively close to one another in economic standing, status, and power.

white-collar: referring to office work or workers.

blue-collar: referring to manual work or workers.

social inheritance: the transmission of family social position to offspring, particularly important because it almost inevitably involves transmission of unequal social opportunity.

social position: one's place in the stratification system of society; one's ranking on the three stratification variables of class (economic standing), prestige (status), and power.

---

tus, and power inqualities were present in ancient societies such as the Greek and Persian, and there are archeological indications that early preliterate societies were far from equalitarian. Moreover, stratification was and is found all over the world. The antiquity and universality of social stratification make us wonder if some form of inequality isn't a *necessary* fact of social life.

In a classic functional interpretation of stratification, Kingsley Davis and Wilbert Moore argued that stratification is necessary in a society with a complex division of labor.[3] Stratification arises out of the distribution of unequal rewards for different occupational positions in the society. Why are positions unequally rewarded? Because some positions are more important than others. The same positions will not be the most important in every society, because the needs and requirements of societies differ, and any one society can change over time. In some societies, the priestly function may be deemed the most essential; in others, the captain of industry may be defined as occupying the most vital position.

A society can insure that critically important positions are taken by the most capable persons by rewarding such positions highly. It is assumed that the most highly rewarded positions will be those most sought after, both by the capable and the incapable. Who will win the competition for the position? Generally, the most able and qualified competitor. Unequal rewards, then, are necessary in order to motivate qualified persons to assume

Figure 8-2
Mean income of men by level of education and age, 1972

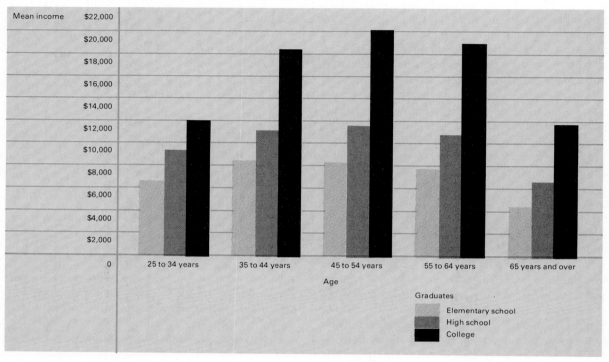

important positions. In societies that rely on **ascription**, or assignment of positions by the society, unequal rewards are necessary to motivate those individuals assigned to important positions to perform their duties well.

Another condition that determines the rewards associated with positions is the scarcity of people capable of performing them. When a position is important and there is a scarcity of qualified personnel, we can be sure a high reward will be attached to it. On the other hand, a less important position may be more highly rewarded if there is a greater scarcity of people willing and able to fulfill its requirements. Few people would argue that truck driving, as a *kind* of position or occupation, is more important to society than, say, the practice of law. And most truck drivers probably make less than most lawyers. But few people are willing or able to drive nitroglycerin trucks in the oil fields, and the drivers of such trucks are very well paid indeed. What is vital is that the generally less important positions do not compete so successful-

ly for personnel that the more important positions are not adequately filled.

A number of criticisms have been leveled at the Davis and Moore functionalist interpretation. It has been labeled a rationalization of present divisions of power, property, and prestige, an argument that present inequalities are justified because they are necessary to the survival of society. For example, some have contended that the stratification system artificially creates scarcity of personnel and therefore is dysfunctional rather than functional. Artificial scarcity occurs when privileged groups limit entry to their position (physicians, for example), and when financial, status, and power advantages resulting from unequally rewarded positions are passed on to the next generation in the form of special opportunities for the development of talent. This criticism arises from the fact that stratification includes more than just ranking and unequal rewards. Davis and Moore do ignore social inheritance, which creates special opportunities for some as well as artificial scarcity.

Another problem with the Davis and Moore argument is that it is impossible to demonstrate empirically just what positions *are* functionally the most important in a society. Therefore, it is also impossible to prove the necessity of unequal rewards for attracting persons to such positions. In addition, the functionalist theory omits consideration of many important aspects of stratification, such as job discrimination on the basis of race.

All of these critiques are important, but the functional theory of stratification nevertheless has an important place in the study of social differentiation. Aside from Marxist explanations—which would be applicable only in industrialized societies—it is a rare attempt to explain the universality of stratification systems, and would, presumably, be applicable to any kind of society from the simplest to the most complex. As such, it has been widely adopted by Western sociologists.

Indicators of Economic and Status Position: Education, Occupation, Income

The term *social position*, we noted earlier, refers to one's place in the stratification system of society, as indicated by one's economic (class), status (prestige), and power ranking. Three variables, level of *education*, amount of *income*, and type of *occupation*, are frequently used as indicators of economic and status ranking, or socioeconomic status, as the combination is often called. (We shall discuss indicators of power in a later section.) Income is a direct but inadequate measure of class or economic standing. Occupations do have prestige rankings, as we have seen, and so are an indirect measure of a person's prestige or social status in the community. Educational level is a factor determining occupation and itself brings prestige.

Levels of education, occupation, and income are related to one another, as well as to the stratification variables. For example, occupations can be ranked according to the incomes associated with them and the educational levels of persons occupying them. The incomes of persons are also associated with their educational levels, so that those with more education tend to have higher incomes. Let us look more closely at these relationships.

Figures 8-2 and 8-3 demonstrate some relationships between income and educational level. Fig-

ascription: assignment of positions by society on the basis of selected criteria not directly relevant to the performance of the duties of the position. Criteria often used are race, family lineage, religion, wealth, and ethnicity. The ugly American phrase *nigger work* exemplifies positional ascription: the restriction of certain difficult or unpleasant occupations to members of a racial group solely on the basis of race. The notion of "banker's hours" is similar: presumably as a consequence of wealth, some persons are permitted to engage in short work days. The opposite of filling positions by ascription is filling them on the basis of *achievement,* in which case people compete for positions on the basis of skill, talent, and so on.

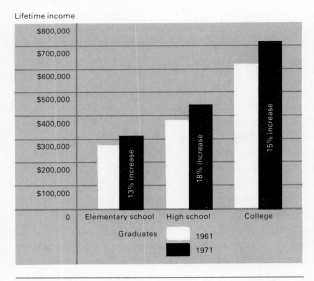

Figure 8-3
Estimated lifetime income in 1961 and 1971 for men 18 and over, by level of education (constant 1972 dollars)

Table 8-1 Median earnings of employed men 25 to 64 years old, by occupation, 1969

Occupational category	Income
White-collar	
Professional, technical, and kindred workers	$12,237
Managers and administrators, except farm	12,101
Sales workers	10,093
Clerical and kindred workers	8,536
Blue-collar	
Craftsmen and kindred workers	9,034
Operatives, except transport	7,863
Transport equipment operatives	7,955
Laborers, except farm	6,076
Other	
Farmers and farm managers	5,561
Service workers, except private household	6,857
Private household workers	3,549

Table 8-2 Median school years completed by occupation and sex, 1970

Occupation	Male	Female
White-collar		
Professional, technical, and kindred workers	16.3	16.1
Managers and administrators, except farm	12.9	12.6
Sales workers	12.7	12.2
Clerical and kindred workers	12.5	12.5
Blue-collar		
Craftsmen and kindred workers	12.0	12.0
Operatives, except transport	11.1	10.6
Transport equipment operators	10.9	12.0
Laborers, except farm	10.4	11.0
Other		
Farmers and farm managers	10.8	11.5
Farm laborers and farm foremen	8.9	9.5
Service workers, except private household	11.2	11.5
Private household workers	9.3	9.0

ure 8-2 shows the 1972 mean income of males by level of schooling. The figure is further broken down by age groups so that men at the peak of their earning power can be distinguished from those both younger and older. Within each age grouping, the mean income of high school graduates is higher than the mean income of graduates of elementary school. Likewise, the mean income of college graduates is higher than that of high school graduates. Estimates of *lifetime income* (Figure 8-3) show that high school graduates could expect to receive $135,000 more than elementary school graduates between the ages of eighteen and death, and that four-year college graduates could expect to receive $279,000 more than high school graduates.

Income levels also vary by occupation. Table 8-1 shows the 1969 median earnings for men associated with various occupations. Among white-collar workers, those in professional, technical, managerial, and administrative categories had generally higher earnings than sales and clerical workers. Among the blue-collar categories, craft workers and operatives received the highest incomes.

Even within the same occupational categories, educational level makes a difference in earnings.

Data on income by years of schooling for specific occupations, like plumber, bus driver, and typist, support the conclusion that education pays off, no matter what the occupation. For example, the 1969 median earnings of plumbers and pipe fitters with one to three years of high school was $9,626, whereas the median earnings of plumbers and pipe fitters with one to three years of college was $10,709.[4]

The higher-paying occupations also tend to employ persons with a higher level of education. Table 8-2 shows the median years of school completed for persons in various occupational categories. White-collar workers tend to have higher educational levels than blue-collar workers, and unskilled laborers tend to have the least education.

We have seen that the three usual indicators of socioeconomic status are related. Educational level is positively associated with income level. Occupations vary in the general educational level of workers in them and in amount of earnings, but even within occupations, education and earnings are positively associated. One way of conceptualizing the relationships between these variables is to view education as preparation for occupation and income as a reward for fulfilling an occupational role; see Figure 8-4. High-status occupations are highly rewarded (with earnings) and require more preparation (in the form of education).

The Consequences of Stratification

Life and health Studies have shown that socioeconomic status is associated with many other aspects of people's lives. In such essential areas as life and health, for example, socioeconomic standing makes a difference. In fact, rates of infant mortality and life expectancy are often used as indicators of the socioeconomic condition of a group. There is evidence that persons with low family income are more likely to have poor health and decayed teeth than those with high incomes.[5] Lower-income persons have also been found to have higher rates of pulmonary and heart disease, arthritis, whooping cough, diptheria, and polio.[6]

These differences are not surprising when we consider the differences in access to health care that are associated with income. The poor are less likely to visit the doctor and dentist. When they do visit the dentist, they are more likely to need extractions, and when they do go to the hospital, they are likely to stay longer than high-income persons.[7] Long life and good health are not solely associated with access to medical aid, however. It is, after all, better to be healthy in the first place. Proper diet, sanitation, and exercise, a clean environment, and freedom from undue stress are important to physical and mental health. Socioeconomic status is vitally related to where and how one lives. It is thus related to one's chances for life and good health, and perhaps for happiness, at least insofar as happiness is related to life and health.

Fertility Fertility also varies by socioeconomic status. Table 8-3 shows the number of children born to American women ages thirty-five to forty-four by level of education. You can see that, in general, as educational level rises, the number of births decline. Income is also related to number of births. For both younger married women who can still bear children and for older women for whom

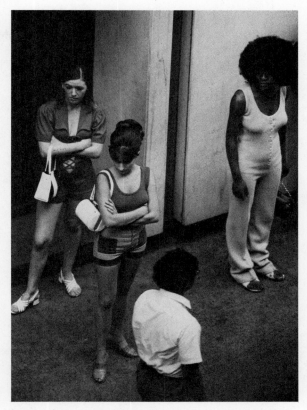

Income is not completely adequate as a measure of social position. These prostitutes may have very high incomes, but their tabooed occupation has low prestige.

Figure 8-4
The relationship between education, occupation, and income

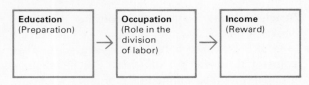

| Education (Preparation) | → | Occupation (Role in the division of labor) | → | Income (Reward) |

Table 8-3   Children born to U.S. women 35 to 44
years old, by education, 1973

Years of school completed	Children born per 1,000 women
Elementary	
Less than 8 years	3,710
8 years	3,447
High school	
1–3 years	3,557
4 years	2,852
College	
1–3 years	2,827
4 years or more	2,345

fertility is complete, lower income is associated with higher fertility. In short, the lower socioeconomic groups have more children than the higher groups.

The dynamics of this situation in Western society are not completely clear. Different value systems among the social classes, knowledge of contraception measures, and middle-class desires to limit family size in order to achieve material aspirations have all been suggested as reasons for the relationship. Differences in fertility between classes have been decreasing, and some sociologists suggest that we may eventually witness the disappearance or reversal of the traditional relationship. If children become status symbols, the upper class may begin to have proportionately more children than the lower class.

Religion Many Americans consider religious choice a particularly personal matter. Even in the area of church membership, however, social class appears to have an influence. Some religious groups draw their membership primarily from the upper and middle classes, while others are composed predominantly of lower-class people. In general Jews tend to rank highest on income, education, and occupational status measures in the United States; white Protestants occupy a middle position; and Catholics rank lowest. Within the Protestant group, however, there are significant variations as well. For example, Episcopalians and Pres-

byterians tend to rank high in social class, while fundamentalists tend to occupy lower social positions (see Figure 8-5). Even within the same religious denomination, moreover, there may be systematic differences in the type of religious involvement and style of participation according to the social class of members.

Politics Political preferences, too, are associated with social class. Both major parties draw some membership from all classes, but the working class has traditionally supported the Democratic party, and upper-income groups have generally aligned themselves with the Republican party. Attitudes toward major political and economic issues vary by social class. In 1949 Richard Centers found striking differences in attitude between the professional, business, and white-collar group, on the one hand, and manual workers, on the other, in regard to such issues as the government's role in the economy and the value of greater influence of workers on government. A significantly higher proportion of the business, professional, and white-collar workers were ultra-conservative on the political and economic issues he raised.[8] A study done three years later found essentially the same relationships.[9]

Membership in associations Differences in associational membership by social class have long been noted. Studies have shown that persons in the professions and business and those with higher incomes are more likely than others to belong to formal organizations.[10] Persons of lower socioeconomic position are less likely to participate in voluntary associations.[11] There are also differences in the *type* of associational life engaged in by social class. Upper-income persons are more likely to be found on the rosters of social clubs, charitable groups, professional associations, and such organizations as the Rotary and Kiwanis, whereas working-class persons tend to join labor unions and religious groups.

The interactional needs of working-class persons appear to be met mainly in kin groupings.[12] Albert Cohen and Harold Hodges interpret this dependence on kin relationships as an adaptation to financial insecurity and lack of status in the work world.[13] In the kin grouping, mutual obligation

Figure 8-5
Class and religion in the United States

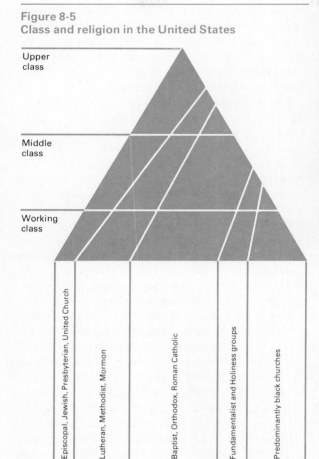

Upper class

Middle class

Working class

Episcopal, Jewish, Presbyterian, United Church

Lutheran, Methodist, Mormon

Baptist, Orthodox, Roman Catholic

Fundamentalist and Holiness groups

Predominantly black churches

The areas are roughly proportional to membership. The pyramidal shape may misrepresent the American class distribution, which, by many criteria, approximates a diamond shape, with the largest numbers in the lower-middle and upper working classes.

One of the consequences of poverty is inadequate access to medical care. For many poorer Americans, endless waiting in public health clinics like this one is a standard feature of "health care."

does not depend on occupational position, but on family relationship. The kin grouping provides security and status irrespective of occupational position.

Marital and family patterns A number of investigations of family life have focused on social-class differences. One important finding is that the female-dominated family structure is more characteristic of the lower class and affects the socialization of males in lower-class households.[14] Another finding is that strict differentiation of male and female roles and structured barriers to communication between husband and wife are characteristic of blue-collar marriages.[15]

The socialization of working-class children to different roles according to their sex may account for the particular pattern of family relationships found in working-class households. Melvin Kohn's study of socialization and its goals led him to conclude that working-class mothers set different standards of acceptable behavior for girls and for boys. Thus, what they consider punishable behavior also differs. Middle-class mothers, on the other hand, tend to punish boys and girls for the same kinds of misbehavior.[16] *Reasons* for punishment also differ by social class. Kohn points out that middle-class children tend to be punished when it can be determined that their intentions were bad. Working-class children tend to be punished when behavior has disruptive consequences, regardless of the child's intention.

That socialization of children may be different because parents' values are different is one widely accepted interpretation of findings like those discussed above. Self-control and self-direction may be more highly valued by the middle class and may thus become an objective of the socialization of their children. If social classes do indeed tend to differ in attitudes, values, and behavior, the socialization process may be an integral component in the perpetuation of these differences.

Values   Values can be defined as the principles or standards that people use in determining their behavior. People express their values when they do what they feel they *ought* do do, when they act according to their standards. It is generally held that values develop as a response to the situation in which a group finds itself. For example, societies that must constantly defend themselves against unfriendly neighbors are likely to develop values oriented toward defense of their territory. Military leadership and service are likely to be favorably looked upon and rewarded. Social and economic groups develop values that are appropriate to the circumstances in which they find themselves, and different social and economic circumstances elicit different beliefs about what should be done and how one should act. For example, families whose prestige and fortunes are built on the accomplishments of their forebears are likely to value the past and to act to preserve traditional elegance.

Differences in behavior between the various social strata suggest possible underlying value differences. Joseph Kahl has distinguished five social classes and the values associated with each.[17] Although some would disagree with his distinctions, he offers an interesting and useful framework within which to discuss these differences. It is important to note that the values are presented only as typical; not every member of a particular social class will share the value described.

The *upper class*, those who rank highest in prestige, economic standing, and power in the community, value gracious living. Making money is not as important as spending it well. One aspect of spending is not to invest too much in modern objects, because appreciation of the past and antiques is considered important to the refined way of life. The family lineage is significant; ancestors are revered for their accomplishments, and any bad behavior on the part of present members is seen as a disgrace to all.

The *upper middle class* is composed of career people in the professions and in business who are college educated and well-to-do. They value initiative, planning, and good organization. Unlike the upper class, they look mainly to the future and are not overly concerned with tradition. Their own accomplishments rather than those of their forebears are most significant to them.

Those in the *lower middle class,* the high school–educated, middle-income businesspeople, professionals, government employees, and manual workers who have been more successful than average, tend to value respectability. In their view, it is respectability that distinguishes them from the lowest group, the chronically unemployed. Education, religious affiliation, and home ownership are the marks of their respectability.

The *working class* is composed of factory and semiskilled laborers. They value "getting by," just making a living. Chances of occupational advancement are slim, and so the worker relies on seniority to bring income increases and a reduced probability of being laid off. S. M. Miller and Frank Riessman propose that a key to understanding the behavior of working-class people is their search for security and stability.[18] This accounts for their reliance on the seniority system and their attachment to the extended family. Other orientations, such as traditionalism, utilitarianism, and anti-intellectualism, are also attributed to the working class. Unlike the upper-middle-class career person, the worker does not tend to find the job satisfying and gets through the work day in order to get home.

The *lower class* is composed of the unstably employed and those in the lowest-paid manual positions. They often have little schooling. Because they view their situation as hopeless, they become apathetic and tend to rely on and expect help from their family and friends in times of economic hardship.

Class: Two Major Theories

At the beginning of the chapter, we referred to class, status, and power as the chief dimensions of stratification. Class was defined simply as income and property position. Let us now look more closely at the meaning and significance of class as presented by two of the intellectual giants of stratification theory, Karl Marx and Max Weber. You have, of course, been introduced to these men earlier.

Karl Marx According to Marx, individuals who share the same economic situation constitute an "objective" class, the word *objective* signifying that no *consciousness* of class position is involved. Each society must organize itself to supply basic goods and services to its members, and it does this through the *system of production*. The system of production in a society generates differences in economic position.

The system of production includes both the *forces* of production, such as technology and science, and the *relations* of production. The basic relations of production, as you will recall from earlier discussions, are that one group owns and controls the means by which goods and services are produced and distributed, whereas another group has only its labor to offer in the productive process. These two groups form the two major classes in most societies. The master and the slave, the feudal lord and the serf, and more recently the bourgeoisie and the proletariat in the capitalistic system of production all represented for Marx this important class division.

Marx believed that the economic system and the class relations that sprang from it were the foundations on which other social structures were built. Class position therefore accounted not only for inequalities in economic position, but also for other inequalities, especially in regard to power. Those who owned and controlled the means of production were also able to control the actions of others. Not only were they the exploiters of labor, but they were also oppressors in other areas of life. They controlled the major institutions of the society, and their ideas influenced the philosophy, literature, and art of the period.

Marx's theory of the dynamics of social change was based on his understanding of class. The two major classes were potentially political communities organized around their own economic interests. The upper or ruling class had already structured the institutions of the society to serve its economic ends. When members of the objective lower class perceived themselves to be a group with common interests flowing from their econom-

ic position, they would organize. This perception is called *class consciousness,* and results in what sociologists term a *subjective* class.

In Marx's theoretical framework, revolution against capitalist relations of production would lead to a classless society. The workers would assume control of the means of production. For a time, a "dictatorship of the proletariat" would have to operate to divest the capitalists of their control. When ownership of the means of production was completely in the hands of the people, there would no longer be any exploiters and exploited. There would be no classes, because class position is dependent on position in the relations of production, and in the new society all would own the means of production. Productive forces could then be developed without opposition or conflict, and "the free development of each [would be] the condition for the free development of all."[19]

The kind of consciousness of a common position and destiny needed for the solidarity of the proletariat did not materialize in Western industrial society, for a number of reasons. Instead of becoming more simple and well-defined, the class structure became more and more complex. As Marx predicted, the petite bourgeoisie, or owners of small means of production, like small businesses and craft shops, decreased in number. They were absorbed, for the most part, into the mass of wage laborers. The rise of the new middle class of managers and white-collar workers and the creation of the stock-held corporation radically changed the meaning of ownership and led to new complexities that made the Marxian distinction between bourgeoisie and proletariat seem less relevant. Differences in income and life-style within the so-called proletariat inhibited the consciousness of any commonality of interest. One can logically divide persons into capitalist and proletariat, but if that distinction is not perceived to be relevant by the proletariat, the kind of revolution Marx envisioned will not occur. Revolutions with a Marxist theme have occurred, but not in the Western industrialized societies, where Marx thought the proper conditions were present.

Max Weber Weber's concept of class was similar to, but not identical with, that of Marx. For both,

class refers to a group of persons who share a common situation in regard to their chances in the marketplace, but for Weber the important economic chances included not only ownership and control of the means of production or property, but also the services one could offer. Scarce skills, such as administrative or technical capabilities, could gain high returns in the marketplace. Weber's notion of class was particularly important in placing the growing number of professionals, technical experts, and entrepreneurs within the framework of stratification theory. It was also important in accounting for a variety of class interests and conflicts, not simply the all-important conflict of interest between the capitalists and the proletariat that Marx had proposed.

Weber also differed from Marx in that he did not make class position the single dominant reality promoting social change. For Weber, common economic position does not necessarily lead to class consciousness and a political community capable

Status groups or communities are distinguished from one another primarily by style of life, often expressed through consumption. Photos of a hot day in the city as experienced by the children of two different status groups.

of acting to change the society. In particular, the proletariat were unlikely to achieve such organization, he felt, because of their great numbers and because they lacked the skills necessary to achieve power in the marketplace.

Marx had been criticized for proposing a strictly economic theory and for ignoring other dimensions of social standing. Weber proposed that class is only one dimension of a complex stratification structure. Status and the political order, along with class, need to be given full consideration. Whereas Marx insisted on the primacy of class in accounting for status and power differentials, Weber, without denying the importance of class, stressed the distinctions between the three dimensions. Economic situation (class), social honor accorded by the community (status), and power exercised in the political or legal realm are often closely interrelated, but not necessarily so.

Weber pointed out analytical distinctions between the three dimensions of stratification, the differences in ranking of these dimensions that are observed in the real world and the different patterns of influence possible in each. Instead of attempting to reduce the complexities of stratification by tracing them to a single economic cause, Weber constructed a useful framework for analyzing them. We shall continue to discuss Weber's ideas in the sections below.

Social Status: Prestige and Life-Style

Weber defined status as honor accorded by a community. There are innumerable bases for the conferral of social honor: royal or aristocratic family background, ethnicity, occupation, property, education, and so on. A status group is a community of persons granted a certain level of *prestige* on the basis of the criteria operating in their larger community, for example, property, race, or religion. Members of a status group consider each other social equals and interact socially in a somewhat exclusive manner; they also pursue similar *life-styles* that set them apart from others.[20] Weber suggested that, in a sense, class was determined by relation to the *production* of goods, while status was a matter of their *consumption.*

Status groups are distinguished from one another primarily by their styles of life, and style of life is expressed through one's activities and consumption of goods and services. For example, a brownstone off Central Park in New York City has more status value than a tenement on the Lower East Side. Likewise, attendance at the Metropolitan Opera carries more status value than a night at the Demolition Derby. Status is also often indicated in work settings by differences in furniture and appurtenances, as Table 8-4 shows.

In American society, where mass production has made possible the imitation of luxury items (as when Detroit imitates the body design of expensive foreign cars), we might expect status differences to diminish. This is not the case. Fake furs and economy tours may represent a general advance in consumption levels, but they are not comparable in status value to ermine or a cruise on a private yacht. Many advertisements contain appeals based on the prestige value of their products. This is probably one reflection of the preoccupation with status in a society that, in its inception, did away with hereditary titles and an aristocracy based on family lineage.

Class and status   For Weber, class and status were vitally linked. Class position, or one's market situation, was a prime determinant of what one was able to consume. Of course, one could choose unwisely and so ruin any chance of being accepted into a status community. The farmer who strikes oil may purchase many expensive items but still remain outside prestigious social circles because he has not acquired the "right" items or does not consume them in acceptable ways. In the long run, however, class position and status position tend to become comparable. Moreover, proper manipulation of status symbols and opportunities for interaction in status communities can be extremely useful in maintaining and improving one's situation with respect to the market. The foundations for lucrative business deals may be established over cocktails or on the golf course at the country club.

Although class and status are closely associated, they are two different realities. Possession of wealth does not automatically insure acceptance into a status community. Likewise, loss of wealth does not inevitably lead to rejection and loss of status, at least not in the short run. Especially in areas of the country where families of old wealth reside, families with the same class standing may not share the same social status.

Power

Power, class, and status   Not only are there structured inequalities in the stratification variables of economic standing and status, but there are inequalities in the capacity to impose direction and control over events and people. Weber proposed that social *power* is expressed in political groups or parties. He was careful to distinguish position in the political order from status and class; for example, people could wield power in the community

Table 8-4 The system of status symbols in a large corporation

Visible appurtenances	Top dogs	V.I.P's	Brass	No. 2s	Eager beavers	Hoi polloi
Brief cases	None—they ask the questions	Use backs of envelopes	Someone goes along to carry theirs	Carry their own —empty	Daily carry their own—filled with work	Too poor to own one
Desks, office	Custom made (to order)	Executive style (to order)	Type A, "Director"	Type B, "Manager"	Castoffs from no. 2s	Yellow oak—or castoffs from eager beavers
Tables, office	Coffee tables	End or decorative wall tables	Matching tables, type A	Matching tables, type B	Plain work table	None—lucky to have own desk
Carpeting	Nylon—1 inch pile	Nylon—1 inch pile	Wool-twist (with pad)	Wool-twist (without pad)	Used wool pieces —sewed	Asphalt tile
Plant stands	Several—filled with strange exotic plants	Several—filled with strange exotic plants	Two—repotted whenever they take a trip	One medium-sized; repotted annually during vacation	Small; replaced when plant dies	May have one in the department or bring their own from home
Vacuum water bottles	Silver	Silver	Chromium	Plain painted	Coke machine	Water fountains
Library	Private collection	Autographed or complimentary books and reports	Selected references	Impressive titles on covers	Books everywhere	Dictionary
Shoe shine service	Every morning at 10:00	Every morning at 10:15	Every day at 9:00 or 11:00	Every other day	Once a week	Shine their own
Parking space	Private in front of office	In plant garage	In company garage—if enough seniority	In company properties—somewhere	On the parking lot	Anywhere they can find a space —if they can afford a car
Luncheon menu	Cream cheese on whole wheat, buttermilk, and indigestion tablets	Cream of celery soup, chicken sandwich (white meat), milk	Fruit cup, spinach, lamb chop, peas, ice cream, tea	Orange juice, minute steak, French fries, salad, fruit cup, coffee	Tomato juice, chicken croquettes, mashed potatoes, peas, bread, chocolate cream pie, coffee	Clam chowder, frankfurter and beans, rolls and butter, raisin pie à la mode, two cups of coffee

even though they did not have high status or much wealth. But the three dimensions of stratification are related. For example, political parties may draw their adherents from and work for the goals of particular economic and status groups in the community.

Attempts have been made to document the association between power and status and power and class. G. William Domhoff concluded that members of the upper social class, the business aristocracy, hold more than their share of important decision-making positions and do in fact form a governing class. "A governing class is a social upper class which owns a disproportionate amount of the country's wealth, receives a disproportionate amount of the country's yearly income, and contributes a disproportionate number of its members

to the controlling institutions and key decision-making groups of the country."[21] In his study, Domhoff presented evidence that a governing class does control the economy, federal, state, and local government, foundations, universities, and the military.

The predominance of persons from upper-class backgrounds in government is an indication that class and power are associated. One study of the class backgrounds of 180 U.S. senators serving between 1947 and 1957 showed that they were recruited disproportionately from the top of the class scale.[22] Other studies demonstrating the relationship between power and class have focused on the national and multinational corporation. The power of the corporation to influence political decisions at home and abroad is discussed not only in the stratification literature but also in the daily news.

Approaches to the study of power It can be very difficult to discover who actually holds power in a community. First we must ask: power over what kinds of events and actions? Many kinds of decisions are made in a community. City ordinances are made and interpreted, workers are hired and fired, and the date for the local church bazaar is set. In studying the distribution of power, we can first define areas or spheres of decision making, like civic, business, and religious, and then determine who in each category are the major decision makers. But not all spheres of decision making are equally important, and the isolation of various hierarchies of power does not tell us which is most important in a community. Further, there is often considerable overlap. Consequently, researchers have developed several other ways of measuring power, the most important of which we will discuss here.

The reputational approach In a study of Atlanta, Floyd Hunter developed a method of discovering leadership in community affairs by means of assessing reputation: the *reputational* approach.[23] Lists of leaders nominated by persons active in the community were narrowed down by a panel of judges to about forty. These forty, who did indeed have the reputation of being influential, were then asked to choose the ten top leaders from the list. Through this method, Hunter identified a small group of influential people who were predominantly from one sphere of community life—business. One advantage of the reputational method is that it does not prejudge which institutional domains are most likely to supply community leaders. The method has been criticized, however, on the grounds that a reputation for power is not at all the same as the actual possession of power.

The positional approach Another way of deciding who has power in the community is to study the official positions held in each area considered important in influencing community affairs. This is called the *positional* approach. Of course, we cannot be sure that those *persons* holding the official positions in community organizations or govern-

ment are actually making the decisions. What happens "behind the scenes" may be more crucial than what occurs publicly. The difficulty involved in confirming the suspicion that more has gone into the decision-making process than what is publicly observable has always plagued the study of power.

The decision-making approach Some students of community power contend that the only way to determine who has power is to observe the actual exercise of influence in community issues. This *deicision-making* approach to the study of power involves the selection of several issues and careful observation of the actions of all concerned parties. The positional and the decision-making approach share a common problem, however: How can researchers be sure that they are observing everything that is significant in terms of the final outcome? If influence is being exercised behind closed doors, the doors are closed for a reason. It is unlikely that the social scientist will be invited in to record the exercise of influence and then tell the world. There are other methodological problems as well. How do we decide which issues to analyze? If a sufficient number of representative issues can be determined, the time and research staffing involved might become prohibitive.

The structure of power: Elitist or pluralist? Given the difficulties of discovering who has power and who exercises it, what does research suggest concerning the *structure* of community power? Is there a group of persons in the community who do or could exercise disproportionate influence over events, no matter what the issue? In other words, is the structure of power *elitist*? Hunter's famous study of Atlanta suggested that there was such a group of persons in that community, but his particular use of the reputational approach may have biased his findings. Critics have suggested that Hunter's list of influential people may actually have been a collection of names of people who were influential in various spheres of community life, but did not represent a coalition capable of collectively determining all or most major community decisions.

Robert Dahl, using the decision-making approach, found evidence of another kind of power structure in New Haven.[24] Here there appeared to be various groups exercising influence over different spheres of community life. Like Dahl, a number of social scientists have proposed that the structure of power in communities is *pluralistic*, that power is exercised not by a small group of very powerful persons who influence the outcome of all important community decisions, but by groups organized around their own interests in various aspects of community life. Coalitions form and dissolve depending on the issue at hand, and individuals shift allegiances according to their interests. In this view, power is much more diffused than the elitist model suggests, and the outcome of issues is dependent on the balance of power among competing interest groups rather than on the collective will of a single elite power bloc.

There has been much controversy over the relative merits of the elitist and pluralist perspectives. It is becoming clear, however, that the way in which power is structured differs from one community to another and that comparative studies of communities are more useful than generalizations drawn from a single study. Large industrialized urban centers appear to have more pluralistic power structures, whereas the smaller and older urban centers, particularly in the southern United States, are more likely to have an elite power group composed of businessmen.[25]

One of the best-known analyses of power on the national level is that of C. Wright Mills.[26] Mills argued that three spheres of decision making, economic, political, and military, became critical in American society after World War II, and that there are relatively few persons in each of these spheres dominating the decision-making process. These persons occupy "the strategic command posts" of the social structure. Moreover, the top leaders in each of the dominant domains take each other into account in making major decisions. Together, they form a *power elite*.

Coordination of decision is made easier, and perhaps even possible, by the formation of status communities. The corporate, political, and military elites tend to regard each other as status equals. They form the American upper crust or social elite, an exclusive community within which both business and social calendars are coordinated and from which friends and marriage partners are selected. Thus, power position and status position are close-

ly associated. Power and economic standing are also related. The acquisition of wealth and the ability to employ the means of retaining and increasing it are highly dependent on power position in the economic, political, or military institution.

For Mills, class, status, and power are inevitably linked to institutional position, and some institutions in society are dominant. High institutional positions in religion or education, for example, do not provide high class, status, and power to incumbents. Mills viewed these institutions not as policy setters, but as entities controlled and even manipulated by the economic, political, and military power elite.

Types of Stratification Systems

The principal types of stratification systems are *estate*, *caste*, and *class*. These may be distinguished from each other in three ways. First, they may be distinguished by the nature of their chief stratification inequality, that is, the dimension (economic, status, or power) that determines other inequalities. Second, they may be distinguished by how much movement between social groupings is permitted or preferred, in other words, by how normatively *open or closed* they are. Third, they may be distinguished by the extent to which positions are filled by *ascription* or *achievement*. (*Ascription*, you recall, refers to the placing of persons in social positions using criteria over which they have no control, like race or national background; *achievement* refers to the placing of persons in social positions according to the success of their competitive efforts.) Let us consider how the principal types of stratification systems differ from each other on the basis of these three criteria.

The estate system The estate system arose in Europe in the Middle Ages following the collapse of the Roman Empire, a series of Germanic invasions, and the rise of the Islamic state. As a result of these events, strong and stable government disappeared, and urban life, dependent on merchant activities, declined. The estate system that developed in these circumstances was essentially agricultural; the new social groupings, called estates, were dependent on the land and those who controlled it.

The three medieval estates were the nobility, the clergy, and the peasants. These were social and legal groupings that had both rights and responsibilities relative to one another. In the early feudal period, the noble was essentially a warrior whose authority derived from the protection he was able to extend in a society in which government had broken down. He also served to maintain social order by performing a judicial function in disputes among his social subordinates. The noble derived economic benefit from the land he was able to control, but his status or prestige was determined not so much by his economic standing as by his *power.* Of the three estates, the peasants ranked lowest in economic standing, social status, and power. The clergy were more difficult to categorize, because they ranged from high-ranking bishops who were themselves nobles to rural clergy who were little better off than the peasants.

The estate system was relatively closed in a normative sense; that is, the norms called for little movement from one social grouping to another. However, some **social mobility** was sanctioned, so it was not a completely closed system.

The estate system relied heavily on ascription based on the estate into which one was born, although some limited achievement of social position was allowed. What we mean here by "ascription based on the estate into which one was born" is simply that the social system attributed specific characteristics to, and prescribed behaviors or activities for, people on the basis of birth. Thus nobles had "blue" blood, were expected to be brave, and had to conform to a well-understood set of social conventions for relating to others. Peasants, to the contrary, were defined as stupid and childlike, were not permitted to ride horses, and could not engage in many activities, such as hawking. Some few persons of common birth were permitted to rise somewhat in social rank, however, chiefly in the church or through prowess in war, although top social positions were denied them.

The caste system   Caste stratification involves the attribution of superiority and inferiority to various permanent and hereditary groupings in the society. Caste is the most extreme form taken by status communities. A caste is, in fact, a closed status grouping, membership in which is hereditary. In a

> **estate system:** the type of stratification system, characterizing medieval Europe, in which social position was based on relationship to land. There were three estates, the nobility, the clergy, and the peasantry, and social position was largely ascribed, although some mobility was possible.
>
> **social mobility:** movement of persons from one social group or position to another.
>
> **caste system:** the type of stratification system in which social position is based on birth (family position) and is entirely ascribed; no social mobility is possible. Traditional India is an example.

caste system, the status inequality of permanent and hereditary groupings is the major inequality from which economic and power differences flow; that is, caste status determines access to economic resources and power.

A caste system is normatively closed and relies exclusively on ascription based on caste membership. Thus, there is no socially acceptable way for individuals to achieve a higher social position through their own efforts, not even through marriage. Marriage between members of different castes is usually forbidden, and when it is allowed, the child usually takes the status of the lower-caste parent. This closure of castes is reinforced by tradition and ritual. In the traditional caste society of India, for example, certain types of intercaste contact render the higher-caste person "unclean" and in need of ritual purification.

Such extreme closure is probably possible only when built on differences considered to be ethnic or racial. Weber suggested that caste is the usual arrangement by which different ethnic groups live in the same community. They do not intermarry or interact socially and have only those forms of contact necessary for the sharing of life in the same general territory. If one group is considered more honorable than the other, then their relationship takes the form of a caste structure.

Occupational specialization is characteristic of a caste system. Those occupations considered least desirable are assigned to the lower castes. In traditional India, for example, the Shudra, the lowest caste, are confined to such occupations as craft work, farm labor, and water carrying, whereas the highest caste, the Brahmins, are the priests and

Brahmins and Untouchables.

often own land as well. The Kshatriya, or warrior caste, fall below the Brahmins in the traditional status ordering; they also tend to be landowners and engage in farming. The third major caste grouping is the Vaisya, or yeoman farmers, many of whom are now merchants. Besides these four major castes, which have hundreds of subgroups, there are individuals who fall outside any caste grouping. These are the "untouchables," the lowest-status group of all. Their assigned occupations are those considered most detestable: jobs associated with human and animal carnage and waste. Such tasks include cleaning latrines, washing clothes, cutting hair, sweeping, and butchering.

Traditional India is not the only society characterized by a caste form of stratification. Caste or castelike systems appear around the world. Gerald Berreman, who has studied the operation of caste in present-day village India, has also cited caste

features in other societies: among the Tutsi, Hutu, and Twa tribes in Ruanda, East Africa; among the Japanese, the outcaste Burakumin, a minority group of some 3 million; and, perhaps most well-known, in colonial situations like that of South Africa, where the colonizers have established themselves as an exclusive and nonintermarrying ethnic group.[27] Some have suggested that blacks and whites in the United States have castelike relationships insofar as they form two distinct groups that do not usually intermarry, whites having higher status than blacks.

There are two essential differences between an estate system and a caste system, although they may appear quite similar in some respects. First, power, wealth, and so forth, in an estate system are based on relationship to *land*, whereas *birth alone* determines them in a caste system. Second, no social mobility is possible in a caste system. People can change their estate, but they cannot change their caste.

The class system We have already discussed the meaning and significance of class, and class systems show important differences from estate and caste systems. You will recall that a class is a category of persons sharing a common economic situation. A class system, as the name implies, is one in which the chief dimension of stratification is economic and the other dimensions, such as social status and power, are based on economic position.

A class system is normatively open in an absolute sense; that is, individual mobility is not defined as improper. Of course, this is only the norm and not the reality, as we shall see. Nevertheless, there is more possibility for individual social mobility in class societies than in caste or estate systems. Theoretically, a class system relies totally on achievement to fill positions, but as we will see in the following sections, ethnic-racial and sexual differentiation limit people's ability to achieve. Thus, in reality, class systems do not meet their norms: mobility is limited, and ascriptive criteria like race and sex are often used along with achievement to fill occupational positions and to determine social status, class standing, and power.

Ethnic-Racial Differentiation

The United States is composed of many different ethnic and racial groups. There are blacks, Chicanos, Native Americans, Irish Catholics, Jews, "white ethnics," Asians, and of course the celebrated white Anglo-Saxon Protestant, or WASP; and this list is not exhaustive. Membership in some of these groups is associated with class, status, and power ranking and may be a key factor *determining* rank on these dimensions of stratification. We proposed in Figure 8-1 a model relating ethnic and racial differences to role in the division of labor. Ethnic-racial differentiation can operate to determine class, status, and power by determining the role taken in the division of labor, which in turn determines class, status, and power ranking. We

> **class system:** the type of stratification system where social position is based on possession of income or property, is largely achieved, and in which considerable social mobility is possible. Most contemporary industrial nations have a class system.

also discussed such differences as a basis for the development of status distinctions and caste relationships.

Chapter 9 on minority groups will discuss these matters in considerable detail, but we can indicate the point here briefly by considering the roles generally allocated to black Americans by the division of labor in the United States and the effects of that allocation on blacks' stratification rankings. Economically, the class standing of blacks is generally markedly below that of whites. In 1972, approximately 33 percent of the black population had incomes below the poverty level, as compared with only 9 percent of the white population. More whites than blacks occupy white-collar occupations, and fewer blacks than whites complete either high school or college. Even mortality statistics favor whites; black people of both sexes have lower life expectancies than whites.

With regard to the other two stratification variables, status and power, we have only to search the social register or other honors lists, such as *Who's Who*, to know that black Americans are less valued socially than whites by the majority white population. No one with any knowledge of the United States would hold that black men and women occupy many significant positions of power in the country. In most communities, and certainly on the national scene, Black Power remains an ideal rather than a reality.

Sexual Differentiation

Early in this chapter, we commented that sexual differences are related to the division of labor insofar as task assignment in the division of labor is often determined by whether one is male or female. Here we will look closely at some data on occupational and income differences between the

Figure 8-6
Representation of women in various occupational categories

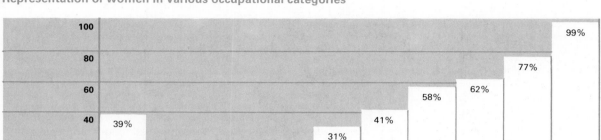

sexes, concentrating particularly on women. Then we will consider the important issue of how sexual differentiation develops.

Occupation and Income

The proportion of the American female population participating in the labor force has increased steadily in this century. In 1900, 20 percent of women eighteen through sixty-four years of age were working; in 1940, the proportion was 30 percent; and by 1970, half were in the labor force. The stage of life when women enter the labor force has also changed. Before 1940, women tended to work before marriage and childbirth. After 1940, the proportion of women over thirty-five who were working showed significant increases. In 1970, 33 percent of married women aged twenty to twenty-four, with husbands present in the home and with preschool children, were working. Compare this with the 20 percent of all American women eighteen through sixty-four years of age, both married and unmarried, who were working in 1900.[28] The change in labor force participation of women has been great.

The occupational distribution of women in the labor force differs markedly from that of men. A higher proportion of women are white-collar workers, but women tend to be concentrated in the lower-paid white-collar occupations, especially in clerical and sales work. Some occupations, usually low-status ones, like household work, are overwhelmingly filled by women. Figure 8-6 shows both the overrepresentation of women in some occupations and their underrepresentation in others.

Differences in male and female income are partially accounted for by differences in occupational distribution by sex. There are, however, income differentials for males and females in the same occupations. For example, the median income of women teaching in primary and secondary schools in 1969 was $7,200. The median figure for males in this occupational category was $10,000.[29]

What accounts for sex-based income differentials, given the same occupation and comparable levels of education? The obvious answer is that qualified women are not paid as much as qualified men for doing the same work simply because they are women. This is discrimination comparable to discrimination based on race or color. As with all forms of discrimination, many rationalizations are given for practicing sex discrimination: women are inherently inferior; woman's place is in the home;

"*I closed a three-hundred-thousand-dollar export deal. You had Mrs. Muncie polish all the silver. I see we both had a productive day.*"

New Yorker, August 19, 1974. Drawing by Weber; © 1974 The New Yorker Magazine, Inc.

Does a woman's biology determine which roles and tasks she is capable of?

in a tight job market, women should not take jobs that men need; men are more often heads of households. Another explanation for sex-based income differentials is that women as a class are not as qualified as men, even if they have the same education, because they do not have as much work experience. However unobjective and unfair many of these views are, they are widespread enough to set limits on what women can achieve.

Nature or Nurture?

There is controversy concerning the relative effects of biological differences and of socialization on observed sex differentials in occupations and roles. In every society, one task of women is bearing

Researchers Find Pay Gap Widens for Men, Women

The earnings gap between men and women has continued to widen during the last 20 years, despite some effort toward equal pay for both.

As a group, women working full-time now average only $6,800 a year, or 43 per cent below the $11,800 average earnings of men holding full-time jobs.

Twenty years ago, working women were earning only 36 per cent less than their male counterparts, according to a report by The Conference Board of New York, a private business research group.

Fabien Linden, a Conference Board economist, said the widening gap is largely explained by "a change in the occupational mix of working women" over the last 20 years and the fact that women generally are paid less because of less experience in the labor force.

Even among the college-trained there is a sizable earnings gap between men and women workers, he said.

College-trained women working full-time earned an average of $9,300 last year, compared with $15,200 for men. Among college graduates, women earned $10,400 compared with $17,200 for men.

Women college graduates, in fact, earned less on the average than men who did not finish high school.

Twenty years ago, most working women were either well-educated or worked because of a need to support themselves. Since then, however, because of changing attitudes toward work, a much broader base of women has entered the labor force, representing virtually all ages and all levels of education.

By contrast, males who have entered the labor force traditionally have come from the younger age brackets, since most men in the older age categories are already working. These young workers are increasingly better educated that those who preceded them into the work force.

The number of college-trained working women has risen significantly, but they account for only 42 per cent of the growth in the total female work force. Women with a high school education or less made up 58 per cent of the increase over the last 20 years, the majority taking relatively low-paying jobs. . . .

Chicago Tribune, November 30, 1975. Reprinted courtesy of the Chicago Tribune.

children. This, of course, is a function of the biological structure of females. The important question is whether further differentiation of tasks and roles is inherently linked to the performance of this biological function and to the genetic structure of women. Does a woman's biology determine which roles and tasks she is capable of assuming and performing well in society? (We could, of course, ask the same question about men.)

As we saw in Chapter 4, some sex differences in intellectual achievements have been documented. Girls generally tend to score higher than boys on tests of verbal ability, whereas boys at the high school and college levels tend to excel at arithmetical tasks. Likewise, adolescent and adult males tend to excel at tasks involving the perception of objects in space and their relationships. Sexual differences in personality have also been reported. Ratings by teachers and self-reports indicate that girls tend to be more anxious than boys.[30] Some research shows boys at early ages attempting to be more dominant in peer groups and with adults than are girls in similar situations. And young girls are reported to be more compliant with adults than young boys.[31]

But what is the source of these differences? The case for socialization, rather than genetics, as the cause of these differences is impressive. Recent research, for example, suggests that sex-role socialization begins as early as the delivery room. Parents asked to describe their newly born infants tended to describe girls as smaller, softer, more delicately featured, and more inattentive than boys, whereas doctors' ratings showed no significant differences.[32] In another study, mothers tended to offer a doll rather than a train to a six-month-old child dressed as a girl. The same child, when dressed as a boy, was more frequently offered the train. What is also interesting is that the women participating in the study did not perceive that they treated male and female children differently.[33] Leading children's books also reinforce traditional sex-role distinctions. Women tend to be portrayed as wives and mothers, whereas men are shown performing a variety of tasks.

In general, there is considerable consistency in the sex-role messages transmitted to children by the major socialization agents—parents, teachers, friends, books, and other media.[34] Boys should be active, achieving, aggressive, independent, ambitious, rational. They are encouraged to succeed, to attain higher education, higher prestige, and higher-income jobs. They are, in short, socialized to compete for the occupational goals and to adopt the attitudes and personality traits that exemplify the values most prized and rewarded in American society.

By contrast, girls are socialized to be passive, nurturing, dependent, pretty, responsive, emotional, and "nice," all traits that are not so highly valued in society and that do not lead to positions and occupations of high prestige, power, and material benefits. If a woman does seek gainful employment, in general she will be limited in her choice to the occupational categories considered acceptable for women. These consist principally of occupations like nursing, teaching, secretarial and clerical work, and household help—all areas involving caring for other people or performing low-status tasks. True, there are a few female executives in business and a few women who hold political office, but compared with men, not many. There are relatively few high-paying and high-status occupations for which female competition is sanctioned by the society as a whole. And many of these, such as fashion model and movie star, are generally open only to women of outstanding physical attractiveness. This is hardly a criterion applied equally to males.

Needless to say, discrimination also operates against males who desire social and occupational roles deemed inappropriate. Male nurses are still a rarity, and men who perform jobs traditionally associated with female activities, such as dress design or hair styling, are often considered "queer." And men who manifest personality traits associated with femininity, such as emotional sensitivity and tenderness, are unlikely ever to occupy positions of high social reward.

But sex discrimination is predominantly a female problem, principally because people accept the socialization that society offers. Despite the fact that certain individual women have achieved jobs, pay, and status equal to those of men, *women as a class* are still largely confined to lower-paid, lower-status occupations; denied equal access to professional training; discouraged from competing with men for positions of power and prestige; and, in almost every occupational category, receive less pay for the same job than a man would receive. (Who do you think is more likely to become the first "minority" Vice President of the United States—the Presidency remains unthinkable—a black male or a white female?)

Even today, despite the remarkable gains made by the female emancipation movement, the typical American woman continues to be socialized to internalize and display "feminine" passivity, dependence, and emotionality in a culture that values and rewards "masculine" aggressiveness, achievement, rationality, and self-sufficiency. She is socialized to take home economics rather than shop, become a cheerleader rather than an athlete, and marry a doctor rather than become one. If, despite all this, she elects the traditional masculine achievement goals, she is likely to experience social disapproval and the pain of self-doubt for pursuing a deviant pattern. If she succeeds in entering the male-dominated occupational world, she will be subjected to educational, occupational, and income discrimination and will not be able reasonably to expect the same levels of success and reward as her male counterparts. Although a numerical majority of the American population, women remain a minority group in the sense in which that word is used in Chapter 9: a group socially dominated by another.

"Why don't WE try this 'role reversal' business, and I'll be the domineering one for a while."

Reprinted by permission of Newspaper Enterprise Association.

Most, though apparently not all, women are raised to be passive, dependent, nurturing, pretty, responsive, emotional, and "nice."

Stability and Change within the Stratification System

Continuity of Rankings

What makes for stability within a stratification system—the maintenance of same relative class, status, and power rankings for families from one generation to the next? Earlier we called this *social inheritance*, the passing on of social position. Many social scientists contend that the desire to pass on the benefits one has received or acquired to one's own children is the key to understanding continuity of social rank through the generations. Let us examine this theory.

Direct inheritance Direct inheritance of money, title, family business, or, in some countries, a throne is one way of maintaining continuity of social position from one generation to the next. Little more need be said concerning this form of social inheritance. The benefits received are direct, and it only remains for the individual receiving them to be able to hold onto and use them to advantage.

Inheritance of unequal opportunities   Another form of social inheritance—probably the more important one in American society—is the *inheritance of unequal opportunities.* What we mean by this is that while, indeed, a relative few may directly inherit great wealth, industrial corporations, or the like, most of us do not. Rather we inherit *differential access to the opportunity* to attain high class, status, or power as a consequence of family position and home environment. Although it may be legally true that any native-born citizen of the United States has the opportunity to become President, for example, we all know that it also helps to be Protestant, white, male, well-educated, and reasonably wealthy. Nonwhites, females, Jews, and the poor have inherited from their families a reduced chance of attaining that particular goal. Or, to use a similar example, a law degree from Harvard or Yale is very useful in attaining a position with a Wall Street law firm. And, while there are certainly graduates of those schools who came from poor neighborhoods and families, the opportunity for admission to them is much reduced for the working-class teenager from a midwestern or southern industrial city. The inheritance of unequal opportunity is most marked with respect to occupational and educational attainment.

Occupational attainment   Occupational achievement may be passed on from generation to generation as a form of social inheritance, as shown in Figure 8-7. Families with high social position are able to give their offspring financial, behavioral, and attitudinal advantages that enable them to attain occupations associated with high class, status, and power. As a result, their offspring (the second generation) are likely to become adults with high social position. They in turn establish families of their own, giving the same advantages in the occupational world to *their* children (the third generation). And so the dynamics of social inheritance

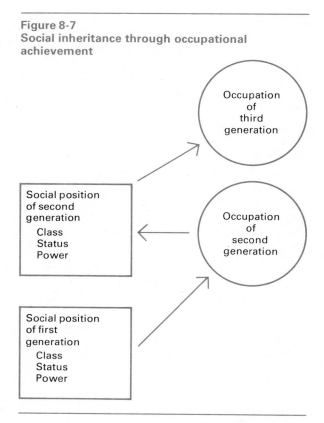

Figure 8-7
Social inheritance through occupational achievement

can continue through the generations, with the result that great-grandchildren may find themselves in the same relative social rank as their great-grandparents were eighty years ago. Of course, social inheritance does not operate perfectly in American society; family rankings may change somewhat over time—in either direction.

Educational attainment   Education is an important qualification for many highly rewarded occupations. In fact, as we have seen, research shows that educational level is highly related to occupational position and earnings. But what determines the educational level one attains? Intelligence is one factor. The results of a study by William Sewell and Vimal Shah indicate that intelligence, as measured by IQ tests, is a significant predictor of who will complete four years of college.[35] But they also found another important indicator: the socioeconomic position of the family of origin. Sewell and Shah used four categories for both IQ and socio-

Table 8-5   Socioeconomic status and IQ

Socioeconomic status	IQ	
	Lowest	Highest
Lowest	0.3	17.0
Highest	9.2	57.6

This table compares the lowest and highest categories of IQ and socioeconomic status for one sample of college graduates. Figures shown are percentages of the total sample. Read the table vertically to compare the effects of socioeconomic status within I.Q. groupings.

Poverty: A city play area.

economic classifications: low, lower middle, upper middle, and high. A higher proportion of high school seniors who scored low on IQ tests but high on the socioeconomic indicators completed college than did seniors who were low in IQ scores and low in socioeconomic status (see Table 8-5). In each IQ category, socioeconomic status was an important predictor of plans to attend college and actual completion of college. Likewise, IQ made a difference in plans to attend college and college completion in each socioeconomic level. Other research strongly supports the link between family background and the amount of education received, although other factors, such as sex, may also affect educational attainment.

Social inheritance and the functional interpretation of stratification   You will recall our earlier discussion of the functional theory of stratification, the most popular explanation in American sociology for the existence of stratification. The functional theory has been widely criticized, as we noted, but it is important to realize that the existence of social inheritance—which the theory ignores entirely—flatly contradicts a functional interpretation.

The functional theory proposes that unequal rewards are necessary to motivate the most qualified persons to assume the most important occupational and social positions. But the fact of social inheritance means that persons from families with high social positions, on the average, will *be* the most qualified. How do individuals acquire their respective abilities and qualifications? Some can be classified as *natural*, such as musical genius, and some as *acquired,* such as administrative skills. The acquired abilities presume some native intelligence and ability to learn, but we know that such levels of

intelligence and aptitude are widespread in the population in comparison to genius-level aptitude for music.

Now if appropriate aptitudes are widespread, but relatively few people achieve the highly rewarded positions that require some special qualification, three conclusions are possible. First, only a relative few *want* the most highly rewarded positions. We can dismiss this possibility as nonsensical on its face. Second, there is direct discrimination on the basis of ethnicity, religion, race, sex, and so forth. This, of course, is true, but cannot account for all of those who are not discriminated against but who still fail to attain highly rewarded positions. All of those who are poorly rewarded are not members of groups discriminated against.

Third, and the most reasonable explanation, some persons have acquired better qualifications and thus have achieved higher position. Many children growing up in humble socioeconomic circumstances have the basic intelligence and aptitudes to perform almost any common task or occupation, medicine, for example. But as a consequence of their social inheritance, they do not have the opportunity to acquire the specific qualifications necessary for performing highly rewarded tasks. They are, therefore, beaten out in the competition by those who have had better opportunities to become qualified. This pattern becomes especially apparent at the extreme, within what has come to be called the *culture of poverty.*

The culture of poverty Social characteristics passed on to the next generation through the socialization process promote stability of social rank. The *culture of poverty,* as Oscar Lewis points out, is a response to a marginal position in a society that stresses free enterprise and achievement.[36] It is characterized by apathy, hopelessness, female-dominated homes, and distrust of institutions, such as education and government. By means of the socialization process, the culture of poverty is passed on to succeeding generations. Thus, the children of the poor share the characteristics of the culture of poverty even though they may have better economic opportunities than their parents. These characteristics prevent them from taking advantage of opportunities for advancement.

The culture of poverty exerts an especially strong influence on attitudes and values. As noted earlier, the lowest social classes are frequently characterized by attitudes of apathy and cynicism. And thus children who have been brought up by their family and neighborhood culture to believe that they are helpless billiard balls propelled hither and yon by a fate they are powerless to control, and that all important aspects of life are determined by others ("the bosses" or "the big guys"), are less likely to attempt to change their lot than children with more optimistic views. For example, even if a boy from a poor family is told by a high school counselor that he has the ability to go to college, his cynicism may prompt him to believe that "college is for rich guys and sissies," and his apathy may prevent him from applying for an available scholarship.

Social Mobility

Social mobility, as was implied earlier in the chapter, refers to the movement of persons from one social group or position to another. Social mobility operates in a number of ways, on both individual and group levels, and can be classified by certain characteristics discussed below.

Horizontal and vertical mobility Movement between groups on the same social level is called *horizontal;* movement between different levels is called *vertical.* When a company transfers a plant manager from one large city to another, the manager moves from one social grouping to another but remains in the same relative social position or rank because his occupational status has remained the same. This is a case of horizontal mobility. Vertical mobility, by contrast, does involve a change in social rank, as when a salesperson is promoted to personnel manager or when an executive becomes a tramp.

Vertical mobility is either *upward* or *downward.* Persons moving to a higher level experience upward mobility, while persons moving to a lower level are downwardly mobile. Pitirim Sorokin called this *ascending and descending mobility,* or, more colorfully, *social climbing and social sinking.*[37] Climbing presumably takes some effort whereas social descent is perceived as passive, probably caused by forces outside one's control or by not making an active effort to retain one's position. High economic standing, status, and power are valued in the United States. Social climbing, then, is for the purpose of attaining generally valued social ends, while social sinking probably represents either the repudiation of these ends or the inability to attain or retain them.

Group mobility Not only *individuals* but also whole *groups* may experience upward or downward mobility. For instance, the early Christian clergy had relatively low social status because the Church was not recognized by the state. After the recognition given by Constantine the Great, the Church gained importance and prestige, and the clergy as a group experienced upward social mobility. To take a current example, there is evidence that scientists in the United States now have somewhat higher social status than they did in 1947; so we can say that scientists as a group have changed in status position in relation to other occupational groups.[38]

Status inconsistency An individual or a group may experience mobility along any one of the three dimensions of stratification (class, status, or power). A person may come into a great deal of money, for example, and still be denied higher social evaluation and access to power in the community. Mobility on a single dimension of stratification may result in *status inconsistency:* the situation of an individual or group that has inconsistent rankings in the stratification differentials. The inconsistency between ethnic status and class standing is a good example. A doctor may rank high in economic standing, but be accorded low social status because of his ethnicity.

Status inconsistency can have several effects. It may cause people to seek political change, as when members of groups of declining social significance, such as WASPS, join reactionary movements like the John Birch Society. It can also affect interpersonal relations. The person experiencing status inconsistency may interact with others on the basis of the highest status he possesses. But others may choose to interact with him in terms of his lowest status. A classic example is the case of the black doctor and the white laborer. If each operates out of a desire to establish himself or herself as socially superior, the doctor will strive to make occupational standing most important in the relationship and the laborer will try to make race primary. There is also evidence that status-inconsistent people commit suicide more often than others.[39]

Intragenerational and intergenerational mobility
Social mobility may be experienced by a single individual within his lifetime or by a family line over a number of generations. The former case is called *intragenerational* mobility and the latter, *intergenerational*. Sociologists have used the amount of intergenerational mobility in a given society as an indicator of the strength of social inheritance in that society and of how open or closed it is.

Measures of mobility: Amount and distance Both the *amount* of social mobility and the *distance* moved are measures of social mobility in a society. The proportion of persons moving up or down the socioeconomic scale indicates the amount of social mobility in a society. The amount or degree of their increases or decreases in income and property, social status, and power indicates the distance moved. Together, these two measures give us some idea of how open or closed a society is.

Social mobility in industrial societies The amount of social mobility varies from one society to another and within the same society at different periods.

"I just hope it drops in a decent neighbourhood."

© 1975 Punch (Rothco).

Aspirations for social mobility.

Factors like economic stability, prevailing ideologies, and the political situation may account for the variations. A classic study of social mobility in industrial nations done by Seymour Martin Lipset and Reinhard Bendix in 1959 revealed similarities in the amount of actual upward mobility between generations.[40] The authors suggest that similar occupational structures in industrialized societies coupled with the desire of individuals to rise in status are responsible for the similarities. Another cross-national analysis of intergenerational mobility, done by S. M. Miller, concludes that the United States, France, and the Soviet Union have similar upward mobility rates.[41] In only five of the seventeen nations Miller studied did upward mobility exceed downward mobility, however. These were the United States, France, Brazil, India, and the Soviet Union. Miller characterizes the United States and the Soviet Union as having a general pattern of upward mobility with limited downward mobility.

In regard to the United States alone, another study of over 20,000 American men found more upward than downward mobility both within and between generations. The distance moved, however, did not tend to be great. In general, sons were not far removed from their fathers, and persons at

Table 8-6   Distribution of family income in the U.S., 1947–1972 (percent)

Income rank	1947	1950	1955	1960	1965	1970	1972
Lowest fifth	5.1	4.5	4.8	4.8	5.2	5.4	5.4
Second fifth	11.8	11.9	12.2	12.2	12.2	12.2	11.9
Middle fifth	16.7	17.4	17.7	17.8	17.8	17.6	17.5
Fourth fifth	23.2	23.6	23.4	24.0	23.9	23.8	23.9
Highest fifth	43.3	42.7	41.8	41.3	40.9	40.9	41.4

the end of their occupational careers were not greatly advanced from their first occupations.[42]

Change in the distribution of income over the years is a good indicator of how equalitarian or stratified a society is and whether it is changing. Table 8-16 shows the distribution of income for each fifth of the U.S. population, beginning with the fifth that has the lowest income. You can see that there has been very little change in the distribution of income among segments of the population between 1947 and 1972. Using this indicator, we can say that the United States has become neither greatly more equalitarian nor more highly stratified in recent years.

Factors affecting social mobility A number of factors affect social mobility. Some of these operate on the societal level and some on the individual level. Those on the societal level affect the objective opportunities of all or some groups for upward mobility; those on the individual level affect who will benefit from the opportunities and actually achieve a higher social position. On the societal level, when the supply of highly ranked occupations expands or when the upper strata do not reproduce in sufficient numbers to fill the highly ranked positions, the possibilities for upward social mobility are increased. Migration of unskilled workers to cities may improve the competitive position of the native-born and established urban dwellers. Likewise, the degree of ethnic discrimination in the society hinders some groups and enhances the competitive positions of others. The state of the economy and the stability of the

government are also factors that can influence the opportunity structure.

On the individual level, such factors as *family size* and *sibling position* appear to affect occupational achievement and thus social mobility. Individuals who come from small families tend to achieve higher-status occupations than those coming from large families, even when the socioeconomic standing of the families is the same. Family size is important mainly because it affects the amount of education received. The higher educational attainments of children from smaller families may be a result of there being fewer persons to share in the financial, emotional, and time resources of the parents.

The *amount of education attained* is, as previously noted, a significant factor affecting socioeconomic status. Access to education can function as a gateway to upward social mobility. Earlier, we saw that attainment of a high level of education is related to ability as expressed through IQ scores and to the socioeconomic position of the family of origin. Educational attainment is also related to sex and race. Women are less likely than men and blacks are less likely than whites to receive a higher education.

Aspirations are important factors accounting for social mobility. If aspiration to achieve is lacking, all the opportunity and ability in the world will not advance the individual. There is evidence that members of the working class who do move upward in class ranking tend to be the most highly motivated.[43] Socialization in the home and by peers seems to be decisive. For example, one study found that among working-class boys with high IQs those whose families gave more direct encouragement to get a higher education in order to advance were the boys who did indeed intend to attend college.[44] Other research suggests that parents have the greatest effect on aspirations to attain a high level of education and a high-status occupation; friends have slightly less effect than parents; and teachers have less effect than friends.[45]

We have seen that there is by no means a perfect correlation between the socioeconomic standing of parents and that of their children in the United States and other industrialized nations. In other words, there is intergenerational social mobility, and much of it is upward. It is evident that there are opportunities to advance, although many factors affect the extent of these opportunities and who benefits from them.

Summary

Social differentiation is the practice of ranking individuals or groups on the basis of assigned criteria—criteria that are assigned socially a significance that they do not possess intrinsically. Social differentiation is sociologically important for two reasons: (1) it distributes life chances differentially among a population; (2) it is likely to influence almost every facet of life from fertility and mortality to taste in clothing and recreation.

There are three basic types of social differentiation: social stratification, sexual differentiation, and ethnic-racial differentiation. Sexual and ethnic-racial differentiation are important because they often determine what roles an individual is permitted to hold in the division of labor in society. Social stratification is related to division of labor because it determines the degree of reward an individual receives from a role and influences role allocation. These relationships may be summarized as follows: social differentiation in the form of stratification and sexual and ethnic-racial differentiation fixes roles in the division of labor, which, in turn, fixes basic social rewards, class standing, status, and power.

Social differentiation is different in preindustrial societies than in industrialized societies. Because they exist on a bare subsistence level, hunting and gathering societies are likely to show little differentiation beyond a sexual division of labor and some differences in prestige. Some differentiation based on economic inequality can occur in horticultural societies because their greater stability in food supply permits the accumulation of some economic surplus and the elaboration of ceremony. Agrarian societies may be expected to exhibit considerable differentiation based on greater surplus, refined technology, and a money economy. Industrial societies are characterized by new energy forms, advanced technology, occupational specialization, and considerable social differentiation.

Social stratification refers to social distinctions among persons based on differences in the stratification variables of class, status, and power. People may be ranked relative to one another with regard to any of these, and ranking is an essential element in stratification. Occupational positions may be ranked as well as individuals; and, in industrial societies at least, positions are likely to be accorded different rewards as well as different prestige. Why particular positions or kinds of positions are ranked as they are may be a matter of historical accident, although the functional interpretation of stratification argues that positional ranking is associated with the value of the position to the society as a whole and is necessary to insure that important activities will be fulfilled by persons with the talents or training to perform them. Social inheritance is an important part of all stratification systems. This is the transmission of social ranking from one generation to the next and is accomplished in the family, primarily through the transmission of unequal opportunities, education, and occupational position.

The term social position is used to indicate the class, status, and power ranking of an individual or social group. Class and status are commonly gauged by education, occupation, and income, in which it is possible to rank people individually or collectively. The three are deeply interrelated, the level attained on any one relating to levels attained on the others. The usual relationship among the three is that education in part determines occupation, which largely fixes income.

The reason that sociologists are deeply interested in social stratification in industrialized societies is that it strongly influences life chances. Stratification has serious consequences for a large variety of social phenomena, among them life and health, fertility, religious membership and behavior, political behavior, membership in voluntary associations, marital, sexual, and family behavior patterns, and social values.

Of the three stratification variables, *class* is the major stratification dimension in industrial societies. For this reason it has been of special interest to sociologists, and two of the classical theorists, Marx and Weber, paid considerable attention to it. Marx thought that all Western industrial societies tended to produce a split of class structure into two *objective* classes: the proletariat and the bourgeoisie. In time, Marx believed, the objective relations of class would produce subjective awareness, or *class consciousness,* among the proletariat, who would then recognize their exploitation by the bourgeoisie, unite, and overthrow the capitalist economic system to produce a classless society. Weber's theory of class is similar to Marx's in that class is defined as the collectivity of those with common market positions. It is more sophisticated, however, in recognizing the significance of skill in affecting bargaining power and the multiplicity of interest groups in the stratification system. Weber also denied Marx's emphasis on economic position as the sole dimension of stratification, insisting on the importance as well of status and power.

Status, another stratification variable, has to do with the *social honor* that others are willing to accord an individual, and it is manifested through life-style. Groups with similar life-styles based on status are called *status communities.* Class is importantly related to status in that it has a dominating influence on what one is able to consume, which, in turn, determines life-style.

Social *power,* the third stratification variable, refers to the ability to direct people and events. It is closely interwoven with class and status. The study of power is difficult because power is diffused and often invisible in application. Researchers have devised three approaches to this problem: the *reputational, positional,* and *decision-making.* Under the reputational approach, people involved in a community are asked who the influential or powerful members are. In the positional approach,

prominent institutional positions are studied. And in the decision-making approach, actual events are surveyed to determine who made the decisions that influenced them.

Such studies have led to two different concepts of the nature of social power: that it is (1) *elitist,* exercised by relatively small groups over the entire population concerned; or (2) *pluralistic,* diffused widely through the population concerned and exercised by many different groups. This could be called a debate over whether social power is centralized or decentralized. The question has not been settled, and the truth may be that power is more or less centralized with regard to some kinds of issues and decentralized with regard to others. In the United States, for example, great issues of foreign policy are probably decided in an essentially elitist manner, while great issues of domestic policy may have to respond to pluralistic pressures.

Stratification systems appear in three major varieties: *estate systems, caste systems,* and *class systems.* The principal dimensions by which the three may be compared have to do with the degree of social mobility possible (how much the system is open or closed to movement between groups or levels) and the extent to which social position is *ascribed* or *achieved.* The medieval estate system was based on land ownership; position in it was largely ascribed and the possibilities for mobility largely closed. In the traditional Indian caste system, social position is based on birth and thus is entirely ascribed; mobility is impossible. In a class system, social position is based on economic position and is to a considerable degree achieved (although never entirely so, owing to social inheritance); social mobility is more or less open.

The second major form of social differentiation is *ethnic-racial differentiation.* In societies where one or both of these operate, ethnic or racial status may influence stratification by determining role in the division of labor, as well as status and caste position. The significance and possible impact of ethnic differentiation may be seen by examining the social position of black people in the United States, where blacks are economically discriminated against and socially segregated.

Sexual differentiation, the third form of social differentiation, is also significant in all societies in regard to division of labor. In the United States, the proportion of women in the labor force has increased steadily in this century, as has the proportion of married women who work. Despite these facts, the distribution of women throughout the labor force differs markedly from that of men. Women tend to be concentrated in the lower white-collar occupations, traditionally female occupations such as nursing and elementary school teaching, and lower-paid industrial jobs. This distribution in part accounts for generally lower female incomes, but sexual discrimination also operates, since on the average women are paid less than men for the same jobs. There is still controversy over the effects of biological differences on the allocation and performance of social and occupational roles. Some real biological differences do appear to exist, but socialization to sex-role behavior exerts a very strong influence. Regardless of what biological material it has to start with, socialization produces sex differences.

The problem of *stability and change* within a stratification system is inevitably linked with the topic of *social mobility*. To the degree that a system is stable and unchanging, mobility will be inhibited. The chief factors making for stability in stratification systems are *direct inheritance* of wealth, property, or social position and the *inheritance of unequal opportunities*, particularly for education and occupational position. The latter is particularly apparent when we examine the *culture of poverty*, which acts upon people born into it to perpetuate their location there through generations. One of the major logical flaws in the functional theory of stratification is that it does not take into account the fact of the inheritance of unequal opportunity. The effect of direct inheritance and the inheritance of unequal opportunity is to produce stability in the stratification system, which means that existing rankings tend to be perpetuated and social mobility between ranks is reduced.

Social mobility may be *horizontal* (within a social rank) or *vertical* (between ranks). It may occur for *individuals* or for entire social *groups,* within a single lifetime or across generations (*intra* and *intergenerational* mobility). One frequent effect of individual mobility is to produce *status inconsistency*, the situation where an individual has experienced mobility along one of the three dimensions of stratification (class, status, or power) but has not

moved equally in the others, or where ethnic-racial or sexual status is inconsistent with attainment in other areas.

The amount and direction of social mobility is influenced by a number of factors, some societal and some individual. Societal factors include such things as the relative *proportion of different kinds of jobs in the labor force* and changes in that distribution, *geographic migration, prejudice and discrimination,* and the state of the *economy*. Individual factors include such things as *family size, education,* and *aspiration.*

Review Questions

1. Describe some of the dominant values and outlooks on life found in the different social classes discussed in this chapter: upper, upper middle, lower middle, working and lower classes.

2. Compare some of the patterns typical of a working-class marriage and family with those in a middle-class counterpart. Note such things as power structure, sex role, socialization, family size, and punishment of children.

3. Contrast the social differentiation found in different types of societies: hunting and gathering, horticultural, agrarian, and industrial. What role is played by specialization?

4. Explain the three basic systems of stratification discussed in this chapter: estate, caste, and class. How open or closed is each? How much mobility occurs in each?

5. Karl Marx has been called an economic determinist. What does this mean? How was Marx's perspective different from others, such as Max Weber?

Suggestions for Research

1. As the most pervasive sociological variable, social class and its consequences may be studied by looking at television programs. Many situation comedies such as "All in the Family" and "Upstairs, Downstairs" carry themes of social class. Select one or two such programs and watch these over a period of several weeks. Describe the role of social class in the life-styles of the persons in these shows. Then, make a personal evaluation of how social class is treated by the producers and writers.

2. Devote a term paper to studying sexual differentiation and inequality. Consider discrimination against women in education, in the occupational arena, in income and

government benefits such as social security payments. On what are such inequalities founded? Are the stereotyped differences between the sexes biologically based? One rich source for this project is Judith Bardwick's *Readings on the Psychology of Women.*

3.   India has long been used as an example of a caste society in which persons are born into rigidly stratified groups and mobility is considered improper. Study India's caste system. Is change evident in how the different castes have coexisted over time? How do persons in the lower castes accept their social position? What role is played by religion in justifying the caste system?

4.   Social differentiation varies greatly, depending on the degree of complexity in a society. Study differentiation in a simple society such as a hunting and gathering band or a horticultural society. Which persons enjoy wealth, prestige, and power? How is differentiation different than in the U.S.? You may want to turn to anthropological ethnographies for your data.

5.   Although sociologists are aware of many inconsistencies, most agree that persons in similar social classes or economic positions share similar life-styles. Select one social stratum for study: upper, upper middle, lower middle, working or lower class. Describe such things as consumption behavior, leisure patterns, religious behavior, values, and outlook on life.

CHAPTER 9
MINORITY GROUP RELATIONS

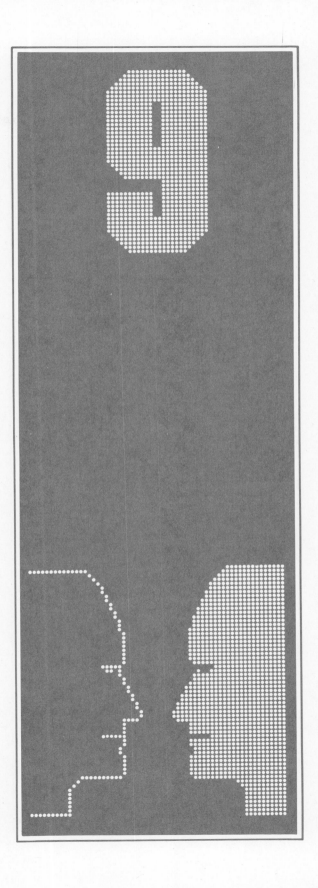

Navy Is Enlisting Filipino Servants

Washington—The Navy, continuing a practice that dates back to the American Colonial days in the Philippines, will recruit 1,860 Filipinos this year as servants for its officers.

In the process, the Navy obtains men who are willing to serve as stewards, messboys, houseboys and servants for the officers—jobs that both white and black American recruits have been reluctant to take.

The practice also provides free military servants for the White House. About 50 Filipino messboys are assigned by the Navy to work in the White House dining room, aboard the Presidential yacht Sequoia and at the Presidential retreat in Maryland. At times, the messboys are required to work at private parties of White House officials.

New York Times, November 24, 1974

Job Discrimination, 10 Years Later

Last September, the Jersey Central Power and Light Company decided to lay off 200 employees in a cost-cutting program. It asked a Federal Court to decide which of two contracts took precedence, its collective bargaining agreement with locals of the International Brotherhood of Electrical Workers (with its strict seniority provisions) or a contract signed with the E.E.O.C. (Equal Employment Opportunities Commission) last December in which the utility promised to bring its minority and female work force representation up to 15 percent.

New York Times, November 10, 1974

Requiem for the American Dream

And Jimmie D. said, "I tell the guys on the job people ought to live together—I'm not better than him, he's not better than me. And they call me a nigger-lover. I don't want my kids bussed—and they call me a racist. So what am I?"

Village Voice, November 7, 1974

The three newspaper reports quoted above illustrate several themes concerning minority group relations in the United States in the 1970s. The navy recruits officers' servants from a former American colonial dependency, the Philippines, because American citizens, black and white, are reluctant to serve in such a capacity. In the second account, a great corporation finds itself caught between two measures designed to protect minority groups: a law providing collective bargaining protection for industrial workers and a contract with the Equal Employment Opportunities Commission providing more jobs for racial and ethnic minorities and women. In the third account, a man on the street finds himself bewildered by inconsistent attitudes among his peers. Together the three stories are a montage of the American racial and ethnic scene.

The sociologist viewing these reports will read into them a great deal more than appears on the surface. The first story, for example, raises several questions: Are there racial or ethnic segments of the labor market—jobs somehow defined as particularly appropriate for members of specific racial or ethnic groups? How does such assignment of labor come about? How does a group come to occupy a "place" in society that others deem appropriate for it? Can such placement be altered? How?

The second story poses the dilemma of conflicting rights to employment and job security. How are such problems to be resolved? Indeed, how could these rights have come into conflict in the first place? What permitted the seniority systems of the labor unions to exclude women and racial and ethnic minorities so that equal employment measures conflict with union-oriented protective legislation? How do such seniority systems perpetuate racial or other inequalities?

The third quotation concerns a personal dilemma, but again reflects social issues as well. How can Jimmie D.'s work environment and his home environment operate on such incompatible principles? What choices are actually open to him, and what costs will he pay for the ones he makes? Why are those the only choices he has? Which ones is he likely to make and why? What is the probable shape of his future and that of his children?

In this chapter, we will explore a vitally important, and therefore an emotionally charged, aspect of the social structure of the United States: its racial and ethnic composition and the relationships between minority groups socially defined by race and ethnicity. Each of the issues related to the newspaper stories will be discussed, plus a variety of others. We will concentrate on racial and ethnic relations in the United States because of their fundamental importance in our society. However, the basic principles underlying American minority group relations can to some extent be generalized and applied to other societies, even though each society's racial and ethnic composition is strongly influenced by its own history. Thus, studying the American experience can help us understand minority group relations in, say, South Africa, the Soviet Union, or Canada.

Most Americans have difficulty putting even the American picture together. How does their situation fit in with—or differ from—the experience of other groups in the United States or elsewhere? Why does ethnic and racial discrimination reappear each generation despite attempts to eliminate it? Why is there so much conflict? These are questions the sociology of minority group relations attempts to answer.

But first it is crucial to define the concepts sociologists use to analyze racial relations: minority group, ethnic group, and race. We will pay special attention to what race is and is not because it is so important a social phenomenon in the United States and in certain other nations in the world. After that, we will turn to the essence of minority group relations in the United States: structured social inequality. Then we will discuss the major racial and ethnic groups in the United States and, finally, consider how best to describe American society with regard to minority group relations.

Key Concepts

Minority Group

The essence of the sociological understanding of a minority group is that it is a group that is *socially dominated* by another. What a minority is may be distinguished by other dimensions, such as size, citizenship, culture, or religion, and these are important determining characteristics; but the ultimate meaning of minority group status is social subordination.

The *size* of a group is one obvious way people define what is and what isn't a minority group. According to this criterion, a minority is a small group; it is "minor" in comparison to groups with more members. But the size of a group is not nearly as important in determining what a minority group is as are other considerations. In South Africa, for example, the native black population is sociologically a minority group, although blacks constitute about 75 percent of the total population.

Minority group status is sometimes determined by reference to *citizenship.* If minority status is the result of birth in another country, majority group status is achieved when people become citizens. But the difficulties some minority groups face in the United States do not cease once they achieve citizenship and the privileges that accompany it, such as the right to vote. Minority group status is more than a legal issue.

A distinctive way of life, or *culture,* is another feature that may distinguish minorities from other groups in a heterogeneous society. Minorities are defined as groups that are culturally different from the dominant group; they form subcultures. People who define minority groups this way may expect them to disappear once minorities adopt the culture of the so-called majority groups. But this viewpoint assumes that heterogeneous societies have unified cultures and that the majority of their citizens practice and believe in them. This assumption is open to serious question in countries such as the United States, where instead of one culture there are many. If we defined minority groups in this way, we would find no majority groups.

Minority groups can also be distinguished by the criterion of *religious affiliation.* Religion and national origin often overlap: Puerto Ricans and Italians tend to be Roman Catholics; the English tend to be Protestants. The association between national origins and religious affiliation is strong, and religion has often been used as a means of characterizing minorities. When we speak of Anglo-Saxons in the United States, we implicitly refer to Protestants, in speaking of the Irish, we usually imply Catholicism.

Size, citizenship, culture, and religion are all

features that can make a group a minority in comparison with some other group or groups, and if we looked only for these characteristics, we would call every group a minority group. But by doing so, we would miss what is crucial about being a minority group. The essential *sociological* feature of being a minority group is being *disadvantaged in power,* not having the resources or ability to do things according to one's desire. A sociological minority cannot choose widely among alternative kinds of work, cultural expression, or politics, because it has little power in relation to the social majority in society, regardless of its relative numerical size.

To make the definition more explicitly sociological, a **minority group** is any social category of individuals that is dominated socially, politically, or economically by those who control the institutions of a society. Interestingly enough, the characteristics of the dominant group are often the basis for singling out a given group as a minority, although the social characteristics of the minority will appear to be the criteria used. What this apparent paradox means is that if we know the racial, religious, or ethnic characteristics of the dominant group, we can predict that any group not sharing those characteristics may be singled out for treatment as a minority. In the United States the socially dominant group has been white, Protestant, Anglo-Saxon, and male. Those in the population who do not share these characteristics may be treated as minorities because they are not white, not Protestant, not Anglo-Saxon, or not male.

A minority group is one dominated socially, politically, or economically by those who control the society's institutions. Consequences of minority status: black and white residential neighborhoods in Fort Myers, Florida.

Ethnic Group

When we think about minorities, it is useful to distinguish between ethnic groups and races. An **ethnic group** is a population socially identified according to cultural criteria, such as language, religion, or national origin. The social identification of ethnicity may be either imposed by others or self-generated from within the group in question. In the United States, any adherent of Judaism is likely to be classified by others as a Jew, that is, a member of a single ethnic group. In Israel, important distinctions are drawn among Sabras (native-born Israelis), Sephardim (Jews of Spain and Portigal and their descendants), and Ashkenazim (Jews of western, central, and eastern European origins).

Another way of making the point would be to say that ethnics are people who share a common cultural origin, real or imagined. If people think of themselves as having a common origin, they are defining themselves as ethnics. If others perceive them that way, they are being defined as ethnic. To the extent that a fourth-generation Italian-American man identifies with Italian ancestry and cultural practices, for example, he is emphasizing his ethnic heritage, although he might be unable to speak the language, hate Italian food, and have anglicized the spelling of his name. But even if he personally felt no tie with Italian culture, he might still be treated by others as if he did.

Race

The phenomenon of **race** is widely misunderstood, mainly because, in the Western world at least, it has a peculiar double character. There are popular views of what race is and what it means and a biological definition of race. The popular concepts are largely wrong. In studying minority groups, sociologists must consider both the biological aspects of race and the popular—social—interpretations of race.

The biological meaning of race   The term *race* first appeared in scientific literature in 1749. At first, skin color was used as an index for classifying human differences. But biologists soon realized that skin color was not a sufficient criterion for classifying races because there is no sharp dividing line between one color and another. In looking for other characteristics that they could use to define racial types, scientists developed categories that included the shape of the head, lips, and nose, the texture and shape of hair, and the predominant blood type. But with most of these characteristics, too, there is no clear division between one group and another.

Biologists have now recognized that racial classification based on physical type is arbitrary—that is, it depends on the criteria chosen, and different scientists choose different criteria. Some biologists define three or four races, some twenty to thirty, depending on which characteristics they use to construct racial categories.

However, underlying all these racial classifications is the basic biological definition of race, perhaps best stated by the noted population geneticist and biologist Theodosius Dobzhansky. Dobzhansky defines races as "Mendelian (interbreeding) populations which differ in the incidences of some genetic variants in their gene pools."[1] Put more simply, this means: All human beings belong to one species, because they share the same *basic* genetic makeup (which is what allows them to interbreed). But different populations of human beings show different amounts of *specific* genetic

minority group: any social category of individuals dominated socially, politically, or economically by those who control the social institutions of a society. The minority group may be distinguished by size, citizenship, culture or religion, but the essence of minority status is social subordination.

ethnic group: a population socially identified according to cultural criteria, such as language, religion, or national origin.

race: technically and biologically, Mendelian (interbreeding) populations that differ in the incidence (frequency) of some genetic variants in their gene pools. More simply, a race is a population in which certain genetic characteristics appear with greater frequency than they do among other populations.

"My daughter tells me you're ethnic. I assume this means that your children will also be ethnic."

New Yorker, April 21, 1973. Drawing by Handelsman; © 1973 The New Yorker Magazine, Inc.

variants, such as differences in skin color and other physical characteristics. Thus, if you pick a set of physical characteristics that occur variably, some groups exhibit the collection more frequently than others. For example, light eyes, light, wavy hair, light skin, and narrow noses and lips occur among all people, everywhere. But they are found occurring together, *in combination,* more frequently among the so-called white race than among other peoples.

The difficulty, of course, as was shown above, is deciding which characteristics can best be used to categorize races. It is easy to see that if scientists have trouble defining race, the public is likely to hold confused and wrong ideas about race. And indeed popular views of race are largely inaccurate.

Popular misconceptions Among the many erroneous interpretations of race, none is more pervasive than the tendency to call ethnic, cultural, and linguistic groups racial groups. This is clearly seen in Nazi mythologies about the Aryan and Jewish ''races.'' Neither of these groups is a biological category, which became apparent during the Nazi regime when Jews were identified by clothing that displayed the Star of David, which they were required to wear. Since they had no unique physical characteristics, an observable basis for discrimination had to be constructed.

Perhaps as widespread as the error attributing racial characteristics to ethnic, cultural, or linguistic groups is the error ascribing particular attributes to all members of given racial groups. For example, whites are often thought to be mechanically gifted and warlike; Asians weak-eyed and crafty; and blacks emotionally childlike, lazy, stupid. There is no factual basis for any such beliefs.

A third popular error concerns the nature of race itself. In common American usage, the word *race* is often used as an equivalent to the biological term *species,* and the different races are assumed to be as biologically distinct as different species of animals, say, dogs and cats. (It is probably this misconception that permits the second error mentioned above, the attribution of individual characteristics to all members of a racial group.) This idea, too, is wrong. All human beings, as we said previously, are members of a single species, *Homo sapiens.*

The sociological concept of the social race The biological and social components of the concept of race outlined above provide the basis for the sociological study of race. Sociologically, race is interesting because physical differences, defined either biologically or popularly, are often used as grounds for social differentiation, prejudice, and discrimination. What is important to the sociologist is the way races are defined by *society.* For the sociologist, the significance of racial concepts is not their scientific accuracy, but their social reality: whether people believe in and act on their concepts of race.

For this reason, many sociologists have adopted and defined a category called the **social race.** A social race is a population whose members share certain inherited physical traits by which they are socially identified. The essence of this definition is that it is *social.* Thus, skin, eye, and hair color are considered socially significant as indicating race membership, while other inherited physical traits, such as a tendency to freckles, are not. We speak of races of a given skin color, but do not talk about a freckled race. Like the biological definition of race, the definition of a particular social race depends on the criteria chosen by the definers—in this case, society. For the remainder of this chapter, when we refer to race, we will use the term in the sociological sense of social race.

Although racial and ethnic groups may both constitute minorities, they are often treated quite differently, as we can see in the United States. In order to understand why this happens and how such differences are created, it is necessary to look at the ways in which American society is organized.

Structured Social Inequality

Social inequality means that some persons or groups have greater access to the rewards and benefits of social life; they are privileged. Privilege and inequality are expressed in various ways: politically, economically, and socially. We are most familiar with inequalities and privileges among individuals. All of us know, for example, that the Kennedy and Rockefeller children are born into positions of almost unlimited opportunity. They may be no more competent and ambitious than anyone else, but they have access to resources and opportunities that most people can only dream of. This is how inequality among individuals is expressed, but the notion of inequality and privilege goes beyond individuals.

When social inequality is built into societies and affects entire social groups, it is structured. *Structured social inequality* is the creation of inequalities in life chances by the social organization of a society without regard to the capabilities of individuals. All societies are structured along *some* lines, and all establish basic divisions among their members. The criteria used to make these divisions differ according to what is valued in a particular society. In feudal Europe, and in modern England, there is a division that separates the aristocracy from commoners. This basic division is built into British society, and members of the aristocracy have certain special privileges and rewards. A commoner can only share in these rewards by earning them; but for the aristocracy, they are an inherited privilege.

Some societies are organized and structured on the basis of racial or ethnic ancestry. These societies are organized so that one race (or ethnic group) occupies a superior position and others are subordinated. Physical and cultural characteristics are the basis of participation and exclusion. When race, usually signified by skin color, is the factor determining subordination, **racism** is the organizing principle of the society. Currently, the most obvious example of such a society is the apartheid system in South Africa. The African population occupies a subservient position politically and economically. One set of rules exists for the white population and different sets for the black and mulatto populations. In an economically stratified society, privileged members may acquire or lose the resources that have placed them above the rest of the population. But in a racially stratified society members cannot change their skin color, the basis of reward or deprivation, and so they cannot change their position in society. In South Africa, neither the whites nor the blacks can change their positions, because racial divisions are part of the basic organization of South African society, a closed system with inescapable effects.

social race: a population whose members share certain inherited physical traits by which they are socially identified.

racism: discrimination based on "racial characteristics," usually skin color.

Jews wearing the Star of David in Nazi Germany. The Nazis were unable to distinguish Jews from other people on the basis of the "racial" characteristics they believed in. Thus they had to resort to artificial distinctions, principally the yellow Star of David sewn on clothing.

'Waars U Pas?'—Black Man's Constant Dread

The black man in South Africa dreads being stopped by the white policeman who demands in Afrikaans, "Waars u pas?"—Where's your passbook?

Every black who lives in an area "prescribed" by the government—in effect, nearly 90 per cent of the nation—must carry his multipaged passbook at all times.

Issued at the age of 16, it contains the bearer's name, address, sex, photograph, vaccination record, government identity number, and proof of tax payments.

His employer must sign it monthly. It also must include stamped approval to live outside one of the nation's 10 small tribal homelands.

The passbook is the cornerstone of the detailed pass laws by which South Africa's 4 million whites exercise rigid control over its 18 million nonwhites.

Thus it is unquestionably the most immediate—and most deeply hated—symbol of white authority.

Running afoul of the complicated law is not difficult. If the passbook is missing or not in perfect order, a black person faces a trial as short as 30 seconds and a jail term as long as six months.

Police records show more than 500,000 pass law violations a year. It is estimated that since 1950, there have been more than 10 million arrests.

Chicago Tribune, June 27, 1976. Reprinted courtesy of the Chicago Tribune. Photo by Ernie Cox, Jr.

Whites in South Africa do not have to carry passes.

In each of the above examples, privilege and inequality are organizing principles of the societies described. Participation and reward are distributed in such societies in much the same way as a playground teeter-totter operates. For one group in the system to be elevated or rewarded, another is pushed down or depressed. It is difficult for a person with characteristics of either the privileged or the oppressed group to escape the mechanism. Privilege and inequality are not a function of individual determination, but a reflection of group position.

Group Subordination in the United States

Every measure of socioeconomic status indicates that certain racially defined groups are consistently at the bottom of the American ladder. The *structural* basis for this group subordination lies, at least in part, in the history of the United States as a host nation to various immigrant groups. All host nations establish a pattern of acceptance or rejection of newly arriving groups. One way to understand the past and present subordinate position of various racial and ethnic groups in the United States is to distinguish between the *absorption* and *inclusion* of those groups.

Absorption versus inclusion In an ideal sense, *inclusion* implies that incoming groups can participate fully in developing new cultural, political, and economic realities. But rather than participating equally in the creation of a new society, racial and ethnic groups in the United States tended to be *absorbed* into a preexisting Anglo-Saxon structure. In all cases, the dominant groups in the host society controlled the absorption of the incoming groups so that preexisting social relationships and organizations would be altered as little as possible. Absorption ranged, with varying degrees of success, from dispersion throughout the various layers of society to total subordination to the position of slave.

The differences between racial and white ethnic groups In the United States, white ethnic and racial groups have experienced widely different degrees of absorption. In the early years of this nation, there was no intention of fully including the African slaves within the fabric of American society. A graphic example of this is the section in the U.S. Constitution, now superseded, stating that black slaves were to be enumerated as three fifths of a man for the purpose of apportioning representatives. While racial groups were placed in a subordinate position based on physical type, white ethnic groups were placed in a subordinate status based on economic position.

The implications of these differences between racial and white ethnic groups have been developed by Robert Blauner.[2] He compares the experiences of these groups along three dimensions: the nature of *entry* into the dominant society; the experience within the *labor market*; and the degree of *control exerted over the entering group's culture.*

Entry into society   The most obvious difference in the experience of racial and white ethnic groups is how they *entered* American society. Most racial minorities—blacks, Native Americans (American Indians), and Chicanos (or Mexican-Americans)— were brought or absorbed into the United States involuntarily. (We treat Chicanos as a racial group because that is the way they have popularly been defined in the United States, even though the U.S. Census classifies them as white.)

Black Africans were taken by force from their homelands and brought to the United States as slaves. During the eighteenth and nineteenth centuries, the Native Americans and Chicanos were forcibly incorporated into this country by westward territorial expansion. For both groups, entry into the dominant society was involuntary and was experienced by the group in question more or less en masse. By contrast, most European white immigrants entered the United States voluntarily and individually, or at least in small groups such as the family. Their differences in entry into American society contributed significantly to the different treatment later accorded these groups.

Labor market   Racial and white ethnic groups were also treated differently in the labor market. Europeans in the United States found themselves in a developing capitalist economy and could enter

relatively freely into the wage-labor system. As the American economy developed, so did their mobility and occupational prestige. Racial minorities were treated differently and worked in other sectors of the labor market. The involuntary, unpaid labor done by slaves is the clearest example of this difference. A somewhat mixed case would be provided by the early Chinese immigrants, who were often brought over en masse by labor contractors to work for specific employers at fixed wages.

As a consequence of slavery, the black American was not absorbed into the economy until the beginning of the twentieth century. Slavery also led to the development of a dual labor market, a labor market split into two kinds of employment. In the advanced sectors of the labor market— industrial work—entry was voluntary, wages were paid, and there was some mobility across occupational lines. At the opposite end of the spectrum, in the least developed sectors of the economy, labor was often not voluntary, wages were not paid or were very low, and there was little or no opportunity for mobility. Until recently, superior positions in the voluntary labor market have been reserved for the white population. Throughout the periods of increased immigration and absorption of white Europeans into the voluntary labor market, the society largely excluded other racial groups from participating in the advanced sectors of the economy.

Control of culture   Another major difference in the experience of these groups is the amount of control they were allowed to exercise over their lives and culture. The white European immigrants faced prejudice, discrimination, and ridicule, but they were allowed to maintain a sanctuary where they could express their cultural traditions. This was the ethnic community. Ethnic newspapers, schools, churches, and theaters grew in these communities; and life, culture, and people were respected within them, if not by the dominant society. The situation of racial minorities was different. Their culture was not tolerated; it was attacked. Slave families were often forcibly dislocated, and slaves were prohibited from speaking their native languages. Both slaves and Native Americans were prohibited from practicing their religions. Native Americans and

A Biography

Crow, James ("Jim"). (No photograph available.)
Born about 1870 (exact date and place uncertain).
Nationality: American; originally southern.
Parents: unknown, but multiple, white, Protestant,
probably of Anglo-Saxon stock. Education: public
institutions. Widely traveled, Crow became a
turn-of-the-century man of affairs. Always
particularly active in law as well as national and
local politics, he also engaged in medicine, the
arts, science, education, religion, sports and
entertainment, industry and labor in addition to
long service in the armed forces. By middle-age
his influence had been felt on almost every
aspect of the American scene and there were few
places in the United States which he had not
visited. His death has been prematurely
announced on many occasions but latest reports
indicate that, although enfeebled with age and
practically incapacitated by *civil rightis,* he is still
alive and endeavoring to keep up with his lifelong
pursuits. For detailed biographical information,
see C. Vann Woodward, *The Strange Career of
Jim Crow* (New York: Oxford University Press,
1955).

Chicanos were forced off ancestral homelands that often had deep cultural and religious significance.

These are the structural bases of group subordination in the United States. They represent the lines along which American society is divided. Since these divisions are basic to the social structure of American society, they are re-created each generation. In this respect, subordination of racial and ethnic groups is reproduced over time. The mechanisms through which this occurs are discussed below.

Mechanisms of Subordination

Americans typically express great concern about prejudice when confronted with the persistence of racial subordination. But prejudice is only one mechanism of subordination. Discrimination, stereotypes, and segregation are other ways in which minority subordination is maintained.

Prejudice   What is prejudice? Sociologists generally accept the classic definition of Gordon Allport, understanding prejudice as a hostile attitude toward an individual because he is a member of a particular group.[3] The hostility is based on false beliefs or misjudgments about the group as a whole and attributes beliefs held about the group to any member of it. Because prejudice is an attitude, not an act, and is aimed at individuals, we cannot explain subordination in terms of prejudice alone. Groups do not become socially subordinated only because people hold hostile feelings about them. Groups become socially subordinated when people *do something* about their feelings. Nevertheless, prejudice is pervasive enough to merit further consideration here.

Prejudice is often described as being irrational because it involves misjudgments and prejudgments. Many Americans feel that these incorrect judgments are the heart of racial and ethnic subordination in the United States. Gunnar Myrdahl's *An American Dilemma,* one of the classic studies of race relations, takes this view.[4]

It has also been held that racial prejudice is a pathology, or sickness, and that if this psychological malfunction is eliminated, racial subordination will disappear.[5] Another way of looking at prejudice is to see it not as a sickness, but as a reflection of the position of one's group in society. Since society is organized around the distribution of rewards, any gains racial and ethnic minorities achieve may very well mean that the dominant community will lose some privileges. Thus, resistance to equality need not be irrational. It may reflect, instead, the height of rationality in a situation of structured inequality. It may even be that people sometimes develop prejudices against others in order to justify exploiting them.

Discrimination   When people *act* on prejudiced attitudes, their behavior is called discrimination. While prejudice is an attitude, discrimination is actual behavior. The distinction is important. It clarifies the difference between inequality in thought and inequality in deed. In many cases the two are linked together, but prejudiced attitudes are neither a necessary nor a sufficient condition of discriminatory acts. Thus, an employer might be prejudiced against members of a minority but at the same time be unwilling to risk discriminating against them by paying them less than others for fear of legal retaliation. Or an employer might pay less if he believed he could get away with it, simply as an economic measure and without any personal feelings of hostility toward the group involved.

Stereotypes   Like prejudice, a stereotype is a belief or attitude. Specifically, a stereotype is an exaggerated belief about a group. (Prejudice is based on stereotypes.) A stereotype may be either positive or negative and is used to justify behavior toward the particular group involved. In a stereotype, specific individual characteristics, such as laziness or dishonesty, lust or greed, are attributed to all members of the group. Stereotypes of racial and ethnic groups have been widespread: Jews are money-hungry; Italians are criminal; the Irish are drunkards; blacks are lazy. People often use stereotypes as a justification for establishing a separate place for specific groups in society.

Segregation   *Segregation* means holding apart, or keeping separate. Social segregation exists in two forms. **De jure segregation** is segregation sanctioned by law. **De facto segregation** is simply segregation that exists without legal sanction. De jure segregation existed in the American South as recently as the 1950s. When in 1954 the Supreme Court ruled that segregation in publicly supported educational facilities was unconstitutional, many Americans thought the problem of racial subordination had ended. But de facto segregation of racial minorities has not ended. A recent study based on census data indicates that the situation of racial minorities relative to that of whites has not been dramatically altered in many areas of life by the Supreme Court ruling on education.[6] Segregation in both the labor force and in residential housing continues much as before, although some changes have occurred as a consequence of recent court rulings and decisions. Thus, in most cities, the degree of residential segregation by race has not altered much; and although blacks have made some inroads into professional occupations, managerial jobs are still largely denied them, and except for the college-educated, they are nowhere represented proportionally in the upper-status occupations. This de facto segregation exists and continues because of the structural basis of group subor-

prejudice: hostility toward an individual because he is a member of a particular group, resulting from the attribution to him of false or mistaken beliefs about the group as a whole.

discrimination: acting or behaving on the basis of prejudice. Prejudice is an attitude, a belief or set of beliefs; acting it out in real life toward real individuals is discrimination.

stereotype: an exaggerated belief about a group, arising from the attribution of specific individual characteristics, such as laziness or dishonesty, to all members of the group. Prejudice is based on stereotyping.

de jure segregation: segregation required or permitted by law. (Normally used only with regard to *racial* segregation.) The best-known American example is school segregation before 1954.

de facto segregation: segregation as a consequence of fact or circumstance rather than law (normally used only with regard to racial segregation). The best-known American example is racial segregation in the schools resulting from the neighborhood school concept in public education. If children are required to attend only schools in their own neighborhoods and the neighborhoods are racially segregated as a result of *residential* segregation, the schools will also be segregated *in fact* even though the law may not require it.

dination; it is a by-product of a group's position in society.

The Social Consequences of Structured Social Inequality

Structured social inequality has two important consequences. The most obvious is the subordination of certain groups. The second consequence is usually neglected: dominant groups gain privileges from their position. Subordination and privilege, then, are consequences of structured social inequality. We can see these consequences more clearly by looking at the costs for racial minorities in the United States.

Life chances for racial minorities are less than for members of the dominant white society. Perhaps the greatest cost is the most crucial of life chances: life itself. The average life expectancy of blacks is six years less than for whites. Native Americans have the lowest life expectancy (forty-

Copyright, 1972, G. B. Trudeau. Distributed by Universal Press Syndicate.

Stereotyping.

seven years) of any group in American society. The rate of tuberculosis is three times higher in the black population than in the white, and the infant mortality rate among blacks is six times the national average.[7] In sum, the expectation of life itself is better if one is born with white skin.

The quality of life is also affected by minority status. Very often, the position of subordinate groups is considered a reflection of their lack of educational achievement. But the median education of blacks has dramatically increased from 5.8 years in 1940 to 9.9 in 1970.[8] We would expect, then, that their educational efforts would benefit or increase their life chances, but they have not done so proportionally. One study indicates that inner-city blacks with a high school diploma earn, on the average, only seventeen cents more an hour than white high school dropouts.[9] This study also shows that additional education from grade 9 to grade 12 has no effect on the probability of unemployment for blacks. But for the white inner-city resident, this additional education reduces the probability of unemployment by 3.5 percent.

The way racial minorities are distributed in the labor force is another consequence of social inequality. Harold M. Baron and Bennett Hymer maintain that racial minorities exist in three distinct sectors of the labor market.[10] The first of these is the *standard labor market*. It is dominated by the white population but includes some workers from racially defined groups. The second division is the *racial service sector*. This includes occupations such as domestic and field workers and a number of other jobs almost always performed by racial minorities. The third sector is often called the *surplus labor sector.* This includes a large number of black, brown, and red people who are either unemployed or underemployed. During times of economic growth and prosperity, they are called upon to fill positions in the labor force. At other times they are unemployed.

Who profits from the way racial minorities are distributed in the labor market? There are at least two views on the subject. The first maintains that it is in the best interests of employers to end discrimination in the labor force. By allowing discrimination, employers are forced to pay higher wages than efficiency dictates. In this view, discrimination is a disadvantage to the employer and works to the advantage of the white worker.[11] A second view argues that racial subordination provides gains not for individual employees, but rather for the owners of businesses. Michael Reich maintains that the divisiveness of race weakens the bargaining power of all workers. Using data from forty-eight metropolitan areas, he argues that racism does not help the white worker very much because it leads to unequal income distribution among whites. Reich maintains that the most direct benefit of racial subordination is increased income for "the richest one percent of white families."[12] Though these two views conflict as to who specifically profits from racial subordination, they agree that profit and privilege coexist.

Minority Reactions to Dominance

Minority groups may respond to domination in several ways. According to the sociologist Louis Wirth, there are four basic types of reaction to domination: *pluralist, assimilationist, secessionist,* and *militant.*[13] In addition, minority groups often form subcultures in response to the dominant culture.

Pluralist response   Sometimes minority groups want to keep parts of their culture that are important to them. They want a share of social power, but they do not want to blend in with other groups. They wish to maintain what is distinctive about themselves. This is a *pluralist* response to domination. Pluralists want to be both part of a larger society *and* unique. The American Indian Movement is a current example.

Assimilationist response   When members of a minority group wish to give up what is distinctive about them and become just like the majority, they take an *assimilationist* position. An example is the Urban League.

Secessionist response   When members of a minority group try to remove themselves from society, they adopt a *secessionist* response to domination. Sometimes it is called *separatism* or *nationalism.* Unlike the pluralist and assimilationist, both of whom wish to be part of the society, the secessionist wants nothing to do with it. The idea is literally to secede, or separate, from the dominant group, as is urged, for example, by the Republic of New Africa.

Militant response   Minority group members who attempt to transform or change societies in basic and thoroughgoing ways are responding to domination in a *militant* fashion. This kind of response is also called radical or revolutionary. Unlike secessionists, the militant wants to stay in society and change it. But unlike the assimilationist and pluralist, who also want to stay in society, although on different terms, the militant insists that the situation be altered drastically. The Puerto Rican activist group The Young Lords is an example.

These four categories help us see the different ways minority groups respond to their situation. But unless we say some other things, the categories are misleading. For one thing, minority groups do not respond to domination in unified or cohesive ways. Each of the four responses may be expressed in a given minority group at the same time. Although it is probably true that certain kinds of responses are more appropriate for some groups than others, no one minority group has a monopoly on a particular type of response. During different periods in a minority group's history, certain responses are more appropriate than others, but we can find examples of each type of response during a group's history. The Black Muslims, for example, began as a secessionist movement, went through a militant period, and now, since the death of Elijah Muhammad, appear to be moving toward pluralism.

But the key to understanding how minority groups handle domination is the dominant society, for how minority groups cope with their situation is largely influenced by what they are *allowed* to do. A modern example makes this point dramatically. Various federal, state, and municipal agencies effectively destroyed the militant response of Black Panthers by killing some of their leaders, driving others into exile, and jailing the rest. At the same time the national government encouraged pluralism among black people by offering financial aid to organizations that were politically acceptable to it. The ways in which minority groups come to grips with domination, then, are heavily influenced by circumstances beyond their control.

Minority subcultures   A subculture, as we saw in Chapter 3, is a set of unique customs, rituals, and ways of associating that make a group different from the larger society and other groups in it. Often, as in the case of ethnic minorities, these customs are rooted in a foreign cultural tradition. But in many cases, the customs are mostly developed in response to conditions imposed on the group by the dominant elements of society. The Italians who reached American shores at the turn of the century were often as strange to each other as they were to the Americans who met them. They spoke different dialects, came from feuding villages and families,

Hoover Feared Panther Meals
Richard Philbrick

J. Edgar Hoover viewed the Black Panther Party's free breakfast program for children as a threat to attempts by the FBI to "neutralize the Black Panther Party and destroy what it stands for," a jury learned Friday in Federal District Court.

The late FBI director's opinion of the program was disclosed in an official memorandum by Hoover which was read to a six-member jury hearing evidence in the $47-million suit against the city and various agencies and individuals stemming from a Dec. 4, 1969 police raid on a Black Panther apartment on the West Side.

Fred Hampton, Illinois head of the party, and Mark Clark, a Panther organizer from Peoria, were killed in the raid and some other occupants of the apartment were injured or wounded by gunfire.

Hoover's 1969 memorandum to several dozen FBI field offices was one of a number of government documents surrendered to attorneys for the plaintiffs in the case, survivors of the raid and relatives of Hampton and Clark.

Hoover instructed FBI agents to investigate funding of the free breakfast program in a way that it would "insure that no implication is created we are investigating the BCP [Breakfast for Children Program] itself or the church where it is being held."

Hoover advised FBI agents there was some indication that donations to the program were being used for other Black Panther activities. Of the breakfast program itself, he wrote in the memorandum:

"The resulting publicity tends to portray the Black Panther Party in a favorable light and clouds the violent nature of the group and its ultimate aim of insurrection."

In his memorandum, Hoover ordered FBI bureaus to consider "appropriate counterintelligence action" which included investigating the source of funds for the program.

Chicago Tribune, May 8, 1976. Reprinted courtesy of the Chicago Tribune.

How minority groups cope with their situation is in part a matter of what the majority allows them to do. Federal, state, and local authorities all responded violently to the Black Panthers' early aggressiveness. Later, when the Panthers turned to such innocuous activities as feeding inadequately nourished children, that too was viewed with suspicion.

and expected different things. It was their common experience in America that transformed them into a group called Italian-Americans. And it was the shared expectations they developed that became the Italian-American subculture. The same is true for the black subculture. The Africans brought to America as slaves came from many different tribes. Often they did not even speak the same language. What is known today as black culture was largely created in the United States.

Although minority subcultures have frequently developed as the result of conditions forced on groups, they often become prized possessions. Many minority group members wish to maintain their subculture. They see themselves as different from the majority of society, and they like their differences. They reject the idea of becoming like the majority. This sentiment is captured by rhythm and blues star James Brown in "I'm Black and I'm Proud."

Minorities In American Society

To this point, we have developed concepts and ideas that help us understand the nature of ethnic and racial relations. Now we can anchor these abstract ideas in concrete realities by focusing on the different experiences of specific minority groups in America (see Figure 9-1). (This discussion will not include women as a minority group. The status of women in American society is discussed in Chapter 8.)

Black Americans

Historical experience If the essential feature of minority group status is social subordination, black people are the classic minority in the United States. Brought to this country against their will and forced to work without compensation, black people experienced the ultimate subordination: slavery. Slavery ensured the minority status of black people and determined that they would relate to the nation from a position of weakness rather than strength. While minority white groups inched slowly up the occupational ladder of success, developing sources of strength that they could apply to dominant groups, blacks were forcibly restricted to the edges of the social structure. Slavery warped all aspects of black life, not simply issues related to work. The culture Africans brought with them was systematically undercut. People from the same tribe were placed on different plantations so communication would be impossible unless they learned English. Black families had no legal status and family members could be sold when economic necessity dictated.

The late nineteenth century When slavery was abolished in 1865, it became legally possible for black and white people to compete with each other on an equal footing. But circumstances prevented this. Reconstruction of the South along democratic lines was defeated by compromises worked out between southern reactionaries and northern political interests. Sharecropping replaced slavery. The state disciplined blacks instead of the slave owners, and not much changed in the lives of southern black people.

Legally, the former slaves worked for themselves. But in fact they were still enslaved in many ways. Sharecropping was simply a new kind of bondage. By the time sharecroppers paid the farm owner for the use of his land, housing, and food and seed, they had very little left. In some cases, they owed the owner more at the end of the year than at the beginning.

Legally, blacks were free, but by 1900 a new structure of law had emerged to keep them powerless. "Jim Crow" laws restricted blacks to "separate but equal" public facilities. Vagrancy laws sprang up that effectively regulated the physical movement of blacks in the South. Blacks needed passes to travel, and if they did not have a certain amount of money they could be declared vagrants and thrown in jail. When laws proved ineffective, extralegal and illegal ways were developed to keep blacks in a subordinate position. Riding at night and hiding behind sheets, the Ku Klux Klan would sometimes murder black people who took freedom seriously.

The twentieth century The situation of black people changed significantly in the twentieth century. Scholars have interpreted this period of achievement in two ways. Some have pointed to ad-

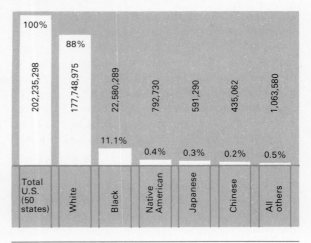

Figure 9-1
Distribution of the U.S. population by race

100%	88%					
202,235,298	177,748,975	22,580,289	792,730	591,290	435,062	1,063,580
		11.1%	0.4%	0.3%	0.2%	0.5%
Total U.S. (50 states)	White	Black	Native American	Japanese	Chinese	All others

vances in education, income, and occupational status as proof of real progress. Others argue that progress is a relative concept. They suggest that black people only make progress when the gap between themselves and white people is narrowed.

Black people began moving north at the turn of the century. Pushed by poverty in the South and industrialization in the North, between 400,000 and 1,000,000 black people migrated northward.[14] Blacks entered the labor force during this period as service workers and unskilled laborers. While their incomes increased, their participation in the labor force was not complete. Black people were excluded from many unions on the basis of their skin color. The areas in which they could work were also limited as racial ghettos began to emerge in the North.[15]

Residential segregation had two somewhat contradictory but related effects on the black experience. Because of gerrymandering and outside political control, blacks could not control the political affairs of their own communities. But they turned the liability of residential segregation to advantage. Prevented from wider participation, black people turned their cultural efforts inward. The 1920s saw an explosion of black literary and musical talent, a period known as the Negro Renaissance.

Black advances to this point were effectively checked by the Depression in the 1930s. Migration essentially ceased. And by the mid-1930s in some sections of the country nearly 80 percent of black people were on public assistance.[16] Nevertheless, President Franklin Roosevelt's New Deal efforts to deal with the Depression and his appointment of a "Black Cabinet" were especially beneficial to black people. But despite these efforts, segregation and discrimination were not eliminated. There was discrimination in federal works projects, and housing financed by the Federal Housing Administration was segregated.[17]

The concern for the position of black Americans that began with the New Deal carried over to the period between 1940 and 1955. Pressured by a march on Washington threatened by black leaders, Roosevelt issued an executive order on fair employment practices in the early 1940s. The combined effects of this order and the wartime economy led to further social and economic gains by black people. By 1948, the armed forces were desegregated and President Truman had issued an executive order banning discrimination. In 1954 the Supreme Court declared unconstitutional the doctrine of separate but equal facilities in public education. The efforts begun in the 1940s culminated in the birth of the modern civil rights movement. On December 1, 1955, Rosa Parks, a black seamstress living in Montgomery, Alabama, refused to sit in the back of a public bus. Her refusal sparked a massive boycott that was eventually led by Dr. Martin Luther King.

The 1960s were marked by hope and optimism. A highly visible civil rights movement resulted in the passage of civil rights legislation in many states, and a national voting rights act was passed in 1965. Urban rebellions were answered in part with federal aid. President Lyndon Johnson declared a War on Poverty. Although it provoked serious internal dissensions, the war in Vietnam provided jobs for many unemployed people. The National Alliance of Businessmen, in conjunction with the federal government, promised programs to employ the "hard-core" unemployed.

Three wartime economies contributed to the economic progress of black people. Per capita cash income increased threefold between 1940 and 1955. Between 1945 and 1961, black families earn-

Table 9-1 Median family income in the U.S., nonwhites and whites, 1950–1972

Year	Nonwhite	White	Ratio of nonwhite to white
1950	$1869	$ 3445	0.54
1951	2032	3859	0.53
1952	2338	4114	0.57
1953	2461	4392	0.56
1954	2410	4339	0.56
1955	2549	4605	0.55
1956	2628	4993	0.53
1957	2764	5166	0.54
1958	2711	5300	0.51
1959	3161	5893	0.54
1960	3233	5835	0.55
1961	3191	5981	0.53
1962	3330	6237	0.53
1963	3465	6548	0.53
1964	3839	6858	0.56
1965	3994	7251	0.55
1966	4674	7792	0.60
1967	5094	8234	0.62
1968	5590	8937	0.63
1969	6191	9794	0.63
1970	5516	10236	0.64
1971	6714	10672	0.63
1972	7106	11549	0.62

Note that the figures given here are for all nonwhites, not just blacks. It is often impossible to obtain separate statistics for blacks and other nonwhites, but because blacks constitute so high a proportion of the nonwhite population, about 88 percent, figures for all nonwhites are a close approximation to figures for blacks. Figures for blacks are often even lower than figures for all nonwhites; the median income in 1972 was $7106 for all nonwhites, $6864 for blacks.

ing $6,000 or more a year increased five times, from 4 percent in 1945 to 20 percent in 1961.[18] The median annual income of black families went from approximately $1,869 in 1950 to $6,864 in 1972 (see Table 9-1). There was also progress in the black housing situation. Between the years 1940 and 1955, blacks owning their own homes increased 137 percent.[19] This resulted in one-third of all black families being home owners by 1955.

These figures indicate that relative to the past situation progress has occurred within the black community. But is *equality*—a narrowing of the gap between the black and white life situation—occurring? While the median black family income did rise between 1950 and 1972, the ratio of non-white to white income increased only eight percentage points in twenty-two years. In 1950, for every $100 a white family made, a black family earned $54; and in 1972, for every $100 earned by a white family, a black family made $62. The issue of income equality is complicated by two factors. First, the ratio of nonwhite to white incomes traditionally increases during periods of war and drops in peacetime. The ratio dropped 2 percent between 1970 and 1972 when the Vietnam war was winding down. It is reasonable to assume that it has dropped even more since then. Second, black family incomes are often the result of the efforts of two breadwinners. A study conducted in 1968 showed that 90 percent of black families earning over $10,000 a year had at least two wage earners.[20]

The housing situation is similarly complicated. Between 1950 and 1960, for instance, black home ownership increased, but the difference in the median *value* of black-owned and white-owned homes went from $4,700 to $5,530. This means that the gap between the value of white- and black-owned homes *increased* 17.7 percent. During this same period, 1950–1960, overcrowded housing decreased for whites by almost one-third but increased for the black population.[21]

Compared with what has been, blacks have made progress. Compared with the position of whites, however, the status of blacks is less clear. The gap between the races has narrowed somewhat in certain respects but has remained the same in others.

Present status: The consequences of racism The essence of the black experience in the United States has been *racism:* exclusion from the society and its social resources on the basis of skin color. Inclusion, at best, has been reluctant. American society has been organized around the principle that there is a special place for black people, a place not equivalent to that occupied by whites. The special limits put on the opportunities available to black people have insured that whites will have advantages.

Racism operates on two levels: the individual and the institutional. *Individual racism* consists of

Census Bureau Stats Show Black Progress

Washington (AP)—Blacks have made mixed progress during the past year, gaining in college enrollments but losing ground in actual spending power, a Census Bureau report says.

The report, released Sunday, also said that about 40 per cent of all food stamp purchases were made by black families during at least a portion of 1974.

In addition, the number of black families headed by women has continued to grow, rising to 35 per cent this year from 28 per cent in 1970.

The report, the eighth and most extensive in an annual series on the nation's black population, said enrollment of blacks in colleges increased 56 per cent during the 1970's, compared with an increase of 25 per cent for whites.

But while the median black family income in 1974 was $7,800, an increase of 7.4 per cent over 1973; real spending power, after adjustment for inflation, for black families decreased by 3.2 per cent.

Other findings in the report included:

—There has been a slowdown in the growth of black population to 1.6 per cent compared with 1.8 per cent annual growth during the 1960's. The total black population of 24 million last year was 11.4 per cent of the total U.S. population of 211 million.

—Reversing the trend of past decades, the black population in the South stabilized at about 53 per cent, with as many blacks moving into the area as moved out.

—The jobless rate for blacks was 13.7 per cent, compared with 7.6 per cent for whites.

—Blacks holding elective office totaled 3,503 in May of this year, an increase of 1,643, or 88 per cent in four years, although the total was still less than 1 per cent of all elected officials. Illinois and Louisiana have the largest number of black elected officials.

Blacks in jail during 1972—the last year for which figures were available—numbered 59,000, which was 42 per cent of the total jail population of 142,000.

Life expectancy for blacks still trailed that of whites, but there was a "striking reduction" in black mortality rates under one year, with the death rate of infants declining 19 per cent for males and 16 per cent for females, the report said.

Among blacks, the average life expectancy in 1973 was 61.9 years for males and 70.1 years for females, compared with 68.4 years for white males and 76.1 years for white females.

Lafayette (Ind.) Journal-Courier, July 28, 1975. Reprinted by permission of AP Newsfeatures.

The status of black Americans continues to change. Some improvement has occurred, but in many areas of life little change is visible.

Table 9-2   Levels of education by race for persons 25 years or older, 1971

| Race | Years of school completed | | | | | | | |
| | Elementary | | | High school | | College | | |
	Less than 5	5–7	8	1–3	4	1–3	4	Median years completed
All	5.0%	8.7%	13.0%	16.8%	34.4%	10.7%	11.4%	12.2
White	4.1	7.8	13.3	16.2	35.5	11.1	12.0	12.2
Black	13.5	17.4	10.8	23.5	24.2	6.2	4.3	10.1

individual attitudes and actions that are recognized as prejudice and discrimination. **Institutional racism** is less open and more subtle. It is the operation of impersonal, social institutional forces or policies in such a way as to produce outcomes consistent with racial discrimination. Examples of institutional racism include the long history of exclusion of blacks from the craft unions; the reluctance, until recently, to admit black people to colleges and universities or the professions; and the limits placed on participation in professional organizations.

Education   Institutional racism is quite apparent in the field of education. In the past, blacks were held back educationally by de jure segregation. Culturally biased IQ tests and tracking systems based on "ability groupings" presently result in similar consequences. In 1971, 13.5 percent of all blacks over the age of twenty-five had completed less than five years of school—more than three times the rate for whites.[22] Table 9-2 shows this and other educational differentials between blacks and whites. Examining the elementary school columns further, for example, we can see that more than twice as many blacks as whites complete only five to seven years of schooling. (The modest differential between proportions who complete eight years is accounted for by the fact that so many more whites go on to further education.) Looking at those who have only elementary schooling, whether the full eight years or less, we see that only 25.2 percent of the white population is so handicapped, as compared with 41.7 percent of the black population.

Similar contrasts can be made for high school and college education: 35.5 percent of whites finish high school, compared with 24.2 percent of blacks; almost twice as many whites complete one to three years of college and almost three times as many finish four. Whites *attend* college more than twice as frequently.

Occupation   The job situation of black people also reflects institutional racism. Even though the occupational outlook has changed during the past thirty years, and despite a highly publicized civil rights movement, job opportunities remain restricted for black people. Although the number of blacks in white-collar occupations has almost doubled since 1960, only about one-third of the black work force holds white-collar jobs, compared with 50 percent of the white workers.[23] "Black workers," writes Alphonso Pinckney, "continue to be overrepresented in lower-paying, less-skilled jobs and underrepresented in better-paying, higher-skilled occupations."[24] As in the past, work that offers opportunities for advancement, authority, and mobility is often reserved for whites. This situation is frequently the result of seniority systems and "father-son" unions. Although such practices were not originally set up to exclude racial minorities, they have had the effect of keeping racial minorities occupationally subordinate.

The occupational subordination of blacks is also reflected in their rate of unemployment. As the figures in Table 9-3 suggest, the ratio of black to white unemployment remained basically the same over the eighteen-year period between 1954 and

Table 9-3 Nonwhite and white unemployment rates in the U.S., 1954–1972

Year	Nonwhite	White	Ratio of nonwhite to white
1954	8.8	4.5	2.0
1955	8.0	3.6	2.2
1956	7.5	3.3	2.3
1957	8.0	3.9	2.1
1958	12.6	6.1	2.1
1959	10.7	4.9	2.2
1960	10.2	4.9	2.1
1961	12.4	6.0	2.1
1962	10.9	4.9	2.2
1963	10.8	5.0	2.2
1964	9.6	4.6	2.1
1965	8.1	4.1	2.0
1966	7.3	3.3	2.2
1967	7.4	3.4	2.2
1968	6.7	3.2	2.1
1969	6.4	3.1	2.1
1970	8.2	4.5	1.8
1971	9.9	5.4	1.8
1972	10.0	5.0	2.0

As in Table 9-1, figures are for all nonwhites, not just blacks, but the nonwhite figures closely approximate those for blacks.

1972. In 1972 as in 1954, the unemployment rate for blacks was still about double the rate for whites.

Income Paul Siegel's 1965 study of income, occupation, and education indicates that blacks within the same occupational category as whites, regardless of education, consistently earn less than whites. Indeed, Siegel shows that the *differences in income* between blacks and whites (as opposed to gross amount of income) *increase with the amount of education.* Comparing blacks and whites with similar education and from the same geographic regions of the country, Siegel found that on the average whites make $1,000 more than blacks. He describes this income differential as the "cost of being Negro."[25] The data from 1969 in Figure 9-2 show that this trend of disparity between black and white incomes, fostered by institutional racism, continues with only slow diminution. The income discrepancy between blacks and whites is well

institutional racism: the operation of impersonal, social institutional forces or policies in such a way as to produce outcomes consistent with racial discrimination. The use of standard IQ tests, which are strongly biased toward middle-class values and verbal behavior, as the basis for pupil assignment and classification in schools, for example, in fact discriminates against the lower-class black child although that may not be the purpose of the school's policy.

Figure 9-2
Median income of men 25-54 years of age, by level of educational attainment, 1969

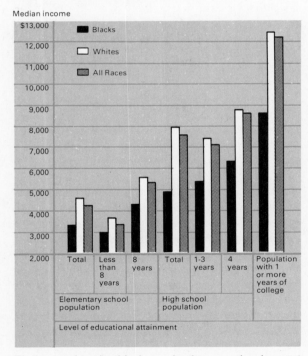

The more education blacks attain, the more they lose out economically in relation to whites.

Martin Luther King leads the March on Washington, August 28, 1963.

illustrated by Rashi Fein's observation that "the Negro college graduate earns but slightly more than does the white high school graduate."[26]

Black protest and present conditions   Black people have rarely accepted their place in American society willingly. Slave owners were constantly on guard for slave rebellions. Sometimes slaves protested their status by pretending to be incompetent. In this way, they got out of work and made the master pay for it. Black protest in the twentieth century has been more dramatic. When black soldiers returning from World War I were attacked by whites in Washington, D.C., St. Louis, and Chicago, they fought back, and riots ensued. The National Association for the Advancement of Colored People (NAACP) was organized in 1909 to protest lynching and make sure that the Constitution was applied to blacks as well as whites. At the same time, some urban blacks protested their situation by demanding that they be allowed to return to Africa, and many proclaimed their pride in blackness.

The modern civil rights movement worked within this tradition of militance and protest. At first the focus was on the South, where the issues were obvious. Sit-ins, marches, and voter registration drives were some of the techniques used to force the South to live up to the law of the land as stated by the 1954 Supreme Court decision that schools must be desegregated. Civil rights activists soon found out that the problems blacks faced were not restricted to the South. Urban unrest between 1965 and 1968 pointed to problems in the North. Blacks were able to vote there, but the schools they attended, the jobs they held, and the houses they lived in were inferior to those available to whites. Militant nationalists like Malcolm X articulated the grievances of northern black people. Organizations like the Black Panthers and the Black Muslims developed to meet the needs of northern ghetto blacks in the latter half of the twentieth century.

Events in the first half of the 1970s have been considerably less dramatic than in the 1960s. Black majorities have emerged in some large cities, and black elected officials are no longer news. Certain cities have black mayors. But in those areas where blacks have achieved political power, they often lack economic power. Wealth surrounds many black communities but is not a part of them. Until black people combine economic with political power, they will remain a sociological minority group.

Asian-Americans

Asian-Americans are a unique minority group. According to popular mythology, they have overcome racial adversity; they are proof the American Dream delivers on its promises. In many ways, however, the treatment received by Asian-Americans duplicates the experiences of other racial minorities. To complicate matters, there are important differences *between* Asian-American groups. The experiences of Japanese- and Chinese-Americans highlight these issues.

Chinese-American historical experience   The first large-scale immigration of Chinese began in the 1850s. During the next thirty years, more than 300,000 Chinese made the difficult voyage across the Pacific to America. They left China because of floods, famines, and revolution, and came to the United States because of the discovery of gold in California, cheap passage, and the possibility of indentured labor. The Chinese were not universally welcomed. White miners in California, fearing unfair competition from the cheap Chinese labor, organized to keep the Chinese out of the mines. White businessmen tried to legalize serfdom by making the Chinese "contract laborers." The Chinese faced harassment of all sorts, including mob violence, miners' "taxes," and expulsion from some towns. By the time they began to migrate to the Midwest and East, they were the focus of a full-scale anti-Chinese movement.

This movement resulted in three types of anti-Chinese legislation.[27] The first restricted or excluded Chinese immigration to the United States. After years of trying to limit Chinese immigration through state taxes, the Congress in 1882 passed a measure that suspended the immigration of Chinese laborers for ten years and made Chinese born in China ineligible for American citizenship. The Geary Act of 1892 extended the restriction another ten years, and in 1904 Congress extended the exclusion of the Chinese indefinitely and unconditionally. That was the situation until 1943, when the Chinese exclusion act was repealed. In 1968, a new immigration act was signed that repealed quotas based on national origins.

A second kind of legislation was used to eliminate the Chinese from occupations in which they competed with whites. California levied taxes on Chinese miners and fishermen. A "police tax" required that all "mongolians" who had not paid the miners' tax pay the state $2.50 a month. Such legislation was not completely effective in restricting Chinese labor because it usually proved to be unconstitutional, but it stimulated other ways of keeping the Chinese from competing with white workers. With the exception of the International Workers of the World (IWW), the labor movement organized to push Chinese workers out of the mines. Racially based strikes, riots, and boycotts evicted the Chinese from numerous occupations and forced them into crowded Chinatowns.

The third type of legislation harassed the Chinese community and attacked its culture. The Chinese queue, or braid—a badge of citizenship worn by males in China—was effectively eliminated by an ordinance specifying that male prisoners have hair only one inch long. Since the Chinese were frequently arrested, few braids survived. Similarly,

An anti-Chinese riot in Denver, Colorado, 1880.

the Chinese tradition of burying the ashes of the dead in the home village in China was virtually eliminated by an ordinance that required permission from coroners to remove the dead from cemeteries; permission was seldom granted. By 1910, the Chinese population was effectively limited, restricted to marginal occupations, and powerless. Their status remained basically unchanged until the 1940s.

Japanese-American historical experience Japanese immigrants began arriving on the mainland, usually California, in the 1880s. The anti-Oriental sentiment directed at the Chinese quickly focused on them as well. In the opening years of the 1900s, business and labor leaders in San Francisco organized an anti-Japanese movement intended to exclude them from the United States. The agitation proved largely successful in 1906, when the San

Francisco school board directed all Asian school-children to attend one school designated the Oriental School. When the Japanese government protested this treatment, President Theodore Roosevelt negotiated a bargain with them that came to be known as the Gentlemen's Agreement. Japan agreed to stop the emigration of its workers, and the President agreed to discourage a law limiting Japanese immigration.

In 1922, the Supreme Court ruled that Japanese born in Japan could not become citizens of the United States. The Court based its decision on the first naturalization act of 1790, which stated that citizenship was available, under certain conditions, "to any alien, being a free white person." This decision was later cited to sanction legislation that made it impossible for the Japanese to own or lease property. Led by California, many states in the West and Southwest passed laws specifying that people who were not eligible to become citizens could not own or lease land. Thus, the Japanese were prevented from voting, and their chances for competing with white farmers were severely limited.

This was not the last time the Japanese received harsh treatment based solely on their color and national origin. Three months after Pearl Harbor was attacked, President Franklin Roosevelt signed Executive Order 9066. The order gave military authorities the power to designate certain parts of the country as military areas and to remove "any or all persons" from such locations. Despite the fact that the United States was at war with Germany and Italy as well as Japan, and despite the fact that there were numerous instances of German subversion on the East Coast and none on the part of Japanese in the West, General John L. DeWitt ordered *all* mainland Japanese—aliens and citizens alike—to leave the west coast and move inland. One month later, he ordered them placed in relocation centers for the duration of the war.

The Japanese internment or relocation camps of World War II are sometimes referred to as concentration camps, but the implications of that term are inaccurate, conjuring up images of mass deaths and brutal treatment from the Nazi camps of that name. The Japanese-Americans were neither starved nor physically mistreated by the authorities. It *is* important to remember, however, that they had been unconstitutionally interned and deported from their homes, which they were forced to dispose of with losses estimated to average $10,000 per family,[28] and that they were kept confined against their will without due process of law. A final irony is that the threat they supposedly represented never materialized. No Japanese-American in the continental United States or in Hawaii was ever convicted of sabotage or espionage during World War II. Financial restitution was made by the U.S. government only years later, and then it was only partial.

Present status and condition The status of Asian-Americans can only be described, at least until very recently, as second class. The consequences of second-class status were dramatic. Most of the Chinese who came to America were men who intended to bring families later. The exclusion acts made that impossible, and it was illegal for Chinese men to marry white women. Thus, the Chinese were for a long time essentially a community of men; they were not able to reproduce to any notable degree until the 1930s. Because there were few American-born Chinese until that time, the Chinese were effectively restricted to the edges of society. Ineligible for citizenship because of race and lacking citizens among their ranks, they could change their status neither politically nor economically. Isolated and without power, they were controlled and exploited by elites who used them as cheap labor in laundries, restaurants, and garment factories.

The Japanese were subject to the same legal harassment and restrictions as the Chinese. Unlike the Chinese, however, the Japanese successfully imported women from Japan, despite the ban on Asian immigration. The Gentlemen's Agreement permitted the Japanese government to issue passports to the wives of Japanese men living in America. Japanese custom encouraged marriages arranged by go-betweens. A marriage broker in Japan would find a suitable woman and stand in for the future husband at the Japanese wedding. Legally married, the woman could then come to America.

In this way, the Japanese developed a community of families and could produce children who, being born in the United States, would be citizens.

The children helped the Japanese get around another restriction. Asians born overseas could not own property, but their American-born children could; and so many Japanese families bought land in their children's names and in this way got an economic start in America. But the Japanese could not completely avoid American racism, as their imprisonment during World War II shows. During those four years Japanese-Americans lost most of what they had gained, and when the war ended, most had to start again almost from scratch.

Today, Asian communities are still treated in some of the same ways as they were in the past. In 1960, San Francisco's Chinatown was on the verge of crisis. The median education in English of people over twenty-five was 1.7 years. The unemployment rate was 12.8 percent, compared with 6.7 percent for the rest of the city. The population density was 885 people per residential acre—second only to Harlem and ten times higher than the density in the surrounding city. Sixty-seven percent of the housing was substandard.[29]

Although the Japanese community is not in a crisis state, Japanese-Americans are still not treated equally with whites. A study in 1959 showed that, despite educational and occupational success, the Japanese had not achieved income equality with whites. Japanese were paid less than whites for the same work, even when their educational level was the same.[30] As Figure 9-3 shows, Japanese-Americans actually exceed white Americans in average educational attainment and occupational status, but still fall slightly below them in income, while Chinese-Americans fall markedly below whites in both income and educational attainment.

Despite the persistence of some carryovers from the past of the kinds cited above, in general it is fair to say that Asian-Americans—particularly the Japanese—have made extraordinary progress over the past thirty years. Blatant discrimination rarely occurs anymore, education is almost entirely open to them, and they have made remarkable strides in climbing the occupational ladder. (These generalizations are less true for Korean- and Filipino-Americans, whose numbers are smaller and who arrived more recently, than it is for the Chinese and Japanese.)

The relative success of these racial minority

Figure 9-3
Socioeconomic profiles for nonwhite males in the U.S., 1960

Transformed score (percent)

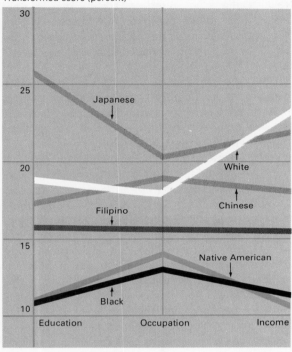

Interned Japanese-Americans being loaded into trucks and buses for "relocation" in 1942.

groups in the struggle for power in American society is something of a sociological puzzle when compared with the experience of Native Americans, Chicanos, and blacks. No present theory of race relations in American society can entirely account for it. We can hypothesize some factors that may have made the difference or contributed to it, but no completely adequate explanation exists.

Both the Chinese and Japanese immigrants came from societies of high, ancient culture and may have found it easier to fit into the dominant Anglo-Saxon culture of the United States than other minority groups. Many of both peoples were already literate in their own languages and thus did not have a tradition of illiteracy to overcome as well as a cultural adjustment to make. Both groups brought from their home countries strong traditions of local social organization, and both were used to working together, as a group, for the welfare of the group. Both had ancient traditions encouraging education, ambition, and hard work, all ideas valued by the dominant culture of the United States. And finally, unlike the blacks, the Native Americans, and the Spanish-speaking, the Asians had never been defined in the dominant society as political enemies. (The Native Americans, of course, had been considered an enemy for two centuries; blacks had had a great civil war fought, in part, over their future; and Catholic Spanish-Mexican influence in the hemisphere had for many years been perceived as a threat to Americans.)

Native Americans

Historical experience Before whites came, the Americas were a land of small nations and tribes. They were organized as political units with territorial boundaries. Some nations were full-blown civilizations (the Aztecs and Mayans of Mesoamerica and the Incas of South America); others were small farmers and agriculturalists (the Hopi and the Zuni of the Southwest). Some were successful fishermen (the Tlingit of the Canadian Northwest); others were hunters and gatherers. The diversity of Native American tribes extends to their social orga-

nization and cultural beliefs. Each tribe had its own religious beliefs, art forms, and family structure.

There were three major periods of contact between the Native Americans of the Northern Hemisphere and the Western world: the period of Spanish conquest throughout Mexico and the American Southwest; the early settlement of the eastern seaboard of the United States and Canada; and the period of western expansion from the California gold rush to the end of the nineteenth century.

The first major thrust of Western contact came with the relatively rapid movement of the Spanish conquistadors in the sixteenth century and later. The Spaniards used a superior technology (including horses, armor, and gun powder) and a political policy of divide and conquer. Moving into the Southwest, they subjugated the Pueblo tribes and placed them in servitude. The Pueblo tribes revolted and forced the Spaniards out of the area for a short while, but after a decade of resistance, the Pueblos finally succumbed to superior Spanish force. Other pockets of resistance appeared in the Southwest among the more mobile Navaho, Comanche, and Apache tribes. The Comanche and Apache were never militarily subjugated.

The pattern of contact in the colonial Northeast differed in several ways. First, the tribes were caught in the vice of competition between the Western powers of France and England, each of which tried to make allies out of them. Second, there was no cohesive movement of conquerors against them, only a gradual encroachment of settlers into their territory. This process began with the earliest settlements of the English in Virginia and at Plymouth, Massachusetts. In many cases, the first contact between Native Americans and white settlers was open and friendly. But this spirit of cooperation soon gave way to resistance and hostility as the settlers demanded more and more land to support their settlements.

The Nation of the Iroquois is perhaps a prime example of this pattern of encroachment and hostility. Initially admired by the settlers, the various tribes of the Iroquois nation were soon caught in the struggle between France and England. The tribes managed to maintain their unity up to the American Revolution, but shortly after 1800, torn by internal rivalry, the Iroquois nation disintegrated.

The period from 1849 to the turn of the century marked the opening of the American West. This is the period of the great Indian wars. The Sioux, the Cheyenne, and the Apache each attempted to resist the massive migration across tribal lands. In the Plains states, the Sioux and the Cheyenne waged long and costly campaigns against the American army. In the Southwest, the Apache and the Comanche used hit-and-run tactics to resist the invader. In the Northwest, the Nez Perce, who had been known as peaceful and compromising, finally retaliated in 1877.

Had the nomadic and highly individualistic tribesmen been able in 1850 to achieve the level of organization and intergroup cooperation finally attained under Crazy Horse of the Sioux at the Battle of the Little Bighorn in 1876, Indian history might have been very different. But the culture of the Plains tribes did not permit this. After Custer's decisive defeat in that battle, intertribal coordination broke down. And in Washington the decision was final: the Plains tribes would be subdued or exterminated.[31]

By 1890, the major campaigns were over. A half century of upheaval and bloody warfare had resulted in the defeat and subjugation of the Native Americans. Domination proved expensive: perhaps as much as $1 million dollars for every dead Native American.[32] A new policy emerged for physical and cultural control of the tribes. Demoralized and defeated, they were made wards of the state and were placed on reservations.

Three key legislative events made this possible. The first was the Indian Removal Act of 1830, which resulted in the removal of the Cherokee people from their ancestral lands in the mountain country of Georgia, Tennessee, and North Carolina. The congressional declaration of 1871 carried the process one step further. Not only could Native Americans be removed by the will of the American government, but they would no longer be "acknowledged and recognized as an independent nation, tribe, or power with whom the United States may contract by treaty."[33] The last step in the policy was the Dawes Act of 1887. In order to "civilize" the Native Americans, tribal lands were

"This damn teepee leaks."

Copyright © 1976 The Chicago Sun-Times. Reproduced by courtesy of Wil-Jo Associates, Inc. and Bill Mauldin

divided among the members of the tribe to fit the pattern of Western private ownership. Native Americans lost 90,000,000 acres of land within forty-five years, as white farmers and real estate speculators bought their holdings or swindled them away from individual Native Americans who often did not understand what their land sale implied.[34]

Present status and condition The past history of the Native American is one of exploitation and oppression, and the present situation is little better. Modern Native Americans today live in the depths of poverty. Fifty percent of Native American families have an income under $2,000 per year, 75 percent below $3,000. In 1970, the unemployment rate was 40 percent, or, at that time, ten times the national average. Suicide among teenagers is three times the national average. Infant mortality is twelve points above the national average. The

average life expectancy is close to twenty years below that of most Americans.

The educational outlook for Native Americans is bleak. Forty-two percent of Native American children drop out of school before completing high school, almost double the national average. The Bureau of Indian Affairs dominates the education of Native Americans, and its record is one of failure. Nearly 60 percent of all Native Americans have less than an eighth-grade education. Shipped to boarding schools, sometimes thousands of miles from their homes, children are often not permitted to use their native languages. When they attend public schools, the school boards are often controlled by whites.

There are over 600,000 Native Americans in the United States today, and the majority of them live in urban communities. Cities like Chicago, Minneapolis, San Francisco, and Los Angeles all have sizable Indian populations. Two factors have contributed to this urban movement. The first is the termination of tribal reservations: the offer of a cash settlement to certain tribes in exchange for withdrawing their rights and claims to ancestral lands. The second factor is the desire to find a better life than can be achieved on the reservations. Driven by poverty, Native Americans moved to the urban centers only to find conditions as harsh as those on the reservations. In many cases, they merely shifted their dependency from the federal government (which administers reservations) to local and state agencies.

Though the urban environment has offered the Native American little in the way of new opportunities, it has provided an impetus for the development of a pan-Indian consciousness. Two factors account for this: (1) the clash between city life and the land-centered cultural traditions of all tribes and (2) the bringing together of members of different tribes in urban ghettos. Through this recent common experience in the urban environment, members of diverse tribes have come to recognize that politically, culturally, and economically they have much in common. The development of social movements like the American Indian Movement (AIM) is an important first step in providing a link between urban Native Americans and traditional reservation life. For many years, Native Americans have been "forgotten Americans." By dramatic action they are now reminding the society of the long overdue debt that is owed them.

Chicanos and Puerto Ricans

We suggested earlier that minority groups are created and defined by their historical experience. Chicanos and Puerto Ricans are the most obvious example of this process. These two groups, though geographically and culturally distinct, share two important experiences. The early explorations of Spanish conquistadors in both Mexico and Puerto Rico resulted in a merger of Hispanic with indigenous Indian culture. This merger created a distinct cultural unit. The other element these groups share in common is their proximity to their territorial homeland.

Chicano historical experience The initial absorption of Chicanos into American society resulted from the Texan Revolution and the Mexican-American War of 1846. When English-speaking "Texicans" successfully revolted against Mexico and then a few years later brought Texas into the Union, thousands of Spanish-speaking Texans became American too. Later, the American victory over Mexico led to great portions of the Southwest and California being included within the dominion of the United States.

The treaty that ended the conflict between Mexico and the United States in 1848 contained specific guarantees regarding the property rights, political rights, and cultural autonomy of the Chicano population. These, however, were quickly violated, particularly in two important ways. First, the treaty promised early statehood, but while California and Nevada were quickly admitted to the Union, New Mexico and Arizona did not become states until some sixty-four years after the treaty was ratified.

The second violation revolved around the question of land. According to the treaty, original land grants made to individuals by the Republic of Mexico were to be honored by the United States. However, the growing westward migration of "Anglos" (English-speakers) made it increasingly difficult to uphold the treaty. By the close of the nineteenth century, the Chicano population, once a numerical majority holding parcels of land in the Southwest, was reduced to the status of a disenfranchised minority.

In the twentieth century, the experience of farm labor has played a particularly significant role in Chicano life. At the close of World War I and again during World War II, the United States actively recruited farm labor from Mexico. This bracero program was supposed to guarantee good working conditions and reasonable payment for employment. But as Carey McWilliams points out, these guarantees were largely farcical.[35] At least one aspect of the agreement, however, was rigidly enforced: the braceros were not allowed to accept employment in the industrialized sector of the economy. This provision had the effect of forcing them to compete at fixed low wages against Chicano agricultural workers who were United States citizens. The result was that the braceros drove the Chicanos out of the market.

Puerto Rican historical experience Puerto Rico became an occupied territory of the United States at the end of the Spanish-American War (1898). A civil government was established, but the President of the United States appointed all government officials, including the governor of the island. Then at the onset of World War I, Puerto Ricans were made citizens of the United States. On the island, Puerto Rican nationalism began to assert itself, and two important factions developed within the nationalist movement. One segment sought full independence for Puerto Rico and an end to U.S. rule. A second group was willing to accept a position as a sort of commonwealth nation under the dominion of the United States. In 1948, the first free elections were held in Puerto Rico, and Luiz Munoz Marin, a supporter of the commonwealth, was elected governor. In 1952, the Puerto Rican people voted in favor of accepting the status of an "associated free state."

Because of the poverty and limited economic base of the island, many Puerto Ricans migrated to the mainland with the hope of bettering their life chances. First as inhabitants of a territory, and later as citizens of an associated free state, they were able to migrate without restriction. The impact of this migration was felt within a relatively short period of time. In the 1930s, there were less than 55,000 Puerto Ricans in the United States. With the end of World War II and the development of air travel, large-scale migration began. Today, there are approximately 1.4 million Puerto Ricans in the United States.

Many Puerto Ricans came to the mainland under contract farm labor programs. One sociologist estimates that "an average of 20,000 contract farm laborers have been coming to the mainland each year."[36] The Puerto Rican government has attempted to negotiate and control basic protection for these laborers, but guarantees notwithstanding, the conditions of employment are often exploitive and harsh. Many Puerto Ricans leave farm labor as soon as they can.

Present status and condition   The exploitation of farm labor so familiar to Chicanos and Puerto Ricans is now a national issue. The recent efforts by the United Farm Workers and the publicity of the national boycotts have reminded all Americans that the problems have not disappeared. Farm labor still offers few guarantees, low wages, and little security. The housing provided for farm laborers usually meets only the barest standards for human existence. In 1970, the Puerto Rican Congress of New Jersey argued that half of the migrant labor camps in that state were in violation of the law.[37]

Although much national attention has been focused on farm workers, they represent a distinct minority of the Spanish-speaking. Both Puerto Ricans and Chicanos are overwhelmingly urban populations. The great mass of the Puerto Rican population is concentrated in New York City. The Chicano population, 80 percent of which is urban, is spread throughout the Southwest, California, and Midwest urban centers. In the urban areas, their experience parallels that of the black population. A recent study by the U.S. Census Bureau indicates that the Spanish-speaking people lost more real income than any other group in the United States during the recession of the early 1970s.[38]

Like other racial minorities, Chicanos and Puerto Ricans have used dramatic methods to get white Americans to recognize their situation. A Puerto Rican group called The Young Lords have changed themselves from a street gang into political activists. Though controversial, they have raised impor-

tant issues such as health care, unemployment, and the numerous housing problems faced by Puerto Ricans. Within the Chicano community, there is a wide variety of organizations protesting inequality. The United Farm Workers, led by Cesar Chavez, is the most widely publicized of these groups. Some Chicanos express their growing resistance to "Anglo domination" by promoting the concept of *la raza* (the race)—the idea that all Chicanos have a common heritage, culture, and experience.

White Ethnics

Historical experience   From the very beginning of the American republic, "foreigners" have often been regarded with suspicion and treated with prejudice and discrimination. The Irish, among the first immigrants, were not welcomed. The Alien and Sedition acts, passed in 1798, helped discourage easy naturalization for the new immigrants, for example, by requiring them to live in the United States before they could become citizens. The first half of the nineteenth century saw the largest number of immigrants arriving from Great Britain, Ireland, and Germany. As more and more came, resistance began to develop. The phrase "No Irish Need Apply" appeared on many job notices.

As the twentieth century approached, the tide of immigration changed. New immigrants began to arrive from southern and eastern Europe. The Italians, Polish, and Russians arrived in time to catch the last glimmers of the great urban-industrial expansion, but unskilled labor was still needed. This last major wave of immigration was confronted by renewed Anglo ethnocentrism. By the turn of the century, some Bostonians had formed the Immigration Restriction League, a group aimed at excluding southern and eastern Europeans because of their alleged racial inferiority. One of the influential spokesmen for this movement was Madison Grant, the author of *The Passing of the Great Race in America*. The great race was, of course, the "Nordic race."

The southern and eastern Europeans were portrayed as mentally defective, criminal, and vulgar. An early federal commission, the Dillingham Commission, concluded that these immigrants' high rate of illiteracy was the product of "inherent racial tendencies." This prompted the adoption in 1914 of a restrictive immigration policy based on a quota system. The system favored immigrants from Great Britain and the Scandinavian countries at the expense of the newer immigrants from southern and eastern Europe. The quotas were based on the population figures of the 1890s, which meant that "twelve out of fifteen newcomers had to be from Britain, Ireland, Germany, The Netherlands, and Scandinavia. Victory had gone to the Nordics."[39]

Religion and ethnicity   There is no way to understand adequately the experience and the development of ethnic life outside the context of religious affiliation. America was not only a nation dominated by an Anglo-Saxon elite; it was also a predominantly Protestant nation. Significantly, many immigrants to the United States were members of two important religious minorities: Roman Catholicism and Judaism.

Much of the early discrimination faced by the Irish immigrants stemmed from hostility to Roman Catholicism. In the 1840s and 1850s, the Know-Nothing party gained many adherents because of its antiforeign stance and the fears it expressed about Catholic loyalty to the papacy. The Ku Klux Klan also expressed strong anti-Catholic sentiment.[40] This recurrent fear of papal loyalty appeared as late as 1960, when some Americans questioned John Kennedy's loyalties. Was he Catholic or American?

Anti-Semitism has been even stronger. As late as the 1880s, the American Jewish community, made up largely of German Jews, was not singled out for harassment. But with the growing migration of eastern European Jews, anti-Semitism began to flourish in America, gaining strength in the first quarter of the twentieth century. In the 1920s, the Ku Klux Klan expanded its horizons to include Jews in its diatribe of hate. Jews were described as belonging to the "Semitic race," which was obviously supposed to be different from and inferior to the "Aryan race." Jews were associated with radical and foreign ideologies, such as Bolshevism and anarchy. In the same period, many notable Americans expressed anti-Semitic views, including Henry Ford, publisher of the *Dearborn Independent,* who warned his readers of the "Jewish menace." He

Jose Angel Gutierrez, founder of La Raza Unida, a Mexican-American political party.

publicized a discredited document known as *Protocols of the Elders of Zion*, allegedly developed by Jewish leaders, that outlined a conspiratorial plan to enslave the Christian world. Discrimination against Jews remained widespread until after World War II, with many organizations excluding Jews and some universities limiting the number of Jewish students.[41]

While religion was the basis for discrimination and persecution on the part of the dominant society, it also acted as a basis of solidarity for ethnic communities of both Jews and Roman Catholics for a century after 1850. In the case of the Jews, religion was the common bond for three distinct groups of immigrants: the Sephardic Jews from Spain and Portugal who arrived with America's earliest settlers; the German Jews who arrived between the 1820s and the 1870s; and the eastern European Jews who followed them. Each of these groups had a distinct national culture, but their religion bound them together. Within the framework of religion, they established numerous projects to aid newly arriving immigrants. And as anti-Semitism grew, American Jewry consolidated its ranks and resources in order to survive.

Religion played a similar role in the transition from immigrant group to ethnic group among Roman Catholics. In an attempt to maintain its hold on the newly arrived immigrants, the Roman Catholic church allowed the development of ethnically defined local parishes, and the church became a center for social and recreational activities within the ethnic community. Perhaps the most significant contribution was the development of a Catholic educational system, which provided mobility for generations of white ethnic groups. By encouraging the ethnic parish, the church not only helped define the meaning of ethnic identification, but also provided a structure that tied various ethnic groups together.[42]

Contemporary ethnic groups We said earlier that an ethnic group was a population socially identified according to cultural criteria, and that the "social identification" in question might be self-generated or imposed by others. Thus, more informally, ethnics could be called people who share a common ancestral origin, real or imagined. Until very recently, sociologists generally assumed that in the United States, at least, ethnic origins would become less and less important socially as time passed and that ethnicity would diminish in significance as a sociological variable, perhaps eventually disappearing altogether. This, however, has not occurred. Several factors seem to have contributed to the persistence of ethnicity in American life, all having to do with the quality of social identification.

One is the matter of self-identification. If people *think of themselves* as ethnics, they will remain ethnics. Ethnicity arises from and is continually re-created by shared experience and cultural tradition and may be expressed in political and marital patterns, social practices, and so forth. Another factor is the reactions of others. If other people persist in treating a group as ethnic, and the others are in a position of social dominance, the definition will persist. The subordinated group may even adopt and cling to this definition in fierce defiance, thus reinforcing the continuing ethnic identification. Ethnicity also has political uses. Many of the immigrant groups used ethnicity as a basis for political power and advancement. The rise of political machines throughout the East and Midwest is often directly tied to specific ethnic communities and alliances.

A final factor is that white ethnic groups are not totally dispersed throughout the hierarchy of American life. Ethnic stratification, as we saw in Chapter 8, still exists. White ethnics, for instance, constitute a disproportionately high percentage of the blue-collar labor force. According to a survey conducted in 1969 by the Bureau of the Census, close to half of all male workers of Irish, Polish, and Italian origin were employed in blue-collar occupations: 44.8 percent of the Irish, 49.1 percent of the Poles, and 50.2 percent of the Italians.[43] Ethnic stratification is also manifested in government personnel practices in many large cities. There may be Jewish, Italian, and Polish "seats" on the city council; and minor government employees, such as building inspectors, may be hired according to ethnic quotas.

The late 1960s saw a rise in social consciousness and social political action on the part of white ethnics. Italian-Americans, for example, began to protest stereotyping of people of Italian extraction as gangsters in the movies and on television and to demand that the media cease to refer to The Mafia as a synonym for organized crime. Such reassertions of ethnic politics remind us that ethnicity remains a vital element in American society.

The United States: Melting Pot or Pluralistic Society?

What is the most adequate way to describe the United States with regard to racial and ethnic relations? This question typically has been answered in one of two ways: America has been called either a melting pot or a pluralistic society. As we shall see, there are serious limitations to each of these concepts.

The Melting Pot

In popular theory People who consider America a **melting pot** mean just that. They say America is like a giant pot full of all sorts of races and nationalities. As the pot boils, it reduces—melts down—the differences between racial and ethnic groups. Out of this process develops a *new* nationality: an American nationality that is unique and has never before existed. The new nationality is a combination or distillation of all the nationalities in the pot. People cease being ethnics and are melted into Americans.

In practice   Contrary to popular theory, if America ever was a melting pot, the pot failed to melt its ingredients into an entirely new substance. As we have seen, racial minorities do not have the same life chances as do ethnic minorities. Ethnic minorities have not all attained complete equality with Anglo-Saxon groups. And racial and ethnic background is an important factor in determining what share each group has in America's social resources. In short, ethnicity and race still survive as social forces.

Racial and Ethnic Pluralism

Because of its poor fit with certain American realities, the melting pot theory has been challenged by a different conception of racial and ethnic relations: **pluralism**. This theory recognizes the persistence of ethnic and racial diversity. Pluralists argue that America is not a melting pot, but a society made up of numerous ethnic and racial subcultures, a *plurality* of subcultures.

Pluralist theorists hold that ethnic and racial minorities can maintain distinctive cultures, forms of organization, and identities and at the same time participate in the larger American community. Individual members of ethnic and racial groups interact among themselves on a face-to-face level; they live in well-defined communities, marry within their own group, work at similar occupations. This interaction sustains and promotes their ethnic identity and subculture. At the same time, minority group members also interact with people outside their own group. This interaction is often less intimate and occurs in the areas of politics, economics, and education.

Pluralist theorists argue that this can happen because all Americans—regardless of racial or ethnic ancestry—agree on certain basic values. These

> **melting pot:**   the belief that the plurality of racial and ethnic minorities in the United States would eventually blend into a new and different "American" compound, their differences disappearing in the process.
>
> **pluralism:**   with regard to minority group relations, the belief that racial and ethnic minorities can maintain distinctive subcultures and at the same time participate with relative equality in the larger society.

values are contained in the Constitution and the Declaration of Independence and are sometimes referred to as the American Creed. Agreement on these values makes it possible for people to be ethnics *and* Americans without contradiction. Pluralists contend that the ethnic and racial diversity that is so obvious in America does not mean that people in the United States do not share things in common.

Horace Kallen, the man who introduced the concept of cultural pluralism into the American vocabulary, used the image of the orchestra to describe the United States. Just as each instrument in the orchestra makes a distinct contribution to the musical composition, each minority group makes its particular contribution to American society. Kallen conceived each instrument—each group—as participating equally in this orchestration of social life.[44] But the image of an orchestra and the pluralist perspective derived from it are misleading. There is a tendency toward pluralism in America, but all groups have not shared equally in the society. Equality in America is a goal, not a fact. The relationship between minority and majority groups has not been based on equality; it has been based on power.

The concept of pluralism has to be modified to be faithful to American realities. There seem to be two kinds of pluralism: a pluralism of equality and a pluralism of subordination. In pluralism of equality subcultural groups would interact in harmony, like the instrumentalists in the orchestra to which Kallen refers. Ethnic and racial subcultures would coexist on an equal basis, and no group would be able to force its way of life on others. Power and status would not be a function of ethnic or racial ancestry, and groups would be able to choose

© King Features Syndicate 1971.

What it means to be an ethnic has obviously changed.

which, if any, aspects of another group's culture they wished to adopt. There would be agreement on who conducted the orchestra and how that conductor was chosen. The criterion for being conductor would not be ethnic or racial ancestry.

A different picture emerges from the pluralism of subordination. In this situation, ethnic and racial subcultures are not treated equally, and the relationship between them is not harmonious. Some subcultures are encouraged or permitted to flourish; others are attacked or coopted. Perhaps more important, a group's ethnic or racial background is crucial in determining how it will share in a society's social resources. Some groups are included in, and others excluded from, full participation in society on the basis of their racial or ethnic ancestry. Subordination is not a random occurrence; it is systematically related to a group's race or ethnic background. Finally, to return to the orchestra analogy, consensus does not determine the conductor or the music to be played; power does. And that power is derived in large part from ethnic and racial status.

Pluralism in the United States is often a pluralism of subordination. The persistence of racial and ethnic distinctiveness does not occur in an egalitarian setting, despite an ideology to the contrary. As we have seen throughout this chapter, racial and ethnic differences have traditionally structured the basis of social reward. Racial minorities have been either excluded or restricted to the margins of society. Some ethnic minorities are isolated and often work at low-status occupations. Only ethnic groups whose cultures resemble Anglo-Saxon values—or at least do not conflict with them—have managed to excel.

Assimilation The tendency toward some sort of pluralism in the United States is accompanied by a push toward **assimilation**. There are certain standards and values by which American society operates: American ways of doing things. The common language is English; the predominant religion is Christianity; clothing is basically Western European in style. Americans place great value on work, being successful, being on time. These are cultural standards to which groups must adjust and by which they are evaluated. If a group adopts these standards, it is considered assimilated. Assimilation is essential to a group's success in the United States, and groups that are not assimilated do not gain an equal share in many of America's benefits.

Racial and ethnic groups in the United States are thus pushed in two conflicting directions at the same time. If people in ethnic and racial groups wish to be successful on American terms they must operate in part outside their ethnic or racial context, and "act like Americans" rather than ethnics. This is the push toward assimilation. Nevertheless, there are some advantages to maintaining a distinctive ethnic identity, living in ethnic communities, and speaking native languages. Ethnic communities provide support for their members, offer some self-sufficiency, and can develop political power that other groups must take seriously. This is the push toward pluralism.

The move toward assimilation has serious implications. On certain levels, it represents a denial of an ethnic's community and self. To be fully assimilated means one is no longer an ethnic. This is why there is a conflict between the pluralist and assimilationist directions.

Amalgamation   Racial minorities confront a problem greater than a conflict in directions, for in some respects they have little choice: complete assimilation in a predominantly white society is very difficult because it would also require **amalgamation**—racial mixing by interbreeding. Historically, racial minorities have not been given the option of assimilation, and short of amalgamation in intermarriage, they can never be completely assimilated. The restrictions placed on racial minorities have other implications for assimilation. Because they have been excluded from full social participation, distinct subcultures have emerged among racial minorities. Thus, even if skin color did not prevent full assimilation, some racial minority group members might refuse to assimilate because to do so would mean giving up their subculture.

Separatism   This state of affairs has led some groups among racial minorities to advocate *separatism* on the grounds that since they cannot be completely assimilated into American society, the most reasonable option is to remove themselves from it. There have always been separatist tendencies among racial minorities in the United States. Some blacks were advocating return to Africa prior to the Civil War. Present-day separatists advocate various strategies. Some blacks want to return to Africa. Other black groups, like the Republic of New Africa, seek cession to them of a number of southern states so they can establish a separate nation of black people. Chicano activists like Ries Tijerina make similar demands concerning southwestern states. Probably, few separatists expect such demands to be fulfilled, but instead regard them as political talking points.

Subcultures and supercultures   The pluralists are correct in pointing out that ethnic and racial subcultures persist. But their contention that people can be both ethnics and Americans minimizes the costs and consequences involved. They do not take seriously enough the push toward assimilation. In this regard, the melting pot notion is instructive, for it does suggest that there is a culture with which all

assimilation: the process by which members of one group discard their unique cultural traits and adopt those of another group.

amalgamation: racial mixing by interbreeding.

The New Colossus
Emma Lazarus

Not like the brazen giant of Greek fame,
  With conquering limbs astride from land to
    land;
  Here at our sea-washed, sunset gates shall
    stand
A mighty woman with a torch, whose flame
Is the imprisoned lightning, and her name
  Mother of Exiles. From her beacon-hand
  Glows world-wide welcome; her mild eyes
    command
The air-bridged harbor that twin cities frame.
"Keep ancient lands, your storied pomp!" cries
  she
  With silent lips. "Give me your tired, your poor,
Your huddled masses yearning to breathe free;
  The wretched refuse of your teeming shore.
Send these, the homeless, tempest-tost to me,
  I lift my lamp beside the golden door!"

Inscribed on the pedestal of the Statue of Liberty, 1903.

Americans have to contend. This culture might be called an American superculture: a culture that crosses racial and ethnic boundaries and that must be accepted if one is to operate in the larger society, even when acceptance means the end of ethnic identity.

The superculture that pervades American life is not the new nationality to which the melting pot referred. Nor is it the American Creed assumed by the pluralists. Essentially, it is a culture rooted in the Western European tradition. Unless groups are willing and able to accept crucial aspects of this culture, they are denied complete access to American life. In this respect, the black essayist Harold Cruse has a more accurate perception of the American superculture than either the melting pot advocates or the pluralists. "America," he says, "has grown up planlessly and chaotically, leaving her racial and ethnic minorities to shift for themselves while she cultivates the idea that America is an all white Anglo-Saxon nation."[45]

Cruse is correct. But in fact the United States is neither all white nor all Anglo-Saxon. Indeed, the WASPS who dominated American social, political, and economic life for so long are numerically a small minority in the American population. The great promises of the Declaration of Independence and Emma Lazarus's poem enshrined on the Statue of Liberty have not yet been kept, but it is too early to conclude they never will be. Structured social inequality is under attack on many fronts in the United States and may yet be overcome.

Summary

The chapter covered four major topics: (1) the key concepts of minority group, ethnic group, and race; (2) the nature of structured social inequality; (3) various minority groups in contemporary American society; and (4) the United States as a pluralistic society.

Sociologically, *a minority group* is one disadvantaged in terms of social power relative to some other group(s). Membership in a minority group may be defined by legal, cultural, linguistic, religious, or numerical criteria; but the basis of the group's existence as a sociological minority group is subordination to some other group or groups.

The two major kinds of minority groups are ethnic groups and races. *Ethnic groups* are socially identified according to cultural criteria. *Races* are more difficult to define because of disagreement about which characteristics to use as criteria and particularly because of the many popular misconceptions about race. For sociologists, the most useful racial concept is the *social race,* a group socially identified by inherited physical characteristics.

Structured social inequality is inequality in life chances created by the social organization of a society. The dominant group in society has greater social privileges or rewards than the subordinate minority groups. Subordination is maintained through the mechanisms of *prejudice, discrimination, stereotypes,* and *segregation.* The social consequences of subordination for minority group members are reduced or disadvantaged life chances and lack of social and competitive equality. Minority reactions to domination can take the forms of *pluralism, assimilationism, secessionism,* or *militancy.* Most minority groups have taken all four postures at one time or another in their histories, and all four may exist within a given group at one time.

The principal minority groups in American society at the present time (women excluded) are blacks, Asian-Americans, Native Americans, Chicanos and Puerto Ricans, and white ethnics. The present circumstances of each group may only be understood in the light of their different histories in the United States. *Black Americans* remain the most disadvantaged, most frequently discriminated against, and most segregated. Even though the conditions of life for blacks have improved dramatically in the past twenty-five years, perhaps in large part in response to black protest, the *gaps* between whites and blacks on such measures as education and income remain roughly the same as in the past.

Asian-Americans have in the past suffered from many of the same kinds of inequities as blacks. But since World War II, they have gained much ground and seem to be attaining a kind of social equality with whites. Some inequalities still remain, however. The differences in their experience as a group may be attributable to their very different history in the United States and to their cultural background.

The *Native Americans* occupy a social position in American society roughly equivalent to that of black Americans, and they suffer as badly from poverty, lack of education, and occupational disadvantage. Their status, too, is related to their historical experience. From the beginning of their contact with whites, they were perceived as an alien culture and usually defined as enemies. Thus they were not absorbed by the general society even in the ways in which blacks were. The removal and reservation policies of the federal government have contributed to their isolation.

Like the Native Americans, many *Chicanos* were the original occupants of land that came to be part of the United States. Although the treaty ending the Mexican War promised that their land rights would be respected, following years saw much of it transferred to Anglo ownership. Originally concentrated in the rural Southwest, Chicanos have recently begun to enter the Midwest in large numbers and are now predominantly urban. They still suffer from high rates of poverty, unemployment or underemployment, and illiteracy. In these conditions they are joined by the other major group of American Spanish-speakers, the *Puerto Ricans,* who are now immigrating to the mainland, principally the East Coast, in large numbers.

White ethnics form minority groups based on former immigrant status and the maintenance of subcultures rooted in Old World practices. In many cases, they have suffered from segregation and discrimination, and consequently their subcultural identification may be strong. Many ethnics use their subculture as a political power base from which to work for improved group status.

Popular conceptions of the United States depict it as possessing a unified culture based on essentially Anglo-Saxon values and practices, and these certainly are national norms. But the United States is, in fact, a *plural* society composed of a great variety of racial and ethnic minorities. To a considerable extent, although in varying degree, these groups remain separate but unequal in the social structure. The idea of the nation as a *melting pot* implies that racial and ethnic groups have been blended into a *new* cultural compound, but in fact this has not occurred. Some partial blending has occurred, particularly in white groups, but it results from the acculturation of minority group members to the dominant Anglo culture. Subcultures still coexist uneasily with the American superculture,

and minority group members experience varying strains toward both *assimilation* and *separatism.* Social inequalities—some of them severe—persist on the basis of minority group membership. And although many of these have been notably reduced in the past half century, the promise of equality has not yet been fulfilled.

Review Questions

1. At their entrance into American society, Asian-Americans were welcomed little more than blacks had been. Yet the former have recently far surpassed the latter in terms of success in the U.S. Explain why.

2. Differentiate among the various forms of subordination discussed in this chapter: prejudice, discrimination, stereotyping, and segregation. Which do you think is most pervasive today? Why?

3. Discuss the various ways in which a minority group can place itself in a larger society: assimilation, inclusion, absorption, pluralism, secession, and militance.

4. Which European nationalities were considered most desirable as America was flooded by immigrants in the nineteenth century? Which were most disliked? Which religious groups were most liked? Which were most disliked? Why?

5. Discuss the plight of black Americans from the time of emancipation to the recent decades of civil rights movements. In what sense have blacks continued to be enslaved?

Suggestions for Research

1. Ask your librarian to help you find census data or statistics compiled by the Bureau of the Census. Contrast whites with blacks, Indians, Asian-Americans, and other minority groups in terms of basic demographic data. What is the mean income of each group? What types of occupations are filled by the majority of each group? What is the life expectancy of each group? How about the average level of education? What other aspects or life chances can you describe? Chart your findings and present them to the class.

2. Investigate how your community tries to assist minority groups. What types of agencies, private and public, have been organized toward this end? What services do they provide? How successful have they been? Other than

funding, what are the main problems of these organizations? How receptive are various minorities to such assistance? How well informed are minorities about available help?

3. Watch several situation comedies that deal with families of racial minorities, such as "The Jeffersons" and "Sanford and Son." In your opinion, are these programs primarily humorous creations, or do they make meaningful comments about race in the U.S.? If the latter, what is the theme of each program? How realistic do you feel these comedies are in general? What attitude does each take toward racial minorities? Toward whites? Summarize your observations and conclusions.

4. Select a magazine that is popular among minority groups, such as *Ebony*. Carefully read several issues, giving attention to any element that seems significantly different from most magazines. What is the general tone of the publication? How can you tell? What appears to be the overall purpose or theme? Do you find that this magazine is significantly different from others? If so, in what ways?

5. Analyze how different ethnic groups have adapted to American society, starting with the earliest immigrants. Which nationalities merged quickly and successfully with the larger society? Which had the most difficulty? Why? Has the general attitude toward immigrants changed over the last three centuries? If so, how? Were the earliest settlers from northern and western Europe hostile toward other immigrating peoples?

CHAPTER 10
CITIES
AND
URBANISM

I saw the skyline grow, and I saw the city grow, and sometimes I wonder if it was worth the price we paid. In those days we did not need interracial movements or good-will groups. Then a neighborhood meant so much.

Here in the most cosmopolitan community since the beginning of time, a city composed of sons and daughters of every one of the forty-eight states, and with men and women from every country in the civilized world, we worked together. Here where there were and are more Irishmen than in Dublin, more Italians than in Rome, more Germans than in any other city than Berlin, and more Jews than in Palestine—here we lived together in peace, like one great family, and should so live today and tomorrow.

We all went to school and to the fields of sport—with little rancor, no real hatred. We lived like human beings, who asked only the opportunity to work out our earthly existence and worship our God according to the dictates of our conscience.

This I hold to be humanity. This is democracy. This was New York of the yon days.

James J. Walker, former mayor of New York, speech, 1946

How is the faithful city become an harlot! it was full of judgement; righteousness lodged in it; but now murderers! Thy silver is become dross, thy wine mixed with water: Thy princes are rebellious and companions of thieves: everyone loveth gifts and followest after rewards: they judge not the fatherless, neither doth the cause of the widow come unto them.

Isaiah 1:21-23

These very different commentaries introduce the subject of this chapter: the intriguing, complex, dangerous, and perhaps ungovernable phenomenon we call the city, where it came from, where it is now, and where it may be going. Cities are as old as civilization (the two words have the same linguistic roots). They have always been its glory and its despair. It is not unlikely that city people have often looked back on their childhoods with the kind of nostalgia displayed by Mayor Walker in the quotation above. And it has only been in this century that the ancient division of the human population into city people and rural dwellers that is mirrored in Isaiah's lament has disappeared among the Western industrial nations. (The United States did not see more than 50 percent of its population become urban until between 1910 and 1920.) By the year 2000, much of the population of the world will live in sprawling urban concatenations like Calcutta, India, which already has 177,000 people to the square mile, roughly three times the number crowded into Manhattan. What that life will be like—whether it will even be *possible*—is not at this time clear.

But that cities themselves will be with us, we may be sure. They have been on the scene for 6000 years or more, and in their essence are probably not much changed. They have tended to dominate the thought and life-style of every society in which they have occurred, and they dominate the entire world today. Such peace as there is between the major nations is bought by holding one another's cities hostage to the threat of thermonuclear holocaust; and every advance in science, art, literature, medicine, music, philosophy, and even theology is the product of urban minds and urban ideas. No matter where we live, we are the people of the city and its captives.

In this chapter we will only scratch the surface of understanding the city. But the urban sociologist has come to know a great deal about cities, and it can be outlined here. Each of the major topics to be discussed has immediate relevance for each of us, even the seemingly abstract subject of the different definitions of what a city is. The three great "urban revolutions" have present significance in that the first created the city, the second shaped it in its present form, and you will have to live through the third. The echoes of an older world—made plain by

Isaiah—haunt us yet, and help to shape our notions of what the city ought to be. And the growth of the city, how it happens and where it will lead, will affect us in one way or another every day of our lives.

Before we may explore these things with profit, however, we must have the conceptual tools to do so, the keys to the urban kingdom, so to speak. And that is where we shall start.

Basic Concepts

Tools for Description

The urban sociologist, like most others, faces two challenging problems. The first is that cities are so complex and so filled with diversity it seems impossible to reduce the colorful variety to coherent patterns without losing awareness of all the differences that really do exist. The line between oversimplification and a description so detailed that it becomes unique is narrow. The second problem is that patterns and changes stem from multiple decisions made by many persons but result in movements that are characteristic of groups sharing similar social traits. To describe such patterns and change, a variety of conceptual tools are used. Three appear regularly in this chapter: the ideal type, the continuum, and the descriptive model.

The ideal type The *ideal*, or *constructed*, type is a mental image created to describe some process or event by listing distinctive characteristics generalized from the examination of a large number of similar phenomena. From the many cases, the social scientist selects those characteristics that appear typical. The ideal exists only as a concept, and no one example will be found that has all of the characteristics.

The continuum If two ideal types that are opposites are constructed, the space between the two can be conceived in terms of small units of gradual change from one type to the other. When this has been done, as we saw in Chapter 7, a *continuum* has been constructed. For example, if the most and least populous counties of the United States are

Panel 1: NOW FROM WILDERNESS TV, A SPECIAL REPORT ON NEWS FROM THE OUTSIDE WORLD

Panel 2: SCIENTISTS STUDYING HUMAN BEHAVIOR PATTERNS OF SUBJECTS PLACED IN SPECIALLY CONSTRUCTED MAZES ARE CONCERNED ABOUT TEST RESULTS...

Panel 3: THE CROWDED CONDITION OF THE MAZES CAUSES TENSION, ANGER, FEAR AND FRUSTRATION IN THE HUMAN SUBJECTS.

Panel 4: THE MAZES, AS REPORTED BY THE SCIENTISTS ARE CALLED CITIES...

© 1976 First Communications; by permission.

hypothesized or actually identified, all other counties could then be arranged by size of population in the space between the two. The continuum would demonstrate both the range of the counties and their distribution by size.

The model As you have no doubt gathered from earlier references, a *model* is a series of statements that define concepts and link them in some relationship to one another so that some part of the real world is described. Models may be simple or complex and may be stated as verbal descriptions or mathematical relationships. Although it is not possible to include every detail in a model, the task in constructing one is to find those features that give the most insight into the reality the model describes. The test of the model is its usefulness in explanation and prediction.

In this chapter, several ideal types are discussed, such as urban society and preindustrial society. These, and others, have been particularly useful to the urban sociologist in describing urbanization and urban areas. Several continua are used, sometimes implicitly. The concentric-zone, sector, and multiple-nuclei theories of land use are models that appear and then reappear in various forms in the urban literature; they will be defined and discussed later in this chapter.

Definitions of the City

Urban terminology presents problems for the sociologist because words used with carefully developed technical meaning in urban literature are also used daily by others with different meanings at-

Population density produces almost psychotic behavior in laboratory animals. What effects does it have on humans?

tached. The word *city*, for example, may mean that the speaker is referring to the core of the urbanized area, to a community of 10,000, 100,000, or 1,000,000 persons. *Greater metropolitan area* and *inner city* have meanings bestowed by business groups and local understandings. But the urban sociologist needs a working vocabulary in which there is general agreement about what phenomena the words describe. The terminology introduced here is the core vocabulary needed in a sociological discussion of urbanization.

The legal city Very frequently when the term *city* is used in the media, the city referred to is the *legal city.* The legal definition of what a city is varies from state to state and is formulated by individual state legislatures. But legal definitions of the city usually include that it is a municipal corporation occupying a defined geographic area and meeting the regulations and rules developed by the state. Because legal definitions vary, they do not provide comparable units from state to state and thus are not very useful for research purposes.

The geographic city Another concept is the *geographic city*, a definition used mostly by urban geographers. Because a U.S. Census term, *urbanized area*, closely approximates it, the geographic city is an alternative definition used in urban research. The geographic city is the continuously built-up area in and around a legal city and extending in all directions until significantly interrupted by farms, forest, bodies of water, or other nonurban land use. It is the city as one would see it from an airplane and includes the legal city and numerous surrounding suburban communities and densely settled unincorporated areas.

The city as a sociological entity The definition that most urban sociologists use as a beginning for more sophisticated treatment of the city was formulated by Louis Wirth in an essay called "Urbanism as a Way of Life."[1] Wirth defined the **sociological city** as a *relatively large, relatively dense, and permanent settlement of socially heterogeneous individuals.* He realized that using size alone as a defining characteristic would be inadequate, because size itself does not necessarily produce the hustle, bustle, and amenities of life recognized as urban. Therefore, he added **density** to his definition, thus removing sparsely populated large villages and clusters of farmhouses from consideration.

The third element in the definition is the most important, the social heterogeneity of the population. Because *heterogeneity* usually implies only diversity, many modern sociologists would prefer the term *differentiation,* which, as we saw in Chapter 8, suggests the *unequal* distribution of power, wealth, education, and skills among a population. In the city, education, skills, and knowledge vary from basic skills to technical expertise. Wealth varies from subsistence to the luxurious life-style of the few. And power varies from the disenfranchised with no vote to the very influential who decide on the development of acres of land and the expenditure of millions of dollars. In an agricultural community, the population is differentiated only by a few occupational roles and sex and age status.

A fourth element added by other writers to the three above is that the city performs special functions for the **hinterland**, or the rural area surrounding the city. Those specialized functions include (1) maintaining a permanent marketplace for the exchange of the hinterland's surplus for the goods produced by the city; (2) providing the locus of government and law and order for the hinterland; and (3) providing the religious center for the hinterland. To say that the city performs these functions is not to say that towns and villages of the hinter-

legal city: a municipal corporation occupying a defined geographical area subject to the legal control of the state.

geographic city: the continuously built-up area in and around a legal city; almost identical in meaning to the U.S. Census term *urbanized area.*

sociological city: a relatively large, dense, permanent settlement of socially heterogeneous persons.

density: the number of people per unit of land area, for instance, the number per square mile.

hinterland: the rural area surrounding the city.

urbanized area: A U.S. Census term covering three kinds of urban "place": (1) legally incorporated areas with populations of 2,500 or more; (2) legally unincorporated areas with populations of at least 1,000 and located adjacent to large urban areas; (3) legally incorporated places with populations below 1,000 when they possess a closely settled dwelling area of 100 or more dwelling units.

Standard Metropolitan Statistical Area (SMSA): A U.S. Census term meaning a county or adjacent counties containing at least one central city with a population of 50,000 or more.

land do not provide any such services. But the city provides them at a highly specialized level, and the hinterland is dependent on the specialized goods and knowledge as well as the coordinating functions of the city. The village may have a grammar school and the larger market town a high school, but to acquire college and professional training you have to go to the city. A village may have a doctor and a dentist, but the doctor and the dentist were trained in the city and refer patients to hospitals and doctors in the city for complicated care. The city dominates and influences the small towns, villages, and isolated settlements; and in doing so, it distinguishes itself from them by the direction of the flow of influence, from city to hinterland.

The city in the U.S. Census Two important U.S. Census Bureau terms have been formulated: one to describe the geographic city, called the **urbanized area**; and a second, useful in the collection of statistics, called the **Standard Metropolitan Statistical Area (SMSA)**. Both incorporate major elements of the sociological definition of the city: size,

Figure 10-1
Standard Metropolitan Statistical Areas

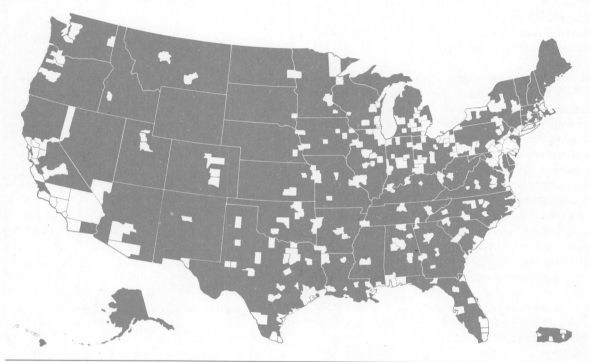

density, and a dominant relationship with the surrounding hinterland.

The urbanized area   The U.S. Census term *urbanized area* covers three kinds of urban places: (1) any incorporated place with a population of 2,500 or more; (2) any unincorporated area having a population of at least 1,000 per square mile and located on the fringe of a large urban area; and (3) any incorporated place with a population under 1,000 that has a closely settled area of 100 or more dwelling units. The population of urban places varies from as low as 200 in some countries to as high as 10,000 in other countries, a fact that complicates research across national boundaries. The urbanized area should correspond very closely to the geographic city.

The SMSA   The U.S. Census defines a *Standard Metropolitan Statistical Area (SMSA)* as a county or

SMSAs (shown in white) cross state boundaries as well as local governmental boundaries. The size of the SMSAs reflects the size of counties. Note the large Phoenix-Tucson area, which covers more land area than any of the Atlantic seaboard SMSAs, which have much larger populations.

adjacent counties with at least one central city of at least 50,000 population (see Figure 10-1). Because the building block of the SMSA is the county, the SMSA is a useful research definition. Although the county unit may include some areas that are not urban, most vital statistics are maintained by counties and, where they exist, their subdivisions, the townships. The fact that statistics for SMSAs are compatible with other data groupings makes SMSAs useful to the urban researcher. What this means is that the county or township is a "natural" enumeration unit and thus is comparable to other natural units.

Which definitions we use in discussing cities makes a difference in how we rank them, as you can see in Table 10-1. In the following discussion, *city* will be used to refer to legal entities and *urbanized area* to refer to the larger area consisting of a central city and its surrounding urban fringe.

Urbanization and Urbanism

Urbanization is a *process*, a movement of population from rural areas of agricultural activity to city areas of manufacturing and service activities. Because urbanization is a process, it is appropriate to devise measures of rates and talk about degrees of urbanization. How urbanization has proceeded in the United States is shown in Table 10-2.

Urbanism is the patterns of behavior, relationships, and modes of thought that characterize persons living in urban areas. *Urbanization* is also sometimes used to refer to the process by which urban patterns of behavior, relationships, and modes of thought spread and dominate until they become the characteristic patterns of a national society and are shared even by people living far removed from urban areas. Urbanism as a way of life is discussed later on in the chapter.

The Urban Revolutions

Urbanization did not occur once but has recurred over and over in history as societies have urbanized at different times. It is an ongoing process that has never stopped and has rarely slowed since its beginning. The initial appearance of cities, then the dominance of urbanism as a life-style, and finally the total urbanization of the world's population are three high points in this process. They are such prominent stages that they are often called urban revolutions. Two of these revolutions have occurred, and the third is yet to occur but is so certain and so near that it will be part of your experience. The first urban revolution is characterized by the emergence of the first preindustrial cities. The second is characterized by the emergence of the industrial city and the urbanization of the populations of the industrial nations. The third is characterized by the further growth of urban

> **urbanization:** the process of population movement from rural areas and activities to urban areas and activities.
>
> **urbanism:** the patterns of behavior, relationships, and modes of thought characteristic of urban life.
>
> **first urban revolution:** the historical emergence of cities and urbanism.

areas in industrial nations, the development of urban areas in the developing nations, and the urbanization of over one-half of the world's population.

Very little of the time that human beings have been on earth has been characterized by urban life. Human beings have existed for about a million and a quarter years (40,000 years in their present physical form), but they have only lived in cities about 6,000 years, or less than 0.5 percent of that time. But all our written history stems from the period in which urban life characterized most human societies to some degree. Many of the complex social institutions that constrain and channel our social life were developed in urbanized societies. In all societies, urban populations, while usually not the numerical equal of rural populations, have dominated thought and the creative arts as producers, consumers, and trend setters. U.S. history, in particular, has been an urban-dominated history. The original pattern of settlement was to plot towns first. Only after the establishment of a town or a city did farmers spread into the hinterland.

The First Urban Revolution

The **first urban revolution** occurred when cities first appeared and the urban life-style first emerged. To call the appearance of cities a revolution is to draw attention to the dramatic change in the nature of society they created, not to imply that urbanization and the appearance of cities was a sudden and violent event. The appearance of the first cities was a gradual accumulation of changes and movements that took place over a long period of time. Archeological evidence indicates that in many cases a settlement existed in an area for a thousand years before it reached the point where it could be

Table 10-1   Rank orderings of the twenty-five largest cities in the U.S. according to three different definitions, 1970

Legal city	Population	Urbanized area	Population	The SMSA	Population
1 New York, N.Y.	7,894,862	1 New York, N.Y.-Northeastern New Jersey	16,206,841	1 New York, N.Y.	11,571,899
2 Chicago, Ill.	3,366,957	2 Los Angeles-Long Beach, Calif.	8,351,266	2 Los Angeles-Long Beach, Calif.	7,032,075
3 Los Angeles, Calif.	2,816,061	3 Chicago, Ill.-Northwestern Indiana	6,714,578	3 Chicago, Ill.	6,978,947
4 Philadelphia, Pa.	1,948,609	4 Philadelphia, Pa.-N.J.	4,021,066	4 Philadelphia, Pa.-N.J.	4,817,914
5 Detroit, Mich.	1,511,482	5 Detroit, Mich.	3,970,584	5 Detroit, Mich.	4,199,931
6 Houston, Tex.	1,232,802	6 San Francisco-Oakland, Calif.	2,987,850	6 San Francisco-Oakland, Calif.	3,109,519
7 Baltimore, Md.	905,759	7 Boston, Mass.	2,652,575	7 Washington, D.C.-Md.-Va.	2,861,123
8 Dallas, Tex.	844,401	8 Washington, D.C.-Md.-Va.	2,481,489	8 Boston, Mass.	2,753,700
9 Washington, D.C.	756,510	9 Cleveland, Ohio	1,959,880	9 Pittsburgh, Pa.	2,401,245
10 Cleveland, Ohio	750,903	10 St. Louis, Mo.-Ill.	1,882,944	10 St. Louis, Mo.-Ill.	2,363,017
11 Indianapolis, Ind.	744,624	11 Pittsburgh, Pa.	1,846,042	11 Baltimore, Md.	2,070,670
12 Milwaukee, Wis.	717,099	12 Minneapolis-St. Paul, Minn.	1,704,423	12 Cleveland, Ohio	2,064,194
13 San Francisco, Calif.	715,674	13 Houston, Tex.	1,677,863	13 Houston, Tex.	1,985,031
14 San Diego, Calif.	696,769	14 Baltimore, Md.	1,579,781	14 Newark, N.J.	1,856,556
15 San Antonio, Tex.	654,153	15 Dallas, Tex.	1,338,684	15 Minneapolis-St. Paul, Minn.	1,813,647
16 Boston, Mass.	641,071	16 Milwaukee, Wis.	1,252,457	16 Dallas, Tex.	1,555,950
17 Memphis, Tenn.	623,530	17 Seattle-Everett, Wash.	1,238,107	17 Seattle-Everett, Wash.	1,421,869
18 St. Louis, Mo.	622,236	18 Miami, Fla.	1,219,661	18 Anaheim-Santa Ana-Garden Grove, Calif.	1,420,386
19 New Orleans, La.	593,471	19 San Diego, Calif.	1,198,323	19 Milwaukee, Wis.	1,403,688
20 Phoenix, Ariz.	581,562	20 Atlanta, Ga.	1,172,778	20 Atlanta, Ga.	1,390,164
21 Columbus, Ohio	539,677	21 Cincinnati, Ohio-Ky.	1,110,514	21 Cincinnati, Ohio-Ky.-Ind.	1,384,851
22 Seattle, Wash.	530,831	22 Kansas City, Mo.-Kans.	1,101,787	22 Paterson-Clifton-Passaic, N.J.	1,358,794
23 Jacksonville, Fla.	528,865	23 Buffalo, N.Y.	1,086,594	23 San Diego, Calif.	1,357,854
24 Pittsburgh, Pa.	520,117	24 Denver, Colo.	1,047,311	24 Buffalo, N.Y.	1,349,211
25 Denver, Colo.	514,678	25 San Jose, Calif.	1,025,273	25 Miami, Fla.	1,267,792

called a city rather than a large village or rural settlement.

The first urban revolution is associated with the process we call **civilization**. Definitions of civilization usually include the criteria of the development of writing, the domestication of animals, the development of seed grain, and the formation of stable areas of settlement. To these a social scientist might add complex division of labor, advanced technology, advanced political systems, and sophisticated religious systems, philosophical thought, and artistic institutions. The historian Arnold Toynbee defines civilization in terms of the institutionalization of relatively enduring and stable patterns of ethical and religious tradition that dominate a society or a number of related societies. Whether civilization is necessary for urbanization to occur or whether urbanization is necessary for civilization to occur is unclear and probably unresolvable, but it is certain that the two interacted and are historically related in time. The elements of civilization, coupled with advances in agriculture and surplus population, are the determining conditions for ubanization.

Determinants   Urban scholars agree that before urbanization could occur, *agricultural development* had to reach the point where domesticated animals and grains replaced wild animals and grasses as the principal source of food. This made possible the development of fixed communities in place of a nomadic existence. But a food supply that allowed a group to settle permanently was not enough to allow the development of urban areas, for such areas depend on agricultural surplus from the hinterland to feed the urban population. The *intensification* of agriculture also had to occur, requiring inventions that allowed the production of more food in a given land area by use of improved grains, irrigation, fertilization, and systematic crop rotation. For example, Rome at its height denuded the hills of Italy in an attempt to provide food for the city and then imported grain from captured territories.

In addition to a surplus of food, urbanization required a *surplus of population*, produced either by increases in the population within the city or by rural displacement, absorption of population from the territory surrounding the urban area. (Urban areas, as we know them, at least, tend to have lower fertility and higher mortality than rural areas, consuming people just as they consume food.)

Once a food and population supply was established, the future urban dwellers needed some *source of livelihood* that would be feasible in the urban area. The emergence of specialized crafts served this purpose for the new urban population. Handicrafts were consumed not by producers of food, but by the elite of the city. *Marketing and trade mechanisms* were needed if cities were to survive. Goods produced had to be sold and raw materials had to be purchased, because the urban craft worker was often far removed from both raw materials and markets. Distribution mechanisms had to be developed, because personal exchange was not sufficient to distribute food to all members of the urban community when much of the food supply was acquired as payment of taxes and stored by the state. Civilization's contribution of writing became essential to the task of taxation, to the maintenance of these market institutions, and to the distribution of food.

Exchange beyond the city's own surrounding territory became necessary because some products and raw materials had to come from other cities and from long distances. Thus, the urban

civilization: the life-style characterized by possession of literacy, domestic animals, seed grain, stable settlement, complex division of labor, advanced technology and political systems, and sophisticated religious, philosophical, and artistic institutions.

Table 10-2   Urban population of the U.S., 1790–1970

Year	Percent of total population
Current urban definition[a]	
1970	73.5
1960	69.9
1950	64.0
Previous urban definition[b]	
1960	63.0
1950	59.6
1940	56.5
1930	56.1
1920 Transitional	51.2 Turnover
1910 years	45.6 point
1900	39.6
1890	35.1
1880	28.2
1870	25.7
1860	19.8
1850	15.3
1840	10.8
1830	8.8
1820	7.2
1810	7.3
1800	6.1
1790	5.1

[a]Includes persons living in rural portions of extended cities.
[b]Excludes persons living in rural portions of extended cities.

Note the decades 1910–1920—the period in which the U.S. became an urban nation.

area had to provide protection not only for the persons within its walls, but also for those some distance from the city, to insure its food supply, its trade routes, and its supply of raw materials. *Military institutions*, therefore, became an important part of urban life. Markets, distribution of goods, and military activities need the coordination of *government*. Without some form of government, cities could not have grown to a decent size. Governmental functions were also required beyond the city to keep peace and to tax in the hinterland.

In summary, the roots of urbanization lie in a combination of technological changes that produced surplus food and in the development of social institutions which coordinated the activities necessary for the maintenance of surplus populations in cities. One without the other could not have allowed the emergence of cities or the first urban revolution. That first urban revolution was a gradual accumulation of far-reaching changes that allowed the concentration of population in large, dense, heterogeneous settlements.

The emergence of cities   Until very recently, cities were believed to have begun in the period 3500 B.C. to 3000 B.C., in the area of the Near East called the Fertile Crescent, encompassing modern Jordan, Syria, and Iraq. Then at a later time, cities emerged in the Nile Valley, in the Indus Valley, on the Mediterranean coast, and in Europe (2400 B.C.), and then in China and Mesoamerica. The links between the development of cities in various parts of the world are still not clear, but it is probable that cities developed in China (1500 B.C.) and Mesoamerica (500 B.C.) independently of other cities because of these regions' geographic isolation.

Early cities were small by modern standards, 5,000 to 10,000 in population, though historians and archeologists think some may have been as large as 100,000. A few could have been larger. For example, the population of ancient Rome, one of the largest preindustrial cities, has been variously estimated at 250,000 to 1,000,000 at the height of its power and development.

New archeological discoveries have shown that cities in the area stretching from modern Turkey to northwest India are far older than earlier believed and were larger than previous estimates. It is now known, for instance, that Jericho—which may have been the first walled city in the world—dates back at least to 8000 and perhaps 10,000 B.C., while a new site in Turkey, Catal Hüyük, had a well-developed, bustling life by 7000 B.C.[2]

Catal Hüyük is located in an area not previously known to have been urbanized, but the evidence from burial sites, foundations, and trash deposits indicates that Catal Hüyük was a community with extensive economic development, specialized crafts, a rich religious life, high attainment in the arts, and an impressive social organization. The variation in amount and quality of burial gifts and the size of the residential foundations shows that the society was stratified, and that wealth and power were unequally distributed among the population. From the grain remains it is clear that sophisticated grains had been developed, such as barley and threshing wheat. In addition, food supplies included peas, lentils, fruits, berries, domesticated sheep, cows, goats, and wild cattle, red deer, boar, and leopard.

Craft remains indicate the presence of weavers, basketmakers, carpenters, joiners, tool makers, bead makers, jewelry makers, merchants of skin, leather, and fur, workers of bone, wood carvers, and painters. The city wealth indicates that it is likely that a fairly extensive trade network existed, particularly in mirrors, jewelry, and obsidian, a volcanic glass used for cutting tools. A variety of ceremonial sites and objects convey the impression that the religious institutions were well developed and went beyond the rather crude fertility worship found in many rural village sites of the same time period. By 7000 B.C., the settlement covered thirty-two acres and met all the qualifications of size, density, and heterogeneity for classification as a city.

The Second Urban Revolution

The **second urban revolution** was produced by the combination of *industrialization* with *urbanization*. The Industrial Revolution is characterized by (1) the replacement of hand production in a craft worker's home or small shop by machine production centered in factories; (2) the production of standardized goods with interchangeable parts; (3) the rise of a class of factory labor who work for wages and do not own the tools they use or the products they produce; (4) a great increase in the proportion of the population engaged in nonagricultural occupations; and (5) the availability of a vast quantity of goods at low cost.

As in the first urban revolution, the changes were both technological and social. The immense reorganization of work into factories required the reorganization of families and kinship structures, of the relations between producers and consumers, and of the relations between government and owners of factories. The rapid growth of cities that was characteristic of the second urban revolution could not have occurred without technological advances in transportation and in the production of goods and the techniques of food storage. These changes gave the city of the second urban revolution a much greater hinterland than that of the first urban revolution.

Rapidity of city growth   The second urban revolution produced cities larger than the first, climaxing with cities in several parts of the world with a population of over a million. Unlike the earlier revolution, the second saw over half of the population of industrialized nations relocated in cities, with only a minority of persons left in agricultural labor. The second urban revolution was more revolutionary in that, rather than taking place over thousands of years, cities doubled and tripled populations decade after decade for a period of from thirty to sixty years.

The growth of Chicago and London demonstrates the rapidity of the urbanization that came with industrialization. In 1811, the population of London was 864,000; in 1891, eighty years later, it was 4,232,000, an increase of almost 500 percent. London's growth increased until, in 1970, the Greater London Metropolitan Area had a population of 7,400,000. About 87 percent of England's population is classified as urban, with about 3 percent of the population in agricultural employment, making England one of the most urban nations in the world. Such growth was not limited to London; other industrial areas grew in Manchester and Birmingham. Between those same years of 1811 and 1891, the population of England's cities of over 100,000 grew from 1.2 million to 9.2 million.

Chicago was incorporated in 1833, with less than

> **second urban revolution:**   the historical transformation of the city accomplished by the Industrial Revolution, which turned the city into an industrial center.

Above: The walls of Jericho. These may be the first city walls ever built.
Below: Ancient Jericho as it appears today.

a thousand citizens. By 1837, the population was still only about 4,100; by 1840, 4,500; but by 1850 it was 28,000.[3] The 1860 census must have been unbelievable: the population figure was 109,206. But the large growth decades for Chicago were still to come; in 1870 the population was almost 300,000; and by 1880, Chicago had passed the half million mark with a population of 503,298. In 1890, Chicago had a population of over 1 million; in 1910, over 2 million; and in 1930, over 3 million.

Rural to urban migration   The growth of the typical city of the second urban revolution was nourished by a steady rural-to-urban, farm-to-factory movement of the population. In Chicago, as in many other cities on the eastern seaboard and the Great Lakes, the farm-to-city movement had two sources: the farms of the United States and the farms of Europe. In 1930, over 800,000 of the white population of Chicago were foreign-born: 150,000 Poles, 110,000 Germans, 78,000 Russians, 74,000 Italians, 66,000 Swedes, 49,000 Czechs, 47,000 Free Irish, 7,000 Northern Irish, 31,000 Lithuanians, 30,000 Canadians, and 26,000 British. (These numbers do not include small children born immediately after arrival in the United States.) It was possible to walk blocks in the city and never hear English spoken. Many of the rural Americans in Chicago in 1930 were black, some 230,000. By 1893, Chicago housed the largest Bohemian community

Chicago then and now. State Street (the principal artery of the Loop) looking north from Washington Street in the late 1880s and in 1976.

in the world; and by World War II, Chicago ranked only behind Warsaw and Lodz as the largest community of Poles.

Chicago was not alone. In 1890, New York City had half as many Italians as Naples, as many Germans as Hamburg, twice as many Irish as Dublin, and two and a half times as many Jews as Warsaw. Boston had still more Irish than New York. Ireland's population had dropped by 1900 to almost half of the 1850 population, and a great deal of that drop could be accounted for by the movement from rural Ireland to urban America.

In the midst of this rapid growth, sometime between 1910 and 1920, half the population of the United States became urban, and by 1970, 75 percent was urban. The urban population grew not by natural increase, but by movement of persons, individual by individual, first away from the farms, then to small towns, and finally to the large cities. In every decade since the first census in 1790, the urban population of the United States has grown more rapidly than its rural population; and beginning in 1860, in every census, the numerical growth of the urban population has exceeded the growth of the rural population, with the single exception of the census of 1870.

The preindustrial and industrial city compared
The characteristics of the city of the first urban revolution, or preindustrial city, and the city of the second urban revolution, or industrial city, have been summarized by Gideon Sjoberg in *The Preindustrial City*.[4] As Sjoberg points out, preindustrial cities everywhere, like industrial cities, display strikingly similar social and ecological structures. The key variable in the change from preindustrial to industrial city is technology, which profoundly affects every aspect of society. Table 10-3 compares the two city types. Both descriptions are ideal types, and any city in transition, or industrializing city, would lie somewhere on the continuum between these types.

Urbanism as a way of life As a result of the second urban revolution, urbanism, the characteristic way of life of city people, became the way of life not only of the residents of cities, but also of the remaining population in the rural areas and farms surrounding the city and dominated by it. The area of dominance of the industrial city was greater than the area dominated by the older city, because advanced methods of transportation and rapid communication transmitted products, events, news, fads, fashions, and crazes of the city to every corner of the hinterland.

Urbanism as a way of life was given its classic statement by Louis Wirth in his essay with that title, mentioned previously. Wirth, you recall, abstracted three characteristics that defined a city: size, density, and heterogeneity. He then linked these with the general body of sociological knowledge about behavior of groups, particularly small groups, and produced a picture of the urban life-style. Wirth says that an increase in the size of an urban area produces changes in how people relate to each other on a daily basis, and that these changes are further reinforced by increasing density. With increased size, the number of daily interactions increases and the potential for differentiation increases. Wirth, like Durkheim before him, believed that specialization occurs in order to meet the problems of increased population in a given land area. Urbanites become less dependent on any one individual for goods and services as they are able to find substitute goods or producers in the growing urban complex. As associations and interactions with people increase, knowledge about each person decreases, and the relationships between people become less intimate. Contacts between people become impersonal, transitory, and segmental. The individual is freed from the personal and emotional control of personal relationships and intimate groups.

With increased density, the differentiation created by increases in size is reinforced, and the social structure becomes more complex. Just as the occupations and livelihoods of the people who use any given piece of land become specialized, so does the use of the land itself. Places of residence and work become separate. Certain areas of the city develop specialized functions: retail shopping, wholesaling, manufacturing, produce marketing, banking, recreation, entertainment, and vice.

Heterogeneity of the cities produced by the migration of peoples of diverse origins further reinforces the differentiation of occupational groups. Because people are so different and because some of the differences are characteristic of large groups of people, segregated groups emerge in the urban area. A cluster of ethnic, religious, or occupational groups replaces the rural cluster of family and kin. People recognize others by their dress and uniforms and take them at face value. Money becomes the agreed-upon measure of the value of things, because personal standards of value vary with every individual and group. Formal control is needed to replace the control of family and intimate relationships. The economic base leaves little room for personal workmanship but instead emphasizes standardization and interchangeability of parts.

Despite Wirth's affection for cities, his description of urbanism clearly conveys feelings of lack of emotional fulfillment in urban life. His portrait of the highly fragmented, individualistic, and free-floating urban dweller has its critics. Studies of neighborliness have presented mixed results, from descriptions of high-rise apartments in which no one knew neighbors to accounts in which the residents of such apartments knew and depended on each other for a variety of daily happenings. Many studies have described ethnic neighborhoods as characterized by closeness and a sense of community: Wirth's own on the Chicago Jewish

Table 10-3   The preindustrial and industrial city compared

Preindustrial city	Industrial city
Physical characteristics	**Physical characteristics**
A small, walled, densely populated city housing a small percent of the population of the society	A large, sprawling, open city housing a large percent of the population of the society
Highly segregated by occupation; ethnic or religious group membership made visible by a vast number of status symbols	Relatively low segregation; few outward symbols; segregation based on race
Streets are narrow, designed for foot travel; internal communication is slow	Space for streets is given priority; internal transportation is good; communication is rapid
Functions	**Functions**
The political capital, the marketplace, the religious center	A manufacturing, finance, and coordinating center of an industrial society
Social structure	**Social structure**
A rigid class structure with an elite composed of holders of high office, landlords, and a few merchants	A fluid class structure with an elite of businessmen, professionals, and scientists
A small middle class, a vast underclass	A large middle class with technologically related jobs
Abhorrence of manual work	A general elevation of science, few unskilled jobs, glorification of work
Economic institutions	**Economic institutions**
Wealth by land holding	Wealth by salaries, fees, investment
Low status of business activity	High status of business activity
An extensive guild system	Unionization at a national level
A small, limited market; small daily inventories; production and marketing by one person	Large, worldwide markets; large yearly inventories; specialization of production and marketing
A small service sector haggling for price	Large service sector, fixed price
No concern for time and an irregular work schedule	Time important and a regular work schedule
Lack of standardization	Standardization of processes and quality
Political structure	**Political structure**
A ruling family with a government of sovereign and ministers and a bureaucracy based on tradition and an appeal to the absolute	Formal public opinion, with a bureaucracy based on technical criteria; government based on appeals to experts and public opinion
Government functions to provide social control and public works and to extract tribute	Government functions to provide social control via police power and the courts, public services, and welfare, and to impose rational taxation
Religious institutions	**Religious institutions**
A dominant institution with strong ties to other institutions	A weak religious institution separate from other institutions
Dominated by the elite and reflecting the divisions of the class structure, used to justify the rule of the elite	Dominated by the middle class; standardization of religious experience marked by the disappearance of magic
Education and communication	**Education and communication**
Religious and sacred education for the few	Technical and secular education for the masses
Oral communication with little emphasis on record keeping	Emphasis on written communication and extensive record keeping
Class dialects cut across national language; writing is an art form; books are religious art objects	A standardized language and a utilitarian use of printing
	A mass media and a popular culture

community (1928), Herbert Gans's on Boston's Italian neighborhoods (1962), and Jane Jacobs's on Greenwich Village (1961).[5]

The growth of the metropolis   The **metropolis**, or metropolitan area, consists of a legal city and the surrounding built-up territory that is linked with it by transportation and communication and is economically integrated with it. The surrounding area usually includes other incorporated communities, some recently established as a result of expansion of the urban population and some older settlements swallowed up by the growing metropolis.

Charles Glaab, an urban historian, gives 1890 as the year that marked the beginning of the growth of metropolitan areas in the United States. No new major city was founded after that date, according to Glaab. Instead, large cities were to grow still larger, and smaller cities were to remain small, receiving less of the urban growth of the twentieth century than the larger cities.[6] Census terminology finally reflected this change in growth patterns in 1950 by initiating the terms *standard metropolitan area* and *urbanized area* in that year's census. The standard metropolitan area was retitled SMSA in the 1960 and 1970 census reports. The United States has three of the fourteen largest metropolitan areas in the world (see Table 10-4).

Metropolitan government   There are no standard governmental units for defining the existence of metropolitan areas. Some have regional planning programs and provide some services on a regional basis, but usually the area is politically fragmented, literally into hundreds or even thousands of subdivisions: cities, towns, fire protection districts, sewer districts, police districts, and school districts. Some notable examples of metropolitan areas that have initiated metropolitan governmental structures are: Toronto, which in 1953 organized the city, five townships, four towns, and three villages into a regional government called Metro; Miami and Dade County, Florida, which in 1957 organized twenty-six municipalities into a regional government also called Metro; and Indianapolis and Marion County, Indiana, which organized a unit called UNIGOV in 1970. In these examples, the municipalities retained their identity, varying numbers of functions and amounts of power.

metropolis: the legal city together with the built-up area surrounding it. Almost identical in meaning to the U.S. Census term *Standard Metropolitan Statistical Area.*

Table 10-4   The world's largest metropolitan areas

Area	Population
New York, New York	16,206,841
Tokyo, Japan	11,324,417
Shanghai, China	10,820,000
Paris, France	9,250,647
Mexico City, Mexico	8,589,630
Buenos Aires, Argentina	8,352,900
Los Angeles–Long Beach, California	8,351,266
Osaka, Japan	7,838,722
São Paulo, Brazil	7,693,000
Peking, China	7,570,000
London, England	7,418,020
Moscow, USSR	7,300,000
Calcutta, India	7,031,382
Chicago, Illinois	6,714,578

Figure 10-2
A metropolitan service area

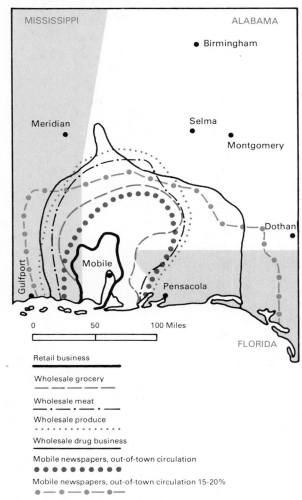

Retail business

Wholesale grocery

Wholesale meat

Wholesale produce

Wholesale drug business

Mobile newspapers, out-of-town circulation

Mobile newspapers, out-of-town circulation 15-20%

The figure shows seven different measures of the influence of Mobile, Alabama, over its service area. Each measure contains differing amounts of land area, but the shape remains much the same. Each of the boundaries encloses an area in which 50 percent or more of the transactions are done in Mobile with the exception of the last, which includes an area of 15 to 20 percent of out-of-town newspaper circulation.

Metropolitan service areas The influence of the metropolitan area extends beyond its own geographic area into the hinterland surrounding it, forming a **metropolitan service area**. The influence of the metropolitan service area has been measured with a variety of indicators, mostly economic: the distance people drive to shop; the frequency of purchases from stores in the central city; the circulation of newspapers; the movement of perishable food commodities, such as milk, eggs, and produce; checking account deposits; department store delivery zones; and radio listening patterns (see Figure 10-2). Each of these measures produces different boundaries of metropolitan influence, but together they give a rough idea of the economic influence and domination of the metropolitan area. In general, as the distance from the center of the metropolitan area increases, its influence decreases; but some functions, such as urban-based credit and banking, may extend over huge service areas.[7]

The area within the zone of metropolitan influence includes other smaller cities and towns that are hubs of regional activity. Each metropolitan service area has within it a large number of small communities that meet daily needs: small stores that sell eggs, butter, bread, and milk, pins and needles, and other frequently purchased items; grade schools; and barber shops. A smaller number of medium-size communities serve more specialized needs for which a larger service area is needed: weekly supermarket shopping, lumberyard and hardware stores, appliance stores, shopping for brand-name articles, high schools, and medical services. All of these communities are under the influence of the metropolis, which serves persons in outlying communities with medical care for serious illness, shopping for expensive items, schools for trade and professional education, credit for the family business, entertainment by nationally known artists, major league sports, symphony, opera, the art museum, and the zoo.[8]

The national network of metropolitan areas Just as the growth of metropolitan areas has meant the expansion of their hinterlands and influence, intimately linking all communities into regional interdependence, so metropolitan areas have become linked in a national network of interdependence.

Metropolitan areas depend on other metropolitan areas for the raw materials, markets, specialized services, and specialized products without which they could not grow. New York and Chicago provide stock exchanges, money markets, and wholesale markets for goods that give them a national hinterland.

Charles Glaab and Theodore Brown trace the emergence of a national network of metropolitan areas to the emergence of a national system of transportation.[9] At first, cities were connected by waterways, which limited their location. As the railroads appeared, they, too, followed established water routes, which often provided the most direct route over the most accessible terrain. At first, railroads connected existing cities, insuring their future growth and enlarging their hinterlands. With advances in technology, tunneling, and bridging, railroads were freed from early construction constraints and could choose the most advantageous routes. City building and railroad building became linked. Railroad networks gave cities trade and commercial advantages; and cities, in turn, offered the railroad incentives of land and money to insure their inclusion in the network.

With the advent of the automobile and the establishment of rubber-wheeled transportation, the first cities to be linked by roads were those already linked by railroad. Often, new roads ran alongside the railroad tracks, a pattern still visible on older highways today. With every new transportation link, the cities' hinterlands grew and their influence spread. Cities that were established after the railroad network was completed or that were bypassed by the railroad were, with few exceptions, unable to maintain significant growth. With the end of railroad building came the end of city building. The era of the metropolis had begun.

The Third Urban Revolution

The discussion now moves to three trends that can be called the **third urban revolution**. They are: (1) the urbanization of over half of the world's population by the year 2000; (2) the emergence of cities in the developing and industrializing nations; and (3) the emergence of a new form of urbanization in the already urbanized industrial societies, the megalopolis.

> **metropolitan service area:** the geographic area or hinterland surrounding a city and dependent on it for various services: commercial, educational, informational, etc.
>
> **third urban revolution:** in general, the urbanization of the entire world population, but sometimes specifically used to include the special form of city emerging in the developing nations (the primate city) and the growth of megalopolitan forms, or supercities.

Growth of the world urban population Urbanization has been a world phenomenon, but urban growth rates have varied considerably from region to region. In 1900, the percentage of the population in cities of over 100,000 varied from a low of 1.1 percent in Africa to a high of 21.7 percent in Oceania (the Central and South Pacific, including Australia), with 12.8 percent in America, 11.9 percent in Europe, 2.1 percent in Asia, and 5.5 percent for the world population as a whole. By 1950 those figures were: for Africa, still lowest, 5.2 percent; Oceania, 39.2 percent; America, 22.6 percent; Europe, 19.9 percent; Asia, 7.5 percent; and for the world population as a whole, 13.1 percent. By 1950, 20.9 percent of the world's population was urban.

As well as illustrating the varied rate of world urbanization, these figures demonstrate that as late as 1950 a great deal of the world's population still resided in rural areas. But this picture is about to change rapidly. If present trends continue, it is generally agreed that half of the world's population will live in cities of over 20,000 by the year 1980, and that by the year 2000, 90 percent of the world's population will live in cities of that size or larger. Much of this urbanization will take place in the least urbanized areas of the world: China, south and southeastern Asia, the Middle East, and southwest tropical Africa. Urban growth is expected to slow in regions that became urbanized early: England, the United States, western and northern Europe, parts of South America, Australia and New Zealand.

Two recent examples of rapid urban growth are China and the U.S.S.R. Between 1949 and 1956, the per annum urban growth rate in China was estimated at 6.5 percent. It is estimated that in this period 20 million Chinese migrated from rural villages to urban areas. China's urban growth has been concentrated in its larger cities. In 1953, 103 cities of 100,000 or over housed 49 million people, or about 63 percent of the urban population. Two of the world's ten largest cities are in China: Peking and Shanghai.

Between 1950 and 1959, the per annum urban growth rate of the U.S.S.R. was estimated at 4 percent. In 1920, 15 percent of the population of the U.S.S.R. lived in cities; by 1959, the figure was 48 percent. In the twenty-year interval between 1939 and 1959, the urban population grew by 40 million people. By 1970, an estimated 56 percent of the population lived in cities. This rapid urban growth paralleled rapid industrial development. In 1970, there were ten Soviet cities of over 1 million inhabitants, including Moscow with almost 7 million and Leningrad with slightly less than 4 million inhabitants.

Urban growth in developing societies Some differences are clear between the early growth of industrial cities in Western nations and the later growth of industrial cities in developing nations. *Subsistence agriculture*, agriculture that satisfies only the immediate needs of the population and produces no surplus, characterizes urbanization in developing nations. With the population barely above subsistence level, unpredictable events affecting the precarious economy can bring on a famine. *Subsistence urbanization* describes the fact that a large number of residents of cities in developing societies live at the subsistence level in occupations only such a society can afford: collecting and selling used shoestrings, for example, or collecting the scraps and refuse of the better fed and housed. These two conditions lead to the development of *overurbanization*, a situation in which more persons live in urban areas than can be justified by the development of the industrial sector of the society.

Probably one of the most significant differences between urbanization in the past and urbanization now is that rapidly increasing populations exist in *both* the rural and the urban areas of the developing nations (see Figure 10-3). Rural dwellers are pushed to the city by pressures of overpopulation created by high birthrates and falling death rates, rather than pulled by the attraction of urban life.

Figure 10-3
Rural and urban population growth projected to the year 2000

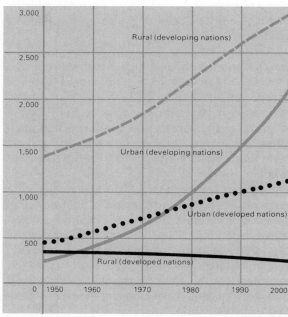

Population growth, both rural and urban, will be greater in developing nations than in the already developed nations.

During urbanization and industrialization in North America and Europe, by contrast, urban populations increased faster than rural populations and birthrates generally declined. In these areas, urban growth and industrial expansion accompanied each other, but the developing nations find themselves with ready-made technological bases waiting. Growth is not postponed until industrialization makes further development possible.

Unlike urbanization in North America and Western Europe, urbanization in many of the developing national societies is accompanied by the process of detribalization. Urban migrants must become acclimated to the urban areas and undergo a socialization process in which their loyalty is transferred from clan chieftan and tribe to the less personal concept of nation. To complete the process of detribalization, urban migrants must establish permanent residence in the city and sever allegiances to their chief. They must become independent of rural relatives for support during periods of unemployment and illness. But as long as tribal loyalties outweigh urban attachments, the migrant urban population of developing nations will be constantly shifting, coming to the city to work for awhile and then returning home when they have earned enough cash to meet their needs for the time being.

Another problem of urbanization in developing nations has been the appearance of **primate cities**: single cities that dominate the national society economically, socially, and culturally. The growth of such centers surpasses the growth of all other cities, absorbing so much of the nation's natural resources that no regional balance or network of urban areas can develop. Lagos, Nigeria, and São Paulo, Brazil, are examples.

Megalopolis In the already urbanized and industrialized nations, a new urban configuration has begun to emerge, the *megalopolis*. The term was coined by Jean Gottmann, a French geographer, in a book of the same name in 1961.[10] It refers to the greater urbanized area created by the growth of metropolitan areas until two or more merge into a great sprawl for hundreds of miles, creating new problems of organization and coordination beyond those of the metropolitan region. Gottmann cites as a major example the northeastern coastal urban region of the United States that stretches from southern New Hampshire to Virginia and includes New York, Baltimore, Philadelphia, Boston, Washington, and other major cities. It extends inland from the coast from 30 to 100 miles at various points, containing a total area of over 53,000 square miles with a population of about 37 million persons in 1960.

Sociologists with an eye to the future have predicted the development of more U.S. megalopolises. The three largest would stretch from southern California to the San Francisco Bay Area and Sacramento; across the Florida peninsula joining both Florida coastal urban concentrations; and from Green Bay, Wisconsin, to Syracuse, New York, along the coast of the Great Lakes in the states of Wisconsin, Illinois, Indiana, Michigan, Ohio, Pennsylvania, and New York (see Figure 10-4).

The question now asked by urban sociologists is whether a megalopolis is largely undifferentiated

primate city: an urban form, now emerging in developing nations, where one city dominates the entire national society. Lagos, Nigeria, is an example.

megalopolis: the supercity, or sprawling greater urbanized *area*, created by the merging of two or more metropolitan areas. The San Diego–Los Angeles–Santa Barbara complex is one example and the eastern coast of the United States from Boston to Norfolk, Virginia, another.

Figure 10-4
The future of megalopolis

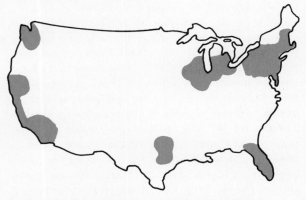

By the year 2000, approximately 70 percent of the American population will live in just six megalopolitan areas: The northeastern seaboard, the Florida complex, the Houston-Dallas complex, the Great Lakes complex, the California complex, and the Northwest complex.

urban sprawl or whether it represents a new urban *structure*. Such a structure would consist of a group of metropolitan areas, each specialized and functionally related to the others, the whole structure dominating a national rather than a regional hinterland. In a study of the northeastern seaboard concentration, Robert Weller found that as yet there is only limited evidence for the existence of interdependence and specialization among the metropolitan areas of that urban concentration.[11] He concluded that until there is more evidence, a megalopolis must be regarded simply as large adjacent clusters of urban sprawl.

Urban Growth in the United States: Patterns and Characteristics

As indicated earlier, American cities exploded in size and social significance in the latter part of the last century and the beginning of this century. That phenomenon still continues, and today the city's impact on our society is overwhelming. In this section, we will discuss first the models of urban growth developed by early urban sociologists to describe the explosive growth of cities and then two striking characteristics of urbanization in the United States: suburbanization and the urbanization of black Americans.

Ecological Processes and Models of Growth

The urban sociologists working in the first half of the twentieth century were concerned with the variety of **ecological** processes operating in the expanding cities, that is, the processes that resulted from the relationship between human groups and their environment in the bounded area formed by the city. These sociologists developed several classic models to explain and describe how ecological processes operated in the cities as they knew them. To some extent, all of these models have been rendered obsolescent by the largely automobile-based, sprawling American city of the post-World War II period (much of what follows, for example, would not apply to Los Angeles). Nonetheless, they are worth exploring for their ideas on urban growth and for their usefulness in under-

standing how the older central city in the United States grew and operated before it deteriorated into its present condition.

All of the theoretical models of the city we will discuss below, and all of the ecological processes associated with them, assumed the existence of the "downtown," the **central business district (CBD)**, which was the city's heart and which, in some older American cities such as Chicago, New York, and Washington, D.C., still is. To a great degree, the classic ecological models remain valid in the United States only to the extent that the CBD has remained vital in a given city. We begin the discussion, therefore, with a description of the CBD and its function for the city when it was at the height of its significance for American society.

The central business district The central business district (CBD), classically described by Earl S. Johnson in 1942, marked the ecological center of the metropolitan area, the point most easily reached in terms of time and money.[12] The CBD was often also the geographical center and therefore the location of market institutions that depended on extensive regional markets for the sale of their goods. It was the area of the metropolis where highly specialized persons and institutions, especially financial institutions, exerted a directing and coordinating influence on the market activities of the entire region.

Ground transportation systems terminated in the CBD, and in the 1930s and 1940s, air terminals were often adjacent. These termination points created what urban sociologists called *breaks in transportation*. A break in transportation means that goods are off-loaded from one form of transportation and loaded onto another, from river barges to trucks, or from rail cars to river barges. It was hypothesized that cities developed at points of breaks in transportation. As the CBD was the locus of transportation, it was also the locus of communication, with more telephone calls originating and terminating there than in any other set of exchanges. It was the focus of information, the office site of radio stations and newspapers. It was the most heavily trafficked part of the metropolitan area, in terms of both wheeled and pedestrian traffic, and the money market of the area, home of the principal federal reserve and commercial banks and the stock and commodities markets.

Although industrial plants were located elsewhere, their headquarters remained in the CBD, where they were close to financial institutions and communication channels. The supporting services needed by financial institutions also clustered there: legal, secretarial, food, janitor, and other personal services for the working population.

The CBD also functioned as a retail shopping center housing large department stores, specialized shops, and luxury shops. In addition, hotels in the CBD housed a regional and national clientele of wholesale buyers and sellers, out-of-town shoppers, tourists, and others. The area was also the location of large, influential churches, specialized medical services, theaters, and entertainment districts.

Since Johnson's description of the CBD in 1942, many changes have occurred to alter his conceptualization of the area: suburbanization of office buildings in industrial parks and shopping centers, movement of luxury hotels to the outerbelt highways and airport sites, the capture of retail shopping by suburban centers. But still the basic, primary functions of the CBD remain: the credit and money market. Decentralization has challenged the CBD, but no city yet has seen all its principal activities removed to outlying centers.

The future of the CBD seems in doubt at the present time. In the United States, at least, few urban residents have much cause to be hopeful about the vitality of the CBD, although some cities (Minneapolis, for example) seem to have saved it from blight. But successful salvage operations are few in number. Urban blight is the far more common fate of the CBD. Even in cities where the heart of the "downtown" continues to pulse, it is often surrounded by massive decay. (Indianapolis serves the point.)

Few urban sociologists expect the CBD to disappear entirely; the least hopeful think that retailing will continue to move outward to alternative shopping centers, with the CBD maintaining only its financial and communicative functions. Others see it losing its dominance but remaining one of several such centers in the urban area. As a consequence of urban redevelopment and federal monetary poli-

ecological: In general, pertaining to the study of organisms and their environment. In urban research, pertaining to the study of human groups and their relation to the bounded area formed by the city.

central business district (CBD): a city's "downtown"; the ecological center of the metropolis.

cy, however, many CBDs have recently enjoyed a boom in construction of new office buildings, convention centers, hotels, and the like, and it is too early to forecast their future.

Urban ecological processes Early urban sociologists identified five ecological processes that explain change in their models of urban growth and land use. These are centralization, decentralization, invasion, succession, and segregation. *Centralization* is the tendency for people to gather at a central point to carry out some specialized social or economic function. The CBD is an example of the centralization of credit and communication functions in an urbanized area. *Decentralization* is the tendency for like functions to move away from a central point. The rapid growth of suburban shopping centers demonstrates the decentralization of the function of retail shopping from a single focal point in the CBD to many points in the urban area.

Segregation, of course, is the tendency of urban residents who share common social, ethnic, or racial characteristics to live near each other. The creation of neighborhoods characterized by a high percentage of Jewish or Catholic residents illustrates the process of segregation, as does the more familiar segregation of black neighborhoods. Segregation may be voluntary, the result of a group's desire to live together, or involuntary, the result of social or economic discrimination. The process of *invasion* occurs when one group abandons an area and enters another area in which the occupying groups are different in key social and economic characteristics. If all of the original residents of the area are replaced by the newcomers, then the process is labeled *succession*.

Each of the following three models consists of a series of statements that construct ideal types and

Figure 10-5
The concentric-zone model of urban growth

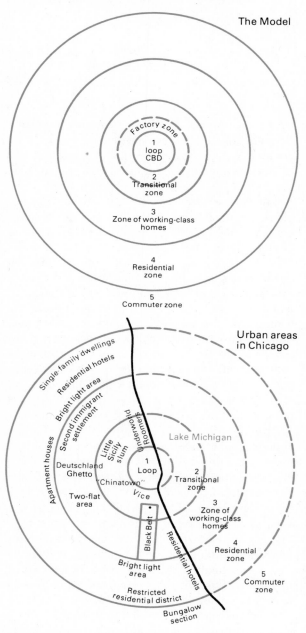

The concentric-zone model is illustrated first as an ideal type, then as applied to Chicago in 1925. The Chicago area actually appears as a series of semi-circles because Lake Michigan influences its shape. As the model is applied to other cities, the width of the circles changes to conform to land use in those cities.

a set of generalizations that try to explain changes by ecological processes.

The concentric-zone model The *concentric-zone model* was developed by Ernest W. Burgess and Robert T. Park, sociologists at the University of Chicago, in the 1920s.[13] This model of city structure proposes five concentric circles with the center zone as the CBD; see Figure 10-5.

Zone 2, surrounding the CBD, is also called the transitional zone because it is in the process of being invaded by the CBD as it pushes outward. The inner boundary of the transitional zone, indicated in the upper diagram of Figure 10-5 by a circle of dashes, is likely to be occupied by light manufacturing and warehousing. The residential housing here is the oldest still in use in the metropolitan area. Originally the business elite's, this housing is large and is easily partitioned into apartments and rooms. Some buildings in this zone, called tenements, were originally built to house the poor in small apartments, rather than being converted to that use in later years. The residential buildings in this zone rent more cheaply than any others in the urban area and quickly become the home of those least able to pay, although ghettoized minorities may have to pay ''what the traffic will bear.'' Landlords adjust standards of maintenance to maximize their profits. Old residential buildings in this zone thus often offer very high rates of return on dollar investment. Because the land itself has value, the landlord can let the building deteriorate until nothing but a shell remains. This practice is encouraged by tax laws based on use and condition of property rather than on market value.

The transitional zone is the location of the metropolitan area's principal slum, occupied first by one, then by another immigrant group. This zone has the highest density of persons per block and per room, as well as the highest rates of crime, infant mortality, venereal and other diseases, the greatest number of commitments to mental hospitals, the lowest per capita income, and the highest unemployment rate.

The third zone is that part of the city occupied by working-class, or blue-collar, homes. Here, second- and third-generation immigrants who have found steady jobs and escaped the slums have bought small homes. The rate of home ownership is high. The houses are well maintained and set on small, neat lots. Here and there, one sees signs of ethnic culture: athletic societies, national clubs, ethnic churches, and architecture. There are some flats or duplexes, perhaps four-family buildings. The area has neighborhood shopping blocks situated at the intersections of main arteries from the CBD. In a contemporary American city, this zone often displays ornate birdbaths, shrines, madonnas, and wrought-iron trim. The average age of the population is high, consisting of adults who either cannot face leaving the old neighborhood or cannot afford to move from a home paid for during peak earning periods. Some of these areas have been able to capture new young couples, but many have not.

Zone 4, called the residential zone, is the location of more expensive residences, in which assimilated ethnic families or native-born white Americans make their homes. The lots are larger, the houses are further from the streets, and side drives, green lawns, and large trees dot the zone. Clusters of high-rise apartments and residential hotels house members of the urban middle class who do not choose home ownership. The residents include owners of small businesses, professional people, clerks and sales personnel, and the educated middle class who live comfortably but not luxuriously. Streets and main arteries are pleasant, and shopping districts have attractive architectural themes. Community agencies, large churches of conventional denominations, and similar institutions break the residential pattern at points.

The fifth zone is the commuter zone; and at this point, the pattern becomes less clear and the model less detailed. This is the point at which drivers use expressways rather than city streets to reach the CBD. The growth is spotty, with houses of similar architectural style and price range clustering together in clumps between commercial areas. Occasional rural slums and segregated communities survive, surrounded by suburban housing tracts.

The city as described in the concentric-zone model grows like a ripple in the water. Change occurs as one zone's population and land-use pattern first invades and then replaces or succeeds the original population of that zone. For example, the

concentric-zone model: an ecological model of the city, developed by Park and Burgess, depicting it as a series of five concentric rings of specialized characteristics and functions.

Figure 10-6
The sector model of urban growth

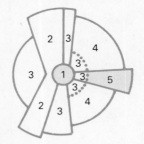

1. CBD
2. Wholesale, light manufacturing
3. Lower-class residential
4. Middle-class residential
5. High-class residential

The sector model of urban growth is based upon a pattern of land use in which pie-shaped sectors radiate from the CBD. The areas of high rent, indicated by shading, are the key determining factors in the configuration of sectors.

Figure 10-7
The sector model applied to land-use patterns in Calgary, Canada, 1961

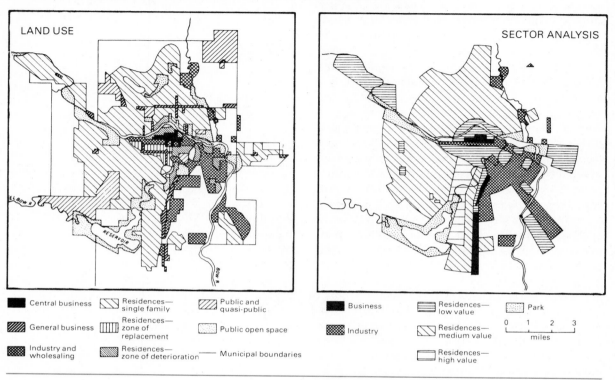

■ Central business	⬛ Residences—single family	⬛ Public and quasi-public
⬛ General business	⬛ Residences—zone of replacement	⬛ Public open space
⬛ Industry and wholesaling	⬛ Residences—zone of deterioration	— Municipal boundaries

■ Business	⬛ Residences—low value	⬛ Park
⬛ Industry	⬛ Residences—medium value	0 1 2 3 miles
	⬛ Residences—high value	

CBD must grow at the expense of the transitional zone, invading it at its inner edge. Then the zone of transition expands by invading the inner edge of the next adjacent zone. Only the outer ring, the commuter zone, is free to develop outward into open land.

The sector model The *sector model* of urban growth was developed by Homer Hoyt, on the basis of data he collected about sixty-four American cities during 1934.[14] These cities were mostly of medium or small size, but the data were supplemented by surveys of New York, Chicago, Detroit, Washington, and Philadelphia. Hoyt first plotted average rents and other data on maps. Then he tried to perceive patterns and make generalizations about the ecological structure of cities and, once patterns were established, to find a key variable to explain variations and changes. He found that *rent*

The figure on the left shows actual land use; the one on the right shows the same land use organized according to the sector theory.

was that variable and was generally a good indicator of other characteristics of an area.

Hoyt also found that maps of rental patterns, rather than forming concentric zones, looked like a pie cut into pieces of various sizes; see Figure 10-6. Within each pie-shaped sector, rental values and land use were constant. Rental value, according to Hoyt, determines land use, and land use in the city is a direct or indirect function of profitability. Because the nonresidential land in the CBD is almost exclusively put to commercial, or profit-making, purposes, these tend to set the market price for all land. Thus, the value of a particular plot is principally determined by the profit-making use to which it can be put, and the use that will return the highest profit is likely to be the one adopted. These considerations fix land use and price.

Manufacturers, for example, must have access to either truck or rail transportation and so must be located close to highways or rail lines. But manufacturing requires a large amount of land and thus cannot compete for it on a cost-per-foot basis with such intensive (rather than extensive) activities as specialty retailing or banking. The latter concerns, as a consequence, flourish in the CBD, where land is very expensive, because they require little of it. It is no accident that at least one bank occupies the central intersection of virtually every American city. Of all urban activities, finance returns the greatest profit per square foot of land, and banks and stock and commodity exchanges are always at the very heart of the downtown. Activities that require more space, such as parking lots, bus depots, and auto salesrooms are at the edge of the CBD and along adjacent arteries.

Users who can afford high costs select the best parcels of land and the best general terrain. The key to the whole configuration is the sector that contains the highest rental values. That sector usually begins near the center of the city and extends toward the edge of the metropolitan area. Immediately adjacent, often on both sides, are sectors that contain the second highest rentals, and next to these are the sectors of the third highest rent. Low-rent areas are located in their own sectors and are as far from the high-rent area as possible. The center of the configuration is the CBD.

Growth, Hoyt thought, moves toward open and less expensive land. The key high-rent district influences the movement in all other sectors by attracting the growth of the urban area in its direction and thus causing other rental areas to try to buttress themselves against this pull. The model assumes that nearness to the high-rent areas has some value in terms of prestige of location.

Hoyt listed a number of factors involved in the movement of high-rent areas: First, such areas tend to grow along established lines of transportation. Second, they gravitate toward high ground free from flooding, or to waterfronts, beachfronts, and riverbanks where these are not used for industrial purposes, or toward free and open country and

sector model: the ecological model of the city, developed by Hoyt, depicting its major characteristics and functions as distributing themselves geographically in somewhat pie-shaped pieces.

multiple-nuclei model: the ecological model of the city, developed by Harris and Ullman, depicting it as developing a variety of growth centers with specialized functions and appearing geographically somewhat like a molecular model in biology.

away from natural barriers to expansion. Third, they move toward the homes of influential members of the community who have already established themselves at some distance from the CBD. Fourth, office buildings, banks, and stores tend to pull high rental areas toward them. Fifth, high-grade residential areas tend to develop along the fastest existing commuter lines. Sixth, growth continues in the same direction for long periods of time.

For an application of the sector model to a real city, see Figure 10-7. The map on the left shows actual land use in Calgary, Alberta, Canada, in 1961. The map on the right shows the same land use when organized according to the principles suggested above. The correspondence between the two is an indication of the model's accuracy.

The sector model explains many things that the concentric-zone model could not explain. In the concentric model, for example, high-rent residential buildings in the CBD were always treated as an exception. In the sector theory, such buildings become the focal point of a sector radiating from the CBD. The sector theory provides a better explanation of the continued outward development created by widespread automobile ownership through its attention to the effect of traffic arteries. Like the concentric-zone model, however, the sector model does not explain suburban patterns as well as it explains patterns of older sections of the metropolitan area.

The multiple-nuclei model The last of the three models that have become classics is the *multiple-nuclei model* developed by Chauncy D. Harris and Edward Ullman in 1945.[15] In this model of land use, the city is seen as consisting of numerous areas, each built around separate centers that attract growth to them; see Figure 10-8. Growth around any particular attracting element, any nucleus, is all of one kind. Some of the nuclei have existed since the origin of the city, persisting as growth from other nuclei have filled the space between them and merged all into the urban area. Each nucleus is an island or clustering of similar land uses. A large hospital may be the attracting nucleus around which cluster a medical school, other hospitals, research laboratories, doctors' offices, medical suppliers, restaurants, and other service activities for the people who work there or who come as patients. An urban university may attract other small colleges, private schools, libraries, bookstores, research institutes, semiacademic organizations, and businesses that serve student needs.

The location of nuclei, according to Harris and Ullman, is the result of four factors: First, certain activities require special facilities, such as access to railheads or water in large quantities. Second, certain similar activities group together because they profit from cohesion—lawyers' offices and real estate offices cluster around municipal buildings, stockbrokers and financial advisors near banks. Third, unlike activities are detrimental to each other—the noise of manufacturing, for example, is not compatible with private housing. Fourth, certain activities requiring large amounts of land must be located where rents are low, for example, factories.

The multiple-nuclei model is the most recently developed of the three models we have examined, and it is best able to account for the pattern of growth, the expansion of shopping centers, the growth of industrial parks, and the clusters of suburban apartment developments. This model allows for many aspects of urban growth that we see going on today, such as the expansion of airports and the formation of new clusters of motels, restaurants, and light manufacturing.

Probably no one model adequately explains the configurations of a particular city. The models are most useful when used in various combinations or when all three are applied, using those elements or patterns that each model illustrates best. For example, researchers have often found that certain variables, such as family characteristics, housing

Figure 10-8
The multiple-nuclei model of urban growth

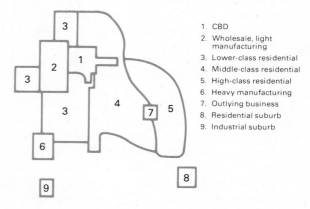

1. CBD
2. Wholesale, light manufacturing
3. Lower-class residential
4. Middle-class residential
5. High-class residential
6. Heavy manufacturing
7. Outlying business
8. Residential suburb
9. Industrial suburb

The multiple-nuclei model of urban growth shows a CBD not necessarily located in the center of the urban area and not circular. Unlike the concentric-zone theory, the multiple-nuclei theory postulates growth from many centers.

patterns, or educational level, produce concentric-zone patterns, while other characteristics, such as prestige, conform to a sector pattern.

As indicated earlier, none of these models foresaw, or can entirely accommodate, the post–World War II exploding sprawl the American city has become. The sprawl, of course, resulted from a variety of phenomena: government-backed cheap credit for the construction of private residences, the rabbitlike multiplication of the automobile, and the development of the freeway (also government-financed) to accommodate it, the changing racial character of the city, and many more. But the city of today developed from and out of the city of yesterday, and it would be impossible to comprehend its present nature if we did not know the past from which it sprang. The classic ecological models explain that past, and the process variables they employ (invasion, succession, and so on) are just as valid today as when they were first described.

Suburbanization

Because most American cities were not even plotted until after the Civil War, their history has been one of continuous, sometimes explosive, growth.

The contemporary manifestation of that phenomenon is, of course, what we called *sprawl* in the paragraph above. The formal name for it is *suburbanization.*

Outward movement from the city's center is almost as old as American cities. This movement, called *flight from the city* by journalists and politicians and *decentralization* by sociologists, reflects the fact that the fastest growing part of any metropolitan area is the *fringe,* a belt of land around the edge of the city that is characterized by lower population densities than the central city and pockets of open, undeveloped land.

The outward movement of the population involves two very different processes: decentralization and deconcentration. *Decentralization* is the movement away from a single focus to growth around several focal points or seemingly focusless growth. **Deconcentration** is the decrease in the *density* of the population in a fixed land area. The effect of these two processes is **suburbanization**: the creation of a ring of relatively small communities, some of which are independent legal entities, that are adjacent to and dependent on the central city.

The movement to the edge of cities and growth in the fringe area began as cities entered their period of rapid growth shortly after the Civil War. Outward movement was made possible by a series of improvements in transportation that extended the possible commuting distance of those who travel to work daily. Before such improvements, cities could only grow by increasing their density of concentration. In 1832, the horse car expanded daily commuting distance to five or six miles; in 1887, the electric streetcar expanded that distance even more; and with the modern commuter train, sixty miles is not an unusual daily commuting trip. But in the first half of the century, moving to the suburbs was so expensive that relatively few people made the shift. Construction was difficult and expensive; down payments on homes were at least a third of the purchase price; and loan periods were no longer than ten years. After World War II, however, changes in the financing of suburban housing, including small down payments, long loan repayment periods, government loans and insurance, coupled with mass automobile ownership, put suburban homes within the reach of

deconcentration: a reduction in population density in an area.

suburbanization: the growth of a ring of relatively small communities around the central city and the movement of urban population to them. Contemporarily associated with urban sprawl and the deterioration of the central city.

Suburbanization: Nassau County, New York.

increasing numbers of people, blue-collar as well as white-collar workers.

How much of the resulting growth can accurately be called flight from the central city is unclear. A review of growth patterns of 160 SMSAs between the period of 1940 to 1950 indicated that suburbanization is the natural outgrowth of rapid increases in the population of urban areas.[16] Cities that had the greatest growth in the suburban ring were those that had the most overall growth and the densest central city populations. Cities that experienced the least population growth in their suburban fringes were those whose land area was already large. This may indicate that when the spread of a city begins to be a barrier to good internal transportation and communication, the growth is contained.

Residential suburbs and satellite suburbs All **suburbs** are not alike, either in their functions or in the composition of their populations. Two fairly common distinctions divide the urban fringe area into two kinds of communities, *residential* suburbs and *satellite* suburbs. The residential, or bedroom suburb, often called just *suburb,* is mainly composed of homes for urban workers. These communities tend to be newer and smaller than satellite suburbs, closer to the central city, and to have higher rents. The average age of the resident tends to be higher, and the community tends to have higher socioeconomic status. On the average, residential suburbs are growing rapidly in all metropolitan areas.

Examination of the socioeconomic characteristics of residential suburbs indicates that once the socioeconomic status of the community is established, it remains constant through time. The socioeconomic status of an area is often fixed by the developer, who prices a development's units in a narrow range, believing that the property values of units are protected by surrounding them with similarly priced units. Empirical evidence indicates that ethnic groups do not scatter over the suburban area, but concentrate in certain communities in the fringe and remain almost as segregated as in the central city, though not as visibly.

Satellite suburbs, usually called just *satellites*, are employment and industrial subcenters whose main activity is manufacturing. In general, satellites tend to be found in the heavy industrial areas of the

Northeast and the north central metropolitan areas. Rents for homes in satellites tend to be lower than in other communities, probably because of the nearness of industry. The industrial basis of the satellites is usually highly specialized production of a narrow range of goods, such as automobiles or appliances.

The effect of suburbanization on central cities The suburbanization of the population and the resulting growth of suburban areas has had several effects on central cities. One important result of suburbanization has been a net decrease in the population of central cities (see Figure 10-9). For example, the land area of the city of St. Louis was basically filled by 1910 with a population of 690,000. By 1930, the population of the city had reached 820,000, with no annexations and the same land area. By 1970, the population had fallen

Figure 10-9
U.S. population by place of residence, 1910-1970

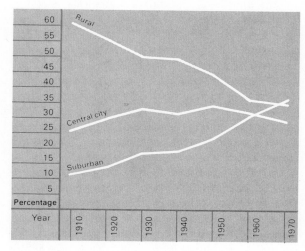

The percentage of the population living in rural areas declined drastically during the period shown. The percentage in central cities rose steadily until 1950, except for a slight decline during the Depression of the 1930s. The percentage in suburban areas grew throughout this period, and particularly so after 1940. Since 1940, suburban living has gained so steadily at the expense of both central city and rural living that by 1970 there were more suburbanites than either of the other two groups.

to about 630,000, about the same as when the land area was originally filled.

Although reduced numbers may bruise civic pride, they can bring welcome relief to overburdened cities and their facilities, particularly schools. Population reduction can also be a mark of one kind of progress: expansion or renovation of the CBD and the construction of parking lots and highway exchanges removes marginal residential property from the cities' inventories.

Unhappily, however, the overall decrease in population density in central cities has meant the creation of pockets of increased density and the dislocation of many people. The removal of substandard housing, particularly under the banner of urban redevelopment, means the removal of people. Because of the conventional politics of redevelopment, such projects have often proved enormously profitable to the redeveloper and enormously painful to the populations—usually poor and ethnic or nonwhite—who are displaced. Since they are poor, they often have no place to go but to whatever substandard housing may remain elsewhere in the city, thus further crowding surviving older residential areas.

Suburbanization is also associated with the changing racial composition of the population of the central city, and thus with segregation and poverty and the other problems they bring. And the changing population base has created economic disaster for the cities. The suburban explosion, as we have seen, is in part explained as a flight *from* the central city. For many white suburbanites, that meant flight from the new black city dwellers. The departing whites were largely middle-class, and the incoming blacks were largely lower-class. Often fleeing rural poverty themselves, the new immigrants had few skills to offer the urban labor market, and they came at a time when the demand for manual labor in industry and commerce was dropping to a vanishing point. They were doomed to poverty in the city as well.

Any urban poverty population places a disproportionate financial burden on the resources of the city. The poor have greater needs for fire and police protection, public health care, day-care centers, and social services than the middle or upper classes. Because the black population is younger than the white, with a higher proportion of women

> **suburb**: a community on the urban fringe. Suburbs tend to be of two general types, the *residential*, or bedroom, suburb, which simply *houses* urban workers, and the *satellite* suburb, which employs them as well. Satellite suburbs are usually industrial.

in the childbearing years, the fertility of blacks is higher; and so there are more children to require schools, medical services, and appropriate housing as well. The costs of maintaining the public welfare increased for the cities in part simply as a result of the change in population composition.

But another phenomenon operated at the same time. With the departure of much of the middle class, often accompanied by business and industry as well, the city lost a significant fraction of its tax base. The poor cannot bear the tax burden conventionally assessed corporations and the middle and upper classes. So at the same time that the demands for civic services were being increased by the increasing proportions of the poor among the population, the city's ability to meet those demands was being reduced by the departure of those able to support them. The result, for almost all American cities of any size, has been bankruptcy or near bankruptcy. In the meantime, just beyond the city's legal borders (and beyond the reach of its taxation power), the new suburbanites are free of any immediate responsibility for helping to solve or bear the city's problems, although they remain residents of the metropolitan area.

The Urbanization of Black Americans

The phenomenon of suburbanization in the United States is inextricably bound up today with a final feature of urban growth, the increasing urbanization of black citizens. One hundred years ago, black Americans were overwhelmingly a rural population; today, like most other Americans, they are largely urban. But because of the special position that black people have unenviably occupied in American society, and because the migrants to the city were often semiskilled agriculturists who came at a time when the urban labor market had little use for their skills, the changing racial composition of

Sellout in Detroit

The city of Detroit is in parlous condition these days, facing a $44 million deficit, continuing layoffs of city employees and a general sagging of the civic spirit. But a sprightly, 50-year-old city publicity staffer named Patti Knox came up with an idea not long ago: to gather all the white elephants from the government basements and stage "the world's largest garage sale" in cavernous Cobo Hall last week. Bureau chief James C. Jones filed this report:

"What if nobody comes?" fretted Patti Knox. She needn't have worried. People were lining up outside at 5:30 a.m.; by midmorning, the traffic jam stretched for 2 miles. Knox had assembled about 100,000 artifacts ranging from an 1833 segment of wooden water conduit to an electric guitar with two strings missing. But the supply wasn't enough. By nightfall, an estimated 50,000 Detroiters had picked Cobo Hall so clean that little but junk was left—and the promoters had no choice but to cut the sale from the scheduled three days to two.

'Trampolines!' It was a classic garage sale, with buying fever making everything seem like treasure. "Look at those life nets from the fire department," somebody burbled. "They'd make great trampolines." Anybody might expect to find typewriters, calculators and park benches among a city's leftovers. But there were also hospital beds, animal cages, food-conveyor systems, sewing machines, tire rims, urinals, fire-department sliding poles, the hood from a Buick and a plastic canoe. Knox herself was sufficiently infected to pay $22 for two kittens; later she couldn't imagine why. "I've already got two," she said. . . .

Despite the overwhelming signs of success, a few cynics maintained that the whole affair was a symptom

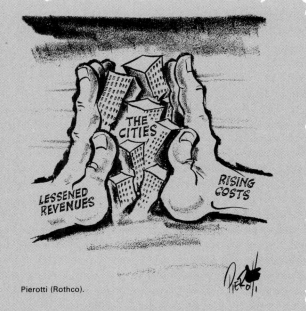

Pierotti (Rothco).

of urban decay—what one of them called "the world's largest going-out-of-business sale." At the weekend, city officials were still counting the take. But they had already banked a welcome lift to the long-depressed civic morale. "People like themselves today," Knox concluded. The world's largest garage sale may not ease the financial pressure on Detroit one whit, but it did provide a kind of spiritual respite.

the city created new problems that suburbanization only helped increase.

As we noted in Chapter 9, the urbanization of blacks in the United States did not begin in earnest until well after the Civil War, when the vast majority of black people lived in the southern states. Immediately after the war, no discernible urban migration pattern developed, but there was some slow and confused movement of blacks into southern cities, with a reverse trend at the end of the Reconstruction period. Not until 1910 did a pattern of movement to northern cities emerge.

Migration patterns often found a black migrant moving first from the rural area to a southern city, then to a northern city. The early migration was called the migration of the "talented tenth," because blacks with skills, training, and talent were

The cities are caught in a desperate financial crisis which they are powerless to relieve. This news article describes a unique attempt to alleviate the situation.

the first to leave the South. But in the period 1935-1940, the pattern changed, and more direct migration occurred from rural areas by persons without urban job skills. The first northern cities affected were those of the eastern seaboard and those rimming the lower edges of the Great Lakes. Black migration to western coastal cities began with the growth of war industries in 1940 and, once begun, continued at a rapid pace (see Table 10-5).

The movement of blacks to the city has been characterized as consisting of too many too late. By the time blacks moved in numbers to American cities, the cities were old and had already housed several generations of immigrants. Cities were beginning to reel under financial liabilities incurred during periods of rapid growth. The 1950s saw halting industrial growth, several recessions, and mild dips in the job market. Reform government was the goal of most cities, and the big city political machines that had employed immigrants to sweep streets and clean city hall were gone. Food stamps, aid to dependent children, and legal aid had replaced the neighborhood politician and his food basket. When blacks began to hold city office, there was little in the way of favors to dispense, and the most pessimistic saw black mayors elected only to preside over the doom and death of American cities. They had offices no one else wanted.

For blacks urbanization resulted in the creation of large inner-city residential areas characterized by high rates of unemployment, crime, poor health, and similar problems associated with other groups who had occupied those same quarters. The growth of segregated residential areas led to de facto segregation of public schools, playgrounds, clinics, hospitals, and all other public facilities. The economic conditions of black Americans have been discussed in Chapter 9. But since housing is a major urban concern, we take up that aspect of segregation as it has affected black people here.

Ghettos and slums   Segregated black residential areas and their accompanying service businesses have been labeled *ghettos,* a word that until the 1960s had been applied almost solely to Jewish communities. The word **ghetto** was introduced to sociology in 1928 by Louis Wirth in a book about the Jewish community in which he traced the social history of Jewish residential segregation from early Italy to Spain, England, Central and Eastern Europe, and finally to American cities.[17] Wirth defined a ghetto as a segregated community that had its own social institutions, its own social structure, and its own version of the law, but was economically and politically dependent on the larger national society. It was not a slum. The ghetto population included rich and poor, merchants, bankers, scholars, and craft workers whose ties were ethnic and religious, buttressed by kinship.

Unlike a ghetto, a **slum** is the outgrowth of *economic* forces. It is a residential area populated

> **ghetto**: an urban ethnic or racial *community.* Often confused with *slum.* A ghetto may also be a slum; a slum need not be a ghetto. The ghetto is the product of segregation, the slum, of economics.
>
> **slum**: an urban residential area characterized by poverty, overcrowding, and substandard housing.

Table 10-5   Black population of the U.S. in millions, 1960–1970, by place of residence

Area	1960 Number	Percent	1970 Number	Percent
Metropolitan	12.8	68	16.8	74
In central cities	9.9	53	13.1	58
Outside central cities	2.8	15	3.7	16
Nonmetropolitan	6.1	32	5.8	26
Total	18.9		22.7	

American blacks are a highly urbanized population. Note that in the ten years following 1960, not only did the nonurban black population decrease and the metropolitan increase, but the urban portion of the population became even more concentrated in the central city despite a 1 percent increase in suburban residence.

Left: A racial ghetto—San Francisco's Chinatown.
Right: Uptown Chicago slum.

by low-income groups characterized by over-crowding and substandard housing. Some writers have characterized slums by the absence of social organization. Others dispute this and contend that the slum has a distinctive pattern of social organization that has been overlooked by those trying to find patterns similar to community patterns with which they were more familiar, such as middle-class white patterns.

Some segregated black areas have been both ghetto and slum at various times in their histories. Several interesting studies of Harlem and the Chicago Black Belt in the 1910-1920 period indicate that these were black ghettos with a full range of social institutions, a black press, black hospitals, banks, and other social institutions.[18] In these communities, the Urban League, the NAACP, and the black churches were founded and black politicians began careers. Black musicians and writers migrated to early Harlem. Black talent drew white audi-ences to black theaters and restaurants. But when large numbers of new black migrants entered these communities, they segregated by income, creating both slums and ghettos.

All segregated black communities in contemporary American cities are not slums. Major American cities have middle-class black neighborhoods with established patterns of social life and institutions. Many areas in American cities in which both blacks and whites live can be classified simply as low-income. Although poor, these communities remain socially intact and have a minimum of social problems.

An empirical study of housing segregation   A detailed empirical study of housing segregation in

207 American cities by Karl and Anna Taeuber destroyed many myths about the residential segregation of black Americans, for example that it was a function of poverty, that it was worse in southern than in northern cities, and that it resulted only when large numbers of black people were present in a city's population.[19]

Using a "segregation index" in which total integration would produce a value of 0 while complete segregation produced a score of 100, the Taeubers calculated indices for all cities with at least 1,000 black households and for which data on black residents were available in 1960. The scores ranged from a low of 60.4 in San Jose, California, to a high of 98.1 in Fort Lauderdale, Florida. The median score for the 207 cities based on the 1960 census was 87.8. The scores were high regardless of the regional location of the city, the size of the city, the size of the black population, and the attitude of the community toward employment practices and civil rights.

The Taeubers also investigated the role of poverty in creating patterns of residential segregation. If poverty were the cause, then as black incomes increased, segregation should decrease; and programs that increase black incomes should at the same time decrease segregation. The Chicago census of 1960 showed that while blacks on the average were poorer than whites, they paid about the same rent for apartments and about the same price for houses. On the basis of rent figures, then, rental housing in Chicago should be segregated only to the extent that the rent structure varies; there should be integrated areas of like income groups able to pay the same market rent. Calculations of segregation based on income were developed. Residential segregation scores based on income produced indices between 13 and 33, but the *actual* segregation index for Chicago was 83. The same pattern was found in fifteen other cities. The conclusion is that poverty is *not* the explanation for segregation; actual rates of segregation are much higher than income differences alone would produce.

We know from Chapter 9, of course, what the true causes of racial segregation are, but in the case of the urban housing market, where a great deal of misinformation has been spread (for example, that house values decline when a black person moves into a formerly all-white neighborhood), accurate facts of this kind are useful. Beyond such brute facts, however, the larger phenomenon of racial segregation prevails and will not be substantially altered in the foreseeable future: the growth of the American city has always mirrored change and growth in the society as a whole.

When the immigration of Asians and European whites was a major feature of the social landscape, the city accepted the new arrivals and changed in meeting them. In the same way, as black Americans came to the city in large numbers, the city altered in response to them. Like the earlier immigrants, they brought some problems with them, and their particular social characteristics created others upon arrival. Unlike the Europeans, however, they came at a time when the city was being transformed by other forces as well, and these have imposed many problems on black urbanites that are in no sense of their own making. For the problems of the American city, at least (and the city in many other nations too), are in fact the problems of the society as a whole. The United States is an urban society, and change and trouble in the cities means change and trouble throughout the total society. The city *is* the society, and until that fact is properly appreciated, its future will remain unclear.

Summary

This chapter has explored three major topics: (1) ways of defining and understanding the city and the phenomenon of urbanism; (2) the great urban revolutions of history; and (3) the nature of urban growth in the United States, especially as sociologists have learned to understand it utilizing the three classic ecological models.

In the matter of defining the city, we looked at the notions of ideal types, continua, and models and explored the implications of the legal, geographic, sociological, and census definitions of what a city is. The *legal city* is defined by the laws of the state, province, or nation in which it exists and is a precisely boundaried geographic entity. The *geographic city* is simply the continuously built-up area surrounding a legal city, what one might see as the city from an airplane. Louis Wirth offered a far more *sociological definition* of the city (in the sense of its focus on social interaction) by calling it a relatively large, relatively dense, and permanent settlement of socially heterogeneous individuals.

The basic U.S. Census definition of an *urbanized area* is that it is an incorporated place with a population of 2,500 or more. And although the census adds some qualifications that would include other places, this is the conception used by most sociologists in urban research. Another census term frequently used is the *Standard Metropolitan Statistical Area (SMSA)*: a county or adjacent counties with at least one central city of 50,000 or more people.

Two other important concepts were discussed: urbanization and urbanism. *Urbanization* was defined as the process of movement or change in a rural population to city areas, activities, and functions. *Urbanism* means the patterns of behavior, relationships, and thought typical of urban people, as distinguished from rural people.

We then turned to the three urban revolutions. The *first urban revolution*, of course, was the one that created the city in the first place. The *second urban revolution* accompanied the Industrial Revolution and saw the cities grow immensely in size. In industrialized societies, the majority of the population began to live in cities. The second urban revolution also saw the emergence of a new form of city, the contemporary *metropolis*. The *third urban revolution* has really only begun to occur and will go on until at least the year 2000. This is the urbanization of the developing nations of the world and the whole world population. It will also see the emergence of a new city form, the *megalopolis*, or supercity, the larger urbanized area connecting large geographic regions, such as all of coastal southern California from Santa Barbara to the Mexican border, and even beyond.

Consideration of the second and third urban revolutions led us to the topic of urban growth and its patterns and characteristics, for increase in size has been one of the chief characteristics of cities in both phases. American sociologists, studying the history of American cities during the second urban revolution, developed three ecological models of growth that have become classic: the concentric-zone model, the sector model, and the multiple-nuclei model. Each presumes as a major element the nature and significance of the *Central Business*

District (CBD). The CBD is the central focus of transportation, communication, and finance, not only for the city itself but for the surrounding metropolitan service area and rural hinterland. The immense significance that the CBD assumed in the classic ecological models of urban growth has been diminished since World War II by the phenomenon of suburbanization.

All three classic models of urban growth use the conceptions of five *ecological processes* to describe the growth or change of population and activities. These are centralization and decentralization, invasion, succession, and segregation. *Centralization* is the tendency for people to gather at a geographically central point to carry out specialized activities; *decentralization* refers to the opposite tendency. *Segregation* is the separation of certain people or activities from others of unlike nature. *Invasion* means entrance into an area of people or activities unlike those that have been there before, while *succession* means the successful occupation of an area by new people or activities. Although the three classic models are to some degree unable to describe accurately the contemporary American city, these processes remain valid descriptions of the ways in which change takes place in them.

The *concentric-zone model* of urban growth was the first ecological attempt to describe it. It conceives the city as consisting of five concentric circles, or zones, of differing habitation and function. Zone 1, the inner circle, is the CBD. It is surrounded by zone 2, often called the transitional zone, which has multiple and diverse functions: light manufacturing and warehousing, residence for the poor, often in ghettos and slums, rooming house and vice districts. Zone 3 is a working-class residential area, and zone 4 the middle-class residential zone. Zone 5 has vague outer boundaries and may include upper-class residential suburbs, rural slums, truck farming, and manufacturing.

The *sector model* of urban growth uses somewhat pie-shaped map references rather than concentric circles and is based on land rental value. Its hypothesis is that land use is determined by cost and that, therefore, like uses tend to cluster together along required lines of communication and transportation. In general, users who can afford high costs, or whose use will return high profits, select the best pieces of land in the best general terrain for their use. But all will seek to be as near as financially feasible to the CBD because of the functions it performs for the city. Urban growth tends to extend to open, less expensive land as activities that can afford higher costs push out those that cannot.

The *multiple-nuclei model*, developed in the 1940s, is the most recent of the classic ecological models of urban growth. This model sees the city not as a single organic entity, as the others do, but as a series of separable centers around which specific functions cluster. Growth around a particular center, or nucleus, tends to be all of the same kind. Thus a hospital, for example, may expand to become a general medical complex in an area, producing pharmacies and medical supply stores, physicians' offices, and so forth. The place where particular nuclei occur tends to be determined by access to any special facilities required, such as railheads, by the fact that some activities (like hospitals and pharmacies) profit from cohesion, by land cost, and by the fact that dissimilar activities are often detrimental to each other.

The principal feature of urban growth in the United States in recent decades has been the phenomenon called *suburbanization.* Although this had been occurring somewhat almost from the time of the Civil War, its major impact came after World War II with mass ownership of the automobile, good economic times, government subsidies for housing, and a number of other phenomena. City populations exploded at this time, with the major growth occurring in the suburban fringes surrounding them.

There are basically two different kinds of suburb, those called simply *suburbs* by sociologists, and those called *satellites.* The first are residential communities for city workers. Satellites are employment centers adjacent to and dependent on the larger city. Manufacturing is their typical function, and they are often narrowly specialized.

The general effect of suburbanization on the central city has been harsh, sometimes disastrous, as a result of its economic consequences. The typical American suburbanite is a middle-class worker, and his removal to the suburb has meant the removal of a tax resource for the city. This has been exaggerated by the coincidental movement of many commercial activities to the suburban fringe as well. The physical deterioration of many American central cities can be largely laid to this phenomenon.

Accompanying this process, and in part related to it, has been the changing racial composition of the central city that has resulted from the general urbanization of black Americans. Black Americans started migrating to the city in large numbers in about the first third of this century. Most were poor, and many were unskilled laborers. Not having the skills needed in the city, they often remained poor. They also came to the city at the same time its wealthier population was suburbanizing, thus reducing the city's tax base, while the new poor increased its needs for tax funds for social services. These matters have much to do with the plight of the cities today.

Black housing in the cities has typically been segregated, often in the form of ghettos and slums. A *ghetto* is an ethnic, racial, or religious *community*, a residence area of people of some particular type but one that embraces the full range of urban life, with its own social structure and social life within the city. A *slum*, by contrast, is an economic phenomenon, a residence area for the poor characterized by overcrowding, deteriorated housing, and, often, social problems. Contrary to popular white belief, not all segregated black residential areas in the American city are slums, although some are. An empirical study of housing segregation for blacks showed that as of 1960 segregation was still the norm in American cities, and that it was unrelated to poverty, national region, city size, or local attitudes toward fair employment or civil rights.

Review Questions

1. Describe the three models of urban ecological processes. Who formulated each model? Which do you find most applicable to the cities with which you are acquainted? Least applicable? Why?

2. The chapter notes four different definitions of the city (legal, geographic, sociological, and that of the U.S. Census, the last with sub-categories). What are they and how do they differ? If you were a Martian trying to

understand the American city what differences would it make to you which definition you picked to use?

3. Explain the five processes comprising human ecology discussed in this chapter: centralization, decentralization, invasion, succession, and segregation.

4. What conditions are necessary before urbanization can take place? Approximately when were these conditions first met?

5. Discuss the relationship between industrialization and urbanization. Did one appear to have caused the other? If so, how?

Suggestions for Research

1. Explore the role of community, as defined in this chapter, in your own home environment. Which everyday needs are filled in the neighborhood area? For which others do you drive to a more central urban area? Generally, how dependent do you consider yourself on the greater urban areas? Draw up your conclusions and observations in a paper.

2. Spend a day in a town with a population less than 10,000 and another day in a city with a population over 100,000. Compare the various leisure opportunities and facilities in each, noting the degree of specialization. From your observations, what assumptions can you make, if any, about the differences in the respective life-styles of the inhabitants of these areas?

3. Study in depth the three models of human ecology discussed in this chapter: Robert T. Park and Ernest Burgess's concentric-zone theory, Homer Hoyt's sector theory, and Chauncy Harris and Edward Ullman's multiple-nuclei theory. In what ways, if any, are they similar? Different? What are the strong and the weak aspects in each theory? Which seems most applicable to today's cities?

4. Choose a rural area in which to take an hour's drive along country roads (as opposed to busy highways). Analyze the houses you pass. How many appear to be reasonably or very modern? What proportion are of the traditional farmhouse variety? What other material traits did you notice that indicate something about contemporary rural life-styles? You may want to sketch or photograph some of the more interesting structures and share them with your classmates.

CHAPTER 11
POPULATION AND DEMOGRAPHY

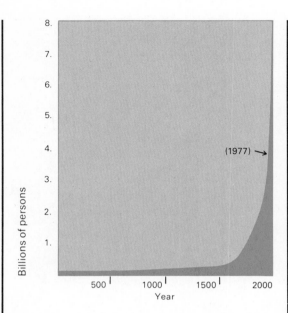

It took more than a million years for the world's human population to reach about a quarter billion at the year 1 A.D.

It took an additional 1,650 years for that population to double to about one-half billion.

But it took only about 200 years for it to double again to a billion in 1850.

Less than 100 years after that, it reached 2 billion in 1930.

It doubled again to 4 billion only 36 years later in 1976.

And there will be more than 8 billion people living on this planet in only another 23 years, by the year 2000!

Thousands will die of starvation this year. Ten years from now, they may number tens of thousands.

What will your world be like when you are fifty?

The facts in the first column are stark. For any reader at all thoughtful, they may also be frightening. There are more than 4 billion people alive in the world today; many of them are already starving or on the verge of starvation. And within twenty-five years, the world population will more than double its present size.

How are so many people to be fed? What will happen if they cannot be fed? Will tens, hundreds, or thousands of human beings passively accept death by starvation? Will their governments stand by and watch them starve? Will the starving masses rebel against their fate? What might this mean for those populations and countries where food is still in good supply?

You have undoubtedly confronted the problem of projected world population growth before. Newspapers and television programs discuss the effect of the population explosion on the quality of life and debate whether advanced farming methods can be exported to the developing countries (which have the highest population growth rates) in such a way as to make them self-sufficient in food production. Presidential panels are commissioned to set population policy for the United States, the findings of one often conflicting with those of the panel that preceded it. Other nations, like India, devote even more time, energy, and money to problems associated with massive population growth. Various experts forecast unrelievable famine for much of the world before the end of the century if population continues to grow at its current rate. On the other hand, the Roman Catholic church continues its traditional stand against artificial birth control, and some American technocrats hope that as-yet-undiscovered techniques for farming the sea and increasing agricultural yields will solve any food shortage that might develop. And finally, spokespeople for some of the nations that have or will have the greatest population–food supply problems reject suggestions that they should limit their population growth as stemming from selfish or even genocidal motives on the part of the already developed countries.

The reason that population growth and change have aroused so much attention and controversy is that population has a critical relationship, of a reciprocal nature, with the social organization of society. Population phenomena to a large degree determine the nature of a society and its future; while the nature of the society and its past to a large degree determine the characteristics of its population. What these characteristics are, and why they have so important a relation to social phenomena, is the subject of this chapter.

Demography is the scientific study of population, its structural characteristics and its processes. The demographic phenomena most directly related to the structure and functioning of human societies are the *structural* aspects of populations: their *size and rate of growth, spatial distribution,* and *composition,* which includes characteristics like sex, race, occupation, and education. The population *processes*—fertility, mortality, migration, and social mobility—will be discussed only within the context of these structural features. Because population problems clearly have great international significance (you may die in a nuclear war as a consequence of them), we will not limit our discussion to only one or a few nations, but will consider worldwide population trends.

Before starting our examination of population phenomena, we will briefly survey the principal sources of demographic information and the basic techniques of demographic analysis. Then we will discuss population size and growth, distribution, and composition. Finally, we will consider some of the consequences of contemporary world population: the major societal and international problems that have resulted from recent demographic trends and various solutions that have been proposed for these problems.

Demographic Data and Methods

Types of Demographic Data

The population census The primary source of demographic data is the *population census,* an inventory of selected facts about the people falling within the jurisdiction of a given administrative unit, such as a nation, county, or city. Most population censuses are conducted periodically by national governments in order to assess the needs of the population and to determine how national resources can best be used.

> **demography:** the study of population, including the structural characteristics of size and rate of growth, spatial distribution, and composition and the population processes of fertility, mortality, migration, and social mobility.

Table 11-1   Information typically covered in a national population census

A. *Geographic items*
1. Location at time of census and/or place of usual residence

B. *Household or family information*
2. Relationship to head of household or family

C. *Personal characteristics*
3. Sex
4. Age
5. Marital status
6. Place of birth
7. Citizenship

D. *Economic characteristics*
8. Type of activity
9. Occupation
10. Industry
11. Status (as employer, employee, etc.)

E. *Cultural characteristics*
12. Language
13. Ethnic or nationality characteristics

F. *Educational characteristics*
14. Literacy
15. Level of education
16. School attendance

G. *Fertility data*
17. Children—total live born

H. *Topics derived from the questionnaire*
18. Total population
19. Population by size of locality
20. Urban-rural classification
21. Household or family composition

Censuses have been taken since ancient times, but only within this century have censuses been taken of the majority of the *world's* population. In the decade 1955-1964, eighty-five national censuses were taken, including an estimated 68 percent of the earth's inhabitants. All four of the population giants—China, India, the Soviet Union, and the United States, which contain nearly half of the world's population—had censuses around 1960 and 1970. In the U.S., a census of the population has been taken every ten years since 1790.

Data collected The information collected for a population census varies from one nation to the next. Table 11-1 lists the information usually obtained in a national census. Additional facts that may be available include income, place of work, number of times married, age at marriage, and religion. In general, the questions asked are determined by what the government needs to know, and alterations in a nation's census reflect new problems confronting state and society.

Errors Population censuses are not always free from error. Occasionally, census results are purposely falsified to serve political aims. More often, though, such errors are due to methodological inadequacies in collecting and processing census information. These can be classified as either errors of coverage or errors of classification.

Errors of coverage involve either incomplete enumeration, the most frequent mistake, or duplicate counting. Isolated households or communities are likely to be overlooked; and some categories of persons, such as very young children, sometimes go unreported. Further complicating the enumeration issue is the fact that population counts may be based on two different criteria. The **de facto census method** counts the population according to where it is on the night preceding the census, while the **de jure census method** distributes people on the basis of their usual place of residence. Under the de facto system, a traveling salesman would be counted at his location for the night regardless of whether that was his permanent residence. Each method has advantages and disadvantages, and both are widely used. In the United States, the de jure definition is the main method used, although de facto statistics are also collected.

Errors of classification result from the incorrect recording of population characteristics. Some of these inaccuracies are due to misreporting by the informant; others occur when the enumerator has to guess about a particular piece of information because the appropriate question was not asked, or was not answered, or was answered incorrectly. Age, income, marital status, and occupation are particularly likely to be erroneously reported.

Vital registration systems While the population census provides a record of the characteristics of a population at a given time and is taken only periodically, *vital registration systems* are designed to record selected population events as they occur. Under ideal conditions, summaries are published monthly or annually. Events registered may include births, deaths, marriages, divorces, adoptions, and legitimations of minor children.

Not all of these types of information are recorded in all countries, and the accuracy of such statistics varies widely. For each event recorded, supplementary information is also obtained, such as race, age, occupation, place of birth, and place of residence. Although errors in reporting and recording sometimes occur, the major problems with vital registration data are incomplete coverage and the vast amount of data to be recorded and analyzed. In 1965, for instance, complete birth registration statistics were available for only about 35 percent of the world's population.[1]

Population registers Comprehensive procedures for continuously recording individual events and characteristics have been developed by many countries, including several European countries, Japan, and the Soviet Union, but not the United States. Any change of characteristics, like occupation and place of residence, or any vital event must be reported within a specified time. Although such *population registers* are usually established for purposes of policing or social control, they are often used for compilation of demographic statistics as well.

Sample surveys In recent years, *sample surveys* have been used increasingly to supplement census and registration data. In developing countries, they provide a means of supplementing the otherwise erroneous data stemming from incomplete census and registration coverage. The major advantage of sample surveys is that they allow the investigator to obtain a wider range of information than is available from census or vital registration sources. Surveys also permit more detailed analysis of the social and psychological factors associated with demographic events.

Publication of Demographic Data

The main published sources of demographic information are the census and vital statistics prepared by individual nations. Because of the need to insure the anonymity of respondents, these data are reported only for units, such as states and counties, and broad population categories, such as sex, race, occupation, education, and income.

Census data, especially for the developing countries, are subject to several limitations beyond those already discussed. First, there are long periods (usually ten years) between censuses, during which population characteristics are changing, often rapidly and at unknown rates.

Second, it is often many years from the time a census is conducted until the analyzed data are published. In the developing nations, where governmental resources of personnel and money are already severely limited, all but the most basic analyses may never be published. In the last decade, however, technical and financial assistance provided by the United Nations and other organizations has increased the availability and quality of census information for many such countries. International vital statistics data are even less accessible, and probably subject to greater error as well.

A major source of international data is the United Nations *Demographic Yearbook,* published annually since 1948. Included are basic population figures from censuses or estimates, vital statistics data, and special topics presented in more detail, for instance, births and deaths, marriage and divorce, and population trends. For the relatively few countries having population registers, reports are available and can be quite useful. Other sources of demographic data are the records of various national programs and services: social security, military conscription, voter registration, and school enrollment programs, among others.

---

de facto census method: counting people for census purposes as residing in the place they spent the night preceding the day they are enumerated.

de jure census method: counting people for census purposes as residing in their usual or normal place of residence.

balancing, or demographic, equation: the basic equation used by demographers to analyze population size or distribution. The equation is

$$P_t = P_0 + (B - D) + (I - E) + e,$$

where P_t = population size at the end of some specified time interval; P_0 = population size at the beginning of that interval; B = number of births; D = number of deaths; I = number of immigrants; E = number of emigrants; and e = the residual error resulting from inaccuracies in census and vital registration statistics.

Demographic Analysis

Although the analysis of demographic data often involves the quantitative techniques common to most types of social research, certain unique procedures are particularly important in dealing with population variables. Of fundamental importance are the basic indicators of population growth, distribution, and composition, as well as fertility, mortality, and migration.

The balancing, or demographic, equation The fundamental model underlying the study of population is the *balancing equation,* sometimes called the demographic equation. For determining changes in population size or distribution, the equation is:

$$P_t = P_o + (B - D) + (I - E) + e$$

P_t is the population at the end of some specified interval; P_o is the population at the beginning of the interval; B is the number of births; D is the number of deaths; I, the number of immigrants (in-migrants); E, the number of emigrants (out-migrants); and e, the residual error due to inaccuracies in census and vital registration statistics. The importance of the demographic equation for population analysis cannot be overstated. Its principal use is to further understanding of the factors that contribute to population change. In addition, the demographer can use it to project future population figures by making assumptions about future births, deaths, migration, and compositional changes.

Frequently, the demographer focuses on particular subgroups within a population, such as blacks or workers. In these cases, the components of the balancing equation have to be specified accordingly. For some subgroups, such as those differentiated by sex or place of residence, it is only necessary to collect the appropriate statistics on births, deaths, migration, and so on. But with age groups, special considerations are necessary. Because age by definition varies with time, persons who were age X at the time t are age $(X + i)$ at time $(t + i)$, i being the length of the interval. Persons sharing such a common property in a population subgroup are said to constitute a **cohort.** In addition to age, cohorts may be defined in terms of a number of other properties, such as marriage or termination of formal education during a particular year.

Many demographic analyses are focused on cohorts, particularly when changes over time are being studied. For instance, it might be useful to project to the year 2020 the effect on American society of high survival rates among the present cohort of those aged twenty to thirty. At the present time, this group is the largest single age category in the American population. This means that, if they survive in large numbers (as they are expected to do), and present birth rates do not change much, in 2020 they will still be the largest group. But at that time, of course, instead of being young, economically productive workers, they will be elderly, with all that *that* implies for the labor force, medical care needs, social security, and so forth, all of which must be planned for ahead of time.

Rates and ratios Demographic statistics are frequently presented in terms of *rates:* the number of events in a given period of time divided by the population in question during that period. The period of time used is usually a year, and in order to avoid awkwardly large numbers, rates are expressed per 100, 1,000, or even 10,000 members of the population. There are two types of rates: crude and refined. **Crude rates** measure the frequency of an event per unit of the whole population. **Refined rates** measure the frequency of an event per unit of the population that is relevant to the event in question. Crude rates are not very useful because the denominator includes all members of the population, some of whom are not at risk of experiencing the event in question. The crude birthrate, for example, includes in the denominator women above and below the childbearing ages, as well as men of all ages. Refined rates are more valuable because in them the denominator is limited to population members who actually do risk experiencing the event being measured. Examples are birthrates for women of childbearing age and marriage rates for the previously unmarried population.

Other types of demographic statistics are presented in terms of *ratios,* for instance, the **dependency ratio,** which is the number of persons in the nonworking ages divided by those in the working ages. Generally, rates are used in the analysis of population change, while ratios are employed for descriptive purposes.

Population Size and Growth

Historical and Modern Views

Not until the eighteenth century did anyone consider population problems in a systematic and more or less scientific way. The most important of these early writers were Thomas Malthus and Karl Marx and his followers. In modern times, the dominant view of population size and growth has been based on the theory of the demographic transition.

Thomas Malthus The first person to write systematically about the dangers of population growth was Thomas Malthus, an English clergyman and economist. In 1798, he published an analysis of population growth in which he argued that a "natural law" governed the growth of populations.[2] Population, Malthus thought, would always increase faster than the subsistence—food production—unless prevented by certain moral restraints, "vice," or natural disasters and disease. According to Malthus, methods of subsistence grow only in arithmetic progression (1, 2, 3, 4, 5) because, at a given level of food-producing technology, the only way to increase the food supply is to increase the number of acres under cultivation, fish caught, and so on. Population, however, increases in geometric progression (1, 2, 4, 8, 16), because two individuals can and normally do produce more children than the 2.1 required to replace themselves. (Any married couple must produce more than two children in order statistically to reproduce themselves because, in any population, some people will never marry and some will be infertile.) Thus, if unchecked, population would soon outstrip the resources necessary for sustaining it, leading to widespread famine.

Malthus foresaw only two effective means of curbing the growth of population. The first was *preventive checks,* including deferral of marriage (which would reduce the number of children who could be born before the wife became infertile) and "vice" (extramarital sexual relations and prostitution, which would allegedly avoid the birth of children). The second was *positive checks,* including epidemics, wars, plague, and famine, all of which reduce the normal duration of life. Voluntary methods of preventing conception within wedlock, other than abstinence, would probably have been designated as immoral in Malthus's time and, consequently, would have been labeled vice. Thus, for Malthus, only individual human decisions and natural disaster could curb population growth. No amount of social or governmental reorganization could affect it.

The Marxian view The Malthusian doctrine created a great deal of controversy and alerted followers and opponents alike to the need for a better understanding of population trends. An opposing view was presented by Marx and other socialist writers. They argued that there is no natural law of population, but rather that population size and growth are determined by existing social and economic conditions, particularly the capitalist mode of production. The Marxian thesis is that capitalism not only creates unemployment or underemployment because of its inability to provide jobs for all, but furthermore depends on a readily available labor force that can be guaranteed only if there is surplus population. And because capitalism requires consumers for its products, there is further

cohort: a group of persons within a given population sharing a common property, for example, a specific age or degree of formal education.

crude rate: the frequency of an event per unit of total population, usually per 1,000 or 10,000.

refined rate: the frequency of an event per unit of population at risk of experiencing that event, for example, births per women of child-bearing age.

dependency ratio: the ratio of people in the non-working ages in a population to those of working age.

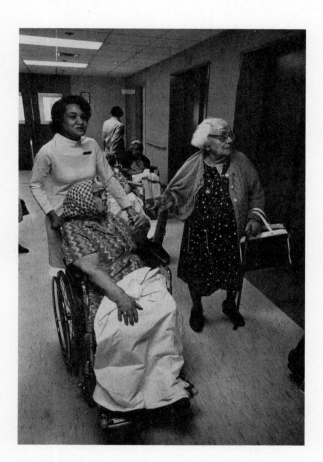

As significant numbers of people age, special services must be provided for them. This care used to be given by the extended family system. Now we confine the elderly to high-cost nursing homes.

necessity for a large population. Population problems, therefore, are due to prevailing social and economic conditions rather than any lack of moral restraint in human beings, and they can be resolved only through a reorganization of the social and economic bases of society.[3]

The demographic transition Modern views on population growth are largely based on the observed decline in rates of growth in Europe following the Industrial Revolution. The most prominent of these is the **demographic transition theory** (see Figure 11-1). This theory argues that populations pass through a series of stages, initially typified by high birth and death rates, producing a stationary condition of little or no net growth (period A on Figure 11-1). This is followed by a series of transitional stages: In the first, (period B), mortality is reduced, generating a period of expanding growth. Then (period C) fertility declines, causing a downward swing in the rate of growth. Finally (period D), with birth and death rates both low, the rate of growth becomes relatively stable; depending on the balance between mortality and fertility, the population may increase or even decrease slightly.

The factors causing these declines in mortality and fertility are the processes of social and economic modernization. Mortality declines when improvements occur in public health, medical care, and the general standard of living. Fertility decline, by contrast, results from a more complex interaction of social, psychological, cultural, economic, and demographic processes. Some of them are urbanization, growing individualism and rising levels of aspiration, the declining influence of traditional norms governing familial organization and the status of women, industrialization, and increasing geographic mobility.

Refinements in the demographic transition theory The demographic transition theory provides a convenient explanation of the historical experience of European nations, but it has not proved very useful for predicting growth trends in the currently developing countries. Although mortality rates have decreased, as expected, in many developing countries, fertility has not declined in the predicted manner. Recent attempts to reformulate transition theory have therefore focused on specifying the biological, social, and cultural factors that affect human decisions regarding reproduction.

Basic Measures

The quantitative indicator of population size is obvious: the absolute number of inhabitants occupying a specified area at a given time, although it should be remembered that this number may vary according to whether the count is based on a de jure or a de facto definition. It is also important to recognize that except when census-year data are used, population size is based on estimates. Population change, which may reflect a net increase or decrease in population size, can be represented in a variety of ways.

The simplest indicator is the absolute difference between two dates. More useful are measures that reflect the amount of growth relative to the size of the population. One often used is the *intercensal percent change* (IPC): the relative amount of growth of a population between census periods. It is computed by dividing the amount of intercensal change by the population at the earlier census and converting the resulting number to a percent. For example, the U.S. population between 1960 and 1970 increased from 179,323,175 to 203,211,926, or about 13.3 percent; while the population of the world in the same period increased from about 2,982,000,000 to 3,632,000,000, or 21.8 percent. In order for comparisons among different populations to be meaningful, the *interval* between censuses must be equivalent, though it does not necessarily have to refer to the same years.

It is also frequently useful to express population change in terms of the components of the basic balancing equation, discussed earlier. **Natural increase** (or decrease) is the net difference between births and deaths and is typically expressed as a rate per 1,000 population during a specified period. *Net migration* is the absolute difference between in-migration (immigration) and out-migration (emigration) and can also be expressed as a rate.

Trends and Differences

Considering the length of time human beings have been on earth, the so-called population explosion

Table 11-2   Estimates of historical population growth

	Population (millions)	Average annual increase since preceding date (percent) [a]	Approximate number of years required for population to double at given rate
B.C.			
7000–6000	5–10		
A.D.			
1	200–400	0.0	
1650	470–545	0.0	
1750	629–961	0.4	173
1800	813–1,125	0.4	173
1850	1,128–1,402	0.5	139
1900	1,550–1,762	0.5	139
1950	2,486	0.8	86
1975	4,147	2.2	32

[a]Rates for periods prior to 1975 are calculated on the basis of population at midpoint of range. The 1975 rate is a mid-year estimate.

demographic transition theory: the idea that societies go through a set of stages in population growth and decline, from stability in size based on high rates of both birth and death, through a population explosion resulting from a rapidly lowered death rate while birth rates remain high, through a downswing in population growth as birthrates decline, and finally reach a relatively stable size characterized by low rates of both birth and death.

natural increase: the net difference between births and deaths.

**Figure 11-1
The demographic transition**

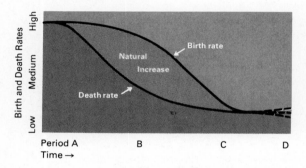

The theory of demographic transition, based largely on the European experience with industrialization, assumes that societies go through similar population stages as a consequence of modernization. In the original preindustrial stage, both birth and death rates are high and the population is usually relatively small, and stable (period A). With the beginnings of industrialization, improvements in medicine, sanitation, and so forth, death rates drop rapidly while, for a time, birth rates remain high. This results in a population explosion (Period B). After a time, however, birth rates drop too, with the result that the rate of population growth decreases (period C), and population size becomes relatively stable once more, although it is larger. The relation of births to deaths may vary somewhat thereafter, resulting in a steady state, a slight increase over a long period of time, or even a slight decline in size (period D).

is a very recent event. It is estimated that the human population did not reach 1 billion until approximately 1800-1860, but the second billion was reached around 1925, the third by 1960, and the fourth by 1975. As Table 11-2 shows, this trend is directly associated with an increasingly high rate of growth from about 1750 to the present and is uniform in one respect: *absolute size has continually increased.*

But the long-term trend in average annual rates of growth is not uniform among regions. In the period since 1750, the population growth rate declined in North America, remained stable in Europe, fluctuated in the U.S.S.R. and China, and increased in the remainder of Asia, Latin America, and Africa.[4] Paradoxically, then, the most rapidly growing nations are those that can least afford numbers of people. For developing countries (in Africa, Latin America, and Asia excluding Japan), annual growth rates averaged 0.3 percent during the period 1850-1900, 0.9 percent for 1900-1950, and 2.1 percent in the years 1950-1965. Corresponding figures for the developed nations (Europe, the Soviet Union, North America, Oceania, and Japan) are 1.0 percent, 0.8 percent, and 1.2 percent, respectively.[5] If the most recent rates continue, the population of the developing nations will double in approximately thirty-three years, while for the developed nations the doubling time would be about fifty-eight years.

The first national census taken in the United States (1790) showed a total population of just under 4 million. By 1850, this figure had grown to a little more than 23 million; for 1900, it was 76 million; and in 1950, it was just over 151 million. The most recent census, conducted in 1970, reported the population was 203,211,926. The average annual rate of growth in the U.S. has declined considerably during the past two and a half centuries, the peak being approximately 3.2 percent in 1820, while the lowest rate, near 0.6 percent, was recorded during the mid-1930s. The overall trend shows a sharp decline from the end of the Civil War to the beginning of World War II, followed by an equally sharp increase to the late 1950s. Since then, annual rates of growth have steadily fallen.

Causes and Consequences

Causes Population size and rates of growth are direct results of interaction between the components of the demographic equation—fertility, mortality, immigration, and emigration. These are in turn related to a wide variety of biological, social-structural, cultural, and additional demographic factors. It should now be evident that the pattern of world population growth prior to the eighteenth century was characterized by *gradual* increase. Following the Industrial Revolution, the world rate began to climb more *steeply,* but sizable differences developed between nations directly and immediately affected by industrialization and those that did not begin to industrialize until the twentieth century. These differences were due to changing relationships between fertility, mortality, and, less obviously, migration.

For both categories of nations, however, a decline in death rates initiated the increase in population. With the now-developed nations, the death rate began to fall in the early eighteenth century and continued to decline gradually for a period of 75-150 years, after which it stabilized at the current level. Although lagging behind the falling death rate, the birthrate also declined. The result has been that natural increase remained relatively low and stable, averaging between 0.5 and 1.5 percent. Contrasting with this pattern, the death rate in Asia, Africa, and Latin America did not begin to fall sharply until about 1940, but then it declined dramatically, becoming comparable to, or even lower than, the death rate in the industrialized nations in 15-30 years. At the same time, the birth rate has remained at a level *above* that prevailing in Western Europe in the early 1800s.

It is important to recognize that the reduced mortality brought about by the industrialized nations during the Industrial Revolution was associated with increased productivity, whereas the dramatic reduction of death rates in the developing nations since 1940 has been primarily due to medical technology exported from the more industrial nations, without the associated increase in internal economic productivity experienced by the industrial nations in prior centuries. The result of this drastic shift in the balance between births and deaths has been a spectacular acceleration in the overall increase of people in the developing world during the past three decades—in short, *the population explosion.*

The contribution of migration to population increase has varied widely among different nations and historical periods. For example, the growth of European nations was curtailed somewhat by heavy emigration, primarily to the United States, between 1880 and 1930. But in the contemporary world, net migration has relatively little influence on population growth, except in a few nations like Australia, Brazil, Canada, Israel, and New Zealand.

Consequences The consequences of variations in population size and growth can be viewed from two perspectives. In the short run, some distinct advantages can be seen in relatively large size and rapid growth. If a nation has abundant natural resources, food supply, and habitable land area, then an increasing population can make a positive contribution to national development. People are needed to settle the land, to produce and consume goods, to provide and utilize services, and to coordinate the activities of groups and institutions. Such was the case with many, if not most, nations prior to the twentieth century, the United States being an obvious example.

But when land, food, and other resources are not abundant, continued population growth can be detrimental to national development, and sometimes even disastrous. Unfortunately, this situation prevails for the vast majority of the contemporary world. Natural resources have been depleted far beyond our present capacity to replace them, millions of people are suffering from malnutrition, and the numbers dying from starvation increase annually. In short, the era when rapid population growth was advantageous to national development has passed and is unlikely to be repeated in the foreseeable future.

Increasing growth presents more problems for some populations than others. Consider two of the developing nations, India and Nigeria, which in 1970 showed roughly similar levels of economic development (about $80-$90 gross national product per capita) and annual rates of population growth (2.6 percent). United Nations population projections for 1985 show that each country would increase its total population by about the same proportion, 46-48 percent. But, in absolute terms, Nigeria would be adding only about 30 million persons, while for India the comparable figure would be 253 million!

Problems of population growth are not, however, limited to developing nations. The United States, for example, has the highest per capita standard of living in the world and is the world's leading food exporter. But many of the problems facing it today are directly or indirectly a consequence of population size. The "baby boom" after World War II produced a tidal wave of children. School buildings had to be dramatically enlarged to accommodate them, as did the teaching profession. As the cohort aged, however, it left behind empty grammar and high schools, some still unpaid for, and teachers with empty classrooms, while it overwhelmed the colleges, creating a now-diminished demand for college teachers. Surely, some of the dissension today characterizing the teaching profession is related to the fact that too many people are trying to retain jobs unnecessary now that the children born in the baby boom have grown up and received their education. Similarly, the increasing energy shortage, deterioration of the national park system,

unemployment, pollution, and water-shortage problems are also in part problems stemming from population growth. The United States now has too many people to maintain the standard of living that became conventional in the 1940s and 1950s. Today's American college students probably cannot expect in maturity to enjoy the affluence to which most became accustomed in childhood.

To a large, although as yet unspecified extent, the social chaos that characterizes the contemporary world is a product of population growth. Increasing numbers of people mean that social institutions are increasingly unable to meet societal needs. Political systems are unable to govern, educational systems to educate, economic systems to produce and distribute goods and services. But workable solutions to current problems of excessive population growth themselves depend heavily on a reorganization of these same collapsing social institutions.[6] That is the dilemma presented by increasing population growth.

Summary

Although problems of population size and growth have been debated for centuries, recent concerns have focused on the implications stemming from the dire predictions of Malthus. Historical evidence shows that the turning point in demographic evolution for the now-developed nations was the Industrial Revolution in Europe, while for the currently developing nations it can be dated around 1940. In both cases, the key factor was a decline in the death rate. In those nations experiencing early industrialization, a drop in the birth rate followed relatively soon, resulting in a return to a low rate of growth. In contrast, reproduction in the developing nations has remained at a high level, the consequence being increasingly high rates of growth. Current levels of population increase cannot be maintained without serious and undesirable social consequences.

Population Distribution

Accompanying the increased size and rate of growth of the human population has been an alteration in its pattern of distribution over the

Table 11-3   Estimated distribution of the world's population 1750–1975 (percent)

Area	1750	1800	1850	1900	1950	1965	1970	1975	Net change 1750–1975
World[a]	100.1	99.9	100.1	100.1	99.9	99.9	100.1	99.9	
Africa	13.4	10.9	8.8	8.1	8.7	9.2	9.5	10.1	−3.3
Asia	63.0	64.4	63.5	56.1	54.5	55.7	56.6	56.8	−6.2
Latin America	2.0	2.5	3.0	4.5	6.5	7.5	7.8	8.2	+6.2
North America	0.3	0.7	2.1	5.0	6.7	6.5	6.3	6.0	+5.7
Europe	15.8	15.5	16.5	17.9	15.8	13.5	12.7	11.9	−3.9
USSR	5.3	5.7	6.0	8.1	7.2	7.0	6.7	6.4	+1.1
Oceania	0.3	0.2	0.2	0.4	0.5	0.5	0.5	0.5	+0.2

[a] Deviations from 100 percent are due to rounding.

earth's surface. A number of factors have contributed to changes in this pattern, but the major recent shifts in population distribution are largely a result of the increasing urbanization of the world.

Basic Measures

A variety of indicators have been developed for measuring population distribution. *Population density,* as we saw in Chapter 10, is the number of people per unit of land area (per square mile or kilometer, for instance). Density ratios, however, are crude measures because they do not reflect variations in the habitability or "support potential" of the land.

   More useful and more frequently used are measures of population distribution within and between specified geographic areas, usually defined by political boundaries. The most important criterion of population distribution within or between major political areas of the world is the *urban-rural distinction.* Although everybody recognizes that significant differences exist between city and country populations, there are no universally agreed-upon criteria for the definition of an urban locality. Definitions vary widely among the nations of the world, but typically, urban residence is associated with predominantly nonagricultural employment and a lower limit of around 5,000 total population. Obviously, there are drastic differences *among* those localities classified as urban, many more than exist between rural areas.

Trends and Differences

The pattern of distribution of the world's population according to major regions has changed somewhat, though not greatly, over the past two centuries. As Table 11-3 shows, slightly more than half of the world's population has been in Asia, ranging from 64.4 percent in 1800 to 54.5 percent in 1950. The remainder has been relatively equally dispersed among the other major land areas. But the proportion residing in the Americas has increased from 2.3 percent in 1750 to 14.2 percent in 1975, while moderate declines have occurred in Asia, Europe, and Africa.

   Population densities are highly variable, as shown in Table 11-4. Although high densities are evident for some of the more industrialized nations, *average* densities are generally higher among the developing countries. As world population continues to grow, overall density must inevitably increase. One researcher concludes that even by a *conservative* estimate the population density of the world will double between 1960 and 2000, resulting in over 7 billion people on the earth.[7] Furthermore, the data shown in Table 11-4 indicate that the density differential between developing and developed nations will increase on the order of sevenfold. Once again, evidence suggests that the pattern of population change in the contemporary world will continue to present grave problems for those nations least able to cope with the resulting pressures.

Table 11-4   Population, area, and density for the world, major areas, and regions, 1970.

Area	Estimated mid-year population (millions)	Area (km² in thousands)	Density (population per km²)
World total	3,632	135,781	27
Developing regions	2,542	74,468	34
More developed regions	1,090	61,312	18
Africa	344	30,319	11
Western Africa	101	6,142	16
Eastern Africa	98	6,338	15
Middle Africa	36	6,613	5
Northern Africa	87	8,525	10
Southern Africa	23	2,701	8
Asia (excluding USSR)	2,056	27,532	75
East Asia	930	11,757	79
Mainland region	765	11,129	69
Japan	103	370	280
Other East Asia	61	258	237
South Asia	1,126	15,775	71
Middle South Asia	762	6,771	113
Southeast Asia	287	4,498	64
Southwest Asia	77	4,506	17
Europe (excluding USSR)	462	4,936	94
Western Europe	149	995	149
Southern Europe	128	1,315	98
Eastern Europe	104	990	105
Northern Europe	81	1,636	49
Latin America	283	20,566	14
Tropical South America	151	13,700	11
Middle America (mainland)	67	2,496	27
Temperate South America	39	4,134	10
Caribbean	26	236	109
Northern America	228	21,515	11
USSR	243	22,402	11
Oceania	19	8,511	2
Australia and New Zealand	15	7,955	2
Melanesia	3	525	5
Polynesia and Micronesia	1	30	41

Note: Because of rounding, totals are not in all cases the exact sum of the parts. Population totals for the world, developing, and more developed regions have been adjusted to take into account discrepancies between regional assumptions of immigration and emigration.

The most dramatic shift in the distribution of the human population in modern times is reflected in the growth of cities, as we saw in Chapter 10. By 1800 no more than 3 percent of the world's people could be considered urban (5,000 or more inhabitants), and it is questionable whether any single city contained a million inhabitants.[8] During the past 175 years, the proportion of people living in cities has steadily increased, as has the number of localities classified as urban. For example, while only about 2 percent of the world's inhabitants lived in cities of 20,000 or more population in 1800, this figure had increased to 4 percent by 1850, 9 percent by 1900, and 21.2 percent by 1950. Recent figures for the world and selected regions are shown in Table 11-5.

The pace of urbanization differs considerably from one region to the next. The 1920-1970 increase for world urbanization as a whole is 97 percent; it is 72 percent for the developed regions and 219 percent for those that are less developed. Not only is the world's population becoming more

Table 11-5 Percentage of total population in cities of 20,000 or more for major areas of the world, 1920–1970.

Area	1920	1930	1940	1950	1960	1970[a]
World total	14.3	16.3	18.8	21.2	25.4	28.2
Developing regions	5.8	7.0	8.7	11.4	15.4	18.5
More developed regions	29.4	32.6	37.0	40.0	46.0	50.5
Africa	4.8	5.9	7.2	9.7	13.4	16.5
East Asia	7.2	9.1	11.6	13.8	18.5	21.7
South Asia	5.7	6.5	8.3	11.1	13.7	16.0
Europe	34.7	37.2	39.5	40.7	44.2	47.1
Latin America	14.4	16.8	19.6	25.1	32.8	37.8
Northern America	41.4	46.5	46.2	50.8	58.0	62.6
USSR	10.3	13.4	24.1	27.8	36.4	42.7
Oceania	36.5	38.0	40.9	45.7	52.9	57.9

[a]Projected.

urbanized; it is also increasingly concentrated in *large* cities (see Table 11-6). Although residence in large cities is still more characteristic of the developed countries, *the rate of increase is higher for the developing nations.*

Changes in population distribution within the United States reflect the world pattern and, more precisely, that for the industrialized countries. Population density at the time of the first census in 1790 was 4.5 persons per square mile; this figure increased to 7.9 in 1850, 21.5 in 1900, 50.5 in 1960, and 57.5 in 1970.[9] The increasing urbanization of the United States also reflects world trends. As we saw in Chapter 10, the urban component of this country has been growing steadily since the beginning of this century, and 73.5 percent of the population is now urban, according to the U.S. Census definition of the term.

Causes and Consequences

Causes Population distribution is influenced by a wide range of factors. *Geographical elements* include climate, terrain, the quality of the soil, the presence of energy and mineral resources, and location in relation to other areas and to routes of transportation. But, in general, the more complex a society becomes, the less directly such physical factors influence the distribution of its population. Since the Industrial Revolution, the significant de-

terminants of population distribution have increasingly come to be associated with changes in *demographic and social organization.*

The most direct causes of population distribution are, of course, levels of natural increase and net migration. To the extent that births exceed deaths and immigration is greater than emigration, a given spatial unit will grow and will become more densely populated. In addition, under normal conditions population distribution changes relatively slowly, and thus the pattern of distribution existing at a given time has important consequences for future changes. At the international level, population distribution is largely a consequence of differences in rates of natural increase, although in some countries, international migration, plus alterations in national boundaries, continues to play a significant role.

Less direct yet equally important causes of population distribution are social organizational factors that influence natural increase, migration, and administrative decisions concerning classification of people and places. Types of economic activities, production technology, and social policy have an important bearing on population distribution. The Soviet Union, for example, has deliberately populated Siberia through forced emigration as well as incentive plans.

Generally, the greater the variety of economic activities located in a particular area, the greater

Table 11-6   Percent of total population in large cities for selected years, 1920–1970

	Cities of 100,000 or more				Cities of 1,000,000 or more			
	1920	1950	1960	1970	1920	1950	1960	1970
World	9.1	15.6	16.4	22.9	3.6	7.1	9.4	11.6
Less developed regions	2.6	7.9	11.5	14.9	0.1	2.9	5.0	7.2
More developed regions	22.8	30.5	36.4	41.8	10.0	15.1	18.5	21.8

the population density. The link between technological change, industrialization, and population concentration is relatively obvious. But it should also be noted that technological advance may serve to open up new areas for human habitation. For example, irrigation of desert areas may disperse rather than concentrate population by making more territory available for living and working.

Finally, political decisions influence patterns of population distribution. All national governments have laws that regulate migration to and from other countries, and some have developed policies affecting the internal distribution of population. Examples of the latter are the rural colonization schemes established in recent years in several Latin American countries, government programs designed to encourage the decentralization of industry, and the development of "new towns," such as Brasilia, aimed at relieving demographic pressure on large cities. (Brasilia, in fact, is an interesting example because it hasn't worked. Intended as an administrative city, like Washington, D.C., it was built so far from other centers that few Brazilians moved there voluntarily, and it remains relatively empty.)

Consequences   Variations in population distribution have effects at both international and national levels. As Table 11-3 showed, the distribution of population around the world has not changed greatly in modern times, and it has varied only slightly more within individual countries. However, population distribution of individual countries, especially around borders shared with other nations, has important social, political, and economic consequences for international relations.

Larger, more densely populated nations are often under pressure, or have imperialistic intentions, to expand their territorial boundaries at the expense of smaller, less densely populated ones. Indeed, one of the major causes of international conflict is population pressure, examples being the recent Chinese movements into India and the Soviet Union, and the extended conflict in Indochina during the past quarter century. People are viewed not only as producers and consumers of material goods but also as the basis of national security. Territorial expansion is not, however, usually a feasible way to relieve population pressure, and so many nations are currently facing demands for social reorganization.

At the national level, the principal trend in population distribution has been urbanization, and social consequences are evident for both urban and rural segments. Philip Hauser refers to this process as *population implosion*, and argues that as size and density increase, a multiplier effect is produced whereby the *potential* for human interaction in any fixed land area is drastically increased.[10] For example, if we assumed an average density of 1 person per square mile for the U.S. in 1500, there would have been 314 persons within any circular area with a ten-mile radius. Then if we assume a density of 8,000 persons per square mile for the average central city in 1970 metropolitan America, the number of persons within the same circular area would be 2,512,000. And, finally, an extreme case would be Manhattan Island, with a density of approximately 75,000 persons per square mile and 23,550,000 potential contacts within a circle having a ten-mile radius! See Figure 11-2.

As populations become increasingly urbanized and social density is multiplied as illustrated above, conditions may be created that generate behavioral, psychological, and organic pathology, although the evidence presently available is not totally compelling. As yet no one has determined the optimum density for human settlements, but Hauser suggests that contemporary trends point to increasing confusion and social disorder—in short, "the chaotic society," with no establishment of, or planning for, optimum population density.

Although many of the problems associated with urbanization are more directly a consequence of population diversification than population concentration, others result directly or indirectly from the sheer numbers and density of urban inhabitants. For example, in many cities in the more affluent nations, unemployment is on the increase, land values and the costs of housing are skyrocketing, and pollution of the environment is reaching a level such that life itself may be endangered.

In the developing countries, the major problems of urban living are housing, employment, education, and poverty. More generally, the problem throughout the world is one of too many people concentrated in relatively small areas lacking the necessary resources to satisfy collective expectations regarding human welfare. Whether cities continue to be the focus of civilization and the more creative aspects of human culture, or degenerate into a modified version of Hobbes's state of nature—where life would not only be poor, nasty, brutish, and short, as Hobbes said, but also *crowded*—will depend upon our ability to develop new and improved modes of urban social organization.

Although the major trend in population distribution in the modern world is reflected in the growth of cities, this does not mean that rural areas have been unaffected. While the proportion of people living outside cities has been declining, absolute numbers of rural dwellers have been increasing in the developing nations. The result has been an excess of rural population relative to the land cultivated, and thus considerable underemployment. This problem is made worse by the inequitable distribution of land ownership in many rural areas. Rural poverty is a significant problem in the developed as well as the developing nations of the world. Furthermore, rural-to-urban migration is selective: migrants more frequently come from the younger, better-educated, and more ambitious segments of the rural population, leaving behind on the land the aged, the illiterate, and the apathetic.

Summary

Data for the last hundred years clearly indicate a trend toward increasing density of population, as well as increasing concentration in cities. The major factors currently influencing population distribution are demographic, economic, technological, and political.

Although urbanization certainly has positive consequences, such as the centralization of commercial and administrative institutions and the creation of a diversified labor force, these appear to be overshadowed by the problems of large and densely populated settlements. Unemployment, slums, traffic congestion, pollution of the natural environment—these are but some of the more obvious difficulties associated with rapid, often uncontrolled, urbanization. Whether this trend can be reversed or even arrested is as yet uncertain, but whatever the outcome, it will have far-reaching implications for the quality of life.

Population Composition

In addition to size and territorial distribution, populations differ in terms of a third structural feature, the distribution of personal characteristics among members. This component of demographic analysis is called **population composition**. The characteristics considered are of two basic types. *Ascribed characteristics,* as you will recall from Chapter 8, include attributes such as age, kinship, sex, race, ethnic status, and place of birth, that are assigned to individuals by reason of the circumstances of their birth; and they are, except under unusual conditions, not subject to change. *Achieved characteristics,* by contrast, are determined by a person's efforts and social experience and are more clearly subject to change. Examples include marital status, nationality, language, religion, place of residence, occupation, education, and income.

Variations in population composition influence the basic population processes of fertility, mortality, migration, and social mobility. If large numbers of males have been killed in a war, for example, many women will have to remain single, and fertility will be affected, as well as the composition of the labor force. (The German population will show the effects of World War II for decades yet, as will the British.) Similarly, the mortality rate will be diminished by a baby boom; migration is enhanced by large proportions of young people; and social mobility, as we saw in Chapter 8, is likely to be easier in a society with a small-but-growing population than an overpopulated one. Variations in population composition are also significantly related to patterns of social and economic organization. To illustrate the importance of compositional characteristics, we will discuss in some detail two ascribed characteristics: age and sex.

Basic Measures

A fundamental technique for representing age and sex composition is the **population pyramid**, which is constructed by plotting the age distribution of a population, differentiated by sex, at a given time. The pyramidal shape results from the fact that the number of people in the population is typically somewhat less in the older than in the younger age groups, although the degree of variation is highly dependent on fertility and, to a lesser extent, mortality rates. Figure 11-3 (p. 343) shows various population pyramids. The pyramids of the Philippines and Mexico are typical of populations with high and fairly constant fertility. Sweden and the United Kingdom exhibit patterns associated with long-standing low fertility. And the pyramids of Japan and Singapore reflect a more recent decline in fertility.

Two additional measures of age and sex composition are available. For the former, as we saw earlier, there is the *dependency ratio,* the ratio of people of nonworking ages (generally those below fifteen and over sixty-four) to those of working age (fifteen to sixty-four). It is usually computed in terms of number of persons of nonworking age per 100 of working age. For some purposes, it is useful to calculate youth and old-age dependency ratios separately.

An important measure of sex composition is the **sex ratio,** the number of males in the population per 100 females. At birth, this ratio is approximately 105 for the human population in general, indicating a higher proportion of male births. But because men have higher death rates than women, the

population composition: the distribution in a population of both ascribed characteristics (age, sex, race) and achieved characteristics (marital status, education, and occupation).

population pyramid: a graphic representation of a population's age-sex distribution.

sex ratio: the number of males in a population per 100 females.

Figure 11-2
Increasing population density

1 person per square mile = 314 in a 10-mile radius (U.S. in the year 1500)

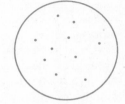

8,000 per square mile = 2,512,000 in 10-mile radius (average density of American central city in 1970)

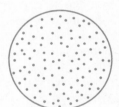

75,000 per square mile = 23,500,000 in 10-mile radius (Manhattan Island in 1970)

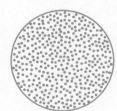

initial higher proportion of males is gradually reduced until the sex ratio is approximately even near middle age. From that point onward, females are in the majority. As will be seen later, social and cultural factors can influence the sex ratio for any given population.

Trends and Differences

Until about 1850, most of the world's populations had similar age structures, reflected by the classical pyramidal age-sex distribution seen in the Philippines or Mexico in Figure 11-3. Since that time, substantial changes have occurred in the age structures of the now-developed countries, with a decrease in the proportion of youth and an increased representation of the older age groups. In the developing countries, where fertility remains relatively high, the pyramidal shape of the age structure has been maintained. Abbreviated age distributions for various regions of the world are shown in Table 11-7. One important consequence of the differences in these data is a variation in the dependency measures, shown in the last three columns. Generally, the total and youth dependency ratios are considerably higher for the developing countries, which means these countries must devote a substantial proportion of their resources simply to caring for their dependents. But the old-age dependency ratios are higher for the more developed populations, reflecting their lower fertility as well as longer life expectancy. In these countries, there will be increasing demand for services for the elderly, such as extended medical care.

Trends in the United States have closely paralleled those in other developed countries. In 1900, the U.S. showed the classical pyramid-shaped population, but by 1970 it had begun to shift toward a more rectangular shape. In 1970, 28 percent of the population was under fifteen, 62 percent between fifteen and sixty-four, and 10 percent sixty-five or over. The resulting dependency ratios are 61.5 (total), 45.6 (youth), and 15.9 (old-age).[11] Comparison with the figures in Table 11-7 indicates that the U.S. currently exhibits an age structure that is clearly representative of the developed countries, but one with a higher dependency ratio than the European countries or Japan.

Sex ratios typically do not vary much over time,

but they do differ somewhat among the nations of the world, and considerably among the various age groups in a population. Generally, sex ratios are lower—that is, there is a higher proportion of females—in the developed nations and in successively older age categories. Comparative data are presented in Table 11-8 (p. 344). In 1970, the U.S. showed a sex ratio for the population under fifteen of 105.0, while it was 94.6 for those Americans aged fifteen to sixty-four, and 72.1 for those sixty-five years of age or more. The total sex ratio for the population was 95.8.[12]

Causes and Consequences

Causes Trends and differences in age and sex characteristics have a number of causes. As indicated earlier, the sex ratio at birth is approximately 105 males for every 100 females. Explanations for this difference have been proposed in terms of race, rural-urban residence, age of the mother, legitimacy status of the child, frequency of pregnancy, birth order, and the influence of war on the age structure of a population. But the evidence is often contradictory and is by no means comprehensive. Differences in sex composition at later ages are much better understood and are largely due to sex differences in mortality and migration, as well as differences in the composite age structure of a population.

Higher mortality rates for males result in a gradual reduction in the sex ratio, such that it reaches 100 males for every 100 females approximately during the fifth decade of life and continues to fall with advancing age. Because migration is frequently more likely for one or the other of the two sexes, the sex compositions of migrant and native populations tend to differ. The direction of the difference, however, is highly dependent on factors influencing the pattern of migration. For example, the sex ratio is often lower in urban areas than in rural areas, reflecting the greater in-migration of young females. This situation appears to be true of many Latin American cities.[13] Some African cities, however, exhibit an excess of males, largely due to the movement of younger men to the city from rural areas.[14] Finally, populations with a young age structure will have higher sex ratios than those with a larger representation of older persons.

A population's age structure is potentially affected by variations in mortality, fertility, and migration, as well as a few nondemographic events, the most prominent of which is war. Clearly, the most significant of these factors are mortality and fertility. The differential effects of birth and death rates on the age composition of a population are best illustrated by using **stable population models**: hypothetical populations of the same size for which assumed levels of mortality *or* fertility are held constant while the other is allowed to vary. If, for example, we hold fertility constant in both, we can observe the effects of differential mortality rates. The population of lower mortality will have larger proportions of its members in the childhood and elderly groups because more will survive the traumas of childhood and the winnowing of aging. But it will have smaller proportions of members in the middle-aged groups. (If there are larger proportions at the extremes, the middle must be smaller because the total cannot exceed 100 percent.) The influence of lowered mortality decreases as life expectancy increases, however, particularly beyond the age of sixty, when age begins to "catch up with" almost everyone.

The precise impact of mortality change depends on the mortality rates in different age groups. Where mortality is reduced more significantly in the younger age groups, the proportion of children and youth in the population will increase, and where the reduction is concentrated in later life, the proportion of old people will be greater. During the past century, the pattern of change for most of the industrialized countries shows much greater reduction of mortality in the younger age groups, thus reducing the average age of the population. But mortality in infancy and early childhood cannot be expected to go much lower, and so future changes in the age structure of these populations can be expected to show an increase in the proportion of older persons.

Fertility is even more important in determining composition than mortality, because much more *extreme* differences in age structure occur between stable populations having similar mortality rates but different levels of fertility. High fertility results in a much greater proportion of younger people, and therefore lowered fertility will eventually increase the proportion of older persons.

> **stable population models:** hypothetical populations of the same size in which assumed levels of mortality *or* fertility are held constant while the other varies. For example, two populations might be hypothesized with identical mortality rates but with very different fertility rates. Such population models aid in the analysis of the influence of fertility or mortality on the age composition of a population.

The effects of migration are more difficult to pinpoint. Generally, it is agreed that migration does not typically exert a significant influence on age composition. Exceptions are cases of sizable and long-lasting migratory movements that are highly age-specific. In Latin America during the past quarter-century, for example, most of those migrating from rural to urban areas have been young, thus affecting the age composition in both areas.

Finally, war affects the age distributions of certain countries. Heavy losses in particular age groups, such as men of military age, affect age composition directly. There is also an indirect effect in the form of lowered fertility in succeeding years. Recent population pyramids for France, Czechoslovakia, and West Germany show irregularities in age structure that reflect the effects of World War II.

Consequences Variations in age structure have dramatic effects on mortality, because death occurs more frequently at the youngest and oldest ages. They have a lesser, yet significant, impact on fertility and migration, because very young and very old people tend not to be migrants. Age composition also has a determining effect on natural increase, because fertility increases with numbers in the childbearing ages. For example, if the age distribution of the United Kingdom for 1961 were standardized to reflect that of Mexico in 1960, the crude birthrate would increase from 17.6 to 21.0, the crude death rate would decrease from 11.8 to 4.8, and the rate of natural increase would climb from 5.8 to 16.2. If we reversed the procedure so that the Mexican age structure reflected that of the United Kingdom, Mexico's crude birthrate would fall from 46.1 to 41.5, the crude death rate would increase from 11.3 to 16.8, and the rate of

Table 11-7   Estimated age distribution and dependency ratios of the population of major areas of the world, 1965.

Area	Percentage distribution by age			Dependency ratio (number of persons in dependent age groups per 100 aged 15–64 years)		
	Under 15 years	15–64 years	65 years and over	Under 15 years	65 years and over	Total (under 15 plus 65 and over)
World Total	37.4	57.6	5.0	64.8	8.7	73.5
Developing regions	41.6	55.1	3.3	75.4	5.9	81.3
More developed regions	28.1	63.0	8.9	44.6	14.2	58.8
Africa	43.5	53.7	2.8	81.0	5.2	86.2
Western Africa	44.3	53.3	2.4	83.1	4.4	87.5
Eastern Africa	43.6	53.6	2.8	81.2	5.2	86.4
Middle Africa	41.7	55.3	3.1	75.4	5.5	80.9
Northern Africa	44.2	52.7	3.0	83.9	5.7	89.6
Southern Africa	39.8	56.5	3.7	70.5	6.6	77.1
Asia (excluding USSR)						
East Asia	36.9	59.0	4.1	62.5	6.9	69.4
Mainland region	37.9	58.3	3.8	65.0	6.6	71.6
Japan	25.8	68.0	6.3	38.0	9.2	47.2
Other East Asia	44.2	52.6	3.3	84.1	6.2	90.3
South Asia	43.0	54.0	3.0	79.5	5.5	85.0
Middle South Asia	42.7	54.3	3.0	78.8	5.6	84.4
Southeast Asia	43.5	53.8	2.8	80.9	5.1	86.0
Southwest Asia	43.1	53.3	3.6	80.9	6.7	87.6
Europe (excluding USSR)	25.4	64.1	10.5	39.6	16.3	55.9
Western Europe	24.1	63.9	11.8	37.7	18.5	56.2
Southern Europe	26.9	64.2	8.9	42.0	13.9	55.9
Eastern Europe	26.8	63.9	9.3	41.8	14.5	56.3
Northern Europe	23.6	64.7	11.8	36.6	18.2	54.8
Latin America	42.5	53.9	3.6	78.9	6.8	85.7
Tropical South America	43.8	53.2	3.1	82.3	5.9	88.2
Middle America (mainland)	46.3	50.5	3.2	91.7	6.4	98.1
Temperate South America	33.3	60.8	5.9	54.7	9.7	64.6
Caribbean	40.7	55.2	4.0	73.7	7.3	81.0
Northern America	31.0	59.8	9.2	51.9	15.3	67.2
USSR	30.5	62.1	7.4	49.2	11.9	61.1
Oceania	32.8	59.9	7.3	54.7	12.2	66.9
Australia and New Zealand	30.2	61.4	8.4	49.2	13.7	62.9
Melanesia	41.6	55.5	2.9	75.1	5.3	80.4
Polynesia and Micronesia	46.5	50.8	2.6	91.8	5.2	97.0

Figure 11-3
Population pyramids for six countries, 1965

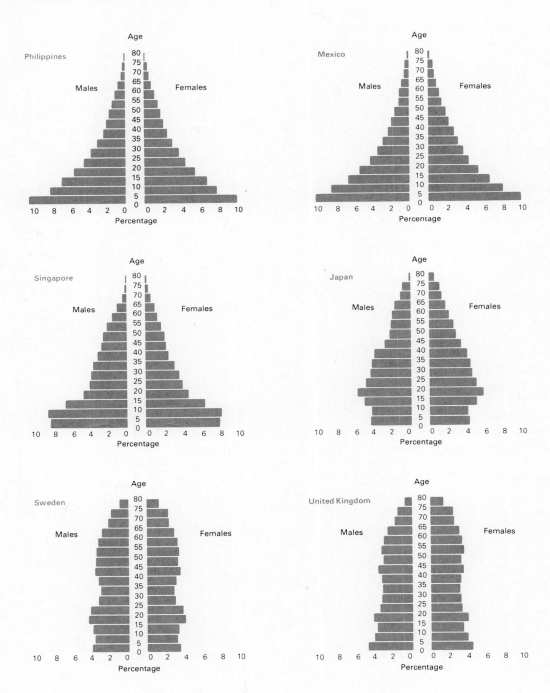

Table 11-8   Estimated sex ratios (males per 100 females) for major areas of the world by selected age categories, 1965

Area	Under 15 years	15–64 years	65 years and over	Total
World total	103.5	98.9	74.8	99.2
Developing regions	103.2	102.3	87.8	102.2
More developed regions	104.3	92.8	65.6	93.0
Africa	100.3	99.6	82.6	99.4
Western Africa	99.5	102.9	84.8	100.9
Eastern Africa	99.3	96.9	79.1	97.4
Middle Africa	97.8	93.6	77.7	94.8
Northern Africa	103.6	100.8	88.1	101.6
Southern Africa	99.4	102.4	78.8	100.2
Asia (excluding USSR)				
East Asia	102.8	100.2	80.9	100.3
Mainland region	102.7	100.9	82.1	100.8
Japan	103.7	95.6	78.6	96.4
Other East Asia	103.3	101.1	70.8	100.9
South Asia	104.6	104.8	95.7	104.4
Middle South Asia	105.5	107.2	103.2	106.3
Southeast Asia	102.0	98.7	81.3	99.6
Southwest Asia	104.6	105.4	80.5	104.1
Europe (excluding USSR)	104.8	95.3	66.6	94.1
Western Europe	104.5	96.0	63.7	93.4
Southern Europe	105.0	93.8	71.8	94.4
Eastern Europe	104.7	93.2	66.6	93.2
Northern Europe	105.1	99.4	65.9	96.0
Latin America	103.0	99.4	89.2	100.5
Tropical South America	102.3	99.9	86.9	100.5
Middle America (mainland)	104.4	97.8	93.4	100.7
Temperate South America	103.1	99.9	87.7	100.2
Caribbean	102.7	99.0	93.7	100.3
Northern America	103.8	97.6	78.4	97.5
USSR	104.2	81.3	45.1	84.3
Oceania	105.3	105.3	74.6	102.8
Australia and Polynesia	104.9	104.3	72.5	101.4
Melanesia	107.1	112.3	105.7	109.9
Polynesia and Micronesia	105.4	108.2	107.7	106.9

natural increase would decline from 34.8 to 24.7.[15] Mexico's age composition is typical of that of most of the developing world, and these calculations therefore illustrate how youthful age structures contribute to high rates of population growth.

Age composition can affect social organization in a number of ways. First, changes in age composition can lead to the redistribution of political power and hence to changes in government policies, such as employment and welfare programs. Second, a concentration of persons in the younger age groups means that personnel and resources will have to be devoted to education and the creation of new employment opportunities. Third, populations with a relatively high proportion of older people are faced with the problems of managing the society so that the elderly are not excluded from employment and participation in social and political activities. Furthermore, providing adequate housing and leisure-time activities for the elderly has become a matter of public concern in many of the more industrialized societies.

Summary

Human societies show wide variation in terms of ascribed and achieved characteristics of their members, and these differences are, in turn, related to a number of social and demographic processes. Age and sex are two important compositional characteristics. Perhaps the most evident differences in them, as in other characteristics, are between the developing and the developed nations. In developing nations, nearly half the population tends to be in the younger age groups, and large numbers of women are in the reproductive ages. In the more industrialized countries, age distributions are more balanced, with a higher proportion of persons over sixty. The higher total and youth dependency ratios in the developing nations means they must devote much of their resources simply to caring for their dependents, while the higher old-age dependency ratios in the developed countries means they must provide more services for the elderly. Overall, age, sex, and other compositional features of the less developed countries tend to foster continued high rates of growth.

Population Problems

During the past quarter-century, we have come to recognize that many of the problems faced by contemporary societies are, directly or indirectly, the result of demographic conditions. Perhaps the most universal concern in the modern world is improving the quality of life. Basically, the emphasis is on guaranteeing that all human beings have sufficient amounts of food, clothing, and shelter, opportunities for employment and recreation, and the freedom to pursue their interests with a minimum of external constraint. Definitions of the "good life" differ among societies and cultures, but these basic features are generally agreed upon.

The argument of this section is that current population conditions, more serious in some areas of the world than others, constitute barriers that inhibit attempts to improve the quality of life. Rapid rates of population growth (and the absolute number of people in some countries), increasing population densities, and imbalances in population composition seriously limit the success of attempts to achieve more desirable conditions for human existence. The issues discussed below represent some of the basic features of the population problem.

Food for the World

Malthus defined the population problem largely in terms of an increasing imbalance between food supplies and numbers of people and foresaw a time when the world would be faced with the threat of widespread famine. Although this gloomy prediction has not yet come true, there is cause for concern, or perhaps alarm, over the current world food situation. The major problems include an imbalance in the growth of food production between the developing and the developed nations, insufficient reserves to insure against widespread disruption in food production, malnutrition, and the lack of coordination in national food policies.

Although gross food production has increased during the past decade by about the same amount (30 percent) in both developed and developing countries, inequities in rates of population growth have resulted in a sizable difference in per capita

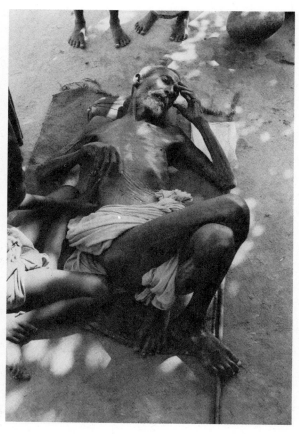

food production. For the developed countries, the increase in per capita production has been about 15 percent, but in the less developed nations there has been virtually no improvement in per capita food production.[16]

Approximately 60 percent of our food energy is supplied by grains, including roots and tubers, with wheat and rice accounting for about 40 percent of total food consumption.[17] Available grain stocks therefore provide a useful index of world food reserves, with 100 million tons generally considered to be a lower limit beyond which prices increase sharply and severe shortages develop. In 1961, world grain reserves totaled 222 million metric tons, equivalent to ninety days of consumption; 1974 estimates showed only 90 million tons of reserves, sufficient for only twenty-six days.[18] The vast majority of these reserves is concentrated in the more developed nations.

Estimates of the extent of chronic hunger in the world are highly variable and unreliable. In 1967, the United Nations Food and Agricultural Organization (FAO) indicated that 2 billion people were malnourished. In the same year, the President's Science Advisory Committee Panel on the World Food Supply speculated that the figure could more realistically be set at a billion and a half. A more recent estimate (1974) puts the figure at a billion or more.[19] In spite of the differences in these figures, it is clear that a sizable proportion of the world's population (a quarter to a third), concentrated in Asia, Africa, and Latin America, suffers from an inadequate diet.

National food policies frequently conflict with one another, and this conflict seriously impedes resolution of world food problems. The issues at stake include government price supports for farm products, restrictions on grain imports and exports, international support for agricultural development in the poorer nations, fishing rights in national and international waters, and the establishment of a world food reserve. Clearly, increased international cooperation is necessary if we are to improve the quantity and quality of food resources.

Viewed quite simply, population growth can be directly translated into additional food demand. A population that increases by 2 percent during a given period must increase food supplies by an equal amount, whether through internal production or imports, if per capita consumption is to remain unchanged. Any increase in per capita consumption, of course, depends on a greater gain in food supplies than in population.

Analysts of the contemporary world food situation can be placed in two opposing camps. Some are optimistic about increasing food production through the application of modern technology.[20] They point to the great reservoir of unexploited food potential in the developing countries and to the recent increases in grain production achieved through the use of new high-yield seeds and improved fertilizers. The latter development, known popularly as the "Green Revolution," was heralded as the answer to world food problems in the early 1970s.

But a growing number of scientists recognize that technological solutions, including the Green Revolution, are themselves subject to a number of constraints.[21] A major concern is the serious shortage of four basic agricultural resources: land, water, energy, and fertilizer. In addition, some critics have pointed to ecological stresses—soil erosion, pollution of lakes and streams from overfertilization, depletion of fish stocks—that have resulted from technological innovations aimed at increasing food production. Finally, institutional factors governing the diffusion of knowledge necessary for using new technology, the extension of credit, and the distribution of profits and products can influence the outcome of technological solutions to food problems.

In short, the world is faced with potential worsening of an already serious imbalance between population and food supply. Solutions based on improvements in food-producing technology have

Environmental pollution is often an indirect consequence of overpopulation.

been explored. However, as one observer indicates, "that there is a vast technological opportunity for expanding food supplies is not debatable, but this is not the real problem. The critical issue is *at what price* the additional resources will be brought into use."[22] The costs involved, as evidenced by dwindling resources, environmental pollution, and ineffective governmental policies, are high. The ultimate solution must be a reduction in population rather than an increase in food supplies.

Natural Resources and the Environment

The food problem is only one aspect of a larger issue. The survival of human populations depends on a continued supply of natural resources—everything from air, water, and land to minerals and animals—and the maintenance of a habitable environment.

Resource problems can be understood in terms of (1) current and projected supplies and (2) rates and patterns of consumption. It is also useful to distinguish between two types of resources: those that are potentially renewable, such as water and forest products, and those that are nonrenewable, like minerals and fossil fuels. Present concern is highest over the future availability of nonrenewable resources, but in the long run, both types may be in danger of falling short of world demands.

Unfortunately, reliable estimates of ultimate reserves are not available for most natural resources, especially those that are ordinarily replenished by natural processes. Nonetheless, it is generally conceded that the earth's supply of natural resources is limited. Moreover, most resources are unequally distributed among the regions and nations of the world.

The stock of natural resources available to any population is affected by several factors in addition to natural endowment, including the level of technological development achieved and patterns of international trade. Advanced technology can potentially result in the discovery of new supplies, increased efficiency in extracting and processing resources, and the capacity to recycle resources for continued use. Through international trade, populations deficient in a given resource can theoretically maintain a supply sufficient to meet their needs, if they can obtain foreign exchange with which to purchase it. But technological development thus far has contributed more to the depletion of natural resources than to their increase, and equalization through international trade has been prevented by political and economic factors.

Although it is impossible to estimate accurately the absolute stock of world resources, trends and patterns of consumption are relatively well-documented. A few examples suffice to indicate the overall trend toward increased resource utilization. For nonfuel minerals, world output rose by about 74 percent during the period 1953-1966, while population increased by only 28 percent.[23] In the United States, per capita water consumption increased from approximately 10 gallons per day at the beginning of this century to the current average of 160 gallons, and this figure is two or three times higher in some large cities.[24] Finally, between 1950 and 1968 the average annual rate of increase in energy consumption per capita for the world was 3.5 percent.[25] Clearly, with few exceptions, the human population is consuming an increasingly large proportion of the natural resources available, and projections for the foreseeable future show no indication of any significant change in this trend.

Furthermore, resources are consumed disproportionately by the various nations of the world. Generally, the higher the level of technological and economic development, the greater the share of resources utilized. For example, a 1970 estimate showed that the United States consumes 42 percent of the world total of aluminum, 44 percent of the coal, 28 percent of the iron, 25 percent of the lead, 63 percent of the natural gas, 38 percent of the nickel, and 33 percent of the petroleum.[26]

The increased utilization of natural resources has been accompanied by a trend toward environmental deterioration, as evidenced by the great increase of various waste products in the air, land, fresh waters, and oceans. Human activities of all kinds—residential, recreational, agricultural, industrial, military—contribute to the build-up of pollutants. The manifestations of pollution can be usefully divided into four categories:

1. Direct assaults on human health (e.g., lead poisoning or aggravation of lung disease by air pollution).
2. Damage to goods and services that society provides for itself (e.g., the corrosive effects of air pollution on buildings and crops).
3. Other direct effects on what people perceive as their "quality of life" (e.g., congestion and litter).
4. Indirect effects on society through interference with services that are provided for society by natural ecosystems, such as ocean fish production and control of erosion by vegetation. Examples of such indirect effects are destruction of vegetation by overgrazing and logging, and poisoning of coastal water with oil and heavy metals.[27]

Environmental deterioration is most evident in the highly industrialized nations of the world, and only these countries have developed organized measures to deal with pollution and its consequences, such as the U.S. Environmental Protection Agency. In the developing nations, pollution is often viewed as an unavoidable consequence of efforts to raise the standard of living through the exploitation of natural resources.[28]

Growing pressures on resources and the environment are directly related to two dominant population trends: increased size and concentration in cities. A growing population means a greater demand for resources of all kinds, and, with the exception of land, urban populations consume more resources per capita than those in rural areas. Furthermore, because environmental deterioration is largely a result of human activities, continued growth and concentration of population can hinder the preservation of natural habitats unless measures are taken to counteract or control destructive practices.

Although there is some disagreement over the extent of resource scarcity and environmental pollution, most observers agree that unless measures are taken to reduce the rate at which resources are consumed and natural processes disrupted, the quality of human life will sooner or later be threatened. Several solutions have been proposed. First, population growth and distribution could be controlled. Second, advanced technology might provide substitutes for natural resources and more efficient means of waste disposal. The difficulty with these solutions is that each takes a considerable amount of time to implement, and neither deals with resource and environment problems directly.

A third solution involves organized efforts to conserve the supply of natural resources and to maintain the quality of the environment. This strategy can be viewed in terms of two related stages.[29] *Resource management* involves attempts to optimize the yield from a particular resource process through governmental influence. Resource utilization and economic growth continue, but under rational guidance aimed at minimizing harmful effects, as in government control of the extraction of natural gas. *Environmental management* goes further in recognizing that further exploitation of resources is ultimately limited by the planet's bio-environmental system. The underlying goal of this stage is to produce resources while simultaneously maintaining environmental quality and ecological stability. Recent American attempts to restrict porpoise kills by tuna fishermen is an example.

The relationship between population, resources, and the environment is complex. Population growth and urbanization increase the pressures on available resources and the life-supporting environment, and thus any reduction in these trends would conceivably be beneficial. But even if the human population could somehow be frozen at its current level of development, existing rates of resource use and environmental deterioration would threaten the quality of human life within a few centuries. Although some optimists continue to anticipate technological solutions to these prob-

Another effect of overpopulation is the depletion of nonrenewable natural resources. Strip mining in Arizona.

This Objiway Indian suffers from mercury poisoning he contracted from consuming fish caught in a polluted lake.

lems, the more likely prospect is that we will have to adopt rather stringent environmental conservation measures.

Economic Development

Without doubt, the most universal national goal in the world today is to raise the material living standard and improve the quality of human life. Although the means for achieving this goal are diverse, relative success is usually measured in terms of economic criteria. Standard indicators of economic development include per capita income, gross national product, the industrial distribution of the labor force, and levels of savings and investment.

Since about 1850, economic growth has increased at very high rates, compared with advances in earlier times. But not all nations have shared equally in this trend toward affluence. In fact, the economic gap between the rich and poor nations is increasing. In 1958, for instance, the developed nations produced about 82 percent of the world's goods and services; by 1968 this figure had increased to 87 percent.[30] Furthermore, incomes have increased much more in rich nations than in poor ones. The estimated ratio between incomes in the industrializing countries and all other nations in 1850 was about 2 to 1. By 1950, this ratio had increased to 10 to 1, and by 1960, it was close to 15 to 1. If recent trends continue, a ratio of 30 to 1 could well be reached by the end of this century.[31]

Economic development is affected by many factors, but few have as much significance as population growth. It is important to recognize that until the 1930s population and economic growth were positively related: the more developed countries grew more rapidly than the rest of the world. The past four decades, however, have produced a reversal in this relationship. Rapid population growth now appears to be an obstacle, rather than a stimulus, to economic development.

How does rapid population growth impede economic development? Answers to this question are complex and necessitate numerous qualifications. Nevertheless, it is possible to identify several aspects of this relationship generally agreed upon by demographers and economists. First, prolonged high fertility results in a youthful age structure, thus creating a "dependency burden." This means a lower proportion of the population will be available for the work force. Second, in a country with a rapidly growing population, available resources and capital must be used to meet subsistence requirements, and therefore cannot be used for investment and upgrading of production technology and the educational system. Third, many people in a rapidly growing population will be unable to find work (unemployment) or will work at tasks that are relatively unproductive (underemployment).

Not only does high fertility impede economic growth, but a low level of economic development hinders significant reduction of fertility. Two factors are especially important. First, a stagnant economy offers few opportunities for women to enter the labor force. The principal alternative for them is early marriage and motherhood. Second, slow economic growth inhibits attempts to raise levels of educational attainment, and education shows a significant inverse relationship to fertility. Almost everywhere, the educated have lower fertility rates than the uneducated.

It should now be evident that problems of population and economic development constitute a vicious circle. Rapid population growth impedes economic improvement, and the latter is made considerably more difficult by the strains generated by growing populations. The problem now facing the developing countries is where efforts to break this potentially catastrophic relationship should be concentrated: on population, the economy, or both? Although opinions are divided, there is some evidence that the most crucial immediate task is somehow to control the rate of population growth.[32]

Political Conflict

Under certain conditions, changes in a population system can produce political and governmental problems. In the modern world, these conditions are characterized by the growing scarcity of resources that populations need for survival and material welfare—food, land, water, minerals, and sources of energy. Changes in a variety of population variables, such as size, density, and composition, can have political consequences, but rates of growth are currently the most important factor.

The political effects of rapid population growth are evident at both national and international levels. Problems on a national scale are more severe in the developing countries, where governments typically lack the resources necessary to satisfy citizens' rising expectations for improvements in the quality of life. Jobs are scarce, hunger is a way of life, the supply of housing is inadequate, and public services are often disorganized. Under these conditions, there is little public confidence in government officials, and the resulting social and political unrest often leads to political instability, social disintegration, and even civil war.

Of much greater significance, in the long run, are the international problems generated by rapid population growth. As we saw earlier, large and growing populations were thought until recently to be necessary for power in international relations; consequently, many governments adopted policies favoring high birthrates. The resulting rapid population growth is currently causing a number of strains in the international political system. Imbalances in population and resources often generate border wars, such as the recent conflicts in the Middle East and Central America. Competition for resources influences international trade relations. Nations with a relative advantage in the supply of key resources can "blackmail" other members of the international community as continued world population growth increases the demand for these necessities. The current activities of the oil-producing countries of the Middle East are a prominent case in point.

As the advantages of controlling population growth become more apparent to world leaders, those nations possessing the technology, personnel, and knowledge necessary for accomplishing this task are increasingly placed in a politically delicate position. On the one hand, they may be viewed as "imperialist villains," interested only in minimizing the strength of potential competitors for world power. On the other hand, because these nations can withhold assistance for reducing population growth, they may be charged with attempting to impede the social and economic development of the developing nations. In either case, the potential for international conflict is great.

Robert Heilbroner has argued that we are currently faced with three principal external dangers:

Landscape: American state park.

In countries with rapidly growing populations, available resources must often be devoted to subsistence rather than development. Slum housing slated for replacement in India.

runaway population growth, massively destructive war, and potential environmental collapse.[33] To a large extent, the latter two are consequences of the first. Rapid population growth creates conditions under which international conflict and environmental deterioration become increasingly likely, if not inevitable. Because of the widespread implications of population growth, its control may be the most important political issue in the world today.

Prospects for Population Control

Despite widespread agreement that rapid population growth is a major world problem, there is little consensus as to what the optimum size or rate of growth of population is, or the means by which population goals, however defined, might be achieved most effectively. Although the following discussion focuses on the developing nations, the issues are relevant to all countries of the world. The difference is a matter of time: population growth is an immediate problem for the developing countries; developed countries are not yet under such pressure to devise solutions.

Family Planning

Earlier, we saw that high fertility is the major contributor to rapid population growth. Recognition of this fact has led to national programs to reduce birthrates as the principal means for combating runaway growth. These efforts, generally known as **family planning** programs, involve limiting family size by distributing efficient contraceptives on a national basis, usually through the public health services. There are also many private family planning programs, such as Planned Parenthood in the United States. Underlying this strategy are several assumptions.

First, it is assumed that contraceptives are technically efficient—in other words, that by using them correctly people can prevent births. Second, there is the expectation that contraceptives can be distributed widely and economically. Third, supporters of the family planning approach assume a demand for contraceptives among that segment of the population having the greatest risk of producing children, primarily women in the fifteen to

Oil monopolists: Two Saudi Arabian oil barons at a recent OPEC conference. As population pressures increase world demand for scarce resources, suppliers find they can exploit the situation.

twenty-nine age range. Finally, it is believed that participation in family planning programs must be voluntary.

As you can see, some of these are big assumptions indeed. Although it is certainly true that modern contraceptives are technically quite efficient, for example, the assumption that people will use them, and use them properly, is clearly weak. Even many American college girls believe that the Pill may be used as "morning-after" protection, and many pregnancies occur on college campuses every year as a consequence of people, usually girls, avoiding the use of contraception because it is "unnatural" or appears preplanned and, therefore, "immoral." (It is not "immoral," apparently, to engage in coitus spontaneously when swept off one's feet by romance; but the regular ingestion of the Pill, or the insertion of a diaphragm, must occur *before* a date, thus demonstrating that one is consciously planning to "do it.")

Despite problems such as these, the number of countries with family planning programs has increased steadily since the early 1950s. Of 118 developing countries surveyed in a 1974 Population Council publication, 63 provided financial support for family planning activities, and many of those that didn't at least tolerated such programs under the auspices of private organizations.[34]

Assessment of the success of family planning

programs is hindered by the lack of adequate data. Nevertheless, several studies have been attempted. One early evaluation by Donald Bogue (1967) heralded "the end of the population explosion." Bogue concluded that "from 1965 onward the rate of world population growth may be expected to decline with each passing year. The growth will slacken to such a pace that it will be zero or near zero at about the year 2000, so that population will not be regarded as a major social problem except in isolated and small 'retarded' areas."[35] The major justification for this optimism was a belief that family planning programs were becoming increasingly widespread and effective in the developing countries of the world.

In the same year, 1967, Kingsley Davis presented an alternative viewpoint: that fertility control programs limited to family planning are not sufficiently effective. He criticized several features of the family planning approach, including the emphasis on allowing couples to have the number of children they want, failure to take reproductive motivation into account, and lack of attention to institutional factors that reinforce the large-family pattern. In particular, he maintained that socioeconomic changes are more effective in changing fertility patterns than family planning efforts.[36]

In 1975, Walter Watson and Robert Lapham classified changes in the birthrate during 1970-1974 for eighty-one developing countries according to a crude socioeconomic index. They concluded that declines in fertility were not likely among those living at very low socioeconomic levels, unless determined, sustained efforts to reduce fertility were carried out.[37] Of the thirty-one countries included in the "low" category, many of which had very active family planning programs, only India and Indonesia showed a possible or probable decline in the birthrate over the four-year period. This conclusion reinforces Davis's argument that changes in patterns of social and economic organization have a much greater influence on change in birthrates than do contraceptive programs.

Population Policy

The relative lack of success of family planning programs suggests that we need a more comprehensive approach to problems of population

family planning: the general name for publicly or privately sponsored programs to reduce birthrates through encouraging individual citizens to limit family size.

Family planning programs often assume that the people in high birth population categories will want to limit births. This assumption is frequently erroneous.

"I feel a little hypocritical doing a fertility dance so soon after my vasectomy."

Playboy, November 1973. Reproduced by special permission of PLAYBOY Magazine; copyright © 1973 by Playboy.

growth. Essentially, this means that national governments and international organizations must develop and carry through population policies.

The United Nations defines *population policy* as "programs designed to contribute to the achievement of economic, social, demographic, political and other collective goals through affecting critical demographic variables, namely the size and growth of the population, its geographic distribution (national and international) and its demographic characteristics."[38] Although all nations have implicit policies along at least some of these lines, few have taken explicit stands that provide mechanisms for enforcement.

Of the 118 countries whose official views on population were evaluated in the 1974 Population Council study cited earlier, only 33 show policies aimed at reducing the population growth rate.[39] But some of these are among the world's most populous nations—Egypt, Bangladesh, China, India, Indonesia, Mexico, Pakistan, the Philippines, Thailand, and Turkey.

Almost without exception, population policies are concentrated on fertility. But recently a few countries, such as Colombia and Venezuela, have specified policies aimed at obtaining a better territorial distribution of the population. And China's population policy seeks to maximize female labor force participation.

The idea that population policies should go beyond family planning is certainly not new. A wide variety of alternative measures have been suggested, including postponement of marriage, encouraging women to seek rewards from nonfamilial roles (primarily in the labor force), substantial fees for marriage licenses, taxes on children, legalization of abortion and mandatory abortion for illegitimate pregnancies, and compulsory sterilization for men with two or three children, to mention just a few. Some of these suggestions are now being incorporated into official population policies. For example, there has been a slow trend toward legalizing abortion in developing countries, especially those that have attained a higher level of socioeconomic development. In a few countries, such as Colombia, there is some evidence of efforts to improve the status of women. Various incentive programs have been tried in India in an attempt to

The earth can't handle many more birthday parties.

ZPG poster. The Zero Population Growth movement offers a radical solution to the problem of overpopulation. It may be the *only* solution.

increase voluntary sterilization. In short, efforts to develop national population policies are increasing, with some apparently positive results. But it is not clear whether the problems created by rapidly growing and densely concentrated populations can be resolved in time to avoid disaster.

There is a growing movement, based in the United States, but slowly spreading to other countries, that is highly critical of current population policies in the developing as well as the developed countries. This movement, generally called Zero Population Growth (ZPG), has as its major goal stopping world population growth as soon as this is demographically feasible—that is, within the limitations of existing age structures. The principal mechanism suggested for achieving zero growth is social regulation of rights and obligations concerning childbearing. This would involve reordering people's view of personal freedom. Emphasis would be placed on a person's obligations to society rather than the rights derived as a member of society. Private interests would be given a lower priority than those of the social unit. In effect, people would be socially restrained from having children, or would be limited to one or two, in order to allow available services and resources to be used for raising the standard of living of the earth's existing population.

Ultimately, the choice is up to us. Population policies are no different from any other guidelines for human conduct. If they are to be effective, they must call forth a sense of obligation and a recognition that compliance offers many benefits. If population control is to be seen in this light, however, the social definition of parenthood will have to undergo some drastic changes. How that might be accomplished remains to be seen.

Summary

Demography is the study of human population. It is of importance to sociologists because of its close, reciprocal relation with social organization. That is to say, the principal demographic variables—*birth, death, migration,* and *social mobility,* population *distribution* and *composition*—both deeply influence a society's social organization and are influenced by it.

The fundamental demographic data are simply pieces of factual information about a given population: at a particular time or in a particular time period, their number, ages, sex distribution, marital statuses, number of children, occupations, educational characteristics, places of residence and employment, numbers of births and deaths. This information is obtained in a variety of ways, the most common of which are: (1) the *population census*; (2) *vital registration systems,* which record births and deaths, marriages and annulments, divorces, adoptions, and so forth; (3) *population registers,*

No Easy Way Out?

MYTH: **WARS, DISEASE, AND NATURAL DISASTERS WILL CONTROL POPULATION SURPLUS.**

FACT: IN FIVE YEARS OF TERRIBLE WAR, POPULATION OF NORTH AND SOUTH VIETNAM HAS GROWN MORE THAN 3 MILLION

FACT: GIANT TIDAL WAVE KILLED MORE THAN 500,000 IN EAST PAKISTAN IN 1970, BUT THIS NUMBER WAS REPLACED IN JUST 35 DAYS

FACT: IMPROVED HEALTH CARE AND MODERN MEDICINES HAVE LENGTHENED WESTERN MAN'S LIFE-SPAN BY TWO DECADES SINCE 1900

MYTH: **TECHNOLOGY AND OCEANS WILL FEED WORLD**

FACT: GREEN REVOLUTION IS SHOT IN ARM, BUT POPULATION GROWTH IS NEUTRALIZING FOOD PRODUCTION GAINS.

FACT: OCEANS ARE 90% BIOLOGICAL DESERTS, WITH OTHER 10% IN DANGER OF BEING OVER-EXPLOITED

MYTH: **PLENTY OF ROOM—MAN IS ONLY USING A FRACTION OF THE LAND**

FACT: MUCH OF LAND IS TOO HOT, TOO COLD, TOO WET OR TOO DRY FOR AGRICULTURE OR HUMAN HABITATION.

The population problem will neither go away nor resolve itself. It can only become worse if we do not attack it systematically in the near future. Wishful thinking is not enough.

which, in some countries, require citizens to enter such information as occupation and residence and any changes in them; and (4) *sample surveys* of populations or segments thereof. These data are published in many ways, usually by national governments or the United Nations.

The three major areas of demographic interest are: (1) population size and growth, (2) population distribution, and (3) population composition. *Population size and growth* did not become a matter of public and scientific concern until the writings of Thomas Malthus in the late eighteenth century. Malthus argued that population growth would always increase faster than the means of subsistence. If unchecked by certain moral restraints, "vice," or natural disasters and disease, population growth would inevitably lead to widespread famine. This general view remains popular today, although Marxians deny it, arguing that there are no natural laws of population growth, but that it is determined, rather, by social and economic conditions.

Modern scientific views do not particularly reflect either of these positions, being much more deeply influenced by the conception of the *demographic transition*, derived from the observation that rates of population growth, in European history, at least, were profoundly affected by the Industrial Revolution. The demographic transition involves moving from a situation of high birth and death rates and relatively stable population through a transitional stage of continued high birthrates together with lowered death rates, resulting in a population explosion, to a final stage of much reduced rates of both birth and death, resulting in a relatively stable population size once again.

Population size is essentially calculated by counting, of course, and although there are many ways of measuring changes in it, all basically compare births to deaths with allowance for changes due to migration. For the world population as a whole, size has continually increased in a geometric fashion, although there are important regional differences. In general, in recent times the least industrially developed countries have been increasing at the greatest rate. Perhaps the fundamental cause of the rapidity with which world population has been increasing in the past century is a general decline in mortality rates. In many areas of the world, birthrates have remained high while death rates have dropped steeply. Where this condition is coupled with lack of technological development, the resulting problems have seriously interfered with efforts at further development.

The basic measure of *population distribution* is density, usually calculated as the number of persons per square mile or kilometer. An important concept of distribution has been the rural-urban distinction. This calls attention to the fact that the principal and most important change in population distribution in recent years has been the increasing urbanism of the world's population, with consequent increases in the number and sizes of cities everywhere. Particularly in the developing countries, the rapid rate of increasing urbanization is producing social dislocations and a decline in quality of life.

Population composition has to do with both *ascribed* characteristics, such as age, sex, race, ethnicity, and place of birth, and *achieved* characteristics, such as labor force status, marital status, nationality, education, and income. Age and sex are particularly important compositional variables. A basic measure of population composition is the *population pyramid,* which is simply a plot of the age and sex distribution in the population at a given time. Population pyramids are significant because the shape of the pyramid in a given society has a great deal to do with its fertility and mortality and such things as the *dependency ratio*: the ratio of those in the nonworking ages to those in the working ages. A society with a high dependency ratio will have to devote significant proportions of its resources simply to caring for its dependents, with important proportions of what work force it has laboring to that end. In general in the world today, dependency ratios are higher in the underdeveloped countries than in the more developed. The *sex ratio,* the proportion of men to women, is also an important measure of population, as is age structure.

The social significance of these matters is apparent when we examine a number of worldwide social problems for which population is an important contributor or, in some instances, cause. Perhaps most evident of these is simply the problem of *food supply*. It is mathematically inevitable that if world population continues to grow at its present rate, the world will run out of food. Even if new technologies made an adequate food supply available, numerous problems of distribution and preference would remain. The depletion of *natural resources* and *environmental problems* are also clearly and inescapably related to population size and increase. In the developing nations of the world, *economic and technical progress* is hindered, and sometimes crippled, by very high birthrates and dependency ratios, so that expectations for improvements in the quality of life cannot be met. *Political turmoil and conflict* would appear to be the inevitable result.

Population control of some kind appears to many to be the only possible answer to problems of this kind. The two basic categories in which proposals for control can be classified are *family planning* and *national population policy*. The former refers to efforts by governments and private organizations to encourage individuals to reduce family size, thus diminishing the birthrate and, eventually, maintaining population at levels capable of permitting a desirable quality of life. The latter refers to rational programs for manipulating variables that national governments can control, such as distribution, employment, education, and so forth, all of which affect fundamental demographic variables like birth and death. A private organization in the United States that has taken a forthright population policy stand is Zero Population Growth, which advocates social regulation of childbearing.

Review Questions

1. Discuss Thomas Malthus's theory which first drew attention to population as a problem. How does arithmetic growth differ from geometric growth? How do these different kinds of growth relate to Malthus's logic? What are preventive checks? Positive checks?

2. List and briefly describe the chief sources of population information available in the U.S. today. Consider the census as one important source and note both its advantages and disadvantages as a pool of statistics.

3. Explain several possible sources of error that demographers confront when dealing with population statistics. What are errors of coverage? Errors of classification?

4. Some demographers who express concern over the present population condition promote what is known as population policy. How could such a policy possibly alleviate the current population problems?

5. What changes in marriage and family patterns might help or already have helped in reducing population growth? That is, what factors help bring about smaller families?

Suggestions for Research

1. Further your understanding of population composition by studying the impact of a high proportion of dependent persons upon the economy. You will need to acknowledge both older persons and youth. What social problems arise when retirement is mandatory at age sixty-five? When many young people are not self-sufficient, financially, until their middle twenties? What are some of the proposed solutions? What shape does the dependency ratio in the U.S. appear to be taking?

2. Study the impact of the women's movement upon family size; some of the literature on this topic will be primarily speculative because this issue is young. Explain the relation between broadening female role options and family size. What other factors, aside from the movement, appear to be influencing family size? How strong do you feel the association is between these two variables?

3. Conduct a small sample survey among your peers to discover whether or not they have been influenced by exposure to recent population problems. Interview your respondents about their personal desires and plans (these may be very tentative at this point) regarding future family size. Are their goals based on personal desires or what they feel is best for their society? To what extent do they feel influenced by reading and hearing about a population problem?

4. Select one particular environmental problem such as air or water pollution, overcrowding, depleted energy supplies, food supplies or another you may prefer for study. In a paper, report on the current condition of this resource, prospects for the future and possible solutions. Then, add your personal evaluation of various proposals to improve the situation.

5. Explore the concept known as quality of life—one that has received new attention since population problems have been recognized. What specific areas of human life are seriously threatened by population growth? Can these problems be solved by modern technology in itself? You may want to include these references in your reading: Nathan Keyfitz's article entitled ''Population Density and

the Style of Social Life," in *Bioscience* 16 (December 1966): 868–873, and J.E. Meade, "Population Explosion, the Standard of Living, and Social Conflict" in *The Economic Journal* 77 (June 1967): 233–255.

PART FOUR
SOCIAL INSTITUTIONS

Part three talked about what sociologists call *social structure.* In the five chapters that follow we examine what are probably the most significant structural elements of any society anywhere, its major social institutions. These are the *family, education, religion,* the *polity (politics and government),* and *economics.* Although most societies have social structural elements beside these that could properly be called institutions, these five are certainly universal; no society can exist without them.

You will recall from Chapter 5 that a social institution was defined as a form of social organization relationship—a set of organizational relations—that had become so conventionalized as to be normative. A social *structure,* say, a class system, is just "how things are done" by most people in a society. A social *institution* has normative values attached: it is the right, just, moral, and proper way to do them.

Most sociological analysts of social institutions adopt a functional approach to them, perceiving them as existing to fulfill imperative social needs, things that must be accomplished if the society in which they exist is to survive. (The rearing of children and the production and distribution of food would be classic examples.) The argument is simply that some activities are so essential to a society that specific arrangements for getting them accomplished *must be* established and followed, and that institutions are the product of this necessity. All five chapters in this part adopt this view.

CHAPTER 12
THE FAMILY

You might think that this photo is obviously a picture of a young family. After all, you would expect the opening illustration of a chapter about the family to depict one. But if you consider a moment, you'll probably agree that there's nothing in the picture that makes it clear the group shown is a family. There's no way we can tell from looking at the picture, for instance, that the people illustrated are not a babysitter and a friend taking their charges for a walk.

What Is a Family?

The point here, of course, is that a family is not just a group of people. That is why we cannot tell whether the group pictured is a family or not. A family is a group of people with a certain very special kind of relationship to one another, and it is that relationship which you may have inferred from the photo, but which is not, in fact, illustrated there, and cannot be.

But what exactly is that relationship and what exactly is a family? Many of us, if asked what a family is, might say something like, "Well, obviously, a family at minimum is a mother, father, and their children." But if you think about it for a moment, you'll realize that a commonsense definition like that is inadequate. There are too many situations that we recognize as representing families which that doesn't cover. That's a good start at a working definition, but it leaves some important things out. (What about adopted children? What about old Aunt Minnie who lived with your mother and dad for years? And your married sister and her husband and baby; is she a part of your family now, or has "having a family of her own" somehow changed that relationship?) Defining a family is not as simple as it may first have appeared.

Let's start with a minimum sociological definition of the family and then go on from there. For our purposes, we can say that, at minimum, a **family** is an adult male and female living, together with any offspring, in a more or less permanent relationship of the kind approved by their society as "marriage." This still leaves many matters undefined, but it points out the basics, the minimum essentials, of the family as a special kind of *social* grouping: (1) it involves a sexual relationship between adults of opposite sexes; (2) it involves their

cohabitation, living together; (3) it involves at least the expectation of relative permanence of the relationship between them; and (4), most important of all, the relationship is culturally defined and societally sanctioned—it is a marriage. The roles the people involved play with regard to each other, their rights, duties, and interactions concerning each other, are defined by the society. Marriage and the family are not just something people become involved in on their own. Some of the ways in which they must relate to each other are decided for them by their society.

Marriage and the Family

Both of the definitions of the family given above (the commonsense and the sociological) distinguished between marriage and the group called the family, and recognized that the first is the basis for the second. It is worth taking a moment to draw that distinction more clearly. Anywhere in the world, the phenomenon we call **marriage** involves a stable set of socially recognized relationships between husband and wife. Universally, these include sexual relations, although it is relatively rare for a society to restrict all sexual activity to marriage. But a stable heterosexual relationship in itself does not constitute a marriage; marriage also involves the stability of a number of other kinds of social activities.

Marriage in all societies is distinguished from sexual activity per se in that marriage is involved with parenthood and the legitimacy of offspring. Legitimacy, in turn, is involved with the transmission of goods and social position to the younger generation. Marriage, then, is recognized as a special kind of relationship because it is the one in which families are created and perpetuated, and the family is the ultimate basis of human society.

Biological parenthood, of course, is possible outside of marriage and is hardly unusual there, but no society permits promiscuous parenthood; and in many the offspring of nonmarital unions are not recognized as **kin** (relatives), so that the inheritance of social position from the parents is denied the illegitimate child. The family is everywhere recognized as the appropriate place for reproduction, although many societies reverse American practice and regard pregnancy or birth as the appropriate

> **family:** at minimum, an adult male and female living together with any offspring, in a more or less permanent relationship of the kind approved by their society as "marriage."
>
> **cohabitation:** living together, sharing a habitation.
>
> **marriage:** a stable relationship between adults of opposite sexes in which certain rights, duties, and interactions are socially prescribed and supported and in which any children born are legitimate in the eyes of society. More technically, a contract between spouses of the opposite sex that legitimates their offspring.
>
> **kin:** all those socially defined by a given society as "related."

occasion for marriage rather than vice versa. A plausible reason for the demand that parenthood occur only within marriage is simply the necessity for locating responsibility for children and their care. The long period of dependence of the human young demands that adults accept responsibility for rearing them. By making marriage a condition for the creation of families (that is, by insisting that parenthood be accompanied by marriage), human societies provide for their own perpetuation.

With this introduction, we are ready to turn to the examination of the family as a social institution. It is, without question, the oldest of all human institutions, and may even have arisen among prehumans before the species as we now know it evolved. It is universal. It is impossible to conceive realistically of a society surviving without the family, and the few that have tried to experiment along such lines have had to give up or face dissolution.

Following a discussion of the family's functions for us and for society, we will examine some of the ways in which families may be organized and arranged (for the American system is not typical) and then look more closely at American family arrangements. In this regard, we will examine our practices of mate selection, changing marital roles in American society, marital dissolution and remarriage, and some of the alternatives to traditional marriage and family styles now being experimented with in the United States.

Social Functions of the Family

The reasons for the endurance and universality of the family are largely grounded in the functions that it performs for individuals and for society. The major functions the family accomplishes are: (1) member replacement for the society and physical maintenance for individuals, (2) socialization of children, (3) regulation of sexual behavior, (4) transmission of social status from parents to offspring, (5) economic support, (6) social-emotional support of individuals, and (7) linkage with other social institutions.

Member Replacement and Physical Maintenance

In order to survive, every society must replace members who die and keep the survivors alive. Any society that consistently neglects these vital activities becomes a subject for archeological investigation. The regulation of reproduction is centered in the institution of the family in practically all societies, as are cooking and eating and care for the sick. Once children are born, they are almost always nurtured and protected within the family. It is the family that feeds, clothes, and shelters them. Of course, not all families provide the same amount, or quality, of physical care and maintenance, but virtually all provide some. Only rarely are the newborn cast into the river.

Socialization of Children

Not only does the family create and physically maintain children, but it carries out the serious responsibility of socializing each child. Although in American society there is a tendency to think that children will largely determine their social development, the process of socialization does not really proceed along such free and open pathways. Children are largely taught by their families to conform to socially approved patterns of behavior.

Learning to conform may or may not result in individual happiness, but few question the legitimacy of the social demand that children should not learn and display social patterns injurious to themselves or others, whatever such standards may be

for a given community. The fact that some parents fail to socialize children effectively does not diminish the persistent demands of society for proper performance. Exactly what behavior constitutes proper performance, of course, differs according to social-class, religious, racial, ethnic, and other factors. Therefore, societal demands for conformity tend to be somewhat generalized, but they are nevertheless powerful and pervasive.

Socialization is not totally a process of learning to conform, however. Socialization also teaches us how *not* to conform to some general societal rules or how to bend them in particular situations.

Regulation of Sexual Behavior

The family also functions to regulate sexual behavior. Some husbands, wives, and the unmarried may not *feel* regulated in this respect, but everyone's sexual behavior is influenced to some extent by what is learned in the family setting. The sexual attitudes and patterns of behavior we learn in the family reflect societal norms and regulate our sexual behavior in both direct and indirect ways.

The sociological notion of sexual *regulation* should not be confused with *repression*. No society has norms forbidding sexual expression; rather, the norms specify under what conditions and with what partners sexual needs may be satisfied. The traditional American norm, which until very recently defined marriage as the only appropriate condition for sexual expression, *regulated* sexual behavior in that sense. But marriage also allows the possibility of virtually unlimited sexuality, so it cannot be viewed as repressing it. Similarly, current norms forbid sexual contact with animals, but encourage it with members of the opposite sex and to some degree even permit homosexuality.

Through interaction with parents and other family members throughout childhood, adolescence, and even adulthood, all of us form sexual attitudes and feelings that equip us to participate in sexual activities. Children learn much sexual behavior relatively early in their lives: how to feel about the body, especially the sex organs; how to relate to the opposite sex with respect to sex differences and similarities; and how to deal with the experiences of sexual sensation and arousal. This kind of learning experience is the making of sexual regulation in any society. Sexual controls on personal behavior are actually a matter of internal control for the most part. Although there are, of course, individual variations in sexual behavior, in most cases our sexual attitudes and patterns are generally consistent with what we learned through socialization in the family.

Sexual patterns have a relationship to many other cultural variables. Generally, the forms of sexual regulation that prevail reflect such influences as the way in which sex roles determine nonsexual patterns and interaction. Sexual practices often mirror differences of social status between the sexes and also are influenced by differences in social class. The family is important in imparting a kind of *sexual ideology*, even when avoiding activities such as formal sex education in the home. The typical avoidance of direct teaching of sexual knowledge by American parents is in fact a kind of social learning that may be very important in determining how their children will behave sexually.

Status Transmission

Family life in most societies has another function, one that is sometimes overlooked, but is nevertheless extremely important, as we saw in Chapter 8: the intergenerational transmission of social status. As most of us have observed in our own lives, American family practices seek to provide members with competitive advantage. Parents are expected to do everything they can to equip their children with the benefits of their own socioeconomic position.

The transmission of social status in and by the family is much more than a matter of parents' determination to "do their best by the children," however. In American society, *social identity* is initially fixed by family membership—by being born to parents of given status characteristics. Children take on the socioeconomic class standing of their parents and the culture of the class into which they are born, including its values, attitudes, and definitions of reality. The foundry worker's children do not share the outlook of the banker's children. Further, in addition to internalizing family attitudes and beliefs, children are treated and defined *by others* as extensions of the social identity of their parents. The children of "the best family in

Socialization in the family. Who taught *you* how to fly a kite?

town" are treated as such; the children of Scandinavian Lutherans are not treated like Irish Catholics. And we saw in Chapter 8 that even occupational position or level—and sometimes role—is "inherited" from parents by both sons and daughters. Thus, the family in modern societies is the principal agent for the transmission of social status from generation to generation.

Economic Activity

Until recent times, the family was an important—if not the central—unit of both production and consumption, producing most of what it consumed and consuming most of what it produced. The American family today, of course, is no longer an important source of the production of goods; even the last bastion of family production, family agriculture, is giving way to corporate farming. Economically, families today are producers only of income, which means that their principal function is that of the *consumption* of goods and services. Through its choices in this activity, each family manifests a *style of life* that in some respects

Copyright, 1976, G. B. Trudeau. Distributed by Universal Press Syndicate.

establishes its status and identity in the community.

Because the production of income—the provision of economic support for family members—is a major function of the modern family, the role of the breadwinner or breadwinners becomes crucial. Underemployment or unemployment can have very serious consequences indeed, perhaps similar to the effects of flood or drought on the family of colonial times. When family income is reduced or cut off, the family's power to survive is diminished, and the insecurities people experience under such conditions can have serious effects on family relationships. Additionally, the problems facing the worker who is displaced by technological advances, age, or limitations in learning ability, which remain unsolved in our society, can cause great distress for all members of the family.

Social-Emotional Support

Ordinarily, the family functions as a group to fulfill a wide range of social and psychological needs. Caring for family members does not end with infancy and childhood. It is seemingly the nature of human beings to establish social interdependencies, not only to meet physical needs, but to gratify psychological needs for response and affection as well. The family as a primary group is an

The family imparts a sexual ideology to the child. In the American white middle class, it is often one of avoidance.

important source of affection, love, and social interaction. Those who lack family interaction and must depend on other experiences for fulfilling emotional needs, perhaps vicariously, still tend to search for the kind of stable and enduring relationships found in the family. Such people often rely on friends, office-mates, date bureaus, and so forth. The pages of Ann Landers and Dear Abby columns attest to the strength and endurance of such needs throughout life.

Interinstitutional Linkage

Finally, we note some other functions of the family, those that have a relationship to the activities of other institutions. Each newborn child is a potential participant in the group life of the society. Family membership in a church, political group, economic interest group, recreational organization, or other kinds of voluntary association typically gives individuals at least the opportunity to participate in activities that might otherwise be closed to them. The family, then, not only prepares the individual to fill social roles and occupy a status in the community, but also provides the *opportunities* for such activity.

Some institutions appear to depend on the way the family functions in this regard to insure their own continuity and survival. Religious groups are probably the prime example. "The family that prays together" not only "stays together," but stays in the church and supports *it*. Similarly, although political behavior is supposed to be highly individualized, especially with regard to voting, the family unit functions in many respects as a political unit. Studies of political socialization show that children tend to "inherit" the political attitudes and habits of their parents. Similar links can be established between the family and educational institutions.

Patterns of Family Organization

The ways in which families may be organized are not all obvious. You are, of course, familiar with the family in the United States and probably know that there are ethnic differences in the way people *regard* their families, or how much authority parents exercise over their children, how weddings are celebrated, and so forth. You are probably aware as well that people in other cultures follow practices of their own that are very different from the American pattern. (Who hasn't heard tales of wild goings-on in the bushes of Samoa?) In the following section, we will describe a few of the major organizational forms that families may take, beginning with the basic distinction between the *nuclear* and the *extended* family, going on to consider forms of marriage, and finally discussing patterns of descent and authority.

Nuclear and Extended Families

The **nuclear family** consists of a married couple and their children. This is the basic building block of most kinship systems, and in contemporary Western civilization, it is the most important unit in terms of the social functions of the family. The **extended family** is commonly defined as the nuclear family plus all kin living together beyond the immediate parent-offspring group: grandparents, uncles, aunts, in-laws, and so forth.[1]

The extended family form is probably the most common one in the world, and until about the year

> **nuclear family:** the kinship unit consisting of a married pair and their children.
>
> **extended family:** the nuclear family plus all kin living together beyond the immediate parent-offspring group. In the most typical form of extended family, the kin live together in a single household or adjacent households and function as an integrated economic unit.

Children tend to inherit the politics of their families. We can be quite sure this young man's parents didn't vote for Ford in 1976.

Family portaits, then and now. The degree to which the extended family has disappeared in America is a measure of the radical degree of recent social change.

1900, it typified the American family as well, particularly in rural areas. Although there are many variations of it in different societies, the form it most typically takes is that of a married pair with their children, both married and unmarried, and grandchildren, married and unmarried, plus spouses and offspring of children and grandchildren, living together in one household or adjacent households and functioning as an integrated economic unit. The economic function may be the reason for the frequency of the extended family throughout the world; for most societies throughout history, the extended family was a more efficient economic unit than the nuclear family.

The degree to which the extended family has disappeared from American life is a measure of social change in the society and structural change within the family. Today, the typical American does not identify the extended family as an important focus of activity or personal identity. Nowadays, the extended kinship network is usually significant only on ceremonial occasions: births, weddings, funerals, and, perhaps, major holidays, such as Thanksgiving—"Over the river and through the woods, *to Grandmother's house we go . . .*" (But note, in this jingle from the last century, that grandmother's house is only "over the river and through the woods" and is accessible by sleigh; one needn't take a jet to Miami or Los Angeles.) Otherwise, the extended family is usually ignored except by those fascinated with the intricacies of family trees. Most Americans recognize a difference between their nuclear families and their "relatives," and resist being drawn into the activities and responsibilities of the latter. ("Why should I help bail my brother-in-law out of his financial difficulties?")

Forms of Marriage: Monogamy and Polygamy

It would be difficult to list, and impossible to describe, each of the specific forms that the marriage relation has taken in human societies. Earlier, we defined marriage as a stable set of socially approved relations between husband and wife, including, but not limited to, sexual relations. A more technical definition would be that marriage is

**Figure 12-1
Monogamy and polygamy**

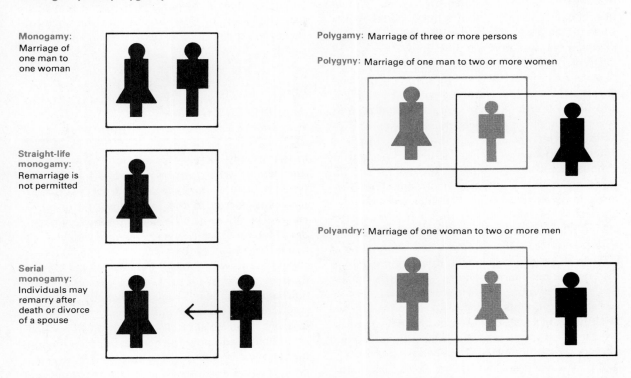

Monogamy:
Marriage of
one man to
one woman

**Straight-life
monogamy:**
Remarriage is
not permitted

**Serial
monogamy:**
Individuals may
remarry after
death or divorce
of a spouse

Polygamy: Marriage of three or more persons

Polygyny: Marriage of one man to two or more women

Polyandry: Marriage of one woman to two or more men

a contract between spouses of the opposite sex that makes children born to them legitimate. (The legitimation, of course, is provided or accorded by the society, not the parent couple.) But note two other elements of the definition. First, a marriage is a contract. It is a legally recognized and, hence, public agreement between people for an exchange of goods and/or services. Americans might find such an understanding of marriage unromantic, even pedestrian, but that is, when we come right down to it, what marriage is all about. Quarrels between husband and wife about how money is to be spent or who should take out the garbage are stereotypical because they are so important: in such minutia of living together is a marriage made. Second, the definition just offered says the contract is between spouses, but does not say one spouse of each sex. This raises the distinction between the

two basic marriage forms, monogamy and polygamy.

Monogamy means the marriage of one man to one woman. It is the basic marital form practiced by most people throughout the world and is virtually universal in industrial societies. *Polygamy* is the marriage of three or more persons. It is not uncommon in preindustrial societies, and in fact, more cultures around the world permit polygamy than restrict marriage to the monogamous form.[2] The explanation for the apparent contradiction between this statement and the previous one that monogamy is practiced by most people is simple. Even in societies that permit polygamy, most people do not practice it because they cannot afford to.

Each of the two basic marital forms has a number of possible subtypes that are practiced in one society or another (see Figure 12-1). A monogamous society may practice **serial monogamy**, in which individuals may remarry after an original marriage has been terminated by death or divorce; this, of course, is the custom in the United States. A society may also practice **straight-life monogamy**, in which remarriage is not permitted.

The variations of polygamy are **polygyny**: marriage of one man to two or more women; **polyandry**: marriage of one woman to two or more men; and **group marriage**: marriage of several men to several women simultaneously, all of one sex regarding all of the other sex equally as spouses. Polygyny and polyandry have been practiced in various societies throughout the world and in some societies are still practiced today. The Mormons in nineteenth-century America were polygynous. It is unclear whether group marriage ever occurred among preliterate peoples, although early anthropologists believed they had found some instances of it. None is known to exist now, and it may be that nineteenth-century reports of the practice were incorrect, mistaking other conventional social arrangements or ceremonials for marriage. The American press, however, occasionally reports the existence of the practice in the United States, often in connection with group living experiments. And at least one sociologist, Ira Reiss, has documented it in a few instances.[3] No such "marriages" are recognized as legal by any American jurisdiction, of course, nor are they ever solemnified by religious authority.

This discussion has thus far kept to the formal definition of marriage as a contract between spouses that legitimates children. But two things are happening in the United States at the present time that may eventually require a somewhat broader definition. One is the trend toward eliminating the distinction between legitimate and illegitimate births. The other is the trend toward living together: persons not legally wed live together as if they were married. Because both of these practices seem to be increasing in frequency, we may find Americans coming to conceive of marriage as a pattern that encompasses possibilities now outside the roles legally sanctioned as husband and wife. And the advent of the Pill, which for the first time in history truly gives *women* the power to determine whether they will conceive, seems certain in the long run to destroy the distinction between legiti-

macy and illegitimacy. After all, we always know who a baby's mother is, but with the kinds of sexual freedom made possible by simple and effective contraception for females, the possibility of determining fatherhood will become ever more remote.

The Structure of Marriage: Patterns of Descent and Authority

In any society, family organization involves more than simply what form of marriage is practiced. Given the fact of marriage, a whole set of structural problems comes to the fore: How is the newly created family unit to be set up? Where will children fit in the kinship system, to whom will they be related? How will problems be solved and quarrels settled? Who will "wear the pants" in the family? Each of these issues is a major element in any marriage, and every society develops structural solutions to the questions they raise.

Descent The issue of descent—who will be related to whom and how—is not as simple as it might first appear. On first sight, it may seem that you're either related to someone or you're not, but it isn't that easy. The point involved is what *constitutes* kin relationship. Who gets *counted as* kin in a given culture? Is a woman, for instance, related to her cousin's husband? The answer would depend on the kinship system in her society.

There are three different systems for reckoning descent: **matriliny** (through the female line), **patriliny** (through the male line), and **bilaterality** (through both lines). The United States uses a bilateral system, and we see ourselves as descended from (related to) the families of both our parents. We have grandparents, for example, on both our mother's and our father's side of the family. But if we were a matrilineal society, we would not have paternal grandparents; that is, you would not recognize your father's family as related to you. Your father, of course, would be related to you, but upon birth, you would have joined your mother's family tree, not his. (And you would take her family name too, not his.) Descent, then, is a social, not a biological relationship, although in this country we define it as the latter.

Authority Another major structural element in marriage is *authority*, the pattern of dominance and subordination in marital decision making. The American folk phrase "wearing the pants in the family" pinpoints the issue. (It also implies, through the use of "pants"—traditionally an item of male attire—the conventional American value of male dominance in family decision making.) Authority is an important issue in families or any other human group for a simple sociological reason: for any group to work or live together, decisions must be made, and people must be convinced or coerced to carry them out. Thus, authority or leadership of some kind has to be exercised. *Someone* must plan, initiate, and decide.

It need not, however, be any particular someone, and three different patterns for the distribution of authority in the family are visible in different societies around the world. These are **patriarchy**: male dominant; **matriarchy**: female dominant; and the **equalitarian pattern**: authority shared between the sexes. Pure forms of any are probably rare; even in the patriarchal or matriarchal forms, there is often some division of labor. For example, a family system that is essentially patriarchal may still acknowledge female authority in many domestic matters, as did nineteenth-century American society. Further, in heterogeneous societies, different tendencies may appear among different social classes, ethnic groups, educational levels, and so forth. In the United States, for instance, working-class people still tend to hold to patriarchal patterns, as seen in Archie Bunker, while the middle and upper classes in general tend to be equalitarian. Some Native American groups are distinctly matriarchal.[4]

Most of the world's cultures have more or less followed the patriarchal pattern. In modern societies everywhere, however, social and cultural change is tending to establish more equalitarian patterns of decision making in which the expression of authority is not linked to gender. (The American military service academies admitted female cadets for the first time in the summer of 1976, thus opening the possibility that women could attain the high prestige afforded "regular" officers who are academy graduates.) Such changes are visible in almost all of the institutions of the modern world and are particularly evident, in the

serial monogamy: monogamous marriage with the possibility of remarriage after divorce or death of a spouse.

straight-life monogamy: monogamous marriage without the possibility of remarriage.

polygyny: marriage of one man to two or more women.

polyandry: marriage of one woman to two or more men.

group marriage: marriage of several men to several women in which all persons of one sex regard all of the other sex as spouses.

matriliny: the practice of tracing descent or kinship through the female line.

patriliny: the practice of tracing descent or kinship through the male line.

bilaterality: the practice of tracing descent or kinship through both male and female lines.

patriarchy: the dominance of the male in marital decision making.

matriarchy: the dominance of the female in marital decision making.

equalitarian pattern: in regard to marital decision making, the pattern in which authority is shared between the sexes.

"You can usually tell when he's annoyed about something."

Punch, October 17, 1973. © Punch (Rothco).

Authority is always an important structural element in marriage and the family.

United States at least, in the primary relationships of contemporary marriage. Decision making is no longer considered the sole province of the male, and the subordination of wives in the American family is rapidly ending.

Principles of Mate Selection

We have thus far discussed marriage and the family as *given,* as existent facts, without considering the processes that produce marriage in the first place. Common sense would seem to indicate that there is little to understand and certainly that sociological factors must be largely irrelevant. People fall in love, decide to marry, and do so, and the whole process is intimate and personal to the couple involved. As in the preceding discussions, however, we shall find that this commonsense approach is inadequate. The following discussion will tend to concentrate on the American experience of getting married, but there are lots of other ways of going about it, and some of these will be noted for contrast.

The process whereby people choose marriage partners is called **mate selection**. It operates according to two sociological principles usually credited to the work of G. P. Murdock and Robert F. Winch.[5] These are, respectively, **preferential mating** and **marriage arrangement**. Preferential mating refers to the cultural and behavior patterns that define the field of eligible mates for a given individual. Marriage arrangement refers to the processes through which *persons other than the nuptial couple* influence or control the selection of a mate by an individual.

Preferential Mating

Every society possesses a number of values dictating who is eligible to marry whom and, among eligibles, what characteristics are to be considered desirable or undesirable. But all societies share in common two great principles of preferential mating that narrow the field considerably for everyone. These are the principles of *heterosexuality* and *the incest taboo.*

Heterosexuality   Every society requires as a first and elemental precondition of marriage that persons to be married be of opposite sexes. Although homosexuality has often been permitted at various times and places and even seems to have been celebrated as a special condition of male friendship among the ancient Greeks, it has never been defined as a *marital* relation among either men or women. Marriage, by apparently universal definition, must require the possibility of parenthood, which, of course, demands a heterosexual union. The effect of the heterosexuality requirement on the field of eligibles for any given individual, obviously, is to reduce it by approximately 50 percent.

The incest taboo   Sexual interaction with someone closely related—**incest**—is forbidden in all human societies, although exactly what behaviors are defined as constituting it, and who is defined as a close relative, vary considerably. In some American states, for instance, one is permitted to marry anyone not a parent or sibling; other states prohibit marriage between second cousins or persons more closely related. Parent-child and brother-sister contact, however, is forbidden in all societies, at least for the great bulk of the population. (Some societies have historically required such marriages for specific individuals, usually for religious reasons. The Pharoah and the Inca, for instance, were defined as gods and therefore had to marry close relatives, sometimes their sisters, in order to avoid the contamination of their line with mortal blood.)

The commonly accepted sociological explanation for the universality of the incest taboo is that it avoids social conflicts that would destroy the family and kinship group. If daughters could compete with mothers for their father's sexual attention, and sons with fathers for their mother's, and brothers with each other for their sister's, the family could not endure. The effect of the taboo is to remove whole classes of familiar people from the field of eligible mates. In some societies, such as our own, this may not involve a large number. In others, whole clans and other kinship units may be eliminated.

Endogamy and exogamy   Rules of **endogamy** and **exogamy** specifically define the field of marriage

The Rupee Knot

The advertisement in last week's issue of the New Delhi *Hindustan Times* was clearly designed to catch the eye of marriage-minded Indian males: MATCH FOR TALL, CONVENT-EDUCATED, LEGALLY DIVORCED 27-YEAR-OLD GIRL DRAWING FOUR-FIGURE SALARY, FOREIGN FIRM. FATHER SENIOR OFFICIAL. FAMILY RESPECTABLE AND HIGHLY CONNECTED. If the "legally divorced" line discouraged bachelor readers, they could scan hundreds of other announcements in the *Times's* nine columns of "matrimonial" ads. The ads discreetly avoided the subject of dowries. Yet the real nuptial knot in India—where 90% of marriages are still arranged—is not love but rupees.

The dowry system, which crosses all caste lines, is now a major target of government reform. Technically, dowries were outlawed under a 1961 law that proved impossible to enforce. Now the reformers are relying on social pressure. The 5 million-member Youth Congress is urging its male members to sign a pledge that they will not accept a dowry when they marry; female members are asked to have their families turn down requests for dowry payments. Plans are under way for sit-ins and picketing at ostentatious weddings where parents brag about their daughter's dowry. . . .

The burden hits hard at every level. Upper-class families in the cities demand steep cash payments from a bride's family in return for a well-educated, well-connected bridegroom. A young man who holds a job in the prestigious Indian adminstrative service or the Indian foreign service, for example, can command $10,000 or more in dowry payment. Valuable consumer goods such as refrigerators, television sets and automobiles are commonly tossed in as part of the deal.

Lower-class families, in turn, demand that their son's new in-laws hand over transistor radios, motor scooters and sewing machines as well as cash. Fathers of the bride quickly learn that the local moneylender is their best friend. In rural areas, farmers frequently borrow bank money for "agricultural development," then spend it on their daughter's dowry. For generations, family savings have been wiped out by the dowry payments. . . .

Time, March 22, 1976. Reprinted by permission of TIME, The Weekly Newsmagazine; copyright Time Inc.

The business side of marriage.

---

mate selection: the process of locating and securing a mate defined as socially suitable for a given person.

preferential mating: the cultural and behavior patterns that define the field of eligible mates for a given person.

marriage arrangement: the process through which persons other than the nuptial couple influence or control mate selection.

incest: sexual interaction with close relatives.

endogamy: the requirement that a member of a given culturally defined group marry within that group.

exogamy: the requirement that a member of a given culturally defined group marry outside of that group.

---

eligibles and ineligibles further. *Endogamy* requires an individual to marry *within* some culturally defined group of which that individual is already a member. *Exogamy* is the reverse of this rule, requiring the individual to marry *outside of* his or her own kind.

Both the heterosexual marital requirement and the incest taboo are examples of a kind of exogamy, but the terms *endogamy* and *exogamy* are more usually applied to kinship units, such as clans, and racial, ethnic, and religious groupings. All of these requirements are typically learned in early childhood through the socialization process and become so firmly internalized as right and proper that most people never perceive them as limiting or determining their marital choices, and few ever seriously consider violating them.

Marriage Arrangement

Marriage arrangement is, of course, the source of the term *arranged marriage,* which causes most young Americans to shudder. "Let someone else pick my spouse for me?" we think, "Never! What an awful way to have to marry." It may surprise you to learn that many people who practice marriage arrangement are perfectly satisfied with the results. Indeed, women from cultures where arranged marriage is a way of life often pity American women for having no assistance in seeking a husband. It may surprise you even more to learn the degree to which our own marriages are arranged (in the sense of *influenced* by others), a matter discussed in the following section. In fact, in all societies, not only are individuals constrained by the norms defining the field of eligibles, but seldom is the specific choice to be made from this field left to the individual entirely. Some influence and control is almost always exerted by persons other than those being paired.

It is not uncommon in non-Western societies for the participants in a marriage to have little or nothing to say about the selection of a spouse, with the eventual decision being made by their respective kinship groups. Some consideration may be given to the characteristics and needs of the potential mates, but the final judgment will be made by the families involved, acting to support family interests. Affection between the spouses, if relevant at all, will be expected to occur as a product of the marriage—just the reverse of the expectation that we regard as normal.

The business of marriage (and often it is business) is much too important to be left to the whims of the participants. Significant social-status and economic considerations structure the process of mate selection as the family strives to arrange unions advantageous to itself. Similar *kinds* of consideration are not unknown in the United States either, as a matter of fact. Many a young man has sought to "marry the boss's daughter," and more than one young woman has been advised by a parent or relative that "it is just as easy to marry a rich man as a poor one."

Mate Selection in the United States

Despite the American habit of viewing mate selection as a psychological phenomenon, it is predominantly a *social* process, even in the United States. Clearly it has some psychological components, but the factors that in fact influence one's mate selection through the process of excluding other possibilities are overwhelmingly social. Principal among these are two general phenomena called *homogamy* and *heterogamy*.

Homogamy and Heterogamy

Marital homogamy refers to the possession of similar attributes or characteristics in husband and wife. **Marital heterogamy** refers to their possession of differing characteristics. The terms may be applied to either social or psychological attributes.

In American mate-selection patterns, homogamy tends to prevail, particularly with regard to social characteristics. Most people marry others like themselves in age, residence, racial and ethnic group membership, religion, education, and social class. And in all of these matters, marriage arrangement, in the sense of family influence, may have considerable influence. Only in the matter of the psychological characteristics of the mate is there evidence of heterogamy in American mate-selection patterns.

Social Factors

Age In general in the United States, people marry others very close to their own ages. When the partners differ in age, the general pattern is for the man to be older. Although men marrying at eighteen tend to be a few months younger than their brides, those marrying at twenty-five are three years older, on the average. And men marrying at thirty-seven are six years older than their brides.[6] Thus, the difference in ages becomes somewhat wider as age at marriage increases. (Note also that our norms permit, if they do not encourage, marriage between young women and rich old men. But the sexual reverse is subject to severe informal sanction.)

Residence It is obvious that in a society where people more or less select their own mates, you cannot marry someone you have never met. And, in general, whom do you meet? Those who live nearby. "Nearby," of course, is relative to the kind and availability of transportation, school patterns, and so forth. And the increase in personal mobility that came with the widespread use of the automobile and the airplane has reduced the influence of proximity (technically called *propinquity*) as a feature of American mate selection. Nevertheless, people who live in small towns still tend to marry others from the same town, and one study done in Columbus, Ohio, in 1961 (1960 population, 471,316) showed that about half of the people who married in that year lived within walking distance of each other before marriage.[7]

Race and ethnicity Although racial barriers have been struck down in almost every area of American life in recent years and legal prohibitions against cross-racial marriage were declared unconstitutional by the Supreme Court in 1948, the societal norm against biracial marriage, particularly marriage between blacks and whites, is not often violated. In 1966, only about 1 percent of all American marriages were cross-racial, and the incidence of Asian-white marriage was higher than that of black-white marriage.[8] With increasing racial freedom in the United States, and reported increases in cross-racial dating on college campuses, we may expect the incidence of cross-racial marriage to increase somewhat. But the racial endogamy requirements are strong among all racial groups in America, and there seems no reason to believe that biracial partnerships will become common in the foreseeable future.

Ethnic endogamy tends to have similar, although less pronounced, effects. Research on the matter is scarce, owing to the difficulty of determining ethnicity from marriage records. But we do know that many American ethnic groups still hold strong values about marrying "one's own kind," and some ethnics who retain close ties to old country ways still hold funerals for a group member who marries an outsider. It is probably accurate to say that in general persons defining themselves as ethnic marry others of the same ethnicity more often than they do other people. As the duration of a particular group's residence in the United States increases, however, such tendencies diminish.

Education The educational homogamy of marriage partners is clear at all levels of schooling. As a general rule, those with grammar school educations marry others with no greater educational attainment; high school graduates marry other high school graduates; and college graduates, as a class, marry others with college experience. Male

marital homogamy: the possession of similar characteristics by husband and wife.

marital heterogamy: the possession of dissimilar characteristics by husband and wife.

An aspect of mate selection in America. Most computer dating services function to select homogamous partners.

college graduates are a partial exception to the generalization. Because fewer women graduate from college than do men, some male graduates marry somewhat less well educated women, but marriages across wide educational gaps are uncommon. We can expect this phenomenon to become less frequent in the future as more women attend and complete college. The consistency shown by educational homogamy is probably the result of several factors, not the least of which is simple propinquity. Most Americans attend coeducational schools and thus are kept for a number of years in the company of persons of the opposite sex who are having similar educational experiences.

Social class   While there is a certain degree of concern shown in some segments of American society about people marrying "up" or "down" in class standing (marrying "for money" or "beneath oneself"), research indicates that the actual number of such marriages is small.[9] Julius Roth and Robert F. Peck, surveying 396 couples, found that 55 percent of their marriages were between persons of the same social class, another 40 percent were between people in adjacent classes, and only 5 percent were between persons in nonadjacent classes.[10]

Class homogamy is related to educational homogamy, since schools tend to sort people by class. Further, the free-choice system of mate selection in the United States gives each class the option of selecting as mates others like themselves: the wealthy and better educated choose those who are well educated and well off, and so on at all class levels.[11]

Religion   Religious homogamy in marriage is still the general rule among Americans, but it is declining as social mobility, extensive education, and other factors increasingly homogenize the population. Interfaith marriages, in other words, are increasing, but not rapidly. As in so many other things, the general tendency remains that "like marries like."

One reason for this, of course, is that all major religious groups oppose mixed marriages. Some are concerned with losing from the faith any children born to a marriage where one parent is of

another religion. Some hold that differences between spouses on religious values can threaten the endurance of the marriage. In other cases, particularly among ethnics, interfaith marriage is viewed as constituting a possible conflict between loyalty to church and loyalty to kin.

Different studies disagree somewhat concerning the actual incidence of mixed marriage among Americans, but most concur that it is least frequent among Jews, next most infrequent among Catholics, and most common among Protestants. According to one prominent religious researcher's 1962 study, only 7 percent of Jews married non-Jews, and only 9 percent of Catholics married non-Catholics, while 32 percent of Protestant marriages crossed religious lines.[12]

The influence of the family   A final social factor in mate selection in the United States that most of us ignore at our peril is the influence of the individual's family on his or her choice of mate. This is probably exercised most significantly in the early socialization process, when the basic rules of racial, religious, and ethnic endogamy are transmitted; but for most Americans, it continues up to the marriage itself. Interest in who the children are dating, casual or pointed remarks about one's friends, their dress, language, work habits, spending behaviors, drinking, and so forth, all operate on the child to clarify and specify who is and is not suitable as an associate or mate. If such tactics fail to keep the child from choosing a "suitable" mate, others may be brought in to influence the child: relatives, friends of the family, religious counselors, or even, among the middle classes, psychiatrists. Economic threats may be leveled ("We won't help you!"), and persons below the age of consent can be denied parental permission to marry. Those who are of legal age may be threatened with disinheritance or family excommunication if they marry someone not of the family's choosing.

Psychological Factors

Here we will consider two psychological factors in mate selection that have been extensively studied. One is **complementarity**, the tendency of like to marry unlike, a pattern in which heterogamy, rather than the homogamy we have seen operative in

Table 12-1   Kinds of marital complementarity.

If the husband is high in:	The wife tends to be:
Achievement-oriented independence	High in submissiveness High in self-deprecation Low in dominance
Nurturance	High in succorance High in need for approval
Status-oriented dominance	High in submissiveness Low in dominance
Hostile dominance	High in yielding dependence
Yielding dependence	Low in self-deprecation

complementarity: with regard to marriage, the hypothesis that individuals with one characteristic or attribute are attracted to and complemented (made perfect or whole) by different or opposite traits in a spouse. Complementarity is supposed to increase marital happiness.

Figure 12-2
Complementarity represented in the yin-yang symbol.

social factors, is the general rule. The other, you may have guessed, is that great American obsession, the belief in *romantic love*. For many, falling in love or being in love is the only important basis of marriage, and we will look into why that is so.

Complementarity   Complementarity can be defined as a condition in which two or more things fit together to make a complete or perfect whole, each part in itself being incomplete and imperfect. The familiar yin-yang symbol (Figure 12-2) is a classic example. The hypothesis of marital complementarity, often associated with the work of Robert F. Winch, is that people marry each other to make up for some lack in themselves, that we seek spouses who possess qualities we lack or have only in a small degree.[13] Very aggressive women are often observed to have passive, timid husbands, for example, while noisy, talkative men may have withdrawn and reticent wives. Such popular perceptions are probably the basis for the folk belief that "opposites attract each other," the complementarity hypothesis in simplified form. Table 12-1 illustrates some of Winch's findings regarding complementarity in twenty-five instances of what he regarded as normal marriages.

One assumption of Winch's complementarity hypothesis is that the complementarity makes for marital compatibility: an imperfect or inadequate personality is made whole or perfect through union th another that fulfills it. But some researchers have found that certain complementary combinations lead not to fulfillment, but to the acting out of neurotic tendencies in the marital relationship. For instance, Bela Mittelmann found that (1) if one partner is dominant and aggressive, the other is submissive, passive, and masochistic; (2) if one partner is emotionally detached, the other craves affection; (3) if one partner is helpless, craving to be dependent on the mate, the other is endlessly supportive; (4) if one partner alternates between periods of dependency and self-assertion, the other responds with periods of helpfulness and unsatisfied needs for affection.[14]

There seems little question that complementarity exists in many marriages, and certainly popular belief in it is widespread. But recent research, based on both married and dating couples, has not always revealed complementarity. J. Richard Urdry suggests that the reason for this may be that complementarity operates in mate selection at the *perceptual* level; prospective mates see in each other qualities that do not really exist. The complementarity is real only in their eyes.[15] That it exists with regard to husband and wife *roles* in marriage is, of course, obvious. The roles are necessarily different, but must complement each other for the marriage to work at all.

Romantic love Romantic love is both a complex emotion, that is, a psychological phenomenon, and a culture complex as defined in Chapter 3. The latter aspect of it can be traced back to the early Middle Ages, where some of its psychological manifestations would appear familiar enough to modern Americans, but where it had very different outcomes and was differently understood. The female object of a knight's romantic affections—and romance was a prerogative of the aristocracy—was usually married, and it was understood by all parties, including the lady's husband, that sex had nothing to do with the matter. Sex was much too practical a business to be left to the nonsense of romance. Volumes have been written about romance and the translation of the medieval ideal into its present reality in American life, but we are here concerned with it only as a psychological factor in mate selection.

The dictionary defines the relevant meanings of the word *romance* as (1) a tale depicting heroic or marvelous achievements, colorful events or scenes, unusual or even supernatural experiences, or other matters of a kind to appeal to the imagination; (2) a made-up story, a fanciful or extravagant invention or exaggeration. The essence of romance, in other words, is *unreality*. It is a useful understanding to keep in mind when we ponder romantic love.

The skepticism of the dictionary does not change the fact that Americans believe in romantic love, however, and in general regard it as the proper basis for a happy marriage, if not the only basis for one. We talk, sing, and write about it endlessly, or did until very recently. The American understanding of **romantic love** is difficult to define exactly, but most of us would probably agree that it is a kind of ecstasy, a mixture of excitement about, sexual attraction for, and idealization of the loved one, who is perceived as the "one and only" person with whom we could live happily.

Popular music of the 1940s and 1950s sometimes even suggested that love was a kind of disease as well. Symptoms commonly attributed to it in this period often included sleeplessness, loss of appetite, absent-mindedness, vague pains, heart tremor, and muscular weakness. "You're Not Sick, You're Just in Love" by Irving Berlin is a classic example.[16]

I hear singing and there's no one there
I smell blossoms and the trees are bare
. . . .
I keep tossing in my sleep at night
And what's more I've lost my appetite

The problem with romantic love as a basis of mate selection is that it is not love at all; it is an infatuation, what the dictionary calls "a foolish and unreasoning passion." Further, it is defined in the United States as something that happens *to* you, not something you do yourself. One is struck with love as if by lightning, one falls into love as into a mud puddle; it is something one *is*, not something one *does*. It is, then, a condition, not an act. Further, it is perceived as a condition over which we have no control. It happens to us, and we are helpless.

The reason this is a problem, of course, is that if we can fall into love without volition, if it falls upon us like rain from heaven, we can also fall out of it again, also without volition. The rain dries up. And if the basis for marriage was the presence of the condition, then its absence becomes a reason for divorce. The attribution of marvelous qualities to the loved one is also a problematic feature of romantic love as a basis for marriage. Blinded by love, we perceive the loved one as perfect, possessing all desirable qualities, especially that most magical of all attributes; the ability to make *us happy*. For people who marry on such a basis, the aftermath of the ceremonial—including cooking, cleaning, making a living, and the routines of living together—often reduces the longed-for bliss to the ordinary business of life. But if we are not happy, it is obviously the other's fault, since that person, we believe, has the ability to make us happy. If he or she were truly the "one and only," we would be happy. Since we are not, it must be that we made a mistake. The Beckoning Fair One is still "out there" somewhere, and so we dispose of the mate we have to continue the search. That a large number of marriages conceived on such romantic notions fail should surprise no one.

There is some evidence that the ideal of romantic love has declined somewhat in popularity in the past decade or so. Among young people, the alteration in sexual customs that has made premarital sex with affection permissible has also had the inevitable effect of bringing greater reality into interpersonal relations, since romantic love is based on unattainability. It is possible to romanticize knightly lovers-from-afar and unattainable virgin beauties in ways that are difficult when we share a bed and bathroom with a lover. And the current decline of 1940s "moon-June" songs suggests that romantic love may be losing its hold on us as a basis of mate selection.[17]

Research on marital adjustment supports the notion that successful marriages are built on practical factors: the perceived happiness of parents' marriages, adequate length of courtship and engagement, similar (and mature) age, adequate sex information, and so on.[18] The importance of practicality for successful mate selection should not surprise us, particularly if we consider some ways in which other cultures have worked out the process that contrast markedly with American practice. Many societies have marriage and family systems in which the social roles of wife, husband,

romantic love: an emotion involving ecstasy, excitement about, idealization of, and sexual attraction for the loved one, who is perceived as the "one and only" person with whom the lover can be happy.

The idea of "romantic love" is medieval in origin. Only aristocrats could afford it.

father, and mother prescribe clear criteria for judging human performance. Life is without romantic fantasy. Marriage partners interact with each other through the exchange of necessary life skills: cooking and child care, hunting, fishing, and farming. Such marriages sometimes fail, of course (although much less frequently than ours, as a rule), but when they do, they are likely to fail because one partner does not adequately fulfill role expectations, not because complex, subjective requirements for emotional gratification are unsatisfied.

Changing Marital Roles in American Society

My marriage was in 1973. Beverly and I rented an apartment after our honeymoon, and we settled down buying furniture, a stereo, and began our payments on the new car . . . [19]

After the honeymoon Fred became so bossy. He wouldn't let me get my hair done every week. He was always picking on the way I would keep the house. He complained about the cooking. We never went to the movies or out to dinner. He spent all our money on the car, but we never went anywhere I wanted to go. I had no freedom at all. He was just like his father . . . [20]

These quotations from case histories of recent American marriages illuminate two important aspects of marital roles. In the first, we see a young couple responding to conventional social expectations about how one goes about setting up housekeeping: buying what are regarded as essential elements for a newly created, independent household. In the second, we see a young wife relating how her husband failed to meet *her* expectations through acting out his own, which she thinks he learned in his own home from his father. (She may well be correct. Most of us learn the particular details of how to act like a wife or husband from the people closest to us who have those roles: our parents.)

The second quotation may also be an example of something else. Role conflicts between husband and wife within the marriage relationship are sometimes the result of social change. If we infer that Fred is acting out typical lower-middle-class American male behavior, we can also conclude that either he violated class homogamy by marrying a

girl from a higher class (unlikely), or that his ideas about marriage and marital roles have remained traditional while hers have changed. The latter seems a reasonable hypothesis.

In our rapidly changing society, many people have altered or are beginning to alter their ideas about role expectations in marriage. And sometimes these changing conceptions lead to marital strife and disappointment, as they did for Fred's wife. How far such changes have gone, and who is most affected by them, is the subject of the following section. We will focus on five aspects of marital roles: authority and decision making, allocation of responsibility, procreation and child rearing, social and occupational status, and sexual behavior.

Authority and Decision Making

One of the most important aspects of marital relationships is how decision making is divided between husband and wife. The couple is usually influenced by a number of factors besides their individual feelings. There are many social-class, racial, and ethnic differences in how husbands and wives allot decision-making power, and in some cases other members of the family may be involved. But in general, the American family has until recently followed a patriarchal pattern in assigning the husband the major share of authority and decision making.

In the last decade or so, however, there have been several indications that the patriarchal pattern is being deeply eroded. The major force in challenging the male supremacy is, of course, the women's liberation movement. As a legally enforceable code for marital authority in decision making, patriarchy is dead. Women in most jurisdictions now have the right to retain their own family names upon marriage, to work for the same wages as men, to hold property in their own right and obtain credit on the same terms, and so forth. Although research data are scanty, it seems unlikely that role expectations for female behavior in marriage have remained unchanged while alterations of this magnitude were going on in the society.

And changes in role expectations for the wife's contribution to decision making in the family necessarily imply changes in the husband's role as well. Among the middle and upper classes, at least (for the women's liberation movement remains largely a class-related social movement), the companionable, equalitarian marriage is probably the rule today. Studies of college students suggest that expectations for such equalitarian marriages are now widely shared by educated persons of both sexes. No longer does father always know best.

Responsibility

Marriage necessarily entails some division of labor, with each partner being responsible for certain activities. Although it is logically possible to maintain a marriage built around a strict rotation of all family duties (except that of birth itself), it seems unlikely that most families will adopt such a system. For reasons of talent, training, convenience, and aptitude, most people will probably continue to divide up the labor into "my job" and "yours."

But the allocation of *who* is to do what is certainly changing. In many modern marriages, husbands and wives exchange or share some responsibilities that not long ago would have been traditionally the husband's or wife's. Employment outside the home is a clear example, and many domestic routines, such as cooking or child care, are now exchanged far more frequently than they were in the traditional family. There are probably few American fathers below the age of fifty who have never changed a diaper.

This state of unclear or changing role expectations may cause some problems in the early years of marriage when family circumstances are apt to change rapidly. (What alterations in expectation for the woman's earnings are to be made when the first child is born, and how is the increased labor a baby creates to be divided?) Once a couple has determined by trial and error—and perhaps constructive quarreling—who can do what, they are likely to settle into a routine of reciprocally shared role expectations, however. This makes for family and marital stability so long as role responsibilities are responsibly accepted and shared. There is always work to be done in a family, and *someone* must do it. Misunderstandings and role conflicts arise when responsibilities are unfairly divided or shirked.

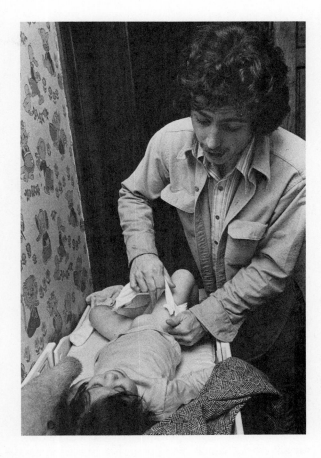

Male role expectations with regard to child rearing are clearly changing, particularly among the more educated. Few husbands below the age of fifty are unfamiliar with the chore shown here.

Procreation and Child Rearing

Although a great deal of premarital and extramarital sexual expression prevails in American society, there is still a high degree of consensus that *procreation* ought to occur within marriage. And the marital unit is still generally considered the best environment for raising children. But there is a new trend, still statistically insignificant, although growing, for birth or adoption outside of marriage: single parenthood. No one yet knows how this practice will work out in the long run. But we do know that it is important for children to have adult sex-role models of both sexes in the home, and this fact suggests that single parenthood is capable of creating considerable psychological damage.

Of more widespread significance are the changes in child-care responsibilities within marriage suggested in the discussion above. Traditional wife and husband roles are altering. Women are taking greater responsibility outside the home than was ever true in the past, adopting role responsibilities once considered exclusively male. But since marital roles are reciprocal, men will have to accept greater responsibility in the home if family stability is to be maintained. Among the educated, at least, there is evidence that men are indeed assuming more responsibility for child care; and it is probably safe to say that more and more men among the population as a whole will be assuming some child-care responsibilities. This is part of a shift toward more equalitarian roles for men and women: men will be doing *more* of the cooking, cleaning, laundry, shopping, and child care; and women will more often be employed outside the home and will perform more physical maintenance chores. But the role *reversal* advocated by some feminists has not caught the imagination of most Americans.

Social and Occupational Status

Probably all of you have been affected by the women's liberation movement. The thrust of it, of course, is to secure for women the same social status in the society traditionally granted men. This great collective effort to redefine the meaning of being female outside of the traditional role prescription of inferiority to and dominance by men has deep implications for modern marriage and family life.

As remarked earlier, changes in female roles necessarily imply and require adaptive changes in male roles. How will men respond to increasing pressures for sharing traditional statuses? If they are eventually required to give up prerogatives that were important sources of self-identity, what new bases for self-approval may they find? We noted earlier that the American service academies admitted female cadets for the first time in 1976. The public seems to be generally unaware of it, but there is also pressure on the services from women to open even combat roles to females. If pride in toughness and virility is one of the few rewards available to the "grunts" of the infantry, what would be the effect of permitting it to be shared with female "sharpshooters" and grenadiers? And we may equally ask what may be the effect on a generation of women instructed that they, too, may be architects, engineers, or airline pilots, when they discover that most of them, like most men, are doomed to jobs that are dull, repetitive, and psychologically unrewarding?

The latter question may be particularly important because, of course, the changes we have been describing do not represent a universal pattern in American life. Although data are scarce, it is clear that the greatest amount of sex-role change has occurred among the educated middle class, where women are more likely to be equipped educationally for professional or managerial careers in which they may compete with men. And a college-educated, middle-class woman might find it psychologically easier to adapt to actual role reversal—herself as wage earner and her spouse as househusband—than a lower-class woman would, the latter being more deeply imbued with a self-evaluation based on traditional roles.

For women locked into socioeconomic situations that cannot promise financial independence, liberation is relatively meaningless and sometimes suggests the denial of femininity as a goal. The lower-class female is at the mercy of a combination of traditional social, cultural, and economic forces that operate to maintain conventional sex-role patterns. Because of her class background, she lacks education for any jobs except those

Narrative of Sojourner Truth, 1878

"Slowly from her seat in the corner rose Sojourner Truth, who til now, had scarcely lifted her head. . . . She moved slowly and solemnly to the front, laid her old bonnet at her feet, and turned her great, speaking eyes to me. . . .

"'Well, chilern, whar dar is so much racket dar must be something out o'kilter. I tink dat 'twixt de niggers of de Souf and de women at de Norf all a talkin' 'bout rights, de white men will be in a fix pretty soon. But what's all dis here talkin' 'bout? Dat man ober dar say dat women needs to be helped into carriages, and lifted ober ditches, and to have de best place every whar. Nobody eber help me into carriages, or ober mud puddles, or gives me any best place [and raising herself to her full hight and her voice to a pitch like rolling thunder, she asked], and ar'n't I a woman? Look at me! Look at my arm! [And she bared her right arm to the shoulder, showing her tremendous muscular power.] I have plowed, and planted, and gathered into barns, and no man could head me—and ar'n't I a woman? I could work as much and eat as much as a man (when I could get it), and bear de lash as well—and ar'n't I a woman? I have borne thirteen chilern and seen 'em mos' all sold off into slavery, and when I cried out with a mother's grief, none but Jesus heard—and ar'n't I a woman? Den dey talks 'bout dis ting in de head—what dis dey call it?' 'Intellect,' whispered some one near. 'Dat's it honey. What's dat got to do with women's rights or niggers' rights? If my cup won't hold but a pint and yourn holds a quart, wouldn't ye be mean not to let me have my little half-measure full?' . . .

The movement for female equality has been gathering force for a long time.

As women take on more and more of the traditionally male roles, men will have to adapt to the situation. What the outcome will be is not yet foreseeable.

low-paying ones traditionally reserved for women (dime store clerk, beautician, assembly-line worker) or those in which she might have to face discrimination from male-dominated labor unions or occupational associations. (Female jockeys are an example.) Because of her own socialization, she may not believe it possible or appropriate to compete with men, thinking it unfeminine even to try. Thus, traditional sex-role patterns are preserved in the lower classes. A recent comment from a lower-middle-class white female illustrates the general point:

I really don't care much for it [women's liberation] because I want to have a man who can make decisions and take care of a wife. I'm looking forward to keeping house, having children, and making a nice life for my husband when I get married. I don't want to drive a truck or pour cement like my father.[21]

Sexual Behavior

The changes in sex and marital roles we have been talking about obviously will have effects on sexual behavior in marriage. The continuing trend toward greater sexual freedom for both men and women, increasing acceptance of premarital sexual experience, and the increased control over fertility offered the female by the Pill, all are altering the traditional ways in which men and women relate to each other sexually. Women are now permitted to be the initiators of cross-sexual interaction and do not have to wait demurely to be pursued. Men no longer are expected always to be tough and authoritative, and the old "macho" figure of the stupendously virile male is often subject to ridicule.

Unfortunately, we know little about the relationship between sex roles and sex behavior, and much of the research on sexual behavior that has been conducted in recent decades has been performed by physicians and is sociologically inadequate, such as the clinical findings of Masters and Johnson. The relation between sex roles and sexual behavior deserves a great deal more sociological attention than it has thus far received. It is likely to get it in the near future as the problems for sex behavior that alterations in sex roles are producing become more and more apparent. The so-called sexual revolution is more than an increase in the frequency and freedom of sexual intercourse; sexual attitudes and behavior affect much more than the prevailing norms in a society. They are the consequences of many years of learning and experience, and changes in the direction of sexual equality involve problems at the interpersonal level not likely to appear in other forms of social interaction between men and women. The new ideas are welcomed by some, but many others have difficulty reconciling them with the traditional sexual attitudes and behavior expectations they learned while growing up. Traditional social conditioning, after all, prepared both sexes to feel, think, and act

in accord with sexual scripts that are not based on ideas of sexual equality.

The traditional gender roles in sexual activity, for example, are those of hunter and hunted. The sexually aggressive, dominant, almost rapacious male is supposed to pursue and subdue the passive, submissive female. She may permit him to chase her until she decides it is time to let him catch her, but the male is supposed to initiate the pursuit and the female to do nothing active or forward to encourage it. (It's OK to bat your eyes and look breathless at his approach, but you don't imitate Lauren Bacall in *To Have and Have Not*, leaning against Bogart's door jamb and saying in a sultry voice, "If you want anything, just whistle.")

For persons whose gender identities have been molded by role expectations such as these, what will be the effect on sexual performance, for example, of greater male passiveness and female assertiveness or aggression? If women are supposed to be virginal upon marriage, how many men—regardless of their own sexual experience—will be able totally to ignore it if their brides have sexual histories as long and as erotic as their own? What is the typical effect of female sexual initiation or assertiveness on male *potency*, the simple ability to have an erection? These are profoundly important questions which have yet to be answered for the public at large.

Marital Disruption and Remarriage

Marriages may be disrupted through divorce or dissolution, desertion, or death. Desertion among Americans is difficult to quantify because it rarely gets into vital statistics records and is often followed by divorce. Marriages actually disrupted by desertion, therefore, may appear statistically *as* divorces. In the past, the male partner was typically the one who deserted, but the practice seems now to be growing among females as well.

Death of a partner will sooner or later interrupt any marriage not previously broken in other ways, of course, and we will treat widowhood as a separate topic of discussion.

Many marriages are disrupted by divorce, and we will discuss that phenomenon below, but it is worthwhile here to note the technical distinction

"*It was thanks to you that my first marriage was a flop and it's thanks to you that this one's a flop!*"

© Punch (Rothco).

Divorcing couples usually blame each other, not social factors. Research on divorce, however, shows the strong influence of a number of social variables.

divorce: a legal action by a plaintiff against a defendant seeking the termination of a marriage as a remedy for a wrongful condition.

marital dissolution (no-fault divorce): a legal action through which a marriage may be terminated without legal sanction against either party.

Figure 12-3
The divorce trend in the United States.

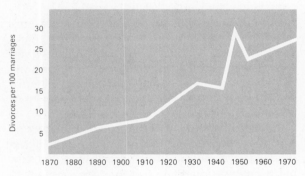

between **divorce** and **marital dissolution**. A *divorce* is a legal transaction, with a plaintiff making a complaint against a defendant and seeking a divorce as a remedy. One party must be shown to be at fault for the divorce to be granted and may be required to make restitution for "guilt" or misbehavior. *Marital dissolution*, or no-fault divorce, is also a legal transaction. But in states such as California and Washington, where no-fault laws are in effect, there is neither plaintiff nor defendant, but merely two married people who wish to be made unmarried once again and petition the court to terminate their marriage. Traditional divorce proceedings remain possible in these states, of course, for those who cannot separate amicably.

For many people, marital disruption, regardless of cause, is often followed by remarriage. This is a significant phenomenon in its own right among Americans, and we will discuss it separately below.

Divorce

The American divorce rate is higher than that of any other major nation in the world except the

Soviet Union, and is still climbing. There are more than 16 million divorced people in the population, about 8 percent of the total, and three or four divorces occur each year for every ten marriages performed. Figure 12-3 shows the trend in divorces since the early part of the century.

It seems reasonable to believe that few people get married with any expectation that the marriage will end with divorce. It may be, however, that today more people than previously marry with the reservation in their minds that if the marriage doesn't work out, it can be escaped. There are no complete explanations for the high divorce rate in the United States, but the greater social acceptability of divorce that now exists may well have something to do with it. Divorce was once a scandal and was viewed as reflecting badly upon the persons involved. It is today accepted, if not as matter of fact, at least as a misfortune that could happen to anyone.

Most people today still tend to look on divorce as a matter of personal failure on the part of the individuals involved, stressing psychological tensions between marriage partners: they fell out of love; they couldn't get along; she was too aggressive; he was too stingy. And the kinds of complaints that divorcing people make about each other support such an essentially psychological interpretation. In a study of divorcing couples in Cleveland, for example, George Levinger found them citing the following reasons for seeking the action: physical and verbal abuse, financial problems, drinking, neglect of home or children, mental cruelty, in-law trouble, excessive demands, infidelity or sexual incompatibility, and lack of love.[22]

Sociological studies of divorce, however, tend to use somewhat different categories of explanation. Causes frequently cited include: changes in divorce laws making divorce easier to obtain, changes in financial support for divorce action, religious identity or practice, social class and mobility, ethnicity and race, education, age at marriage and dissolution, length of engagement, rural-urban differences, economics, change in sex norms and roles and expectations for marriage, and number and age of children.

What are we to make of the apparent inconsistency between these sociological findings and the reasons people often give for seeking divorce? To

be sure, the reasons given by divorcing couples in the Levinger study make sense, but this does not mean that sociocultural factors are not involved. The social factors that influence divorce are quite real and have been observed with dismal regularity. What accounts for the seeming inconsistency is that people do not experience social factors *directly*. Responding to the stresses introduced into the marital relationship by such factors, they develop strong personal *feelings* about them. Thus, when asked directly why they want a divorce, they report their feelings as the *cause* of the breakup.

A lower-middle-class wife, for example, might report distress over her lower-class husband's drinking and gambling and consequent "neglect" of herself and the children as the reason for seeking divorce. Her husband, in turn, might regard himself as having been a reasonably dutiful mate whose nagging spouse would not permit him to enjoy his usual male prerogatives. A sociologist observing the situation would see the cause of the divorce as being neither neglect nor nagging, but inconsistent expectations for marital role behavior based on different, class-related value systems. The two lists of factors, in other words, are merely the objective and subjective sides of the same coin.

Much marital behavior is a matter of having learned to think, feel, and behave according to sociocultural patterns. But in a heterogeneous society like the United States, not everyone an individual meets will be socialized to the same norms and values. While marital homogamy still operates, as we saw earlier, it is far less powerful than it was fifty years ago. We can, thus, continue to expect that millions of Americans will find their marriages insufferable and seek to end them.

Current trends in the society make divorce far more acceptable and easier to obtain than it ever was in the past. What effects this situation will have on the family of the future cannot be clearly discerned today. Many commentators have viewed the high American divorce rate with dismay and foretold the destruction of the family as a result, but no clear trends in that direction are visible. People still marry—and remarry—in the United States at very high rates. *Marriage*, at least, is still in good repute. *The family* is a different phenomenon, however, and only the future will tell us what is in store for it.

Widowhood

Today, about 11 million Americans are widows or widowers (about 5 percent of the total population and about 14 percent of the population fourteen years old or older). Eighty percent of these are women. The very high proportion of women among the widowed is accounted for by several facts of the human life-cycle and social custom. Males have higher mortality rates at almost all ages, so that women typically outlive men of the same age. Widowed women are also less likely to remarry than are widowers. Additionally, in the United States women usually marry men somewhat older than themselves, thus increasing their chance of becoming widows. If this practice remains common (and there is no reason to believe it will not), and if longevity continues to increase among the population at large, we can expect the proportion of widowed women to increase in the future, particularly as the population "bulge" of twenty-five to forty-year-olds ages.

Widowhood in the United States is thus essentially a female problem. Both because of the highly unbalanced sex ratio among the widowed and because of the status of women in American society, it is an unfortunate, and often distressing, social status. Simply making a living, for example, is likely to be much harder for the widowed female than the widowed male. Insurance, if any, is likely to be inadequate for years of continued survival, and there are always funeral expenses to be paid. The widow, unless she is one of the relatively small minority who have always worked, may find herself unemployable through lack of experience or job skills, through obsolescence, or simply because of age. If the widowed woman also has children to support and educate, her problems are compounded.

For the widowed of either sex, loneliness and social isolation are severe and common problems. Given the disappearance from the American scene of the extended family, the children may have left home years ago, perhaps moving to distant locations. If the individual is a city-dweller (as most Americans are), he or she may have few friends or relatives in the vicinity. For women, particularly, being middle-aged or elderly and once again single is socially difficult. Even if a widow has friends

California Split, in Style

LOS ANGELES [AP] — Everyone had such a good time at the Smiths' wedding 15 months ago, the couple decided to invite all the guests back for another party.

The champagne they received as a wedding gift was opened, and the best man was there to perform the honors—this time removing the wedding bands from the fingers of Ed and Mari Smith.

Ed and Mari filed divorce papers on July 9. Under California law, the final decree will be issued in six months.

The couple hugged—Ed called her "Babe" and Mari called him "Honey"—and everybody cheered.

Invitations to Saturday night's party read: "You are cordially invited to join us in celebrating our divorce."

Ed, 44, said the party was thrown "to show our friends that Mari and I are not mad at each other."

Mari, 24, agreed: "Ed and I are still buddies. Ed's awfully nice, but we just couldn't stand living together."

The party was Ed's idea, Mari said.

"Everybody thinks that divorce is some kind of terrible thing, like a funeral. But if two people are not getting along, it is good to find out quickly. Then it's nice to celebrate," she explained.

Chicago Tribune, July 15, 1975. Reprinted by permission of AP Newsfeatures.

Divorce is far more acceptable in American society today than ever before.

Loneliness and isolation are common in widowhood.

nearby, if they are still married, an extra woman friend around is often a social liability, whereas an extra man at a party or recreational event is usually welcome. Further, women are not customarily expected to travel, play golf, and so on, alone, which men are free to do. (Most American social phenomena are built on the assumption that the participants will be either couples or single males.)

Finally, widowhood for either sex involves major demands for resocialization. The problems of living alone, when one has spent years as a family member or as half of a married couple, are severe. Some, as we have seen, are essentially practical. But the subjective stresses in becoming an "I" again, after perhaps decades of being a part of a "we," are immense. Our heterogeneous, footloose, youth-oriented society does not do much to relieve them. We may expect greater attention to be paid to the widowed in coming years, as the majority age group in the population alters from young to "old." But until that time, widowhood will continue to be, for most Americans, an undesirable and unhappy social condition.

Remarriage

The proportion of remarriages is increasing, as you can see in Figure 12-4. The latest U.S. Census figures indicate that of Americans who ever married, about 14 percent of whites and 21 percent of blacks have been married two or more times.[23]

Remarriage of the widowed has a greater statistical chance of succeeding than the remarriage of the previously divorced. Presumably, the reason for this is that people who have remained married until the death of a spouse are better able to adjust to the marital state than are the previously divorced, and they therefore have greater chances for success in second marriages.

People who have been divorced tend to remarry at a *higher* rate than either single or widowed persons of similar ages.[24] As we might expect from those who were unable to maintain a satisfactory first marital relationship, the remarriages of formerly divorced persons have a higher failure rate than do first marriages, but most second marriages do endure. Chances for a successful second marriage are considerably reduced, however, when both partners to it have been previously divorced.

Remarriage after divorce is also class-related. Lower-class persons have the highest divorce rates for both first and second marriages, while remarriages among the upper class have almost as high a chance of succeeding as first marriages do.[25]

It is possible to conclude from the facts discussed here that the American marital system is clearly one of serial monogamy, and that the pattern of divorce and remarriage, while a minority practice, is completely accepted in American life. Divorced people are no longer considered odd or immoral. It is probably also permissible to guess from the higher rates of failure among second marriages that a statistical minority of people do have personal characteristics that make them unsuited for stable marital relationships. Two-or-more-time losers in marriage should probably look to themselves for the explanation of their troubles. But the significantly higher rates of marital failure among the lower class also suggest that the conditions of life do make a difference in the probability of success in marriage. Poverty and lack of education have a destructive effect on marriage and family relationships as they do on so much else.

Alternatives to Traditional Marriage and Family Systems

In nineteenth-century America, there were few alternatives to life within the traditional marriage and family system. Most people got married, some starting households of their own and some living in extended families in or adjacent to their parents' households. Women who did not marry remained in their fathers' homes, often assuming headship of any remaining family upon the death of their parents. Only men who did not marry were free to "go it alone." These alternatives to traditional marriage, of course, remain open to Americans, but recent years have seen changes both in the definition of remaining single (the Old Maid has become the Bachelor Girl) and in the creation of other possibilities.

Remaining Single

The most common alternative to marriage for millions of Americans is not getting or not staying married—remaining single. The greatest number of those remaining single live alone. Others choose living together as a couple, and a few experiment with communal living. Probably all single persons suffer some social handicaps, and even discrimination, in a society in which marriage is *the* socially expected and "desirable" state. The tax laws, for example, discriminate severely against single persons for their choice of marital status.

Living alone   Living alone is a common life-style, but it has not been much studied by sociologists, and we know little about it in a technical sense. For some people, clearly, living alone is a matter of choice and preference. For others, it may be a result of lack of alternatives and a condition of loneliness and despair. And the definitions and reactions of other people to the single person who lives alone may have considerable effect on the individual. The young single woman living alone is often regarded by males as sexually available by definition, while the single man living alone may be perceived as either sexually rapacious or potentially homosexual.

Living together   Staying single does not always mean staying alone. Expecially, although not exclusively, among young people today, there is developing a hard-to-measure pattern of "living together." It could loosely be called common-law marriage, but that dull label is rarely attached, either by the law or the participants. More colorful labels like "shacking up" are rejected as derogatory, and "trial marriage" suggests a potential for permanence that many wish to avoid. Perhaps a relationship designed to last only so long as it works out is the best description we can offer at this time. "Living-together-for-awhile" is beginning to be studied by marriage and family researchers, but little is actually known of it as yet. What data do exist suggest that many young couples who practice it eventually marry.

Interestingly enough, living together is also becoming common among the elderly who are widowed, apparently as an adjustment to Social Security regulations that have the effect of reducing the total income of elderly pensioners if they remarry.

Figure 12-4
The increasing proportion of remarriages.

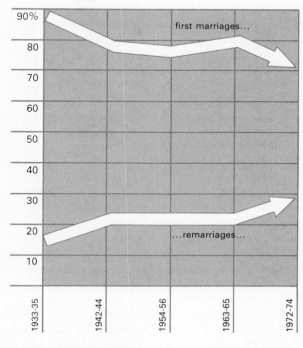

Communal living A third alternative to traditional marriage is represented by a variety of forms of communal living. Living together with others has for some time been a common experience for college students, but what seems to be new in recent years is that sexual behavior is now an accepted part of the interactional patterns of some of these collective households. Although some such experiments have a utopian plan to follow, probably most lack sophisticated intellectual and philosophical direction. Some are built around avoidance of the group structures for work or decision making that sociologists usually regard as essential for group functioning and survival.

The popular press has made two rather different kinds of commune familiar to the public: the rural and the urban. The rural commune, popularly associated with the hippie phenomenon of the 1960s, is in some senses a return to the family farm of the last century, with various members of the group taking responsibility for the handicrafts and agricultural chores associated with rural life in that period. Often associated with consumerism, environmental protection, and so forth, the rural commune movement also contributed to, or was associated with, the popularity of such phenomena as the *Whole Earth Catalogue* and the "return to nature" movement. Many such communes practice organic farming, eat only health foods, and in general, try to stay close to the land.

The urban commune or collective often shares a single multiple dwelling—a large house or apartment building—while many or all of its members are employed in conventional jobs or child care and other domestic duties. Sometimes made up in whole or in part of parents without partners, such arrangements ease the financial burden any single person has in maintaining a separate household as well as providing companionship, security, emotional support, and an efficient division of labor.

"Self-Realization" in Marriage

Recently, a new social movement seeking alternatives to traditional marriage has evolved, directed at individuals who are already married. Often the emphasis is on "self-realization" in marriage. Marriage manuals of this persuasion not only provide instructions on sexual behavior but also offer advice on how to change traditional marriage patterns to make the marital experience more gratifying and enjoyable. Almost all such books ask the reader to think in terms of personal liberation from the traditional sociosexual norms of society. Much of the focus is on discovering *emotional intimacy*, said to be denied by the traditional patterns of society. Part of the critique is also directed against traditional sexual restraints; extramarital sex is sometimes encouraged if it offers the promise of being "meaningful." The best-selling book *Open Marriage*, by Nena and George O'Neil, is a good example of this trend in thinking about marriage.[26] But, of course, what people think and what they do are not always the same. Idealized images do not always work out in practice. (Newspapers report that the authors of *Open Marriage* are now divorced.)

Summary

The *family* is the basic social institution of all societies. It involves a social and cultural system, a set of norms for individual behavior, and a network of social roles for human activity. It is specifically defined as an adult male and female living, together with any offspring, in a more or less permanent relationship of the kind approved by their society as "marriage." The family is a universal institution; there are no societies where it is not recognized, honored, and practiced, and it may be that there could be none. So far as we know, none has ever existed. The family is based on *marriage*, a stable relationship between opposite sexes that, among other things, legitimates offspring.

The family serves a variety of social functions in all societies: (1) *member replacement and physical maintenance*, (2) *care and socialization of children*, (3) *regulation of sexual behavior*, (4) *transmission of social status* to offspring, (5) *economic activity*, (6) *provision of social-emotional support* to individuals; and (7) *linkage between other social institutions*.

Families may be organized in an amazing variety of ways. One major distinction is between nuclear and extended families: the *nuclear family* is the kinship unit consisting of only the married couple and their offspring; the *extended family* includes the nuclear family plus all other kin that live with them.

The *form of marriage* is another widely varied aspect of family organization. The basic forms are *monogamy* and *polygamy*. Possible variations of the first are *serial monogamy* and *straight-life monogamy*. Polygamy may take the form of *polygyny*, *polyandry*, or *group marriage*.

The *division of power and authority* in the family between male and female is often the basis of aspects of family organization. In many societies, this is tied to kinship structure by practices relating to the tracing of relationship. Descent can be traced through the male or female lines (*patriliny* or *matriliny*), or it can be traced through both, the *bilateral* system we use in the United States.

Mate selection, sociologically considered, operates through two processes: preferential mating and marriage arrangement. *Preferential* mating refers to societal norms defining possible and desirable marriage partners, and often involves norms prohibiting marriages between some categories of people as well: rules for *endogamy* and *exogamy*. Such rules reflect social definitions of kinship (as in the *incest taboo*) and kin relations (what groups are defined as kin). In the United States, for example, "most desirable" partners will be seen as being *homogamous* (alike) in race, religion, and social class. Marriages between members of different races are disapproved but not forbidden, while "marriages" between persons of the same sex are not legally recognized and are strongly disapproved.

Marriage arrangement refers to the process through which two individuals actually come to be married—including the participation of others in the nuptial process. In many societies, the decision is made by parents or other kin, and the wishes of the couple, or considerations of romantic love, are secondary or even irrelevant. Arrangement may also be the consequence of purely social phenomena, however, as in the United States, and reflect norms and practices regarding such *social factors* as age, race, religion, residence, education, social class, occupation, and so forth. *Psychological factors* also operate in mate selection in "free-choice-of-mate" systems like that of the United States, and include as major elements *complementarity* of needs and personality traits and the whole cultural complex called *romantic love*.

Once a marriage has been consummated, what happens in it afterward is deeply influenced by *marital roles* and the role conceptions that husband and wife have learned while they were growing up. What constitutes being or acting like a husband or wife is a matter of individual socialization and is deeply affected by social change as well. In the United States at the present time, marital role definitions that have been conventional for a long time are undergoing serious change. Perhaps the most fundamental of these changes regards *marital authority and decision making*. The older norms of male dominance in marriage are altering in many areas of American life as women become better-educated, economically more active, and politically more aware. The patriarchal family is on the decline.

Whether or not change in marital roles can be adapted to is in part a function of the *responsibility* with which couples play their roles. If both partners recognize the complementarity of marital roles, the necessity for some division of labor, and are committed to maintaining the marriage, change in conventional role behavior may require nothing more than agreement. Attitudes toward such changes may become especially important in allotting responsibilities for *child care*.

Another set of problems highlighted by the change in marital roles is the relationship between *marital roles*, the *social and occupational statuses* of both partners, and *sexual behavior*. As the social definitions of what it means to be male or female change, such alterations have obvious implications for the ways in which people play out the roles of husband or wife. Such role changes also influence specific *sexual behavior*. Sexual behavior expectations and patterns are deeply conditioned, and are inextricably interwoven with sexual or gender identity. As standards of sexual behavior change in the society as a whole, their application in marriage and the family must alter as well.

Study of marriage and the family is incomplete without consideration of the phenomena of *marital disruption*, through divorce or dissolution, desertion, or death, and *remarriage*, although these subjects have not received the sociological attention they deserve. A variety of social factors have been shown to influence *divorce*, although these may appear to the couples in question to be psychological or behavioral rather than social. Discordant role expectations are often a factor. Remarriages, except those contracted by people who have been widowed, are less stable than original marriages, but survival rates vary with social factors such as class and previous experience with divorce. *Widowhood* is a problem for both sexes, but particularly for women, who constitute 80 percent of the widowed.

Alternatives to traditional marriage include *living alone, living together, communal living*, and the search for *self-realization in marriage*. While remaining single and living alone is the most common, it has been little studied. "Living together" has only recently come to be more or less accepted as an alternative to traditional marriage, and still seems to be most practiced by the very young adult and the very old under some circumstances. For the young, it often consists of a period of experiment before traditional marriage. Communal living, while not at all new, has only recently come to be practiced in the United States between the sexes. Some sociological information is being generated on this practice now, but it is too early to generalize about it. The movement for "self-realization" in marriage is also new, and it remains to be seen whether it is a true alternative to traditional marriage.

Review Questions

1. Based on your general comprehension from media coverage in addition to the material in the chapter, explain the position taken by the women's liberation movement. What changes do they advocate for women? For men? What would you personally predict will be the future implications of the movement?

2. Explain and describe changing bases for marriage, from that of economics to one stressing companionship. How does each form fit in with the specific type of culture in its society? What are the advantages and the disadvantages of each form?

3. The chapter covered several ways in which American marriage is vastly different from that in many other cultures. List at least two of these and explain.

4. Discuss the various functions of the modern family. Which, if any, seem to be increasing in importance? Declining in importance? Why? Which function strikes you as the most necessary? Why?

5. Under what conditions is divorce more common? In other words, what specific attributes of a person's life predispose him or her to divorce? Why is divorce more probable under these conditions?

Suggestions for Research

1. Schedule an interview with a marriage counselor; for your convenience, you may have to look no further than the child development and family living or related departments at your university. Ask the counselor to acquaint you with his or her profession. What is a typical problem plaguing many clients? What type of therapy or approach is usually most successful? How effective is marriage counseling? Why? You may want to broaden your perspective by interviewing more than one counselor or a local member of the clergy who deals with similar situations.

2. *MS.* magazine is generally recognized as an important voice for modern feminists. Examine several issues of this publication and organize your observations and reactions in a paper. You may want to include imagery through photographs. What appear to be main themes running through the different issues? Give attention to both content and style. What is your evaluation of this magazine?

3. Sociologists have devoted considerable study to the effects of social class upon the marriage institution. Explore this relationship. In general, how do typical lower-class marriages and families differ from those in the middle classes? Consider such variables as authority, sex roles, occupations, education, divorce, socialization of children, family size, and overall happiness.

4. Interview a couple living together without marriage. If you do not personally know such persons, ask your friends and classmates if they can suggest anyone. In your interview(s), discuss such things as why the couple decided to live together, why they preferred not to marry, what they plan for the future, and how they feel their relationship would be different if they were married. You may want to compare your observations with those of married couples you know. After organizing your findings, would you be interested in such a pattern of living for yourself? Would you recommend it to your friends? Why or why not?

CHAPTER 13
EDUCATION

Nineteen fifty-four was a landmark year in the history of education in the United States. That was the year the Supreme Court ruled in *Brown* v. *Board of Education,* a decision hailed by many as the greatest step forward by black Americans since the Emancipation Proclamation. The issue in the Brown case was whether "separate but equal" facilities could be maintained by public funds for the purpose of segregating black and white children in the public schools. In a unanimous opinion, reversing a ruling made more than half a century before, the Court held that segregated facilities were discriminatory and, therefore, unconstitutional. In that and subsequent rulings, the public school systems of the United States were ordered to insure that students would not be assigned to schools on the basis of race.

But racial segregation in the schools was not, and is not, a simple issue. The public schools in many southern states had been segregated by law. In many areas in the North, racial segregation in the schools was almost as complete, reflecting the existence of the neighborhood school system operating in communities with overwhelmingly segregated neighborhoods. Southern schools, thus, had been segregated de jure (by law), while northern schools were segregated de facto (as a matter of fact or circumstance). Later court decisions also held de facto segregation to be unconstitutional, and the schools were required to institute plans to achieve "racial balance." In most instances, school systems faced with the problem elected to meet it by *busing,* the practice of transporting some students from largely black or largely white schools by bus to attend schools "overbalanced" in favor of the other race, thereby achieving a more equal mixture.

The various Supreme Court rulings on these issues have created conflicts among several fundamental American educational values. The ideas of equal opportunity and the "melting pot" approach to culture, for instance, are inconsistent with racial discrimination and segregation as reflected in the neighborhood school. Not surprisingly, these value conflicts have produced considerable hostility and frustration among the parents of schoolchildren, both black and white. Many black parents have supported busing as a means of securing education of higher quality for their children than that perceived as possible in ghetto schools, although some have resisted having their offspring removed from the neighborhood to strange locations and white peer groups. Many white parents have resisted busing out of fear for their children's safety if they were removed to "poor" neighborhoods or from fear of declining educational standards if large numbers of black children appeared in "their" schools. And simple racism itself has probably never been absent from the dispute.

In 1974, the Supreme Court ruled that, except in special cases, students could not be transported from one school *district* to another in order to achieve racial balance, although busing within a single district was still upheld. Whether or not that was the Court's intention, this decision appeared to have the effect of limiting busing to urban centers, the inner cities of the great metropolitan areas, from which many whites had already fled. Thus, the predominantly white and more affluent suburbs surrounding the cities, with their separate school systems, seemed to be relieved of any responsibility for helping the cities integrate their public school systems. The urban schools, already suffering from lack of funds and deteriorating facilities, were apparently left to face the full burden of the problem, while the continuing white exodus to the suburbs went on reducing the number of white children remaining.

If this trend were to continue, many urban schools would eventually have largely black student populations again, while the suburban schools remained largely white. But in 1975, the Court once more ruled (by refusing to alter lower-court decisions) that interdistrict busing was permissible. The effects on racial integration in public education remain to be seen, and further court tests will surely follow, for the Supreme Court itself has so far not taken a definitive stand. Whether, in the face of strong, continuing resistance, school districts will be able to continue to bus, whether whites will permit their children to remain enrolled in public schools where busing is extensive, and even what the long-range consequences of forced integration are for the educational process, are questions that remain unanswered. Behind them

stands an even larger one: Are the schools the appropriate agency with which to try to solve one of America's most pressing and painful domestic problems?

The busing problem outlined above dramatically highlights the importance of the educational institution in American society. It also touches on a number of themes we will explore in this chapter. Most basically, the busing controversy involves the question of what education is or can achieve, a question on which no firm agreement has yet been reached. Further, it reflects questions about the *functions* of schools. One of the functions of schools in all societies is to help achieve socialization, and clearly how children will be socialized is influenced by whether they attend segregated or integrated schools. Moreover, specific functions American schools have been asked to perform, such as to insure equality of opportunity, are clearly related to the type of education offered in segregated and integrated schools.

Even the *organization* of American schools has been affected by the busing controversy. The United States has always had public and private schools at every level, but certainly private institutions in some areas of the country have benefited from, or even been created in response to, white fears of integration in the public schools. And in part, the busing problem results from the very structure of public education in the United States, with its emphasis on community control and neighborhood schools. In this chapter, we will examine these and other issues relative to schools in general and in the United States in particular.

What Is Education?

Education is an extremely difficult term to define precisely. Indeed, different views about education are at the heart of the problems that schools in many societies face. Education does, of course, imply learning of one sort or another, but exactly what kinds of learning qualify as education is a matter of some debate, as we shall see throughout the chapter.

The Educational Institution

Whatever its concept of education, every society has some form of **educational institution**: the culturally standardized forms of *deliberate* instruction. In modern societies, this instruction is largely, though not entirely, performed by the formal bodies we call schools, and in this chapter we will concern ourselves only with education as it is enacted by the schools. But we should note that in preindustrial societies without formal schools, there are certain standardized methods of instruction, as when fathers teach their male children how to skin an animal. Indeed, even in modern societies, some education is carried on outside the schools; children, for instance, learn certain expectations about the role of a child in their culture largely from their parents.

Education in the Schools

Let us return to the schools and explore some different concepts of what *education* in the schools means. Schools are institutions created by many social systems in order to provide a specific, planned, and graded kind of learning. They have an identifiable structure, with relatively permanent roles, and a number of socially approved functions. But precisely what education in the schools is or should be is not by any means completely clear.

To some, education is something a person has after receiving passing grades in the courses required for a particular certificate, diploma, or degree. If, however, people complete all of their courses, but remember little of what they studied and apply still less to their daily lives, can we still say they are educated? Has their thinking been changed in a permanent way as the result of their experience?

Education has also been defined as preparation for worthwhile, practical, or financially rewarding work. A physician probably fits this concept of an educated person, but this definition also has its limitations. Take an extreme example to illustrate the problem. Consider the doctors in Nazi concentration camps who conducted experiments using prisoners in the same way as mice and guinea pigs are traditionally used. It seems safe to assume these doctors were technically compe-

tent: they had passed their courses, were awarded degrees—and they were murderers. Do we really wish to refer to them as educated?

These questions about the meaning of education in the schools are not rhetorical. They have always been subjects of considerable debate in the United States, and the rather different answers that people have given to them have greatly influenced, and continue to influence, the institution of education in America. We will see some of how this has worked below.

Because people disagree about the definition and purpose of education, it is difficult to evaluate the effectiveness of the schools. They could be judged by the number of people who receive diplomas or degrees. Such data would provide an indication of how many students pass through these institutions. Researchers could also examine the schools by looking at the kind of work obtained by their graduates. They would then have an indication of the vocational implications of education. But this information would hardly be sufficient to make judgments about the overall impact of formal education. All of these data are useful, but it seems clear that other factors must be included in the analysis.

When we try to identify these additional elements, we get to the heart of the problem of analyzing schools. We must begin to make an evaluation of the kind of people they are trying to create and the way in which they would like students to live. In the process, we run the risk of controversy, because these kinds of questions usually require responses that are ideological, philosophical, or subjective. Short of this, we are faced with a rather sterile analysis of degrees, occupations, and income levels that cannot completely describe the reality of schools.

Over the years, educators, psychologists, and sociologists have devised many definitions of the nature and purpose of schools. Here we will examine some of the major viewpoints that have emerged. Robert Hutchins suggests that "the aim of an educational system is the same in every age and in every society where such a system can exist: It is to improve man as man."[1] On this basis, he reasons: "If the object of education is the improvement of man, then any system of education that is without values is a contradiction in terms. A system that seeks bad values is bad. A system that denies the existence of values denies the possibility of education."[2] Those who agree with Hutchins are, according to Theodore Brameld's terminology, "perennialists." They believe education should deal with universal concepts such as truth, beauty, justice, and goodness. This view has been criticized for failing to address the more immediate, or day-to-day, problems of both students and their societies.

Brameld calls the great American educator John Dewey a *progressivist.* Dewey emphasized the importance of method, as opposed to content. He viewed education as a vehicle for developing an inquisitive and flexible mind that seeks solutions to everyday problems using the scientific method of inquiry. This view has been criticized for failing to identify the goals toward which intellectual energies are to be directed. In other words, it lacks, according to its opponents, a commitment to some vision of the future or of what constitutes a "good" society.

Brameld, a *reconstructionist,* believes that education should attempt to restructure society with specific goals in mind. He argues that "education in its comprehensive sense should become the co-partner of politics—the politics of comprehending and implementing popular government on a world-wide scale."[3] Critics of this definition of education point out that it is difficult to get broad agreement on how to proceed toward the goals Brameld has identified. In addition, there are serious doubts about the schools' ability to exert the influence Brameld envisions. Educational organizations are products of their cultures, and as a result, it is difficult for them to initiate social changes.

Although these men spent much of their lives in schools, they have noticeably different views of education. As we continue our discussion, it will be helpful to remember some of the uncertainties associated with the definition of formal education and, therefore, with educational organizations.

The Functions of Formal Education

The evolution of formal educational institutions over the past hundred years is best explained by the growth of technology, bureaucracies, and mass

educational institution: the culturally standardized forms for *deliberate* instruction. The concept includes all organized types of learning, whether or not these are embodied in formal organizations like schools.

While formal education has become immensely important in industrialized societies, a great deal of "extracurricular" educating still goes on informally in the family.

production. The transition from nomadic or agrarian societies means that the more informal, traditional methods of socialization are no longer adequate. No longer can family and friends teach the young the skills they need to deal with the complex social arrangements required by industrialization. In addition to the vocational skills required, a basic change in life-style is necessary before the new system will function efficiently. For example, instead of measuring time in days or seasons, as agrarian societies do, industrial societies must use precise units of hours and minutes. Everyone on the seven o'clock shift at the General Motors factory begins work at the same time.

The division of labor is more sophisticated in industrialized societies. No longer do all members of one sex or age group perform essentially the same tasks. Rather than assuming general roles associated with providing food and shelter and child rearing, people must take on the more specialized and segmented roles that accompany increased social complexity, such as Certified Public Accountant.

Not only is the family unable to transmit all of this knowledge, but the schools require more and more time to prepare the young for adult roles. Because nearly all contemporary schools have ties to industrialization and the complex social relationships it inevitably entails, they tend to fulfill similar functions. In fact, educational institutions throughout the world are remarkably similar considering the variety of social, economic, and political environments within which they operate. There are at least four functions that are common to all formal school systems: *socialization, social integration through cultural transmission, vocational sorting,* and the achievement or denial of *social mobility.*

Socialization

Educational institutions provide a formal setting within which socially desired skills, values, and attitudes are instilled. In other words, socialization, as it takes place in the schools, includes not only the transmission of technical knowledge but also the teaching of moral and political principles. In a relatively stable society, this function usually enjoys wide public support. But in societies experiencing significant change or instability, it is likely to

be controversial. Conflict may be generated by economic or political factors as well as changes in norms and values.

Schools in developing countries like Uganda, Kenya, Malawi, and Zambia are currently subjected to criticism for their role in changing traditional patterns of life. These societies are beginning to adopt some of the organizational patterns of industrialized societies. An African graduate student describes how many inhabitants feel about people who have been socialized in the schools:

They say, you have taken your child to school, you have educated him, and he is not improved. They also complain of lack of respect. They also distrust the position the educated man occupies between the European and his own people. The educated man is often the interpreter, the liaison, and is easily bribed. They associate the educated with cunning, with people who swindle in organizations, with people who know how to manipulate books. This comes from experience. They feel that we are an appendage to the Whites and would go with the Whites.[4]

Aside from the racial implications, which may not be common to all societies, the student is describing breaks with cultural tradition. And when these occur, the schools are likely to be criticized.

In industrialized societies, controversy in the schools usually centers on changes in life-styles created by the maturation of industrialization rather than its emergence. Thus, schools are rarely criticized for their career-oriented curricula, but there is recurring conflict over nonvocational issues like sex education, sex-role stereotyping, religious beliefs, and political philosophy. Parental and church groups occasionally mount substantial opposition to courses dealing with human sexuality. Atheists and members of unusual religious sects are often not considered competent teachers. (About fifteen years ago, the Texas state legislature very nearly passed a bill requiring teachers to sign an oath affirming their belief in a "supreme being" before they could be employed in state-supported schools.) Faculty who advocate unpopular political ideologies, values, or life-styles have, on occasion, been hounded out of educational systems. And periodically, there are attempts to have certain books banned from the classroom, usually books that some consider immoral or politically dangerous. At the root of these protests is an objection to how the schools are socializing students. The intensity of the hostility indicates the importance of this function.

How the schools transmit knowledge and shape values and attitudes is also important. Students are influenced by both the *formal* and the *informal* school curricula. The **formal curriculum** is composed of the content of the various subjects taught—history, biology, mathematics, and so on. Here the impact on the student is obvious and easily understood. The **informal curriculum** consists of the values, norms, and social relationships that are encouraged by the schools. Consciously or not, the schools try to teach the students to obey rules and individuals in positions of authority, to follow a predictable routine, and to be evaluated by impersonal criteria. This process has been referred to as the development of a "bureaucratic personality" or an "organizational mentality."

School personnel have the power to reward students who respond "appropriately" to both curricula with high grades and personal privileges. These students may be designated class leaders and be allowed to participate in valued extracurricular activities. Conversely, students who do not respond "appropriately" to the school environment may be assigned extra work, be made to remain after normal hours, or be disciplined in other ways. To school personnel, these students are "problems," and they are normally assigned low grades and status. Students who are particularly resistant to the socialization process may be expelled from the schools. They are "failures"—they have not responded to the demands of their culture as reflected in educational institutions.

Although most people support both the formal and informal socialization that occurs in the schools, a minority question the wisdom of the schools' influence on socialization. Some fear that those aspects of the informal curriculum that teach obedience and the acceptance of routine will hamper the students' intellectual independence and curiosity. As a result, these critics say, societies may be deprived of the advantages of critical analysis and innovative thinking. Interestingly, some of the most outstanding individuals of our time have not done well in school. Winston Churchill was considered extremely dull by his secondary school teachers; and Albert Einstein

formal curriculum: the curriculum composed of the content of the various subjects taught, e.g., history, biology, mathematics.

informal curriculum: the curriculum which consists of the values, norms, and social relationships that are encouraged by the schools.

once recalled that he had had great difficulty learning arithmetic and, as an adult, was still not good at it. And we probably all know successful and capable individuals who have not gone to college. But these exceptions do not, of course, prove that the schools are useless.

Should schools train students to fit into the existing social structure or help them develop the capacity to evaluate it and develop alternatives to the status quo? How much of what you have come to believe about the nature of your society is a reflection of your school experience? What is the distinction between education, socialization, and indoctrination?

Social Integration and Cultural Transmission

One of the aims of socialization in many schools is the social integration of students from varying linguistic, racial, ethnic, and socioeconomic groups into the common culture. This process includes the teaching of a common language and instruction in the skills necessary to participate in the economic and political life of the society. In addition, the schools attempt to develop a broad sense of national identity and loyalty. Countries such as the Soviet Union and the People's Republic of China are composed of many different ethnic and racial groups. These subcultures frequently have their own language, customs, and values. The schools attempt to forge a national identity out of this cultural diversity. Switzerland faces a similar situation, having at least three major language and cultural groups within its borders. Schools in American urban centers, especially around the turn of the century, were asked to help integrate waves of immigrants from Europe.

Obviously, the more a society's subcultures have in common, the greater the chance of successful

扫除文盲. 普及小学和中学教

integration. Beyond this, in most cultures there is some concept of the ideal, or "good," citizen. This ideal is usually defined rather vaguely by tradition or by dominant economic or political groups. Generally, the more a subculture differs from this concept, the greater the adaptation it is expected to make in order to enter the mainstream of the society. In England, for example, the children of Pakistani immigrants have great difficulty adjusting to the English culture as it is reflected in the schools. Students from subcultures that vary significantly from the ideal also run the risk of having their characteristics perceived in a negative way. If their culture is considered less desirable, they may be discriminated against. As a result, these students may be handicapped in two different ways.

First, the more alien the culture being promoted by the schools, the more difficult the adjustments expected of the students. The more difficulty these students have in coping with the school environment, the more likely they are to be categorized as slow or ignorant. Once certain students are identified as being "different" their teachers' expectations for them may change and they will not be treated like other students. When this happens, the

Heterogeneous societies like the United States and China are likely to use their schools—and other agencies of the state—to transmit a common culture. Here kindergarten-age children in the People's Republic of China pass a government wall poster on an outing. Part of the poster says, "When you finish school and go home, you meet your mother coming out. Where is mama going? Mamas are all going to school."

Pygmalion effect we discussed in Chapter 4 is likely to occur. Students may respond to their teachers' attitudes by acting as they are expected to. The differential treatment these students receive, coupled with the difficulty of adjusting to an alien school environment, is likely to reduce academic success.

This phenomenon is common in most societies. In South Dakota, male children of the rural Oglala Sioux at the Pine Ridge reservation lack many of the traits highly valued by school personnel. They have little respect for institutional rules and rebel against the repetition, discipline, and persistence demanded by many academic activities. It is not surprising that about 35 percent of these children drop out of school before the end of the ninth grade. Most of the boys value reckless, daring, or impetuous actions. In their own environment, these defiant activities are equated with masculinity. In the schools, these acts are disruptive and are likely to get the students labeled "troublemakers."[5]

The second handicap results from the schools' frequent assumption that members of minority groups should rid themselves of at least some of the characteristics of their subcultures. This process may include changes in language or dialect and dress, and, more important, changes in values and living patterns. Certain minorities resist this transformation. At times, their reluctance is tied to a distrust of "progress" or modernization. In other instances, pride in the traditional life-style may not be offset by the advantages of integration. Occasionally, the very survival of the subculture may be at stake. For example, Cherokee children of northeastern Oklahoma have historically been confronted with the culture of Anglo-Saxon America when they enter the schools. In some cases, these children eventually find themselves caught between the two cultures. Their faith in traditional tribal ways has been eroded by their school experience, yet they cannot fully adapt to, nor are they fully accepted by, the dominant white culture. This problem is frequently cited as one source of the decreasing tribal loyalty and increasing juvenile delinquency among these Native American adolescents. Thus, it is not clear that the kinds of adaptations the schools expect some students to make always work to the advantage of either the individual or the subculture.

The cultural-integrative function of the school may provide members of various groups with a way to participate in, and enjoy the benefits of, the larger society. But at the same time, it may subject young people to humiliation and weaken the cultural bond of the group. Each social system and subculture must be examined separately in order to determine what advantages, at what price, are produced by the common experience provided by the schools.

Exactly such an examination is going on right now within the American black subcultural group. The Reverend Jesse Jackson of Chicago, a nationally prominent black leader, has recently spoken out strongly against other blacks who argue that black people should regard themselves as victims

Caught between two cultures, Native American children (as well as those of other ethnic groups) find their own culture eroded by the schools while they are not fully accepted into the American common culture they are taught about.

of American society, people who are owed something. Jackson urges that if radical change in the social condition of black people is to occur, a lot of it will have to be effected by blacks themselves, and that formal schooling is an important vehicle to this end.[6]

Vocational Sorting

Educational institutions usually engage in a systematic process of grading, labeling, or evaluating students. The express purpose of this process is to direct students of varying abilities into those vocations for which they are best suited. This occupational sorting function usually receives wide public support. For some students, it presents an opportunity to improve their socioeconomic position. In many instances, the better their academic performance, the greater their opportunity to enter higher-status work situations. This relationship often creates intense competition for admission to curricula that prepare students for the more prestigious occupations.

Economic, political, and social institutions also benefit from this function. The schools provide these organizations with a continuous flow of recruits who have, to some extent, been screened and placed in various categories. Often, the criteria used in job placement roughly coincide with those used by the schools. Through this process of matching job requirements with the grading criteria of the schools, the new work force is channeled into the appropriate occupations.

For years students have been academically segregated at an early age. For example, since 1944 England has rigorously tested all pupils at the age of eleven to determine their future schooling, if any. The results of intelligence tests and examinations in English and arithmetic, together with report cards and the headmaster's appraisal, determine the student's educational fate. Under this system, most children receive no further schooling at all, or else attend trade schools. Only a few are permitted to continue to college preparatory curricula.[7]

In recent years, the formal sorting, or "tracking," of young children has come under increased criticism in both Europe and North America. Many schools are now reluctant to assign students to specific curricula on the basis of previous academic performance. Although overt labeling is declining, a covert and subtle process tends to assure that many students' educational goals will be generally consistent with their school performance. Academically superior students usually choose college preparatory programs, average students are likely to opt for vocational curricula, and poor students either drop out or do not go beyond high school. The schools say that this is more a result of students' social and economic background than of official school policies. The end result, however, tends to be the same. Peer pressure, grades, teachers' expectations, and parental attitudes all have an effect on the classroom performance of the student. This performance, in turn, shapes their vocational goals and aspirations. Some degree of self-fulfilling prophecy is evident.

This raises a question about whether the schools are primarily established to meet student needs or the needs of other institutions. If the schools act as representatives of other institutions and see their role as preparing students to serve them, then the schools seem to be placing the interests of these institutions ahead of the needs of the students. In this case, students may be encouraged to set aside their own aspirations and fit themselves into already established vocational positions. Conversely, if the schools are primarily concerned with helping students attain their own vocational goals, then the schools would be meeting the students' needs. The issue is whether the schools act as agents for other institutions or help individual students identify and develop their own vocational talents. For example, does a school that gives a student the skills to become a bookkeeper serve the student or the business that utilizes his skills?

Although a majority of people in most societies still seem to support this latent kind of sorting, some criticize its impact on young people. The educational sociologist Edgar Z. Friedenberg argues that the granting or withholding of a certificate, diploma, or degree often has a significant effect on the student's life chances.[8] Thus, the criteria by which the schools decide who will be granted various credentials are important. Often, according to Friedenberg, vocational competence is not the sole determinant of student suitability. The school's evaluation may also include judgments about life-style, behavior, and habits, as well as intellectual capacity. Those identified as troublemakers may be prevented from obtaining certain credentials in spite of their intelligence. Often students are considered disruptive if they disagree with the values of the school and, consequently, with the dominant social definition of the "good" citizen. The penalty for their dissent may be the withholding of the diplomas or degrees that would enable them to enter certain occupations.

The difficulty here, of course, is that the judgment the school renders concerning style, manners, and behavior is often a judgment concerning class, race, or ethnicity. Like the adolescent Sioux mentioned earlier, lower-class students are often rowdy, noisy, and aggressive and may use "bad" language in public. To the extent that the school responds to such phenomena by "tracking," or even expulsion, they operate as a class-sorting device. Tables 13-1 and 13-2 show the relationship between "tracking" and social class.

Social Mobility

Contrary to some popular beliefs, the schools do not *create* social mobility. Mobility is determined primarily by economic and political factors in the larger society, which in turn effect the operations of the schools. Usually economic growth, generated by industrialization and advances in technology, increases the demand for specialized skills. Where this occurs, traditional methods of socialization become inadequate, and educational institutions are called upon to assume the responsibility for training the young. The number of students who can become upwardly mobile as a result of formal education is determined by the demand for skilled personnel in other sectors of the social system— not by the schools.

A sophisticated and complex division of labor requires social mobility. The schools determine who, not how many, will receive the educational credentials necessary to qualify for the more lucrative positions available in the society. If schools were to train and graduate computer programers in a society that had no computers, the social mobility of those students would be nil. The schools would merely have created a pool of unemployed computer programers.

Table 13-1 Students eligible by achievement level for upper track and their placement

Socioeconomic level	Number qualified for top track	Percent qualified for top track and placed in top track	Error of placement (percent)
Upper class	333	80	20
Middle class	894	65	35
Lower class	408	47	53

Table 13-2 Students eligible by achievement level for lower track and their placement

Socioeconomic level	Number qualified for low track	Percent qualified for low track and placed in low track	Error of placement (percent)
Upper class	22	2	98
Middle class	187	63	35
Lower class	283	85	15

There are serious doubts about whether the schools provide every student with an equal opportunity to be successful. Even when lower-class students qualify for advanced standing on the basis of their achievement test scores, there is a good chance that they will not be placed in this group. Table 13-1 indicates that 53 percent of these students were not placed in the top track. Upper-class students are rarely placed in the low track. Table 13-2 shows that only 2 percent of these students were actually placed in this track as a result of their low achievement test scores.

Reprinted by permission of Newspaper Enterprise Association.

This concept of the relationship between the schools and social mobility is important. If the schools actually created mobility, teachers could directly assist students in improving their socioeconomic status, and society would have to respond to the decisions of teachers by establishing appropriate positions for students. But in reality, teachers can only decide *which* students will be allowed to compete for the positions that society makes available. This means that the teacher's role is primarily screening students and determining which will be eligible for the more privileged positions and which will not. Thus, rather than being in a position to help all students, the teachers stand between many students and the various opportunities existing at any point in time. One consequence of this "gate-keeping" function is that students, especially mediocre and poor students, are likely to view teachers not as helpers but rather as potential threats to their life chances.

One of the consequences of industrialization has been the breaking down of rigid class distinctions, giving at least some students from the lower classes an opportunity for upward mobility. As a society becomes more complex, it usually generates greater social mobility because the upper classes are not large enough to staff and manage growing institutions. Even lower-level jobs require some specialized training. In most instances, the middle class must be expanded in order to meet the growing demand for skilled and specialized labor. The schools provide such societies with a vehicle for determining which members of the lower social classes will be recruited to the ranks of the middle class. In general, the faster the pace of economic

Schools determine who becomes "credentialed" for high-status positions in the society but not how many will actually achieve such positions.

growth, the greater the need for a mobile society and the more central the role of the school in identifying those who will become upwardly mobile.

The schools are often viewed as providing all members of a society with an opportunity to rise above their class origins and to advance on the basis of their individual merit. It is becoming more apparent, however, that the ability of the schools to eliminate the built-in advantages of high socioeconomic status has been overstated.[9] Although some lower-class students have been successful in obtaining good educational credentials, there is still a strong correlation between social class and the likelihood of achieving high socioeconomic status. In general, the lower the status of the student, the lower his chances of obtaining worldly success regardless of his school experience.

Many factors contribute to this relationship, but family background seems to be the most important. The kind of environment created in the home affects the performance of the children in the schools, and there is little the schools can do to alter this relationship. For example, students from intellectually stimulating home environments tend to do well in the schools. But schools cannot create intellectually stimulating home environments. The kind of socialization that occurs in the home is, to a large extent, determined by the social class of the parents. This explains some of the relationship between social class and the social mobility achieved through educational institutions. Middle- and upper-class families are more likely to provide their children with a home environment that is conducive to high educational achievement than are working-class, rural, or poor families.

The more similar the values of the parents to the values promoted by the schools, the greater the child's probability of educational success. If parents emphasize the value of reading, conceptual thinking, and articulate speech, their children's early socialization will reflect these characteristics. Students entering the schools with this background are more likely to be successful than those coming from families where reading is neither encouraged nor highly valued, where conformity takes precedence over intellectual activity, and where linguistic patterns vary significantly from those used in the schools. Those children who have had little exposure to books are probably not going to learn to read as quickly as those who have been surrounded by them since birth. A student who declares that he "ain't got no pencil" is not likely to make much of an impression on his English teacher.

Although industrialization has moved many societies toward a more open stratification system, mass education has not been able to eliminate the effects of social class. The schools, if they are to provide students with a comparable opportunity for success, would have to create an educational environment that is *equitable* rather than one that treats students *identically*. An equitable approach to education would be one that takes into account the socioeconomic background of the student; it would provide different learning environments for different kinds of students. You might be interested in trying to understand how your academic performance may have been affected by your socioeconomic background. How closely do your parents' values reflect the values of your instructors?

Poverty and home environments which do not value intellectual achievement handicap children in school performance. This youngster may be fortunate. She has a pair of scissors, something to cut out, and a background which gives her an interest in doing something creative.

The Functions of American Schools

Like all formal educational systems, American schools perform the general functions we have described above. In addition, schools in the United States reflect the social, political, and economic forces characteristic of *American* society and culture. In the remainder of the chapter, we will consider the way in which American schools have been affected by and, in turn, have helped shape their society.

The character of the modern school in the United States has been molded primarily by a combination of the waves of immigrants that swept into the country during the nineteenth and early twentieth centuries; by the demands of constitutional government; and, except during sporadic economic downturns, by a shortage of certain vocational skills that persisted up to the 1960s. Responding to these conditions, the schools concentrated on three functions: *Americanization* of all students, providing *"equal opportunity,"* and supplying *vocational training.* These three factors influenced the kind of socialization that still occurs in many American schools, socialization emphasizing good citizenship, practical or useful education, and the traditional American values of success, competition, hard work, deferred pleasure, and sexual modesty.

Americanization

To the extent that the schools were successful, the children of certain immigrant groups were Americanized and integrated into the economic and political life of the nation. At a minimum level, the schools were able to accomplish these objectives. The economy developed at a rapid pace, democracy survived, and the melting pot theory of American culture, whether accurate or not, gained wide acceptance. Further, thousands of people did develop a common language, learn the rudiments of American government and historical experience, and become socialized into some of the essential meanings and values of the society (accepting the "Founding Fathers," for example, as *their* political ancestors too.)

But the Americanization fostered by the schools has also had negative consequences that, until recently, received very little attention. For one thing, the conventional image that the schools project of the ideal, or "good," American is not, as the melting pot theory implies, a composite of the diverse groups who make up this society. Instead,

this model American obviously embodies the characteristics of a single group, the white Anglo-Saxons. Southern and eastern European white ethnics, coming from a rural and lower socioeconomic background than the early colonists, found that the price of Americanization was often a denial of their own heritage. For them, Americanization meant the loss of a sense of their place in history, a tendency to feel self-conscious about their names, and the equation of their traditions with out-dated provincialism. Michael Novak, a Slovak-American, expressed his school experience this way:

Nowhere in my schooling do I recall an attempt to put me in touch with my own history. The strategy was clearly to make an American of me. English literature, American literature; and even the history books, as I recall them, were peopled mainly by Anglo-Saxons from Boston (where most historians seemed to live) . . . I don't remember feeling envy or regret: a feeling, perhaps, of unimportance, of remoteness, of not having heft enough to count.[10]

Nonwhite children have found schools even more inhospitable. Black, Native American, and Spanish-speaking young people have been exposed to discrimination based on skin color as well as discrimination associated with low socioeconomic status and a different cultural orientation. School personnel often have a poorly disguised contempt for their physical and cultural characteristics. Part of this contempt has been reflected in many teachers' attitudes toward the learning abilities of nonwhite children. These teachers, including some who mean well, simply do not expect such children to learn at a pace comparable to white students and have given up trying to teach them. Of course, children will not learn if they are not taught—particularly once they discover that the teacher really does not expect a great deal from them. Once more, a self-fulfilling prophecy.

Although the white ethnics paid a price for the Americanization of their children, the mobility created by an expanding economy did create at least the possiblity of improved socioeconomic status for them. But for nonwhite children, the schools have often been more a source of humiliation, frustration, and defeat than a vehicle for upward mobility. As a result, Americanization by the school has had an uneven effect in spite of the myth of

Table 13-3   Lifetime earnings by years of school completed for whites and nonwhites, 1960

Years of school completed	Lifetime earnings (thousands of dollars)		
	White	Non-white	Nonwhite as percent of white
Elementary			
Under 8 years	157	95	61
8 years	191	123	64
High school			
1 to 3 years	221	132	60
4 years	253	151	60
College			
1 to 3 years	301	162	54
4 years or more	427	215	50
Total	241	122	51

In 1960, the average nonwhite college graduate had slightly less lifetime earnings than the average white high school dropout. These results suggest that the personal characteristics of the individual holding an educational credential may be more important than the credential itself.

The Americanization function of the schools. Fifth graders reenact the World War II flag-raising on Iwo Jima.

equal treatment. First, there is still a relationship between socioeconomic class and life income; and second, there is a correlation between race and material success, especially income (see Table 13-3). White ethnics suffer from the first handicap, nonwhites from both.

Equality of Opportunity

Most Americans believe that all people should have an equal opportunity to realize their full potential. They do not, however, believe that all are equal when it comes to results.

It seems reasonable to argue that a boy born into a wealthy family would have to work hard at being a failure. He will attend expensive schools, have tutors available, and will not have a great deal of difficulty finding work once his education is completed. To help him over the rough spots, he may

Table 13-4   Mobility from father's occupation to son's first occupation for U.S. males 25 to 64 years old (in percent), 1967

Father's occupation	Son's first occupation					
	Higher white-collar	Lower white-collar	Higher manual	Mid manual	Lower manual	Farm
Higher white-collar (professionals, managers, proprietors)	28.6	28.2	9.8	22.6	8.5	2.4
Lower white-collar (sales and clerical)	21.1	33.3	7.9	25.1	9.6	3.0
Higher manual (craftsmen and foremen)	7.4	20.5	17.4	36.0	14.0	4.6
Mid manual (operative and service workers)	6.6	17.3	9.6	47.5	14.8	4.1
Low manual (laborers)	4.6	13.6	6.8	37.2	30.3	7.6
Farm	4.1	6.7	5.8	21.0	12.0	50.3

Note: The entry in each cell is the percentage of sons whose fathers were in the occupational category listed at left whose first job was in the category listed at the top. For instance, 28.2 percent of the sons whose fathers were in higher white-collar occupations were first employed in lower white-collar occupations.

come into a considerable amount of money once he reaches legal age. A boy born into a poor family invariably will attend poor schools, will not have the luxury of private tutors, and certainly will not be able to move into the offices of dad's company upon graduation. His chances for success are as remote as the chance of failure among rich children.

The schools, then, rather than providing equal opportunity, merely legitimize the inequalities that exist between children from different families. Just as the schools do not create social mobility, but merely help determine which students will be eligible to take advantage of whatever mobility exists in the larger society, so too they do not create equal opportunity, but rather formalize the inequalities that already exist. Although there has been some upward mobility from manual occupations to white-collar work, this movement is due more to changing economic needs than to schooling (see Table 13-4). To some extent, social stability in the United States is dependent on the assumption of equal opportunity. The present distribution of wealth and power might be widely questioned if large numbers of Americans no longer felt they could rely on the schools to provide their children with a chance to prove themselves and get ahead.

While there is a distinct relationship between the occupational status of the father and the likelihood that the son will enter a higher white-collar occupation, some upward mobility is reflected in this table. This mobility is more a reflection of the changing nature of the American economy than a creation of the educational system.

Vocational Training

Secondary school curricula are frequently divided into precollege (liberal arts), mathematics or science programs, and vocational programs. Although all these programs are vocational in the sense that practically all students eventually become involved in some kind of work, *vocational curricula* emphasize immediate employment after a relatively short period of formal education. The liberal arts, mathematics, and science programs, by contrast, aim toward future employment that nearly always requires more years of schooling, law or medical school, for instance.

Because jobs that require advanced academic credentials have traditionally been high-paying and prestigious, they have attracted the more academically able students. Students who experience difficulty in the secondary schools have been encouraged to enroll in curricula teaching secretarial skills and automobile repair, rather than to prepare for college or to attend trade schools and community colleges for post–high school education. Thus, the difference in status between these programs is based not on vocational orientation, but rather on the number of years of additional education required, the kind and background of students they recruit, and the prestige of the occupation for which they provide training.

For over a century, people have argued and worried about the kind of vocational training the schools provide. Different programs have different statuses. The "tracking" of less able students into "skill courses" has lowered the prestige of such vocational curricula. The precollege curricula have had more prestige, but usually only so long as they lead to more advanced study and eventual white-collar employment. Parents, relatives, and even teachers frequently question liberal arts students who have no clear-cut employment objectives, asking what the students will do with their education once they graduate and why they are wasting their time on such impractical activities.

We can gain some insight into the source of these attitudes by looking at American conceptions of academic activity. In his study of anti-intellectualism, Richard Hofstadter argues that most Americans make an implicit distinction between an intelligent individual and an intellectual.[11] An intelligent person is usually defined in vocational terms. People who have become engineers, computer systems analysts, accountants, or lawyers are considered intelligent because they have been successful in school and can apply what they have learned. Because the schools determine who will be eligible to enter these occupations, the schools reward intelligence with advanced degrees. In this view, the function of the schools is the identification, nurturing, and certification of bright students.

Intellectuals are usually not widely respected, occasionally arouse suspicion, and are often ridiculed. An individual who is devoted to the life of the mind, to knowledge for knowledge's sake, may not be considered intelligent. The stereotype of the absent-minded professor, lost in his ivory tower, unable to deal with the realities of life, exemplifies

this attitude. The essense of this view is captured in the opinion of one of the people quoted in Robert Coles's book on *Middle Americans*:

Going to college can be like drinking. Take a lot of beer, take a few shots of whiskey, and you get high. You lose your judgment. You overestimate yourself and you forget about the most obvious and important things. Likewise, one can read and read and read, and get lost in a world of theories, an unreal world.[12]

Part of the ambivalence toward the liberal arts is attributable to their future vocational value, on the one hand, and their relationship to intellectualism, on the other. Conflict today centers around the kind of vocational training that ought to be offered. Few question the proposition that the schools ought to prepare doctors, but the consensus is less clear when it comes to training automobile mechanics.

Some critics of vocational curricula argue that students in such programs are unfairly pressured into curricula that lead to low-paying jobs with limited opportunities for advancement. Students may opt for these programs before they have an opportunity to identify their own interests and skills. In some instances, opponents argue, the schools may be merely creating a semiskilled labor pool that can be exploited by business and industry. Why, they ask, don't the institutions employing these young people train them in the specific skills necessary for their work.

Because less able students make up a large part of the enrollment in such curricula, and because academic performance and social class are related, the schools are accused of assuring that low-status students are prepared for low-status jobs; the beautician's daughter, for example, is trained to be a typist. In addition, those opposed to programs leading directly to employment suggest that these students' personal lives would be enriched if they developed an understanding of art, music, and literature in school. In other words, these critics assume that there is more to education than merely learning skills; the school should assist people to live stimulating and fulfilling *lives* as well. This argument brings us back to our earlier discussion of the lack of agreement over the nature and purposes of education.

Educators who support vocational programs suggest that many courses in the arts, humanities, and social sciences do not meet these students' needs, that many students find these courses irrelevant and seek the more immediate and visible rewards of early employment. In this view, the main purpose of education is to provide students with the practical skills necessary to find decent work. Intellectual activity per se is considered to be of secondary importance.

These two positions by and large parallel the distinction between the intelligent individual and the intellectual discussed above. Those who support early vocational education are inclined to think in terms of intelligence as reflected through work. Those who are more intellectually oriented are critical of these programs and think of occupational training as secondary to the prime function of the schools—the development of the intellect. At the heart of this dispute is a disagreement over the basic content and purpose of formal education.

To date, there is no agreement among educators about the role, nature, and extent of vocational training in the schools. Clearly, there is danger in limiting education to vocational training. An educated person is more than someone who possesses a marketable skill. The problem is to determine how much and what kind of vocational emphasis ought to be incorporated into educational programs. The dominant life-style of a society will be influenced by the extent to which vocational training is perceived as the essence of education. When a vocational orientation prevails, individual and group identity tends to be tied to the occupational hierarchy of the society. That is, people define themselves in terms of what they do rather than what they are.

This makes for obvious problems when, for reasons of unemployment or obsolescence, people can no longer do what they were trained for. Hundreds of Seattle engineers, for instance, experienced major emotional crises when layoffs at Boeing turned them from skilled professionals into "welfare bums." But vocationalism has even more profound consequences for the society as a whole. When people value only the practical, the readily useful, much of what makes life interesting, exciting, and rewarding is discarded: music, art, the theater, literature, even love. The ultimate end result can be read in a remark made by the Nazi Hermann Goering about intellectuals: "When I hear the word 'culture,' I reach for my gun."

The Organization of American Schools

Primary and Secondary Education

There are many ways in which a society can organize its school system. One is implied in the (probably apocryphal) story that, at one time in France, the Minister of Education could tell by looking at his watch exactly what every French child in every grade in school was reading at that instant. The United States has chosen a much more decentralized system, in which the states are responsible for setting standards of education and local communities are responsible for establishing and supporting public schools that meet those standards. Private school systems are also permitted, so long as they meet state requirements. In the following section, we take up elementary and secondary education (generally kindergarten through eighth grade and grades nine through twelve, respectively) and higher education in both their public and private forms. In the process, we will see that the educational establishment exerts a strong and pervasive force in American society.

Public schools The fundamental organizational principle of public primary and secondary schools is control by the *local* community or school district. This control is usually exercised through an elected board of education, although a few school systems have boards appointed by political bodies. The board of education, made up of citizens from the school district, raises and allocates the money to finance schools. Almost everywhere, this money is raised through special school taxes. Before the tax is levied, citizens vote either to accept or to reject the proposed budget as it is translated into a property tax or bond issue. The states also allocate some funds to schools, and special federal monies are also available. The bulk of support, however, is usually local.

The board of education also appoints the school superintendent, who is responsible for the functioning of all of the schools in the district. On his recommendation, the board also appoints the principals who direct the activities of each school. In addition, the board of education establishes guidelines for teacher behavior and is usually responsible for negotiating teacher contracts and salaries. In most instances, the board has the final say in granting or withholding tenure (job security) for eligible faculty. Finally, this group establishes the rules of conduct for students and approves any changes in school curricula.

The concept of local community control is intended to make the schools responsive to the wishes of the parents and other adults in the community. It is assumed that these adults have and should have the ultimate responsibility for determining the kind of education children will receive. The board operates as the representative of the people in the district. Although parents and other interested residents may have considerable influence when they deal directly with principals and teachers, it is the knowledge that the board of education has far-reaching powers that makes most school personnel sensitive to outside pressure. Complaints made by the board are likely to be heeded.

Majorities and minorities In general, the structure of the public schools, particularly the board of education, will be responsive to the sentiments of local *majorities*; but in responding to the majority, it may ride roughshod over *minority* opinions. Control by locally elected boards tends to make school personnel sensitive to the wishes of the larger community about how children are to be socialized in school, while those who think otherwise may find teachers and principals afraid to respond to them. The inability of minority groups to influence school policies has become a heated issue in many areas. In Bedford-Stuyvesant, New York, for example, black parents tried to make the school system more responsive to *their* perceived needs by redefining the concept of *community* control of the schools to mean *neighborhood* control. (They were in part successful.) More recently, Louisville, Kentucky, and Boston, Massachusetts, have experienced prolonged unrest (and, in the latter instance, rioting and violence) over the issue

Early Out?

At the height of the recession just three years ago, a national commission set off a furor when it proposed that 14-year-olds should be allowed to leave school and go to work. The proposed reform, with its vast economic and educational implications, has been a focus of debate ever since, and as a result, some state legislatures have begun to revise their laws. . . .

The most compelling argument for lowering the mandatory-schooling age is that current statutes are unenforceable—and sometimes counterproductive. "It's impossible to get a truancy case before the courts these days, so students flout the laws with full knowledge that nothing will happen to them," explains B. Frank Brown, who chaired the commission. Forcing unwilling students to stay on in the classrooms, says Brown, invites disruptive behavior. "Our high schools are in a serious state of intellectual disrepair because of compulsory schooling," he argues. "They cannot be custodial institutions and still excel at teaching." Brown suggests that minimum-wage laws could be modified in the case of young dropouts so that businesses could train them inexpensively for work in apprentice programs.

Ranged against Brown are a number of educators who think that more schooling, not less, is the answer. "The solution doesn't lie in getting rid of the problem," says Owen Kiernan of the National Association of Secondary School Principals, which has recommended that the minimum age be set at 18. "We think that the schools should be *solving* problems." Kiernan advocates more and better vocational education. "Dumping millions of 14-year-olds on the streets, especially when their parents couldn't care less about them, is dynamite," says Kiernan. "What will they do? They'll get into trouble, and it will cost society many times the money it costs to educate them to correct it." . . .

One alternative to either vocational or liberal education is simply dropping out—with or without the consent of the law. But if even vocationally trained persons have difficulty finding employment, where does the dropout drop *to?* The argument about what the schools should do, and how, is not likely to be resolved soon.

of racial busing. In both cases, it required the National Guard to restore order to the streets.

At issue in all of these situations is the concept of community control of education. The American system assumes that the local community *should* exercise the dominant control of the schools, subject to meeting state minimum standards, and that this may be done effectively through an elected board of education. But the cases we cited above, and multitudes of recent others, raise two questions to which local school boards have no clear answer: First, who is the relevant community? And second, how can a board represent more than one community if the interests involved are inconsistent or contradictory? In recent years, both of these questions have often translated themselves into a third: How can the board represent and protect the rights or wishes of a community minority while still representing the majority?

The busing issue has focused national attention on these questions. In general, the courts have held that the rights of the majority of the American people are best upheld by busing to achieve racial integration. But many local communities or groups within them, both black and white, think that *their* rights—to segregated education, to neighborhood schools, to schools largely black and with black teachers, and so on—are withheld by this interpretation. Different boards have leaned both toward and away from busing in different places in attempts to serve their perceptions of the best interests of their constituents. To compound the confusion, recent data seem to show that integration does not bring about the large-scale improvement in the *quality* of education that many people predicted.[13]

The cost of education   Many Americans have an inconsistent attitude toward the schools. They believe that education is important, but they do not want it to be too costly. Urban centers, for example, have woefully inadequate school financing, and yet encounter little difficulty raising funds for the construction of new sports arenas. And even in·communities where citizens really want to support the schools, the funding levels requested are more than many tax payers feel they should have to bear. Local financing of schools places a very great burden on middle- and lower-income neighborhoods, which are already hard-hit by other taxes. When confronted with a proposal to raise school taxes, many people may reluctantly vote against it, because this is the only tax over which they have some control.

The problem of how to pay for spiraling school costs appears to be insoluble within the framework of local support. As inflation and governmental expenditures have increased, taxes have risen and the purchasing power of personal income has decreased. People feel their taxes are too high already and resist anything that would raise them further. But it is, in essence, the public's problem, one that the public has created for itself. For at the same time that people refuse to support bond issues or higher tax rates for education, they clamor for the schools to take on ever-greater responsibilities.

At one time, the typical American public school was a one- or two-room building in which children remained until sixth or eighth grade to learn to read, write, and do sums. The schools today, high schools in particular, are now expected to provide community entertainment in the form of sports contests, theatrical events, and musicals, teach students to swim, bowl, care for babies, have satisfactory sex lives, revere God, stay off drugs, prepare for hundreds of occupations, balance their checkbooks, and appreciate music and literature, as well as become patriotic Americans. The school has replaced the home and church in the public mind as the place where an immense variety of socialization should take place. Until the public is willing to pay for it through some national system of educational support, or else reduce its expectations, it is difficult to see how the cost of doing—or attempting to do—it all will be borne.

Private schools   Private schools can be divided between those based on a religious philosophy and those with a secular orientation. They differ from the public schools in several ways (see Table 13-5). Most obviously, they are administered and financed by groups outside the public service system. As a result, they are often faced with financial difficulties and have problems obtaining state and federal funding. They also are, of course, more

Table 13-5   The organization of American primary and secondary schools

Organizational characteristic	Public primary and secondary schools	Private primary and secondary schools	
		Secular[a]	Religious
Source of control	Local community	Private corporation	Religious corporation or church
Finance	Local taxation	Tuition, donations	Tuition, donations
Responsiveness to public	Moderate to high for majority groups, low for minorities	Low	Low to moderate
Clientele	The lower- and middle-class public	The upper and upper-middle classes	All classes
Primary functions	Socialization, cultural transmission, vocational sorting, social nonmobility	Socialization, transmission of WASP culture, class endogamy, upward mobility	Socialization, religious indoctrination, some vocational sorting, social mobility
Social orientation	"High school civics conservative"	Educationally liberal, politically conservative	Moderate to conservative

[a] Excludes storefront schools, alternative schools, and so on.

selective in which pupils they accept, and tend to have somewhat different orientations than do the public schools, as we will see below.

Religious schools   All major religious denominations have some church or temple-related schools, but the Catholics have developed the most extensive private educational system. Supported primarily by the financial contributions of church members, these parochial schools usually have a traditional orientation that appeals to many parents.

In the past, religious denominational schools were often more concerned with maintaining religious orthodoxy, or even ethnic identity, than with the quality of education they provided. Particularly since World War II, however, this tendency has diminished considerably. The Catholic school system, for example, once famous for dogmatic theological indoctrination, strict discipline, and memorization as the basic learning device, has flowered, sometimes producing excellent institutions indeed.

The cost squeeze of recent years has tended to hit the Christian school systems hard, in part be-

cause they have erected duplicates of the public schools to be maintained at their own cost. Many, both Catholic and Protestant, have had to close. The Jewish schools, which normally were established to maintain religious and ethnic practices, did not attempt this duplication and have not been as strangulated by rising expenses. (The Hebrew school is typically an after-public-school-hours institution.)

Secular schools   Private secular schools run the gamut from expensive institutions for the upper socioeconomic classes to schools operating in urban store-fronts and rural communes. Schools like Exeter, Choate, Groton, and St. Mark's cater to students from elite families and provide a luxurious academic setting. Their exclusiveness may be measured by the fact that many middle- and lower-class Americans have never heard of them. In addition to providing an education, they assure that students will associate with others of similar socioeconomic background. Every large urban area has several such schools to serve the local elite. These schools are financed by a combination of

tuition charges and contributions from wealthy supporters.

There are also private schools that have an ideological rather than a socioeconomic orientation. These are relatively new, are not numerous, and often have difficulty staying open because they are financed only by their tuition charges. But some at least persist because they represent an alternative to the public schools, on the one hand, and the more expensive private schools, on the other. The Montessori school system may be the most familiar example. Usually, the philosophy of these "alternative" or "free" schools is based on psychoanalytic theory and definitions of education that differ from those of the larger society. For example, most public schools offer group instruction that relies heavily on a teacher-dominated learning environment. Some "free"-school advocates assume that instruction must be individualized and center on the specific needs and interests of the student. Although such schools provide alternatives to traditional education, they often lack the facilities and equipment found in the public schools. At this time, it would be risky to assume that they are capable of developing and maintaining successful programs on a scale large enough to challenge traditional institutions.

Some private schools have been established and continue to operate primarily for racial reasons. These are concentrated in parts of the South, particularly Louisiana, and in some northern cities, like Boston, where integration has become a heated issue. When in 1954 the Supreme Court ruled that public schools must be integrated, many white groups established all-white private elementary and secondary schools. Supposedly, these schools are financed exclusively by parents, but in some cases publicized in Mississippi and Alabama, local government funds were channeled into them. Although parents claim that they are not racists and are only concerned about quality education, there is little doubt that opposition to integration is the real reason for establishing these schools. In spite of legal and financial pressure, many persist.

Higher Education

Changes in higher education Beginning around the turn of the century and accelerating since the end of World War II, an important change occurred in the attitudes of some Americans toward higher education. Before the 1940s, a college education was not generally considered essential for a white-collar occupation or for participation in the material benefits of American life. People thought a high school diploma was adequate preparation for a productive adulthood and considered it a substantial educational achievement. Few people went to college, and most of those who did either came from the more privileged social classes or were highly motivated and academically able.

The postwar economic boom brought greatly expanded job opportunities in businesses that were becoming more technologically sophisticated. Led by almost 4 million World War II veterans, more and more people began to recognize the importance of college education. A growing economy meant that there was increased social mobility and a continually rising standard of living. A high school education no longer seemed adequate, and the concept of the good life came to be equated with, and dependent on, higher education. In the process, the opportunity to enter college came to be viewed more as a right of all Americans than as a privilege extended to a social or academic elite. Mass education, which began in the elementary and secondary schools, came to the American college and university. As a result, colleges and universities underwent many changes, including spectacular growth and changes in admission policies, and a new status system evolved for ranking institutions of higher learning.

Increases in size and number of institutions Changing perceptions of higher education resulted in a dramatic expansion in the size of colleges and universities. In 1962, Frederick Rudolph, looking back over almost a century of American education, observed:

In 1870 American institutions of higher learning enrolled somewhat over 50,000 young men and women; a hundred years later the City University of New York alone would be enrolling almost four times that number. In 1870 but 1.7 percent of the young people aged 18-21 were enrolled in colleges and universities; by 1970 half of the age group 18-21 would be at college. In 1960 approximately 3,500,000 young men and women attended institutions of higher learning; by 1970 that figure would be doubled. In 1876 there were 311 colleges and universities; in 1960 there were 2,026.[14]

Open admission Recently, traditional admission requirements have come under increased scrutiny. In the late 1960s, groups who had been excluded from institutions of higher education pressed administrators to formulate policies that would give all an equal opportunity to "prove themselves," regardless of their previous academic performance. The idea that a college education was a right rather than a privilege led to the opening of college doors to millions of students, particularly from black and lower-middle-class white families, who previously would not have gone beyond high school. The concept of open admissions gained popular support.

The phrase *open admissions* is popularly associ-

Blacks Bused 107 Miles—to All-Black Schools

Boykin, Ala. [AP]—It's 6:30 a.m., and the black children are lining up for the school bus to begin a 10-hour school day burdened by their 107-mile roundtrip bus ride through Wilcox County.

And though the busing was ordered by the federal courts to achieve racial integration, the 120 or so black pupils get off the buses to attend almost all-black public schools—most of the white pupils have switched to private academies.

The Wilcox County students are not alone. In Choctaw County black pupils ride the school bus 104 miles each day to and from classes.

And state school officials say there are several other rural Alabama districts where pupils sandwich classroom time around bus rides of about 80 miles—rides which anger many parents and which one teacher says can "decimate the whole school system." . . .

The two longest bus routes, in Wilcox and Choctaw counties, are through rural south Alabama school districts under federal court orders to achieve integration and improve education for blacks.

It is ironic that all of the children on those longest bus rides are black.

There is a move for change in Choctaw County. School Supt. Edward Woods says the federal court will be asked for an informal hearing to discuss a rezoning plan to cut the bus ride in half. . . .

Chicago Tribune, October 11, 1976. Reprinted by permission of AP Newsfeatures.

ated with the city college system of the city of New York. It implies that any resident of the community taxed to support the school has the civic right at least to enter it without fee to see how well he fares. It is, in other words, an extention to college of the public school concept. Various ethnic and racial minority groups, who previously had been collectively excluded from college opportunities by inability to pay for them, tended to support open admissions strongly. In New York City, this policy led to the bankruptcy of the system, as the schools floundered in the attempt to handle vastly increased loads of students, many requiring special remedial classes to prepare them for college-level work. Although not known as open admissions, the general idea has, in fact, been around American higher education for a long time, particularly among the community colleges. Most of these have minimal fees and will admit, at least on a probationary status, almost anyone, regardless of previous school experience.

The status system The rapid growth in college enrollments has raised concerns about whether academic excellence can be maintained. Some educators feared that academic standards were being sacrificed in order to respond to the needs of a less select student population. One consequence of the question whether quality can be synonymous with quantity was the emergence of a nationwide status system among institutions of higher education. Generally speaking, the relatively small private schools primarily in the Northeast—the Ivy League and the Seven Sisters—are at the top of the collegiate status system. They remain highly selective in their admissions policies, have high tuition charges, and a lingering liberal arts tradition. Next in the hierarchy are a number of large state universities. Among the leaders in this group are the University of California at Berkeley, the Big Ten schools in the Midwest, and many other institutions across the country from Rutgers to the University of Washington. In about the same position are a number of small, select private liberal arts colleges, such as Antioch, Oberlin, and Swarthmore. State colleges, such as teachers colleges, are next in line. These schools have a decidedly more local orientation than the large universities and are not, therefore, well-known outside their regions.

Finally, junior colleges, with their open admissions policies and generally heavy vocational orientation, have the lowest status among the institutions of higher learning.

Public institutions Publicly supported colleges and universities appear in a variety of forms and sizes. The giants are the **multiversities**, universities so large and so complicated as to have multitudes of functions, interests, and effects on the society, as well as multiple ties to a variety of social institutions. They are typically named "The University of . . ." such and such a state. Largest of these is the multicampused University of California system, with a student enrollment of 100,000. Its Berkeley campus is commonly conceded to be one of the finest universities in the world. Other types include state colleges and teachers colleges (often now called "universities" as well), and community (or junior) colleges, typically supported by cities or counties rather than the states. The basic difference between a college and a university is that a college is a four-year institution, while a university offers graduate and professional education as well. A community college, however, is almost always a two-year institution.

Multiversities Most state universities are large enough to qualify as multiversities, with student bodies of well over 10,000, sophisticated administrative and accounting systems, and a multitude of curricula in all academic and vocational areas. In these institutions, undergraduate programs in chemistry, psychology, and history exist alongside vocational curricula like animal husbandry and accounting. They also offer graduate programs leading to masters degrees and doctorates in many fields, often including such advanced professional studies as law, medicine, and dentistry.

Multiversities are frequently rather impersonal and always highly bureaucratized. At the undergraduate level, particularly in the freshman and sophomore years, students may be enrolled in very large classes held in lecture halls. (Introductory sociology at Purdue University is taught in two sections of about 450 each.) In these learning environments, personal contact with faculty is frequently minimal, and the evaluation of students may be based on computerized multiple-choice

Jack Manning-NYT Pictures.

Student demonstration during the financial crisis at the City University of New York (CUNY). The crisis was precipitated in part by the adoption of the "open admissions" policy.

examinations. Critics argue that learning is a highly individual process and cannot be mass-produced in a lecture hall. But educators who are comfortable with large classes suggest that it makes little difference whether a lecturer faces 30 or 300 students. Furthermore, they argue that large lecture halls reduce costs and increase efficiency. (The Purdue sociology course requires one instructor—your editor—and three graduate teaching assistants, for an annual salary cost of approximately $36,500. If taught in sections with enrollments of thirty, it would require ten instructors, each teaching three sections. If these were, say, experienced assistant professors—the lowest of the academic ranks—and each professor had one graduate assistant to help him, the cost would be in the neighborhood of $185,000 annually.)

The multiversity has the advantage of being able to offer a diversity of curricula, students, and faculty that is impossible in most smaller institutions. Although residents of the state in which the institution is located usually make up the largest segment of the student population, there are usually also many foreign students and students from other parts of the country. These schools can attract well-known scholars and teachers and have the financial resources to support extensive extracurric-

---

multiversities: universities so large and so complicated as to have multitudes of functions, interests, and effects on the society, as well as multiple ties to a variety of social institutions.

Lower Minority Standards Hurt Medical Quality
Ronald Kotulak, Science Editor

Academic Standards at the nation's medical schools may be slipping because of programs to enroll minority students, according to a Harvard University educator.

The need to make up for past discriminatory practices is real but it would be wrong for the public to believe that these programs are operating smoothly, said Dr. Bernard D. Davis.

The problem is that some of the minority students cannot meet the academic requirements and medical schools are forced to lower their standards in order to graduate them, he reported in the current issue of the New England Journal of Medicine.

"It is cruel to admit students who have a very low probability of measuring up to reasonable standards," he said. "It is even crueler to abandon those standards and allow the trusting patients to pay for our irresponsibility."

He cited the case of one student who finally was awarded his medical degree despite the fact that he had failed to pass the qualifying exam in five tries. . . .

Better programs are needed to recruit and help students who were formerly excluded from medical schools, Davis said. But any attempt to establish quotas for minority students could further lower standards, he warned.

The number of black students in medical schools has increased nearly five fold in the last eight years. This year a total of 3,456 blacks are enrolled. . . .

Chicago Tribune, May 16, 1976. Reprinted courtesy of the Chicago Tribune.

Rapid growth in college enrollments, particularly among the poor and members of disadvantaged minorities, has caused some educators serious concern about possible negative effects on academic standards. *Can* adequate standards be maintained if significant proportions of the student body cannot meet them? *Should* they be maintained?

ular activities: a variety of guest speakers, athletic programs, cultural events, and student clubs. Their libraries are usually excellent. The basic issue is whether this educational and cultural diversity offsets the impersonality that is almost inevitable in large institutions.

State colleges State colleges are scaled-down versions of the large universities. Usually the student populations are somewhat smaller—somewhere between 3,000 and 15,000 students. The faculty are departmentalized along the same general lines as those in the universities, although there may be fewer academic curricula. Although many state colleges offer some graduate programs, they are usually limited to the master's degree level. The faculty may not be as prominent as some of those in the universities and usually do not engage in as much research and publication.

Admission policies are frequently not as selective as those of the multiversities, and a large percentage of the students are likely to be drawn from the local area. Undergraduate classes are generally smaller, so that students may have slightly more personal contact with teachers than in a multiversity. But these institutions do not offer the social, cultural, and intellectual diversity found in many of the large universities.

Community (or junior) colleges Typically smaller than the state four-year colleges, community (or junior) colleges are tied even more closely to their locality, because some funding is usually provided by city or county political bodies. As a result, these two-year institutions do not have the independence of the four-year school and are almost as dependent on local community support as the elementary and secondary schools.

Community colleges occupy a space between the secondary schools and the four-year colleges. Until recently, the number of these institutions had been increasing rapidly. They are most prevalent in large urban states like California, New York, and Michigan. It is difficult to determine whether they represent two additional years of a high school curriculum or the first two years of a college education. A significant percentage of the faculty have had secondary school teaching experience, and they are often recruited from the local area. Faculty respon-

sibilities center almost exclusively on teaching; there is no emphasis on research and publication.

Community colleges are intended to fulfill the promise of higher education for all who seek it. If access to college is to be perceived as a right rather than a privilege, some arrangements must be made for students who cannot meet the admission requirements of the four-year schools or who must stay at home and work to pay for their educations. The majority of community college students come from the second and third academic quarters of their high school classes.

The community colleges offer the promise of higher education for all, have made that promise a foundation of their existence, and have fulfilled it for some. They are, indeed, open-door institutions. But a common wisecrack among their faculties is that what they truly provide for many students is not an open door to college, but a revolving one—in and out. Their dropout rates are considerably higher than those of other kinds of institutions, and many students are admitted who have little actual hope of graduation. (To be fair, it must also be noted that many dropouts drop back in again after some absence. This pattern may in part be accounted for by the fact that many community college students support themselves in regular jobs while going to school.) But such colleges were essentially established for working-class people who could not afford more expensive education, and many of their students bring with them problems that contribute to low academic motivation and high attrition: poor academic backgrounds, lack of support for education in the home environment, low reading skills, competition from family and job for time and energy. Such phenomena create problems for the community colleges that no other educational institutions have to face. Florissant St. Louis C. C. Florissant Valley, for example, teaches some classes on a "swing shift" to accommodate workers from a nearby aircraft plant.

Private colleges and universities Like the private elementary and secondary schools, private colleges and universities are divided between the religious and the secular. They differ from public institutions principally in funding, administrative control, and student body (see Table 13-6).

Table 13-6   The organization of American institutions of higher learning

Organizational characteristic	Public	Private
Source of control	State	Private corporation
Finance	State and federal taxation	Tuition, donations
Responsiveness to public	Moderate to high	Low to moderate
Clientele	All but highest and lowest classes	Middle to upper classes
Primary functions	Liberal, professional, vocational education; cultural transmission; social mobility	Liberal, professional, vocational education; cultural transmission; social mobility; class endogamy
Social orientation	Moderate to liberal	Moderate to liberal

Among religious schools, the Catholics have established the greatest number of colleges, although all major religious groups are represented. Notre Dame and Georgetown are Catholic institutions; the Protestants have created Valparaiso University; and Yeshiva University represents the Jewish faith. Their funding and administration is similar to that of the religious elementary and secondary schools. The trustees and many of the administrators are professional religious people, although an increasing number of lay people are joining their staffs. Generally, the private religious colleges do not have the academic reputations of some of the private secular schools, but they do provide students with a conservative environment that is consistent with their previous religious training.

Private secular schools, as exemplified by Harvard, Yale, Princeton, and the rest of the Ivy League, Northwestern, and Stanford, have a decidedly elitist orientation. They have a considerably more diverse student population than the exclusive secondary schools, but they are still attractive to families from the upper socioeconomic classes. Tuition charges are high and admission policies selective. This combination assures, consciously or otherwise, that not many students from lower-status families will be admitted. There are also a number of private women's colleges that enjoy a similar social status. Schools like Vassar, Smith, Skidmore, and Radcliffe have relatively small student populations and emphasize the value of small

"What you want is a multiversity or perhaps a polyversity, but I don't think you'll be happy at a megaversity."

classes. In addition to tuition payments, a good deal of these institutions' financial support is derived from contributions by wealthy graduates, large endowments, and grants from private foundations and the federal government. Students who graduate from these institutions often have access to choice positions in business and government.

By and large, the private colleges and universities are attended by upper-class students, while middle- and lower-class students go to public colleges and universities and community colleges. Although this trend has been greatly modified in the past thirty years by the G.I. Bill, scholarship programs for the academically competent poor, and current pressures from minority groups and the federal government for minority admissions, the fact remains that almost all institutions, public and private alike, rely heavily on student tuition for significant portions of their operating funds. Post–high school education remains in large part a commodity for sale to those who can pay for it. Thus, to a discernible degree, higher education mirrors, and to some extent reinforces, the American class structure. It is difficult to see how this feature of the educational institution in the United States might be altered unless and until the public and their representatives undertake almost total support of the colleges and universities through state and federal taxation. As in the case of the elementary and secondary schools, such an increase in tax contribution does not appear to be likely in the foreseeable future.

Some Problems of American Schools

In preceding sections, we have occasionally touched on specific problems in American education associated with the topic under discussion, for example, the controversy over busing and arguments about vocationalism. A number of other problems exist, however, that are not specific to such things as the structure or function of the schools themselves, but that instead span the entire educational system. Two of these are discussed below, the role of the student in the school and the impact of mass education.

Students: Clients or Products?

It takes only a short exposure to a traditional elementary or secondary school classroom (or, many would add, the typical university) to reach the conclusion that, by and large, students are products rather than clients. Schools are run according to bureaucratic principles. Students are moved from room to room according to a schedule that seems to come closer to meeting the demands of efficiency than the needs of specific, unique individuals. Curricula are designed for students in specific age groups in spite of the common knowledge that young people mature at different rates and in different ways.

Within the schools, administrators have overall responsibility for their operation, teachers are in charge of directing activities within their classrooms, and students are asked to respond to the authority vested in both groups. Rules regulating the behavior of students, teachers, and administrators are often not directly required by the demands of their specific jobs. Thus, there are rules governing attendance, tardiness, and conduct in the halls and in the lunchrooms. Schools have not only a fixed division of labor, but also a fixed division of knowledge. Students learn that which has been broken down and compartmentalized into disciplines—English, mathematics, biology, and so forth. Somewhat like products on an assembly line, they move from point to point, on a fixed timetable, and are processed at each stop along the way.

The question here is whether a bureaucratic structure based on principles that emphasize efficiency and predictability is really effective when applied to the teaching-learning process. The majority of students do not respond well to the structure of the school. Many students find schools dull, tedious, frustrating, and unhappy places. High dropout rates, discipline and truancy problems, and vandalism all attest to this dissatisfaction.

Victims of the system?   The central problem facing American educational institutions during the last quarter of the twentieth century is that both students and teachers are, to some extent, victimized by the structure of most contemporary schools. Both groups spend much of their time venting their frustrations on each other. Teachers are frustrated and angered by students who do not respond to their efforts. Discipline is likely to be a problem when students are bored or feel that what they are asked to learn is irrelevant. Student assignments are often not completed, or reflect only the minimum amount of effort, and class discussion may be minimal. Students blame teachers for their boredom, their inability to pursue their own interests, and for the meaningless work they are often asked to do. Both groups have difficulty understanding that the source of much of their unhappiness may be the way in which the schools are organized.

Working within externally established guidelines, the teacher plans, initiates, directs, and evaluates nearly all of the students' activities. After a relatively short period of time, students become dependent on the directions and expectations of the teacher. In the process, they may be stripped of initiative and have their curiosity dampened and their intellectual independence undermined. Learning becomes synonymous with whatever the teacher indicates they are supposed to know. Students discover that it is important to try to produce what they think the teacher wants.

Critics of the dominant-teacher–passive-student relationship argue that true learning can occur only when students consciously decide to participate actively in the process. It is doubtful that students can be forced to learn, in any real sense, although many schools operate on this assumption. Students may be coerced into going through the motions of learning—taking notes, completing assignments, memorizing information for tests—but there seems to be no way to make them remember what they have supposedly learned once they leave school. They may pass all their courses, but they will gain little if they have not improved their ability to reason or do not apply what they have learned to their daily lives. In a society that is characterized by relatively rapid social and economic change, failure to remain educable throughout life can lead to rapid obsolescence.

Functional illiteracy Each year American high schools graduate millions of students who are

Vandalism is one reaction high school students have to boredom in school. This Akron, Ohio, junior high was one of three hit the same weekend. All but seven rooms in the three-story building received the same treatment as the art room shown here.

Making Diplomas Count

Early last month, Albert A. Briggs, superintendent of schools for Chicago's West Side, began to review the reading scores of eighth graders scheduled to enter the district's high schools this fall. By the time he had finished, Briggs was appalled. Of 296 students headed for one high school, 270 were reading well below the appropriate achievement level; 38 could not even read as well as the average American third grader. Briggs issued an order unprecedented in the Chicago school system: starting this June, no student on the West Side will graduate from eighth grade until he or she has mastered at least sixth-grade reading skills.

Until recently, promotion from grade to grade through high school was almost automatic—making the diploma hardly more than a certificate of twelve years' attendance. In 1973, just one major system, Denver, Colo., required students to pass proficiency tests in English and mathematics in order to graduate from high school. Now, schools from Dade County, Fla., to Craig, Alaska, demand that their pupils meet minimal standards of competence before they are advanced through the schools. . . .

Most of the competency standards are fairly low. When students are required to pass exams in order to graduate from high school, they usually must demonstrate the ability to read and compute at approximately eighth-grade level. . . .

Some parents fear that if the schools are required to enforce only rock-bottom standards, teachers will stop demanding the best of their students. Other critics object that the competence tests put the whole burden of success on the students, without forcing the schools to improve their teaching. . . .

Despite the difficulties that accompany the creation of new standards, educators seem convinced that setting minimal goals—and enforcing them—is essential to making a public-school diploma mean more than a certificate of attendance. "We cannot allow schools to be as bad as they want to be," says Victor Taber of New York State's Division of Educational Testing. Putting a "floor" under the requirements for graduation can help prod the schools to improve.

Every year American high schools graduate large numbers of students who are functionally illiterate. Some states are responding to the problem.

functionally illiterate: they cannot read or write well enough to function effectively in a complex, technologically oriented society. These students have woefully inadequate reading and writing skills—some may be reading as low as the fifth grade level—yet they are awarded diplomas. Often, these students blame themselves for their marginal position in American life and do not question the legitimacy of the schools or how they are organized. If they failed to receive an adequate education, it must be their fault—not the schools' responsibility.

The Triumph of Mass Education?

The idea of American mass education is at least partially rooted in the need for educated citizens to fulfill the responsibilities of democratic government. Thomas Jefferson argued that liberty and self-determination could be maintained only by an educated populace. The growth of the American economy and its development into a world power has added a vocational emphasis to education. Finally, the schools were also used to bring substance to the belief in the equality of opportunity. No other society in the world has placed so much faith in the schools to prevent the development of a rigid system of social classes. In some ways, the educational system has been America's answer to Karl Marx. Theoretically, the schools would prevent the development of a rigid class system based on the ownership of the means of production. Mass education, it was supposed, would allow the fittest members of society, regardless of social origin, to rise to the limits of their potential.

Beginning in the 1960s, attempts were made to extend the assumed benefits of education to the poor and members of minority groups who had been excluded because of lack of financial resources or racial discrimination. This was one of the main purposes of Lyndon Johnson's much ballyhooed War on Poverty, the Head Start program, and even "Sesame Street." It was thought that once the poor had the advantages of quality education, the fittest among them would move into the mainstream of American life. It was presumed that the schools could overcome the disfiguring consequences of generations of economic and social deprivation. At the same time, the racial prob-

lems that had plagued American society for centuries would be reduced. As the educational sociologist Christopher Jencks pointed out:

The basic strategy of the war on poverty during the 1960s was to try to give everyone entering the job market or any other competitive arena comparable skills. This meant placing great emphasis on education. Many people imagined that if schools could equalize people's cognitive skills this would equalize their bargaining power as adults. In such a system nobody would end up very poor—or, presumably, very rich.[15]

Thus, the schools were to assure that democracy flourished, provide training in the specialized work skills needed by an industrialized society, prevent the development of a class structure, reduce racial hostility, and, at the same time, help students develop an appreciation for great art and literature. Could a single institution possibly accomplish all of these objectives?

Some successes   The American schools produced a series of contradictions. In some ways, they have been remarkably successful. At least three out of

Black pride in the classroom. In addition to their other functions, some schools now attempt to reduce or eliminate many of the negative psychological consequences of minority status in the United States.

every four students now graduate from high school. The proportion of nonwhite and poor students completing secondary school has increased dramatically. In 1973, for example, the proportion of nonwhites twenty to twenty-one years old who had completed less than four years of high school was only 27.9 percent, as compared to 62.7 percent of those forty-five to fifty-four years old. Proportions completing college for the same age cohorts were 27.0 and 12.1 percent, respectively.

Federal, state, and local per capita expenditures for education have steadily increased since the end of World War II. In 1946, total federal, state, and local expenditures for all public schools totaled $2.9 billion; by 1973, this had reached $67.2 billion. Suburban building programs have greatly increased the number of elementary and secondary schools. More than 50 percent of the college-age population is now enrolled in institutions of higher learning. Today, almost any person who wishes to attend college has the opportunity to do so. Tuition rates at state-supported institutions are within reach of many lower-income people, and government-guaranteed student loans are available for those who cannot afford the tuition charges. At this level, American mass education would appear to be highly successful.

Many failures   But from another perspective, the results are not so pleasing. Many schools are grossly underfinanced. Teachers, particularly in the urban centers, often work under deplorable conditions. Even residents of the more affluent suburbs are voting down school budgets when they mean an increase in local taxes. The vitality of many students is drained by the demands of the traditional classroom. Racial tension in urban schools sporadically disrupts the daily routine. Increasingly, colleges and universities are faced with students who, after twelve years of schooling, have not mastered the most basic skills of reading, writing, and arithmetic. Finally, most students do not seem to develop a real appreciation for the arts, music, and great literature. Shakespeare cannot compete with the police and detective shows that monopolize the television screen.

American society is still faced with chronic poverty and a steady deterioration in the quality of life in its metropolitan centers, in spite of the increase in the overall standard of living. Drug abuse and alcoholism continue to plague a disturbingly large segment of the American population. Some people feel alienated and powerless to exercise control over their own lives. Others live with a nagging feeling that "something is missing" in spite of the abundance of consumer products. In each case, educational institutions seem to have contributed little to the solution of these problems, although many in the public seem to assume they should.

To some, it is perplexing how the educational system can be so successful from one perspective and so ineffective from another. Charles Silberman, one of the great critics of the schools, believes that "the question cannot be answered with regard to education alone; it is, in fact, the central paradox of American life. In almost every area,

improvements beyond what anyone thought possible fifty or twenty-five or even ten years ago have produced anger and anxiety rather than satisfaction."[16] The success of American society in some areas, coupled with an insensitivity to and failure to deal with other long-standing social problems, accounts for much of the current trouble. Educational institutions by themselves have not, and cannot, respond effectively to problems with such broad social, economic, and political roots.

A steadily improving standard of living combined with increased educational opportunities resulted in rising expectations among a majority of the population. In many cases, these aspirations exceeded the ability of the society, including the schools, to keep pace. Before World War II, many people were satisfied with steady work and minimum fringe benefits. But in the postwar years, blue-collar factory work became increasingly unacceptable, and more and more young people sought entry into the white-collar managerial and professional occupations. Each generation assumed that it would be better off in terms of working conditions and income than the one preceding it. People viewed the schools and education as the vehicle through which they could fulfill their aspirations. But although mass education was instrumental in helping some people reach some of their goals, it could not, and cannot now, help all of the people do likewise. There is no way every American can achieve material success, no matter how long he stays in school. There simply is no room at the top of the social system for everyone—a competitive system must, by definition, have losers.

The American school has thus become the victim of its own success. Particularly during the decades of the great immigrations, the schools were called upon almost to create a nation. Despite the overapplication of the melting pot metaphor, they succeeded sufficiently well to cause amazement in many places abroad. But that very success, and our overcelebration of it, created further expectations that cannot be fulfilled. The public school—or the more vague conception of "education"—has become the American equivalent of a magic wand: virtually no personal or social problem exists that someone, somewhere—often educators, who ought to know better—has not assured us can be overcome through education. The current crises of our schools, from Head Start through multiversity, are testimony to the falsity of that belief. Social problems are the problems of the society as a whole. No single institution, from school to court, can hope to cope with them. Until that realization becomes widespread, the problems of the schools—and the society—will remain unresolved.

Summary

All societies educate their young. In all but the most simple, this process is likely to occur through some kind of formal educational structure. In industrialized societies, such structures are, of course, schools. Examining the institution of formal education in such societies, we see that everywhere it performs certain universal and presumably basic functions. These are (1) *socialization* of students into their culture beyond that accomplished in the family; (2) *social integration* through indoctrination in a single "official" culture (and, perhaps, ideology) of all the young, regardless of subcultural background; (3) *vocational sorting,* which both trains and targets people for available positions in the society, including, in many cases, those that are culturally defined as socially "suitable" for persons of certain racial, ethnic, and socioeconomic status; and (4) the provision, selectively, of an avenue for *social mobility,* as well as the perpetuation of immobility accomplished by the sorting function. In any industrial society, then, the schools act both to instill culture in the young and to maintain the social structure and order.

In the United States, the publicly supported schools in particular have had imposed on them certain other functions or requirements that might not occur in other societies. These include *Americanization,* the indoctrination of the children of numerous racial and ethnic groupings in what amounts to white Anglo-Saxon culture; the attempt to provide or appear to provide *equality of opportunity* through standard education for all (although as a consequence of racial discrimination, community standards, and regional and socioeconomic differences, this goal has never been attained); and specific *vocational training* (often at odds with more liberal educational goals).

The United States also has what amounts to a double system of educational organizations: those supported by public monies and "private" schools, both secular and religious, supported in other ways. These duplicate each other in many ways from primary level through university, although their student bodies and some minor functions may be quite different.

The structure, problems, goals and controls of schools at different levels are very different. The *public elementary and secondary schools,* for example, confront both problems of finance, as taxpayers refuse to adopt higher bond rates to support them, and the basic issue of *community control,* a standard feature of American public education. Community control is represented by the locally elected school board, but the problems of which people constitute the community to be represented and how it is to be represented remain unsolved. A pressing issue that plagues many boards is that adequate representation of the majority in a community may well result in rejection of things of crucial importance to minorities.

At the *college and university level,* in addition to the ever-present financial difficulties, an overriding problem is that despite the existence of community and state colleges, which do serve the less-than-affluent, the structure tends to reflect the nation's class system. The poor and the nonwhite go to low-status, low-fee institutions, bringing with them the educational problems of disadvantaged backgrounds. The middle class go to state universities—many of them, the immense multiversities—with all of the educational problems *they* entail. And the wealthy go to prestigious, and excellent, private institutions.

The institution of education in the United States, like any social institution in any society, in some respects mirrors that society, reflecting its ideologies and basic assumptions, its problems and promises. The American school may be more beset with dilemmas than other institutionalized agencies, however, because it has often been explicitly charged with the solution of problems that are in fact societal rather than educational. Certainly, some of the crises facing the schools today, like those we saw confronting the family, were born of that condition.

Review Questions

1. This chapter made a distinction between the formal and the informal curricula in the schools as they take an active part in the socialization process. Explain the role of the informal curricula. Compare this influence with that of a student's parents. Is one more pervasive than the other? How do these two forces interact?

2. What would be some of the characteristics of an intellectually stimulating home environment for a student? In your answer, be sure to include the roles of various members of the family which would lead to an enriched environment.

3. Why does the American intellectual receive less respect than the "intelligent person"?

4. What are the main reasons parents would choose to send their son or daughter to a small private college instead of a larger university?

5. What are the various factors accounting for the relatively low level of prestige and salary of teachers in America? Is there any reason to believe the situation is changing? Why or why not?

Suggestions for Research

1. Ask as many American history teachers as are employed in grade schools and high schools in your community to provide you with a list of the ten Americans they consider the most famous and instrumental in the nation's progress. Referring to biographical materials, investigate the amount of formal education enjoyed by the fifteen or twenty persons most frequently selected by the teachers. Do most appear to have been very educated, somewhat schooled, or primarily self-taught? What conclusions can you draw in terms of American educational ideals? How, if at all, would you expect your findings to be changed if these figures had lived in the twentieth century?

2. This project should be particularly enlightening if your early years were confined to white or middle-class elementary schools. Locate an elementary school teacher who works in a lower class or inner-city school who is willing to allow you to observe one full day of school. Write and report on this experience to your class. In your conclusions, compare this school with the one you attended as a child. How significant are the differences? What implications for the future does the lower SES level school hold in terms of the students?

3. For most of you, nursery school was a luxury during your early years; today, however, it is often the rule in comfortable neighborhoods. Observe several classes in a neighborhood nursery school, including different age groups of children. Do you think the nursery school experience is one which gives the child a decided advantage over his peers? If so, how does this affect the lower-class child? Summarize your observations in a paper and discuss the impact of pre-school institutions upon American education.

4. The American college system has often been accused of being archaic, outdated. Devote your term paper to this issue, gathering your data from a sample survey of college students. What are the most common complaints? What aspects of college instruction are the most popular? Is there any apparent relationship between a student's success in college and his level of satisfaction?

5. Prepare a term paper on anti-intellectualism in America. What specifically is anti-intellectualism? How powerful is it today in comparison with two centuries ago? What, if any, changes can Americans expect in the future of this force? In your discussion, you will want to explore the age-old stereotype of the intellectual. How close to reality is the absent-minded professor? What function is served by such a stereotype?

CHAPTER 14
RELIGION

© 1965 United Feature Syndicate, Inc.

The question of meaning is fundamental to religion. Among the Peanuts, Linus is the theologian of the group, the one who repeatedly wrestles with the meaning of life, the forces of good and evil, love and hate. As the leading scholar of the church school set, Linus has just explained to Lucy that one of the social functions of religion is to dispel anxiety by a sound meaning system capable of taking a load off your mind. Yet Linus is sufficiently versed in Scripture and theology to recognize this is not the only function of religion. Like an Old Testament prophet, Linus frequently brings religion to bear in a critical fashion on conventional moral attitudes and behavior patterns. To comfort and to challenge aptly summarizes the major roles of the religion to which Linus subscribes.

We will see in this chapter that, in one larger sense, comforting and challenging are the two basic, and opposing, functions that *all* religions perform. All are both integrative and disintegrative for their societies. Sociological analysis of the institution of religion cannot tell us anything, of course, about the theological-metaphysical *validity* of any religious system. But by scrutinizing religion and religious behavior as social phenomena, we learn a great deal about human society and ourselves.

Mark Twain wrote: "Man is the Religious Animal. He is the only Religious Animal. He is the only animal that has the true religion—several of them."[1] What Twain underscores with this quip is a double-barreled fact that any scientific study of religion must take seriously: religion is universal among human societies, yet the concrete forms through which it is expressed are extremely various. Moreover, these religious forms are regarded with earnest seriousness by those who adhere to them.

The presence of religion in all human societies is an accepted fact of social science. Of course, not all people everywhere are religious. Some individuals, especially in the advanced societies, do resist the call toward religious belief and regular participation in worship. But the presence of religious activities in all known societal systems does suggest, at the very least, that religious experience endures as one of the most highly valued human endeavors.

In this chapter, we will develop a systematic sociological definition of religion, describe the major religions of the world and the functions that religion performs for people and their societies, and, finally, survey the nature and characteristics of religion in the United States.

What Is Religion?

At first glance, this question may appear elementary. For surely all of us have some commonsense knowledge of religion. But many of us are acquainted with only a few world religions, and to form an adequate definition, we need to understand the basic premises of all the major world religions.

The Major World Religions

The religious communities of the world are often distinguished by reference to their central object of worship. Around this sacred reality, belief patterns, ritual practices, ethical systems, and social organization take form. These typical features of religious life have given rise to a set of categories for identifying religious traditions. Hence, we commonly speak of **monotheistic** (believing in one god), **polytheistic** (believing in several gods), **ethical (religions of the way)**, and **ancestral (or nationalistic) religions**. Beyond this assortment, further variety is added by the various primitive religions. Several of these classifications contain more than one religion.

The great monotheisms: Judaism, Christianity, Islam   We tend to be familiar with two of the major monotheistic faiths: *Judaism,* the smallest world religion, with about 14.5 million adherents, which centers on the worship of Yahweh, the God of the Old Testament as revealed to Moses and the prophets; and *Christianity,* whose Protestant, Catholic, and Eastern Orthodox branches form the largest religious body in the world, numbering almost 967.5 million believers (see Table 14-1). Most Christians believe in a trinitarian or three-natured, God, accept the Bible as their sacred scripture, and adhere to the teachings of Jesus. Together, Judaism and Christianity, which sprang from it, make up the Judeo-Christian tradition that has been so influential in both Western civilization and American society.

A third monotheistic faith from the same tradition is *Islam.* This religion originated in the sixth century under the prophet Mohammed, who called for faith in Allah and recorded his revelations in the Koran, the sacred scriptures of Islam. After vigorous expansion, Islam stands today as the second largest world religion; its 513 million members, called Moslems, are located primarily in the Near East, Africa, and Asia.

Polytheism: Hinduism   The most prominent polytheistic faith is Hinduism. It teaches its followers to believe in a hierarchy of gods who increase, somewhat in pyramid fashion, from local deities, to

> **monotheism:** belief in the existence of a single supreme deity.
>
> **polytheism:** belief in the existence of multiple deities.
>
> **ethical religions (religions of the way):** religions that emphasize the practice of an ethical life so as to produce harmony in both social and personal life. They lack belief in a personal god.
>
> **ancestral (nationalistic) religion:** religion that glorifies ancestors and sometimes, by extension, the state as represented by its leader.

regional gods, and eventually to gods associated with larger caste groups. Hinduism is probably the oldest existing religion, coming into being sometime during the late Stone Age. Presently, its almost 516 million members are situated in India, Pakistan, and Bangladesh.

Religions of the way: Buddhism, Confucianism, and Taoism   Three leading world religions—Buddhism, Confucianism, and Taoism—reflect an outlook quite different from that of Western faiths. Because they stress ethics rather than ideas, adjustment more than change, and the past instead of the future, these traditions are often called *religions of the way.* All lack a notion of a personalized god, and their doctrines form around a set of revered principles defining the ultimate order of the universe. These sacred principles encourage followers to practice an ethical life so as to fulfill the ultimate order and produce harmony in both personal and social life.

Buddhism, which is closely related to Hinduism, arose in India during the sixth century B.C. when the "enlightened one," or Buddha, discovered the means for achieving spiritual excellence (Nirvana) through meditation. Gradually over the centuries, Buddhism divided into a number of sects. Each one emphasized different aspects of the sacred texts and developed separate rituals and moral codes. Altogether, these groups today have a following of some 223 million members.

Confucianism is the religion founded on the ethical teachings of Confucius, who lived in China from 551 to 479 B.C. By urging the moral and

Table 14-1   Estimated membership in major world religions by geographic area, 1973

Religion	North America[a]	South America	Europe	Asia	Africa	Oceania[b]	Total
Total Christian	224,933,250	163,567,000	372,425,700	87,396,500	98,862,000	20,609,000	967,793,450
Roman Catholic	128,995,500	157,831,000	179,684,000	46,456,500	34,587,000	4,395,000	551,949,000
Eastern Orthodox	4,117,000	54,000	67,380,700	2,135,000	17,410,000	484,000	91,580,700
Protestant	91,820,750	5,682,000	125,361,000	38,805,000	46,865,000	15,730,000	324,263,750
Jewish[c]	6,344,475	680,700	3,983,750	3,064,050	297,950	73,000	14,443,925
Moslem	205,000	185,000	4,088,000	414,796,000	93,328,500	572,000	513,174,500
Zoroastrian	—	—	—	180,600	450	—	181,050
Shinto	55,000	90,000	—	63,005,000	—	—	63,150,000
Taoist	15,000	12,000	—	31,340,700	—	—	31,367,700
Confucian	92,165	90,000	40,000	275,630,700	500	45,500	275,898,865
Buddhist	142,000	175,000	200,000	223,136,500	2,000	—	223,655,500
Hindu	65,000	470,000	300,000	513,755,500	461,000	529,000	515,580,500
Total	231,851,890	165,269,700	381,037,450	1,612,305,550	192,952,400	21,828,500	2,605,245,490

a. Includes Central America and West Indies.
b. Includes Australia and New Zealand, as well as islands of the South Pacific.
c. Includes total Jewish population, whether or not related to the synagogue.

physical harmony of all things, Confucianism has shown a tremendous capacity for attracting many quite different peoples. Yet Confucianism failed to generate a real priesthood, a distinct theological system, and other features common to religion. Consequently, several interpreters—notably Max Weber and C. K. Yang—have questioned whether Confucianism is really a religion or whether it is not better viewed as a philosophy possessing an ethical system.[2] Although this is a valid question, we shall follow the usual procedure of including Confucianism, with its 275 million adherents, as one of the world religions.

Closely allied with Confucianism is a smaller religious movement known as *Taoism.* Beginning as a philosophical school in China some 2,000 years ago, Taoism gradually developed into a religious community that today includes some 31 million followers. More mystical than Confucianism, Taoism has also developed its own sacred scriptures, ethics, and especially a political theory. Like other religions of the way, however, Taoism continues to stress the quality of one's life in relation to the ultimate order governing the universe and individual destiny.

Ancestral religion: Shintoism   By far the largest ancestral religion is *Shintoism,* almost exclusively a religion of the Japanese peoples. Early in its history, Shintoism emerged as a religion worshipping ancestors. But perhaps the most famous feature of this faith is how it transformed patriotism into a religious virtue. At the height of Shinto growth, just before and during World War II, glorifying one's ancestors became a means for showing loyalty to the state as represented by the emperor. After the war, the nationalistic character of Shinto was rejected in favor of the more ancient practice of honoring the ancestral spirits who guard individual and collective life. There are now about 63 million followers of Shinto in Japan and throughout the world.

Primitive religion   In addition to the major world religions, two leading forms of primitive religion also need to be taken into account. **Animism** is the belief of primitive peoples in spirits and ghosts who move about the world working good and ill in people's everyday lives. Sir Edward Tylor was one of animism's chief interpreters.[3] He suggested that such universal experiences as dream activity, death, visions, and so forth, led primitive people to assume the existence of a soul that was capable of roaming about detached from the body. From this notion, there arose the concept of spiritual beings who could be appeased through some rituals and invoked in times of distress by others. Elaborate religious ceremonial practices grew up around these ideas about spiritual beings as people sought to come to grips with the crisis events of their lives. Although animism still remains a form of religious life investigated by scholars, few today accept Tylor's early conclusion that all religions originated out of animism.

Totemism, often considered a more advanced form of primitive religion, centers on the notion that sacred power, or *mana* (a Melanesian word for the sacred), is represented in specific objects drawn from the immediate environment—usually some common plant or animal. These serve as the focus of religious veneration in ritual activities. Emile Durkheim pioneered the analysis of totemic religion by suggesting that primitive people did not worship the actual snake, bird, or tree that was their totem, but instead regarded these concrete objects as visible symbols of the sacred force standing behind them.[4] By identifying with a totem, one gained a means of access to the realm of the sacred. Durkheim also pointed to the close linkage between totemic religion and the kinship network. Members of the same clan shared a totemic emblem. Hence, when an individual received his totemic symbol within the religious sphere, he simultaneously found his "place" within the family system, the basic social organization of the secular society.

Durkheim believed that he had discovered in this connection the key for understanding the function of religion in primitive and modern societies alike. Symbols such as the cross in Christianity and the star of David in Judaism promote an identification with a particular religious group, just as primitive people identified with their totem to find a place of belonging. This similarity led Durkheim to reason that primitive religion is not as different from modern religion as many interpreters assumed. Indeed, Durkheim theorized that religion everywhere shares a fundamental nature. Although contemporary scholars are not so inclined as Durkheim

animism: the belief that the world and objects in it are "animated," or peopled, with spirits.

totemism: the belief that sacred power exists in or is represented in animals or natural objects.

"It's one of two things—either the great god of the inner earth, Timbuku, is angry with our last virgin sacrifice, or the enormous pressure of a formation of molten rock is breaking through a weak spot in the earth's crust."

to stress the similarity between primitive and modern religions, sociologists do regard primitive religions as significant sources of data for understanding the social and psychological needs fulfilled by religion both yesterday and today.

The Sacred as the Hallmark of Religion

Against the backdrop of this survey of world religions, we are in a better position to address the question: What is religion? Clearly, some responses of the commonsense type must now be judged inadequate. For example, we cannot define religion as a belief in God, because the religions of the way really have no gods as such. Nor will **theology,** the formal study of the divine, always serve as the distinguishing mark of religion, because all religions have not generated a doctrinal system. And neither will defining religion as an activity carried on by priests suffice, because some religions have existed for centuries without ever developing a professionally trained priesthood.

If we cut through the complicated variety of historical religious types, however, there does emerge one outstanding feature that will serve as a touchstone for a minimal definition of religion. This root element may be designated as *sacredness,* the focal center for religious veneration. For theistic religions, the sacred is defined in terms of a **supramundane** deity, that is, a personal God who exists above and beyond the world. In the ethical and primitive religions, the sacred takes on a more abstract character. The sacred is understood as the ultimate structure of the universe, either as symbolized in certain sacred principles or as reflected in totemic objects. However differently religious communities may have perceived the sacred, all of them have some explicit notion of sacredness standing at the center of their tradition.

Durkheim was one of the first to recognize the overriding significance of the sacred for setting religion apart from purely secular—worldly— affairs. Consequently, he defined religion according to the formula: ''A religion is a unified system of beliefs and practices relative to sacred things, that is to say, things set apart and forbidden— beliefs and practices which unite into a single moral community called a church, all those who adhere to them.''[5] Durkheim's primary thrust was to assert that the sacred should be seen in opposition to secular objects and forces. Hence, the sacred became a reality set apart as powerful, extraordinary, awe-inspiring, and *transcendent—* above or beyond the material universe.

Durkheim's ideas were complemented by research on the nature of the sacred undertaken by the German scholar of comparative religion Rudolf Otto. In *The Idea of the Holy,* Otto isolated the major features of the sacred.[6] He included among the traits of the sacred the qualities of otherness, mystery, tremendousness, and the capability of inspiring awe and adoration. Durkheim and Otto stood on common ground in their assumption that the sacred represented the root source of religious sentiment. Yet the sacred remained a general category, with different specific meanings being filled in by each religious community. Historically, religions have typically established themselves around the sacred by developing a specific set of beliefs, practices, and social organization that make up the distinctive characteristics of their religious tradition.

The Basic Dimensions of Religiosity

As Durkheim and Otto suggested, religious movements respond to the sacred by generating belief patterns, ritual practices, ethical codes, and cultic organizations. Each of these separate elements results from people's encounter with the sacred. And while the sacred, being nonempirical, is not available for scientific research, these concrete features of the religious life are susceptible to sociological investigation.

Belief patterns   A sacred content is defined by a set of ideas about the nature of the religious reality people experience through revelation, reflection, or divine illumination. Belief patterns perform the necessary function of defining the nature of sacredness for a given religious community. Of course, religious beliefs vary considerably, not only in terms of their content but also in terms of their clarity and precision. Some belief patterns achieve quite logical organization, such as the medieval Catholic theology of St. Thomas Aquinas. Others, like the legends of primitive religion, remain loosely related collections of myths with only vague doctrinal systems—if doctrinal systems are present at all. Whatever their established form, however, some belief patterns must be developed by a religious body in order to provide direction for the movement as a whole.

Ritual practices   Closely related to belief patterns are the forms of worship oriented toward the sacred called **rituals**. These consist of behavior patterns prescribed for believers as appropriate responses for human relationship with the ultimate source of being or value. Rituals, like the belief patterns from which they spring, display considerable variation, from making deep scars on the face in some primitive rituals to praying five times a day for orthodox Moslems. Variation is determined not only by the nature of religious ideas but also by the occasion for which the ritual is performed. For example, some rituals serve the primary goal of bestowing thanksgiving and praise on the deity; others petition supernatural powers for special blessings; and still others seek to appease the wrath of gods who have been offended by some impious deed. A few rituals are practiced by individuals in isolation from the group, but most tend to foster collective participation and encourage a collective enthusiasm.

Ritual practices also differ in terms of their structure and strict requirements. Some rituals, such as the early Quaker meetings, are largely free and spontaneous; while others, such as the Latin Rite of the Roman Catholic Church, retain a uniformity over long historical periods and across many cultural frontiers. In general, however, rituals serve the basic purpose of reinforcing the commitment of believers to the content of the faith. They provide periodic occasions for remembering and celebrating the central meanings of the religious tradition.

Ethical codes   Ethical codes differ from ritual patterns largely in terms of their orientation. While rituals are behavior patterns directed toward the worship of the deity, ethical action is religiously ordained behavior addressed toward other human beings whom one meets in everyday life. The ethical life is intimately informed by the religious ideas in the belief system. The Roman Catholic emphasis on the sanctity of life, for example, produces an ethical norm prohibiting abortion. Ethical

theology: the formal or scientific study of the divine.

supramundane: above or beyond the natural world.

rituals: the patterns of formal behavior oriented to and reflecting the significance of religious belief.

Moslems at prayer. Religious ritual fosters collective participation.

codes are regarded with seriousness precisely because the sacred stands behind them to bestow legitimacy on their demands. One major consequence of ethical norms is that they mold members belonging to a religious tradition into similar character types. Hence, participants in a single religious tradition often adhere to similar patterns of behavior that help distinguish them from other religious communities. For the sociologist interested in the ways religions control and direct the behavior of their followers, the structure of a group's ethical system is a crucial object of analysis.

Cultic organization The cultic organization of a religious group is its social organization and structure. The **cult** perpetuates and safeguards the central religious experience around which a body of believers has developed. The cult oversees such diverse matters as the conduct of ritual activities; the establishment and maintenance of a place of worship; the selection of specialists in religious affairs—priests, monks, nuns, shamans, seers, prophets, and so forth; and the arrangement of various religious offices relative to one another, as in the hierarchy of priests, bishops, and archbishops. The cult also defines the proper role for laity as opposed to clergy.

Cultic organization, whatever its form, is necessary to give social and institutional expression to religious beliefs. A logical connection, therefore, links the cultic form to the belief and ritual patterns of a given religious group. Sociologists are convinced that no religion can endure very long without cultic organization. Without a cult to maintain order for the group, belief systems would become confused, new members would fail to be adequately indoctrinated into the faith, and places of worship would fall into disuse and disorder, to cite but a few problems.

The overriding significance of cultic organization for insuring the continued life and vitality of a religious tradition has led to the conclusion that religion is preeminently a social phenomenon. Of course, individuals can and do initiate new religious beliefs and transform old religious practices. But personal efforts are not likely to make much of an impact or persist very long if a cultic order fails to arise and transmit these innovations to others. In short, any religion that survives its founder must become a social force complete with a cultic organization. Individual religion can exist, of course, but no religion can survive very long without meeting certain social conditions and taking on an institutional structure.

A Working Definition of Religion

After examining the basic types of world religions and the dimensions of religiosity, we can now suggest a working definition of religion. Essentially, **religion** is the human activity organized around the sacred, that nonempirical source of religious power, transcendence, mystery, and awe. In the process of becoming a social institution, religion creates in relation to this sacred center the several elements of belief systems, ritual practices, ethical codes, and cultic organizations. All religions that endure over time eventually become social movements. Hence, religion is a social phenomenon as well as a reality that bestows meaning and significance on the lives of individuals.

What Religion Is Not

If our definition adequately separates the religious phenomenon from nonreligious activities, then we should be able to identify some endeavors that resemble yet do not actually qualify as religious behavior. Four common activities that belong to this category are magic, science, political ideology, and secular philosophy.

Magic Magic frequently develops ritual practices and leadership roles similar to those of religious communities. Magic also parallels religion in its desire to manipulate the "unknown" for the achievement of certain concrete goals. What distinguishes magic from religion, however, is that magic engages in special and often secretive activities in order to attain specific goals for individual clients. The rituals of magic typically try to produce the defeat of enemies, the healing of sickness, the increase of rainfall, greater fertility of the soil, and so forth.

Religion, by contrast, is oriented toward more spiritual goals, like providing people with an ultimate meaning for life or deepening their commitment to the faith and its ethical standards. Religion is concerned with the question of our relation to the sacred, while magic seeks only to manipulate reality for a specific and limited purpose. There is, however, a point at which the two seem occasionally to blend into each other. Several religious practices—having a priest bless a car, for example, or placing a plastic Jesus on the dashboard—resemble magical activities. Yet, generally, religion addresses issues of ultimate importance rather than questions of merely personal vested interest, and religion also generates a system of myths and rituals more complex and creative than the simple techniques of magic.

Science   Like magic and religion, science is also a mode of human orientation toward the unknown. Where magic attempts to manipulate the world by strange and mysterious rituals, however, science seeks to understand the natural realm by discovering those universal laws that operate independently of human will and supernatural intervention. Consequently, science proceeds by means of a methodological approach that is empirical, quantifiable, and repeatable by other scientists working under similar, controlled circumstances. Not only has scientific advancement in driving back the "unknown" rendered nature more intelligible; it has also made nature more controllable and subject to human manipulation. Furthermore, the growth of scientific knowledge has disenchanted the world so that the need for magic has been decisively reduced. As a part of this disenchantment process, science has also challenged some religious views of long standing. A host of biblical reports, from the creation of the world in seven days to miracles and historical events, have either been refuted by natural science or enshrouded in a cloud of doubt.

The history of the warfare between science and religion—as one writer has characterized this relationship—has not been a wholly negative process, however.[7] Nor has science destroyed religion, as some scholars were predicting only a few decades ago. Instead, natural science has assumed a larger and larger role in describing the nature of the physical order, while religion has continued to concentrate its attention on the moral or spiritual aspects of reality.

cult: a system of worship, in particular its rites and ceremonies. Although the Roman, Anglican, and Orthodox branches of the Catholic Church all share many practices, for example, the particular cult of each is distinguishable as a special social organization and structure. *Cult* is also used more generally to refer to the form of religious organization more properly called a *sect*.

religion: the human activity consisting of belief systems, ritual practices, ethical codes, and cultic organization organized around the idea of the sacred.

Magic, like that practiced by this voodoo priestess, is usually a practical affair directed toward specific objectives for individual clients.

Political ideologies and secular philosophies In recent years, there has been a growing tendency among social scientists to compare political ideologies (such as communism and fascism) and secular philosophies (like the thought of Bertrand Russell, Albert Camus, or Jean-Paul Sartre) with religion. But political and philosophical idea systems typically lack a concept of the sacred. And without this critical element, such movements do not satisfy the most important criterion in our working definition of religion. Indeed, magic, science, and political-philosophical ideologies all stand apart from religion largely because their relationship with the unknown is not organized around a sacred center. Thus, our definition of religion emphasizing the sacred does provide the means for clearly distinguishing between religious and secular movements, even when the two appear to perform almost identical functions in everyday life.

The Social Functions of Religion

Because religion is a complex institution, the social functions it performs are quite diverse. If a religious function produces beneficial consequences, then we normally refer to it as a positive function—as, for example, when religion stimulates tolerance, peaceful cooperation, or love. Religion can also generate harmful, or dysfunctional, effects. The religiously approved human sacrifice practiced by the ancient Aztecs of Mexico is an obvious example. In general, then, as we noted at the beginning of the chapter, religion can exert both a positive, cohesive, and comforting influence and a negative, disintegrating influence.[8] Furthermore, some religious functions are manifest—intended and immediately observable—and some are latent—unintended and not immediately discernible.

Determining precisely what functions are exercised by religions in specific cases and whether they are positive or negative, latent or manifest, is very difficult. To do so requires both skill in empirical observation and knowledge of theoretical alternatives. For this reason, the following discussion of the social functions of religion includes both differing theoretical viewpoints and the empirical research inspired by each perspective. Throughout

The Scopes trial was one of the great U.S. battles in the war between science and religion. John T. Scopes, a high school biology teacher, was tried, and convicted, for violating a Tennessee law forbidding the teaching of evolution in the public schools. While some fundamentalist sects and intradenominational groups still resist the idea of evolution, no established denomination any longer officially disputes this conventional scientific knowledge.

the discussion, we should bear in mind that no one theory can account for all religious behavior.

The Alienating Function: The Marxist Tradition

Karl Marx had a profound influence on the growth of sociological interpretations of religion. Partly because he was one of the first scholars to employ sociological categories, Marx framed the issues to which subsequent interpretors had to respond—whether or not they agreed with him.

Marx's thought Marx opened his analysis of the social functions of religion by adapting the innovations in religious interpretation suggested by Ludwig Feuerbach, a theologian whom Marx admired, even though he felt Feuerbach was not sufficiently radical in his critique of religion. Feuerbach had alleged that the idea of God was of human origin and creation.[9] Human beings projected into the

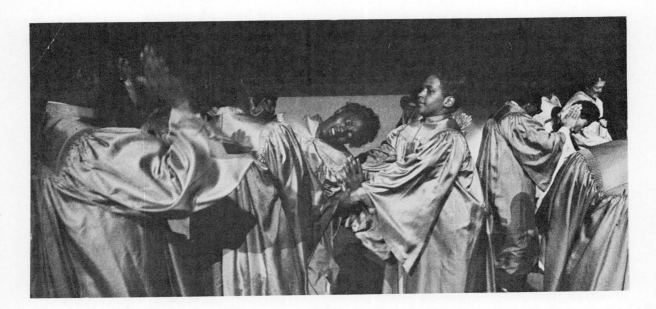

heavens an ideal image composed of the noblest human traits. The purpose of this ideal was to provide individuals with a model of moral excellence toward which they might strive. Before long, however, people lost sight of the fact that this "god" was an object of their own creation. They began to worship and fear this ideal as though it were a supernatural being.

Alienation Marx borrowed this notion from Feuerbach and carried it further. He proposed that because people live in fear of an object they constructed, religion must be perceived as an *alienating force* in human life—perhaps the primal alienating force.[10] By terrorizing people with the fear of a nonexistent god, religion prevented complete self-realization and deprived people of the opportunity to become fully human, thus alienating them from their real selves. In addition, Marx saw religion as alienating clergy from the laity and groups of different faiths from each other. Marx regarded the dehumanization that religion promoted as the distinguishing feature of alienation. He concluded that overcoming the alienating influence of religion required nothing less than the complete rejection of all religion.

Social class From this general outlook on the role of religion in society, Marx turned to an analysis of the concrete functions religion performs. Here the economic factors—the core of any Marxist analysis—came to play a larger role: not only is religion an alienating force, but it serves the special function of sustaining the vested interests of the dominant class within society. Therefore, religion contributes to the exploitation of the lower classes.

Marx grounded this larger proposition in a theoretical notion that separated reality into two major divisions: *ideal* forces and *material* forces. Ideal forces, or the "superstructure" of society, consist of all mental forms, such as legal ideas, values, philosophies, political ideologies, and religious beliefs. The material forces, or "substructure," of society include those economic relations derived from production—in short, one's class position. Marx asserted that the material situation—the social class—one acquires by accident of birth determines one's ideals and values, including one's religious beliefs. Religion, therefore, is first and foremost a reflection of one's socioeconomic situation as established by the economy.

More important, religion *maintains* the prevailing class structure, together with its unequal distribution of economic wealth and social privilege. This role is particularly important for the working classes, who suffer under an exploitive system imposed from above by the ruling class. Religion works to snuff out those fires of anger and resentment kindled against an unfair class arrangement and helps the working classes tolerate their growing misery and "pauperization." Religion accomplishes this by teaching the lower classes that this world is a "vale of tears," to be endured with humility and piety, and that those who remain faithful will receive reward in heaven. A modern jingle states much the same idea: "There will be pie in the sky by and by when we die." Marx used a different metaphor. Religion, he declared, "is an opiate to the people," a tranquilizer that dulls people's senses and lulls them into a passive acceptance of the injustices produced by a capitalist economy.

The legacy of Marx   Much of doctrinaire Marxism has been rejected by contemporary sociologists; few, for example, still subscribe to his view that religion is an illusion. Another problem with Marxian thought was that it violated an important rule of sociological method. Marx could tell you before he began his research that, because religion was *always* an alienating extension of the material substructure, it furthered the injustices of the status quo. Modern sociologists are skeptical about the validity of any analysis where the findings can be reached before the research is undertaken.

Yet Marx has taught us a great deal. He brought into view a succession of insights that had previously gone undetected. With regard to religion, his major contribution was the recognition that material factors—and especially social-class influences—have a dramatic impact on what a religious community believes and how they practice their faith. Marx could readily have understood why some people worship only with Bach and others tolerate nothing but gospel songs. For in each instance, class perspective is the deciding factor in determining what music is appropriate. Indeed, there is ample evidence to uphold the thesis that religion sometimes lends support to the cultural perspective of its adherents. During the American Civil

War, for example, the southern churches condoned slavery, while the northern churches raised their voice to champion the cause of abolition. These facts neatly conform to Marx's idea of the class-bound character of religion.

Yet there is another side to the coin. More recently, the churches of the South sparked the civil rights movement and even provided ministers, like Martin Luther King, for leadership in the drive against segregation. The Southern Baptist Convention was the first leading denomination officially to approve the school desegregation ruling of the Supreme Court in 1954. And the National Council of Churches has received major credit for passage of the Civil Rights acts of 1962 and 1964. In these instances, the religious institution spoke out prophetically against its culture in a manner Marx would have believed impossible. Consequently, sociologists have moved toward a qualification of the Marxist thesis by substituting the statement: religion is *sometimes* a reflection of the class outlook of its members. This revision has retained Marx's major insight without perpetuating its errors. We turn now to some modern studies of the relation between social class and religious denomination based on Marx's insights.

The link between denomination and social class
One of the most scathing critiques of religion's surrender to material factors is a 1929 study by H. Richard Niebuhr, *The Social Sources of Denominationalism.*[11] Niebuhr maintained that material factors played a more significant role than religious doctrines in dividing the church into **denominations**, conventional, widely accepted church organizations. Central in this process was the effect of social class. Members of the lower class—the "disinherited," Niebuhr called them—were in effect barred from participation in middle-class denominations. This forced them to create their own **sects**—smaller, more orthodox groups—to minister to their needs.

Gradually, as the lower-class sect encouraged its members to practice such virtues as honesty, hard work, abstention from alcohol, and responsibility to family obligations, the whole group experienced upward social mobility toward a middle-class lifestyle. As the sect approached the status of a middle-class denomination, extreme features of its theology were modified in favor of more moderate beliefs and practices. This change helped the group attract converts who were already middle-class. But once middle-class status was achieved, the denomination no longer ministered to the disinherited, making necesary the formation of another sect to address the religious needs of the lower class, and the cycle began anew. Niebuhr concluded that churches have a very difficult time overcoming the class divisions of the culture.

Other material or social factors exercise a divisive influence like that of social class. Among them are the elements of race, which split denominations into black and white churches; ethnicity, which perpetuates nationalistic differences carried by immigrant groups into American society, resulting in the German Lutheran Church, the Norwegian Lutheran Church, the Swedish Lutheran Church, and so forth; sectionalism, which divides denominations like Baptists, Methodists, and Presbyterians into northern and southern branches; and the frontier, which fostered rural revivalism in opposition to the urban religion of the commercial East. The common feature running through all these schismatic church structures is their dependence on sociological foundations rather than doctrinal differences. Thus, while Niebuhr was not a Marxist by intellectual persuasion, he nonetheless utilized the Marxist tradition to isolate the force exerted by material factors on church structure and religious behavior.

Recent studies have revealed that we are only beginning to scratch the surface in understanding the links between social class and religious behavior (see Table 14-2 for social-class profiles of American religious groups). In a study done in 1965, N. J. Demerath III discovered that social class affects denominations in varying degrees.[12] For example, religion tends to reinforce the secular values and pursuits of the middle and upper classes, while it has the opposite effect of fostering a withdrawal from the world for lower-class believers. Demerath urged that far more research is needed before we can fully understand the complex links between religion and social class.

In 1970 Rodney Stark and Charles Y. Glock conducted a series of studies designed to fill this void.[13] Among their more significant findings is a curious discovery relating to upward social mobili-

---

denomination: a conventional, widely accepted religious organization without "establishment" in the form of state support; a "respectable," although not "official," church. Methodism or Roman Catholicism in the United States are examples.

sect: a small grouping of great religious orthodoxy characterized by stress on withdrawal from secular society, lay leadership, often of a charismatic nature, informal services, adult conversion, and strict personal ethics. The original Black Muslims were an example.

Table 14-2   The social-class distribution of major American religious denominations (percent)

Denomination	Upper class	Middle class	Lower class
Christian Scientist	24.8	36.5	38.7
Episcopal	24.1	33.7	42.2
Congregational	23.9	42.6	33.5
Presbyterian	21.9	40.0	38.1
Jewish	21.8	32.0	46.2
Reformed	19.1	31.3	49.6
Methodist	12.7	35.6	51.7
Lutheran	10.9	36.1	53.0
Christian	10.0	35.4	54.6
Roman Catholic	8.7	24.7	66.6
Baptist	8.0	24.0	68.0
Mormon	5.1	28.6	66.3
No preference	13.3	26.0	60.7
Atheist, agnostic	33.3	46.7	20.0

ty and the tendency for people to switch their denominational affiliation. Previous research had established that Protestant denominations can be arranged hierarchically in terms of the class status of their members. Fundamentalist or conservative groups tended to minister to the lower class; the majority of denominations were solidly middle-class; and Episcopalianism and Christian Science were the denominations with the highest social-class status among members. Glock and Stark showed that upward social mobility by individual church members was positively correlated with shifts in denominational affiliation. Sect groups (as well as Southern Baptists and Roman Catholics) drew most of their new converts from the un-churched of lower-class standing. Middle-class denominations, such as Methodists, Presbyterians, and Congregationalists, attracted their new members largely from lower-class churches. Episcopalians recruited their converts from the moderate, middle-class churches.

A striking pattern of membership fluidity emerges from this research: conservative churches initially enlist new members from the unchurched, then lose them to more moderate, middle-class churches; the middle-class denominations, in turn, lose members who are upwardly mobile to Episcopalianism; and this liberal denomination loses members to the ranks of the unchurched. Hence, social-class mobility correlates positively with denominational affiliation, switching, and disaffiliation, so that the middle class manifests a stronger commitment to religion than members of other class groups. Moreover, social class mobility, and not religious ideas, appears to be the critical factor in explaining why members switch their denominational affiliation.

The Cohesive Function: The Durkheimian Tradition

Emile Durkheim and Max Weber pioneered the development of *sociological* interpretations of the religious institution. Durkheim discerned the major social function of religion in its immense power to integrate human societies in their symbolic and institutional dimensions, arriving at this conclusion after a searching investigation of the forces that bind people into a unified social order.

Durkheim's thought   The boldest concept introduced by Durkheim to explain the integration of society was the *collective representation,* a kind of conscience, a set of beliefs, values, and norms shared by the average members of the same society. This collective conscience functioned to mold both institutional structures and individual action. Yet Durkheim understood it as a reality beyond human control, a social element that arose spontaneously out of interaction among members of society to define their cultural norms. The collective conscience is the highest moral order, through which members agree on the rules and norms that are essential for cooperative interaction. Although Durkheim intended something more sophisticated than a "group mind" concept, he spoke as though this cultural control center at the heart of society could act and impose its demands in a somewhat suprahuman fashion.

The first problem confronted by the collective conscience in all societies is how people can be made to control their natural egoism and submit to the demands of the collective rules. Durkheim believed that no person voluntarily gives up his own interests in favor of more binding collective requirements. Some overwhelming force is necessary to convince them to obey the rules; religion represents that force. By dressing the moral principles of society in sacred garb and infusing them with awe-inspiring power, the collective conscience created the sacred as a means of fostering commitment to its own values and norms. For in accepting the ideas of religion and following the ethical requirements of the religious community, people unknowingly fulfilled the obligations of the collective conscience. This is the context for Durkheim's famous assertion that religion is actually society worshipping itself.

Like Marx, Durkheim believed religion was a social fiction (for the gods that religion serves do not actually exist). But unlike Marx, Durkheim was not opposed to the religious community and its operations. For, to Durkheim's mind, people's commitment to religion generates a greater degree of cohesiveness in society—and the achievement of social unity was an absolute requirement for social life as far as Durkheim was concerned. Religion should be tolerated as a social fiction, therefore, so long as it promotes social solidarity.

Religion efficiently performs this integrative function because it places human action in a sacred framework of meaning. During the Middle Ages, for example, citizens believed the king ruled by divine right. To challenge the authority of the king was to question the wisdom of God. In a similar fashion, religion bathes secular institutions, ideas, and norms in the legitimating glow of the sacred. It gives them a sense of "rightness," so that people are less likely to question them than rules that are obviously secular. (Many Americans today support democracy not only because they think it is a good political theory, but also because it is the form of government ordained by God as "right for Americans." Consider the phrase "One nation, under God," and the frequent assertion that the United States is a "Christian country.")

Durkheim also perceived other reasons for the effectiveness of religious institutions in promoting social solidarity. In the secular realm, the collective conscience must rely on its coercive power to impose order on society. Religion functions through a different type of motivation. The magnetic charm of the sacred persuades rather than forces people to fulfill the demands of the collective conscience. Religion transforms external pressures into internal compulsions, so that people obey society not because they must but because they feel they should. This explains why, in Durkheim's view, societies strive as swiftly as possible to disguise their social norms as principles stemming from the divine order.

Religious ritual also reinforces social integration. Ritual promotes commitment to the sacred, and through the sacred to the collective conscience standing behind it. But the fires of religious enthusiasm require periodic rekindling, Durkheim reasoned, if they are to keep alive the religious sentiments that support social solidarity. For this reason, public ceremonial occasions assume a preeminent role in religious life. They afford an opportunity for collectively remembering, celebrating, and reasserting the meaning of those sacred events that provide a society's identity. In addition, rituals supply the occasion for voicing the vital concerns of the society and appealing for divine help in the face of disruptive forces. Even today, some farming communities still gather in the church to pray for rain. In the afterglow following a ritual experience,

June 1976: presidential nominee Jimmy Carter is at prayer in the Plains, Georgia, Baptist church. In some societies a fundamentalist religious orientation would be an impediment to social mobility, but in the United States upward mobility is often accompanied by a denominational switch. Will President Carter eventually become an Episcopalian?

societal members feel themselves invigorated, with a newfound sense of power for coping with the realities of life. They are not deceived in these perceptions of increased power, Durkheim observed, for they really *are* more adequately equipped to deal with life's problems. The power that believers encounter under the guise of the sacred is a real power: it is the collective power of society itself.

The legacy of Durkheim Durkheim's general theory of religion has been as influential as that of any other figure in the sociology of religion. Indeed, it is almost impossible to find an active researcher who has not been affected by this tradition. Of course, not all of Durkheim's ideas have been uncritically accepted. The thesis that religion is society worshipping itself has largely been rejected, and sociologists now use the concept of culture where Durkheim spoke of the collective conscience. But Durkheim's emphasis on the role of the sacred, his theory of the close connection between religious beliefs and moral norms, and his stress on ritual in reinforcing commitment to religious and secular values have all weathered the test of critical scrutiny rather well. Above all, Durkheim made us aware of how the religious institution generates loyalty to the authority of secular society. Durkheim would have immediately understood why Americans print "in God we trust" on their currency, Englishmen sing "God Save the Queen," and Nazis of the Third Reich rallied around the slogan "Gott mit uns" (God with us) and tried to replace the Christian cross with the swastika.

Religion and the integration of American society A number of sociologists have perceptively applied Durkheim's insights to an analysis of American society and its religious communities. One of the more fascinating interpretations was produced by W. Lloyd Warner in 1961.[14] He contended that beyond the level of churches there exists a more basic symbolic order where sacred beliefs and rituals oriented toward secular existence function to overcome the tensions and conflicts of communal life. Memorial Day observances serve to bring into focus this higher realm of collective experience, for this holiday—at least in earlier decades of this century—took on the charac-

ter of a religious ceremony. It represented an occasion set aside by secular society for celebrating the sacrifice of those who died so that "the American way of life" might live. Parades, patriotic speeches, and other rites of the day were designed to stimulate a renewed commitment to the ideals of American society. (Do not reject this thesis if the Memorial Day celebrations with which you are familiar do not seem this elaborate. The holocaust of World War II, followed by further bloodletting in Korea and Vietnam, have made it harder for Americans to celebrate death in war as gloriously sacrificial, but the analysis of the *functions* of such ceremonies remains as valid as ever.)

Warner's interpretation of Memorial Day became an opening wedge for understanding a whole series of other semireligious phenomena. Not only do we Americans commemorate the major events of our social history with holidays like Thanksgiving, the Fourth of July, Washington's and Lincoln's birthdays, but we also honor quasi-sacred artifacts such as the flag, the Tomb of the Unknown Soldier, and the original copy of the Constitution.

In addition, we have collected some quasi-sacred scriptures in the form of the Declaration of Independence, the Preamble to the Constitution, and the Gettysburg Address and have elevated men like Washington, Jefferson, and Lincoln to the status of demigods. Throughout his interpretation, Warner viewed the function of the American sacred order in terms quite consistent with the formulations of Durkheim. The similarity was not accidental. Warner specifically acknowledged his dependence on Durkheim in framing this analysis of American social religion. Indeed, Warner believed American civil ceremony sustained the basic norms of society in precisely the manner Durkheim had predicted.

The American way of life as religion An alternative analysis of American religion, still in the Durkheimian tradition, was suggested by Will Herberg in *Protestant-Catholic-Jew* (1960).[15] Initially, this study noted that church membership was increasing in the early 1950s, along with almost all the major forms of social *disorganization,* from crime and delinquency to family disorganization and suicide. Herberg sought to explain this startling state of affairs.

Americans were participating in religion more but heeding its teachings less, Herberg said, because *belonging to* a religious community had become more important than knowing its beliefs or living by its ethics. Individuals needed an organization in which they could establish an identity in their personal life and derive a "place" in American society. Each of the major religious traditions—Protestant, Catholic, Jewish—became separate but equally valid avenues toward identifying as an American and participating in the American way of life. Conversely, not belonging to a religious community was tantamount to being un-American.

Hence, the membership of the three major religious bodies increased substantially, but the average participant was more interested in "having a religion" than in "living the faith." The beliefs and morals informing everyday life were the secular principles of the American way of life, not the teachings of a religious community. In short, the primary function of religion had become more social than religious. This led Herberg to denounce American religion as idolatrous and to raise the critical question of whether religion can serve two masters, whether it can faithfully perform its religious function while simultaneously fulfilling a social function.

The civil religion thesis What bearing does religion have on unifying society today? In 1967, Robert Bellah addressed this question in a penetrating essay called "Civil Religion in America."[16] Bellah describes civil religion as a religious sanctification of American political ideals, historical leaders, and the ultimate destiny of the society. Civil religion is not an organized church like Roman Catholicism, but rather a religious dimension to political society that sets American experience within a transcendent frame of reference. No real conflict emerges between this religious aspect of the society and the religion of the churches because civil religion advances no doctrinal statements, apart from the democratic creed, and the god it serves maintains a somewhat "unitarian" character. What civil religion *does* supply is sacred legitimation for the basic ideals of democratic practice. It keeps before the citizenry a vision of their action as "one nation under God." Without the aid of civil religion to bolster allegiance to democratic

President Kennedy's grave has become a quasi-religious shrine. Visited by thousands every year, it is one of the most popular tourist attractions in Washington.

principles, Bellah believes, American society might lose its sense of direction and suffer social disintegration.

The ghost of Durkheim haunts the civil religion thesis. Clearly, Bellah has given modern form to the Durkheimian conception of religion's integrative function. But Bellah goes even further and questions whether any society can endure without a civil religion. Even so secular a society as China elevated Mao Tse-tung to the status of a demigod and attached an almost sacred character to his utterances and political ideology. Only additional research will confirm whether civil religion is a universal feature of all societies. Meanwhile, it is obvious that religion does, as Durkheim suggested, contribute to cohesiveness.

The Creation of Meaning: The Weberian Tradition

Weber's thought Max Weber coined the term "sociology of religion" and, along with Durkheim, helped set the discipline on its current course. Weber stressed other functions than those identified by Durkheim, however, even though their ideas converged at a number of points. Primarily, Weber was concerned with how religious institutions give authority and legitimacy to systems of meaning, which, in turn, both direct the social action of people and exercise some control over their behavior. Through these two modes of influence, religion has been at once a creative and a stabilizing institution within society.

Creation of meaning With respect to the creation-of-meaning role, Weber proposed that religions seek to respond to a basic human need—the need for an understanding of the purpose of life. The Old Testament figure of Job, for example, suffered terrible calamities—the loss of his family, the destruction of his worldly possessions, and the affliction of painful sores from his head to his toes. In all of this, Job's most pressing question was not "How can I regain what I have lost?" but, "Why has all this trouble descended on me?" We can tolerate terrible suffering, Weber observed, if that suffering is meaningful. Otherwise, we are more likely to end it with suicide. Religion typically furnishes the meaning system that convinces us that life is worth living.

Yet, in the process of pursuing this purely religious goal, the religious institution makes an invaluable contribution to secular social life. For in order to impart meaning to personal existence, religion must first define the world where human action is set. Consequently, one of the initial tasks of any religion is to create a *world view* that carefully sets forth the shape of the physical and moral universe. Consider, for example, the world view of the New Testament. Here reality is depicted in terms of a three-story universe with hell below, earth in the middle, and heaven above. Within this reality structure, people are taught what to believe and how to act so as to escape hell and enter heaven. And people take quite seriously the world views constructed by their religions. Because the Bible plainly spoke of "the edges of the earth," the sailors under Columbus were afraid of falling off the edge of the world. Galileo was brought before a court of the Church to answer to charges that he claimed the earth moved around the sun. His claim directly contradicted the Scriptures, which had the sun moving across the face of the earth.

Thus, world views of religious origin establish definitions of social reality whose influence is not confined to religious matters alone. Once religion defined the world as flat, for example, people acted in everyday affairs on the assumption that the world was indeed flat. By the same token, most Americans firmly believe that, by nature, people always strive to get ahead. Actually, this commonplace assumption about the way things are is of religious origin. The early Puritans preached that people should achieve for the glory of God. Later, when the United States was established, the secular value of achievement was institutionalized as a permanent feature of American character. This pattern is not unusual. Very frequently the world view of a civil society is the secularized version of the world view of its major religious tradition. In this manner, the religious institution often lays the foundations of socially accepted meaning on which social orders are constructed.

The Protestant Ethic Under the title *The Protestant Ethic and the Spirit of Capitalism,* Weber elaborated what is now perhaps the most famous hypothesis in the whole of sociological literature.[17] The central theme traced the consequences for secular economic behavior that could flow from a set of religious ideas organized into a world view. Weber concentrated his analysis on Calvinism, the theological doctrines originated by the Geneva reformer John Calvin. The argument fell logically into four parts. Weber proposed that (1) Calvinist doctrine determined the content of a distinctive (2) ethical system, which, in turn, produced a corresponding (3) character type among Calvinists that stimulated the rapid development of (4) modern, rational capitalism. A quick summary of each segment will reveal the connecting links binding the causal sequence together.

The *Calvinist concept of God* emphasized His glory and holiness, His freedom and sovereignty. These attributes fostered the Calvinist belief in predestination, the conviction that God selected certain individuals for heaven and others for hell before they were born. Nothing people did during life could affect God's decision for their salvation or damnation. Now one might expect that such a belief would produce fatalism; if one's eternal destiny is already sealed, what is the point of trying to live righteously? Weber argued that it had the opposite effect. Calvinists were under tremendous psychological pressure to live righteously, not because they believed God's decision could be changed, but in order to convince themselves they might be among the elect marked for salvation.

These doctrines gave birth to a lively set of *ethical standards.* Because of God's holiness and sovereign power, Calvin claimed in the Geneva Catechism that the chief purpose of human life is to glorify God and give Him honor. Calvinists readily understood that this commandment applied to more than Sunday worship. Those other six days when they labored in their secular vocations could also be dedicated to God's glory. Working for the glory of God, however, required nothing less than the believer's best effort. Hence, economic achievement through honest, disciplined, rational labor constituted a major portion of Calvinist ethics. Yet this achievement orientation was not pursued for economic motives, such as making money for money's sake. Rather, the ultimate purpose of achievement was religious, and hard work was dedicated to the glory of God.

John Calvin

John Calvin (1509–1564) was one of the great Protestant theologians. His doctrines, Weber argued, provided an essential and fertile underpinning for the development of capitalism. Calvin preached thrift, hard work, temperance, plain living, and, perhaps most important, the doctrines of calling and predestination. These doctrines implied that all people were ordained to be whatever they were; thus, it became an act of worship and obedience to divine command to do one's job well. From this doctrine also sprang the notion of work as worship. These ideas formed a complex unit which lent itself very easily, according to Weber, to the creation of a capitalist mentality and economic rationality in business. Working hard and thriftily to make a business prosper became a religious activity.

Calvinists who subscribed to this ethical pattern of diligent labor had the *psychological mind-set essential for productive capitalist activity*. For not only did Calvinists work hard, but, more important, they also demonstrated the characteristics of rational, calculating entrepreneurs rather than the patient art of skilled craft workers. Calvinists manifested an adventurous spirit fired by an ambition to give God glory. This fitted them with the proper mental attitude for lively participation in modern, rational capitalism.

With the last variable, *capitalism,* we encounter one of the more subtle elements of Weber's analysis. He was fully aware that capitalism in some form had been present in economic relations for centuries. He contended, however, that *modern, rational capitalism*—which seeks the maximization of profit, keeps double-ledger books, follows cost-accounting procedures, and strives to achieve the highest price the market will afford—is a product of the Reformation era and is qualitatively different from previous forms of capitalist endeavor. Before the expansion of Calvinism, the enterprising attitude required by modern, rational capitalism was lacking, and hence this form of economic activity was prevented from developing. But once the mentality of Calvinist activism was introduced into the social sphere, modern capitalism began to develop. And with great speed, this economic form swiftly overwhelmed all other types of economic practice to become the dominant system of business activity in the Western world.

Later in his career, Weber sought further support for the Protestant Ethic thesis. The result was a set of studies on major world religions—one each on the religions of China, India, and ancient Judaism. The common theme was the question of why the other world religions had failed to stimulate economic rationality as Calvinism had done. Weber's research revealed that in these cultures the patterns established in ethical life, along with tightly interlocking bonds between religion, state, and the family, all actively prevented the development of a business mentality like that found in modern Western economies. With this additional evidence, Weber felt more secure about the accuracy of his original hypothesis regarding the unique relationship between Calvinism and modern capitalism.

The legacy of Weber The central sociological significance of Weber's work remains firmly rooted in his insights concerning the ability of religions to establish world views. Calvinism, quite unintentionally, offered a definition of reality that stimulated rational economic activity. Hinduism, Confucianism, Buddhism, and Judaism, by contrast, developed religious world views that, again quite unintentionally, frustrated the emergence of aggressive business behavior of the Western type. By addressing purely religious questions, therefore, religious institutions frequently generate ideas that later transform the way people think and act in their secular affairs. Indeed, some of a people's most important sentiments—especially those relating to the purpose of life—originally sprang out of religious sources. The significance of religion goes far beyond the institutional limits of the churches; its ideas often penetrate to the foundation of social life to lend direction to numerous activities we tend to regard as thoroughly secular.

Puritanism and science Another area of secular affairs affected by religious ideas is science. In an imaginative essay—actually a spin-off from Weber's Protestant Ethic thesis—Robert K. Merton sketched the latent function of Puritan attitudes toward the world in fostering scientific development.[18] Puritanism, a later branch of Calvinism, stressed inner-worldly activity, which, Merton noted, led to a deepened interest in nature and science. In Britain, where Puritanism was strong in the seventeenth century, the Royal Society for promoting scientific research was heavily populated by Puritans, who emphasized the twin virtues of rationalism and empiricism in the analysis of nature.

As science progressed, however, theories and data were generated that ultimately conflicted with some of the events reported in the Bible—the creation story, Noah's flood, New Testament miracles, and other supernatural events. Ironically, the latent function of Puritan endeavors in natural science was to undercut the credibility of a series of religious beliefs also propagated by the Puritan community. Merton concluded that such a pattern may not be unusual. Secular activities stimulated by a religious orientation may often bear within them the seeds of later strife with the religious community itself. Once new religious ideas and orientations have changed the world, that newly defined world is likely to alter substantially the way the church pursues its purely religious tasks.

The Protestant Ethic in contemporary life Since the initial publication of Weber's thesis, scholars have wondered whether Protestantism still encourages greater economic success among its followers than, say, Catholicism or Judaism. Gerhard Lenski set out to explore this question in a landmark study of metropolitan Detroit.[19] Lenski was not interested in the historical connection between Calvinism and capitalism. Rather, he was concerned with the contemporary influence religious perspectives exert on the attainment of secular success in American life.

Lenski's findings tend to confirm that religious beliefs still play an important role in developing orientations leading toward success in the wider social sphere. For example, Protestantism nurtured individualism and some independence of familial ties, along with a powerful drive toward upward social mobility, while Catholicism reinforced the opposing sentiments of obedience to authority and reliance on members of the extended family. Hence, although the differences between Protestants and Catholics are not excessive in the United States, they are sufficiently large to reduce the ability of Catholics to experience upward social mobility, as compared to their Protestant neighbors. Lenski was able to conclude from these data that, as Weber had suggested, religion is still a significant factor in motivating people in secular activities.

The interrelation of religion and culture: Church, sect, and mysticism The relationship between faith and culture is complex in any age. Weber identified some of the ways religious ideas influence secular processes. Ernst Troeltsch, his colleague and friend, focused attention on the opposite issue: how culture affects religion. Initially, religion can adopt one of three possible attitudes toward culture. The church may embrace a culture, reject it, or dismiss it as religiously irrelevant. According to Troeltsch, each choice results in a

"My Protestant work ethic made me a bundle, but my Puritanical guilt complex won't let me enjoy it."

New Yorker, May 5, 1973. Drawing by H. Martin; © 1973 The New Yorker Magazine, Inc.

Even in modern Japan there are tight links between religion and other institutions. These men are draftsmen, crane operators, and common laborers. But the companies they work for have ordered them to spend the first three days of their jobs living as Buddhist monks.

different form of church structure: *church, sect,* or *mysticism.*[20]

The **church**, to use Troeltsch's technical categories, is an established ecclesiastical system supported by the state and enrolling most of a society's members. At one time, Anglicanism in England, Lutheranism in Sweden, and Roman Catholicism in France all conformed to this pattern. But all religious communities are faced with the hard choice of whether they should maintain high standards of belief and practice, so that the few members who qualify must possess a real depth of faith, or lower standards, in order to impart a modest degree of faith to a large number of people. In many ways, these options are similar to the choices thrust upon a Little League coach: should the athletically gifted members of the team play all the time or should all members of the team play an equal amount of time regardless of their athletic skills? In both baseball and religion, sound arguments exist for both options. But the *church* decides for the masses. It chooses to *embrace* culture along with the state and the ruling classes so that some faith, however limited, may be dispensed to the masses.

The *sect* confronts the same problem, but chooses the other option. The sect limits its members to a small group of believers who adhere to the very rigorous standards established for doctrinal belief and ethical practice. In short, the sect rejects culture. As a consequence, sects tend to stress withdrawal from secular society, lay leadership in the religious fellowship, informal liturgy, membership based on adult conversion experience, and strict ethical discipline in daily life. Church and sect, then, represent two almost mutually exclusive sociological forms of religious expression.

The third form, **mysticism**, declares culture religiously *irrelevant.* It opposes in principle all formal worship and social organization. Believers focus on an inner experience, a vision of God, that is highly individualistic. Compared with this all-important vision of God, culture is unimportant. Thus, mystics remain indifferent toward any compromise with secular affairs. Although they sometimes unite in loosely formed groups, they quickly dissolve these communities when group life appears to threaten the free movement of the spirit.

The universal church characterized medieval Europe, touching every aspect of life, sometimes in ways modern people find grotesque. This is a medieval procession of flagellants (people who tortured themselves in religious mortification).

Hence, church, sect, and mysticism are three mutually exclusive forms of social organization within Christianity. (Troeltsch refrained from applying these categories to religious bodies outside the Christian communion.) Yet Troeltsch believed each form represented a valid expression of the Christian ideal and held great respect for each alternative. He admired the aim of the church to Christianize society by drawing everyone into its membership fold, just as he was impressed by the ethical achievements of the sectarians. Above all, Troeltsch came to appreciate the several ways the religious institution could organize the interplay between faith and culture. In this process, a reciprocal influence emerged; religion modified culture even as culture set the conditions for the course of religious development.

An expansion of the church-sect distinction Troeltsch based his threefold model on the social patterns Christianity had developed through the nineteenth century. Recent innovations have sought to update and expand his basic notions. As we have seen, Niebuhr placed sect and church on a continuum starting with sects of the disinherited and moving toward churches of the middle class.[21] Liston Pope carried this approach further by citing twenty-one separate steps in the process of transition from sectarianism to church status.[22]

A more recent and popular revision by J. Milton Yinger replaces the church-sect distinction with a model constructed around four institutional types: ecclesia, denomination, established sect, and sect.[23] This has the advantage of relating more directly to contemporary patterns in the churches. The **ecclesia,** a concept highly similar to Troeltsch's *church,* reaches out to the boundaries of society and embraces members from all socioeconomic levels. It is likely to be an *established,* or state, church like the Church of England.

The *denomination* is not an established church, nor does it withdraw from society like sect groups. Rather, the denomination allies itself with political and cultural forces, even while it remains somewhat circumscribed by class lines, regional differences, and racial boundaries. A series of American religious bodies fall into this category, such as the United Methodist Church, the American Baptist Church, Roman Catholicism, and other mainline denominations.

The **established sect** is the third type. It is more inclusive and less alienated from secular culture than Troeltsch's *sect.* It does not, however, possess the sophistication and social influence found within denominations. Representatives of this type in North America might include the Church of God, the Jehovah's Witnesses, the Church of Christ, and a number of smaller religious bodies.

The fourth type, the *sect,* represents very small and normally unstable groups striving for success, quite often under a charismatic leader. These sects come and go with some frequency, but if they are able to solve the difficult organizational problems that invariably plague them at the beginning, they usually move into the established sect type. Frequently, storefront churches are of the sect type. (The Black Muslims in the United States began as a sect and have now become an established sect.)

The enormous interpretive power of the original church-sect distinction is demonstrated in these subsequent efforts to enlarge the model. It is likely that further refinement will be forthcoming, because this model has already made an invaluable contribution to our understanding of the religious institution.

church: in Ernst Troeltsch's terms, an established ecclesiastical system supported by the state and enrolling most of a society's members. The Church of England in Britain and Lutheranism in Sweden are examples. More commonly, simply a conventional religious organization.

mysticism: a highly individualistic form of religious behavior focusing on subjective experience and tending to regard both the secular world and religious structures as irrelevant. The search for personal, supernatural experience.

ecclesia: one form of religious organization in Yinger's model; very similar to Troeltsch's "church"; an established, state-supported, national religious organization.

established sect: a sect in the process of becoming a denomination. In the United States, Jehovah's Witnesses and perhaps the Church of Jesus Christ of the Latter Day Saints (Mormon) are examples.

One of the common hallmarks of the sect is the storefront church.

The Social Construction of Religious Reality: The Synthesis of Berger and Luckmann

Fashioning the varied functions of religion into a general framework of analysis is far from a simple task. Two sociologists, Peter Berger and Thomas Luckmann, have recently accomplished this feat in a remarkably sophisticated manner.[24] By combining the insights of Marx, Durkheim, and Weber with some of their own, they have achieved a new synthesis of the many functions performed by religion.

Berger and Luckmann describe their framework as *social construction of reality perspective*. By this they mean that the basic elements of reality—its social meanings and structures—are humanly created and maintained. This perspective is important for understanding the religious institution, they maintain, because we often regard the church as deriving from supernatural forces and discount the role of people in its formation and perpetuation. Using this perspective, they emphasize the objective and subjective aspects of religious reality.

The objective level: Institutions Institutions are created out of habitual patterns of action organized in reference to a common set of social meanings. For the religious institution, therefore, the symbolic realm includes the accepted social meanings through which the nature of sacred reality is defined. Berger and Luckmann refer to this set of meanings as a "sacred cosmos," or world view, that not only establishes an "official version of reality," but also explains and justifies "the truth" as a religious group perceives it. Theology is essentially a "plausibility structure," an organized rationale for attributing believability to a religion's fundamental doctrines.

Social organization arises in response to the need to arrange members in the series of offices and roles required to fulfill the mission of a church. The sacred universe informs the organizational structure. The Lordship of Christ over the church in Catholicism, for example, finds institutional expression in the office of Pope, Christ's vicar on earth. Together the symbolic and organizational features of the religious institution constitute the objective level of reality.

The subjective level: Individual religiosity Vast numbers of people rely heavily on the services of religion. The important events of an individual's life-cycle are typically celebrated by religious ceremonies, from baptism at birth to a funeral at death in Western societies. Churches and synagogues also provide an ever-present source of help during periods of individual crisis, whether the need is for psychological or material aid. And always the church provides individuals with a social life where friendships may be cultivated. Yet religion also ministers to individual needs in other, more spiritual ways. And it is to these spiritual functions that Berger and Luckmann direct their attention in discussing the subjective level of individual religiosity.

When individuals enter society, they begin a long and difficult learning process. In swift order, they must learn a language, master the symbols of their culture, assume roles, accept social norms, and establish an identity. Through the same socialization process, they also acquire a religion, complete with its sacred beliefs, rituals, and ethical requirements. During the early years of religious socialization, individuals accept uncritically the validity of the religious tradition in the form it is given them. But as they approach maturity, they may begin to raise questions about the adequacy of their religious tradition. Once this occurs, the "fit" between the subjective religion of the individual and the objective beliefs and practices of the church can no longer be taken for granted. The religious institution provides a succession of mechanisms to increase the likelihood that believers will conform to the officially sanctioned patterns of the religious community. The most extreme pressure is excommunion, but other, more subtle forms of persuasion and social control are available.

Of course, these mechanisms aimed at aligning subjective religiosity with objective institutional expectations are not always adequate to prevent deviation. The breakdown of social controls may result either in the loss of an individual to another religious community or the death of subjective faith altogether. A good deal of the church's energy is geared toward nurturing the subjective religiosity of its members. Indeed, the success of the religious institution depends to a large degree on its ability to keep individuals committed to its beliefs and practices.

Conclusion

Our analysis of this sample of theorists emphasizes the varied and complex nature of those social functions performed by the religious institution. This variety prevents the reduction of religious activity to one simple set of functions. For example, religion at once creates meaning and destroys other meaning systems. It promotes social change on some occasions, while on others it retards change. Sometimes religion exerts rigorous social control to maintain the status quo, and elsewhere it may legitimize changes in patterns of action. Frequently, religion merely reflects socioeconomic patterns of stratification, yet at other times it chal-

Something all religions do is respond to the major events of the human life cycle.

lenges material inequalities as morally unacceptable. And through all this diversity, religion is constantly affecting secular culture and being affected by it.

We should not conclude from this complicated situation, however, that nothing very intelligible can be said about the social functions religion performs in society today. Actually, the contrary is true: the theoretical options for understanding religion, along with the empirical research generated by each tradition, represent a substantial body of

Women Priests at Last

Unlike most Protestant denominations in the U.S., the Episcopal Church has never suffered schism—although it has come close in recent years over the explosive question of ordaining women as priests. Last week, the church's triennial General Convention voted to ratify that historic step, but it was a reluctant reform that will put a continuing strain on church unity and sharpen the divisions over still more controversial questions yet to be faced.

In the past, Episcopalians—who straddle the Roman Catholic and Reformation traditions—have been able to maintain their unity by a typically Anglican stress on liturgy, style and decorum rather than with dogma and discipline. Significantly, the issues that divided the delegates in Minneapolis, representing nearly 3 million Episcopalians, were more matters of form than theological substance.

Twice before, the House of Bishops had voted in principle to accept women priests, and at the church's last convention, the House of Deputies (divided evenly among clergy and laity) nearly went along. Since then, fifteen women have been "irregularly" ordained; subsequently, three retired bishops involved in the ordinations were censured. As this convention approached, each faction resorted to what, for Anglicans, were unseemly tactics. Both sides organized pressure groups and even went so far as to appear on national television. . . .

As for the women, the church now faces the practical question of how to find employment for nearly 150 women deacons awaiting ordination. Already, there is such a shortage of ecclesiastical jobs that the church has hired an employment agency to find secular work for priests already ordained. What's more, since bishops have the right to approve their own candidates for the priesthood, some undoubtedly will reject any women who apply. If that happens, feminists warn, they may retaliate by taking the recalcitrant bishops into civil court on charges of sex discrimination. . . .

Subjective religiosity and objective institutionalization are only two of the dynamic tensions characterizing contemporary American religions. Their secularity and volunteerism also play into and between the two, creating tensions of the kinds discussed here. Such problems have always haunted the religious institutions of this country.

knowledge that gives us considerable insight into the contribution religion makes to common life. In no small part, the pluralism in sociological interpretations of the religious institution is made necessary by the complicated nature of religion itself.

The Sociology of American Religion

General Traits

The religious institution has always held a prominent place in the American experience. Indeed, few societies have fashioned a better environment for the growth of religious sentiments. The vitality and enthusiasm associated with our religious life has tended to encourage the formation of new denominations and experimentation with new forms of religious expression. With considerable accuracy, one scholar has captured the essence of American religion in the simple phrase: "the lively experiment."[25] We shall employ three basic concepts—*pervasiveness, secularity,* and *voluntarism*—for organizing the interpretation of American religion.[26] These traits serve to distinguish American religion from the religious experience of other societies.

Pervasiveness   Most Americans have never questioned the basic value of religion. The United States has been spared the anticlerical periods experienced by other nations—most notably France in the eighteenth and nineteenth centuries. In part, the continuous support Americans have extended to their religious communities can be explained by the events surrounding the founding of the nation. The first English-speaking settlers fled England in 1620 to escape religious persecution, and their settlement here was motivated by religious sentiments. The second wave of immigrants, the Puritans of 1630, came voluntarily to establish their own style of holy commonwealth in Massachusetts free from the interference of either bishop or king. Other colonies were likewise founded on religious principles: Connecticut was colonized by Thomas Hooker, a Congregationalist; Rhode Island by Roger Williams, a Baptist; Pennsylvania by William Penn, a Quaker; and Maryland by the English Catholic Lord Baltimore.

During the first century of American history, however, the colonies tended to flourish while the vitality of the churches waned. The first newcomers had been devoutly religious, but later immigrants showed greater interest in acquiring land and making money than in developing piety. Thus, the churches of America experienced their darkest days from roughly 1650 to the coming of the Revolution, when church membership slipped to probably no more than one-fifth of the population.[27]

The great revival surges of the 1740s and early 1800s started a long process of recovery for the churches. Membership rolls swelled impressively, and universal identification with some religious community gradually became the norm in American society. Reviewing the data since the 1830s, Seymour Martin Lipset concluded that American religion experienced an almost continuous "boom" after that time.[28] Now, according to the best available data, the following patterns of religious belief and practice prevail: 95-98 percent of Americans report they believe in God; about 60 percent belong to a denomination (see Table 14-3 for religious affiliation of Americans); and about 45 percent regularly participate in worship, more than in other industrialized countries (see Figure 14-1).

These figures are striking when compared to the rates of belief and participation in other Western, industrialized societies. A 1968 Gallup poll taken in a series of Western countries revealed the following numbers who responded affirmatively to the question of whether they believed in God: United States, 98 percent; Greece, 96 percent; Austria, 85 percent; Switzerland, 84 percent; Finland, 83 percent; West Germany, 81 percent; Netherlands, 79 percent; Britain, 77 percent; France, 73 percent; Norway, 73 percent; and Sweden, 60 percent.[29] Sweden, the most secular of European societies, reported levels of participation in weekly worship for the state Church of Sweden at 3.l percent, while the total participation for all groups in Sweden was about 9 percent.[30] In the United States for a similar period (1955–1966), 44 to 49 percent of the population attended church services in an "average" week.[31] The pervasiveness of American religion is clearly demonstrated in these figures. The growth of modern life, often suspected to be hostile to religion, does not yet appear to have eroded the

Table 14-3   Religious affiliation of the American population, 1974

Religious group	Members
Protestant	72,485,146
Roman Catholics	48,701,835
Jewish	6,115,000
Eastern churches	3,695,860
Old Catholic, Polish National Catholic, Armenian	849,052
Buddhist churches of America	60,000
Other	380,557
Total	132,287,450

Figure 14-1
Percentage of adult population that attends church each week in various countries

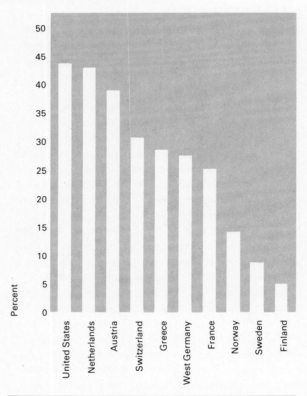

American commitment to religious belief and participation.

Secularity   Against the backdrop of the lively institutional support enjoyed by the American religious community, the second trait of *secularity* may evoke surprise. Yet pervasive religiosity and secularity have been mutually supportive traits in American religion. By secularity, we mean here the religious orientation where denominations are legally separated from the state, regard one another as equals, cooperate on matters of mutual spiritual concern, and readily enter into productive relationships with nonreligious institutions and organizations.

The secular tendency to such institutional behavior received support from the pluralism and moralism conspicuously featured in American religious life. Pluralism has distinguished American religion from the very beginning. The original colonies contained representatives of Congregationalism, Episcopalianism, and Presbyterianism, along with smaller groups of Baptists, Lutherans, Quakers, Roman Catholics, Jews, and, later, Methodists. Today—despite a number of denominational mergers in recent years—there are still some 223 religious organizations in America. Such variety makes it difficult for one denomination to press the claim of being "the true faith" against all others. And the legal barrier against state support of any religion has encouraged American denominations to treat one another as equals. Thus, American society has long emphasized the need for belonging to a church without ever showing much concern over which denomination one joined.

The moralistic bent to American religion has also fostered a secular orientation. Since the early revivalist days, Americans have come to stress ethics over doctrine, right living over right belief. In Europe, rigid doctrinal boundaries segregated religious communities into almost self-contained enclaves. The moralism of American religion has produced the opposite effect. Indeed, the frequent exchange of pulpits by ministers of different denominations, the initiation of union prayer meetings and **ecumenical** organizations, and the relatively common practice of denominational switching have all given American religion a secular

Atheism Lives

"We're here to stay and the religious community had goddam well better find that out. There's no way atheism will die now." So says Madalyn Murray O'Hair, the militant atheist who was instrumental in winning the 1963 Supreme Court ban on prayer in the public schools. As a result of her crusade, O'Hair also won the epithet "the most hated woman in America."

Five Supreme Court suits later—including one asking the White House to ban prayer among the astronauts on Earth or in space—O'Hair, 56, and her band of nonbelievers are finally gaining acceptance. The Society of Separationists, Inc., founded by O'Hair ten years ago to advance the separation of church and state, now claims 60,000 members and last month moved into an $85,000 headquarters in Austin, Texas. With all the zeal of a Billy Graham crusade, the Separationists have launched their own national publicity campaign. Their stated goal is to establish chapters in each state—six states already have chapters, and another three will soon—and to create a network of atheist credit unions under state laws. The American Atheist Book of the Month Club and a weekly radio show heard on 21 stations now help to spread the word, while an atheist-studies college curriculum and an American Atheist Television Service are on the drawing boards.

The reason the group is so successful, says O'Hair, is that atheists are "no longer afraid to admit that they are atheists." Another reason is that O'Hair was able to get a tax exemption on donations to the society and contributions have risen to about $100,000 a year. O'Hair hopes to use some of that money for a summer camp "where an atheist young man can meet an atheist young girl," she reports. "They have problems meeting each other and always seem to be dating Christians."

In addition to being characterized by pervasiveness, secularity, and voluntarism, American religion is also pluralistic, including nonreligion as well.

quality not present in the religious climate of other societies.

The depth of our secular orientation and moralistic cast is vividly revealed in the low levels of religious knowledge prevalent in our society. A Gallup poll of 1954 (and it is unlikely that matters have changed very decisively since then) showed that while virtually every American identifies with a religious community, very few know even the most commonplace facts about their faith. Consider these startling findings: In response to the question, "Who is the mother of Jesus?" some 6 percent of all Catholics and 5 percent of all Protestants could not identify Mary; 67 percent of Protestants and 40 percent of Catholics in the sample could not specify Father, Son, and Holy Spirit as the three persons of the Trinity; 79 percent of Protestants and 86 percent of Catholics could not identify one Old Testament prophet; 78 percent of Protestants and 94 percent of Catholics could not name Paul as the author of the most books in the New Testament (Jews, who do not accept the New Testament as Scripture, did almost three times better than Catholics, with 17 percent answering correctly); and 41 percent of Protestants along with 81 percent of Catholics could not identify Genesis as the first book of the Bible.[32]

These data do not speak well for the effectiveness of the religious education programs carried on by the major denominations in the United States. But something else is also revealed. American church members put a very small premium on serious knowledge about their faiths. Some scholars have interpreted this limited religious knowledge as indicating an increase in socially motivated (or "other-directed")—rather than religiously inspired—church-going in the past few decades. Such a view would be more convincing if the secular, moralistic orientation were something new to American religious life. But observers have noted for almost two centuries that Americans are far more interested in moral issues than in religious knowledge and doctrinal distinctions. This suggests that secularity is an abiding characteristic somehow rooted in the way Americans practice their faiths.

Voluntarism   The final trait, *voluntarism,* synchronizes readily with pervasiveness and secularity to distinguish American religion. By voluntarism, we mean that membership in a religious organization is always a matter of personal choice. One is not legally a member of a given church by accident of birth—as is often the case in societies possessing a state church. Voluntarism deeply affects the social environment in which the churches function. For example, it thrusts all denominations into com-

> **ecumenical:** relating to the movement among Christian churches for a *worldwide* church, the drawing together of separated denominations and worship systems on common grounds of belief.

petition with all other denominations for members. Such a competitive arrangement risks introducing fierce discord into the religious arena as churches vie for new members. However, one sociologist, Talcott Parsons, has argued quite convincingly that denominational competition also serves a positive function.[33] It forces a church to be responsive to the spiritual needs of its members. State churches are not under this sort of pressure because their financial support is guaranteed, and hence members can be taken for granted or even ignored. It may well be, therefore, that denominational competition represents a part of the special genius of American religion and accounts for much of its dynamism.

The churches and politics   The absence of a state church and the ever-present stress of voluntarism have not prevented the churches of America from lively engagement in political issues. In fact, the arrangement has enhanced the efforts of the churches to apply religious principles to political questions. Perhaps because they could not assume their concerns would automatically gain a hearing in the councils of government (an assumption state churches could make, although it was frequently unwarranted), the American churches have for many years spoken out quite strongly on critical political issues.

Political activity has differed, however, for the liberal and conservative churches. The liberals have moved freely into the political realm to lobby for decisions they considered morally significant. Usually, the liberal causes were reform programs, such as the drives against slavery in the 1840s, against industrial abuses at the turn of this century, and against the war in Vietnam in the 1960s. The lower-status churches and more conservative sects have often supported conservative political views. These groups have typically waged political campaigns supporting prohibition, in favor of suppressing natural science findings that conflict with the Scripture, and strongly opposing communism and "un-Americanism," to cite but a few examples. As might be expected, the political activity of churches has frequently reflected their class position.

Voluntarism has also affected the internal politics of the churches. In societies with a state church, the religious institution tends to be hierarchically organized and governs itself through ecclesiastical officials alone. The ordained priesthood normally shares little decision-making power with the laity. From the time of the Puritan experiment, however, American religious institutions have followed an alternative course, with the laity deeply involved in formal policy-making decisions. And because the members at large control the purse strings, they can informally influence church policies and activities. Church leaders understand that if they do not serve the congregation's interests, the members can withhold financial resources.

The central features of pervasiveness, secularity, and voluntarism have combined to generate a dynamic religious community in the United States. Like all religious communities, no doubt, American religion provides ample evidence of saints and sinners, moral earnestness and hypocrisy, good faith and bad. On balance, however, it would be difficult to discover another society where religion as a social institution is so widely regarded as a good thing or personal religiosity is so much a part of the life-style of the people. Certainly, no other industrialized nation approximates the level of commitment to the religious life and support for the religious institution shown in the United States. And if commitment and support represent key factors in any measurement of the strength and vitality of a social institution, then religion must be judged one of the more stable institutions in American society.

Recent Trends

All basic institutions must confront the pressures of social change and adapt themselves to modifications occurring in the other institutions around them. American religion is no exception. It is diffi-

Despite the constitutional separation of church and state, the voluntaristic nature of American religion has always insured the political involvement of the religious. Here, clergy march in support of civil rights in Selma, Alabama.

cult to determine precisely what accommodations churches may make, but some recent trends can be identified: (1) the alleged decline of belief and the emergence of a "post-Christian age," (2) further legal disputes over the meaning of separation of church and state, (3) the resurgence of **evangelicalism,** and (4) the development of new functions.

The emergence of a post-Christian age In the 1960s a group of theologians and social scientists combined to render the judgment that belief in the supernatural was declining at a rapid pace in the modern world. The great cultural era inspired by the Judeo-Christian tradition was drawing to a close, because people no longer required the overarching religious symbols that once helped produce harmonious social life. The evidence supporting this interpretation, still valid today, cites the decline in church and Sunday school attendance (see Figure 14-2), the waning of dogmatic orthodoxy, the rise of interfaith marriages, declining seminary enrollments, declining financial support, and the general relaxation of moral codes—especially those regulating sexual behavior. In addition, scholars suspected that a decline in religious fervor was a natural outcome of the other major features of modernity: urbanization, bureaucratization, and industrialization.

The empirical evidence suggesting a decline in

religious belief was strong, although somewhat mixed and hard to interpret clearly. But before it was all in, the 1970s witnessed a swift resurgence of supernaturalism. Without warning, occultism, spiritualism, and the Jesus movement sprang into existence among youth and middle-class groups—the very people alleged to be the *avant-garde* of encroaching secularization. Whether supernaturalism in its various manifestations will persist among such groups we cannot tell. But the evidence does tend to raise questions about the broad hypothesis that American society is entering an era when people can no longer believe in the sacred.

Separation of church and state   Although American society permanently institutionalized the doctrine of separation of church and state in the Constitution, it is becoming increasingly clear that the two institutions are interrelated in a number of subtle ways. For example, the churches in America, like certain other nonprofit organizations, enjoy tax-free status. A growing chorus of critics both within and outside the churches have charged recently that tax exemption constitutes an informal state support and therefore violates the honored tradition of institutional separation.

Another related issue concerns the question of governmental financial aid (federal, state, and local) for parochial schools. Ironically, when this issue first surfaced in the 1800s, Catholics tended to oppose the practice, while Protestants—who then had more religious schools than Catholics—largely approved the arrangement. Now the sides are very nearly reversed. Catholics, who have a sizable parochial school population, argue most vigorously for state aid to religious schools, while Protestants are more likely to oppose the practice. The courts have until now ruled against parochial aid, but the issue has yet to recede from public discussion, and it does not appear likely to disappear anytime soon.

The resurgence of evangelicalism   *Evangelicalism* refers to the practices of religious groups that embrace a conservative theology and stress immediate religious experience. Historically, evangelicalism in American society has been closely allied with revivalism. In the late 1960s and early 1970s,

evangelicalism: the religious position stressing conservatism or fundamentalism in belief and immediate, personalized religious experience among adherents. Often associated with revivalistic practice.

Figure 14-2
The decline in American church attendance, 1958-1968

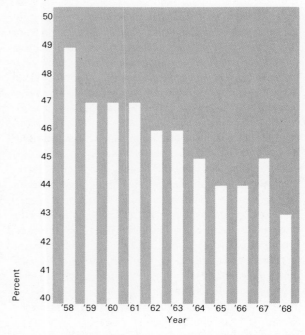

Adult church attendance has declined steadily (except for 1967) from its peak of 49 percent in 1958 to 43 percent in 1968.

revivalism suddenly experienced renewed vigor. In part, this may have been a reaction against the predictions of increasing secularity. The most notable consequence of renewed evangelical fervor to date has been to increase the numbers of those allied with conservative or fundamentalist sect groups. The conservative sects appear to be the fastest-growing segment of American religion. If this is true, American religion may well be entering an era of greater conservatism. Some authorities, however, think that the sect groups may soon lose their new converts to middle-class denominations. This would mean that the resurgence of evangelicalism will probably be less significant in the long run than current data would appear to indicate. Based on previous experience, there is considerable likelihood that this period of enthusiasm will leave the basic structure of American religion reinforced, although essentially unchanged.

New functions   As we approach the year 2000, some commentators predict that some new emphases will emerge within the religious institution. Basically, they say that religion is being displaced by the secular ideologies of nationalism, humanism, and socialism. As these forces conspire to limit the influence of religion within the social realm, the churches are expected to concentrate their attention on family life and personal experience. This will mean an increased role for the churches in celebrating the peak experiences of individual and family life, from birth, to marriage, to death. And, indeed, there are indications that the churches are preparing to address the problems of personal adjustment and mental health more vigorously than they have in the past. Courses in pastoral counseling and small-group therapy for the clergy, along with heightened concern over the quality of community life, are taken as indicators that neighborhood, family, and individuals may soon be religion's main, almost exclusive concern.

If this new strategy is adopted by the American churches, it could have both positive and negative effects. On the one hand, people in industrialized societies genuinely need private refuges from the harsh demands of the marketplace and impersonal relationships. Churches may prove quite effective in helping balance the personalities of those enmeshed in the tensions of modern life. On the other

Despite theological discussions of a post-Christian age, evangelicalism has experienced a sudden upswing in America, particularly among the young.

hand, however, the withdrawal of the churches from social engagement may result in the loss of those social functions of legitimation that religion has historically performed. Not only does religious endorsement lend greater authority to the basic values and norms of a society, but it also provides an arena for the ongoing discussion of the meaning of human existence and the nature of the "good society." Indeed, our analysis of the functions of the religious institution tends to suggest that religion can never fully relinquish its responsibility for both individual and collective needs. Although relative shifts of emphasis may occur during short spans of time, the churches will, no doubt, maintain a lively involvement with the pressing human issues in the private and public spheres of social life.

Summary

The religions of the world may be classified as *monotheistic, polytheistic, ethical,* or *ancestral.* The great monotheisms (Judaism, Christianity, and Islam) include the largest number of religious believers. The central point of all religion, regardless of type, is the *sacred,* a reality set apart as extraordinary and transcendent. Whatever else characterizes a particular religious phenomenon, it necessarily involves something its adherents respond to as sacred. It is the absence of this quality that distinguishes *magic, science, political ideology,* and *humanistic philosophy* from religion, although some of these may sometimes come to resemble it in other ways. (There was clearly a cultic quality, for example, to the role of Chairman Mao in the People's Republic of China.)

In addition to this concern with the sacred, however defined in a particular place and time, most of the practices that might be called religion are also characterized by specific *belief patterns, ritual practices, ethical codes,* and *cultic organization.*

Students of religion have ascribed three great classes of social function to it: the *alienating function,* as seen by Marx; the *cohesive function,* as seen by Durkheim; and the *function of creating meaning,* as seen by Weber. A more recent synthesis by Berger and Luckmann sees religion as having a more overarching function: the construction of reality.

Marx conceived religion as alienating because he believed that *all* belief systems merely reflect material phenomena, particularly the economic order. Thus, an economic order he perceived as exploitive of the masses of people (capitalism) had developed an other-wordly rationalization for the state of affairs on earth in order to justify things, particularly the class system, as they were. The Marxian tradition defines the religious institution as essentially *alienating,* a social structure that has the effect of dividing person from person. Research studies supporting that interpretation have often found, for example, that religious organizational membership follows social-class lines.

Work in the tradition of Durkheim has tended to focus on the *integrative* effects of religious practice and belief, the ways in which the religious institu-

tion supports and solidifies social groups and societies. In American sociology, some excellent examples of this thrust are found in research on "civil religion" in the United States and the way in which "the American way of life" may be said to be a religious belief system for Americans.

Weber was responsible for yet another major emphasis in the study of religion with his great classic work *The Protestant Ethic and the Spirit of Capitalism,* and research in this tradition tends to focus on the function of religion for the *creation of meaning.* Research following Weber has tended to support his contention that each general religious system has a different meaning system and that the form taken by a religion is never independent of the culture in which it appears. Religion and culture and social structure are inextricably intertwined. Stemming from this same tradition in sociology are a variety of research studies on the *form of religious organization* within the Christian religion, such as Troeltsch's, which makes the distinction between *church, sect,* and *denomination.*

Two Americans, Peter Berger and Thomas Luckmann, recently attempted to synthesize all three perspectives in what they call a "social construction of reality" perspective. What they mean by this is that reality is a perception: all we know of the universe is what we perceive of it, and this perception is socially conditioned. With regard to religion, what this means is that, whatever supernatural truths it may tell, it is also a response to human needs and values. *Objectively,* religious *institutions* are reflections of habitual behavior organized by common meanings and values. The sacred is thus defined by reference to accepted social meanings, and theology thus becomes a rationale for imputing believability to religious doctrine. *Subjectively,* religion serves a variety of individual needs, including help in personal crises and social life and spiritual assistance.

The religious institution in the United States has three general social characteristics that, influencing each other reciprocally, may be responsible for the great vitality of religion in American society: *pervasiveness, secularity,* and *voluntarism.* Regarding pervasiveness, 95 to 98 percent of all Americans report a belief in God, and about 60 percent belong to some religious denomination. Secularity is important in the sense that religion is legally separated from the state, which means that the various religious organizations must compete with one another for popular support and that none can make a formal claim of being a "true faith." Voluntarism is important because, in the absence of a state church, religious membership is a personal matter, and thus the churches must compete in offering something the public will wish to have. And since voluntary giving is the source of necessary financial support, responsiveness to individual needs is built into the system. Voluntarism may also be responsible for the very active political role that religion has taken in the United States: the people support the churches and if their members want them to be active—or passive—politically, the churches will probably respond.

It is only within the framework of these three qualities of the American religious institution— pervasiveness, secularity and voluntarism—that we can understand recent trends in American religion: the debate about the "post-Christian age"; the continuing struggle over separation of church and state; the resurgence of evangelicalism; and the possibility that American religion may, in the future, redefine its primary functions.

Review Questions

1.   Divide the major faiths according to the social class they typically serve. Which denomination is the most elite among the Protestant denominations? Which is primarily comprised of lower-class members and very predominant in the South?

2.   Differentiate between these four religious institutions: ecclesia, denomination, established sect, and sect. How do they differ in size?

3.   Explain how religion differs from magic and science. Include a brief definition of each.

4.   List and describe the four dimensions of religiosity discussed in this chapter. Does any one dimension appear to be growing or declining in importance in contemporary society?

5.   Discuss how Puritanism and the Protestant Ethic led to an obsession with science and rationalism as well as to modern capitalism.

Suggestions for Research

1.   Attend a weekly service in a Roman Catholic church, a Protestant church and a Jewish synagogue. You may want to sit in the rear so any note-taking you do will be as inconspicuous as possible. If you have questions, remain after the service and ask a member of the congregation or the clergy to clarify these areas for you. Write a report analyzing each service as well as similarities and differences among the three. Does the congregation take a more active role in one faith than in others? If so, in which? What role does symbolism play in each service? Ostentation?

2.   List and describe community functions served by your local churches. Are specific programs sponsored for the aged? Adolescents? Children? What types of classes are offered to community residents? What forms of counseling are available? Describe any recreational programs provided by the churches. Do the churches sponsor any charitable drives? If so, for whom? How important a role do you believe most churches play in the community in terms of social functions?

3.   Select several of your acquaintances or classmates who do not affiliate with an organized church for a brief interview. What are the main reasons for their lack of church involvement? Do most share similar reasons? Do they express any desire to become involved with a church later? Why? Have they established a personal rapport to replace formal ties with religion? From these interviews, what assumptions, if any, can you make about why many students (and others) have rejected church membership? Does the fault seem to lie in the churches' approach? Or with the students? How does their feeling toward religion tie in with other feelings toward life?

4.   Devote a term paper to studying religious utopian communities in America's past history. You may want to include the following: Robert Owen's New Harmony, Mother Ann Lee's Shaker society, and John Humphrey Noyes's Oneida community. What religious convictions were among the reasons for the establishment of these communities? When were they founded and how long did they last? To what can one attribute their failure or success? What generalizations do they suggest about religious utopias?

5.   Contrast the Puritan faith of early New England settlers with the Anglican faith which pervaded the colonial South. How did these two faiths differ in belief patterns? In rituals? Describe the lifestyles of these two groups in terms of limitations and customs which appeared to be church-related. What fate eventually befell these two groups? Why do you think they succeeded or failed in remaining strong religious communities over time? One source that may prove helpful is Daniel Boorstin's *The Americans: The Colonial Experience*.

CHAPTER 15
POLITICS AND GOVERNMENT

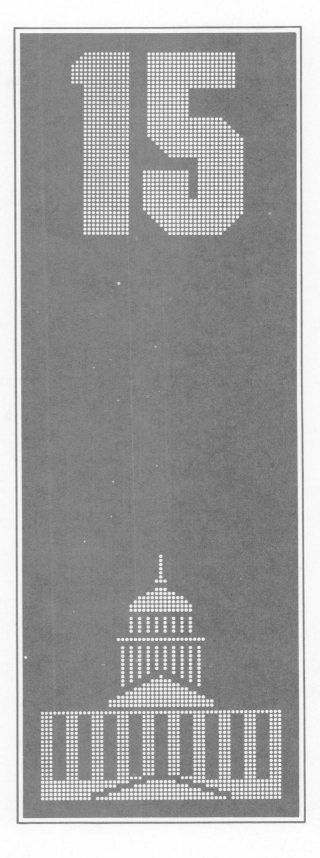

A Joke They Tell in Czechoslovakia

"What is the difference between socialism and capitalism?"

"Under capitalism you are free to write what you like, to read what you like, to telephone to whom you like."

"And socialism?"

"Exactly the same thing, only under capitalism you're still free afterwards."[1]

CIA gained data by burglaries of Yanks abroad

'Guinea pigs' not told during CIA drug tests

Report FBI stole mail during probe of antiwar group

Ex-FBI official 'proud' of '72-'73 break-ins in U.S.

Kelley not positive FBI burglaries have ceased

A Question They Ask in Peoria

"Is the joke they tell in Czechoslovakia still true?"

f, as you realized the meaning of the "question they ask in Peoria," you were momentarily startled, or perhaps suppressed an impulse to shudder, it is because the question confronts one of the gravest problems in politics and governance. *"Quis custodiet ipsos custodes?"* the Romans said. That can be translated into English as "Who keeps custody of the custodians?" or "Who shall watch the watchers?" And wrapped up in that question and implied by it are a number of issues this chapter addresses. What is government? Is it necessary, and, if so, what forms must it take? How does the political process work, and what is its relation to government? What is the relation of the individual to both in different forms of government, and how can that be altered when it is unsatisfactory?

The study of politics and government, of course, is the legitimate domain of one of the social sciences, political science; and to some degree, much of what will be related here will already be familiar to anyone who has taken an introductory course in that field. But the political sociologist (that is, someone interested in the sociology of political behavior) has insights to add to the understanding of politics and government which one gains from political science.

Perhaps the most important sociological "added ingredient" is the familiar concept of social organization. The fact that society is socially organized implies the requirement of leadership—direction or coordination—and that is what government is all about. Politics is how it works. So any consideration of either topic inevitably confronts the fact that government is a kind of social structure and politics a kind of social process.

The utility of having some sociological understanding of politics and government is readily apparent. We live in what earlier chapters have described as a mass society, and in such a society, we feel the influence of government at all levels throughout our lives. What we do in response to that influence—to conform, manipulate, reject, or control it—is likely to be effective only to the extent that it is politically relevant to the governmental process in question. The antiwar students of the 1968-1972 period who sat in at ROTC armories or occupied university administration buildings were engaged in politics. The relevance of their activities to the conduct of the American adventure in Indochina was somewhat tenuous, but they did succeed in calling to the attention of the world the existence of a great deal of political dissent from United States policy.

The young American men who fled to Canada to escape conscription for that war—many of whom remain there still—attest to the terrible impact that politics and government may exert on the lives of even the most indifferent citizen. Finally, of course, it seems beyond much dispute that the 1968 antiwar candidacies of Eugene McCarthy and Robert Kennedy were directly connected to Lyndon Johnson's decision not to seek reelection as President. And those campaigns depended heavily on college students for workers. (McCarthy's campaign was nicknamed "The Children's Crusade" because it was so largely student-staffed.) American policy altered as a result. Whatever his personal inclinations, Richard Nixon could not have been elected in the fall of 1968 on a prowar platform, and since he had seen his predecessor unseated by the antiwar revolt of the young, we may presume he regarded a prowar candidacy as doomed to failure.

Politics and government thus are deeply relevant to all of us, young and old alike. But understanding them requires that we go beyond the legal forms we learned in high school civics courses. They are social phenomena throughout, and it is to that social aspect that we turn our attention in this chapter. The principal topics to be discussed are the nature and functions of political institutions, government as social behavior, the types of government, how governments are changed, and the characteristics of the American political system.

What Is the Political Institution?

The **political institution** (also called polity) refers to the distribution of power, authority, and influence within a society and to the degree of legitimacy granted that distribution by the society's members. **Legitimacy,** in the social-political sense, means the perceived correspondence of a practice, statement, or policy with the cultural values of the society. It may be thought of as social justification, or justifia-

political institution (polity): the social distribution of power, authority, and influence and the degree of legitimacy it is given in organized social life.

legitimacy: in the social-political sense, the perceived correspondence of a practice, statement, or policy with cultural values in a given society; social justification or justifiability.

What we do in response to the immense impact of government on our lives is effective only to the extent that it is politically relevant to the government in question. Here a Selective Service employee requires police help to get by demonstrators who are protesting the Vietnam War and the draft, 1971. This kind of protest clearly had some relevance to the politics of the late sixties and early seventies.

bility, the acceptance of something as right or proper because it is in agreement with underlying values. We grumble about paying taxes, for example, but do not deny the government's right to levy them, and regard it as somehow illegitimate—improper—that some rich people take advantage of tax "loopholes" to evade payment. While no one claims that his behavior is illegal, Ronald Reagan's campaign for the Presidency was undoubtedly flawed by the revelation that he had paid no income taxes for several years while he was governor of California (when he was in office, he consistently scolded welfare "chiselers").

Power is the capacity to "get one's way"; more formally, it is the ability of individuals or a group to exercise their will despite resistance. Governments have the power to enforce the law, and muggers have the power to steal from their victims.

Authority is legitimated power, power that is perceived as right and proper. Thus, in the example given above, a government has the authority to enforce the law because it is perceived as proper that it should do so. The mugger, to the contrary, has only physical power, because his actions are perceived as illegitimate.

Influence is the capacity to change the possible outcome of an event or process. Influence is less conclusive than power. A President, for example, might try to bring about energy conservation by appealing to the public to conserve gasoline and electricity and pressuring the Congress for legislation to that end; but only the Congress has the authority to pass the laws themselves, and the people may not listen. So the President's actions do not make the outcome inevitable; influence is tentative.

At the core of the political institution of any society will be a set of interrelated roles that command legitimate power (authority) and influence in the eyes of the populace. In this sense, the political institution may be thought of as an expansion of the principles underlying leadership. Extending from the legitimate core-leadership roles will be a variety of other roles of power, authority, and influence. Such "outer" roles in the political institution are an important part of it. In the United States, they include racketeers and "Apple Pie" Americans alike.

"*That loophole I found in the tax law turned out not to be a loophole after all!*"

© 1974 by NEA, Inc.

Reprinted by permission of Newspaper Enterprise Association.

Functions of the Political Institution

You already know from the discussion in other chapters that there is rarely agreement on all of the functions that an institution may perform for a society, and thus you will not be surprised to learn that this is true of politics and government as well. Most analysts would probably agree, however, that whatever else it may do in a given case, the political institution always involves (1) *protection of the society from external threat;* (2) *the maintenance of internal order,* and (3) *planning and coordinating for the general welfare.* Before we turn to these, one explanation is in order.

You may recall from Chapter 7 that, in discussing the military institution, we said that *it* always had the protective function, and sometimes the internal order function as well. Why, then, are we now assigning these to politics and government? The answer, of course, is fairly simple; in modern societies the military is always an agency of government, that is, a substructure of the political institution. But it need not be. It can be analyzed as an institution in its own right in any situation, and in some premodern societies the military may be separated from political functions. In feudal Europe, for example, the "government" was the king, but the military aristocracy operated more or less independent of him, and the military *institution,* while owing formal allegiance to the monarch, was in fact completely independent. Each feudal overlord in effect raised and maintained his own private army. But since we are here concerned principally with modern states, the United States in particular, we will assume the military is a subunit of the political institution and discuss its functions in that context.

Protection from External Threat

A society may not endure, and cannot carry on its activities unaltered, if another society invades and conquers it. The conquerors may permit the vanquished to survive (although some, like Genghis Khan, did not), but they are likely to impose their own sociopolitical order or even simply divest the vanquished of their movable resources and depart. In either case, the survival of the invaded society is threatened. And although it is true that modern wars are rarely fought for plunder, are sometimes started by accident, often appear stupid in hindsight, and frequently have outcomes very different from those envisioned by the people who start them, it is also true that they still happen. The only societies that can afford to ignore the necessity for protection from external threat are those (like Mexico, perhaps) that can count on someone else to do their fighting for them.

At a moment of external threat, societal survival and strong social organization become synonymous. The need for government is apparent, and all successful governments for this reason insist upon the power to coerce. Neither conscription nor martial law is a recent historical invention. The morality of such matters has been endlessly debated (which is probably a very good thing for all of us), but for most human societies, the lesson of history appears clear: if a society expects to survive intact, its members need to be able to defend

power: the capacity of individuals or a group to exercise their will despite resistance; the capacity to "get one's way."

authority: legitimated power.

influence: the capacity to change the outcome of an event.

Despite the citylike appearance of the buildings in this medieval painting, it is probably a rendering of some feudal lord's private army engaged in a private dispute.

themselves from external attack. And government is typically charged with that responsibility.

Maintenance of Internal Order

The sociological use of the word *order,* as in "social order" or "internal order" above, should not be confused with the political catchphrase "law and order" that became almost synonymous with racial and political oppression during the first Nixon administration. In sociology, the word *order* refers to the social organization through which all human beings survive, discussed in Chapters 5-7. The function of government in maintaining order within the society, then, is the task of insuring that this crucial pattern does not fall apart. It does this primarily in two ways: (1) through enforcement of the norms that prescribe the expectations that constitute social organization, and (2) through the arbitration of conflict (often about what norms are to be enforced) that could threaten the stability of that organization.

Maintaining order through norm enforcement The government is often in the position of helping to codify norms into law. When new activities occur or old ones cease to occur, the government must either enforce norms existing in the form of law or help create new ones. The widespread adoption of the automobile in the United States, for example, involved government at all levels in deciding whether, when, and where new roads were to be built; in passing new traffic regulatory laws and enforcing them; and in formulating auto liability laws. The rise of automobile insurance companies, in response to the liability laws, enmeshed the government in their regulation.

Maintaining order through arbitrating conflict If governments wish to maintain internal order, they must *arbitrate* conflicts among members of the society, not merely repress them. The conflict must be in some way *resolved.* The word *conflict* often calls up the image of physical violence; but values can also be in conflict, and groups, organizations, or individuals with different values or goals may also conflict in this sense. The enrollment of James Meredith as the first black student at the University of Mississippi in 1962, for example, involved both

Conscription rites of the Civil War and World War I. Conscription by the state for military and other purposes goes back to the beginning of history.

physical and value conflict. And the debate about the proper use of national forests and other government-owned land in the western states pits conservationists, lumber interests, and stock raisers against one another without violence.

In the latter instance, all three groups have aims that they regard as legitimate and that are certainly legal, but are contradictory. In such cases, the government must arbitrate because it is the only authority capable of doing so. Sometimes its role as arbitrator is simply to provide time for a new value to become widely legitimated, as in the Meredith instance. (Federal troops are no longer needed to enroll black students in universities.) Or sometimes the government may seek to accelerate social change by making sure it does not bring about destructive consequences. This is often accomplished through regulatory legislation.

The role of government in controlling social change through arbitration of conflict is an important one. In general, it may choose any one of four responses at a given time, or more than one through time. First, government may *repress change* to avoid conflict, although this tactic, if prolonged, may bring about either social stagnation or revolution. In Czarist Russia, for example, both occurred.

Second, government may *arbitrate and guide change* in such a way that conflict is avoided during the change process. Once Communist domination of the political process had been thoroughly secured in the People's Republic of China, traditional Chinese social life was radically transformed without overwhelming bloodshed or traumatic upheaval.

Third, government may *repress conflict* in order to avoid the social change that often accompanies it. The Nixon administration attempted this tactic to try to stop the antiwar movement of the late 1960s and early 1970s. This response is often unsuccessful, however, as it was in that instance. The American public's attitudes about American involvement in the internal affairs of other countries were shifting during this period, and were clearly affected by the massive conscription for, and casualties in, an unpopular, far-away war. The government repression of dissent may only have hastened and hardened the change.

Fourth, government may *arbitrate social conflict* to bring about guided change. The responses of the Kennedy and Johnson administrations to the civil rights movement are examples in point.

Planning and Coordinating for the General Welfare

Societies vary in the degree to which planning and coordinating the general welfare are considered legitimate tasks of government. The conventional distinction between socialist and capitalist societies turns on the legitimacy of government planning and coordination. Socialist thought is dominated by the conception of having a blueprint for

James Meredith goes to class at the University of Mississippi, 1962.

Mass arrest of antiwar demonstrators, May 3, 1971. The Nixon administration reacted to social change by attempting to repress the conflict it provoked.

society and government action to bring that plan into operation.

Capitalism and socialism **Capitalism** minimally refers to an economic system in which private individuals and groups own and control productive enterprise. Theoretically, the existence of such enterprises stems from the needs or demands of consumers for the products involved. **Socialism** originally referred to a system in which government would own and control at least the major productive enterprises of the economy in accord with specified social values and goals. But these traditional definitions are nineteenth-century European understandings. The political, social, and economic conditions that gave rise to them have altered drastically throughout the world, and the labels now may obscure more than they illuminate.

Both "socialist" and "capitalist" societies have moved toward what John Kenneth Galbraith calls a **mixed economy,** in which the state intervenes in, but does not necessarily own, productive enterprises.[2] In the mixed economy, for example, the government may adopt a number of courses. It may set standards to which privately owned industries must adhere, as in the case of American auto safety equipment. Or government may itself be a customer of private industry; our government annually buys billions of dollars worth of defense equipment from private contractors (when such contractors exist only to supply a government demand, the arrangement is sometimes called "state capitalism"). Or government may own some but not all of the productive enterprises in the society; in Britain, coal mining, railways, and the steel industry are nationalized, but other enterprises are privately owned. Or government may emphasize control of industry only to the degree required to implement social ideals, as suggested by the West German Social Democrats' post–World War II formula: "As much competition as possible; as much planning as necessary."

Planning and regimentation In point of fact, *all* governments plan and coordinate in differing degrees and in different areas of social life—health, unemployment, transportation, monetary policy,

and so forth. But not all governments regiment their populations. **Regimentation** implies the attachment of coercive sanctions to social behavior. In a regimented society, the scope of social behavior subject to legal control is wide; many actions are required or forbidden.

The distinction can be seen in a remark attributed to an American who traveled through pre–World War II Britain and Germany: "In Britain, anything not specifically prohibited is permitted. In Germany, anything not specifically permitted is prohibited." The difference between government planning and coordination of social activity and government regimentation of social activity, then, is this: Is the individual punished if he does not fit into the plan? In Britain, a planned but not regimented society, no one is punished for not using the National Health Service. In the Soviet Union, a regimented society, one is coerced into joining the labor force. Soviet citizens do have some latitude, of course, about what work they do, but work they must, or be imprisoned.

Governments typically plan and coordinate primarily in areas of social life in which it would be difficult or impossible for any other organization or individual to do so: building highways, coordinating air and sea traffic, issuing currency, and so forth. No other institution or organization has the resources required to collect the data necessary to make such decisions, and no other has the power and authority to enforce them for the common good.

Government and Social Behavior

We emphasized earlier that government is a part of social organization and that politics is a social process. In the following section, we will turn our attention specifically to these phenomena and their interrelations by considering three topics: the two fundamental political roles, those of the elite and the nonelite; the distinctions between formal (governmental) power, authority, and influence, both legitimate and illegitimate, and the informal (nongovernmental) expressions of the same phenomena; and the relations among power, authority, and influence.

Elites and Nonelites

We can, from one perspective, divide all political roles into one of two categories: elite and nonelite. These roles make up the political *structure* of a society; its political *functions* (protection, maintaining order, and planning) are performed by people in elite roles. The political elite, then, are the special class of people in a society who perform its political functions. In sociology, the word *elite* is normally used to denote all those in top political decision-making roles, whether they are formally members of the government or not. The famous sociologist C. Wright Mills called such persons a "power elite," as we noted in Chapter 8; and Suzanne Keller has refined and extended Mills's idea in the conception of a "strategic elite."[3]

There is, as we saw in Chapter 8, some debate among sociologists as to whether such elites actually exist as self-conscious social categories. Is there, for example, a strategic elite of persons, largely male, who make decisions for a "military-industrial complex"—generals and admirals, high government officials, and industrial tycoons who know each other, consider each other's interests, and perhaps even collude in planning and coordination? Mills and Keller believe that such elites exist and that their existence is demonstrated. Their critics say that, since such *roles* exist, the possibility of an elite is manifest, but its existence has yet to be demonstrated. For our purposes in this chapter, it is not necessary to try to settle the argument. We will use the term *elite,* or **strategic elite,** to refer to people in top decision-making roles in both the formal and informal political structure and not attempt to answer the question of whether those people form an actual group or groups.

Keller defines *strategic elites* as those having the most comprehensive scope and impact, people who claim or whose roles assign them responsibility for and influence over their society as a whole. Such roles may be either governmental or nongovernmental, what we called earlier formal or informal positions in the social structure. Elite governmental roles, for example, include those of President, Supreme Court justice, members of Congress, Cabinet members, the Joint Chiefs of Staff, and high-level appointees such as the head of

capitalism: the economic system in which ownership and control of production in a society is in the hands of private individuals and groups rather than the state.

socialism: the economic system in which the government owns at least the major productive industries in a society, controlling them in accord with specified social values and goals.

mixed economy: the economic system that combines elements of classical capitalism and socialism, typically with the government intervening in economic production without owning industry.

regimentation: the attachment of coercive sanctions to social behavior.

strategic elite: Suzanne Keller's term for people in roles with responsibility for and influence over the society as a whole.

political process: the exercise of the functions of the political institution by those with elite roles in it.

politics: the process through which people gain access to elite roles in society.

governance: the conduct of the functions of the political institution by the political elite.

government: the elite exercising the legitimate power, authority, and influence of the state.

the Central Intelligence Agency, and so forth. Nonelite governmental roles are numerous and may be exemplified by civil servants holding clerical rank. Elite nongovernmental roles might include lobbyists for powerful organized groups like the American Medical Association, heads of major corporations, retired high-ranking military officers who act as consultants to industry, and so on. The nonelite, nongovernmental political role is that of the average citizen.

We can now see how government is intertwined with social behavior. The **political process** can be conceived as the exercise of the functions of the political institution by those with elite roles within it. What people call **politics** is the activity involved with gaining access to such roles, whether elected or unelected. **Governance** means the conduct of that portion of the political process carried out through the government by those in official, or formal, elite roles.

Government may be formally understood as the elite that at a given time exercise the legitimate

Figure 15-1
The political institution

Formal relationships and structures

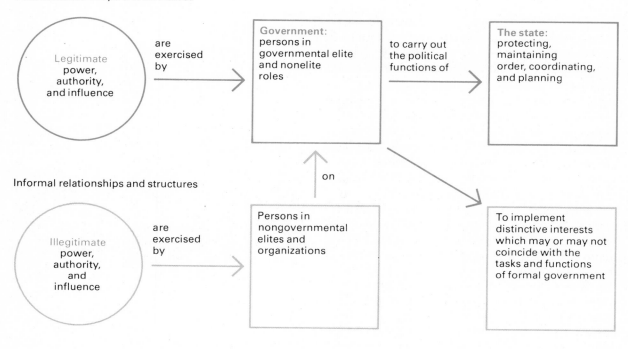

Informal relationships and structures

power, authority, and influence of the **state,** which is, in turn, defined as the highest sovereign (independent) political unit. The state is the political form of which the government at any particular time is the operating embodiment.[4] Figure 15-1 illustrates these relationships.

Formal and Informal Functions and Roles

The social character of the political institution means that power, authority, and influence in government and the political process may be either formal or informal and either legitimate or illegitimate. We may understand *formal* in this context as referring to acts undertaken by officials or agencies of government in the name of government. *Informal* actions are those that influence the process but are undertaken by actors without official position

or through extragovernmental channels, such as lobbying.

Many examples illustrate these points. It is both formal and legitimate, for instance, for the Department of Justice to use its power to enforce the law, but when FBI agents committed burglary in an attempt to gain evidence against Daniel Ellsberg in the Pentagon Papers case, they engaged in an illegitimate use of their formal power. Similarly, it is a legitimate use of informal power for labor unions to impose restrictions on their members specifying the conditions under which they will work. But the murder of insurgent United Mine Worker (UMW) Joseph Yablonsky and his wife in 1969 at the direction of then UMW President Tony Boyle was clearly an illegitimate use of such power. It would take a twelve-cell table to represent all of the possible combinations of these variables (legitimate power, authority, and influence, both formal and informal, and illegitimate examples of the same), but you could easily think of illustrations to put in every cell.

Relations among Power, Authority, and Influence

Power, authority, and influence, and the degree of legitimacy that any of them may possess in a given instance, are not always easy to distinguish. Subtle interplays exist among them, and as we all know from many recent Washington scandals, it sometimes takes a court to determine whether a particular political act was or was not legitimate.

The example of lobbying may provide as good an illustration of the relations among the four variables as any we could offer.[5] **Lobbying** can be defined merely as the attempt to influence public officials in their decision making. It is not illegal and ranges from sending your senator a postcard sounding off about something important to you to the expenditure of thousands of dollars by great corporations to entertain legislators. Lobbying is a characteristic of all political systems, but in the United States some attempt is made to make lobbyists accountable for their acts and legislators accountable for their responses to the lobbyist. The Federal Lobbying Act of 1946 requires professional lobbyists to register as such with the government, but the nature of lobbying makes the act difficult to enforce. Approximately 5,000 full-time lobbyists are now based in Washington, about 10 for each member of Congress.

Some lobbies are more effective than others. A concerned citizen writing an outraged letter is less influential than the organized bodies of special-interest agents employed by the nation's great industries and organizations. Major lobbies permanently based in Washington include oil (perhaps the most mammoth and influential of all), sugar, tobacco, armaments, and automobile interests, as well as special-interest organizations such as the American Medical Association, National Rifle Association, Chamber of Commerce, National Association of Manufacturers, and the National Farm Bureau Federation, which act as lobbies for their members.

state: the highest independent political unit.

lobbying: the attempt to influence decisions to be made by public officials. The conventional use of the word implies that the attempt is made with means other than rational persuasion, but this is not a necessary part of the definition.

This nineteenth century political cartoon illustrates a common perception of the relative importance of lobbyists and legislators in the law making process.

Lobbyists operate by obtaining influence over government officials, which, when effective, transforms itself into a form of power. Influence can be secured in a variety of ways. Good lobbyists pride themselves on knowing how to find anything the official may desire: fine foods and liquors, football tickets, entertainment and travel, the use of company aircraft, or even willing call girls. The lobbyist does favors for the official and for his secretary, who controls the official's mail and appointment book. Campaign funds for elected officials are also important, and there is always what has been called the "deferred bribe": the possibility of a high-paying job with the lobbyist's organization when the official resigns or fails to get reelected.

For legislators in particular, one other form of influence is important: information. Lobbyists operate as an informal intelligence and research network supplying members of Congress with the basic raw material of law making, information about problems the Congress is working on. The information is likely to be slanted to the lobbyist's interest, of course. But with little time and often greatly overworked staffs, it may be the best the legislator can get. The lobbies have the time to draft legislation, gather evidence, and help persuade other members of Congress to "go along with" a particular member's bill, and many acts of both the Senate and the House are originally written in corporate or organizational offices.

Thus, power and influence are deeply meshed in the act of lobbying, and the lobbyist's influence becomes authority when the government official acts on it. But legitimacy is an integral part of authority (which was defined, you will remember, as legitimated power). To remain in office, authority must express the values accepted as proper by the society in which it exists. Max Weber defined the three ways in which legitimacy is conferred on authority in his studies of the types of social action characteristic of different societies throughout history, described in Chapter 1.[6]

Traditional authority is legitimated by the belief that "things have *always* been this way"; that is, legitimacy is conferred by the values of the past.

Charismatic authority is legitimated by the unique personal qualities of the leader, by the belief of others that he or she is someone extraor-

The "Nixon tapes" are delivered to the House Judiciary Committee, April 30, 1974. President Nixon attempted to convince the Congress and the public of the constitutional nature of his behavior by appearing to respond to congressional subpoena of his Watergate tapes. Unfortunately for him, the tapes had been "laundered," and the result was public condemnation rather than praise.

dinary. Jesus, Joan of Arc, and Hitler are outstanding examples.

Rational-legal authority is legitimated by the belief that the official is acting in conformity to an agreed-upon code. The individual member of society gives allegiance to the code—the "rule of law," for example—and so long as officials are perceived as acting in conformity with that code, their actions are perceived as legitimate. In the United States, what could be called *constitutionalism* probably best represents such a rational-legal authority. So long as public officials can convince the public that they are acting in accord with constitutional principles, they are likely to be accepted, if not liked; and it seems probable that it was the failure to maintain that conviction in the public mind that eventually unseated Richard Nixon.

Sometimes, of course, the bases of legitimation may be mixed; John F. Kennedy's Presidency was legitimated by a combination of rational-legal and charismatic authority, as were those of Franklin D. Roosevelt and, to a lesser degree, Dwight Eisenhower. The different forms of authority, and the varying relationships among power, authority, and influence, are important in determining the type of government that a society possesses, and we turn to that subject now.

Types of Government

The government embodies the state, but governments vary as to whether they are primarily autocratic, oligarchic, or democratic.

Autocracy

Under **autocracy**, one individual in the society is the source of law. Aristotle believed that this person ideally would be a virtuous philosopher-king, but the absolute monarchy of Louis XIV, the Sun King, is probably a more common model. Autocracy refers only to the *absoluteness* of the law-making power, not its scope. An autocrat may be limited in his actual power, for example, by power in the hands of others. But within the scope of authority recognized by his society as legitimate, the autocrat's power is perceived as absolute.

The feudal system is an example of such a situation. The temporal power of a feudal king might have been deeply restricted by having to rely on his barons for armies, but so long as he was accepted by the Pope as the rightful monarch, his word was law within certain areas of social life. (This situation also had the effect of giving the Pope considerable *influence* in the state's affairs. Joseph Stalin's satirical question in World War II, "And how many [army] divisions has the Pope?" would not have made sense in feudal Europe.)

Oligarchy

Oligarchy means rule by the few, and it has appealed, among others, to Plato, Aristotle, and the eighteenth-century British statesman Edmund Burke. Burke believed in constitutional government, but thought it could be best implemented by an elite corps of law makers trained and specialized in ruling for the common good. In Burke's opinion, the ordinary citizen did not have sufficient information and judgment to run a society or even to criticize the law makers intelligently. The elite, instead, should run things according to their best

Louis XIV (1638–1715), the absolute autocrat, is reputed to have said, "I am the state."

The Bill of Rights

Amendment I   Congress shall make no law respecting an establishment of religion or prohibiting the free exercise thereof; or abridging the freedom of speech, or of the press; of the right of the people peaceably to assemble, and to petition the Government for a redress of grievances.

Amendment II   A well regulated Militia, being necessary to the security of a free State, the right of the people to keep and bear Arms, shall not be infringed.

Amendment III   No Soldier shall, in time of peace be quartered in any house, without the consent of the Owner, nor in time of war, but in a manner to be prescribed by law.

Amendment IV   The right of the people to be secure in their persons, houses, papers, and effects, against unreasonable searches and seizures, shall not be violated, and no Warrants shall issue, but upon probable cause, supported by Oath or affirmation, and particularly describing the place to be searched, and the persons or things to be seized.

Amendment V   No person shall be held to answer for a capital, or otherwise infamous crime, unless on a presentment or indictment of a Grand Jury, except in cases arising in the land or naval forces, or in the Militia, when in actual service in time of War or public danger; nor shall any person be subject for the same offence to be twice put in jeopardy of life or limb; nor shall be compelled in any criminal case to be a witness against himself, nor be deprived of life, liberty, or property, without due process of law; nor shall private property be taken for public use, without just compensation.

Amendment VI   In all criminal prosecutions, the accused shall enjoy the right to a speedy and public trial, by an impartial jury of the State and district wherein the crime shall have been committed, which district shall have been previously ascertained by law, and to be informed of the nature and cause of the accusation; to be confronted with the witnesses against him; to have compulsory process for obtaining Witnesses in his favor, and to have the Assistance of Counsel for his defence.

Amendment VII   In Suits at common law, where the value in controversy shall exceed twenty dollars, the right of trial by jury shall be preserved, and no fact tried by a jury, shall be otherwise re-examined in any Court of the United States, than according to the rules of the common law.

Amendment VIII   Excessive bail shall not be required, nor excessive fines imposed, nor cruel and unusual punishments inflicted.

Amendment IX   The enumeration in the Constitution, of certain rights, shall not be construed to deny or disparage others retained by the people.

Amendment X   The powers not delegated to the United States by the Constitution, nor prohibited by it to the States, are reserved to the States respectively, or to the people.

judgment, whether it agreed with that of their constituents or not. The source of law in oligarchy, then, is a small group whose legitimacy in authority is conferred by their presumed special training or capabilities.

Democracy

In **democracy,** the citizens of the society are the source of law, either directly or indirectly. Democracy has been practiced in two forms: *direct democracy,* in which all citizens participate in law making; and *representative democracy,* in which the general citizenry delegates the law-making power to elected representatives, but each citizen is eligible for election to that role. Athens under

The first ten Amendments to the Constitution, the Bill of Rights, delineate those areas of social behavior on which the government cannot infringe. The Amendments have always been open to interpretation by the courts, and some of the great legal battles of recent years (such as the right of the defendant to counsel in *all* criminal cases) have been fought on the basis of their provisions.

Pericles (fifth century B.C.) and the New England town meeting are familiar examples of direct democracy. But in both, not all members of the society were considered citizens or allowed to participate. In New England, minors, criminals and nontaxpayers were typically disenfranchised; while in Athens, women, slaves, and foreigners were not allowed to vote.

The contemporary United States, of course, is a representative democracy in which any citizen of majority age who is not a felon or has not been adjudged insane may participate in the electoral process, which, in turn, conveys the law-making power to representatives. The legitimacy of the law-making role is thus conveyed by popular election, while the threat of defeat at the polls insures that elected officials will to some degree be accountable to the electorate. (Officials are also accountable to the law for their acts, of course, and official acts themselves must pass the test of constitutionality.)

---

democracy: government by the many or all; government in which the citizenry has the law-making power. In direct democracy, as in a New England town meeting, all citizens are the actual law makers. In representative democracy, as in the American legislative system, actual law making is delegated by the people to representatives chosen by themselves from among themselves.

Criteria for Assessing Government

We can see from the discussion above that the *type* of government a society has is defined by the nature and number of its legitimate law-making roles: where the power to make law is located and how many people share it. But to call a government autocratic, oligarchic, or democratic does not tell everything about it that it is important to know. In the contemporary West, we tend to think of democracy as "good" and autocracy as "bad" and to use the word *oligarchy* as an insult, despite our knowledge that the Soviet Union calls itself a democracy, that Monaco (which has a real, live American movie star as its princess) is an autocracy, and that Vatican City is an oligarchy. The more important question to ask in assessing whether a particular government is "good" or "bad" is what life under it is like for the typical citizen. Usually, three political dimensions or continua are important in answering this question: *regimentation/voluntarism, partiality/impartiality,* and *tyranny/juridicality.*

Regimentation/Voluntarism

We can judge how regimented or voluntaristic a society is by determining how many social acts, such as writing, speaking, assembling, and so forth, are subject to punishment by the state. A nation's legal code gives some indication of how much regimentation is allowed. The Bill of Rights of the U.S. Constitution, for example, is essentially a set of prohibitions against regimentation and has

been consistently interpreted in that way by the courts.

Besides a society's legal code, there could be a number of empirical or operational indicators of this dimension of political life. The number of newspapers, their circulation in the population, and whether serious criticism of the government appears in their columns would be one such set. The freedom of individuals to form groups to express opposition to the government or attempt to alter it would be another. The role of the police and the scope of their authority over individual life is another important criterion. Even the amount of immigration and emigration that occurs constitutes such a measure. Immigration *to* highly regimented societies is likely to be low, while emigration *from* them may be seriously restricted. The restriction of Jewish emigration from the Soviet Union has been a major issue in world affairs recently, and non-Jewish Soviet citizens seeking to emigrate have been harassed by the police and publicly accused of various character defects and misbehaviors.[7]

Partiality/Impartiality

The dimension of partiality/impartiality is essentially a measure of how much government favoritism exists. Does the government rule in such a way that the opportunities in life are enhanced as much as possible for all citizens, or does the regime favor a few? Such indicators as the literacy rate, the infant mortality rate, life expectancy, the percent of the population with advanced educational degrees, and the proportion of the gross national product spent for general governmental functions, social services, and public enterprises would all give some clue to the government's care for the average citizen. Distribution of ownership of agricultural land and income distribution after taxes are similar indicators. Naturally, a wealthy nation will be able to provide more for its people than a poor one, but the relative distribution of such things across social classes is an important measure. Fulgencio Batista's (pre-1959) Cuba, for example, was notably more partial than contemporary Cuba under Fidel Castro, where the state has taken over the provision of health and educational services, raising the literacy rate and all other indicators of social welfare.[8]

Tyranny/Juridicality

A **tyranny** is a rule, regime, or government that is unchallengeable by the governed, where the only way in which the governed may change the government is to overthrow it. **Juridical rule**, to the contrary, is a rule of law under which provision for changing the law is made within the existing law. Juridical rule has rules for changing the rules.

One empirical indicator of the degree of a society's tyranny or juridicality is the death rate from domestic violence. Societies with high death rates from domestic violence are likely to be more tyrannical than juridical. Where people cannot challenge their laws by peaceable, formal means—through the legal system itself—they are more apt to "take the law into their own hands." And when they do that, domestic violence is likely to follow. In the interval 1950-1962, for example, Cuba (where the constitution had been suspended until 1959) had the highest rates in the world for deaths from domestic violence, while the United Kingdom, a constitutional regime of long standing, had the lowest.[9] Cultural differences are reflected here as well, of course—Latin societies tend to have more domestic violence than the English-speaking nations, regardless of the nature of their governments—but the tyrannical nature of the Batista regime certainly may have contributed to the high death rates.

Note that the question to which the tyranny/juridicality dimension of assessment points is not whether the laws may be *appealed to,* but whether the law itself may be altered or challenged through institutionalized channels. The repeal of the Prohibition Amendment, the current attempt to add the Equal Rights Amendment to the Constitution, and

Many Latin American "palace" revolutions merely change the identities of those who occupy elite roles. Other forms of revolution effect profound alterations in the social structure. Chile, 1973; the American Revolution, 1776.

the revision of drug laws are all evidence of the existence of juridical rule in the United States. That German citizens were imprisoned, or even executed, for so much as questioning the law in Hitler's Germany showed it to be a tyranny.

How Governments Are Changed

To call attention, as the preceding section has done, to the quality of life in society is also to call attention to the fact that people often wish to change their collective quality of life through altering the political structure. This can be done in three ways: (1) by changing the *form* of government, say, from autocracy to democracy; (2) by changing those occupying the elite political roles, as in many recent Latin American revolutions; or (3) by changing both, as in revolutions where colonial regimes are changed for rule by local populations. When changes proceed in institutionalized, juridical ways, they are peaceful; but when they occur in abrupt, uninstitutionalized forms, accompanied by violence, they are, of course, revolutions.

Institutionalized Change

As indicated in the previous section, a government that operates juridically can be changed in regular, institutionalized ways. It has built-in provisions for its own alteration. This is perhaps most apparent in the modern world in parliamentary governments such as that of the United Kingdom. Whenever a British government fails to maintain the parliamentary majority's belief in its capacity to govern effectively (as shown by a vote of no confidence in the House of Commons), it is obliged either to resign or to call for new elections. In either case, a new government will be formed. The government is in this way kept almost absolutely responsible to the people, and alteration in its membership is easy.

In the United States, alteration in governmental form can be accomplished—and has been historically—through constitutional amendment. For instance, the United States became more widely democratic through black and female suffrage, accomplished by amendment, and it would be theoretically possible for it to choose autocracy or oligarchy in the same way. Thoroughly juridical regimes are likely to be long-lasting as a result of this kind of built-in perpetual change mechanism. Many Americans do not appreciate that their "young" country has one of the oldest continuously established governments in the world (only the British and Icelandic parliaments are older) and that our election process has never, even in the midst of civil war, been delayed or canceled. The American system of election every two, four, or six years, plus constitutional juridicality, seems to have satisfactorily institutionalized the possibilities for change.

tyranny: a regime or system of law in which no legitimate channels exist *in* the law for challenge *of* the law. The only way such a government may be changed by the governed is by its overthrow.

juridical rule: a rule of law that provides channels *in* the law for challenge *of* the law.

First black voter. American democracy was fundamentally altered through the constitutional amendments that gave blacks and women the right to vote.

Revolution

Claude Welch and Mavis Taintor suggest that there are four elements that make up a true political revolution: (1) alteration in the means of selecting political elites, which creates new elites, often by nonconstitutional or unsystematic means; (2) the opening of new channels for access to political power; (3) the expansion, sometimes temporary, of political participation in the society; and (4) the creation of a new political order based on new conceptions of political legitimacy.[10]

Revolutions, although dramatic, are not the product of fleeting grievances. Although they may occur suddenly, they take generations to develop. And such movements cannot properly be called politically revolutionary unless a new basis for political legitimacy is created and sustained. The "palace revolution," a frequent occurrence in Latin American politics, is not a true revolution; only the residents of the palace change. Examples of genuine revolutions include those in France in 1789, Russia in 1917, China in 1949, and Cuba in 1959.

Samuel P. Huntington outlined two paths or sequences that revolution may follow: what he calls the Classic (or Western) model and the Modern (or Third World) model.[11] The key events in each type contain the same elements, but in a different time sequence. The Classic model is exemplified by the French, Russian, and Mexican revolutions, while the Modern model is illustrated by most colonial revolutions (of which the American is somewhat representative) and the recent civil war in Vietnam. In the Classic (Western) model, (1) the political institutions of the old regime collapse; (2) new groups are mobilized and brought into the political process; and then (3) new political institutions are created. In the Modern (Third World) model, (1) new groups are mobilized and brought into politics; (2) new political institutions are created; and only then are (3) the political institutions of the old order overthrown.

In the Classic revolutionary model, the government's loss of ability to perform the tasks of the political institution hastens the downfall of the regime, but does not guarantee it. The necessary and immediate cause of the Classic revolution is some event that demonstrates that the regime has lost the capacity to defend itself. The storming of the Bastille, which precipitated the French revolution, is an example. Modern revolutions, which create new national regimes, begin when elite groups adopt ideas about how power could be acquired and used to serve the interests of neglected majorities. Their sense of purpose and appeal to the masses is frequently based on their ability to arouse nationalistic feelings. Nationalism provides the unifying ideal through which a population, even if divided along class, tribal, or racial lines, may be melted into a cohesive force of "citizens." The final task of the new elite in the Modern revolution is to integrate the national economy into the world economy as the means of establishing the better future that was part of the revolutionary program's appeal.[12]

It can be argued that one reason the United States failed so abysmally to achieve its political aims in both the Cuban and Vietnamese revolutions was the failure to distinguish between the two revolutionary models. U.S. government policy treated both as Classic revolutions when, in fact, they were Modern ones. The essential differences between the two are clear in the sequence in which key events occur.[13] In the Classic model, the political mobilization of the population is the *consequence* of the collapse of the old regime, and relatively little action is needed on the part of rebellious groups to overthrow it. Basically, they need only to realize that the state has ceased to exist as an effective force. This is demonstrated by some precipitating event. Bloodshed occurs after the seizure of the capital, in which the revolutionaries first take power and from which they must then struggle to extend their control over the countryside.

In the Modern revolution, the political mobilization of the population is the *cause* of the overthrow of the old regime. There is no specific precipitating event to mark the collapse of the old government; and bloodshed takes place before the seizure of the capital as the revolutionaries fight their way in from the countryside, over which they have gained control through persuasion and terror.

In both the Cuban and Vietnamese cases, political mobilization of the population in support of the revolutionary groups was well under way before the United States made any attempt to intervene massively. American planners apparently assumed that the presence of revolutionaries in or near the respective capitals merely signified the beginnings of the effort, as, indeed, it would have under the Classic model. Instead, of course, it signaled in each case that the issue was already largely decided, and that the time for any intervention to be effective was long past.

Characteristics of American Political Structure

Thus far, we have been discussing the political institution largely in the abstract, referring to specific facts and events only to illustrate general principles. We now turn to the political institution in the United States to examine the characteristics of American political structure. These are (1) a federal system, (2) political pluralism, (3) consensus politics, (4) the two-party system, and (5) the problem of unresponsiveness.

The Federal System

The basic key to American political structure, often missed or misunderstood by people from other nations, is that it is a *federal* political system. The United States, as its name implies, is a federation of partially sovereign political entities. The system originated, of course, at least partially because of the fierce independence of several of the original colonies and the Founding Fathers' fears of giving too much authority to a central government. The controlling clauses of the Constitution are found in Articles IX and X of the Bill of Rights: "The enumeration in the Constitution, of certain rights, shall not be construed to deny or disparage others retained by the people" (IX); "The powers not delegated to the United States by the Constitution, nor prohibited by it to the States, are reserved to the States respectively, or to the people" (X). Article VI, however, declared that laws passed by Congress pursuant to the Constitution "shall be the supreme law of the land," and that state laws and constitutions are to be bound by federal enactments. Thus, while the states were granted certain sovereign powers on which the central government was forbidden to

The Bolshevik uprising that established the Soviet Union was a true revolution, not a palace revolt.

When North Vietnamese and Viet Cong troops seized Saigon in April 1975, it marked the end of the revolution, not the beginning.

intrude, in other areas, federal legislation and authority were made supreme.

This description is deceptively simple, of course, and great bodies of law and precedent have grown up delineating the rights and powers of both the central government and the states; and legal contests between the two sets of authorities still continue. Often, these must be decided by the Supreme Court, which is the final legal authority for all American territory and jurisdictions. The ultimate meaning of the federal system is that power is *shared* between the central and state governments.

Power is also shared, of course, among a mosaic of lesser governmental units. In 1972, the U.S. Census Bureau tabulated a total of 78,268 different governments within the United States: roughly 3,000 counties, 18,500 municipalities, 16,500 townships, 15,500 school districts, 23,500 special districts (for water, fire, mosquito control, and so forth), 50 states, and 1 national government.[14] This complex overlapping and distribution of various authorities is also a part of the federal system as applied in the United States. This feature has two ultimate effects: (1) it qualifies or constrains the power of any one government by checking it against that of others; and (2) it gives individual citizens an opportunity for access to the political structure that they might not have under another system.

Citizen power at the local level It is unquestionably true, as often charged in recent years, that the great complexity of the American political structure and the massive size of federal and state government make for "structural unresponsiveness": the condition in which the average citizen finds it difficult or impossible to make his voice heard. Some of the reasons for this are discussed in a later section. But it is also true that the mosaic of local governments makes it possible for American citizens, individually or collectively, to participate in and influence government, at least on the local level, in ways that often amaze foreign visitors. If you don't like how local taxes or resources are being used, you can attend the meetings of the city council and tell them about it. And if you are not satisfied with their reaction, you can run for membership on the council yourself or back a candidate

who thinks as you do. This possibility is not, in fact, remote. All over the country in recent years, neighborhood groups concerned about taxation, water and air pollution, and similar matters have influenced policy, often with startling results.

Nor is action of this kind limited to influencing local governments. Ralph Nader's Public Interest Research Groups, made up almost entirely of interested volunteers and operating at the local level, have become political forces to be reckoned with not only in state capitals, but even in Washington. And one American President, Lyndon Johnson, was driven from office by grass-roots uprisings led by Senators Eugene McCarthy and Robert Kennedy, while Richard Nixon found his capacity to govern deeply flawed by popular unrest.

Most Americans probably do not realize how easy it is—if you are willing to expend the effort of months of doorbell ringing and giving neighborhood coffees—to create an effective local political organization. And when such citizens' groups are linked to a national organization, as in the McCarthy and Robert Kennedy campaigns, they can become formidable forces indeed. The Eugene McCarthy campaign in Tippecanoe County, Indiana, for example, operated around a hard core of only about a dozen people, six or eight of whom had come together in November 1967 to urge McCarthy to run in Indiana when Robert Kennedy said that he would not contend for the Presidency. The people involved were three university professors, a handful of committed housewives, one businessman, and a few students. By the time of the primary election, in May 1968, this group was being aided by about a hundred part-time workers, mostly students and housewives. Together they had so organized the county as to defeat there resoundingly, in his home district, the popular former governor of the state who was running as President Johnson's stand-in. John Kennedy became President through just such grass-roots action.[15]

Political Pluralism

American society, as we have seen in earlier chapters, is socially heterogeneous and pluralistic. This great diversity among the American people means that they are receptive to membership in groups organized on many different bases: age, sex, race, social class, geographic region, religious preference, income, occupation, and the like. Some of these groups will become politicized—they will focus their group consciousness and activity on political objects or political goals. This is the phenomenon of **political pluralism** so characteristic of American politics: the existence of considerable heterogeneity among political groups and hence the possibility of competition between them.

You can appreciate the full meaning of this political pluralism by recalling the immense diversity of organized groups active in the 1976 election campaign. There were ethnic and racial groups represented; sex groups (women's liberation and gay liberation); people interested in the abortion issue, some from a religious group background, others not; conservationists (of many different stripes and with a number of issues) and industrialists; the pro- and antigun lobbies; urban interests and farmers (often subdivided among themselves); regional interests; and on and on and on. By sampling the news magazines through the spring and summer of the year, you could have identified literally hundreds of different groups and organizations politically active in one way or another, all trying to influence the parties, the campaigns, or the outcomes of the various elections. This political pluralism, within the framework of the two-party system, has a great deal to do with the nature of the parties as well, as we will see later.

Consensus Politics

So that divergent interest groups do not plunge the society into a Hobbesian "war of all against all," it is necessary for there to be political consensus. This means that there must be both public awareness that there are "rules of the game"—the Constitution and the party system—and public willingness to abide by those rules. Political consensus derives from the basic belief that the rules of the game are worth preserving because they will, if only eventually, have desirable results.

Most political commentators seem to agree that in the United States we have a general belief in consensus politics. That is, the vast majority of the common people are sufficiently satisfied with the system and the rules to go along with them. Thus, there is little open conflict, or outright chal-

> **political pluralism:** the condition in which there is considerable heterogeneity among existing political groups and competition among them is possible.

Ralph Nader and teenage "raiders" testify before the Senate Special Committee on Aging, December 1970. Nader's public interest research groups and such citizen organizations as Common Cause have had great impact on government.

lenge of the validity of the political process, in the United States.

The absence of open conflict, however, does not necessarily demonstrate consensus. The silence, or lack of open conflict, of the "Silent Majority" of the late 1960s and early 1970s, for example, could hardly be described as consensus. Conflict may be absent for a number of reasons other than the existence of consensus. People may simply be *apathetic,* not care about political events and outcomes. Or they may be *ignorant* of the true state of affairs, with their silence (lack of conflict) stemming not from satisfaction, but from lack of information with which to judge the situation accurately. People may also be *afraid* to speak for fear of being included on a subversive activities list or being otherwise harassed by the authorities. The Nixon administration's indictment of Daniel Ellsberg for releasing the Pentagon Papers in 1971 is an outstanding example of the unwelcome government attention that can be focused on those who speak out boldly against administration policy. Or people may refrain from engaging in open conflict be-

The Populist party convention in 1896 and the Democratic and Republican party conventions in 1976. Third parties do not fare well in American politics because of the requirement that the President be elected by a majority vote.

cause they see the situation as hopeless and feel they can do nothing to influence it.

The Two-Party System

For all practical purposes, the American political system may be seen to operate within the structure of the two great political parties, the Republican party and the Democratic party, that have dominated American politics for close to a century. No law forbids the formation of new parties, and third (or fourth or fifth) parties, can, sometimes with difficulty, get on the ballot. But most of them are short-lived, often formed by people who are particularly interested in a single special issue that they cannot get either of the major parties to pay sufficient attention to. Both the longevity and the nature of the major parties—and the brief life spans of most others—are related to the requirements of the U.S. Constitution and the pluralism of American political life described previously.

Constitutional provisions The Constitution requires that all candidates be elected by a *majority* vote. Because of this requirement, the number of political parties tends to reduce to two, so that each party has a reasonable chance of amassing the necessary majority. The more parties there were, the more difficult it would be for any one of them to secure a majority for its candidates. Hence, although any number of political parties are permitted to exist in the United States, the two major parties always tend to dominate the political process.

In addition, the Constitution specifies that the executive office can be filled by only one person, the President. All executive authority in the U.S. government is vested in the President. This means, of course, that there is no possibility of coalition government, such as we frequently see in European countries that operate under a parliamentary system. In Italy, France, and the United Kingdom, for example, the government consists not of one person but of the prime minister plus all cabinet ministers; and sometimes, particularly in Italy, these ministers come from two or more different political parties, depending on the strength of the various parties in the legislature.

Coalition parties Since we cannot have coalition government in the United States, the political system has to find some other way of accommodating the vastly different interests represented in American society. It is the existence of pluralistic interests that largely determines the character of the major American parties. They have to appeal to large numbers of people if they are to have success at the polls, and to do that they must offer programs (platforms) that will attract many quite different groups and audiences.

Frequently, of course, people who like some aspects of a party's program or candidate dislike others. In 1976, for example, many people who leaned toward the Democratic party were somewhat alienated by its Presidential candidate's public claim to be a "born-again Christian." For them, however, the party had a variety of other attractions to offer, such as Jimmy Carter's stand on government reorganization, tax reform, and foreign policy; and it seems unlikely that Mr. Carter lost many votes he would otherwise have gained had he possessed a different religious status.

In fact, the political parties in the United States are coalitions of many different audiences, as the saying that "politics makes strange bedfellows" points out. An example of such strange bedfellowship to many Americans is the strong backing given Jimmy Carter, a rural white southerner, by Representative Andrew Young of Georgia, an urban black and one of the most powerful black politicians in the United States today. Asked during the Democratic National Convention in July 1976 what proportion of the black vote Carter was likely to obtain in November, Young replied, "About 99.44 percent [because] Jimmy Carter grew up with black people. He didn't have to study about race and poverty at Harvard. And we have a kind of radar about white people. We know the ones who are in our corner, and we know that Jimmy Carter is comfortable among us." The magazine article in which Young was quoted also notes that Julian Bond, another powerful young black politician from Georgia, was *not* supporting Carter, although Bond is a Democrat too. The explanation Bond offered, according to the article, is that *his* "audience" was different; his political role is that of maverick "outsider" in the party.[16]

Despite Bond's defection from the Carter campaign, the Democratic coalition has traditionally included the blacks, at least since 1930. Other groups that have usually supported the Democrats are labor unions, southerners in general, and, to a lesser degree, white ethnic groups. The Republican party has regularly counted on support from whites of Anglo-Saxon background, northerners, the major Protestant churches, corporations, and the economically advantaged.[17] In recent years, however, the elements in these respective coalitions have been either declining in political significance (as has the farm bloc for the Democrats) or changing their allegiance (as have some parts of the South), bringing about some shifts in party loyalty. More changes in these traditional alignments can

Martin Luther King, Sr., gives the invocation at the 1976 Democratic convention. Many people were amazed at southern white Jimmy Carter's "strange bedfellowship" with black voters.

be expected to occur if the parties alter their stands on major issues.

Abuses and changes within the parties Both major parties have faced and continue to face dissatisfaction from various elements within them. A good deal of this disaffection stems from the procedures that have been used to nominate Presidential candidates, many of which prevent truly democratic participation. Some important examples of procedures that prevent democratic participation are: the "unit rule" of state primary conventions, which allows the winner of the primary to control all of the state's votes at the national convention, thus disenfranchising within the party all those who vote for other candidates; selection of delegates to the national conventions by the state political organization; underrepresentation of women and racial and ethnic minorities.

The rules committee of the 1972 Democratic National Convention instituted several reforms, largely in reaction to the domination of the 1968 convention by forces loyal to Chicago Mayor Richard Daley and President Lyndon Johnson, who had declared he would not run for President again. That domination, you may recall, resulted in fighting in the streets and immense conflict and bitterness on the convention floor. In 1974, the Democrats held a "miniconvention" in which they made reforms such as those adopted for the 1972 convention permanent operating rules of the party.

These reforms included adoption of the "affirmative action rule," meant to insure that minority groups would thereafter be represented in convention delegations in numbers proportional to their numbers in the party. Furthermore, the convention said that caucuses and meetings would henceforth be open to the public and well advertised in advance, with no more secretly called meetings in back rooms. This change was made to insure more open delegate selection to the nominating conventions. Finally, the winner-take-all primary system was abolished: now the winning Democratic candidate controls at the convention only the proportion of electoral votes that he commanded in the primary victory.

The 1976 Democratic National Convention, its proceedings and rules largely dictated by Carter people, was described on television as "less young, less black, and less female" than that of 1972, but its delegates nevertheless were far more widely representative of the Democratic public than the delegates to any convention held before 1972.

The Republicans have also made some changes in their rules in response to dissatisfaction within their party and considered others. Ronald Reagan's announcement of his choice of running mate before the 1976 convention stirred much debate among delegates about the desirability of having knowledge of Vice-Presidential choices before they have to vote on Presidential nominees. Some states have abandoned the unit rule, and in some delegate selection is no longer made by party bosses. The *New York Times* noted, however, that the Republican convention of 1976 was still dominated by white, male, professional politicians, and that women, young people, and nonwhites were notably less well represented there than they had been in the Democratic party convention a month before.[18]

Rep. Barbara Jordan acknowledges applause after giving one of the keynote speeches at the 1976 Democratic convention. Reform of party rules has given women and members of minorities greater prominence in the Democratic party than in the Republican party.

Responsiveness and Unresponsiveness

Political organization is to the political institution as social organization is to the society. A political structure can accomplish for an individual or a group what they could never do alone. This, of course, is one of the fundamental principles of sociology; it is the organization of individuals that makes society itself possible.

Organization, however, is a two-edged sword. The same organizational and structural principles that facilitate political behavior can be used to frustrate and impede it or to monopolize political power, conditions in which government becomes "unresponsive" to the people. Robert Michels, an Italian-German sociologist of the early part of this century, argued that tendencies toward such abuses are inherent in democratic politics, that the nature of democracy (and "human nature") unwittingly produce them.[19] And in the American political "machine" we see a clear example of the deliberate use of political organization to monopolize power. A current attempt to overcome these phenomena in the United States is that collection of attitudes and behavior that goes under the general label *participatory democracy,* which seeks to make the political institution more responsive to the public it serves.

Organization and the iron law of oligarchy
Michels studied the European trade union movement and the political parties it developed in the late nineteenth century, in particular the German Social Democratic party. His first major conclusion was that direct democracy on a large scale is impossible. Large numbers of people cannot effectively govern themselves without leadership to give them direction and focus; some kind of delegation of power, authority, and influence is necessary. Representative democracy, thus, is a practical necessity of any large-scale democratic political structure.

Michels's observations led him to believe that representative leadership would originally arise spontaneously in a group. People (perhaps charismatic personalities) would volunteer to perform necessary activities in getting the group formed, establishing a program and a division of labor to implement it. In time, however, as the group became better established and, perhaps, early enthusiasm waned, leadership duties would become more complex, more time-consuming, and would demand greater or different skills. At this point, the original volunteer leaders would become, or be replaced by, salaried professionals devoting full time to the task. A political elite would thus be created.

As more time passed, the elite would acquire increased freedom of action with regard to the ordinary membership of the group. Their ability to devote all of their time to the political task would put them into a strategic position; they would have the "inside track" and the knowledge of who to know and what to do in order to get things done. They could also use their skills to perpetuate themselves in office; the efficiency of the full-time leaders makes it difficult for the political layperson to compete with or challenge them effectively. The system thus has the makings of its own perpetuation: democratic organization becomes oligarchic as a consequence of social organization among human beings. A political organizational structure

becomes a rigid bureaucracy, entrenched in its own operations, and no longer necessarily responsive to its general membership.

Michels believed that this kind of social evolution was inevitable, and spoke of such developments as an "iron law." The general principle is now called *the iron law of oligarchy.* And although the notion has its critics—Michels may have generalized too broadly from too limited a sample—it is apparent that the phenomenon does operate. Almost any social group has some tendencies toward self-perpetuation. A special instance of such oligarchic political organization is the American political "machine."

The political machine We noted earlier that political parties can provide a variety of appeals to numerous audiences. But when a party is highly organized on the local level, it can also frustrate the goals of representative democracy, becoming largely unresponsive to anyone but its own membership. This is likely to happen when political machines are created, typically in large cities.

A machine, of course, is an artifact, a set of parts assembled for the purpose of accomplishing a set task repetitively. A **political machine** is an organization with roles of varying complexity and importance intermeshed in such ways as to generate *votes.* The purpose of generating votes is the production of political *power* for those who run the machine.

Machines were more common in the last century and the early part of this one than they are now. Historically, they were probably more often found in the Democratic party than the Republican, although neither ever had a monopoly on them. The New York Democratic machine, Tammany Hall, under the infamous Boss Tweed, is the great prototype (it still exists), but contemporary Chicago under Mayor Richard J. Daley is also a classic example.[20] Machines also exist, or have existed, until recently, in Philadelphia, Kansas City, and Boston, and approximations of them are not uncommon elsewhere. For this discussion, we will use the Chicago Democratic machine as illustrative.

Like all political machines, the Cook County (Chicago) machine works through the interaction of two principles: *political reciprocity* (exchange of favors or services) and *hierarchy* (the exchange is usually between people or groups of unequal power, authority, or influence). In order for the hierarchical-reciprocity relation to be maintained, each participant must get something (a "payoff"), or the relationship will be dissolved. For the participant subordinate in power, however, the payoff is rarely greater than that necessary to keep him working with the machine. Sometimes it is simply an omission: *not* getting harassed by building or sanitary inspectors, *not* losing a job, *not* having his taxes reassessed and raised by a factor of ten. The grease that lubricates these hierarchical-reciprocity relationships, which are the working parts of the machine, is resources and money.

The machine is kept in business, of course, by votes. It must have votes to keep itself in power and to bargain with state- and national-level politicians, organizations, and agencies. Producing votes, therefore, is its operative aim. Votes are its product.

But votes are owned by voters, and, although they can occasionally be forged or cast for the dead, in the main, the voter must be convinced to *give* them. The vote must be "gotten out." The crucial point at which the average voter and the machine meet—where in essence the vote is gotten out—is the **political patronage job.** This can be a government job or a position on a public works project, for example, but it is a job given to the individual as a reward for political services. The Cook County Democratic machine controls directly about *25,000* political patronage jobs, an enormously powerful resource. (For voting records are carefully kept. You do not get such a job if you don't vote; you don't keep it if you stop voting, and the job will go to someone else if the machine is not kept in office, so you vote for its candidates.)

Money is an important component in the process. Federal money, for example, can create thousands of jobs building schools or freeways, and these can also be dispensed as patronage jobs. By staying in office and getting out the vote for the candidates it elects to back, the machine can generate such funds when those candidates are in federal office. The machine has other favors to dispense: housing in public projects, preferential treatment in the granting of such things as liquor licenses and

political machine: an organization whose purpose is to generate votes and thus political power for those who run the machine. The word is an epithet implying that the power so generated is not entirely legitimate and/or that some of the machine's operations may not be legal.

political patronage job: a publicly financed position given as a reward for political service. "Plum" patronage jobs may require no actual work from their holders.

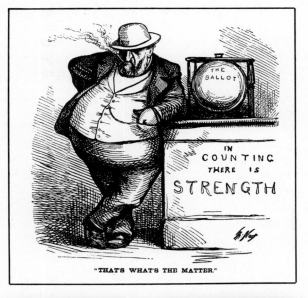

"THAT'S WHAT'S THE MATTER."

Bosses: Boss Tweed, New York, 1871; Richard J. Daley, Chicago, 1968.

Table 15-1   The operation of the political machine in Cook County, Illinois

The actors	What the actors exchange	With whom	The payoff
The ordinary citizen	His vote and those of his family, money for political events and contributions	The precinct captain	Patronage job, assistance in obtaining relief money, licenses, relief from harassment by civic agencies
The precinct captain	Delivery of votes, payment of dues to the ward organization, buying and selling of tickets for political events	The ward committeeman	Patronage job requiring little effort, favors from the party organization and civic agencies (free tickets to ball games, special parking privileges, minor graft, etc.)
The ward committeeman	Delivery of the vote, control over some jobs, some control over police, licensing, etc.	The party subbosses	Well-paid patronage job, influence with political elite and those who must deal with them (lawyers, real estate agents, the police, etc.), direct control over many patronage jobs, some of them important
The party subbosses	Control over law and ordinance enforcement, taxation, award of contracts, permits, and licenses, thousands of jobs, etc.	The party boss and the strategic elite of the city (contractors and builders, unions, real estate interests, churches, banks, businessmen, schools, the courts)	Votes, money, and power; bargaining power with state and national political party, etc.
The party boss	Support for candidates by the machine or its opposition at election time	The governor, candidates for Congress and the Presidency, the President of the U.S.	Freedom from state and federal interference in the machine's domain, state and federal tax monies and grants, etc.; influence in the statehouse and Washington for a "kingmaker"

contracts; tax breaks; amiable relations with the police, ordinance enforcers, and city inspectors; and so on. Table 15-1 describes the operation of the Cook County Machine. The actors are shown in the order of the power they hold, from the ordinary citizen to the party Boss. The hierarchical reciprocity exchange system is evident.

Clearly, the existence of a political machine in a given locality may make for governmental unresponsiveness to those who do not support the machine. There is a Republican party in Cook County, but it rarely wins an office the Democratic machine does not want it to have, and its wealthy contributors may give more campaign funds to the Democratic machine than they do to their own party—they feel they have to in order to stay in business. The rule is, "to get along, go along," and for those who do not want to go along, the only other way to go is *out*.

Participatory democracy   Even in the absence of machine politics, representative democracy may be structurally unresponsive, perhaps as a consequence of such phenomena as those suggested by the iron law of oligarchy. Large-scale government has a complicated structure of roles standing between the ordinary citizen and the official who has the power and authority to do something the citizen needs. It may take a great deal of time for the cumbersome bureaucratic machinery to do its work. (The Japanese-Americans forced to leave their homes and belongings during World War II were not reimbursed for their losses for more than twenty-five years.) Long lags are likely to occur between the formation of needs and desires in the population, their recognition *as* needs and desires, subsequent communication of them to the appropriate representatives, agencies, and policy-making bodies, and their actualization as law or policy.

When unresponsiveness occurs, a number of "solutions" or adjustments may spring into being or be advocated. One of these in the contemporary United States is reflected in the catchphrase *participatory democracy.* The general goal of those who identify themselves with this position is the restoration of communication between the people and the political leadership. This is to be accomplished, proponents say, by the participation of ordinary citizens in decision making or implementation, which will restore genuine representation to the governmental process. Participatory democracy would give the citizen more direct control over the political structure by insuring that decision making occurred at the lowest possible government level, where feasible, at the "grass roots" —in a town or community meeting format—or even in the urban block or neighborhood. Participation is thus substituted, whenever possible, for representation.

At first glance, this seems an appealing program. There are a number of problems with it, however, and some of those most strongly advocating the position have recognized them.[21] How extensive should the *scope* of such decision making be? Decisions made in one neighborhood, city, or state often affect others as well: the Army Corps of Engineers recently suggested solving Chicago's sewage disposal problem by pumping the stuff to northern Indiana for dumping there. Hoosiers were not enthralled. How much expertise is really needed to make effective decisions? To use an example relating to a discussion in Chapter 13, should the citizens of a community have *total* control of their schools? Political democracy is not enhanced to the degree that people participate if their participation systematically results in bad decisions. Should the citizen participate in political decision making or decision implementation, or both, and how? Such questions are valid and complicate easy answers to the problem posed by the idea of participatory

---

> **participatory democracy:** the substitution of political participation for representation.

democracy as an answer to political unresponsiveness.

That the problem has been posed at all, however, points to a significant feature of the American political institution. We have seen throughout this chapter that one aspect of American politics is a series of continuing tensions: between legitimate and illegitimate sources of power, competing visions of what is right for the general welfare, between social and political values, among elites and between elites and nonelites, and so on. Constitutionalism has to some degree institutionalized these tensions in American society. Although they pester and frequently frustrate us, they are never absent and never permanently resolved. This balance among competing tensions is a permanent feature of our political system with which sophisticated people simply have to learn to live. It is a major cost of self-government by free people. But most Americans seem to believe the system is worth its costs. As Winston Churchill once put it, "Democracy is the worst of all possible political systems . . . except for all of the others."

Summary

The term *political institution* refers to the social distribution of power, authority, and influence in a society, and their legitimacy in that society. The fundamental elements of politics and governance are *power*, the ability to work one's will, even despite resistance; *authority*, legitimated power; *influence*, the capacity to alter the outcome of events; and *legitimacy*, the public or social acceptance of something as proper because it is in accord with cultural values. The four elements are obviously deeply interrelated. Legitimacy transforms power into authority, and influence may become either, depending on the degree of its legitimacy.

The functions of the political institution for the society include: (1) *protecting it from external threat* (protection accomplished, as a rule, through the military institution, which is normally subordinate to the polity); (2) *maintaining internal order,* through norm enforcement and conflict arbitration; and (3) *planning and coordinating for the general welfare.* The degree to which modern governments plan and coordinate varies. In general, governments in societies called *capitalist* intervene less in their economies than those called *socialist,* but there are few examples of pure types. Most economies, in fact, are what are called *mixed economies* of one form or another. All governments do plan and coordinate some of the activities of their citizens, of course, but they do so in different degrees and in different areas of life. Planning and coordinating should be distinguished from *regimenting,* however, which involves coercion concerning individual social behavior: travel, speaking, reading and writing, and so on.

The two basic behavioral roles in the political institution are those of the elite and the nonelite. (Political elites are those who perform the political functions.) Within the general elite role, it is possible to identify *strategic elites,* people whose social-political positions give them influence over their society as a whole. Not all of such positions are specifically political, although by definition they all have political impact. That such elites exist is subject to some question, although clearly elite *roles* do exist.

Sociological consideration of government as a form of social organization and governance as a social process provides information of a kind not apt to be revealed by high school civics books. *Politics,* for example, in addition to being the way a government operates, is also a process whereby people gain access to elite roles and influence policy, which means that nongovernmental elites, illegitimate activities, and so forth, are also a portion of the whole. It is apparent, for example, that organized crime is a political force in the United States as well as the major political parties, while oil tycoons constitute a nongovernmental elite with quite a bit of influence on governance. There is considerable interrelation among power, authority, and influence, as shown by the example of *lobbying.* Another way of putting these matters is to distinguish between *formal and informal roles in the political process.* One can be very much in politics without holding government office.

A government is the active embodiment of a state, but governments vary in type. Governments can be *autocratic* (rule by one), *oligarchic* (rule by a few), or *democratic* (rule by all). Democracy may be either *direct* or *representative,* and the latter form is the normal rule in political activity of any scale, as in the United States.

The nature and quality of a government of any kind may be assessed according to its location on three important continua: (1) *regimentation/ voluntarism;* (2) *partiality/impartiality;* (3) *tyranny/ juridicality.* The last dimension may be the most critical, because juridicalism, the provision of channels within the law by means of which the law may be challenged, provides remedies for other abuses.

Juridicality also provides the means with which a government may be changed through institutionalized actions, and such governments are likely to endure. If juridicality does not exist, revolution is the only possible alternative. A political revolution may seek to alter the means through which leaders are selected, the channels for access to elite roles, the nature or extent of political participation, or the definition of political legitimacy. Although dramatic, revolutions are not likely to be the product of fleeting grievances; often they take years or even decades to mature. Revolutions tend to approximate one of two basic types: the Classical (or Western) model and the Modern (or Third World) model. In the Classical revolution, exemplified by the French, Russian, and Mexican outbreaks, old political institutions collapse first, then new groups are mobilized for political action in the ensuing vacuum, and finally new institutions are created. The Modern revolution, typified by outbreaks in Vietnam and Cuba, sees the mobilization of new groups in the political process as a first step, followed by the creation of new political institutions, and then terminated by the overthrow of the old regime.

The American political structure is characterized by the federal system, political pluralism, consensus on the political rules, the two-party system, and continuing problems of responsiveness, exemplified by oligarchic tendencies and machine politics. The *federal system* is prescribed by the Constitution and has resulted in an immense mosaic of governments, which have some effect in creating "citizen power" at the local level. Its primary attribute is shared power among the various levels of government. *Pluralism* implies heterogeneity among competing groups, while *consensus* implies that the groups more or less agree on the rules by which they will compete. The American rules consist of the Constitution and the party system. It is also not uncommon, however, for people to mistake lack of open conflict for consensus, whereas in fact lack of conflict may result from apathy, ignorance, fear, or hopelessness.

Pluralism in American politics is expressed in the *two-party system,* which always tends to dominate because of the constitutional provision for majority rule. Since the more parties there were, the more difficult it would be for any one of them to obtain a majority, third parties tend to die out; and the multitude of political interests in the country are expressed within the two major parties, which seek to be responsive to them in order to secure the elusive majority. The two dominant parties have been much criticized, however, for the nature of the party primaries, the winner-take-all primary, the underrepresentation of women and other minorities among delegates, and the procedures for delegate selection. Major reforms were made in the Democratic party in 1972 in an attempt to eliminate some of these abuses, but it is too soon to be certain exactly what effects these will have. The Republicans have made similar, although less far-reaching, changes.

A final characteristic of the American system is the continuing tension between *responsiveness and unresponsiveness* of the political structure to the people. One reason for unresponsiveness may be the so-called *iron law of oligarchy,* associated with Robert Michels. This is the principle that, even in democratically organized political systems, oligarchy is apt to occur among the professionals in the system because of bureaucratic centralization and specialization and apathy among nonspecialist members. A simpler way of putting the iron law would be to say that political leadership is always necessary, which means that elites are inevitable. *Any* form of organization is thus a two-edged sword; it is essential for political activity, but its very existence makes abuses possible.

A special instance of oligarchy is the *political machine,* an organization invented for the purpose of generating votes and, thus, political power. The basis for the machine is the *patronage system* and the fact that an entrenched machine controls many potential rewards in the form of jobs, licensing, taxation, law and ordinance enforcement, and access to influence. The Democratic Party Organization of Cook County, Illinois, under Chicago Mayor Richard J. Daley, is a classic example of a political machine. So long as a machine can turn out the vote for its candidates, it is very difficult to reform. *Hierarchical reciprocity* is the process that keeps it running. Where machines exist, government is likely to be unresponsive to the needs of the people except as they coincide with the political interests of the machine.

Representative democracy assumes, in order to work as expected, that representatives will indeed be responsive to the will of those they represent. For a variety of reasons, including mere bureaucratic inertia as well as tendencies toward oligarchy and machine politics, this is not always so. One solution to this problem recently advocated is *participatory democracy*, the substitution of more direct democratic forms for representative ones. As yet, however, appropriate means for undertaking this adequately have not been invented, and "participatory democracy" remains more a slogan than a program. Its existence, however, demonstrates the continuing vitality of the present system.

Review Questions

1. Describe and contrast the different forms of government discussed in this chapter: autocracy, oligarchy, aristocracy, direct democracy, and representative democracy. Where does the U.S. fit in?

2. Compare the three types of authority in Weber's scheme. Under what social conditions is each most likely to exist? Give an example of each of the three types in contemporary society.

3. List some of the aspects of political revolution. How does the Classic/Western version differ from the Modern/Third World?

4. Why do you think the U.S. is a representative democracy rather than a direct democracy? Is participatory democracy feasible in this country? What is one potential drawback to the latter?

5. How does a capitalist society differ from a socialist

society? What is a mixed economy? Give an example of each.

Suggestions for Research

1. Make a definitive study of charismatic power by selecting at least ten figures in U.S. history that possessed such a characteristic. Try to select persons whose lifetimes would have coincided with those of your parents or grandparents. Ask a number of people who remember these personalities why they were so compelling. What is charisma in the minds of your informants? A television personality? Good looks? Smooth voice? A unique set of mannerisms? What is sincerity? How closely do your informants agree on the nature of charisma?

2. To gain a better understanding of local legislative processes, attend several sessions of your local city or county council. What steps are taken before an ordinance is passed? How does an ordinance originate? How well, if at all, is the public informed of readings of new ordinances? After discussing your observations with well-informed members of your community, would you say Michels's iron law of oligarchy appears to apply to what you have observed?

3. Devote a term paper to studying Robert A. Dahl's decision-making or issues approach to elites in America. Attempt to answer the question put forth in Dahl's work, *Who Governs?* What does Dahl have to say in regard to ethnic group politics? How do governmental operations change when a new mayor assumes office? Does Dahl challenge what you already knew about community power? How?

4. Using your own knowledge and observations, select those U.S. presidents who seem to have been immortalized. After talking with older persons and referring to histories, can you explain why? What characteristics, if any, did they appear to have in common? Were the times in which they held office similar in any way? Perhaps particularly stressful times? Or do you think it was something to do with these particular persons? Could the answer involve charisma? Why or why not?

5. Study the power structures and relationships within alternative communities such as contemporary communes and/or historic utopian groups. Does Michels' Iron Law of Oligarchy appear to have characterized these communities? Can you find working examples of direct or participatory democracy? Do you think rule by the few or through representation is inevitable? What alternative approaches to power and authority have been most successful, if any?

CHAPTER 16
ECONOMICS

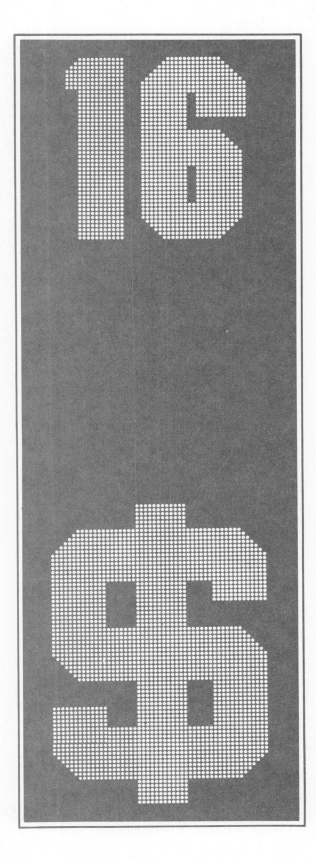

Human beings in their contemporary form have roamed this planet for approximately 100,000 years. But only in the last hundred years have a majority of the people in the most highly industrialized societies been freed from the subsistence worries of obtaining an adequate food supply and protecting themselves from the physical environment with adequate clothes and housing. If you had a book 1,000 pages long, with each page representing 100 years of human social and cultural development, then you could readily see how long it took for the type of economy we have to develop:

You would have to read 910 pages about the nomadic, subsistence-level existence of hunters and food gatherers before reading about the development of a simple horticultural economy based on the hoe or the digging stick.

You would have to read through 950 pages before discovering that an agricultural economy had begun to develop, based on the invention of the plow. It was also in this period that the first written language appeared.

You would have to cover approximately 998 pages before you would read about the Industrial Revolution, around 1800.

The last page of the book, of course, would represent the last 100 years of human history. It would include half of the entire recorded history of the United States. It would only be on this final page, and then only in the most highly industrialized nations of the world, that a majority of the population would not be found preoccupied with the task of basic economic subsistence.

The structure and functioning of the economy affects almost every facet of your life. For example, you may be in school—and reading this book—in part for distinctly economic reasons: to learn skills that will qualify you for a job, or because you cannot obtain the kind of job you want without further education.

You have already read chapters about culture, groups, socialization and personality, social stratification, and the institutions of the family, religion, education, and government. All of these sociological phenomena are so directly related to the structure and functioning of the economy that many seem almost determined by it. It is no wonder that some of the most important theories of human behavior have been based on an economic analysis.

In this chapter, we will briefly survey modern economic evolution and then consider the dramatic effect that industrialization has had on the institutions of education, government, the family, and religion. From there, we will move to an analysis of the central characteristics of the American economy and of the plight of the individual within it. Finally, we will consider the economy and society of the future.

This chapter attempts to skim the entire span of modern economic evolution. This fact, in conjunction with the importance that the economy has for all other facets of social life, necessarily results in a review of some material we have previously mentioned. The sociological significance of the economy lies in the inextricable degree to which this institution is interrelated with almost all other features of the society and culture.

What Is the Economic Institution?

The **economy** is the institution that provides for the production, distribution, and consumption of goods and services for a given population. The economic institution is of such critical importance for society that societies are frequently classified by the types of economies they possess: (1) hunting and gathering, (2) horticultural, (3) agricultural, (4) industrial, and (5) post-industrial.

Although this chapter will focus primarily on the contemporary American economy, it is important that you be able to place in some historic perspective the recency of the industrialization, urbanization, bureaucratization, and secularization that characterize the society of which you are a part. Here we will consider in more detail than in Chapter 8 the major characteristics of societies with the first four of the economic systems just mentioned (post-industrial society will be discussed later in the chapter). Each of them has different effects on the division of labor, institutional differentiation, social stratification, and the types of communities within which people live.

Hunting and Gathering Societies

The *hunting and gathering society* is usually relatively small, with most of its **social bands** having fewer than fifty members. The bands are normally nomadic, having to move where food and game are plentiful. Each band usually moves within a limited territory whose boundaries are recognized by adjacent bands. Members of these societies have few permanent possessions because of their nomadic way of life. Their economy is subsistence-based. All able-bodied children and adults must engage in hunting and/or food-gathering activities. One adult cannot usually obtain more food than he, or he and his family, can consume. Because there is little economic surplus, the stratification system is simple. The most honored member of the band may obtain the choice cuts of meat, be granted a second wife, and receive deference from others, but few other social distinctions are likely to appear.

In hunting and gathering societies, the division of labor is usually based on age and sex. Men tend to do most of the hunting, whereas women and children do most of the food gathering. Although most of the food consumed is obtained through gathering rather than hunting, hunting tends to be a more prized economic activity.

Because hunting is a male-dominated activity, most hunting and gathering societies tend to be *patrilineal* and *patrilocal*: children inherit their kinship group through the father's lineage, and women go to live with their husband upon marrying. Among the Arunta, an Australian hunting and gathering people, for example, a band would usually be composed of a man, his wife and children,

> **economy:** the institution that provides for the production, distribution, and consumption of goods and services for a given population.
>
> **band or social band:** the basic social unit of many hunting and gathering societies. Bands are small, nomadic groups, usually based on kinship, living and traveling together as a subsistence economic and social entity. A number of such kin-related bands may constitute a *clan*, and two or more clans may constitute what is called a *tribe* among Native Americans.

his parents, his brothers and their wives and children, and his unmarried sisters (his married sisters live with their husbands).[1]

Sharing tends to be one of the central economic characteristics of a hunting and gathering society: the individual shares food with other families in the band today so that others will share with him and his nuclear family when necessary in the future. The fact that a sister moves to her husband's kinship group and band upon marriage further contributes to the potential for economic reciprocity in times of scarcity.

For over 90,000 of the 100,000 years of their existence, modern human beings lived in hunting and gathering societies; and *all* pre-modern human beings were hunters and gatherers.

Horticultural Societies

Approximately 9,000 years ago in the Middle East, around Asia Minor and Palestine, people stopped merely harvesting the grains that grew naturally and started *replanting* some of the seeds. In this seemingly modest development lies the beginning of a dramatic change in people's relationship to their environment. Instead of depending entirely on the caprice of nature for game and plant food, people began to produce their own food by cultivation with the digging stick and later the hoe. At first, *horticulture* merely supplemented the food obtained by hunting, fishing, and gathering, but eventually it replaced hunting and gathering as the major form of food acquisition.

The primary distinction between *horticultural* and *agricultural* economic systems lies in the degree to which land tends to be permanently and continuously productive. The agriculturist tends to farm the same land for many years. But the horticulturist tends to open new fields, use them for two to four years, and then abandon them to brush as the yield declines.

In the horticultural society . . . people gain their chief livelihood by planting seeds, roots, or tubers and harvesting the product, but do so without the knowledge of fertilizer, terracing, irrigation, regular rotation of crops, or the use of draft animals. . . . The provision of fertilizer is thus not a conscious act but rather a secondary response to the techniques of clearing. This procedure makes possible the development of more or less permanent villages, but it limits both their size and productivity.[2]

Horticultural communities become more sedentary than hunting societies, because people do not have to move so often as planted crops increasingly become the major source of food. With increasing productivity, these communities increase in size, and dwellings become larger and more permanent. Horticultural societies are usually organized around villages, frequently numbering in the hundreds. Each village is usually composed of various clans, but the **clan** itself is normally the primary unit of economic organization, social control, and religious activity. The increase in economic productivity frees some individuals from food-producing activities and allows them to perform other functions. At this point social and institutional differentiation begins, as some people are able to specialize in economic, political, and religious activities.

Horticultural communities tend to be self-sufficient, and production is for use, not for sale in a market. In general, the women engage in the horticultural activities, while the men clear the bush, hunt, fight, and where there are domestic animals, take care of the livestock.[3] The complexity of the stratification system increases with increases in economic surplus and with increases in specialization in the political, economic, military, and religious institutions.

Agricultural Societies

After approximately 4,000 years during which various societies reached different levels of horticultural development, some groups modified the hoe into a variety of plow. This seemingly modest

Grain harvest in imperial Egypt. The plow, which made large civilizations possible, was invented in the Middle East. The workers shown in this ancient frieze probably used it.

modification of a traditional tool for exploiting the economic environment was in fact a "silent revolution," a development sometimes called "the dawn of civilization." Use of the plow is what distinguishes *the agricultural economy* from the *horticultural* economy. The plow was a great advance over the hoe used by the horticulturists. The hoe could not eradicate weeds or restore nutrients to the soil, and consequently, horticulturists who used it to replant the same land for several seasons found that the land became infertile or choked with weeds. The plow, by contrast, could overturn and kill weeds and could dig deep enough into the soil to restore nutrients to the surface. Unlike horticulturists who had to abandon their land after a few years of use, agriculturists could farm the same land for long periods of time.

The first plows of the Middle East were modified hoes. At first, they were probably drawn by people, but eventually draft animals were used to pull the plow. The use of the plow and draft animals, combined with increasing knowledge of crop rotation and the use of fertilizer, irrigation, and terracing, brought about dramatic changes in society. The greatly increased food productivity freed many more individuals to specialize in commercial, political, military, and religious roles. This increased specialization led to the development of cities, places where specialists could gather to sell their goods and services. The need for a common medium of exchange with which specialists could sell their own goods and services and purchase the goods and service of others led to the development of some form of money. The need for a complex accounting system to record the increasing number of economic, political, and military activities may well have been the chief contributing factor to the development of a written language. (The earliest known specimens of writing are Sumerian "account books" and tax records from between 5000 and 6000 B.C.) As cities increased in size and complexity, bringing increased anonymity and impersonality, it could no longer be assumed that people shared the same values. The political institutions had to construct laws, law-enforcing agencies, and formal penalties to induce a conformity that might not otherwise be forthcoming, because of increasing differences in beliefs, values, and norms.[4]

Advanced agricultural societies had several characteristics in common. Most states were controlled by a small landed aristocracy. Through their control of the government and the military, these aristocrats controlled the farming land and those who worked on it. The ruling elite used the urban areas as their primary center of control over the surrounding hinterland. Often, they used the religious institution as a means of justifying to the illiterate masses their wealth, power, and prestige. These landed aristocrats occupied the top level of the stratification system, with only a small class of merchants and craft workers occupying an intermediate position. At the bottom was the vast bulk of the people, usually around 90 percent of the total population. They were illiterate and lived at the barest level of subsistence, having lives that—as

clan: a number of kin-related bands.

One of the basic elements of the industrial revolution was widespread substitution of machines for human or animal labor. The mechanical reaper shown here replaced hundreds of hours of human work with scythe or sickle.

Hobbes said—were truly "poor, nasty, brutish, and short."

Industrial Societies

Not until 4,800 years or so after the invention of the plow, years in which human societies achieved various levels of agricultural development, did a series of dramatic changes occur in the means of production. These changes were so total in their consequences that they are called the *Industrial Revolution*. The Industrial Revolution began in England in the latter part of the eighteenth century. Many social, cultural, and economic factors contributed to it. The English revolution of 1688 affirmed the ascendancy of Parliament, particularly the House of Commons, over the King. For almost two centuries after that, the property-holding class was dominant in Parliament, and their control of the government meant that these wealthy landowners could improve the techniques of farming and cattle raising. They initiated the use of fertilizers, developed new farming tools and new crops, and improved the system of crop rotation. They also passed a series of "enclosure acts," which forced small tenant farmers to relinquish their ownership or use of the land. The mass of agrarian land thus became concentrated in the hands of a very small class of wealthy landlords. The tenant farmers, no longer tied to the land by law and tradition, often migrated to urban areas and became workers in the factories established during the Industrial Revolution.

Other factors contributed to the development of the Industrial Revolution in England. England had acquired a new set of colonies, developed markets throughout Europe and America, built up the largest navy and merchant marine in the world, and won control of the seas. Thus, England was wealthy from agriculture and commerce and had the capital to invest in the development of the machinery to bring into being the Industrial Revolution.

The first important inventions in the Industrial Revolution were made in the textile industry: the fly shuttle, the spinning jenny, and the water-frame. The newly developed steam engine became the source of energy to drive these machines. In about seventy-five years, the production of textiles increased by more than 500 percent. In the same period, even higher increases in productivity occurred in the production of iron and coal. Steam engines were used to power ships, vehicles, and trains. Thus, the stage was set for changes that would have more profound effects on human beings and their institutions than all of the developments that had occurred in the preceding 100,000 years of human existence.

The Effects of Industrialization on Contemporary Social Institutions

Education

In preindustrial societies, the education of the young for adult economic, political, and military roles took place primarily within the family. Even in advanced agricultural societies, such as those existing in Europe immediately before the Industrial Revolution, the vast bulk of the population received their education for adult roles within the family. Formal education in advanced agricultural societies was only for the children of the nobility and the wealthier merchants. Most people in such societies were illiterate. Only after industrialization occurred did those who controlled the political and economic institutions perceive a need for extending education to the masses. Thus, the development of public education was based less on democratic, humanistic ideals than on the perceived need to train the labor force for the increasingly complex tasks of an industrial society.

Figure 16-1 shows the changing nature of the American labor force. In 1820, 70 percent of the U.S. labor force was in agricultural occupations, and only about 17 percent was in service-oriented occupations. Throughout the next 150 years, we see a continuous decline in the portion of the labor force in farming, with an associated increase in the portion of the population in service-oriented jobs. By 1970, almost as large a portion of the labor force was in service jobs (about 66 percent) as had been in farming in 1820 (70 percent). One of the central educational tasks of the nineteenth and twentieth centuries has been to prepare the children of the less well educated for the increasingly complex occupational roles generated by an industrial economy. You yourself may be an example of this phenomenon, as are several of the authors of this book.

As can be seen from Table 16-1, the population has been given access on a continuing basis to greater and greater amounts of (primarily public) education. First, public elementary education was extended to the masses, then public high school education. In the post–World War II period, the college or university has increasingly become an institution for educating those of the lower middle and working classes, as we saw in Chapter 13. As recently as 1940, only 15 percent of the college-age youth went to college. In the early 1970s, over 50 percent of those of college age were starting college. The number of students attending college more than doubled from 1960 to 1970.

Government

One of the antecedents for the development of a stable democracy is apparently the industrialization of the society. S. M. Lipset found a strong correlation between the level of economic development (industrialization, average wealth, urbanization, and education) and the evolution of democracy.[5] Lipset does not mean by this that the presence of these four characteristics "cause" democracy, but that they may be necessary for the development of a *stable* democracy. In a society where there is little economic surplus, where the vast majority of the population live under conditions of extreme poverty, and where there is no tradition that legitimizes the government, illegal and violent means are likely to be used to change the leadership or structure of the government. The small group composing the elite may be unwilling to compromise with the leaders of the masses because of the small size of the economic surplus, the qualitative differences that appear to exist between the well-educated elite and the illiterate masses, and the often radical nature of the demands made by those leaders.

Figure 16-2 shows the stratification systems in three types of societies. In an agricultural, prein-

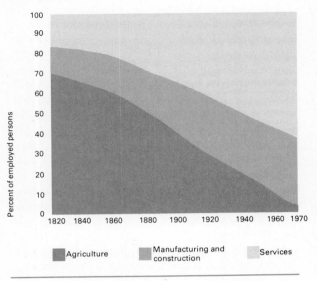

Figure 16-1
The working population of the United States, 1820-1970

Agriculture   Manufacturing and construction   Services

Table 16-1   Enrollments at three educational levels, United States, 1870–1970 (in thousands)

Year	Elementary and kindergarten	Secondary	College and university	Total
1870	7,500	80	52	7,632
1880	9,757	110	116	9,983
1890	14,181	358	157	14,696
1900	16,225	696	238	17,159
1910	18,457	1,111	355	19,923
1920	20,864	2,496	598	23,958
1930	23,739	4,812	1,101	29,652
1940	21,127	7,130	1,494	29,751
1950	22,207	6,453	2,659	31,319
1960	32,441	10,249	3,570	46,259
1970	37,133	14,715	7,413	59,261

dustrial society, there tends to be a very small ruling and middle class, while the rest of the population lives at the subsistence level.

As a society experiences industrialization, the shape of its stratification system changes to that of a pyramid. Elite roles become somewhat more open, and the middle classes expand, so that a smaller proportion of the population remains at the lowest stratification levels.

With industrialization the rural poor are forced or lured to cities, where new forms of employment are being created in the factories and workshops of the new industrial economy.[6] Most of the rural poor are gradually converted into the urban poor—the industrial proletariat. The middle class increases in size as more professionals, managers, and lower white-collar workers are needed to control and service the bureaucracies that run the new industrial activities.

During this "take-off period" of industrialization in the latter half of the nineteenth century and the early part of the twentieth, there was great economic exploitation of the urban work force. The "iron law of wages" prevailed, the philosophy that justified paying employees a bare subsistence wage so that they would have to keep working just to reproduce their own numbers. In 1903, 25,000 children, some as young as five or six years of age, were employed in the cotton mills of the South. They worked twelve hours per day at the machines and received a bare subsistence wage.[7]

Attempts to organize unions and bargain collectively tended to be viewed as illegal during this period. The courts usually sided with management, as did most of the other agencies of government.[8] It was in such an atmosphere that a group of men met in Pittsburgh in 1880 to form the American Federation of Labor (AFL). They wrote the following revolutionary preamble to their constitution:

A struggle is going on in all of the nations of the civilized world between the oppressors and the oppressed of all countries, a struggle between the capitalist and the laborer which grows in intensity from year to year.[9]

In 1955, the men who merged the American Federation of Labor with the Congress of Industrial Organizations (CIO) to form the AFL-CIO wrote a new preamble to their constitution. They proclaimed their allegiance to "our way of life and the

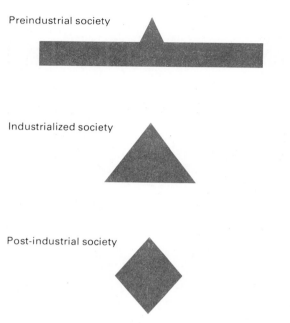

Figure 16-2
Stratification systems in three types of societies

Preindustrial society

Industrialized society

Post-industrial society

fundamental freedoms of our democratic society."[10] The Marxian rhetoric of the 1880 preamble was omitted; there were no terms such as *struggle, oppressed, capitalist,* and *laborer.*

What are the reasons for this deradicalization of labor? The continued industrialization of the American economy has caused great increases in productivity, creating ever greater economic surpluses. The unions and collective bargaining have been legalized, legitimized, and integrated into the structure of the capitalistic economy and into the democratic party system. These changes have brought about dramatic changes in the degree to which workers—union and nonunion—benefit from the economy and thus support democratic capitalist society. In 1890, the average work week was 62 hours;[11] in April 1973, the average work week was 36.9 hours.[12] When the purchasing power of the dollar is kept constant (in 1968 dollars), the following data emerge: (1) in 1913, 61 percent of American families and individuals earned under $3,000, whereas only 17 percent of families and individuals earned under $3,000 in 1967; (2) in 1913, only 4 percent of families and individuals earned $10,000 and over, whereas in 1967, 27 percent of families and individuals earned $10,000 and over.[13] The average income of families and individuals, *after* taxes (in 1968 dollars), was $4,706 in 1929; in 1968, the average income of families and individuals *after* taxes was $8,000.[14]

Increased education and affluence also contribute to the economic security and rationality that enables a population to understand and use the complex instruments of democratic government. The stratification system in highly industrialized—post-industrial—societies tends to become diamond-shaped, as greater and greater proportions of the population share in the affluence and move into middle-class or skilled occupations, and as the *degree* of economic differentiation diminishes.[15] (The typical American worker today lives on a scale *far* superior to that of a European feudal lord, while the difference between his life-style and that of his employer is much less than that distinguishing lord from serf.)

There is now a large middle class: 48 percent of the present labor force is in white-collar jobs.[16] Members of the working class, which is declining in size as a percentage of the total labor force, tend to have stable jobs with incomes and fringe benefits that give them a vested interest in economic stability. Legal and legitimated organizations represent their interests: unions and (usually) the political party of the Left. Thus, there is a reduced probability that the proletariat will consider illegal or violent means necessary to achieve their ends.

If democratic governments tend to induce loyalty to the existing political economy by providing legitimate means through which the great mass of the population benefits, how do they induce loyalty—or at least nonviolent responses—on the part of the 12 percent of the population below the poverty level?[17] One primary way is the provision of various forms of welfare through which the poor may be assisted and controlled. Meeting poor people's minimal needs for subsistence may well be one way of reducing the potential for political and economic radicalism among the disprivileged. Welfare programs give the poor at least a minimal vested interest in the social system.

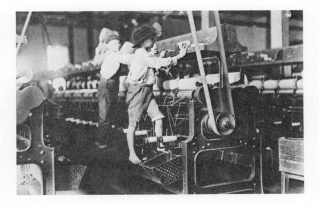

Late nineteenth or early twentieth century industrial workers.

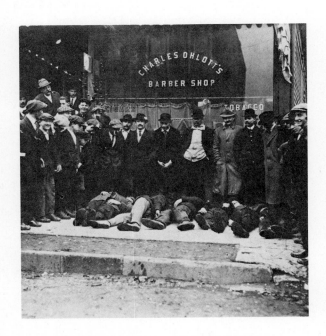

Casualties of the effort to organize labor: Dead strikers, 1915.

The Family

When we look at the diverse forms of family life around us in contemporary America, it is difficult to realize that until the last few hundred years, family life was quite different. For approximately 95,000 years, people depended on the *extended family* for the solution of all problems—economic, political, military, educational, and religious. Even in the most advanced agricultural societies existing immediately before the Industrial Revolution, the family was the primary unit for the production of food, education, religion, protection, and recreation. With industrialization, many of the functions once served only by the family were taken over totally or partially by differentiated and specialized institutions.

The economic function   The production of goods and services, once accomplished within the family, is now almost entirely accomplished by specialized economic institutions. The family no longer works together as an interdependent economic unit of production; only one in twelve persons in the labor force is even self-employed. The bulk of the labor force must leave the home in order to work elsewhere. If the family is composed of both parents and offspring, this usually results in the mother taking over most of the socialization of children.

The educational function   Much of the education of the young is now carried out in formal institutions by trained specialists. The young do not tend to inherit the jobs of their parents in an industrial society. Further, the young require more formal training than the parents would be capable of giving them.

The protective function   Most of the protective functions that were once primarily served by the family have been taken over partially or wholly by other institutions. Government agencies such as the police and fire departments and health and welfare organizations help protect private citizens and their property. Private insurance companies serve similar functions by pooling risks and insuring against ill health, death, and damage to personal and real property.

The religious function   The religious ideology and rituals that permeated all activities within the family in preindustrial societies have been eroded by the processes of secularization within the society. Most of the religious activities that family members participate in now take place within specialized institutions for about an hour per week, on "high holy days," or at births, weddings, and funerals.

Recreational functions   In preindustrial societies, most recreational activities were performed within the family. In modern industrial societies, most recreation occurs outside the home, and children tend to depend on peers, rather than immediate members of the family, for it. Even marital partners may have such specialized recreational preferences that they engage in recreation separately from each other, with the husband playing golf with his co-workers, while the wife plays tennis with her friends. Even the advent of television has not necessarily shifted the focus of recreation to the other members of the family. Given the relative affluence of many families and the specialization of recreational interests, one family may well own more than one television set, so that different family members can watch the programs each is interested in.

Religion

In preindustrial societies, religion was an important part of everyday life. When the extended family had to cope with all of the basic societal problems, it integrated religious ideology and rituals into the everyday activities of the economy, social control, education, and recreation. But with industrialization and the institutional differentiation that accompanied it, religion became less and less important in everyday life. The industrialized economy emphasizes understanding the observable world in order to control it better and thus achieve *secular* ends in the different institutional spheres. Religious status loses most of its importance. In the economy, status is based increasingly on the possession of knowledge and skills that enable one to manipulate land, labor, or capital in order to increase the productivity of organizations. In government, status is increasingly based on the knowledge and skills that enable one to pass or enforce legislation that achieves benefits for a given interest group, a set of interest groups, or for the society at large. The central function of formal education becomes training the population to work in various institutions of the economy, the government, or the military.

One of the predictable consequences of educating and socializing the bulk of the population to understand and manipulate the environment for their own and group goals is secularization, the habit of viewing things in a secular instead of a religious way.[18] **Secularism** is the description and explanation of life in naturalistic terms, terms that refer to observable objects, events, and relationships. Since religious beliefs tend to focus on the supernatural, it is predictable that one result of secularization is to undermine the influence of religious ideology, institutions, and clerical personnel.[19]

Central Characteristics of the American Economy

Changing Composition of the Labor Force

Economists tend to divide the various parts of the economy into the *primary*, *secondary*, and *tertiary* sectors. The **primary sector of the economy** processes raw materials and includes the activities of agriculture, fishing, mining, and forestry. The **secondary sector** deals with manufacturing and construction, the transforming of raw materials into finished products. The **tertiary sector** deals with the economic activities that contribute services to the society, rather than raw materials or manufactured goods.

Reduction of agricultural effort One of the most dramatic effects of industrialization has been to reduce the number of individuals required to feed the population, the primary economic sector. In 1900, 38 percent of the labor force was in farming; in 1972, only 4 percent of the labor force was in farming. In 1940, the average farmer produced enough food to feed 10.7 people; in 1972, the average farmer produced enough food to feed 52.4

secularism: description and explanation of life in naturalistic terms, terms that refer to observable objects, events, and relationships.

primary sector of the economy: the sector that deals with raw materials, including the activities of agriculture, fishing, mining, and forestry.

secondary sector of the economy: the sector dealing with the transformation of raw materials into finished products, including manufacturing and construction activities.

tertiary sector of the economy: the sector dealing with activities that contribute services to the society.

Children today require far more education than can be obtained in the home.

people.[20] Only in the last 200 years in industrial societies have most workers in the primary sector been able consistently to provide more food than their immediate families needed. The great economic surplus of food produced by the average American farm family frees the bulk of the population to engage in other specialized occupations.

The white-collar explosion   There are now over 20,000 different occupational specialties classified by the U.S. Department of Labor. As can be seen in Table 16-2, there has been a dramatic increase in the number of workers in the white-collar occupations. In 1900, only 17 percent of the U.S. labor force was in white-collar occupations; in 1972, 48 percent of the labor force was in white-collar occupations. In 1974, *service workers constituted 67 percent* of the U.S. labor force.[21] The modern worker, then, is likely to be in a service occupation, better-educated than the parent of his or her own sex, and more affluent.

Private Corporations

Separation of ownership and control   An important development in the industrial growth of the United States was the breakup of the family-based capitalism of the nineteenth century. In the nineteenth century, few of the companies that later became national organizations were public corporations. Most began as family-owned businesses with names such as Du Pont, Swift, Armour, Ford, and so on. The shift from family-based capitalism to modern corporate capitalism managed by trained specialists occurred around the turn of the century. Because of a succession of financial crises, the bankers—owing to their control of money and credit—intervened and reorganized many of the largest businesses in the country. They installed professional managers to administer the organizations, thus bringing about a *separation of ownership from control* that was to become an institutionalized practice in the bulk of modern corporations.

The increasing size and complexity of the modern corporation made obsolete the traditional forms of family ownership and control of the nineteenth century. By 1932, the proliferation of shares

Table 16-2   Frequency distribution of the adult population among occupational classes, United States, 1900 and 1972 (in percent)

Occupational class	Both sexes 1900	Both sexes 1972	Males only 1900	Males only 1972
Upper white-collar	10	24	10	27
Lower white-collar	7	24	7	13
Upper blue-collar	11	13	13	21
Middle blue-collar	13	16	10	19
Lower blue-collar (including service workers)	21	19	18	15
Farmer and farm laborer	38	4	42	5
	100	100	100	100

of stock for the major companies and the wide diversification of stock holdings had resulted in a separation of ownership from control in the vast majority of cases.[22] Later studies demonstrated that this separation of ownership from control was even greater in the 1960s: "whereas six of the largest 200 corporations were privately owned (80 percent or more of stock) in 1929, in 1963 there were none, and 84.5 percent of the firms had no group of stockholders owning as much as 10 percent."[23] Paul Samuelson, the Nobel Prize–winning economist, says that "all management together— officers and directors—holds only about 3 percent of the outstanding common stock. The largest single minority ownership groups typically hold about a fifth of all voting stock . . . more than enough to maintain a 'working control.'"[24] Thus, people who own only a small fraction of each corporation exert control over it.

Oligopoly   One of the more visible and controversial developments of the American economy has been the development of **oligopoly**: the domination of industries and markets by fewer and fewer corporations. Table 16-3 shows the degree to which the four largest companies in selected industries dominate the markets for which they produce their goods. In thirteen of the selected industries in Table 16-3, four companies account for 67 to 92 percent of all production. To cite Paul Samuelson:

Table 16-3 Percent of production accounted for by the four largest companies in selected industries in the United States, 1967

Industry	Percent
Motor vehicles	92
Steam engines	88
Cereal preparation	88
Chewing gum	86
Typewriters	81
Cigarettes	81
Woven carpets	76
Metal cans	73
Home refrigerators	73
Tires	70
Soap and detergents	70
Aircraft	69
Explosives	67
Thread mills	62
Synthetic rubber	61
Cookies and crackers	59
Phonograph records	58
Distilled liquor	54
Roasted coffee	53
Radio and TV receivers	49
Steel mills	48
Metal office furniture	38
Petroleum refining	33
Textile machinery	31
Flour products	30
Weaving mills	30
Meat packing	26
Mattresses and bedsprings	26
Pharmaceuticals	24
Frozen fruits and vegetables	24
Fluid milk	22
Paints	22
Dolls	19
Newspapers	16
Soft drinks	13
Wooden home furniture	12
Women's dresses	7
Fur goods	5

oligopoly: the domination of an industry and its market by a small number of sellers.

About 4 percent of the American population now produce food for the rest of us. In 1800 about 95 percent of all Americans were farmers.

Bureaucratic landscape.

The largest 200 corporations hold more than one-fourth of income-producing national wealth. They employ one out of every eight workers. The 500 largest industrial corporations have more than half the sales in manufacturing and mining and get more than 70 percent of the profits. Half-a-dozen industrial corporations each control more money than any one of our 50 states does.[25]

A new class of professional managers has evolved, a few hundred men who control the largest corporations, billions of dollars of resources, and the economic well-being of millions of investors and employees, and even entire communities.[26] These executives are not elected by the American people, nor are they directly accountable to them. The ideology of nineteenth-century capitalism proclaimed that many manufacturers would compete for the purchases of consumers, striving to offer the best-quality product at the lowest price. Consumers would desire certain products and suppliers would respond by supplying them. Thus, according to this ideology, the consumer would be king. This interpretation is challenged by the structure of the oligopolistic market, which shapes consumer tastes for the products it manufactures.[27] Rather than simply responding to the desires of the consumers, the oligopoly attempts to shape consumer attitudes and create a demand for its products by spending billions of dollars for advertising and sales promotions.

Bureaucratization and the "employee society"
Not only do the executives who run the large corporations control huge material reserves, they also control people. Let us look at bureaucratization and employee society. One of the major and most visible characteristics of American society is that every institution in it except the family is bureaucratized—the economy (management and labor), government, the military, education, and religion. A necessary consequence of this bureaucratization is that only 8.7 percent of the workers in the labor force are self-employed.[28] You, upon completing your education, are likely to enter a white-collar occupation in a formal organization that is either a private or a government bureaucracy. The very college or university that you are now attending is probably bureaucratic in structure, and, as remarked earlier, you may be there largely because you want to prepare yourself for bureaucratic participation.

Bureaucracy is frequently associated in the public mind with inefficiency. Yet, whether we like being manipulated by such structures or not, bureaucracy is in fact the *most* efficient way of organizing and coordinating a large number of specialists working to achieve formally defined goals. What other principle of organization could serve to coordinate the activities of the approximately 750,000 people who work for the American Telephone and Telegraph Company, owned by nearly 3 million stockholders? It is not mere coincidence that bureaucratization is a central feature of all industrial societies, be they capitalistic or socialistic.

Labor Unions and Professional Organizations

Unions One of the responses of workers to a society increasingly dominated by large corporate employers has been to form their own organizations in order to bargain effectively for higher wages, better working conditions, job security, and fringe benefits. In 1974, there were approximately 20 million union members in a work force of about 86 million, or 23.3 percent.[29] A list of the eight largest American labor unions appears in Table 16-4. Although there are ninety-four unions with over 25,000 members each in the United States, the fourteen largest unions account for over half of all union members.[30]

The rhetoric of "free enterprise competitive capitalism" aside, unionization or something similar to it is a necessity for many workers. Whereas a single employee would be at a distinct disadvantage in trying to negotiate with a giant corporate employer, a union representing all the employees within the organization—if not within the industry—can negotiate much more effectively. The threat of a single manual worker withholding his services would be unimportant to a large corporate employer. But a union's threat to withhold all truck drivers, machinists, or steelworkers from an employer would constitute such a potential danger to the corporation's activities—public and private—that the employer would probably be willing to negotiate seriously to reconcile differences.

In addition to bringing about negotiations with

Table 16-4   The eight largest labor unions in the United States, 1970

Union	Number of members
Teamsters	1,829,000
Automobile Workers	1,486,000
Steelworkers	1,200,000
Electrical Workers	922,000
Machinists	865,000
Carpenters	820,000
Retail Clerks	605,000
Laborers	580,000
Total	8,307,000

corporate management to improve their members' job conditions and rewards, union leaders also attempt to influence the passage and enforcement of legislation that furthers the interests of union members, as well as the blockage of that which is disadvantageous to them.

Professional organizations   Most professional men and women form occupational groups that they use to protect and further their interests. The American Bar Association represents two-thirds of the 300,000 lawyers in the country; the American Medical Association is composed of 210,000 doctors; and the National Educational Association represents 1,700,000 teachers.[31] These and similar professional associations pursue their members' interests by political endorsements and contributions and by lobbying those who hold executive, legislative, and judiciary positions in federal, state, and local governments.

The Increasing Role of the Government in the Economy

Regulation and control   The nineteenth century in the United States was an era in which there was little intervention in the economy by the government. Those who owned or controlled land, labor, and capital had great freedom to use these resources however they pleased, regardless of the consequences for others. This system however, produced several undesired consequences: recurrent business recessions, the emergence and growth of oligopolies, indiscriminate waste of national resources, extreme racial and sexual discrimination, economic exploitation of the many by the few, and the corruption of government by those who controlled great resources.

In response to these and other problems, the federal government intervened to pass laws, set policies, and create regulatory agencies intended to control the operations of corporate enterprise. The chief regulatory agencies, such as the Interstate Commerce Commission, the Federal Trade Commission, and the Securities and Exchange Commission, have so much power that they have been called the fourth branch of government. Many observers, however, question the effective-

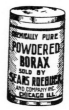

One reason for increasing government intervention in the economy is protection of the population. In this page from an early mail order catalogue, laudanum (tincture of opium) and paregoric (another opiate) are advertised for sale as simple, useful family remedies. Both are available today on prescription only.

ness of regulatory bodies and laws in preventing abuses of the public good by corporations and private persons. The economist Daniel R. Fusfeld, for example, has pointed out the problems brought about by the antitrust laws:

The dilemma of antitrust is that it has permitted the development of an economy dominated in large part by big business and has allowed that economy to structure itself in oligopolistic form. At the same time it has outlawed a variety of specific business practices that are the natural mode of behavior of giant firms and oligopolies. Yet the drive toward market control, price stability, and live-and-let-live attitude is the natural outcome of the oligopolistic structure that antitrust has failed to attack.[32]

Expenditure of tax revenues The federal government now spends over $300 billion per year, $349.3 billion in fiscal (accounting year) 1976. Because almost all of this money is spent directly or indirectly through the privately owned sector of the economy, the distribution of such expenditures has substantial consequences for companies, industries, workers, communities, state and local levels of government, and even entire geographic regions. If, for example, a very large government contract went to Lockheed rather than to Boeing, the entire region that depends heavily on the Boeing Corporation might experience a dramatic increase in unemployment, business failures, regional recession, and a cutback in local government services as public revenues from taxes decline. The State of Washington is still suffering the effects of a recession induced by government cutbacks and contract losses or cancellations to Boeing several years ago.

Control of monetary and fiscal policy In response to many bank failures and financial losses to the public, the federal government passed the Federal Reserve Act in 1913. This act created the Federal Reserve System, which, among other things, controls the money supply by buying or selling Treasury obligations (in the form of notes or bills) to banks. When the Federal Reserve buys, it increases the money supply because it pays the banks in cash, which then becomes available for lending, investment, and so on. Similarly, when the Federal Reserve sells, it takes money out of the system, thus decreasing the money supply. Through its control of the monetary supply and other powers it has to regulate the banking system, such as setting limits on certain interest rates, the Federal Reserve can strongly influence the economic actions of corporations, labor, state and local levels of government, and you as a private consumer. In 1933 the Federal Deposit Insurance Corporation (FDIC) was created to insure bank deposits up to a certain amount and keep the private citizen from being injured by bank failures.

The **fiscal policy** of the government is the way it determines income and expenditures and the relationship between them. The income, of course, comes from taxes. The expenditures are all those expenses listed in the national budget. A *positive*

> **fiscal policy:**   the way the government determines income and expenditures and the relationship between them.

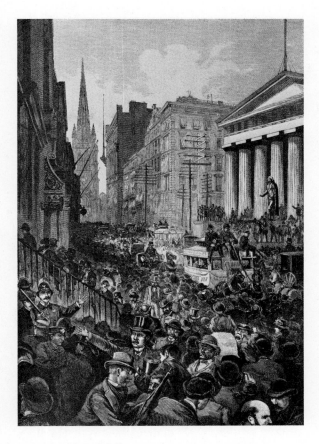

The Panic of 1884. The recurrent financial crises of nineteenth century capitalism eventually led to the separation of corporate ownership from control.

Table 16-5   Taxes as a percent of GNP in various countries, 1976

Developed countries	Recent average tax	Less developed countries	Recent average tax
Sweden	43	Spain	21
France	38	Jamaica	17
West Germany	35	Columbia	16
United Kingdom	35	India	15
Canada	32	Philippines	11
United States	32	Nigeria	9$1/2$
Switzerland	23	Mexico	7
Japan	21	Afghanistan	6

fiscal policy is usually identified as one that prevents extreme fluctuations in the business cycle and that maintains a high level of employment in the economy, without extreme inflation or recession. In time of recession, the government may attempt to stimulate the economy by encouraging corporate and personal spending and by spending more money than it takes in in tax revenues. The government may also temporarily lower income taxes to encourage spending. To ease the burden of the poor, it may increase welfare payments. And to ease unemployment and stimulate the economy further, it may spend money on public works—razing slums and rebuilding central cities, building hospitals, roads, and so on.

Welfare expenditures   Since the New Deal era of the 1930s, there has been almost a continuous increase in the percent of the federal budget allocated to aid the less privileged and disprivileged. In 1976, 43.5 percent of the federal budget ($161.4 billion) was allocated to health, labor, welfare, and education; 4.2 percent of the budget (or $15.6 billion) was allocated for veterans' benefits and services.[33] Although many people, especially those who are the most privileged, may object to such welfare expenditures, these expenditures may well be an indicator of the degree of responsiveness of a democratic government to its electorate.

If you look at Table 16-5, you can see that it is in the industrial democracies that the largest taxes are taken as a percentage of the **gross national product (GNP)**, the total output of goods and services in the economy. As Samuelson wryly pointed out:

And these [industrial democracies] happen to be the kinds of nations which have shown the greatest growth and progress in recent decades. Contrary to the law enunciated by Australia's Colin Clark—taking more than 25 percent of GNP is a guarantee of quick disaster—the modern welfare state has been both humane and solvent.[34]

Government as a tool of group interests   When we look at the major economic functions of the government, it is not difficult to understand why private corporations, labor unions, professional organizations, civil rights organizations, and other interest groups are greatly concerned with the degree to which they can influence the various economic activities the government affects. As we saw in Chapter 15, one of the central functions of a democracy is to translate the potential for conflict among many interest groups into legal and legitimate channels of competition and rivalry. These diverse interest groups are most likely to be loyal to democratic capitalistic institutions if their leaders perceive that they have legitimate means of working to achieve their goals through the existing economic and political institutions. The data in Tables 16-6 and 16-7 show one way in which individuals and interest groups attempt to influence those in legislative positions in the federal government.

Private corporations, labor unions, professional organizations, and other interest groups attempt to

Table 16-6   Special interest group political
             committees, 1974

Total contributions to 1974 congressional candidates

Labor		$6,315,488
Business, professional, agriculture and dairy		4,804,473
Business	$2,506,946	
Health	1,936,487	
Agriculture and dairy	361,040	
Miscellaneous		682,215
Ideological		723,410
Total interest group committees		$12,525,586

Individual interest groups
Largest contributors to 1974 congressional candidates

1.	American Medical Assns.	$1,462,972
2.	AFL-CIO COPEs	1,178,638
3.	UAW	843,938
4.	Maritime Unions	738,314
5.	Machinists	470,353
6.	Financial Institutions	438,428
7.	National Education Assns.	398,991
8.	Steelworkers	361,225
9.	Retail Clerks	291,065
10.	BIPAC (National Assn. of Mfrs.)	272,000
11.	National Assn. of Realtors	260,870

gross national product (GNP):   the total output of goods and services in the economy.

The Poor People's Campaign mule train enters Washington, June 1968. The purpose of the campaign was the encouragement of federal aid to people living in poverty.

create an indebtedness to their interests on the part of those who hold executive and legislative positions in government. For example, in 1971–72 the Committee to Re-Elect the President (Nixon) collected $57.5 million, much of it from large corporations, and spent $55.2 million. Clearly, corporations that made large contributions to the committee hoped that these donations would reduce the likelihood of the President appointing as officials of regulatory agencies people who would control corporations in ways contrary to their interests. Corporations making large contributions also hoped that they would be looked on favorably when the government was deciding which companies to grant government contracts.

Whether fiscal and monetary policies are con-

Table 16-7 Individual contributions of $500 or more to 1974 congressional candidates broken down by occupation of contributor

Occupation	House	Senate	Total
Agriculture	$424,857	$291,988	$716,845
Oil, gas, and other natural resources	688,697	993,923	1,682,620
Construction/real estate	1,270,461	1,197,190	2,467,651
Transportation	131,126	226,909	358,035
Manufacturing	808,345	831,550	1,639,895
Banking	331,177	379,941	711,118
Investments	429,953	583,530	1,013,483
Insurance	225,077	339,756	564,833
Financial industry	986,207	1,303,227	2,289,434
General business	2,145,636	2,312,493	4,458,129
Business total	$6,455,329	$7,157,280	$13,612,609
Doctors	350,110	228,685	578,795
Attorneys	1,123,019	1,528,809	2,651,828
Other professionals	793,369	774,606	1,567,975
Professional	$2,266,498	$2,532,100	$4,798,598
Business/professional total	$8,721,827	$9,689,380	$18,411,207
Housewife	485,982	779,352	1,265,334
Retired	411,183	584,813	995,996
Others	1,262,508	542,566	1,805,074
Miscellaneous total	$2,159,673	$1,906,731	$4,066,404
Grand Total	$10,881,500	$11,596,111	$22,477,611

structed to benefit the entire complex of interest groups or certain groups more than others is likely to be influenced by who the President is, whether he is a Republican or a Democrat, and whether Congress is controlled by a coalition of Republicans and southern Democrats or a majority of Democrats from nonsouthern states. And, obviously, how much welfare legislation is passed often depends heavily on which party controls the Presidency and what coalitions control Congress.

To repeat, political parties tend to represent the interests of the diverse groupings that contribute funds or large blocs of votes to them. We should not be surprised, therefore, at the correlation between the source of a politician's campaign funds and the way that politician votes. In this century, most of the legislation that has benefited the lower and working classes, minorities, and unions has come from the Democratic party. The Republican party has been more likely to oppose legislation to benefit these groups.[35]

Specialization and Economic Interdependence

One of the interesting and frequently painful consequences of the great specialization within the labor force, industries, regions, and countries is the economic interdependence that results. You are likely to specialize in selling a service or goods to others in return for money. With this money, you will have to pay other specialists for your food, clothing, housing, transportation, and so on. A strike, drought, war, recession, or some other catastrophic event—seemingly remote from you—may hamper or prevent you from earning a wage or buying some good or service. For example, a series of poor harvests resulting from bad weather in Latin America has more than doubled the price of coffee in the United States in the past three or four years. When in 1973 the oil-producing nations of the Mideast increased the price of oil by over 300 percent per barrel and imposed an oil embargo on

Courtesy of Chicago Tribune–New York News Syndicate, Inc.

the industrialized world, all of the nations of the world were affected—industrial and nonindustrial alike. The oil embargo was one of the major contributory factors to the worst worldwide economic recession since the 1930s.

People in most preindustrial societies lived in self-sufficient little communities where they provided for all of their needs—economic, political, military, educational, and medical. In industrial societies, we live in complex networks of interdependence with people whom we don't know, but on whose support we depend for survival. This interdependence is as true for corporations, industries, unions, and all levels of government—local and national—as it is for you and me.

The Individual within the American Economy

The American producer-consumer tends to be better educated and more affluent than the parent of the same sex was at the same age. But how satisfied are people throughout various levels of the occupational system? The question is an important one, but it is also very difficult to answer. What is meant by satisfaction? If you believe that you can define satisfaction, then how do you measure its presence in the labor force?

All industrial societies have created ideologies placing a high value on labor within the work force. Russia and Communist China praise the worth of labor for the national good. Manual labor is given

In our society, the loss of one's job often means the loss of one's self-esteem.

high value in both of these nations. In China, programs have been developed to send urban white-collar workers back to rural communes to engage in manual labor in order to regain an understanding of the importance of working with one's hands. In American society, males are socialized to judge their worth in terms of occupational criteria—they are expected to be employed, and their status is largely dependent on their occupational success.[36] One of the first questions that is likely to be asked of an adult male by someone he has just met is, "What do you do?"

The importance of one's work is not judged simply by the quantitative factors of obtaining an income to buy goods and services for oneself and possibly others. In our society, employment is a means by which a man's—and, as more and more women enter the labor force, a woman's—utility to society is judged and his worth as a human being is validated. We can gain an insight into the importance of work for an individual's self-esteem by observing the effects of unemployment on the psychology and physical health of the unemployed. One study found that people who were unemployed for over a year felt stigmatized by the community, friends, and relatives and tended to withdraw from participation in social events, including those with family and friends.[37]

In another study, Nancy Morse and Robert Weiss

Table 16-8 Percent of those in various occupational groups in Detroit who would try to get into a similar type of work if they could start over again

Professional and lower white-collar occupations	Percent	Working-class occupations	Percent
Urban university professors	93	Skilled printers	52
Mathematicians	91	Paper workers	52
Physicists	89	Skilled auto workers	41
Biologists	89	Skilled steelworkers	41
Chemists	86	Textile workers	31
Firm lawyers	85	Blue-collar workers, age 30–55	24
School superintendents	85	Blue-collar workers, age 21–29	23
Lawyers	83	Unskilled steelworkers	21
Journalists (Washington correspondents)	82	Unskilled auto workers	16
Church university professors	77		
Solo lawyers	75		
Diversico engineers	70		
Unico engineers	70		
White-collar workers, age 21–29	46		
White-collar workers, age 30–55	43		

asked a representative sampling of American men the following question: "If by some chance you inherited enough money to live comfortably without working, do you think you would work anyway, or not?"[38] Approximately 80 percent of the sample said that they would continue to work even if they did inherit sufficient funds to live comfortably without working. A majority of the white-collar workers, but nowhere near 80 percent, would continue in the same type of work. A majority of those in the working-class occupations, although preferring to work, would not continue in the same types of jobs.

As Table 16-8 shows clearly, these occupations that require the greatest education and skills and offer the highest status, authority, and income tend to be most satisfying. Those least satisfied with their jobs are those in the occupations that require the least formal education and offer the least status, authority, and income. In an excellent study of satisfaction in the labor force, H. L. Wilensky found that at all occupational levels those who were likely to be most dissatisfied were those who experienced the following: (1) "work situation and organizational setting that provided little discretion in pace and schedule, and a tall hierarchy above (low

freedom, high pressure)"; (2) "career which has been blocked and chaotic"; or (3) "stage in the life cycle that puts the squeeze on," such as having large numbers of children living at home and low amounts of savings and investments.[39]

Conversely, "control over the workplace, opportunity for sociable talk on the job, and an orderly career foster work attachment."[40] The occupations most likely to possess these attributes, of course, are those of the professional and managerial categories. After conducting long interviews with a sampling of 1,354 men in diverse occupational categories and strata, Wilensky concluded that it appeared that "the vast majority of Americans are 'playing it cool,' neither strongly wedded to the job nor feeling it to be an intense threat to their identity."[41]

The Coming of Post-industrial Society

What does the future hold for the American economy and society through the year 2000? A number of prestigious academics have written books on this subject.[42] Let us look at some of their projections.

Table 16-9   Stratification and power in three types of societies

	Preindustrial	Industrial	Postindustrial
Resource	Land	Machinery	Knowledge
Social locus	Farm Plantation	Business firm	University Research institute
Dominant figures	Landowner Military	Businessmen	Scientists Researchers
Means of power	Direct control of force	Indirect influence on politics	Balance of technical- political forces Franchises and rights
Class base	Property Military force	Property Political organization Technical skill	Technical skill Political organization
Access	Inheritance Seizure by armies	Inheritance Patronage Education	Education Mobilization Cooptation

Affluence and Leisure

Herman Kahn and Anthony J. Wiener and others from various academic disciplines project that by the year 2000 affluence and leisure will have increased dramatically in the United States. There is a projected increase in the real per capita gross national product of about 100 percent between 1965 and the year 2000. The projected average work week for the year 2000 is a week composed of four working days per week of 7.5 hours each. There will be thirty-nine working weeks per year, ten legal holidays, three-day weekends, and thirteen weeks of vacation per year.[43]

These projections may not prove to be accurate because of a multiplicity of contingencies that cannot be foreseen. However, let us review some figures from the past, mentioned earlier, in order to gain some perspective on projections into the future. In 1890, the average work week was 62 hours.[44] In April 1973, the average work week was 36.9 hours.[45] In 1913, in 1968 dollars, 61 percent of families and individuals earned under $3,000 per year; in 1967, only 17 percent of families and individuals earned under $3,000 for the year.[46] Just between 1950 and 1972, the per capita income in the United States increased 55.6 percent, the value of the dollar being held constant for purpose of analysis.[47]

Projected Trends

The service occupations   It is projected that there will be a continued increase in the portion of the labor force that is in the service-related occupations. The increased automation of the industrial sector of the economy and the mechanization of the farm sector will further reduce the number of people needed to produce food and manufactured products.

The professional-technical strata   There will be a continued increase in the percent of the labor force that is in the scientific-technical category of workers. Daniel Bell has stated that as America increasingly moves into the postindustrial stage, the way for an individual to gain access to more power and prestige will increasingly be to acquire scientific-technical knowledge and skills.[48] See Table 16-9 for a view of Bell's analysis of the primary means of achieving power in preindustrial, industrial, and postindustrial societies. Rather than the landowners or the businessmen being the dominant figures in postindustrial society, Bell believes that it will be the scientists and professional technocrats.

A person may achieve control of an organization through the inheritance of property. But unless he has the technical skills to manage it, the company will fail to compete successfully with more professionally run organizations. In large private corporations, as we have noted, there has already been a separation of control from ownership, with professional managers administering the complex bureaucracies. Those who use politics as the means to power must either be competent professional technocrats or hire technicians and experts who have the knowledge and skills to make technical judgments on complex issues. What all this adds up to is the increasing dominance of those with technical skills—the emergence of a technocratic elite. In Bell's words:

The members of this new technocratic elite, with their new techniques of decision-making (systems analysis, linear programming, and program budgeting), have now become essential to the formulation and analysis of decisions on which political judgments have to be made, if not to the wielding of power. It is in this broad sense that the spread of education, research, and administration has created a new constituency—the technical and professional intelligentsia.[49]

The increasing role of government An ever-increasing number of people will be employed by all levels of government—federal, state, county, and city. The political institution will come to dominate the postindustrial society as the private corporations dominated the industrial period. In the United States, there is such an inextricable interdependence of economic units that there is an ever-increasing need for government coordination of the relations among corporations, unions, professional organizations, agricultural cooperatives, consumer organizations, and other interest groups. These groups increasingly seek to make their claims known and implement them through politics, to have the economic functions of government serve their interests. In Charles Reich's words:

The valuables dispensed by government take many forms, but they all share one characteristic. They are steadily taking the place of the traditional forms of wealth—forms which are held as private property. Social insurance substitutes for savings, a government contract replaces a businessman's customers and goodwill. . . . Increasingly, Americans live on governmental largess—allocated by government on its own terms, and held by recipients subject to conditions which express "the public interest."[50]

Workers at Social Security headquarters in Baltimore. A projected trend: More and more people will be employed by government.

The future of affluence and leisure We have surveyed a considerable amount of material in this brief chapter. We have seen that only in this century, and only in the most highly industrialized nations, have a majority of the population been freed from the preoccupation of obtaining an adequate food supply and of protecting themselves from the environment with adequate clothing and housing. One might once have thought—naively—that affluence and leisure would have brought us satisfaction and optimism. Yet the national polls document a dissatisfaction with and pessimism toward our institutions and society that is disquieting to many observers. As long ago as 1930, John Maynard Keynes, one of the most prominent economists of our time, anticipated some of the problems of increasing affluence and leisure in a famous essay:

If instead of looking into the future, we look into the past—we find that the economic problem, the struggle for subsistence, always has been hitherto the primary, most pressing problem of the human race—not only of the human race, but of the whole of the biological kingdom from the beginnings of life in its most primitive forms. . . . If the economic problem is solved, mankind will be deprived of its traditional purpose. . . . I think with dread of the readjustment of the habits and instincts of the ordinary man, bred into him for countless generations, which he may be asked to discard within a few decades. . . .

Thus for the first time since his creation man will be faced with his real, his permanent problem—how to use his freedom from pressing economic cares, how to occupy the leisure, which science and compound interest will have won for him, to live wisely and agreeably and well. . . .There are changes in other spheres too which we must expect to come. When the accumulation of wealth is no longer of high social importance, there will be great changes in the code of morals. We shall be able to rid ourselves of many of the pseudo-moral principles which have hag-ridden us for two hundred years, by which we have exalted some of the more distasteful of human qualities into the position of the highest virtues. . . . The love of money as a possession—as distinguished from the love of money as a means to the enjoyments and realities of life—will be recognized for what it is, a somewhat disgusting morbidity, one of those semi-criminal, semi-pathological propensities which one hands over with a shudder to the specialists in mental disease.[51]

Summary

The *economy* is the institution that provides for the production, distribution, and consumption of goods and services for a given population. Of the approximately 100,000 years of human existence, about 90,000 was spent in *hunting and gathering societies*, characterized by small size, absence of social stratification, nomadism, and a subsistence-level economy.

Four thousand years were lived in *horticultural societies*. These societies were larger and village-based, cultivated plants with the hoe or digging stick, and produced some food surplus. Some stratification was likely to exist in them, although the social distance between "rich" and "poor" was not great. In many cases, fields and villages were abandoned every few years as the land wore out.

And 4,800 more years were to pass with people living in *agricultural societies. Agriculture* means tilling with the plow, and it has the capacity to produce considerable surpluses. With the advent of agriculture, there appeared fully developed stratification systems, cities, permanent residences, and great gulfs in social distance between the small, wealthy elite and the mass of peasants, who often lived at a bare subsistence level.

Until the Industrial Revolution of 200 years ago, the vast bulk of the population lived at the subsistence level, leading lives that were harsh and short. Not until this century were a majority of the population freed from subsistence worries, and then only those in the most highly industrialized societies.

The effects of the industrialization of the economy on the other social institutions has been dramatic. The increasingly machine-based economy has reduced the need for unskilled workers and increased the need for those in the skilled manual and white-collar occupations. The educational institution—from the elementary school to the university—has become the instrument for providing people with the knowledge and skills that will enable them to fit into the increasingly complex labor force. The industrialization of the economy has produced a society that is urban, affluent, and well-educated, conditions that appear to be necessary for the development of a stable democracy. The emergence of the contemporary economy has stripped the family of many of its former functions, such as the economic, protective, and recreational functions. The increased emphasis on understanding and manipulating the observable world has brought about a general *secularization* of the society, which has undermined the influence of the religious institution.

The American economy has five central characteristics: (1) the changing composition of the labor force, (2) private corporations, (3) labor unions and professional organizations, (4) the increasing role of government in the economy, and (5) specialization and economic interdependence. The major change in the *composition of the labor force* in this century has been the increasing dominance of service-oriented occupations. Two-thirds of the labor force are in jobs that contribute services to the economy, rather than raw materials or manufactured goods. The proportion of people engaging in agriculture has diminished radically.

Private corporations in the American economy are characterized by *separation of ownership and control*. The control of private corporations has shifted from owners to professional technocrats who possess the new managerial skills needed to coordinate the personnel and resources of the large, complex corporations. Along with corporate growth has come an increasing trend toward *oligopoly,* the domination of an industry by the three or four largest firms. Another characteristic of these large corporations and of our society itself is bureaucratization. Only about one person in twelve is now self-employed, the rest of the labor force working in large bureaucratic organizations, private and governmental.

Workers and professional men and women have formed *labor unions and professional organizations* to protect and further their interests. These groups greatly increase their members' abilities to negotiate with employers and political bodies. The unions have become a major economic and political force in the United States, and almost a quarter of the labor force is unionized.

The *government has played increasingly important roles in the economy* by creating regulatory agencies, allocating expenditures to certain economic sectors, controlling monetary and fiscal policy, and funding welfare programs to aid ever-larger sections of the population. Because of these great economic powers, the government is increasingly viewed as a tool that may be influenced by diverse groups within the society—corporations, unions, professional groups, minorities, and so on.

The *specialization* of the labor force, industries, and regions of the nation and world has created an *economic interdependence* with profound consequences. Events remote from us and possibly unknown to us may affect our ability to obtain the most essential or trivial of goods and services.

The economy has a profound effect on the individual in another way. Work in industrial societies has become one of the central activities by which an individual's worth is judged—by himself as well as by others. In spite of the importance of work in

the occupational system as a basis for self-esteem, most Americans appear to be neither greatly committed to, nor alienated from, their jobs.

Most of the projections concerning the economy and society of the future say that Americans (and those in other highly industrial societies) will have great affluence and leisure. If these projections prove to be accurate, one of our major problems in the future may well be that of having to superimpose meaning upon our lives in ways that are not related to the economic role. Other phenomena expected to occur are a continuing enlargement of the *tertiary*, or service, sector of the labor force, with corresponding reductions in the *primary and secondary sectors* (extraction and manufacture); an increase in numbers and influence in the professional-technical stratum; and an increasing government domination of all economic activities.

Review Questions

1. What is the *economic institution?* Give a formal definition and several examples of each element, drawn from contemporary American society.

2. Societies are often characterized according to the kind of economy they possess. List the four categories discussed in this chapter. Describe the nature of typical economic activities in each category and the social organizational/structural characteristics of each (such as size, division of labor, and basic production tools and methods). With what historical epoch is each associated? Give an example of a particular society, historical or contemporary, which typifies each.

3. Industrialization has had a profound effect on all the social institutions of the Western world. How has it affected education, government, the family, and religion?

4. This chapter described five characteristics of the American economy: the labor force and recent changes in it, the role of private corporations, the role of labor unions and professional organizations, the increasing influence of government, and specialization and interdependence. Jot down everything you can remember about each of the five characteristics; then go back to the text and check your notes against the discussion there.

5. What is meant by the term *post-industrial society?* What are the social structural/organizational characteristics of such a society? To the degree that the United States represents such a society, what economic trends now visible here are likely to be exaggerated or extended in the future?

Suggestions for Research

1.   Using the literature of ethnography (the branch of anthropology that studies preliterate peoples), find detailed studies of a people at the hunting and gathering stage of economic development and a people at the horticultural stage. Compare the two with regard to (1) division of labor, (2) institutional differentiation, (3) social stratification, and (4) typical community form. Explain how the economy of each society affects these four features.

2.   If you are at all familiar with the Bible, you might be interested in doing some sociological analysis utilizing biblical materials. The early Hebrews were pastoral in their economic organization, a stage in some sense midway between hunting and gathering and horticulture. By the time of Solomon and David, however, they had settled in Palestine and become horticulturists; they were probably practicing agriculture by the New Testament period. Go through the Old Testament (or both Old and New) and find all the references you can to the livelihood practiced by people in the different periods and to the social organization of Jewish society in the times in question. In what ways, for example, did the Tribes in the time of the Patriarchs seem to be hunting and gathering societies? In what ways does life in New Testament times sound like the advanced agricultural stage described in this and earlier chapters?

3.   Locate historical census materials for the United States. Chart by census decades the changing composition of the labor force (including education, sex, and proportion in major occupational categories). Then turn to the sections on economic and financial features of the country and chart by census decades such things as government employment, industrial construction, retail sales, number and size of corporations, railway traffic, and so on. (It may be useful to compute dollar entries in constant-value dollars; someone in your economics or business department can probably show you how to do this.) Now write a paper, based on these facts, about the effects of industrialization. If you limit your coverage to the period between 1830 and 1920, you will largely avoid international effects.

4.   Using historical census materials again, make up tables that show the marriage rate, family size, and rural/urban character of the American population. Then make another set for education, showing which people were educated in various periods and how much education they received. Do a paper on the development of specialized institutions of education associated with the decline of the extended family, utilizing the ideas in this and preceding chapters and demonstrating the changes with statistics.

5.   Using library historical materials and, where available, authentic documents of the times (such as newspapers, magazines, the Congressional Record, and party platforms) do a paper or prepare a class presentation on the American labor movement. When were the first unions formed? Where? In what industries? Why? How did the movement grow? What were the sources of resistance to it? Why was there differentiation between craft unions and industrial unions, and how did it affect the movement? Why are some areas of work and some areas of the country still relatively ununionized today? Your local labor council or union headquarters may be able to assist you.

PART FIVE
COLLECTIVE BEHAVIOR AND SOCIAL CHANGE

We saw in Chapter 1 that the great problems and models of sociological analysis have, from the beginning of the field, been concerned with two fundamental issues: social order and social change. These issues could be phrased as questions that appear simple in their formulation but that, as you have seen by now, are immensely complex in their implications. We might ask: (1) What makes social order and regularity possible? How does it happen that things stay so much the same? And: (2) But with the great weight of social order and regularity pressing on us at all times, how does it occur that things do change? What makes social alteration possible, and how does it come about?

The major thrust of earlier sections of this book has been directed to the problem of order, which, in one way or another, is what most sociologists are concerned with most of the time, perhaps because any scientific endeavor must have pattern and regularity with which to work as the subject for observation. The abnormal and unpredictable event is very difficult to study in a scientific manner. The three chapters that make up this last part of the book, however, are concerned with the social phenomena that make for change.

Chapter 17 discusses deviant behavior and social control. *Deviant behavior* is behavior that breaks the social rules, abandoning the conventional pattern; and it is often both the product of, and a force for, change in a society. *Social control*, of course, means all of the forces of a society that are directed toward the regularization of deviance, which means that, even though social control is aimed at the maintenance of order, in reacting to and against deviance, it must often introduce change as well. Chapter 18 is about collective, or group, or mass behavior and a special variety of it called social movements. As we explore these phenomena, we will see that they are often deeply involved in social change, sometimes of a sudden and/or violent variety. And finally, in Chapter 19, we will take up the topic of change itself, the conditions under which it is likely to occur and the various social agents that manifest and promote it.

CHAPTER 17
DEVIANT BEHAVIOR AND SOCIAL CONTROL

Sanity in Bedlam

Newsweek—The plight of the normal person who finds himself committed to a mental institution and unable to convince anyone he is not insane is a standard plot for horror fiction. But in a remarkable study last week, Dr. David L. Rosenhan, professor of psychology and law at Stanford University, and seven associates reported just such a nightmare in real life. To find out how well psychiatric professionals can distinguish the normal from the sick, they had themselves committed to mental institutions. Their experiment, reported in the journal Science, clearly showed that once inside the hospital walls, everyone is judged insane.

The "pseudopatients," five men and three women, included three psychologists, a pediatrician, a psychiatrist, a painter and a housewife, all of whom were certifiably sane. In the course of the three-year study, the volunteers spent an average of nineteen days in a dozen institutions, private and public, in New York, California, Pennsylvania, Oregon and Delaware. Each pseudopatient told admitting doctors that he kept hearing voices that said words like "empty," "hollow" and "void," suggesting that the patient found his life meaningless and futile. But beyond falsifying their names and occupations, all the volunteers described their life histories as they actually were. In so doing, they gave the doctors every chance to discern the truth. "I couldn't believe we wouldn't be found out," Rosenhan told NEWSWEEK's Gerald Lubenow. But they weren't. At eleven hospitals the pseudopatients were promptly diagnosed as schizophrenic and, at the twelfth, as manic-depressive.

As soon as they had gained admission, the volunteers studiously resumed normal behavior. They denied hearing voices and worked hard to convince staff members that they ought to be released. But such efforts were to no avail; doctors and nurses interpreted everything the pseudopatients did in terms of the original diagnosis. When some of the volunteers went about taking notes, the hospital staff made such entries in their records as "patient engages in writing behavior." The only people who realized that the experimenters were normal were some of the patients. "Your're not crazy," said one patient. "You're a journalist or a professor. You're checking up on the hospital."

Crazy: During a psychiatric interview, a pseudopatient noted that he was closer to his mother as a small child, but as he grew up, became more attached to his father. Although this was a perfectly normal alteration of identity figures, it was taken by the psychiatrist as evidence of "unstable relationships in childhood." The hospital, Rosenhan concluded, distorts the perception of behavior. "In a psychiatric hospital," he says, "the place is more important than the person. If you're a patient you must be crazy."

Rosenhan and his colleagues were not exposed to the squalor and degradation of any modern snake pits, but they did witness incidents of abuse and brutality. One patient was beaten for approaching an attendant and saying "I like you."

All this, the Stanford psychologist points out, is part of a pervasive depersonalization and helplessness that afflicts patients in a mental hospital. The experimenters found much additional evidence that the staff didn't regard the patients as people, or even in some cases, acknowledge that they existed. On one occasion, a nurse casually opened her blouse to adjust her brassiere in the midst of a ward full of men. "One did not have the sense she was being seductive," said Rosenhan. "She just didn't notice us."

From their fellow patients, the volunteers quickly learned that they were caught up in a kind of Catch-22 paradox. "Never tell a doctor that you're well," said one patient. "He won't believe you. That's called a 'flight into health.' Tell him you're still sick, but you're feeling a lot better. That's called insight." "You've got to be sick and acknowledge that you're sick," says Rosenhan, "to be considered well enough to be released."

As it was, it took up to 52 days for the volunteers to get out of the hospital, even though most had been admitted voluntarily and the law in many states makes discharge mandatory on request in such instances on 72 hours' notice. Three of the volunteers finally walked out of the hospital. The other nine were ultimately discharged, but with the stigma of the diagnosis "schizophrenia in remission."

Rosenhan bears no ill will against the doctors and nurses who run the institutions he and his associates saw. The staffers' behavior and perceptions, he feels, were controlled by the situation, not by personal malice or stupidity. Perhaps, he hopes, alternate forms of therapy, such as community mental health centers and crisis intervention will increasingly replace the hospital in the treatment of mental illness.

Newsweek, *January 29, 1973. Study originally reported in D. L. Rosenhan, "On Being Sane in Insane Places," Science, 179 (January 19, 1973), pp. 250–258.*

The news report quoted above is both fascinating and frightening. The situation described certainly is a common theme for horror films and nightmares. Sociologically, however, the experiment raises a question with far-reaching implications: if medical specialists trained in a particular variety of deviant behavior, insanity (and a not uncommon one, at that), cannot distinguish between deviance and normality, then who or what can? *What do we mean by deviant behavior, and how is it to be recognized?*

As a matter of popular understanding, people are likely to regard the question itself as "crazy." "Everybody knows" that some kinds of behavior are wrong or immoral or perverted or insane and that the only kind of people who habitually engage in them are the sick or the depraved. (Good folks sometimes go wrong for awhile when under some severe stress, but that is understandable, can be forgiven, and does not mean that they are not essentially "good." What is important is to distinguish between an occasional lapse on the part of someone "like us" and the willfully wrong behavior of people like "common criminals," who are clearly not "like us," or the "crazy" behavior of those who are obviously insane because they act in "bizarre" ways.)

If this interpretation of popular reaction to the concept of deviance is correct, a more formal statement of the understanding of it in American culture might read as follows. "There are two kinds of people and two kinds of behavior, deviant and nondeviant. Deviant people are recognizable by the fact that they engage in deviant behavior, nondeviants by the fact that they do not. Deviant behavior is recognizable because it is wrong, illegal, immoral, or depraved. Any individual who is not a deviant himself would recognize these things because they are just common sense." This interpretation is, in essence, a minitheory in the sociology of deviant behavior. It implies that popular culture is an accurate rendition of the world and that any normal person will accept it as such. A further implication is that deviance is a quality that inheres either in people or in behavior, or in both. Deviant people and deviant acts are different from other people and acts. Deviance is *intrinsic; in their nature* individuals or acts are either deviant or nondeviant.

Deviance is a *quality* of people or actions—and a readily recognizable one, at that.

We can see from the Rosenhan experiment, however, that—as is often the case with "what everybody knows"—things do not seem to be as simple as they first appear. Before exploring some of the problems with the popular conception or looking into the somewhat more complicated sociological understanding of deviance and attempts to control it, let us try to establish an agreement on the meaning of the word itself.

The Meaning of Deviance

The dictionary defines the verb *to deviate* as meaning to turn aside from a way or course, to depart or swerve from a procedure or a line of thought or reasoning. The essential meaning of the word, then, has to do with *departure from* an established way, course, or procedure. Deviance is involved with *variation*. Deviant behavior would be variant or unusual, and a deviant person would be one who was unusual or atypical, "different" from others. To call someone or something deviant thus implies making a judgment that that person has departed from some known standard or norm. *Sociologically,* **deviance** *implies a departure from social norms.*

This would not seem to be inconsistent with the popular understanding until we confront the "two kinds of people and behavior" assumptions on which that understanding rests. When we examine the facts rather than taking them for granted, both assumptions turn out to be wrong. The popular understanding does not, in fact, describe the world accurately at all. Is it true that there are two kinds of people, the deviant and the nondeviant, who *in their natures* are different from one another and are distinguishable? As we will see when we examine some theories of deviant behavior a little later on, this is an old idea and one that even scientists have accepted and attempted to investigate. People have been presumed to be distinguishable as deviant or nondeviant on the basis of their physical characteristics, body types, body chemistry, chromosomal structure, and so forth. But no theory of this kind has been able in fact to distinguish those

Editorial cartoon by Paul Conrad. Copyright © 1976 Los Angeles Times. Reprinted with permission.

What do we mean by deviant behavior? How do we recognize it? Why would many people pick the second group in response to the question?

who were to be called deviants from others, and none has been able successfully to predict deviant behavior.

"But," a defender of the popular understanding might argue, "people have free will; they can *choose* whether to engage in deviant behavior or not. No one makes someone steal. The difference is in motivation." This argument is, of course, a variation on the "different people" assumption. It seems plausible on the surface, but, again, it falls down when confronted with facts. It implies that the essence of deviation is *intended nonconformity,* that deviants are people who want to violate norms. But, as Howard Becker asks, is there any reason to believe that those who have been defined as deviant are the only people around us who have ever experienced the desire to commit a deviant act?[1] Clearly, the answer is no.

All of us have impulses to violate social norms much of the time. Honest appraisal of our fantasy lives would lead most of us to admit that larceny, assault, sexual experimentation, and perhaps even murder were commonly experienced impulses. (Not to mention smoking where forbidden, walking on the grass, cursing in public, and so forth.) Indeed an honest self-inventory would probably show that, for the vast majority of people, impulses to deviate not only are frequently experienced, but are often acted upon! Few of us have never stolen anything, violated a speed law, or engaged in some other illegal or socially forbidden behavior. One classic study of "law-abiding" people showed that, on the average, more than 90 percent had violated the felony code at least once in their adult lives![2] The idea that there are two different kinds of people, the deviant and the nondeviant, simply will not stand up to factual inspection.

The other assumption on which the popular understanding rests, that there are some *behaviors* which are intrinsically deviant, turns out to be equally false when we examine the facts. It is virtually impossible to specify any particular human behavior, any act, that is everywhere and at all times condemned. Murder, for example, is very widely prohibited. But murder is not an act, it is a set of circumstances. The act is the killing of another person, and we recognize immediately that killing is sometimes accepted (as in legal execution) and sometimes even praised and rewarded (as in war). Rape is simply sexual intercourse accomplished under a specific set of circumstances: with threat or violence and without the consent of the victim. Cannibalism may be upheld as the proper outcome of battle or a religious ritual. Incestuous marriage was required among royalty in ancient Egypt and the Inca Empire. Taking property to which one does not have legal title may or may not be theft. Crimes are simply acts that have been prohibited by legislative bodies, and the legal codes are not by any means totally supported by social norms. (Many of us regard some laws as foolish or even morally wrong.)

The popular understanding of deviance, then, is false in both of its underlying assumptions. Deviance is not a quality or characteristic of either people or behavior. It is, rather, as we said earlier, a judgment that an individual is engaging in behavior that departs from social norms.

deviance: behavior that is perceived as departing or varying from the standard described by some social norm.

Shoplifting, a common crime among college students. Almost all of us have at some time committed an act which, if we'd been apprehended, would have been called deviant.

Norms and Deviance

The sociological definition of deviance as a judgment about norm violation seems clear enough, but is immediately complicated when we recall from Chapter 3 that there are two different kinds of norms, real and ideal. Real norms, you will remember, are simply the behavior standards implied by how people *actually* behave: typical behavior. Ideal norms state how we *ought to* behave, whether we do or not.

The traffic laws regulating speed pose a familiar example of the two. A speed limit represents the ideal norm. We ought to conform to it and may be legally sanctioned if we do not. But most of us violate most speed limits (a little bit) most of the time, and, moreover, the police usually do not enforce them exactly. A patrolman with a radar set will not normally pull you over for going thirty-two miles an hour in a thirty-mile zone. A citizen who always observed every speed limit precisely would clearly deviate from the real norms operating in the situation through his observation of the ideal norms. Deviance is *relative.*

The Social Relativity of Deviance

The relative quality of deviance is implied in the sociological perception that deviance is a *judgment* by an individual or group that another individual or group is behaving in nonconforming ways. Judgments are made on the basis of some set of normative standards, which is to say they are cultural; and the social conditions under which they are made vary immensely. It is possible, however, to identify certain conditions that influence the judgment that deviance has occurred. These are as follows:

Deviance is societally relative What is seen as deserving of punishment in one society is ignored or even rewarded in another. A cultural abomination in one society may be a religious observation somewhere else. Even within a given society, different subcultures may have norms quite inconsistent with those of the general culture or other subcultures.

Deviance is temporally relative What is defined as deviant at one time in history is ignored or even encouraged at another. At the turn of the century, opium and morphine additives in patent medicines were used widely and with social approval. Through the efforts of former narcotics chief Harry Anslinger and a number of other "moral entrepreneurs," this social approval was replaced by rather ferocious punishment by the society. Among these turn-of-the-century medicines were such best sellers as Syer's Cherry Pectoral, Mrs. Winslow's Soothing Syrup, and McMunn's Elixir of Opium. These were widely advertised and used for cures for or relief from such different ailments as diarrhea, coughs, and "female complaint." The point of temporal relativity can also be seen in terms of abortions, beer drinking, and many other behaviors that were once viewed as deviant and sanctioned with greater or lesser punishments (indeed, many still view abortion as deviant).

Deviance is spatially relative Sexual intercourse between spouses in the bedroom is encouraged by church and state. Conducted on the front lawn, it will land you in jail. An eighteen-year-old may not purchase liquor in one state, but if he crosses the line to a neighboring jurisdiction, his purchase is legal; and some states have dry counties where the sale of liquor is totally forbidden. The airlines may not serve alcoholic beverages to passengers in flight over Kansas.

Deviance is relative to social status Both the social status of the actor and that of the victim, or the person supposedly harmed by the act, influence the judgment of whether the act is deviant. In many college towns, a professor apprehended by the police for driving while intoxicated may be released with a lecture or even driven home. A student apprehended in the same condition is likely to spend the night in the pokey, and may be expelled from school as well. Richard Nixon directed and was pardoned for actions for which his subordinates went to jail. Corporations may be levied relatively small fines for acts that, if committed by individuals, would result in long prison terms.

The status of victims is also relevant. Sexual

intercourse with a female below the "age of consent" is statutory rape even if she is a prostitute. In former times in the American South, a black who assaulted or killed a white was apt to be treated very harshly, while a white who assaulted or killed a black might never come to trial. White men could and did rape black women with impunity, whereas if a black man raped a white woman, the act would be treated as a hideous crime and the man might not live to be arrested. But blacks who raped or killed other blacks were apt to be treated more leniently than whites who performed such acts against other whites.

Deviance is relative to its consequences Some actions are defined as deviant only when they result in certain consequences; at other times, they are ignored. The classic example is that the social norms forbidding premarital sex are generally enforced for young people only when the female partner becomes pregnant and then, as a rule, only against her. (The male may gain social status in the locker room as a "stud" as a result.) Drunkenness is normally reprimanded only when the resulting behavior becomes flagrantly offensive. Many felonies and misdemeanors among the middle and upper classes, although known to others, are punished only when the offender receives newspaper publicity as a consequence. In one southwestern city not long ago, it was police practice to punish saloon brawls among nonwhites only when someone was hurt badly enough to be taken to the county hospital. In that situation, the victim would be charged with an assault or misdemeanor (presumably as punishment for the extra effort he caused the arresting officers).

We can conclude from this discussion that deviance is a characteristic of neither persons nor actions. It is, rather, like most other human behavior, an interaction process. Most of our behavior is conducted for and before an audience of others, and the example of what is called deviant behavior makes it clear that the meaning of a given act is in large part defined *by* that audience of others. The conditions under which that definition is made—the judgment whether an act was deviant—determine what the definition will be. To understand deviant behavior, then, we must focus nei-

Deviance is societally and temporally relative. *Above:* Marijuana smokers. Specific subcultures sometimes encourage, or at least define as appropriate, behaviors that others—the general culture—define as deviant. *Below:* This ad emphasizes the temporal relativity of the deviant label for marijuana users.

ther on the act itself nor on the individual who committed it, but on the *conditions* under which it occurred and the *reaction* of others to it.

Deviance and Social Control

The concept of deviance is necessarily interwoven with the concept of social control. As we noted in Chapter 4, social control consists of *all of the ways in which social norms are enforced,* the various processes and mechanisms that contribute to the maintenance of normative conformity. Social control may be formal, as with the police, or informal, as in peer pressure within social groups. Its most effective form, however, is the self-control produced by socialization.

Social Control and
Socialization: Self-control

As we saw in Chapter 4, all of us play different roles in which our behavior is to some degree fairly predictable and, thus, reliable: student, teacher, father, daughter, lover, spouse. Certain behavior is expected within each role. There may be a variety of ways to play a given role, but each role has some boundaries. How we come to understand these roles is the subject of socialization, the process whereby we come to internalize those expectations associated with a given role. The socialization process prepares us to behave in accordance with the expectations of the society we are entering. We usually think of this process in terms of children and how they come to internalize the values of a given society. But socialization also operates each time we enter a social situation where we have no precise understanding of what is expected of us. In selecting a career, we are usually socialized into a new language, one peculiar to that occupation. Along with the language come many other norms we are expected to observe in order to function efficiently within that occupation.

Leisure pursuits are another example. If you went to an opera for the first time, you would find that it is perfectly acceptable to leap to your feet and shout BRAVO! when the soprano successfully hits her high notes. Yet this behavior would be inappropriate at a chamber music recital. How to behave as a plumber or an architect, what behavior is expected at an opera or a concert, is generally not learned in childhood. The socialization process is an ongoing one, continuing throughout life, and its end result is the social organization of the entire society.

The form of social control that results from the internalization of social norms through socialization is the most effective form, and it provides the glue that holds society together. The norm we do not wish to violate is far more efficiently enforced than one that requires police surveillance. Few American jurisdictions have laws prohibiting the eating of dogs. They are unnecessary because it is behavior so strongly condemned that legal restraints would be superfluous.

The popular understanding of deviance described above—and the American and British systems of criminal law as well—rest on the idea that deviance results from a failure of this internalization of social controls. Deviants are perceived as people who, for some reason, are not internally controlled in the same ways the rest of us are, for whom the socialization process has not worked properly, since they "choose" to violate social norms. Thus, punishing them for their behavior will help them learn it is improper and harmful to themselves, as well as preventing others from following their example. The deviant is "different," but can be made to conform.

We have seen that this assumption of difference is erroneous. Almost every person raised in a given society has internalized its general norms to some degree. In most instances, the reason for "deviant" behavior is not that the individual has failed to acquire the norms, but that for reasons of *normative conflict* or role requirements he violates a norm in a specific instance. When two or more norms conflict, the actor often has to violate one if he is to abide by the other. Few students will tattle on another who has cheated; they prefer to stick to the norm that says you don't tell on friends and thus violate the norm against condoning cheating.

Social Control and Social
Organization: Informal Control

The type of social control involved with social organization could be called group control, but is more commonly labeled **informal social control.** You will recall that Chapter 5 described social organization as consisting of the web of relations and interactions between individuals in the context of roles in groups, social situations, organizations, social institutions, and society itself. Social organization, thus, is both a structural framework and an ongoing process, and its basis is *reciprocity*. In order to function at all, we must share reciprocal expectations with others for their roles and our own in social situations. Many roles (role sets) are themselves reciprocal, requiring the presence and cooperation of another. Many groups, in turn, exist only as parts of organizations, and both informal groups and organizations operate within institutional and societal frameworks. It is apparent, then, that from the perspective of the individual, both self-interest and need satisfaction are deeply involved in the normal acting out of social organization.

Because we are each so deeply involved in what Georg Simmel called "The Web of Group Affiliation," we must to a considerable degree respond to the expectations that others have for us.[3] To the degree that we do not, we are likely to have satisfactions withheld and punishments applied. Most work situations, for example, require the cooperation of a number of people to be successfully accomplished, even for the self-employed. Physicians in private practice, for instance, are just as dependent on their receptionists, the X-ray technician at the lab, and the pharmacist for the successful outcome of their work as is the assembly-line worker dependent on proper performance by other workers whose contribution to the finished product comes earlier in the process.

To the degree that this cooperation between others in the situation breaks down, all members are likely to experience reduced reward, and those responsible are likely to be called to task by the others. Thus, because we live in social groups and situations, other people exercise an *informal social control* over us by their ability to sanction and their influence on our own behavior. (The "rate buster" on the assembly line can be quite satisfactorily controlled by a "slowdown" on the part of other workers, tardy inspection of his work, delay at the tool crib, and so forth.) The expectations of others, which are a fundamental part of our own roles, are

informal social control: the enforcement of norm conformity through socialization and, particularly, social organizational reciprocity.

"John, you are the best secretary I've ever had, and I would like to confide a personal problem in you. You see, my husband doesn't understand me . . ."

Reprinted by permission of Newspaper Enterprise Association.

We are socialized to believe that while there are many ways to play a particular role, each role has boundaries. This cartoon is funny because it exploits the boundaries of the boss-secretary role relation by switching the genders conventionally associated with it.

a major element in social control. (Remember how, in the description of The Nortons in Chapter 6, the men's social positions in the gang were actually reflected in their bowling scores!)

Social Control and Social Structure: Formal Control

Formal social control is *social structural* rather than *social organizational,* in that it is applied by agencies of the society specifically designated to perform that function. The most obvious illustration of formal social control in Western societies is the apparatus of police, courts, and prisons within the framework of the institution of law. Formal control, then, is specifically and consciously designed for the purpose of securing normative conformity. In terms of sheer effectiveness, it is probably the least efficient of the three varieties of social control, but even momentary consideration will show that it is hardly dispensable. Although formal controls are obviously not 100 percent effective, most people probably *are* sometimes prevented from doing things they might otherwise do by the threat of formal punishment.

The Relation between Deviance and Social Control

A moment's thought about the discussion above might lead you to the sociologist's understanding of the relationship between deviance and social control. Simply stated, it is this: *Deviance is a function of social control. Social control creates deviance.* Essentially, social groups create deviance by creating rules and then labeling those who violate the rules deviant. The perception of the nature of this relation goes back to Durkheim.

You may recall from Chapter 1 that Durkheim devoted his professional career to the study of the social and moral order: what, in this chapter, we have called the social organization and the normative order of society. Crime, the kind of deviance he addressed in *The Division of Labor in Society,* was for Durkheim a natural consequence of the existence of a moral order, a collectively supported morality.[4] It is, thus, a natural part of any society as well, because all society requires a moral order.

Formal social control is applied by agencies of society. While it is probably the least effective of the three agencies, we cannot dispense with it.

Durkheim's perception about crime applies to all kinds of deviance. Society cannot exist without a moral order, and this order is based on rules. But the existence of any rules of any kind makes their violation possible. Thus, deviance is built into the very structure of society itself. The existence of a code or idea of "right" conduct creates the possibility of "wrong" conduct *by definition.* Wrong gives meaning to right.

Later commentators, like Lewis Coser, have pointed out that because in many cases social norms are not entirely precise and clear, the commission of what are later defined as wrongs is necessary to the clarification of what is right.[5] Limits are sometimes established only *after the fact,* when they have been violated. This is, of course, exactly the function of the "test case" in law, the situation where someone deliberately violates a law under circumstances where arrest is certain in order to test the law's constitutionality.

We can see, then, that contrary to the popular (and legal) idea that deviance results from a failure to control individual behavior, deviance actually represents a measure of successful control. Social control creates deviance. The definition of an act as deviant presupposes the existence of norms forbidding it. The amount of deviance in a society, then, is not a measure of the number of deviant persons in it or of the breakdown of its moral order.

Instead, it is a measure of normative conflict, inconsistencies in social organization, or faulty operation of social structure.

Crime and Delinquency as Special Instances of Deviance

Sociologists generally agree that crime and delinquency are simply special instances of deviant behavior rather than a category of acts set off as a unique kind of nonconformity. Illegal acts differ from most other deviance, however, in that they are legislatively defined and thus may *not* be contrary to the social norms that most members of the society support. In a very special and particular sense, the law creates crime (or can "uncreate" it again when laws are rescinded). This makes crime and delinquency special cases of deviance, because some illegal behavior may be considered deviant only because it *is* illegal. We noted earlier that at the beginning of this century the use of opium and morphine was common in the United States. Although drug *addiction* was then considered unfortunate, perhaps on a level with alcoholism, drug *users* were in no sense deemed *criminal.* It was only passage of the Harrison Act in 1915 that turned what had been acceptable (if not praiseworthy) behavior into criminal behavior. A reverse situation is occurring in contemporary American society with the move toward decriminalization of the use of marijuana.

Problems of Definition

One of the problems facing the sociologist of deviance, then, is the problem of adequately defining crime. There is a general social norm that members of the society should obey the law, and in this sense any criminal behavior is deviant. But most so-called law-abiding people in fact violate various restrictions of the legal code much of the time and do not consider themselves, and are not considered by others, either criminal or deviant (see Figure 17-1).

Crime can be defined in a number of ways: it can be considered any violation of law; or it may be defined as behavior thought deserving of punish-

> **formal social control:** the enforcement of norm conformity through formal agencies such as the police, organizational rules, and so forth.

Pot and Glaucoma

Four years ago, Robert Randall, then 24, learned that he had glaucoma, a progressive eye disease that frequently leads to total blindness. The standard medication Randall's doctor prescribed did little to clear up the shimmering halos that had begun to cloud his vision, but by chance, the young teacher discovered something that worked much better: smoking marijuana. Eventually, the police discovered the "therapeutic" plants Randall was growing in his Washington, D.C., apartment. They arrested him, but Randall fought the charge, claiming that he needed the grass for his medical condition, and three Federal agencies have now approved a plan that will provide him with a new—and legal—supply of the drug. . . .

Armed with the results of his medical tests, Randall's attorney applied last spring to the U.S. Drug Enforcement Administration for legal access to marijuana for his client. The petition was referred to the FDA, and while officials were still considering the request, the agency received a coincidental application from a Washington ophthalmologist who wanted to investigate the medicinal effects of marijuana on glaucoma victims.

The FDA approved the application, which was submitted by Dr. John Merritt of Howard University College of Medicine, and arranged for Randall to become part of the new study. The National Institute on Drug Abuse agreed to provide marijuana for the project. . . .

Newsweek, November 8, 1976, p. 53. Copyright © 1976 by Newsweek, Inc. All rights reserved. Reprinted by permission.

The limits of any law (its meaning and intention—and thereby what is deviant) are often established only after it is passed. Here an apparent violation of drug laws may turn out to be legal after all. Deviance is defined not by the law but by its application—a social phenomenon.

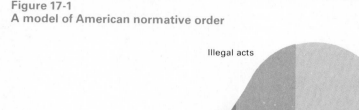

Figure 17-1
A model of American normative order

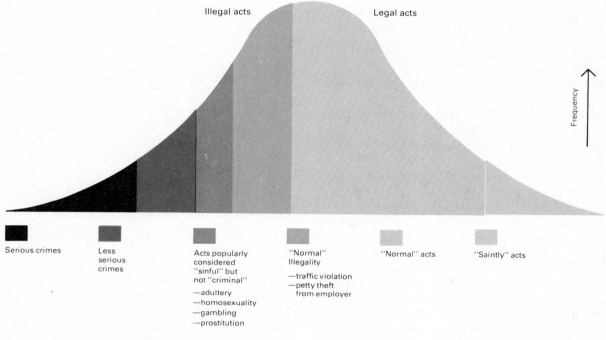

ment; or it may be considered any act deviating from the demands of a given ethical system. One problem in attempting to isolate behavior into the category of "criminal" is that almost any form of human behavior, given the appropriate historical context, can be defined as criminal. Furthermore, since various self-report studies reveal that most Americans have, at one time or another, committed acts that could have qualified as crimes had they been brought to the attention of the authorities, it is difficult even to decide when a criminal is a criminal. Is a person a criminal when he engages in behavior that violates the penal code, or when he is arrested, or when a court finds him guilty?

In the face of these difficulties, there is no overall agreement among sociologists about what constitutes criminal behavior. But most would include at least three elements in a working definition of crime: (1) the actor must violate the penal code either through omission or commission of an act; (2) the actor must be assumed to have acted

Not all violations of the legal code are considered equally serious, and some are not even popularly regarded as crimes. The norms of society distinguish between various types of illegal acts; people view murder, for example, as a serious crime, but don't condemn taking an office pencil for personal use.

voluntarily; and (3) the kind and degree of social injury to the state must usually be specified. This last point helps to distinguish between criminal and civil matters. In criminal matters, the charges are framed in terms of the "People of the State of——," thereby emphasizing the fact that the violator has perpetrated a social injury on the citizens of a given political jurisdiction.

In the case of juvenile delinquency, the problems of definition are multiplied. Many children violate laws in the same way that adults do. Minors murder, rape, rob, burglarize, and steal autos, just as adults do. (Often, in fact, they do it more.) What complicates the issue is that minors come to the

Opium den, late 1800s. Opium use in the last century was not illegal. It became illegal—and deviant—in 1915. If the laws are ever revised, it may become nondeviant again.

attention of the police and the courts for many acts that would be ignored if committed by an adult. These acts include such "children's crimes" as truancy, running away, incorrigibility, and curfew violations. Legally, then, *delinquency* is anything a legislative body has chosen to call delinquent. Sociologically, the term is almost meaningless.

We can see from this discussion that while some crime or delinquency clearly fits the sociological definition of deviance—behavior judged by others to violate norms—some does not. Thus, while crime is popularly conceived to be the best and most obvious example of deviant behavior, and all early theorists addressed deviance *as* crime, many sociologists of deviance have chosen to study other kinds of acts instead. And as we will see when we examine some theories of deviance later on, those that were originally addressed specifically to criminal behavior all fail in explanatory power because they assume that criminals are somehow *different from* other people.

White-collar Crime

The problems of definition discussed above are particularly acute in any consideration of **white-collar crime** as deviant behavior. Originally this notion referred to crime committed by persons in positions of social responsibility and representing

white-collar crime: a violation of criminal law committed in the course of activity of a legitimate occupation, including corporate crime. Includes such things as tax evasion, embezzlement, misrepresentation in advertising, fee splitting, and price fixing.

Children and the Law

Bobby was 9 when he was arrested for shoplifting. As they always do with first offenders, Los Angeles police spoke sternly to him and released him. Three months later, Bobby had graduated to burglary, and was released with a warning. Bobby's sixteenth arrest—he was 12 years old by then—earned him his first jail term, two years at a California Youth Authority Camp, from which he escaped four times. A few days after his release, at age 14, he killed a man. He has been charged with 26 crimes, including murder. But now that he has turned 18, he is, so far as the law is concerned, no longer a juvenile. He is a free man.

Mark's mother was a junkie and he was born in 1965 with heroin withdrawal symptoms. He spent his first six years in a foster home before being returned to his mother, whom he did not know. When she went to work, she regularly tied Mark to a bed. A year later, she told New York juvenile authorities that he was disruptive and uncontrollable, and Mark was institutionalized. Last year he was in court, charged with fighting with his peers and being difficult to control. He is 10 years old.

Bobby and Mark are both products of the American system of juvenile justice. One has compiled an awesome criminal record; the other has never committed a crime. Yet they both have juvenile records and they have been confined in institutions for about the same time. Both are poisoned products of one of the starkest shortcomings of American justice: how to cope with children who fall into trouble with the law....

Delinquency is anything a legislative body has chosen to call delinquent. It is a social, not a natural, phenomenon.

Reprinted by permission of Jules Feiffer.

a violation of trust associated with high-status positions. The term has now been expanded to include all forms of crime committed in the normal course of an otherwise legel *occupation.*

The concept of white-collar crime was conceived by Edwin H. Sutherland.[6] It was through his work that white-collar crime began to be taken seriously by criminologists as a type of crime much the same as robbery, arson, and assault. One of the consequences of coming to grips with this concept was the realization that criminals were not all lower-class. Crimes are committed by the middle and upper classes as well as the lower, but they are likely to be crimes of different kinds. White-collar crime includes a number of offenses, from tax evasion to price fixing.

Tax evasion is a very common white-collar crime that we often read about in the newspapers. One of the most notorious recent cases involved former President Nixon. By backdating certain material he donated to the National Archives, Nixon was able to evade a substantial sum in taxes.

Embezzlement, another frequent white-collar crime, involves manipulation of bookkeeping and accounting systems. If the embezzler is skillful enough, he can even, for a time at least, hide the fact that a crime has been committed. Employee theft comes in all sizes, from the clerk in the small store who steals from the cash register to the

There is some question as to whether much white-collar crime should be considered deviant.

inventory control administrator who diverts merchandise meant for his employer to a third party for the realization of a criminal profit.

Misrepresentation in advertising has been dramatically brought to the attention of the public through the efforts of Ralph Nader and his independent research investigators. This often involves a claim by a company that its product does something that it does not do. A recent example involved a Standard Oil television commercial in which an ex-astronaut conducted a demonstration showing that this brand of gasoline was cleaner than other brands. The demonstration was later revealed to be a fake, and the Federal Trade Commission stopped use of the commercial because it was deceptive advertising.

Fee splitting involves two professionals who are paid by fee rather than salary, such as doctors, lawyers, and writers. The first professional, A, recommends to the client that he needs a particular specialty that is not within A's range of expertise. He supplies the client with a referral to a second professional, B, whose fees are a good deal higher, in line with his allegedly more sophisticated expertise. As a "courtesy" to the first professional, the second rewards the first with an agreed-upon split of the fee for the referral.

Price fixing involves an illegal arrangement between two or more corporations to stifle competition by fixing the lowest bid price in advance of the submission of bids to the prospective customer. In this way, all the participating companies can take turns being the lowest bidder at various times, and at no time will the bids be truly competitive. Thus, the companies' risk is eliminated, and only the unwary customer is victimized. A famous example of price fixing (and bid rigging) was the General Electric–Westinghouse swindle of the 1950s, which resulted in prison terms for some of the executives of these companies. Prison sentences are generally an unusual type of punishment for the white-collar criminal. In this particular instance, the customer happened to be the United States government, which insisted on prosecution for the millions it had been bilked out of.

Other types of occupational crimes include unfair labor practices, padding expense accounts, misappropriation of funds, influence peddling, and corruption in the management of trusts and receiverships.

White-collar crime is made possible for individuals by virtue of their possession of specific occupational positions. Opportunity thus influences both the frequency and the type of white-collar crime. People who never handle cash or keep books in the course of their work are unlikely to commit embezzlement. The decision to hold up a liquor store or gas station may say more about the narrow range of opportunities available to the criminal than about his need for money. If he were in a position to take a bribe instead, he would probably choose to do so, because it might well bring him more money at much lower physical risk. And if he got caught, the possibility of a suspended or much reduced sentence would be greater. (Former Vice President Spiro Agnew, who did not contest his conviction for taking a $2,500 bribe, was sentenced to unsupervised probation.) Thus, the kinds of crimes an individual commits are in some part a function of the kinds of opportunities available to him.

What makes white-collar crimes particularly difficult to deal with as a form of deviance is that many of them are defined by the occupational cultures of

> index crimes: the serious offenses used by the FBI in its *Uniform Crime Reports* as "indexes" or measurements of the overall crime rate.

their perpetrators as legitimate business practices. "Puffing" the client's product is what advertising is about, and so a certain amount of misrepresentation is normal and expected. The practice of not inquiring too deeply into the source of campaign funds appears to be normal among politicians. Thus, although some occupational crimes are clearly committed with criminal intent, others seem to be the consequence of conflicts between the occupational subculture's norms of profit at any price and ruthless competitiveness and the larger culture's norms forbidding law breaking.

The Incidence of Crime in the United States

The FBI is the nation's official recordkeeper of crime. Every year the FBI publishes *Crime in the United States: Uniform Crime Reports,* a collection of statistics about crime rates. These statistics include a compilation of data from approximately 8,000 different police jurisdictions on those crimes known to the police. What is watched closely in this category are what the FBI calls the **index crimes,** those it judges most serious. Table 17-1 shows index crimes for 1970. A somewhat different picture emerges when we look at arrest rates rather than crimes "known to the police." Table 17-2 reveals where police have apparently been concentrating their efforts.

Problems with official reports   The validity of the statistics presented in Tables 17-1 and 17-2 as an accurate reflection of the extent of crime in the United States is problematic. First, these statistics leave out by definition a large number of crimes that go unreported to the police. A murder is much less likely to escape the attention of the police than is a larceny, especially if not much money is involved. And some crimes are by their nature unlikely to be reported. Given all the intervening variables, such as the reluctance of victims to complain, how many forcible rapes do you suppose are committed as opposed to the number reported?

Another problem is dependence on local police jurisdictions for complete reporting. In 1967, the President's Commission on Law Enforcement and Administration of Justice documented cases of some probable errors made by police in their reporting procedures.[7] In some cases, a local police administrator may be self-serving. For example, if the local sheriff wants to run for reelection next year, it may be in his best interest to show that there has been a *decrease* in crime during his tenure. On the other hand, if after election the sheriff wants a computer center or some other expensive hardware from the city council, a *rising* crime rate would be a persuasive bargaining chip for the "fight against crime."

The President's Commission also noted that during the 1960s there was an increasing tendency for ghetto crimes to be included in the statistical compilations. Prior to this period, police were reluctant to involve themselves in the investigation of crimes where both the perpetrator and the victim were black, and often police dismissed reports of all but the most serious crimes in ghetto areas. With the coming of political age of the American black citizen, pressure was exerted for the police to show greater concern for the rights and property of the black ghetto resident.

Unofficial reports Various attempts have been made by social scientists and others to assess the true incidence of criminal behavior in the population, as distinguished from the incidence shown by offical reports. Almost all of these studies have shown that much, much more crime exists than is indicated by official reports, such as the one shown in Table 17-3.[8] For instance, Jay R. Williams and Martin Gold studied the 847 adolescents surveyed in the 1967 National Survey of Youth to examine the differences between self-reported and "official" delinquency. They found that 83 percent had committed a chargeable offense within three years; less than 3 percent of the offenses were discovered by the police.[9] The National Opinion Research Center (NORC) surveyed 10,000 households in 1965 and concluded that the actual crime rate in the United States was about twice as great as the

Table 17-1	Index crimes for 1970
Offense	*Number known to police*
Murder	15,810
Forcible rape	37,270
Robbery	348,380
Aggravated assault	329,940
Burglary	2,169,300
Larceny $50 and over	1,746,100
Auto theft	921,400
Total	5,568,200

Table 17-2	Number of persons arrested for ten most frequent offenses, 1970
Offense	*Number*
Drunkenness	1,097,260
Disorderly conduct	436,862
Larceny (over and under $50)	432,272
Driving while under the influence	281,450
Narcotic drug laws	265,734
Simple assault	208,813
Burglary	200,261
Liquor laws	136,679
Vagrancy	82,311
Gambling	75,325

official crime rate indicated. About half of those interviewed said that they had been victims of crimes they had not reported to the police.[10]

In 1974, the Law Enforcement Assistance Administration (LEAA) released the results of a massive scientific sampling of about 200,000 citizens in eight cities in an attempt to assess the true crime rate. Because people do not always report crimes to the police and the police do not always report them to the FBI, individuals were asked for their own experiences with crime. In general, the citizens reported about twice as much crime as official statistics show.[11] A second LEAA report comparing cities showed that the crime rate as reported by citizens was five times as high in Philadelphia as that shown by the FBI reports; about three times as high in Chicago, Detroit, and Los Angeles; and twice as high in New York.[12]

These reports, however, are not conclusive. Although the NORC and LEAA studies were carefully conducted scientific investigations and may be presumed to be generally accurate, we do not *know* the real state of affairs and perhaps never can in any detail. Statistics on crime rates are notoriously inaccurate, and conclusions based on them must be carefully assessed. But it does seem clear that there is more crime in the United States in recent years than in previous times. And it is clear that there is more than the official statistics show. We do not know exactly how much more there is, however, nor all of the reasons behind the rise in crime rates. Simple explanations should be suspected. There is a great deal more to the explanation of crime—or any other deviant behavior— than such popular explanations as moral breakdown, "mollycoddling," permissiveness, and so forth.

The Matter of Punishment

In the United States, the aspect of the legal system that deals with persons convicted of crimes is called *corrections*. This includes everything that happens to the defendant after conviction: sentencing, fine, probation, imprisonment, parole, execution. As the name suggests, the object or philosophy of the American judicial system is to "correct" a wrongdoer through some kind of punishment. Today, punishment usually means fines or imprisonment. Although capital punishment (execution) was not unusual in the United States in earlier times, the U.S. now seems to be in the process of abandoning it.[13]

The theory that punishment will "correct" a criminal was developed by what is called the **classical school of criminology** (discussed further later on), which flourished in the eighteenth and nineteenth centuries. Classical criminologists believed in the *pleasure-pain principle,* the idea that the fundamental nature of human beings is to seek pleasure and avoid pain. Thus, if someone is made to experience pain as a consequence of some action, he will thereafter avoid repeating the act in order to avoid the pain it caused him the first time. To this

classical school of criminology: the eighteenth- and early nineteenth-century view that crime is willful and morally wrong and is therefore best treated by punishing the criminal to deter him from repeating the act and to make an example of him in order to deter others. The legal code based on this view established an abstract scale of offenses and punishments that "fit" them and applied the punishment regardless of the circumstances of the crime or the accused. (In France in the early nineteenth century, for example, small children and even animals were sometimes tried and, in a few cases, hanged.)

Whether punishment accomplishes "correction" of deviant behavior is open to debate.

Table 17-3   FBI index crimes, 1966–1973

Crime	Rate per 100,000 inhabitants					
	1966	1968	1970	1971	1972	1973
Murder and nonnegligent manslaughter	5.6	6.8	7.8	8.5	8.9	9.3
Forcible rape	12.9	15.5	18.3	20.3	22.3	24.3
Robbery	80.3	131.0	171.5	187.1	179.9	182.4
Aggravated assault	118.4	141.3	162.4	176.8	186.6	198.4
Burglary	708.3	915.1	1,067.7	1,148.3	1,126.1	1,210.8
Larceny ($50 and over)	456.8	636.0	859.4	909.2	882.6	2,051.2
Auto theft	284.4	389.1	453.5	456.5	423.1	440.1
Total crime index	1,666.6	2,234.8	2,740.5	2,906.7	2,829.5	4,116.4

hypothesis, the classical criminologists added the notion of **deterrence**: that others, seeing the pain inflicted on the wrongdoer, would be persuaded not to do the same thing themselves in order to avoid his fate.

Sociologists today are largely convinced that the theory doesn't work. Punishment is not an effective method of reducing the incidence of criminal behavior. Several studies have shown that punishment does not necessarily prevent the convicted criminal from once again engaging in criminal behavior when he has the opportunity. The President's Commission on Law Enforcement and the Administration of Justice, for instance, reported that two-thirds of the persons entering prisons each year had been there before.[14] It seems clear that the "pain" of imprisonment is not sufficient to end criminal behavior. Of course, punishment as a kind of societal retaliation for criminal acts seems to work admirably, but few in the judicial system would maintain that that is punishment's purpose.

The case against the theory of deterrence—that others will be prevented from commiting crimes by observing the fate of criminals—is more difficult to make. The problem is that there is no way to find out whether or not another person has been deterred. If an individual *abstains from* criminal activity, it is extremely difficult to prove that he did so because of fear of punishment. Would the crime rate be even higher than it is if punishments were more mild? Such questions cannot be clearly answered.

But the evidence we do have indicates that the theory of deterrence does not work. Unfortunately,

Some idea of the frequency of serious crime in the United States is given by this table based on FBI reports. All of the crimes shown, except auto theft, which peaked in 1971, have continued to climb since 1966. Social science research puts the actual frequency of crime from two to four times higher than these rates indicate.

most studies on the matter have concentrated on the deterrent effect of capital punishment, which is usually assigned only for murder. Statistically speaking, murder is an unusual crime. It is normally a crime of passion, and until very recently in the United States, was overwhelmingly committed among family members or close friends. Most killings, thus, are spur-of-the-moment acts committed in fits of rage, so that forethought about the consequence, which the idea of deterrence implies, would not occur. In any event, studies of murder rates in American jurisdictions with and without capital punishment have failed to show any relation between the possibility of execution and the incidence of murder.

Most sociologists would probably argue that socialization and social organization are far more effective deterrents to all nonconforming behavior than punishment. As noted earlier, it is extremely doubtful that the reason most of us refrain from eating dogs is that we might be punished for it. And although most states have laws requiring men to assume financial responsibility for their families, it seems probable that most do so out of a desire to conform to internalized norms defining this as proper rather than out of fear of punishment.

Further, deterrence, to be effective, must make punishment *certain*. But few people who commit crimes expect to be caught. At the present time in the United States, only about 5 percent of crimes known to the police are resolved by the conviction of their perpetrators. Punishment for criminal wrongdoing, then, seems far less than certain.

To sum up, if the object of punishment is reduction of the incidence of crime, it is apparent that punishment does not work. This is an extremely complicated matter and involves many variables we cannot take up here (including the whole process of police investigation, arrest, trial, and conviction, and the sociologies of who *gets* arrested, tried, and convicted or released). But beyond this, on a theoretical level, the sociologist would not *expect* punishment to be an effective deterrent to crime or other deviant behavior. Recall that all deviance, and particularly crime, is a matter of definition *by others,* usually after the act in question has been committed. The deviant thus has no control over how his behavior is defined. But if deciding whether a particular action *was* a crime, for example, is something someone else does (typically the district attorney), we cannot expect that punishing the criminal will affect the matter. (And the purpose of trial, remember, is to establish—again after the fact—whether or not a specific individual was "the criminal" once it has been decided that a criminal act has occurred.)

The crime rate in a given society is the creation of the social organization and social structure of that society. Because it is created by that organization and structure (how, we will see below), only that organization and structure can raise or lower it. An obvious example is the way in which the decriminalization of marijuana use will reduce the crime rate for drug-related offenses. By comparison, punishment is irrelevant to the incidence of crime.

Free-Will, Constitutional, and Psychoanalytic Theories of Deviant Behavior

As previously noted, the efforts made to explain deviant behavior are quite numerous. The major types of theories to be reviewed here fall into four main groups, theories based on: *free will, constitutional (or physiological) factors, psychoanalytic*

deterrence: the hypothesis that punishment of one person for a wrongful act persuades others not to behave in the same way out of fear of similar punishment. This belief still widely animates American law and public opinion, but it is largely rejected by social scientists.

Mother Orders Children to Jump; Two Are Killed

MEXICO [UPI]©A despondent young mother threw herself from the top of a three-story building along with her four children, killing two of them.

Authorities said [the mother], 24, had come to the capital in search of a job because her husband is in a hospital with tuberculosis. Unable to find employment, she climbed to the roof of a three-story building, holding her youngest child in her arms, and ordered the three other children to jump with her.

Two of the children . . . died, and the others . . . suffered injuries. Their ages were not revealed.

[The mother,] who survived the leap with undetermined injuries, was charged with homicide and intent to commit suicide.

Chicago Tribune, April 5, 1976. Reprinted by permission of UPI.

Clearly, this young woman would not have been deterred from her act by the threat of capital punishment. Will executing or imprisoning her help anyone?

(psychological and psychiatric) factors, and *sociological factors.* We will discuss the nonsociological theories first.

Free-Will Theory

The *classical school of criminology,* on which American law is based, takes the position that people have *free will* to choose courses of behavior and thus are responsible for the consequences of their acts. Deviance, or norm violation, derives not from personal characteristics or deficiencies but from the individual's deliberate choice of "wrong" over "right."

In modern form, the **free-will theory of crime** reflects the existential notion of choice and the importance of maintaining an environment in which alternatives can be considered and choices made. Essentially this argument is an ancient one: do (or should) we make (or be allowed to make) choices when we live in society? We can observe the two sides of this debate in one of its more recent forms by examining B. F. Skinner's *Beyond Freedom and Dignity* and the Anthony Burgess book and Stanley Kubrick film *A Clockwork Orange.*[15] Burgess and Kubrick argue that the risk society takes in allowing potential deviants to remain free is less than the risk of allowing the state to remove from us our ability to choose between right and wrong. In fact, this ability is what makes us human beings rather than machines or lower animals. Skinner, however, urges us to beware of this argument from two points of view. First, freedom to choose is more often illusory than we would like to admit (a question, incidentally, that lends itself to sociological exploration). Second, the modern state can no longer afford the risk of allowing its deviants freedom of choice.

Under the free-will theory of the classical criminologists, criminals were viewed as lacking will power or a sense of morality and were therefore classified as a menace to society. People had the capacity of making choices, were endowed with free will, and, thus, could be held accountable for their acts.

In order to deter others from criminal behavior, attempts were made to make punishments fit the seriousness of the crime and to apply these punishments equally to similar offenders. Thus, there developed a system of universal and abstract jus-

"The Court takes cognizance of your plea that the very nature of the municipal accounting system invites fraud, and reminds itself that the very nature of the judicial system requires me to slap you in the jug."

New Yorker, October 11, 1976. Drawing by Fisher; © 1976 The New Yorker Magazine, Inc.

The notion of free will holds people responsible for their acts.

tice, abstract in the sense that little consideration was given the individual offender, although much attention was paid to his offensive behavior.

Problems   As we have seen previously, this philosophy of choice is based on the belief that criminal acts and the people who commit them are *different from* other acts and other people. The act is seen as different because it is a "crime," the people, because they commit it. But we noted earlier that neither of these conditions holds true. The *behaviors* involved in crime are usually normal behaviors; only the circumstances in which they are enacted makes them criminal. And if doing things forbidden by law is what differentiates criminals from noncriminals, then there are no noncriminals in the population. Virtually everyone violates the law at one time or another. The free-will theory is not an adequate explanation of deviance.

Constitutional Theories

Constitutional theories of crime are so called because they hold that crime is the result of defects in an individual's physical constitution. The first constitutional theorist was Cesare Lombroso (1836–1909), an Italian criminologist. Lombroso typified the school of **positivism,** a philosophy dominant in his time. Lombroso's brand of positivism rejected free will as a means of explaining behavior and replaced it with biological determinism. People, Lombroso felt, were moved to act as they do as a product of their biology. Criminals were "atavistic anomalies," throwbacks to a type of primeval bestiality. Some people were born criminals, and they could be identified by their body structure and facial features. Indeed, Lombroso provided such information on convicts as the measurement of the length and width of the nose and fingers, the thickness of lips, the height of the brow, and so forth, to prove his point.

Early in the twentieth century, an English criminologist named Charles Goring put Lombroso's hypotheses to the test and found them unsupported by the evidence. Nonetheless, Lombroso's influence remains with us today, certainly much more than Goring's. When we look at the popular literature of the last half century, it is the ugly, the brutish, indeed, the grotesque that we are shown as evildoers. Many of us grew up in a comic-strip world dominated by a straight-jawed, clean-cut hero named Dick Tracy. Dick's enemies were not only grotesque to perceive, but if we missed the point, Chester Gould, the author of the strip, reminded us by giving them names that identified their evil qualities. Arthur Asa Berger points this out in *The Comic Stripped American:*

The grotesque describes someone (or something) fantastically ugly—such as a human being that is part animal. Gould's menagerie involves such creatures as The Mole (and now his daughter Molene), Rhodent, and Piggy. But even his villains who are not animal-like are incredibly ugly: Flattop, Shoulders, The Brow, Flyface, Spots, The Pouch, or Ugly Christine, to name only a few. In addition to having their physical ugliness show their moral ugliness, the grotesques facilitate an easy recognition of "good" and "evil" in general.[16]

But it is not just cartoonists who adhere to constitutional theories. In 1949, William Sheldon, a psychologist and physician, developed a classification of three body types that he maintained were related to behavior. His three types of physique, which he called somatotypes, are: (1) endomorphs, soft and round and usually fat; (2) meso-

free-will theory of crime: the idea that all people have "free will," or complete choice, concerning their behavior and that consequently wrongdoing is the result of the deliberate election of evil over good and deserves stern punishment.

constitutional theories of crime: theories holding that crime is the outcome of physical or "constitutional" defects in the individual. Early views, such as those associated with Lombroso, held that criminals were inherently defective—"born that way." Later versions looked to body types, glandular imbalances, or chromosomes for explanation. Little empirical evidence can be found to support these positions.

positivism: the eighteenth-century philosophy basic to science that the world is explicable by facts and that unobservable phenomena, such as God and free will, should not be used as explanatory variables.

This engraving, from a book published in the late 1800s, shows how little influence the constitutional theory of crime causation had on the New York police of that period. They are photographing a suspect for their Rogue's Gallery, because they believe there is no other way to recognize the criminal in the future. "Nor is physiognamy a safe guide," they say, "but on the contrary it is often a very poor one. In the Rogue's Gallery may be seen photographs of rascals who resemble the best people in the country . . ."

morphs, muscular and athletic; and (3) ecto-morphs, skinny and fragile. Mesomorphs, Sheldon thought, were more often delinquents than the other types.[17]

In 1952, sociologists Sheldon Glueck and Eleanor Glueck, using William Sheldon's ideas and somato-types, tested the theory on samples of delinquent and nondelinquent boys. They claimed to find definite differences in body type between the two groups, the majority of delinquents being domi-nantly mesomorphic: muscular, well-knit, and ath-letic.[18] Like Lombroso's work, the Gluecks' research has been criticized for logical and statistical inade-quacy. More statistically sophisticated reviewers, reworking their data, could not reproduce the Gluecks' results and found simple errors in compu-tation as well. Additionally, many pointed out, adolescent male delinquency is in some respects a *physical* sport, and those who excel at it—thus coming to the attention of authorities—might be expected to be muscular and athletic in build.

The latest entry into the deviance-through-physiology school is the chromosomal-deficiency hypothesis. The Y chromosome represents male traits and the X chromosome female traits. The normal ovum contains one X chromosome. In the uniting of chromosomes at the time of conception, if the ovum is fertilized by a Y-bearing sperm, the baby will have one Y and one X chromosome in its cells and will be male. If the ovum is fertilized by an X-bearing sperm, the baby will have two X chro-mosomes and will be female.

In the early 1960s, a human male was found to have a chromosomal variation in that rather than having an XY combination, he possessed an XYY combination. Within a half-dozen years, some dozen examples had been described as having some manifestations that were to interest criminol-ogists. XYY individuals were described as tall, aggressive, antisocial males, with low IQs and severe acne. They were believed to be found in greater proportions in mental institutions or pris-ons than in the general population, and the public's temptation to embrace the "born criminal" hypoth-esis was once again encouraged. This was strengthened by the types of crimes some of these men had committed, crimes involving murder and rape in rather bizarre forms. The most famous

American example is Richard Speck, who raped and killed eight nurses in one day.

The XYY hypothesis in criminology is not merely an updating of Lombroso. It is, rather, an attempt to explore the possibilities of the field of criminal biology and is a logical extention of the work of Sheldon and the Gluecks on the possible relation-ship between the physiology of the individual and the probability of his acting in a deviant manner. Research in this area is still sparse, and those who have conducted some of the pioneering studies have been reluctant to go much further than to suggest the possibility of the increased risk of a psychopathic personality in the XYY male. Later research has even cast some doubt on this.

Problems   The constitutional approach that postu-lates a "born criminal" has many problems. Mod-ern social science from Durkheim and Freud to the present establishes the ambiguity of the distinction between criminals and noncriminals. The differ-ences between the identified deviant and the non-deviant seem to lie in internalized controls and external constraints that modify the possibility of the deviant act more than any inherited differences. The primary weakness of the constitutional ap-proach to the question of causation is in law and its relativity. An act becomes criminal when it is de-fined as criminal by law. It is not a part of nature or biology, but, rather, a part of the culture, the socially constructed part of our environment. Until a behavior has been defined as illegal by a legisla-tive body, engaging in that behavior cannot be seen as criminal. Thus, an individual *cannot* be constitutionally disposed toward crime commis-sion.

Psychoanalytic Theories

The primary assumption of **psychoanalytic theo-ries of crime** is that deviance is a response to personality problems. Generally, deviants and criminals are considered "sick" or "maladjusted." Crime results from mental illness or psychological abnormality. George B. Vold, a sociologist of crime, summarizes the position as follows:

Criminal behavior . . . is to be understood, simply and directly, as a substitute response, some form of symbolic release of repressed complexes. The conflict in the unconscious mind gives rise to feelings of guilt and anxiety with a consequent desire for punishment to remove the guilt feelings and restore a proper balance of good against evil. The criminal then commits the criminal act in order to be caught and punished. Unconsciously motivated errors (i.e., careless or imprudent ways of committing the crime) leave "clues" so the authorities may more readily apprehend and convict the guilty, and thus administer suitable cleansing punishment.[19]

Much of the psychiatric research conducted early in this century found offenders to be generally "psychopathic" or "emotionally ill." The National Committee for Mental Hygiene published a summary of these studies in 1931 and found there was a large difference in the extent of psychiatric deviation diagnosed in correctional institutions in various parts of the country. The committee concluded that this difference indicated a discrepancy among diagnosticians rather than some definitive description of those being diagnosed.[20]

Problems One of the apparent difficulties in the psychoanalytic approach to deviance is the problem of whether psychological deviation is a cause of deviant behavior or the consequence of it. There is always the temptation to say that anyone acting in a deviant manner is psychologically disturbed, and this is not uncommon among proponents of this approach. This position, however, really explains nothing. It is certainly understandable that someone suffering from psychopathological disorder could commit a crime. It is also conceivable that he could become withdrawn instead. Further, persons not afflicted with these disorders also commit crimes, and not all of those so afflicted do.

More important, despite the occasional assertion of psychiatrists or psychologists to the contrary, there is little empirical evidence that *any* personality trait is associated with deviant behavior. No consistent psychological differences of any kind have been found to differentiate identified deviants from nondeviants. And an overwhelming number of studies have shown that criminals and delinquents, at least, do *not* differ from the normal population in such matters as intelligence, frequency of feeble-mindedness, personality test scores, or neurosis and psychosis.

This accumulation of negative evidence does not

psychoanalytic theories of crime: theories holding that crime is the result of mental illness, psychopathy, or other psychological abnormality. Although they are still popular today, little evidence can be found to support such notions.

social structural theories of deviance: sociological theories holding that crime is a normal reaction on the part of certain individuals to stresses or problems imposed on them by their particular positions in the institutional structure of society.

social process theories of deviance: sociological theories holding that crime is the normal outcome of certain social interaction and social organizational reciprocities, particularly within some subcultural contexts.

surprise sociologists. The psychoanalytic approach to deviance, like the constitutional approach before it, is based on the same wrong assumption about the nature of deviants as is the popular understanding and the law: that they are *different.* We would not expect properly conducted research to show that they are. *Prison populations* in the United States do differ in significant ways from the noninstitutionalized population. As a class, institutionalized criminals and delinquents tend to overrepresent the poor, the nonwhite, and the less educated, and to underrepresent the middle and upper classes, the white, and the highly educated. But these differences are largely reflections of police practice, the judicial process, and cultural definitions of deviance. As noted earlier, nearly everyone violates the law. Not everyone goes to prison for it.

Sociological Theories of Deviant Behavior

A variety of sociological theories have been offered to explain deviant behavior. All can be classified as focusing on either *social structure* or *social process*, although some use both to some degree. **Social structural theories of deviance** hold that institutional arrangements within the society produce deviant behavior on the part of some of its members. Social roles, statuses, and organizations and the way they work are the explanatory variables. **Social process theories of deviance** focus on

When I was very young, my brothers and sisters and aunts and uncles thought I was a big nothing!

So I decided to win their love and respect by working very hard and becoming rich and successful! And... son-of a gun... I DID IT!

Now I have wealth and status and the whole world respects me...

... except my brothers and sisters and aunts and uncles! THEY DESPISE ME!

© 1967 by E. C. Publications, Inc. Reprinted by permission.

interaction in the social group and explain deviant behavior as a product of particular kinds of interaction, group norms, and the responses of individuals to others around them.

Social Structural Theories

Structural theories include *anomie theory* and a number of perspectives that explain deviant behavior in terms of *subcultural norms and practices.*

Anomie theory The word *anomie* was brought into sociology by Durkheim. It means, literally, without norms, and Durkheim used it to describe a social context in which the moral order had broken down for an individual or group, a situation in which normal social structural constraints on behavior became inoperative.

Anomie theory is associated with the work of Robert K. Merton, who modified Durkheim's usage of the word and applied it to explaining deviant behavior. Merton began by identifying two important and related elements in any society, *cultural goals* and *institutionalized means.* Cultural goals are the things a given society defines in its normative system as worth being and having. The institutionalized means are the ways that society accepts as legitimate for attaining the cultural goals. Anomie, in Merton's usage, is the situation that arises when an individual is unable to obtain the goals he has been taught to strive for with the means that the society puts at his disposal. In Merton's view, a common reaction to this situation is to engage in deviant behavior.

This man's relatives may despise him, but most Americans probably don't. Material success is a dominant cultural goal.

In his original statement of anomie theory,[21] Merton used the example of material success in American society. Material success, the possession of money and all it will buy, is an important goal for all Americans; for many, the most important goal they have. (Not because they are necessarily "money mad," but because Americans judge each other as successful or unsuccessful *people* according to material acquisition. Those who can't make it materially don't make it socially either.) In an enormous variety of ways, all of our lives, we are taught that to succeed is crucial. For most of us, our very sense of "self" is derived from the success we have made in society. The society also offers and defines certain means for the attainment of success as acceptable. Typically, these involve hard work, education, thrift, and so forth.

But some people, because of accidents of social position, race or ethnicity, or other factors, will be unable to use the socially acceptable means of goal attainment effectively or will have their access to them blocked. The poor, for example, do not, typically, have effective access to the kinds of education that may lead to success. And the non-white may be denied success no matter how hard they work or even how educated they become. (Many Pullman porters thirty years ago were college graduates, the railroad servant's job being the best they could get.) Such situations Merton defined as conditions of anomie.

Conformity   There are, Merton thought, five possible "modes of adaptation" to the means/goals problem. The first is the "normal" or conventional one that most people in any society will more or less follow most of the time: *conformity.* They adopt the cultural goals offered them as appropriate things to strive for and the approved institutionalized means as the proper way to go about the striving. The other four possible adaptations are anomic reactions to social structural situations by individuals for whom the means don't work or for whom access to them is blocked. These are *innovation, ritualism, retreatism,* and *rebellion.*

Innovation   Those who believe in the legitimacy of the goal of accumulating money and material success but are either unwilling or unable to use the socially approved means to achieve it are *innovators.* The legitimate means may have been blocked for them; perhaps they were denied educational opportunities or entry to the skilled trades on a racial or ethnic basis. But since innovators still want to attain the goal, they will use forbidden means to achieve it. They will, in fact, violate norms and often break the law. This, Merton thought, explained high crime rates among the poor.

Ritualism   People who lose sight of the goal while slavishly adhering to the means are *ritualists.* Some civil service bureaucrats who work in welfare and unemployment offices fall into this category. Ritualistic bureaucrats pay little attention to the real needs of the clients, but instead busy themselves amassing the proper forms, sorting, stamping, and processing them, having the client "stand behind the yellow line," and so forth. Ritualists concentrate on obeying all the rules of the system rigidly and without question.

Retreatism   Rejecting both cultural goals and the institutionalized means for their achievement, *retreatists* are the beats, bohemians, hippies (these terms differ in different historical contexts), alcoholics, and drug addicts: the "losers" of the society. Unwilling or unable to compete, retreatists decide that "the game's not worth the candle" and drop out entirely.

> **anomie theory:** the theory of deviant behavior, identified with Robert K. Merton, that sees deviance as a normal or expectable reaction to a situation in which cultural goals demanded of everyone cannot be attained by some through application of normatively institutionalized means.

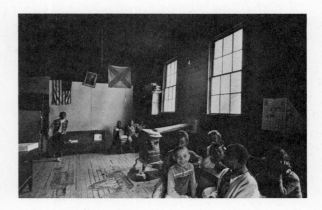

Availability of access to goal attainment mechanisms has a great deal to do with whether people engage in deviant behavior. Do you think you would be in college today if you had gone to this school?

Rebellion   Rebels reject both conventional goals and approved means. They want a new set . . . after *their* revolution. The student radicals of the 1960s are excellent cases in point.

Anomie theory brings us far in understanding the relationship between poverty and crime. In other societies, the demand for financial success is not the same for all social classes. All men were not "created equal" in India, Italy, or England. Thus, in much of the world children of the ghetto are not expected to "rise above," but rather to make do as best they can with what is available to them. In America, as we know, all men (and now all women) are equal, and in America, then, all people are expected to gain economic affluence and are held personally responsible if they do not. The goal is the same for all, despite the castelike and subtle class structures that exist within the society. Thus, if money can't be made through legitimate means, nonlegitimate means often come to be used.

Subcultural approaches   A number of structural theories of deviance dealing with crime and delinquency have focused on subcultures in explaining deviant behavior. They hypothesize that subcultures may develop special sets of norms or behaviors that are contrary to the norms of the general culture as a consequence of the location of the subculture in the social structure of the society. Thus, minority group members or the poor, for example, may exhibit more behavior defined as deviant by the middle-class superculture simply because they are in a minority position or economically depressed. Some of the better-known of these subcultural approaches are described below.

Delinquency as problem-solving behavior   One sociologist of deviance, Albert Cohen, studied deviance in terms of lower-class adolescent male delinquency, which he describes as nonutilitarian, malicious, versatile, and negativistic.[22] This delinquency is not, however, without purpose, Cohen believes, and the purpose is problem solving. Cohen argues that all human activity is related to problem solving of one kind or another and that all problem solving basically involves two variables: *the situation* and *the frame of reference.*

The situation refers to the social and physical

Retreatism.

setting of the actor and the frame of reference to the way in which he perceives it. When confronted with a problem, the actor may solve it by changing either the situation that produces it or the frame of reference, his perception of it as a problem. Cohen uses the example of a boy who is receiving a failing grade in a particular class in school. If he held a positive attitude to the class and wanted to succeed, he could change the situation by working harder to pass. An alternative, however, would be to change his frame of reference toward the class by convincing himself that the class was not worth the bother, or would not be needed for a job. Either solution resolves the original emotional problem. If, in addition, the boy can convince himself that receiving a failing grade in the class will enhance his reputation in the eyes of his peers, failure becomes a positive value.

Lower-class male delinquency, in Cohen's view, is a response of this kind to the differential opportunity structure in American society. Social aspirations may be more or less the same in all strata, but

Subcultures may develop norms contrary to those of the larger society.

opportunity is not. Poverty, race, and ethnicity affect life chances, as we saw in Chapters 8 and 9. The lower-class boy is confronted with a problem. He has been taught by television and the school what amount to middle-class aspirations and values, but his life situation is such that he has little chance of realizing them. And that situation is the product of his society; he cannot alter it.

According to Cohen, the boy's psychological reaction to this dilemma has the effect of "inverting" the frustration-creating middle-class value system. The adjectives characterizing lower-class male delinquency (nonutilitarian, malicious, and so on) represent psychological reversals, mirror images, of middle-class values. In time, these images become a new value system, which, being attainable, creates a reward structure within the framework of the delinquent gang. Actions for which the boy would be punished by middle-class society are rewarded by the gang. Failure according to middle-class standards becomes success according to gang norms.

Delinquency as normative conformity Gresham M. Sykes and David Matza believe that the delinquent, rather than seeing himself *in opposition to* the moral imperatives of middle-class society, devises methods of neutralizing the emotional consequences of his behavior in advance.[23] Thus, instead

The Drowning Pool

It was another dazzling summer day in drought-stricken Britain, and Enrico Sidoli, 15, decided to join his older sister and her two children at a local pool. Like many kids in the poor London suburb of Kentish Town, "Noddy" Sidoli had never learned to swim, but with a protective float strapped around his waist, the slight, dark-haired teen-ager paddled around the pool's shallow end. Then three older boys jumped him, flung him into deeper water and held him under until his body went limp. The attackers fled, and children using a nearby water slide shouted for the lifeguard, but it was too late; Enrico was rushed to a hospital, and eleven days later died of brain damage. The crime itself was bad enough. But what shocked many Britons even more was that by last week not one of the nearly 1,000 people who were in or near the pool at the time had stepped forward to help identify Enrico's killers.

The murder was an ugly echo of New York's 1964 Kitty Genovese case, but such a conspiracy of silence would have been unthinkable in Kentish Town only a few years ago. Its lower-middle-class residents got on well with each other and spent their evenings in amiable, over-the-flowerbox conversation. Recently, however, Greeks, Turks, Italians, blacks, Asians and other immigrants have moved into Kentish Town. Since most of these groups want to protect—and punish—their own, cooperation with the police is frowned upon. Youth gangs brutally enforce the rule of silence. "They have their codes, and one of them is that you must not 'grassin,' which means you mustn't be a snake in the grass and inform," says police Inspector Harry Clement, who is in charge of the case. "It's a children's *omerta*, but in this case it also applies to the adults." . . .

The conspiracy of silence—appeal to higher loyalties.

of creating new norms, the delinquent rationalizes his behavior within the existing normative framework. This involves the use of five major *techniques of neutralization:* (1) denial of responsibility, (2) denial of injury, (3) denial of the victim, (4) condemnation of the condemners, and (5) the appeal to higher loyalties.

The delinquent *denying responsibility* sees himself as a kind of billiard ball, helplessly propelled in various directions by factors beyond his influence. These factors could include a ghetto environment, a broken home, bad companions, low income, and so on. By viewing himself as more acted upon than acting, the delinquent paves the way for deviance from norms without attacking the norms themselves. He simply refuses to be blamed for violating norms.

Denial of injury is a matter of redefining deviant behavior in order to make it more palatable. Vandalism becomes "mischief," auto theft is "borrowing." After all, "there is always insurance available to the injured party," reasons the delinquent. A gang fight is a private quarrel and should not cause the community any concern.

The *denial of the victim* involves either reconstructing the situation so that the victim is perceived as being punished for some transgression (thus deserving injury) or denying that injury resulted. Vandalism can be defined as revenge on an unfair school official or a "crooked" store owner. The delinquent becomes a type of Robin Hood working to right wrongs more quickly than the slow processes of the law.

Condemnation of the condemners involves a redefinition of the accuser as a deviant in disguise, a hypocrite. Police become "pigs," teachers show favoritism, and parents "don't know where it's at." The moral right of others to judge is thus denied. All of these neutralization techniques serve to deflect negative sanctions that would otherwise be associated with deviant acts.

Appeal to higher loyalties is the fifth element of neutralization. Here the norms of the legitimate society are implicitly accepted, but other norms are given precedence for the sake of the subgroup, the peer culture. Choosing between the claims of the law and the claims of loyalty to friends is a classic problem. The delinquent chooses the latter, feeling this is the only truly moral choice open to him.

Delinquency and differential opportunity   Richard Cloward and Lloyd Ohlin, using Merton's anomie theory, suggest some further refinements. They argue that differential opportunities for entering the legitimate social structure (having access to the legitimate "means," in Merton's terms) is not the only problem. In addition, difficulties exist that stand in the way of easy access to the *illegitimate* opportunity structure.[24] They apply this hypothesis to lower-class boys, who, as in the Sykes and Matza formulation, are viewed as sharing the same success ethic as middle-class boys. This ethic is measured primarily through material gain. Whereas middle-class boys have access to legitimate means of attaining material gain, or at least are within reach of the ladder leading to upward mobility, the lower-class boy very soon recognizes the gap between his level of aspiration and the expectation that he will realize it. Thus, he will turn to whatever *illegitimate* opportunities are available to him in his neighborhood.

But if illegal means are not easily available, then adolescents will probably not develop a criminal subculture. Only those who have ready access to illegal and violent means are likely to develop into criminals. In other words, differences in the social structure strongly influence which adolescents of those who have few legitimate means available will adopt illegitimate means to attain their goals.

Similarity of social structural theories   Although the various social structural theories focus attention on different things, or on different aspects of the same thing, all take the position that deviant behavior is a response to or consequence of the institutional arrangements of the society. Their argument is, in one way or another, that the conventional ways in which social arrangements are organized to fulfill individual and collective needs do not work for everyone. There are some individuals or groups who, because of their particular location in the social structure, do not have needs met, or whose abilities to meet their own needs are handicapped. Being located in a racial or ethnic minority is an example of such a position, or being at the bottom of the socioeconomic ladder. People in such social positions are likely to respond to the stresses imposed on them with behavior that others more favorably located may define as deviant.

But that behavior appears to the actors to be a reasonable reaction.

Social Process Theories

Social structural theories look for their explanations to the way in which the society is *organized.* Social process theories look to the ways in which groups work, focusing especially on the interaction patterns that individuals follow within them. What roles are made available to members of particular groups, how they play them out in interaction with each other, and what norms come to be accepted in the process are the variables used in process explanations.

Differential association theory   Edwin H. Sutherland, probably the dean of American criminologists of the mid-century, proposed the theory of *differential association* to explain deviant (specifically criminal) behavior.[25] Its basic assumption is that criminal behavior, like any other social behavior, is learned through association with others. It is not physiological or inherited, and it is not the product of warped psychology.

If criminal behavior is learned exactly as any other behavior is learned, then it is learned through association with others, especially interaction within intimate personal groups. Throughout our lives, association and interaction with others teaches us motives, attitudes, values, and rationalizations. The specific *direction* that these will take—law-abiding or law-violative—will depend on who we learn our behavior from. Thus, *differential* association— differences in who we associate with—will in large part determine how we behave.

In every social group, there are individuals who define adherence to the law as acceptable and, indeed, natural, not really open to question, and others who are otherwise inclined. Often, in our culture, there is a mix. That is, most of us would not think seriously of burglary, yet using the company postage meter to mail our Christmas cards can be justified by saying "everybody does it." If everybody does it, then those "everybodys" are, in a sense, favorably defining the theft of postage from the company. Others would not engage in even this rather minor form of law violation. In our mobile

> **differential association theory:** the theory, associated with Edwin H. Sutherland, holding that criminal behavior, like other behavior, is learned from association with others manifesting it.
>
> **containment theory:** the theory, associated with Walter Reckless, holding that crime is explained by the failure, in some cases, of normal behavioral constraints to operate for specific individuals because of their social position.

and complex society, we have the opportunity to mingle with both types.

Sutherland concludes, therefore, that people may become delinquent (deviant) to the degree that they associate and interact with others whose definitions of reality favor law violation more commonly than they oppose it. Such association varies in frequency, duration, intensity, and priority, and these variables will determine what an individual learns or how well he learns it. Further, while criminal behavior is an expression of general needs and values in the psychoanalytic sense, it cannot be *explained* by such things ("aggressiveness" for example), because noncriminal behavior is also an expression of the same needs and values. It is not "need for money" that explains criminality, but the choices that an individual makes to fulfill that need, and such choices are the product of life-long learning and interaction with others.

Containment theory   Like differential association, *containment theory,* formulated by Walter Reckless, holds that group membership and social interaction determine how individuals will act in particular life situations. But instead of focusing on association, containment theory concentrates on the elements in group life that tend to *prevent* an individual from being "pulled into" a deviant or criminal pattern.[26] In this view, deviance is explained by the failure of normal behavioral constraints to operate in specific individuals because of their social positions. Reckless argues that understanding the social and psychological "buffers" against deviant behavior is more useful than studying deviance-provoking processes. Since most people are nondeviant most of the time, we must understand deviance as a failure of the normal

rather than as something special or abnormal in itself.

There are two kinds of buffers, or containments: (1) the external social structure and organization of society and the groups to which the individual belongs; and (2) the internal, psychological controls that one imposes on oneself. The external constraint is the informal social control a group exerts on its members: role expectations, values, and so forth—all of the conscious and unconscious rules and values about how "people like us" are supposed to behave. The internal constraints are the components of "self" that give the individual the internal strength and motive to resist the deviant impulses that we all experience at one time or another. Normally, the combination of external and internal controls operates to keep us from acting in deviant ways. Internal controls direct our goals toward those that are socially approved and give us a favorable concept of self. We thus gain an ability to react to frustration with an acceptable degree of tolerance and also a strong tendency to identify with the norms in the society that are nondeviant. But once in awhile these controls fail to operate for an individual because of his social position, such as that caused by extreme poverty or severe racial discrimination. In such cases, deviance follows the breakdown of the usual controls.

Labeling theory   The previous discussion of the *relativity* of deviance and the sociological definition of deviance offered (a judgment made by others) stand in the tradition of the *labeling theory* of deviant behavior. It is primarily associated with Howard S. Becker.[27] Labeling is a process theory

"Everybody does it." But where does the kid *get* such ideas?

because it seeks to understand the social interaction process between an individual and others that results in his becoming defined—labeled—as deviant. The basic argument is simple: Out of the enormous diversity of human behaviors, only certain ones are selected by societies or groups within them for definition as deviant. Judgments about what acts are deviant are highly relative and not by any means logically consistent. Not everyone who performs a given act will be called deviant for doing so, and the same act may or may not be called deviant at all times. Ingesting chemicals with the intent of altering our mental or physical condition may or may not be "drug use"—it is sometimes "headache remedy."

In labeling theory, the focus of attention turns to the "normals" who do the labeling, as opposed to the deviant and the deviant act. The labeling theorist studies the process whereby a particular behavior comes to be labeled as deviant. Society is an active partner in the creation of the deviant. "Nuts," "sluts," and "perverts" are not part of the natural world like rocks, rivers, and roosters. The first three are human creations. Our reaction to them plays a critical role in their behavior and our definition of it. Deviance is not an inherent quality of any act, but is conferred by the label.

An interesting refinement of labeling theory was introduced in 1964 by Erving Goffman. He referred to people with "spoiled," or somehow marred, identities as people with a "stigma" attached to them.[28] People react differently to those so stigmatized, and more often than not, the reaction has no basis in logic. Thus, we tend to speak louder to the blind, to be overly courteous to parents of mentally retarded children, and to avoid those with visible physical impairments. Goffman argued that we view such people as "stigmatized," or deviant. Deviance is not a term reserved only for those committing crimes.

Secondary deviance   Edwin Lemert used the term *secondary deviance* to describe those elements of the behavior of the deviant developed as a result of having been labeled deviant in the first place.[29] The most obvious example is that of the drug addict. We define the addict as deviant and criminal and ignore his physiological need for drugs. At the same time, the "normal" society, as a consequence of the application of these labels, represses the addict in many ways. The society claims his addiction is somehow tied to his lack of will power and, in order to strengthen his will, removes all possibility of gaining access to drugs legally.

A probable result of this method of "curing" his deviance is to place him in a position where it becomes necessary for him to resort to street crime to get the drugs he must have to survive. His crimes are a direct consequence of the public reaction to his primary label (drug addict, deviant) and are not the result of the actual physical ingestion of the drug into his body. A secondary deviant is a person whose life and identity are organized around the facts of deviance, someone forced by others to "live up to" his deviant label or identity.

Similarities of social process theories   Two common threads appear in all process theories: (1) that deviant behavior is not intrinsically different from other behavior and (2) that it can be understood only as a consequence of group interaction processes. Differential association theory and containment theory focus on how the interaction process may lead to the learning or enactment of deviant or nondeviant behavior. Labeling theory and the idea of secondary deviance focus on the processes through which the definition of deviance is attached to individuals. All agree that deviance is social, not biological or psychological, and all see it as being in one way or another created by the

labeling theory: the theory, associated with Howard S. Becker, holding that deviance is a label imposed on individuals by others and is not a special, peculiar, or abnormal behavior.

secondary deviance: a term used by Edwin Lemert to describe the deviant behavior that an individual may come to exhibit as a consequence of having been labeled deviant in the first place, as when drug addicts resort to mugging in order to secure funds to purchase drugs only available to them illegally.

Labeling. If these men were Greek warriors of 500 B.C., they would not be considered deviant.

society itself. The latter view, of course, is shared by all sociological approaches, structural as well as process.

A Sociology of Deviance

It is impossible within the limitations of a single chapter to outline a complete statement of the sociological understanding of deviance. Many of the descriptions of different approaches offered above have attempted to summarize whole books—sometimes series of books—devoted to working out the approach. Further, not all of the approaches are entirely consistent with one another. Process theories do not "fit" too well with structural theories. Nonetheless, there is considerable consensus in sociology on a number of general conclusions about the nature of deviant behavior, its causation, and its role in society. These can be summarized as follows:

1. Social organization creates deviance. It is not a specific quality inherent in either persons or actions.

2. Deviance is often functional both for individuals and the society itself. For individuals, it may represent ways of coping with life problems that are otherwise insoluble or intolerable. For the society, its principal functions are the definition and support of the normative structure or moral order.

3. A number of different arguments are advanced concerning the causes of deviant behavior, not all of which are logically consistent with one another. Good cases can be made, however, that specific instances of deviation result from (a) socialization or resocialization to deviant norms; (b) ambiguities and conflicts in the normative order itself that permit subcultural norm structures to coexist with those of the superculture and also permit patterned norm evasion; (c) differences in opportunities and constraints; and (d) labeling phenomena.

As is often the case in any academic field, the question to which we should address ourselves is not which of these interpretations may be "right," but the new ways in which they permit us to understand the world. All withstand better the confrontation with empirical evidence about how human beings really behave than the theories of deviance implicit in the popular and American legal views. Perhaps most important, however, all affirm a conclusion about deviant behavior that radically alters commonsense ideas about reducing it: deviance can never be eliminated from a social order because it is the product *of* social order. Morality in society is defined by the perception of immorality. A conception of "up" is meaningful only when paired with a conception of "down."

Summary

One of the principal problems in the sociology of deviance is obtaining agreement on what *deviance* means. Both American popular culture and American law implicitly assume that deviance is a quality *inherent in* persons or specific behaviors called wrong, immoral, or deviant. But consideration of the evidence shows this cannot be true. The sociological definition of deviance is that it means a *judgment by someone that nonconformity to social norms has occurred.*

This means that deviance is highly relative. It is relative to particular *societies* and *times,* to *place,* to the *social status of actor and victim,* and to *its consequences.* All judgments that a person or act is deviant are made within such contexts. The problem of making or assessing such judgments is complicated by the fact that either *real* or *ideal norms* may be appealed to as legitimating the judgment, and the two do not always coincide. It is sometimes the real norm to violate the ideal norm.

Social control includes all of the ways in which societal norms are enforced. It is conventional to distinguish between formal and informal social control. *Formal social control* is associated with the social structure and specialized agencies of the society such as the police and courts, organizational regulation, and so forth. *Informal social control* is the product of social organization, the individual's involvement in the "web of group affiliation." Social control is also performed by socialization, which produces *internal control,* or *self-control,* as a product of the individual's desire to abide by the norms he has learned. The relationship between deviance and social control is that *social control produces deviance.* Nonconformity to norms is possible only because of their existence in the first place. Because norms exist, they will sometimes be deviated from.

Crime and *delinquency* are special instances of deviant behavior in that they are created by the legal system. Each time a new law is passed, a new crime comes into being; each time an old law is rescinded, a former crime becomes permissible behavior. The fact that criminal behavior is not in a class by itself, but should be treated as simply one form of deviance, is especially indicated by the concept of *white-collar crime:* crime committed as a part of legitimate occupational activity and made possible by the opportunity such activity affords. White-collar crime calls special attention to the criminality of the upper and middle classes, which is apt to be different from that of the lower classes and is much less likely to be defined as deviant.

The *incidence of crime* of all kinds is fairly high in the United States as compared with other nations, but it is impossible to say accurately how high it is or how fast it is growing because of the inadequacy of crime statistics. These are particularly biased because they report largely the crimes of the lower social classes. White-collar crime is almost absent from them.

The American theory of corrections is based on punishment, on the pleasure-pain principle. To the extent that the object of punishment is the reduction of crime, the system does not work. The principal problem is the logical error in the basic assumption that criminals and criminal behavior are intrinsically different from other people and "normal" behavior. Empirically, it is impossible to distinguish either. Further, because punishment for commission of crimes is anything but certain, the principle of *deterrence* cannot usefully be applied. If there is no punishment, there is nothing to act as a deterrent. And even if punishment occurs, we cannot tell whether it has a deterrent effect.

Theories for the explanation of deviant behavior fall into two general categories: (1) those that presume that deviant behavior or people are different from other behavior or people and (2) those that do not. The former appear in the form of *free-will theories, constitutional theories,* and *psychoanalytic theories.* There is little behavioral evidence to support any of them.

Most *sociological theories* of deviant behavior presume that deviant people or actions are just like other people or actions and stem from the same sources and learning. They can be classified as falling into two types, *social structural theories* and *social process theories.* Explanation in structural theories tends to seek ways in which social structural situations impose special strains of one kind or another on individuals or groups, who then respond to these special situations with behavior that others define as deviant. Process theories examine the social situation and social organizational networks of persons called deviant to determine how such behavior was learned or elicited.

Most of both types of sociological theories presume that the deviant individual is "normal" and the deviant behavior a rational response to the social context. Although not all sociological explanations of deviance are entirely consistent with one another, all share two conclusions: that inasmuch as deviance is the product of social structure and organization, it is inevitable; and that neither the behavior nor the persons exhibiting it are "abnormal." Deviance is created by social organization, by society itself. It can be altered by altering social structure and organization, but it can never be eliminated.

Review Questions

1. Discuss some of the popular misconceptions in regard to deviance. What is the sociological meaning given to this concept? How does it differ, if at all, from how most people think of deviance?

2. Contrast the different modes of adaptation provided by Merton in his study of cultural goals and institutionalized means. What special significance is given to the role of innovator in the discussion of deviance?

3. What are some of the dominant cultural goals in the U.S. today? What are some of the institutionalized means for reaching these goals? What are some illegitimate means?

4. What is meant by the constitutional approach? What is the main argument proposed by the school of positivism? What role is played by the somatotype?

5. What is the essence of Becker's labeling theory? What is the role of Goffman's stigma in this perspective?

Suggestions for Research

1.   Schedule an interview with your local probation officer to gain a better insight into how the community deals with minors placed on probation. Gather factual information regarding the meetings between the officer and adolescents on probation. How often do they meet? For how long? Describe how, if at all, the probation officer believes he can/has help/helped his clients. What are the chances of the delinquent committing a subsequent offense? Under what circumstances is probation used instead of reform schooling? How do the two differ? What are the specific advantages of probation? Its particular problems?

2.   Devote a term paper to the study of typical American prisons and the prison system in general. Does it appear to you that rehabilitation is emphasized more or less than punishment? Why? You may want to select a few examples, (such as the incident at Attica), which have received treatment in the media in recent years to illustrate points. Give attention to the structure and authority hierarchy in the prison system in terms of its place and role in society.

3.   Study the relationship between lower social class backgrounds and crime. Why is this relation more complex than simply a matter of material misfortune? In other words, analyze the subculture operating within the impoverished neighborhood, including the role of the peer group. How does their school system operate, if ever, to balance the influence of the environment? In studying subculture, you may want to examine Liebow's *Tally's Corner*.

4.   Select one or more variables to study in its relation to crime: ethnicity, social class, education, religion, marital status, income or others. How is crime affected by the variable? Examine both rates and types of crime in this light. How can you be sure the relationship, if present, is not caused by other intervening variables? Explain why this particular variable is or is not important in the study of crime.

5.   Read and report on Mario Puzo's *The Godfather*. Describe the contraculture of organized crime. In comparison with other subcultures, is it particularly cohesive? Why or why not? How do the values in the contraculture parallel or differ from those in mainstream culture? How does organized crime appear to differ from other criminal behavior? If possible, try to see the film of the same title.

CHAPTER 18
COLLECTIVE BEHAVIOR AND SOCIAL MOVEMENTS

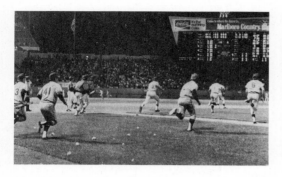

Texas Ranger dugout empties onto field, the players armed with bats, as fans leave the stands and charge Jeff Burroughs in the ninth inning of the game with the Cleveland Indians.

On Tuesday, June 4, 1974, the temperature was in the mid-eighties, and it seemed pretty hot to many of the 23,000 baseball fans filing into Cleveland's Municipal Stadium for a game between the Indians and the Texas Rangers. Perhaps they came a bit earlier and moved a little more quickly than usual, for it was "10¢ beer night." And if the beer was warm by the time it reached them, at least it was cheap and the servings were generous—about ten ounces per cup. Before the night was over, this crowd put away 65,000 cups—plus the game.

"Riots by Indians' Fans in 9th Forfeits Game to Rangers" headlined the sports page of the next day's *New York Times*. With the game tied five to five, part of the crowd had jumped on to the field and charged one of the Ranger outfielders. The fans were quickly pursued by the players from both dugouts. As hundreds of fans surrounded the players, fighting broke out. The game was called, and the Rangers were given the win. That was the initial story.

By the next day, Thursday, however, the facts had changed. Now the *Times* called the event a "near riot." And the same ninth inning took on a milder, more circuslike cast. Both teams did run on to the field, but the number of fans involved had diminished to half a dozen. And some previously missing details appeared. The game had been highlighted by a woman dashing out to kiss an umpire, forty fans running and somersaulting across the field, and smokebombs and firecrackers that

forced the Rangers to abandon their bullpen in the seventh inning. In the midst of all this, a streaker wearing only a sock bolted the outfield fence. And significantly, the second story revealed that some of the fans might have been reacting to a similar fracas between the Rangers and the Indians a week or so earlier in the Rangers' home park at Arlington, Texas.

What did, in fact, happen that night in Cleveland? Certainly something more than a routine baseball game. But was it a riot? Which account was more accurate? Perhaps the story was played down on the second day to please the baseball establishment, or the business people of Cleveland, or some other unknown group or individual. But maybe instead it was the real facts that emerged slowly over the twenty-four hours after the event—the earlier story being the product of speed and emotion on the part of a harried sports writer.

The example of this baseball game points out one of the major problems associated with the study of collective behavior: the analysis is almost always done after the events have begun and often only after they have ended. As we shall see, collective behavior is, by definition, behavior that is somewhat spontaneous, which means it is unpredictable. As a consequence, social scientists rarely are present when such events occur, and must reconstruct them afterward, dealing with the problems of forgotten detail and intentional cover-up of the actual happenings. As with the "riot" in Cleveland, they must piece things together, never being quite certain that they have done so completely and accurately.

The Cleveland baseball game also points to another problem for collective behavior research. Notice that there had apparently been a similar episode in Texas the week before. The *New York Times* writer speculated that perhaps that earlier event had played a part in the activities at Cleveland. Perhaps. But how? Did some of the fans meet before the game and "conspire" to create an incident, hoping to use the frivolity of a drunken crowd as a cover? If so, then researchers would have to shift their analysis to cover the subject of *social movements* as well as collective behavior. If there were conspirators, then researchers want to know how they met, what kind of leadership they had, the degree of permanence of their organization, their link with other groups, and so on. In short, the researchers would try to discover the nature of the social movement and the planning that went into the evening's activities.

Finally, collective behavior research must usually address—and validate, or dismiss—everyday explanations for the episodes examined. Because the researcher is often on the scene only after events are under way or completed, accounts of what happened are almost always accompanied by the explanatory views of the participants, the authorities, and the press. In the case of the baseball incident, the press and many other people simply assumed that the crowd had lost its head as a result of the amount of beer consumed. But was that what really happened? It would be interesting to know, for example, what the typical amount of beer consumed by a baseball crowd of 23,000 is. We

> **collective behavior:** group action that occurs without clear-cut direction from culture.

might well discover that we would have to look elsewhere for an explanation.

As we turn to a more detailed and systematic consideration of the forms and causes of collective behavior, you will soon discover that a great deal more is unknown than is known about it. But the search for understanding continues, for collective behavior seems continually to increase. Many societies today are caught in the grip of riots and terror. What happened in Cleveland was a relatively unimportant event. But the ultimate outcomes of the extraordinary politics of the 1960s in the United States, the civil war and terror in Ireland and Lebanon, and revolution or coup in Chile and Argentina are serious matters indeed.

What Is Collective Behavior?

Over the years theorists have used many different adjectives to describe collective behavior. Each of the words used, such as *extraordinary*, *unstructured*, and *uninstitutionalized*, captures some of the flavor of the baseball episode already discussed, without completely defining it.[1] Perhaps the simplest and least controversial definition of **collective behavior** is: group action that occurs without clear-cut direction from culture.[2] This means that the events that occur, and their consequences, are somewhat surprising to participants as well as observers. The events have been at least in part unplanned and their outcomes unforeseen. Patterns of behavior emerge spontaneously in the process of people interacting together, rather than stemming from the norms and patterned roles that ordinarily direct behavior.

Researchers concerned with collective behavior examine the periodic occurrence of collective action, such as that of crowds, mobs, riots, and social movements. Of these forms of collective behavior, social movements present the most difficult definitional problems. Historically, collective behavior researchers have included social movements in their studies because these researchers are interested in social change. And collective behavior phenomena and social movements are often characteristics of societies undergoing rapid social change. But social movements, as we shall see, differ considerably from other forms of collective behavior. They are more structured, enduring, and predictable, and are increasingly studied by sociologists of organizations and political sociologists. Nevertheless, all of the forms of collective behavior, including social movements, do stand in contrast to the predictable processes and occurrences of everyday life that occupy most of our time.

The Scientific Study of Collective Behavior

Curiously, the scientific study of collective behavior has experienced some of the same processes that students of it work so hard to understand. The literature of this complex field developed in a series of waves of historic interest in the subject, rather than as a result of continuing social scientific research. There have been essentially four major periods of interest in collective behavior.

The First Period

The first of these periods began with the great French Revolution in 1789 and continued through subsequent lesser European revolts in 1848 and 1871. The tone of the studies sparked by these events was largely reactionary. Nineteenth-century historians such as Hippolyte Taine and Edmund Burke and social commentators such as Gustave LeBon were genuinely frightened by the horrors of these revolutions.[3] These writers emphasized the negative consequences of removing restraints upon people, and their work suggests that when the organizations of social control become inoperative, the most brutish of human instincts spring to the fore. Taine and Burke were further convinced that the 1789 revolution in France was the work of riffraff who instigated it as a way of acting out their animosities.

LeBon, however, who is credited with being the first modern theorist of collective behavior, was far more subtle in his analysis. He argued that there was something about *the crowd* that made it qualitatively different from most other human groups. In the crowd, there was a reduction of individual awareness and the capacity to reason. Individuals who alone seemed quite capable of reasonable decisions could sometimes commit outrageously destructive and irrational acts when they became members of a crowd. To account for this, LeBon emphasized the heightened *suggestibility* of individuals in crowds, their increased susceptibility to the influence of others. An individual alone may resist the suggestions of others, but once in a crowd he has difficulty ignoring them. Like a hypnotized person, a person in the crowd usually cannot resist the current of the crowd. As the crowd begins to move toward a goal, the strength of its direction is continually reinforced by the circular and reciprocal nature of the communication within the crowd.

The French revolutions, particularly that of 1848, had an impact on practical students of collective behavior as well as scholars. The great revolutionaries of the day, Marx, Alexander Herzen, Mikhail Bakunin, and many others, studied these events for what they could learn about revolution. In general, the revolutionaries looked at the events in terms of the historical struggle between the proletariat and the bourgeoisie. Although these interests had very little impact on the study of collective behavior in the early days, today we find considerable research developing on large-scale economic processes and the origins of civil turmoil and revolution.

The Second Period

The second great wave of interest in collective behavior came in the 1920s and 1930s. This was a time of very rapid urbanization in the United States, as we saw in Chapter 10. Robert Park, W. I. Thomas, and Ernest Burgess, all of the University of Chicago, were studying various facets of this process. Park, in particular, was interested in the fate of individuals thrown into this new environment. In their introductory sociology text, Park and Burgess argued that rapid urbanization greatly loosened cultural and social bonds, creating ferment and unrest. Individuals cut loose from old associations looked for new ones to join. And amidst the confusion generated by the breakdown of traditional social links, new and unusual political and religious movements sprang up. Thus, rapid urbanization created conditions very favorable for the growth of collective behavior.[4]

One of Park's more enduring contributions to the study of collective behavior was his insistence that while it involved the unusual, there were uniformities within it. He urged his students to examine "natural histories" (objective, sequential case studies) of the episodes and groups they were studying to find out what they shared in common, so that they could isolate the typical characteristics of collective behavior. Two very important legacies, then, emerged from the Chicago tradition: (1) the importance of modern culture in creating a fluid environment where collective behavior is likely to occur and (2) the need to look for uniformities to explain it.

The Third Period

Adolf Hitler's meteoric rise to power fueled yet a third wave of interest in collective behavior. No event in modern history except the Russian Revolution so widely alarmed the Western world. The character, the speed, and the violence associated with the Nazi party and its programs were all so grotesque as to demand attention and explanation. The general question social observers asked was: Is there something about some cultures that create people with a high predisposition to behavior like that of the Nazis?

The great psychoanalyst Erich Fromm argued that "the modern industrial system in general and in its monopolistic phase in particular make[s] for the development of a personality which feels powerless and alone, anxious and insecure." In his view, people who have been freed from external restraints (such as feudal social statuses or the web of the *gemeinschaft*) may suddenly flee into the arms of a dictator in an "escape from freedom."[5] Such people attempt to regain some sense of mastery over their fate by identifying with a powerful leader and movement. Fromm felt that this loss of social structural constraint was so widespread in modern society that the German nightmare might soon befall the democratic states of the West.

In a less grand, but far more systematic way, T. H. Adorno and his associates also attempted to

Execution of Louis XVI, January 21, 1793. The French Revolution sparked the study of collective behavior.

answer the question of what had happened in Nazi Germany. Adorno, while stressing the importance of bad economic conditions as a causative factor, went on to argue that there was in human society something he called the "authoritarian personality." Characterized by "conventionality," "rigidity," and "repressive denial," the authoritarian personality is easy prey in hard times for collective mobilization by the likes of Hitler and Goebbels. Adorno and his associates invested a great deal of energy in developing research instruments that would isolate the authoritarian personality and in relating it to a variety of kinds of human behavior.[6]

Somewhat later, Eric Hoffer argued that mass movements attract and are created by "true believers": individuals who are fanatically devoted to a cause for which they will sacrifice nearly everything and everyone. Like Adorno, Hoffer thought mass movements appealed to a certain type of mind. But Hoffer went further than Adorno. Hoffer said that because mass movements attract the same types of people, it follows that "all mass movements are competitive, and the gain of one in adherents is the loss of all the others." Indeed, "all mass movements are interchangeable."[7] To illustrate his case, Hoffer pointed to the many examples of people who had been fanatical Communists who later became fanatical Nazis. Hoffer argued that rather than such examples being exceptional, they are the rule. Both movements were drawing their adherents from the same pool. Later Milton Rokeach took the ideas of Adorno and Hoffer and others and tried to design research instruments that would measure both left-wing and right-wing authoritarianism.[8]

The Fourth Period

The strength and diversity of collective behavior episodes in the late 1950s and 1960s came as a shock both to the citizens of much of the Western world and to its social scientists. In the United States, there were the nonviolent civil rights movement, the antiwar movement, the ghetto riots, bombings, and mass demonstrations. Student unrest and terrorism were common in Europe and Latin America.

The fourth wave of interest in collective behavior arose in response to this diversity. Researchers

Nazism and its victims pose a special question for students of collective behavior (and for all human beings): Is there something about some cultures that creates people with a predisposition to such behavior? *Above:* "Soldiers" of the German Labor Service, each shouldering a shovel, parade before Hitler in 1937. *Below:* Slave workers shot by S.S. men at Gardelgen Concentration Camp, May 1945.

explored the backgrounds of those involved in civil rights and antiwar protests, and attempted to explain urban riots by contrasting the nature of the cities within which they did or did not occur.[9] There were even efforts to account for all rebellion in terms of some single cause.[10] But more than anything else, the research of the 1960s demonstrated that collective behavior is even more complex than it had previously appeared. There were no convincing answers to the question of how the sons and daughters of the upper middle class of a wealthy, democratic nation could have become locked in a radical duel with a liberal President. Social scientists were faint-voiced and inconsistent when pressed to explain why the urban riots occurred, why destruction was patterned rather than random, and especially why the riots stopped when they did.

The troubles of the 1960s, however horrible in themselves, did produce one sociological benefit. They turned research attention away from preoccupation with illustration and definitional elaboration to a concern with the causes and processes of collective behavior. In the remainder of this chapter, we will examine some of the main forms of collective behavior, like the crowd, the riot, and social movements, and some of the new avenues for explaining collective behavior that the recent period produced. Another day may bring another explosion of collective phenomena for which sociologists are ill-prepared, but it does seem probable now that they are at least beginning to ask the right questions.

Casual crowd.

Crowds, Panics, Mobs, and Riots

Most collective behavior involves crowds of one kind or another. The *crowd*, you will recall from Chapter 5, is a transitory, physically assembled aggregate with minimum social organization. This social organization is the interaction that occurs *as the result* of individuals being in the crowd. Some people in a crowd may have interacted with each other elsewhere, maybe at work, in church, or in school. But the patterns of behavior that have emerged in these regular associations are not activated in the crowd; instead, new ones emerge. Sociologists have identified three different types of crowds: the *casual crowd*, the *audience (conventional crowd)*, and the *acting crowd*. Casual crowds and audiences have the potential for turning into acting crowds, which are characterized by intense interaction among crowd members aimed at accomplishing a specific action.

Casual Crowds

Most of us have at one time or another stood on a street corner waiting for a bus or watching a fire.

Aggregates such as these gather for awhile and then dissolve. The object of attention usually sets the outside limits of the time spent in such collectivities. These are called **casual crowds**: transitory aggregates physically assembled by the accident of a common interest. They are characterized by very low levels of interaction and the absence of specific role expectations for crowd members. In a casual crowd, we have very little involvement either with the object of attention or with the other crowd members.

Casual crowds are interesting to sociologists because few norms operate in them to specify what would be appropriate behavior *if* the crowd members began to interact significantly. In other words, what happens when a casual crowd turns into an acting crowd? The great Watts riot of 1965, which eventually involved thousands of persons and widespread destruction, began as a simple casual crowd gathered to watch an arrest in South Los Angeles.[11] The precipitating event of the arrest was probably important only because of its relation to longstanding and bitter grievances of the blacks in the area. But even in the absence of such historical difficulties, we find casual crowds turning into acting crowds as a result of natural disasters and major accidents.

Audiences (Conventional Crowds)

The **audience**, sometimes called a conventional crowd, is an aggregate temporarily assembled to watch or hear some planned event. It is characterized by fairly low levels of interaction but relatively specific role expectations about how to behave as an audience member. The people who come to the event have planned to do so and have a fair idea of how they will behave when they get there. When we leave for a hockey game, we have very different expectations for the evening than when we leave for a piano concert. At the hockey game we will cheer and howl; the piano concert will end with a bit of polite applause. Thus, behavioral expectations are pretty well defined for a given event. But sometimes there are different expectations depending on where you are sitting during the event. At a baseball game, for example, the kids in the outfield seats are expected to be rather rowdy, but

Conventional crowd or audience.

those in the expensive box seats are supposed to be somewhat more reserved.

Audiences can be conceived as conventional crowds because in them we have a large "shoulder-to-shoulder" gathering with no clear division of labor within it, but with some conventions to guide the behavior of its members. As long as things go as they are expected to, no acting crowd emerges. But if something extraordinary occurs, such as a conflict among the performers, the audience may turn very quickly into an acting crowd.

Acting Crowds

Either a casual crowd or an audience, as we have seen, can turn into an acting crowd. Precisely defined, an **acting crowd** is a temporarily assembled aggregate characterized by emergent social organization, with members intensely interacting with each other to accomplish some common goal or specific action. We can differentiate between threatened, reactionary, and promised acting crowds. The first two are those that involve people who are threatened physically or psychologically or are reacting to the threatened loss of something that they have traditionally possessed or valued. The promised crowd, on the other hand, involves people who are attempting to gain something that they do not yet possess. These crowds react to the promise, or withdrawal of promise, of some thing or value not yet obtained.

Threatened crowds and panic The **threatened crowd** is created by a reasonably sudden shift in the environment around it. Earthquakes, fires, and bomb blasts are merely three of the many events that sometimes turn an everyday association into a threatened crowd. What usually determines how people react in such a situation is whether or not panic develops. And the nature of the association existing before the occurrence has a substantial impact on whether people panic or behave more reasonably. Panics do not occur in large theaters with few patrons. Even many people packed into a dancehall that suddenly bursts into flames may not panic and develop into an acting crowd. Resignation and cooperation are both as common as panic and flight.

In order for panic to develop four conditions appear to be necessary:

1. A feeling of entrapment. There is only one or a very limited number of escape routes.

2. Perceived threat. The people involved perceive a threat, either physical or psychological, and usually feel that there is no time to do anything about it except escape.

3. Blocking of the escape route. The escape route is blocked, inaccessible, or is overlooked.

4. Failure to communicate between front and rear. People at the rear assume that the front exit is still open and push and shove the people in front in their efforts to get to it. As a result, all are crowded together and tend to panic.[12]

At one time, it was common in analyses of panic situations to view the responses of the people involved as representing the triumph of emotion and irrationality over critical judgment and rationality. We must be careful when using such explanations, however, because the assumption of irrationality may be largely unwarranted. Generalizing from laboratory experiments, Alexander Mintz contended that in a fire "if a few uncooperative individuals block the exits by pushing, then any individual who does not push can expect that he will be burned. Pushing becomes the advantageous (or least disadvantageous) form of behavior for individuals, and disorder leading to disastrous conse-

casual crowd: a transitory aggregate physically assembled by the accident of a common interest (such as watching a fire). It is characterized by very low levels of interaction and the absence of specific role expectations for crowd members.

audience (conventional crowd): an aggregate temporarily assembled for the purpose of hearing or seeing some planned event. It is characterized by relatively low levels of interaction but specific role expectations about how to conduct oneself as a member of the audience.

acting crowd: a temporarily assembled aggregate characterized by emergent social organization, with members intensely interacting with each other to accomplish some common goal or specific action. Acting crowds may be distinguished as threatened, reactionary, or promised, depending upon whether the source of their interest and assembly is perceived as danger, threat of loss, or attempted gain.

threatened crowd: an acting crowd responding to perceived threat, usually physical, such as a fire in a theater. Associated with panic.

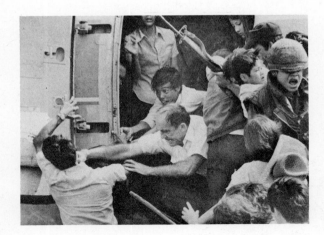

Threatened crowd. South Vietnam, April 4, 1975: An American official punches a man who is trying to climb aboard the already overcrowded evacuation plane.

quences spreads rapidly."[13] Thus, although in after-the-fact analyses we can argue that panic behavior is irrational and nonadaptive, we should understand that the choices people make in any situation are effected by the choices they and others around them have already made. Once a panic has begun, it narrows the range of potential adaptive responses to a very few. Under these conditions, panic spreads, not as the triumph of emotion and irrationality, but as one choice in a limited arena.

Reactionary crowds: Mobs and riots   Economic or historical events that have the effect of threatening people's traditional ways or social positions can sometimes produce **reactionary crowds**. Arthur Raper, for example, found an association between hard economic times and increases in lynching of blacks in the South, as whites reacted to economic threat by traditional scapegoating.[14]

Crowds such as these are sometimes termed **mobs** because of their very narrow and *violent* focus. Where there are many small mobs in action at the same time in the same area, we sometimes speak of **riots**. The period around 1920 in the United States was a time of much mob violence on a scale amounting to rioting, as people responded to the social changes of the new century and World War I. There were major riots of whites against blacks in 1917 in Chester and Philadelphia, Pennsylvania. In 1919, such riots occurred in Washington, D.C.; Omaha; Charleston; Longview, Texas; Knoxville, Tennessee; and Chicago. The report of the National Advisory Commission on Civil Disorders gave the following account of the build-up in this latter riot.

The Chicago riot of 1919 flared from the increase in Negro population, which had more than doubled in 10 years. Jobs were plentiful, but housing was not. Black neighborhoods expanded into white sections of the city and trouble developed. Between July 1917, and March 1921, 58 Negro houses were bombed and recreational areas were sites of racial conflict. The riot itself started on Sunday, July 27, with stone-throwing and sporadic fighting at adjoining white and Negro beaches. A Negro boy swimming off the Negro beach drifted into water reserved for whites and drowned. Young Negroes claimed he had been struck by stones and demanded the arrest of a white man. Instead, police arrested a Negro. Negroes attacked policemen, and news spread to the city. White

and Negro groups clashed in the streets, two persons died and 50 were wounded. On Monday, Negroes coming home from work were attacked; later, when whites drove cars through Negro neighborhoods and fired weapons, Negroes retaliated. Twenty more were killed and hundreds wounded. On Tuesday, a handful more were dead, 129 injured. Rain began to fall; the mayor finally called in the state militia. The city quieted down after nearly a week of violence.[15]

Shifts in the economic institution may also generate conditions from which reactionary crowds emerge. For instance, although the position of many textile workers was improving in industrial England at the turn of the nineteenth century, some jobs were being automated out of existence. Particularly threatened were those who finished fabrics, workers who had for years held a very lucrative place in the industry. These workers (called "Luddites" after the man they took as a model) were instrumental in precipitating a series of machinery-smashing riots designed, in part, to halt the advance of automation—in effect to return to the older practices that the Luddites had benefited from. Similar disturbances occurred in the Manchester brickworks in England from 1859 to 1870.

We even find similar occurrences in such constrained settings as prisons. In 1952, a series of prison riots swept through prisons in Michigan, New Jersey, Idaho, Illinois, Kentucky, Louisiana, Massachusetts, New Mexico, North Carolina, Utah, Ohio, California, Oregon, and Washington. Although some of these riots may have been caused by the appalling conditions within the prisons, Don Gibbons, in reviewing this period, tended to side with those who contended that many of the riots occurred in prisons where reforms had already been instituted. Many of the convicts who had enjoyed advantages under old arrangements began to stir up dissatisfaction among other convicts. After the riot had been triggered by some dramatic event, these convicts were cast in the role of radical supporters of prison reform, when in fact the riot had emerged out of their reactionary desire to return to the system under which they had ruled the convict culture.[16]

Promised crowds   Promised crowds are composed of those who are beginning to benefit from changes within a society. Early American labor unions, the great revolutions in America, France, and Russia, and many political and economic struggles going on in the developing nations today are examples of breeding grounds for crowds that are responding more to promises than threats. Most of what we know about such crowds comes not from sociologists, but from a particularly creative group of historians who in different ways attempted to reconstruct the early history of the French Revolution of 1789 from the point of view of the working classes, the small shopkeepers, craft workers, laborers, and city poor.

Their place in the French Revolution has long been a point of interest and debate among historians and sociologists. George Rudé, in particular, questioned the conventional idea that revolutionary crowds were largely composed of riffraff and went directly to the official records of the revolutionary period to piece the story together. Much like a detective, Rudé sifted what was left of these records to establish facts about arrests, pensions, deaths, and so on. He concentrated on ten major events of the revolutionary days so that he could focus on the relationship between different kinds of events and participants. Through this process, Rudé hoped to determine whether the revolutionary crowds were indeed composed of the most disreputable elements of French society or whether they were composed of people from many different walks of life.

Rudé concluded that the crowds of the revolution were, indeed, composed of many different kinds of people, and most of them were not riffraff. True, some of those arrested, killed, injured, and so on, were unemployed, but unemployment was generally very high during these years. Overall, Rudé concluded, the unemployed played a minor role in the revolution. The same was also true of the criminals of Paris. After a careful study of the number of criminals who participated in the various events of the revolution, Rudé concluded that people in the revolutionary crowds were not more given to crime than the other citizens from whom the crowds were recruited.[17] Thus, rather than the picture of irrational riffraff plundering and raping an old aristocracy, Rudé's research suggests a promised crowd emerging in response to particular problems in the political and economic sectors of the society.

Rudé's findings from a revolution occurring

reactionary crowd: an acting crowd reacting to the threat of loss of something they have traditionally possessed or valued. White parents protesting the busing of their children to other schools to promote racial integration are reacting to such a possible loss. Associated with mobs and riots.

mob: a violent reactionary crowd.

riot: a situation in which a number of mobs are simultaneously active in the same general area.

promised crowd: an acting crowd responding to the promise, or withdrawn promise, of some thing or value not yet attained. The rioting in the United States associated with the assassination of Martin Luther King is an example.

Reactionary crowd. Note the facial expressions of these people. They apparently believe they have resolved their problems.

nearly 200 years ago fit rather nicely with the general conclusions of the 1968 National Advisory Commission on Civil Disorders, which looked into rioting in America's ghettos in the late 1960s. These American riots differed from those of the French Revolution in that they involved blacks attacking the symbols of social inequality rather than a mixed crowd protesting political and economic conditions. Out of the commission's research came a portrait of the black rioter in the summer of 1967 as a person *acting in response to unfulfilled promises*. The typical rioter was male, better-educated than blacks who did not participate in the riots, and most important of all, he was either unemployed or underemployed. He felt that he deserved a better job and that he was prevented from getting it by racial discrimination.[18]

A sociological investigation of American ghetto rioting, published in the same year as the National Commission report, came to similar conclusions: The rioters constituted promised crowds reacting not solely to poverty and low social position, but to the perception of restricted opportunities to change those conditions. In accounting for the general conditions that led to the riots, this researcher, James Hundley, Jr., summarized the precipitating factors as follows:

1) the perception of a crisis in achieving aspirations, 2) the perception that legitimate channels for bringing about changes are blocked, 3) hope on the part of ghettoites that rioting will bring about change, 4) the possibilities that large numbers of people can interact under conditions of reduced social control, and 5) the breakdown of accepted social control mechanisms.[19]

Theories of Collective Behavior

Out of all the historical cases of collective behavior, there have emerged two theories that attempt to account for much of it. These are the explanations of James C. Davies and Neil J. Smelser. These two theories are not really alternatives, but represent different approaches to this complicated field.

Social Needs and Collective Behavior: The Theory of James C. Davies

Davies wanted to explain political turmoil of a rebellious or revolutionary kind.[20] In particular, he

hoped to resolve what he perceived as a difference between the writing of Alexis de Tocqueville, on the one hand, and Karl Marx, on the other. De Tocqueville, in analyzing the French Revolution, had argued that the revolution occurred when the economic position of most Frenchmen was improving. As their position improved, the hunger for change grew into an appetite. In contrast, Marx generally argued that revolutions occur as a result of the growth of class consciousness. Class consciousness would increase most rapidly during times of economic hardship, because it would be during such times that the people would become acutely aware of their shared destiny. From class consciousness would come class action, and from class action would emerge revolution. So, Davies asked, does collective behavior resulting from political instability occur as the position of people improves, or as it worsens?

His answer was a unique synthesis that today stands as an important contribution to the explanation of rebellious and revolutionary collective action. It is shown in Figure 18-1. Davies argues that collective outbursts come when a period of economic prosperity or social development is followed by a sudden reversal. This creates an "intolerable gap" between what people have come to expect and what they then actually receive. Some of the most obvious examples have to do with changes in the economy, but the dimension involved need not be economic. In the case of black Americans in the 1960s, expectations for radical change in social status created by World War II and the civil rights movement were not being met with adequate speed, thus creating the "intolerable gap."

Davies then goes on to illustrate the occurrence of such gaps and the collective outbursts that followed them in such diverse happenings as the Russian Revolution, the Egyptian Revolution of 1952, and Dorr's Rebellion of 1842, an armed insurrection against the government of the state of Rhode Island that had the object of instituting universal male suffrage. Other writers have subsequently argued that such feelings of not receiving what is expected are the inevitable consequence of government policies that promise a great deal more change and improvement than they can, in fact, deliver. This pattern of overoptimistic promises has been referred to as the "revolution of rising

Figure 18-1
Need satisfaction and revolution

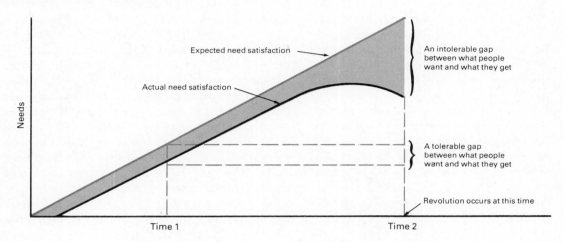

expectations" and is seen by some as a source of worldwide instability.[21]

There are two difficulties with Davies's highly suggestive model. One is the existence of contrary historical examples, most notably the Great Depression of the 1930s in the United States. The other is the lack of elaboration of the "processes" involved in mobilizing people as a consequence of the intolerable gap. The first of these problems is perhaps the easiest to comprehend. Why did not a rebellion or revolution occur in 1929 or 1930 in the United States? Perhaps rebellion was prevented by Franklin Roosevelt's social programs, which, some have argued, led people to feel as if all that could be done was being done. Or perhaps the American people are less inclined to collective radicalism than are some other peoples. Whatever the answer, the fact that rebellion did not occur has serious implications for Davies's theory.

The second criticism is more difficult to deal with. If we assume that the growth of an intolerable gap does cause collective outbursts, *how* does it cause them? Do people rationally perceive their interests and, seeing them threatened, react and mobilize to protect them? If so, is there a difference between the mobilizers and those mobilized? Do some people see the difficulty earlier than others? Does the nature of the gap (size, duration, extent of

At some point in time (time 1) needs and their satisfaction are sufficiently related that people are not distressed; whether times are good or bad, they get most of what they expect. But if good times continue, expectations continue to rise. So long as they can also continue to be satisfied, all goes well. If the economic or social situation deteriorates, however (depression or severe inflation, for example), expectations will not be adjusted accordingly, and an emotionally intolerable gap may appear between what people have come to expect and what they actually receive (time 2). This is a potentially revolutionary situation.

the population affected, and so on) effect the nature of the outburst? All of these questions need attention and are potentially the subject of considerable research effort into historical as well as contemporary episodes of collective action.

"Value-Addition" and Collective Behavior: The Theory of Neil J. Smelser

Neil Smelser's theory of collective behavior is considerably more ambitious than Davies's, both in its formulation and in the extent of the behavior it is designed to explain. Smelser recognized the value of earlier theories of collective behavior, but thought that they had tended to define it by essentially incidental characteristics, such as size of the group, violence of the event, and so on. Smelser defined collective behavior more broadly, as "mobilization on the basis of a belief which redefines social action."[22] As this definition suggests, Smelser is concerned with the *processes* of collective behavior, how people who are involved in normal, everyday activities become involved or mobilized by beliefs that then redefine social action.

Smelser argued that there are determinants of collective behavior that can be laid out abstractly in such a way that they build on one another. He terms this a *value-added scheme*, by which he means that each of the things that go into causing a particular episode of collective behavior further define and limit what kind of behavior it will be. Smelser outlined six parts to his value-added scheme.

Structural conduciveness   First, and underlying all collective behavior episodes, is what Smelser calls *structural conduciveness*, the way the social situation is organized. In assessing whether a financial panic might occur in a society, for example, it makes a difference whether or not bank accounts are guaranteed by the government. We would hypothesize that if they were guaranteed, panics would be less likely than if they were not.

Structural strain   The second determinant of collective behavior episodes is *structural strain*. The structure of a social situation may or may not be conducive to panic, for example, but clearly panic will not occur until a strain or tension is introduced in the situation. Do people feel that the banks have become insolvent? Do they fear the future? Such feelings and fears create strain. It is the addition of strain to structural conduciveness that makes for panic.

Growth of a generalized belief   The third part of the value-added scheme is the *growth and spread of a generalized belief*, for example, the belief that bankers are conspiring against depositors. When a generalized belief develops and is coupled with conduciveness and strain, then possible social action takes on a focus or target that goes beyond simple panic responses. When this occurs, we may find the development of religious sects, reform

movements, or revolutionary movements. Thus, generalized beliefs serve as the mechanism for organizing action in particular directions that are much more complex than panic.

The precipitating factor   The fourth condition is the *precipitating factor*. Smelser argued that the combination of conduciveness, strain, and a generalized belief does not by itself produce a specific episode of collective behavior. For this to occur, there must be a dramatic event that precipitates the episode. A rumor may spread, for example, that a banker has been seen loading his car with money, setting off a hostile outburst. This event would give the generalized belief that bankers are conspiring against depositors concrete, immediate substance. Notice that what makes the precipitating event important is that it occurs within the context of conduciveness, strain, and generalized beliefs. A private car being loaded with packages at a bank is only important to collective behavior when the loading occurs after the other conditions have evolved.

Mobilization for action   Following the precipitating event, there is the fifth condition, the *mobilization of the participants for action*, for example, a spontaneous protest meeting outside the bank by worried depositors. It is here, Smelser argued, that we see the importance of leaders in shaping social action. It seems somewhat unlikely, for instance, that a group of bank depositors would spontaneously decide to break into the bank, or set it on fire, unless someone urgently suggested to them that they should do so.

Type of social control   The sixth and final condition is whether the *type of social control* present in the situation is supportive or repressive. Have the authorities acted to alter structures conducive to strain? How do they react in the face of the hostile outburst? Do they jail protesters or try to accommodate them?

Smelser thinks that these six conditions build up to determine the type of collective episode likely to appear; the more conditions, the more complex the behavior. Structural conduciveness and strain alone may give rise to panic, but not to social movements. For the latter there must be generalized beliefs and precipitating events. In short, each condition increasingly narrows the range of likely outcomes.

Validating Theories of Collective Behavior

The problems of demonstrating the truth or falsity of theories such as Smelser's and Davies's are enormous. We can see immediately how difficult it would be to assess empirically "an intolerable gap" between expectations and reality. What is intolerable? To whom? Under what conditions is public patience likely to be short? Why is it that some expectations may be thwarted for a long time without reaction, while others seem to demand immediate satisfaction?

Likewise, it is very difficult to assess structural conduciveness independently of the strain that it produces. How can we say that something is conducive to strain if no strain has appeared? And how can we be sure that a given event or phenomenon is, in fact, a strain?

Even such an apparently easy task as assessing the consequences of efforts to control collective behavior is fraught with difficulties. Both political liberals and conservatives were quick to propose what they felt were obvious solutions to the problem of urban riots in the late 1960s, but after a careful examination, the National Advisory Commission on Civil Disorders was forced to conclude that it could not clearly discern what the results of various tactics of social control were. The areas of rioting differed greatly from one another. Watts, for example, is an area of low buildings that stretch out for miles, with commercial and residential areas somewhat separated from each other. Harlem, by contrast, is a compressed area of reasonably tall buildings where apartments often sit over commercial establishments. Facts such as these have an unknown effect on rioters as well as the police.

The simultaneous existence of many different control tactics further complicated efforts to assess the usefulness of various kinds of control. Moderate civil rights leaders were appealing for order. Police and military personnel were searching for military solutions. In between were politicians engaging in a variety of tactics, ranging from making conciliatory gestures to issuing "shoot-to-kill" orders. In the dawn of the morning after, it was

Food line during the Great Depression. One objection to Davies's theory is that situations which seem to fit his model do not necessarily produce revolutionary outbursts.

How do authorities react to collective outbursts? Kent State, 1970.

exceedingly difficult to sort out the specific impact of the varying strategies.

Despite such difficulties, Davies's and Smelser's theories are not impossible to work with. More specific propositions can be derived from these more general statements in such a way that they can be researched. And certain aspects of the two theories might be combined to generate new propositions for research. For example, we might hypothesize that certain kinds of generalized beliefs emerge within groups that have recently been financially well-to-do, but that are now faced with loss of their economic position. Perhaps the generalized beliefs produced under such a condition encourage right-wing social movements rather than left-wing ones, as some political thinkers have argued, seeing a relationship between collective behavior and social-political action.[23]

Construction workers attack antiwar demonstrators in 1970.

Collective Behavior and Social-Political Action

It should be clear now that sociologists who study collective behavior have generally been interested in explaining its causes and in describing the actions of the people involved in collective situations. But there is another way to approach the subject distinct from those discussed so far. We might ask: What is the role of collective behavior in the course of history? What part has "the crowd" played in history? In social change? In industrial as opposed to preindustrial societies? In free as opposed to totalitarian societies? This view sees collectivities as active agents in the drama of history. In the 1870s in Russia, for example, there was the famous "Going to the People" movement, in which large numbers of revolutionary youth went into the countryside to try to radicalize the peasantry. In the United States, the Students for a Democratic Society (SDS) engaged in similar activities when they tried to organize ghetto inhabitants for social and political change.

But it is not only those who want change that engage in collective behavior. Many people and organizations, including governments, attempt to use collective action to retard or stop change. Louis XIV encouraged crowd action against the Huguenots, a religious minority whose persecution he

found useful, and the Un-American Activities Committee of the U.S. House of Representatives actively aided radical right groups such as the John Birch Society.[24] During the antiwar activities in the United States in the late 1960s, construction workers attacked demonstrators in New York City; shortly thereafter, President Nixon made a clear bid for such support by inviting the heads of the construction unions to a White House breakfast.

This approach to collective behavior alters the concern from why the people involved in the groups do what they do to *what and how* they do the things they do. We might well compare, for example, the parts played by the crowds in the French and Russian revolutions. From this point of view, then, collectivities are seen as a *social resource* capable of manipulating and being manipulated by others. In this regard, collective behavior is a form of pressure for social and political action.

The People and the Public

All collective behavior takes place within a cultural and social milieu. We often say that certain actions by groups have an impact on the people, or the public. Politicians, philosophers, and social commentators have all tried to define the proper role of the ruled—the public—in relation to the rulers. This very general conception of the public differs, however, from the sense in which sociologists use the term. As you may recall from Chapter 5, *the public*, in its sociological meaning, refers only to a category of people sharing a common concern for some aspect of social life. It differs from the crowd in that its members are not ordinarily physically assembled. Thus, the public as the term is often popularly used, is actually composed of many publics from the sociological perspective.

Publics, Public Opinion, and Social Control

Michael Lipsky has argued that publics (in the sociological sense) play an important part in social control in modern societies.[25] Publics, in his terms *reference publics*, are viewed as a political resource. Ordinarily, reference publics support the leaders within a community or nation. Many members of such publics are also members of formally organized interest groups that try to influence directly the decisions made by authorities. For example, in a city there usually will be a public interested in public health care. Many of the individuals in this public may also be members of a public health association that is trying to influence the passage of a legislative bill relevant to public health. And although their bill may not succeed, some acceptable compromise bill is likely to be passed. But even if the legislation is quite different from what they wanted, they are likely to continue supporting *the way* the system of decision making works, because it did provide them with a way of conveying their views to the authorities. We can think, then, of a community as composed of many publics, most of which normally support the values and procedures of the system.

In any community, however, there are people who are left out of this process. These people are the relatively powerless members of the community. How, then, do the powerless attempt to affect decision making when they desire to do so? One very common technique, Lipsky argues, is protest activity. The powerless might gather for a demonstration concerning *their* health care needs. The popular view of such protests sees the powerless locked in a struggle with the protest target, for example, the public hospital, but Lipsky contends that the process is in fact more complicated.

Figure 18-2 is his diagram of the process, which is actually a rather indirect one. In general, protes-

tors do not communicate directly with the protest target. Instead, they communicate through the mass media. Various media cover and explain the meaning of the protest and through their accounting of the events and issues develop a public in the community with an interest in the protest. This public then interacts with the protest target. It is in this sense that reference publics are a political resource. Protest targets may ignore powerless protestors, but they may well respond to pressure from a reference public in order to relieve the pressure and maintain the public's support.

The press and the powerless   The arrow in Figure 18-2 between the powerless and the press runs in both directions, indicating that the press has access to the powerless and that the powerless usually attempt to manipulate the press to their own ends. Indeed, one of the indicators of a group's social power is its ability to control the access of the press to it. Powerful groups tend to deal with the press through people who are hired for their skill at presenting the desired "image." The powerless, by contrast, must submit to the kind of treatment and amount of access the press wishes to extend to them. Leaders of a powerless group who offer mild solutions for serious grievances may find that the press ignores them, preferring the more colorful and radical solutions suggested by fringe members of the group. Indeed, such groups are often pulled toward more radical positions as the press and the public come to identify them with bizarre solutions. As we shall see, powerful groups in a society often attempt to encourage such activity on the part of the press in an effort to discredit protest groups by making their demands appear irresponsible.

One of the early signs of the growth of power on the part of the powerless is their accumulation of sufficient money to operate their own press or to buy coverage in the national media. To do this well, they also have to develop enough influence over their own membership to control the content of statements made to the press. When the leadership of a heretofore powerless group can afford to place advertising for their organization and its goals in newspapers across the land, they are better able to control the image of the group in the minds of the population. This control, in turn, gives them greater

Figure 18-2
The process of protest by relatively powerless groups

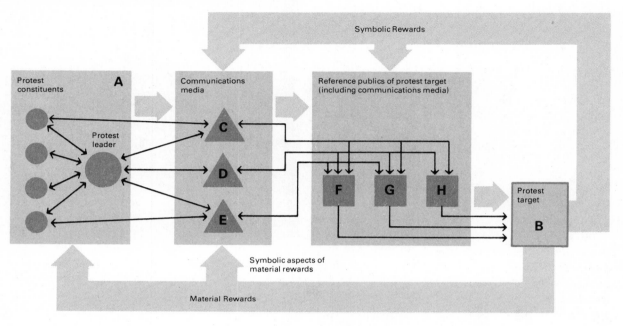

In Lipsky's scheme of protest by the powerless, protesters (A) develop leadership, often spontaneously. The leaders have or make contact with media representatives (C, D, E), reporters, photographers, and TV commentators, who can make the protesters' grievances public. The media representatives, through private contacts and through the media, carry the grievances to the reference publics (F, G, H)—city officials, federal officers, state legislators, agency officials, and so forth. The reference publics then bring pressure to bear on the protest target (B), the person or group thought responsible for the grievance situation. This person or group may then respond to the protest materially—by remedying or improving the situation for the protesters—and this action will provide symbolic rewards for the media agents and the reference publics.

control over both the target and their own group membership.

Strategies for dealing with the powerless   In the beginning stages of the organization of powerless groups, most of the resources lie in the hands of the powerful, who are often their opposition as well. There are six different strategies that protest targets can use to attain their ends.

First, target groups can *deal with the situation on a symbolic level*. Tours can be offered of a blighted area. Comprehensive programs with target dates can be drafted. Research panels can be appointed. All of these give the appearance of action that the protest target hopes will be reported to the reference public through the media.

Second, sometimes the protest target will also choose *to make a token material response*. For example, if the issue is poor housing, then the target group may search for a dramatic case of poor housing and act to remedy it. As Lipsky points out, actions like these may hold some genuine benefits for the protestors. Heretofore "impossi-

ble" technical and bureaucratic barriers may fall overnight as the authorities move for a "good" press at the earliest possible moment.

Third, target groups may also *reorganize their efforts in a way that will blunt the impact of protests*. They may, for instance, decide to organize on a "worst-case" basis to try to solve systematically the most glaring examples of neglect. This effort goes beyond token material responses in that programs such as these do demand reallocation of resources, sometimes on a massive scale. Beyond such quasi-solutions lie more evasive tactics.

Fourth, the protest target may argue, with some truth on occasion, that it *does not have the authority or the resources to solve the problems involved.* The authorities may even admit that the problems are genuine, but still contend that the responsibility for solving them lies elsewhere.

Fifth is the strategy of *postponement.* Protestors, who are quite often novices at politics, do not ordinarily have a great deal of staying power. The target may give verbal assurances that something will be done, or perhaps impanel a prestigious study group. With time, the target group hopes, the problem, or at least the protestors, will simply go away.

The sixth, though not necessarily the last, strategy is *vilification.* The protest target attempts to discredit the protestors in the eyes of the reference publics. Protestors are presented as troublemakers, weirdos, or outside agitators. This strategy is usually coupled with a stern denial of the existence of the problem except as a fiction manufactured by villains trying to stir up trouble. The protest target may attempt to alter press coverage of the events to reflect its own perception of these "deviants." If this technique is successful, the reference publics will be convinced by the press accounts of the situation and stop pressuring the target groups.

Alliance between powerless groups To get around these kinds of responses, the protest group must move to the next level of development: forming alliances with other groups. This is, of course, very difficult to do, because most protest groups are isolated in time and space. Sometimes, however, the reference publics and the protest targets actually aid the formation of alliances. Especially in cases where the protest target adopts the vilification strategy, there is a tendency for the various protest groups to be presented to the reference publics as if they were part of one large conspiracy. This was commonly the case in the American civil rights movement in the late 1950s and early 1960s. Small protest groups scattered all over the South were presented to the press as a monolithic force. The presentation itself helped these protestors to develop a sense of common

Draft card burning: The use of mass media by protest groups.

identity. The same process also worked in the 1870s and 1880s in Russia. In the great trials that followed the "Going to the People" movement, the government argued that the movement was a product of the Socialist Revolutionary party.[26] At the time no such party existed. But once the government had officially "created" it, it did, in fact, come into being.

Direct action by reference publics Up to this point, we have spoken of the role of reference publics in a rather narrow way. Although reference publics rarely go beyond pressuring authorities for "solutions" to problems creating protest, they do occasionally act more directly. They are especially likely to do so if the subject of protest touches one of the normative contradictions in the society, one of the conflicts between aspects of the belief system. The civil rights movement, from the very beginning, always rubbed a raw spot in the American way of life. Most Americans held freedom and equality as virtues. Most Americans also discriminated against blacks. The movement would not let that contradiction persist. As a consequence, it was able to draw resources from the same publics that support the fundamentals of the status quo. These resources permitted the movement to form its own media, to wage protracted civil rights campaigns, and to forge alliances.

Publics and Politics in Modern Society

An issue of continuing debate in sociology is the relationship between publics and the kind of politics that develop within a nation. Some argue that a society characterized by a large number of publics and competing interest groups is more likely to be stable than is one with only a few publics and interest groups.[27] The reasons for the alleged stability of such a system are twofold. First, where there are a large number of competing groups, there are also likely to be many cross-cutting affiliations and loyalties. A Catholic woman, for example, might be a political liberal on many issues, but discover that she parts company with many of her friends on the issues of birth control and abortion. The same person will probably find that many of her allies on birth control and abortion issues take conservative positions on many of the matters

FBI Documents Bare Operation to Harass K.K.K.

WASHINGTON [AP]—The Federal Bureau of Investigation drew and distributed derogatory cartoons, mailed anonymous postcards, and created a dummy citizens' committee in efforts to harass and disrupt the Ku Klux Klan, according to FBI documents disclosed Friday.

FBI agents engaged in a similar harassment campaign against the National States Rights Party and said they caused one Alabama party member to lose his job.

The late J. Edgar Hoover, FBI director at the time of the 10-year counterintelligence program against "white hate groups," said in 1965 that the FBI had informers in all 14 Klan organizations said to be in existence then. He said disruptive tactics were necessary to curb racial violence by the Klan and other anti-black groups such as the States Rights Party.

These disclosures emerged from 125 pages of FBI files on the so-called Cointelpro against white hate groups from Sept. 2, 1961, thru April 28, 1971.

The FBI turned over the documents to a group of reporters who first petitioned for them nine months ago under the Freedom of Information Act.

The documents, censored to delete many names and some other material, provide the first public glimpse of Cointelpro activities against white hate groups. The FBI previously has been forced to disclose documents dealing with Cointelpro operations against the Socialist Workers Party and other Leftist political groups.

The Klan papers show that the FBI in 1966 set its laboratory division to work drawing three cartoons "in an amateurish fashion, suitable for mailing as four-cent postal cards" to known Klan members.

"These cards would be mailed openly to residences and places of business in order to cause embarrassment and dissension in the home," the FBI memo said, adding that 6,000 copies of each of the three drawings had been prepared for distribution. . . .

Chicago Tribune, August 16, 1975. Reprinted by permission of AP Newsfeatures.

An example of the vilification technique.

about which she holds liberal views. Situations such as these are said to increase the likelihood of tolerance of opinions that differ from our own. When enemies are sometimes allies and vice versa, it is difficult for people to conclude that their enemies are "crazy" people undeserving of any respect or tolerance.

The second reason is that large numbers of

publics and interest groups tend to integrate many persons into the decision-making process. This gives them a stake in the system and in observing the rules of the political game. While they may lose today, they may prevail tomorrow.

There can be little quarrel with the *logic* of this position. But arguments begin when it is applied to specific empirical cases. Most of those who hold this theoretical position also argue that American society is one in which decisions are made by the relatively free play of influence between many publics and interest groups. The people who influence a decision will be primarily determined by the nature of the issues involved. One group may be especially interested in the issue of school funding, another in nominating candidates for the U.S. Senate, and so on. There is no elite group of controllers deciding all the major questions.

This perspective is challenged, however, from two directions. One group of critics argues that modern industrial nations are becoming mass societies characterized by increasing homogenization and the leveling of differences between individuals and groups. These critics fear the gray, dull, sterile culture that will develop in such a world, a view that leads them to defend "privilege" as a way of encouraging diversity.[28]

The second group of critics takes the stand of C. Wright Mills in *The Power Elite*. They argue that processes of monopolization of wealth and power in modern society are leading to a mass society characterized, not so much by cultural flatness, as by the pervasive spread of powerlessness. Rather than modern societies being composed of many different small power groups distributed throughout, they are made up of an increasingly small number of elite groups and the masses below them. These writers are led to a defense of the masses, who, they fear, face increasing tyranny from elite groups.[29]

In this debate, there are two central questions: (1) Is massification occurring in modern societies? (2) What is the nature of decision making in modern societies? (We touched on this in Chapter 8.) To date, despite much research, both of these questions remain essentially open. Nobody has been able to answer them with finality. Several researchers have, however, suggested that the idea of a mass society may be more fiction than fact.[30] When

> **general social movement:** a large-scale, long-term shift in cultural values or practices, such as the suffrage movement or the unionization of labor.

we examine attitudes and behavior patterns across categories of people and over time, we do not find the convergence that the concept of mass society suggests we should. Of course, this information does not bear on the question of the nature of power in modern society. Massification as a cultural process may not be working, even though centralization of power resources is occurring. The data on this problem are even more difficult to interpret and more flawed than those on cultural massification.

Those who make the centralization of power argument usually study the concentration of power in certain individuals, such as the overlapping among heads of corporations, trusts, and so on. Certainly, the results from such studies allow us to conclude that a power elite *could* exist. The *potential* is there, but the actual *evidence* of elitist *behavior* is lacking. Without that evidence, anyone suggesting that we know that such people are conspiring together for their advantage as opposed to that of the general population is confusing belief with fact.[31] However, the whole crisis known as Watergate has allowed us to see many aspects of official decision making that were previously barred from public view. It may be that systematic analysis of this newly available information would lead us to a more sophisticated view of the nature of national decision makers and decision making.

Social Movements

We turn now to that special form of collective behavior called social movements. There are two basic types of social movements, first differentiated by Herbert Blumer in the late 1930s.[32] **General social movements** are large-scale, long-term shifts in the culture of a society. An example would be the suffrage movement, which has been going on in the Western world for over three centuries. Many different groups of people have pressed over the years for inclusion within the decision-making process. Barrier after barrier to full suffrage rights for all has been constructed only to be knocked over by those left disenfranchised. Inside of this process of historical change we find many different specific social movements. A **specific social movement** is a collectivity (usually an organization) acting with some continuity in time and direction to promote or resist a change in the society or group of which it is a part.[33] The American Revolution of 1776 was part of a large general social movement that had been advocated by many specific social movement organizations, such as the Sons of Liberty, the John Wilkes Club, and the Palmetto Society, to name only a few.

In discussing social movements, we will consider how they are perceived by the society in which they operate, the role ideology plays in them, and certain developments in their life-cycle.

The Images of Social Movements

We can think of different specific social movements as having an image within a society at any given time. A movement may, for example, be perceived as *revolutionary* because it is immediately threatening to the society. Or a movement may be viewed as simply *peculiar*, in that its members are considered deviant, but nonthreatening. Other movements may be considered *respectable-factional*: the behavior of their members is within the range of acceptability, but they are thought to be rather misguided. Finally, there are *respectable-nonfactional* organizations, which operate by consensus and meet with no organized opposition to their objectives.[34]

But movements need not remain frozen into a given category. Social movements change and in doing so may alter the way they are perceived. Likewise, the social context may change, so that a movement that appeared to be revolutionary suddenly is defined as only peculiar. This latter process seems to have occurred to a number of old-left organizations in the United States. The International Workers of the World (Wobblies), once a center of controversy, now rests in a graveyard of forgotten and peculiar organizations. Some of the anti-Communist organizations that were respectable-

Women's suffrage meeting, 1914. General social movements are large-scale, long-term cultural shifts. This protest is only part of the general suffrage movement.

factional in the 1950s have become peculiar in the 1970s. Few people take the Birchers seriously anymore, and the Christian Anti-Communist Crusade has foundered on the sexual misbehavior of its founder.

The Role of Ideology in Social Movements

As we noted earlier, the sociological study of social movements has often been subsumed under the study of collective behavior. This happened in part because social movements are often movements for social change that arise out of collective behavior relating to protest and grievance. This grouping of the two together as one subject matter is not always completely logical today, however, because modern social movements are numerous and do not always emerge out of collective behavior processes. Some, to the contrary, *create* collective episodes (riots or protest demonstrations, for example) as a part of the ongoing life of the movement itself. The mass rallies of American anti-Communist groups and the Civil Rights March on Washington are examples. The primary difference between modern social movements and many of the earlier variety is the role of ideology in the modern social movement.

An ideology may be defined as the justifying

body of doctrine, myth, symbols, and values associated with a social movement or an organization. Some of the earliest of social movements were little more than social banditry and had no ideology to speak of. Bandit gangs, such as that celebrated in the Robin Hood myth, may have found it advantageous to maintain good relations with the communities within which they operated; and to steal from the rich and give to the poor, as the Merry Men are alleged to have done, would have been tactically wise as well as religiously virtuous. But to the extent that this practice was accompanied by any ideology at all, that ideology was entirely negative, stressing hatred for the rich without offering positive conceptions of how a different social order might be created.

In the West, truly ideological social movements did not emerge on a large scale until the 1700s. One of the fascinating aspects of both the American and French revolutions was their early years, when crowds of people struggled explicitly to create social movements for change. The mechanics and artisans of Charleston, like the French revolutionaries, had to build their movements from the ground up. Later revolutions, like that in Russia in 1917, would profit from the fact that Lenin and Trotsky had learned a great deal about organizing from the study of these earlier struggles. Later still, Mao Tse-tung would apply in China part of what he had learned from Lenin and others, adding texts he had to develop himself (such as that on guerrilla warfare) as he went along.

But unlike early social movements and social movement organizations, the modern movement is under constant scrutiny, both by itself and others. Organizations are routinely watched and assessed by the media and by their own members for ideological purity and the logic of their actions. One of the great radical groups of the 1960s, the Students for a Democratic Society, really had two existences. There was the organization as it presented itself to the world, and there was the organization in actuality. As Roland Warren pointed out, today's social movement exists within a "field" of complicated, interdependent relations with many other organizations and people. Awareness of this fact forces organizations constantly to justify their strategies and goals, so that ideology becomes of primary importance. This need for ideological justification

specific social movement: a collectivity (usually an organization or organizations) acting with some continuity in time and direction to promote or resist change in the society or group of which it is a part. The women's liberation and the civil rights movements are current examples.

Ideology assumes great importance in social movements. *Above:* French Revolution banner shows the people's ideology—patrie, égalité, liberté. *Below:* Sit-in at Tennessee lunch counter—a peaceful effort to bring about social change.

tends to prevent rapid response to new situations that develop unexpectedly. And even when spontaneous action does take place, organization members must worry about its ideological implications afterward.[35]

A fully developed ideology must accomplish three important tasks. First, it must explain why things are as they are in the society. Marxism, for example, explains reality in terms of an inevitable historical conflict between the owners of the means of production and the working class.

Second, the ideology must demand a behavior to effect change. Among the French revolutionaries, "fraternity" was part of an ideology—Liberté, Égalité, Fraternité—but it was also a strategy. When the members of one sectional assembly learned that a key vote was to be taken in another where the reactionaries might win, they would go to the meeting and "fraternize" with their brothers to make sure that the vote would go in the proper radical direction.

Third, a fully developed ideology must justify the actions of the participants within the social movement. A large portion of the American Declaration of Independence is taken up with the justification of radical remedies. Likewise, whole sections of the Port Huron Statement, the primary ideological document of the Students for a Democratic Society, were devoted to justifying the need for new and radical solutions to social ills.

The Life-Cycle of Social Movements

During their life-cycle, social movements undergo some of the same processes we have studied in other organizations, particularly centralization and formalization. And in some cases in the United States at least, social movements tend to become "domesticated," submerged in the popular culture.

Formalization, centralization, and conservatism
Many writers who have studied organizations in general and social movement organizations in particular have pointed out their tendency toward increasing centralization and formalization, as we noted in Chapter 6. We see a change in the kind of leaders that are prominent in the organization and a change in organizational structure. In the early phases, there are leaders who hold authority as a result of their own personal style and its appeal, what Weber called charismatic authority. As the organization matures, there is a "routinization" of charisma as new leaders emerge who hold authority as a result of their position or their technical competence at leadership tasks. Bureaucratization is likely to occur with the appearance of task leaders as opposed to charismatic leaders. The evolution of American labor unions is often used to illustrate these points.

Power becomes more and more centralized as it is increasingly exercised by a very few top leaders. This process leads the organization to become increasingly conservative as the leaders develop vested interests in maintaining power. More and more often, the leaders find themselves in the company of government leaders rather than the rank and file of their organization.

Mayer Zald and Roberta Ash, surveying the literature on these matters, have argued that the conservatizing process is only one of many that may occur as social movement organizations progress and decline. What happens to a movement depends in part on what it set out to do and the methods it used. For example, some movements have open membership policies; nearly anyone can be a member. Other movements have rigid standards specifying who may or may not join. In the first case, we would expect that some members would be highly committed to the organization and its goals, while others would be only marginally involved. This would seem to be a pattern conducive to the development of both bureaucratization and a centralized leadership group within the movement, because the many might willingly abdicate to the few. Where there was greater screening of potential members, however, we might expect everyone in the organization to possess a higher level of commitment and desire for involvement. This fact alone might narrow the range of power between leaders and followers, or at least help prevent the distance from growing larger than when the organization was created.

Finally, from a societal point of view, the conservatizing and formalizing process of centralization may actually have radical consequences. Zald and Ash hypothesize that centralization may itself create factions on the margins that break away to form new social movement organizations (as the Weath-

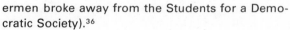

Charismatic leaders: Lenin proclaiming the Soviet Republic, Chavez leading a boycott of nonunion farm products.

ermen broke away from the Students for a Democratic Society).[36]

Domestication One current development in the United States, at least, affects the life-cycle of some social movements: domestication, absorption into the popular culture. This stems from the consequences of what might be called the commercialization of change. Surveying the prospects of the newly born left wing of American politics in the 1960s, Jack Newfield wrote:

To be a radical in America today is like trying to punch your way out of a cage made of marshmallow. Every thrust at the jugular draws not blood, but sweet success; every hack at the roots draws not retaliation, but fame and affluence. The culture's insatiable thirst for novelty and titillation insured LeRoi Jones television interviews, Norman Mailer million-dollar royalties, and Paul Goodman fat paychecks as a government consultant. Yesterday's underground becomes today's vaudeville and tomorrow's cliche.[37]

There is some overstatement here. Harsh repression met many radicals. A number of Black Panther leaders have been killed or driven into exile. Thousands of America's draft resisters remain exiled in Canada. Many SDS stalwarts are in jail or in hiding. But nevertheless, it *is* difficult to sustain a serious critique of a society where utility companies take up the slogan "Power to the People" and a major auto manufacturer urges citizens to join the "rebellion" by buying its kind of car.

In trying to understand why some of the left-wing Students for a Democratic Society turned to terror in the late 1960s and early 1970s, we might ask: how else is a radical to be taken seriously in such circumstances? While many would quarrel with the effectiveness and morality of the SDS's "propaganda of the deed," there is no question that such deeds, especially the violent ones, are taken seriously. It is one thing to see one's efforts within a social movement fail in the face of a strong opposition. It may be quite another to see the movement "disappear" into pop culture.

It is too early yet to tell whether domestication will become a standard fate for many radical social movements in the modern world. That it has occurred for several in the United States in recent years seems inarguable (the hippie phenomenon is another example). Obsolescence (as with the Birch Society) and even success still claim many social movements, of course. But it is possible that cultural processes may succeed in isolating, or submerging, protest when all of the tactics of protest targets fail. We noted earlier that time may change the perception of some social movements; yesterday's radicalism is often today's self-evident truth. But whether any social movement can survive cooptation as media "camp" remains to be seen.

Summary

Collective behavior is group action occurring without clear-cut direction from culture. It is unplanned; its consequences are unforeseen; and participants behave without much guidance from the normal social organization of roles and expectations. It is largely spontaneous, although it is possible for those knowledgeable about crowd behavior, for example, to encourage and direct it to some degree. The principal forms of collective behavior we discussed are (1) *crowds* and (2) *social movements*, a special form of collective behavior that tends to be more highly organized, change-oriented, and long-lived than crowds.

Scientific interest in collective behavior has centered on and been stimulated by four historical epochs: (1) the French Revolution and the European revolutions of the 1840s; (2) the many social changes in the United States in the 1920s and 1930s, particularly urbanization; (3) the rise of Nazism; and (4), most recently, the civil rights and anti–Vietnam War protests in the United States.

Most collective behavior is associated with crowds. Several different kinds of crowds can be distinguished. The *casual crowd* is an accidental gathering with minimum social organization and little temporal duration, such as a collection of people waiting for a bus. *Audiences*, or *conventional crowds*, are not spontaneously formed assemblies and have more social organization than casual gatherings because audience members share cultural expectations about how to behave. *Acting crowds* come in three varieties: the *threatened crowd*, associated with panic in response to danger, usually physical danger; the *reactionary crowd*, associated with mobs and rioting and formed in response to a perceived threat to a possessed value; and the *promised crowd*, which may also be riotous, formed in response to a perceived threat to some value or thing expected or promised but not as yet possessed.

Two sociologists have attempted to formulate theories of collective behavior. James C. Davies sees rebellions and revolutions occurring when a period of good social or economic times is followed by a period of reversal. This creates what he calls an "intolerable gap" between what people have come to expect and what they receive, and people may respond to the gap by attempting to radically alter the social order.

Neil J. Smelser's theory is more ambitious in that it addresses all collective behavior, not just revolutionary and rebellious behavior. Smelser's theory sees six conditions underlying any collective behavior episode. First is *structural conduciveness*; the structure of the social situation must facilitate collective behavior responses or they will not occur. Second is *structural strain*; regardless of the structure of a situation, panics or riots will not occur if no social strain is present. The third condition is the *growth and spread of a generalized belief*; without an organizing belief, people won't respond in a similar way. Fourth is a *precipitating factor*, such as an arrest. Fifth, *participants must be mobilized for action*, brought together under some kind of leadership, whether spontaneous or preexisting. The sixth condition is the *presence and nature of social control devices and agents*. Whether a crowd turns into a riotous mob may well depend on the nature and presence of police power, for example.

A rather different approach to episodes of collective behavior is to place them in their historical context and view them as manifestations of social-political action. In this view, collectivities, from crowds to organizations, are seen as resources for political action, either to be manipulated or to manipulate others. This view makes the concept of the *public*, or the reference public, as one writer calls it, central. Both protest groups and protest targets, for example, conceive the public as the ultimate authority and refer their activities to them, often using the press as an intermediary. Since the public normally supports the social organization of the community or nation, this strategy keeps most collective behavior "in bounds," because activity that deviates too much from accepted norms will be rejected. Both the powerful and the powerless adopt strategies for dealing with the reference publics who will ultimately decide the issue at stake.

Social movements may be either general or specific in character. A *general social movement* is a large-scale, long-term shift in cultural values, such as the movement toward universal suffrage in the West. A *specific social movement* is a collectivity, usually an organization or alliance of organizations, moving to promote or resist change in the society or group of which it is a part. The women's liberation movement is an example of a specific social movement within the framework of the general suffrage movement. Specific social movements tend to have images in their societies that affect what happens to them. These may range from *revolutionary* to *respectable-nonfactional*, and may alter over time.

Historically, social movements often originated, or were believed to have originated, in collective behavior episodes. In modern times, they are more likely to create them. Today's movements also tend to be rather highly self-conscious (aware of reference publics and their relevance), with a consequent emphasis on *ideology*, the necessity for a justifying doctrine for their existence. Because movements are usually change-oriented, ideologies tend to have several functions: criticism of the existing order, suggestions for betterment, and a justification for the actions that the movement takes toward that end.

Social movements also tend to have predictable life-cycles. Early leaders often have power as a result of personal qualities and charismatic style, for example, while later organization tends to produce centralization, formalization, bureaucratization, and conservatism. The nature of the membership and the way in which it is recruited also affects a movement and its likely future. And social movements have some tendency to become domesticated. No matter how they are in inception, if they survive, and particularly if they succeed, they have a tendency to accommodate to the cultural rules of reference publics. A new twist on the life-cycle may be offered in contemporary American society, where some radical social movements have seen their jargon adopted by the mass media and commercial activities so that it becomes "camp."

Review Questions

1. Interest in collective behavior appears to have experienced peaks. List the four main waves of interest in this field, giving attention to important events during those times which served to motivate this interest.

2. Differentiate among the various types of crowds discussed in this chapter: acting, casual, conventional, and mobs. Arrange these in order of intensity of the collective experience.

3. Select two theorists from those studied in this chapter and contrast their orientations toward collective behavior. The list includes LeBon, Park, Fromm, Adorno, Hoffer, Davies, and Smelser.

4. Identify one large scale social movement found in the U.S. during your own lifetime. Explain how this movement meets the definitive requirements of a social movement, as opposed to collective behavior.

5. List and describe at least four strategies that protest targets can use to attain their ends.

Suggestions for Research

1. This chapter gives attention to the concept of mass society. Explore such a society by reading and writing a summary of David Riesman et al., *The Lonely Crowd*. First, give attention to the circumstances necessary for this type of society to exist; then indicate what type of personality is emerging.

2.   Select one of the many examples of collective behavior and social movements which characterized the 1960s as a decade of change and unrest. The civil rights movement, the antiwar movement, and ghetto riots are a few examples. Study one of these events as illustrative of collective behavior or social movements. Integrate your study by using as many of the appropriate concepts from this chapter as you can.

3.   Daniel Bell is one of many who have been concerned with the future of modern society. Read his *The Coming of Post-Industrial Society: A Venture in Social Forecasting*. What is it about this society that differs so considerably from the one in which we are now living? What does Bell foresee as the advantages of a post-industrial society? The problems?

4.   Study the contest for women's rights as a social movement, preferably going back to more historic origins in this country before focusing on recent feminist events. Note the type of leadership in this movement. Does it follow the scheme presented in the last part of this chapter? Give attention to the different phases experienced by this movement.

5.   Communication plays a most important role in social movements. Many schools even offer courses in the rhetoric of social movements. If yours does, interview the course instructor (or the instructor of a similar course). Although your interview will understandably be on a general level, plan some questions in advance. You will want to ask for examples of how communication processes facilitated and also impeded the success of movement goals.

CHAPTER 19
SOCIAL AND CULTURAL CHANGE

This illustration from the Sears, Roebuck catalogue of 1902 shows an object that many of you may never actually have seen: a cast-iron cookstove. Yet such an artifact would have been found in almost any home in the United States only eighty years ago (your grandfather's day), is still in use in a few remote regions, and until recently, at least, was used for cooking in railroad dining cars. What happened to cause the sudden disappearance of so common and utilitarian a device?

Look carefully at the ad, the claims it makes, and the construction of the stove. And consider the price! What are the two round, platterlike protrusions extending from either side of the upright back? Were they ornamental or functional and, if the latter, for what? What was the porcelain-lined reservoir mentioned in the ad? Why was it a major feature of the stove, along with the "high shelf" noted in the box at upper left?

Many of you will be unable to answer these questions. It's not important that you should. The point is, indeed, that most of you probably can't, even though stoves similar to this were everyday fixtures of American life for a century. But in the course of one generation, or at the most two, they have almost completely disappeared, not only from everyday life but from cultural awareness. Oblivion was quick. (The platters held a kerosene lamp or a kettle; the high shelf was for raising homemade bread; and the reservoir stored water that was then kept warm by the heat of the stove until needed.)

We see in this simple exercise an example of one of the major themes of this chapter: the rapidity and scope of social and cultural change in this century. There are many other clues in the ad. For example, the stove is called "world beater, price smasher and the enemy of trusts." You may not be sure of the precise meaning of the last phrase, for it is essentially a political slogan meant to appeal to the populist sentiments held by many of the farmers and rural inhabitants who were the principal clientele of Sears, Roebuck, & Co. in 1902. And while populism of one kind or another may still be found in American politics, and people still live—a few of them—on farms, the antitrust slogans of midwestern turn-of-the-century populism are as irrelevant to farmers in the last quarter of the twentieth century as the war cries of the Whiskey Rebellion.

How do we account for such a rapid rate of social and cultural change, and what are its effects? When the household tools of only yesterday are incomprehensible to us and we are already fearful or quarrelsome about the future, it is clear that sociocultural change has an overwhelming impact on us. We will have to contend with it all our lives, and may, before we are old, see our grandchildren look back on the pages of today's Sears catalogue as uncomprehendingly as we now look on this one.

In the following pages, we will discuss this accelerating rate of change and its implications for the future, the sources of change in any society, the factors that influence acceptance of or resistance to change, the role of technology in change, major social theories of change, and the relation between change and societal disorganization. A final discussion will consider whether planned change is possible.

Throughout the chapter, we will for the most part treat social and cultural changes together. We do this because social and cultural changes occur together and influence each other. But *conceptually*, we may distinguish between social and cultural change. **Cultural change** is a change in normative, cognitive, or material culture (the change from the wood-burning stove to the modern gas stove or even the microwave oven). **Social change** involves transformations in patterns of social organization or activity, such as a change in fertility rates or family patterns. In most cases, however, cultural and social changes are so intertwined with each other that it is difficult to separate them completely. (The change in stoves, for instance, involves changes in family patterns: no longer does the family have to haul in wood or coal for the stove or worry about keeping the fire going, to mention just one connection.) For this reason, we will often refer simply to the phenomenon of change.

Change and the Future

Many recent analysts think that we have entered a new era of unprecedented and accelerated change. In his book *Future Shock*, Alvin Toffler discusses the phenomenal rate of contemporary changes:

cultural change: change in normative, cognitive, or material culture.

social change: alteration in patterns of social organization or activity.

future shock: the sense of bewilderment, frustration, and disorientation produced in some people by very rapid social change. Future shock can be conceived of as resulting from inability to adjust to the *pace* of change.

culture shock: the sense of bewilderment, frustration, and disorientation sometimes experienced by travelers encountering an alien culture.

futurology: an emerging academic discipline devoted to the study of the future and our adjustment to it.

It has been observed, for example, that, if the last 50,000 years of man's existence were divided into lifetimes of approximately sixty-two years each, there have been 800 such lifetimes. Of these 800, fully 650 were spent in caves.

Only during the last seventy lifetimes has it been possible to communicate effectively from one lifetime to another—as writing has made it possible to do. Only during the last six lifetimes did masses of men ever see a printed word. Only during the last four has it been possible to measure time with any precision. Only in the last two has anyone anywhere used an electric motor. And the overwhelming majority of all material goods we use in daily life today has been developed within the present, the 800th lifetime.

This 800th lifetime marks a sharp break with all past human experiences, because during this lifetime man's relationship to resources has reversed itself. This is most evident in the field of economic development. Within a single lifetime, agriculture, the original basis of civilization, has lost its dominance in nation after nation. Today in a dozen major countries, agriculture employs fewer than 15 per cent of the economically active population.[1]

Toffler concludes that the rate of change today is so unusually high that it presents us with the problem of **future shock**, resulting from our inability to adjust to the rapid pace of change. It is akin to **culture shock**—the sense of bewilderment, frustration, and disorientation that people experience when they confront an unfamiliar culture.

The immense magnitude of contemporary change, as well as other factors, has given rise to a new field of study devoted to the future and our adjustment to it: **futurology**. Futurologists have been drawn from a variety of disciplines—social and physical scientists, social planners and theolo-

Culture shock.

gians, business leaders and technologists, science fiction writers and others. Sharing a common fascination with our unknown futures, these thinkers hope to identify trends that will serve to unravel the directions of change in the years ahead. As we continue our discussion of the sources and influence of change, you may want to think about how change will have altered the world by the time you are fifty—and how you will adjust to these changes.

Sources of Change

What prompts change? How does it begin in the first place? We saw in Chapter 3 that *innovation* and *diffusion* were important sources of change for any society, although the latter probably accounts for a much greater share of it. To those two, we may also add *crises and conflicts* as a significant source. Each is discussed below.

Innovation

Innovation, in the form of discovery or invention, is one obvious source of change. Innovations introduce new elements, or new combinations of old elements, into the cultural accumulation. If the new element is truly new, it may be called a *discovery;* if it involves a new combination or use of cultural elements already known, it will probably be called an *invention*. Einstein's theory of relativity and the germ theory of disease were discoveries; the automobile and the computer were inventions. Both inventions and discoveries can be either material or nonmaterial. The discovery of the New World by

European explorers was a true discovery (for them), and cafeterias and coeducation were true inventions.

Innovation is the result of a cumulative process. For example, the invention of a practical steam engine by Watt would not have been possible without the metallurgical techniques that were available at the time it was produced. Watt's invention built on the work of the ancient Greeks, who first applied steam power to driving toys and other mystifying devices; the primitive steam engines that were used for pumping water from houses and mines that developed during the later seventeenth century; and the "atmospheric engine" devised by Thomas Newcomen that first utilized low steam pressure.[2] And the musical genius of Ludwig van Beethoven built upon and could never have occurred without the symphonic contributions and musicianship of Haydn, Mozart, and others.

Diffusion

Another source of change is *diffusion*—the spreading of cultural traits from one society to another. In the last century, the potential for change through diffusion has expanded enormously because of the revolutions in transportation and communications. In assessing the modern transformations in communications, Marshall McLuhan envisioned the possible development of "a global village."[3] And it certainly seems that his prophecy is on the verge of becoming a reality. The nations of the Western world are already extensively interconnected with everything from telephone lines to satellites, and it should not be much longer, perhaps two generations, before the entire world is truly a global village.

In the United States, with its great stress on individualism, rationality, and science, we tend to emphasize innovation as the most fundamental dynamic force in change. But diffusion is far more influential than most people acknowledge. In his portrait of the "100 percent American," quoted in Chapter 3, Ralph Linton estimated that no more than 10 percent of the material objects used by any people represent its own innovations.[4]

Material culture traits diffuse more readily than nonmaterial ones. Thus, people will more readily adopt a new farming implement or other physical object than they will a new religion or different mores. Homer Barnett suggests several reasons why this is so.[5] For one, language differences between cultures more readily impede the flow of nonmaterial items than material ones. Second, the advantages of one cultural form over another are more easily demonstrated when the differences are readily observable. For example, the advantage of a new organizational form would be more difficult to show than the benefits of a steel knife over one made of stone. Finally, Barnett believes that when a physical object is adopted, the recipient less often involves the group by his action. There are likely to be fewer opponents of material objects, because their consequences for the group are less readily forseeable. Thus, physical objects are more socially diffusible than nonmaterial ones. It is easier for missionaries to distribute Bibles, for example, than to alter ritual patterns.

As cultural traits spread from one culture to another, they are not simply accepted or rejected, but often are revised or reinterpreted. A colorful mask originally used as a fertility symbol by a South American tribe may hang on your uncle's wall as a decorative object. And as Europeans adopted the tobacco-smoking habit of the Native American, they transformed its function from serving in ceremonial ritual to providing personal gratification. Tobacco originally smoked in pipes evolved into other forms: chewing tobacco and snuff. There is an unending modification of cultural traits as they circulate among and within cultures.

Mechanical Mom to Coddle Toddlers

Jack Mabley

The Art Institute of Chicago held a Fellowship Show recently and awarded first prize in design to Toddler Coddler 913. It is a capsule-like device intended to hold babies.

It is a nice design, but the concept is so 1984-ish that there was considerable speculation that it might be a put-on.

It looks a little like the cockpit of a fighter plane. The baby is put in and the transparent canopy comes down. Baby's bare bottom rests on pneumatic cushions with provision to carry away wastes.

A baby's bottle with milk hangs within easy reach of baby. Heat control keeps filtered air flowing. A sound system soothes baby with lullabies. If baby complains, a speaker system carries his cry outside the shell. The whole thing is suspended by a spring and chain so baby can rock.

The current price is $1,495, but mass production may bring it down to $300. . . .

Andrew B. Prueher, the designer, sent me a pamphlet describing the Toddler Coddler 913. It could have been written by George Orwell.

"Hello there," it says. "My name is TODDLER CODDLER, but you can call me 'Nanny.' I'm the most innovative convenience in infant care since formula feeding. My designers have packed me chock-full of fascinating features to insure Baby a stimulating and pleasurable environment." . . .

"I've gotten a lot of comment [said Prueher]. Most innovations are laughed at until they succeed. Some people tell me to take my machine and shove it. Others say I am trying to replace parents, that you can't replace a mother's love. I'm not trying to replace a mother's love." . . .

Chicago Tribune, July 7, 1976. Reprinted courtesy of the Chicago Tribune.

Innovation is often a source of social change.

Crises and Conflicts

In addition to innovation and diffusion, *crisis* and *conflict* may serve as important sources of change because they alter social structures and relationships and require adaptation to new conditions. The invasion of South Vietnam by the North Vietnamese and Vietcong forces produced massive changes all over the late Republic of South Vietnam. Mass migrations took place everywhere in an atmosphere of general panic, as many sought refuge from the invading military forces. The South Vietnamese government came under increasing attack by Catholics, Buddhists, and other groups agitating against various government policies. The Thieu government, in response to many pressures demanding a broader-based government, initially removed many cabinet officials and arrested numerous political opponents. Hoarding foodstuffs created shortages in many areas. Shipping companies and air carriers reported full capacity on all ships and planes leaving the country, as many sought to emigrate and send their valuables elsewhere. In the United States, Canada, and Australia, there was an outpouring of offers of rescue and adoption for the country's many orphans.

On a much smaller scale, one might consider the recent crisis caused by a fire in a telephone switching center in New York City that interrupted use of approximately 170,000 telephones for nearly three weeks—the most serious telephone failure in the company's history. Following the shutdown, most businesses in the affected area reported serious production problems and losses of sales. Although some businesses were unimpeded, a few thrived, messenger services, for example. Residents in the affected area who never mingled with some of their neighbors now found occasion to get acquainted; letter writing increased. Many habits and patterns were changed by the loss of the telephones. Had telephone service been unavailable for a longer period, more enduring changes would undoubtedly have resulted.

In the restaurant industry, William F. Whyte reports that interpersonal conflict is likely to produce change resulting in trends toward greater bureaucratization.[6] Whyte observed much conflict between waitresses and male cooks and bartenders. Discord often arose because lower-status waitress-

es gave food and beverage orders to higher-status cooks and bartenders, who resented being bossed by those of lower rank. This status discrepancy often led to emotional outbursts, especially during busy periods. Such status conflict is usually reduced by the use of written orders, placing orders on spindles, and creating physical barriers between the waitresses and food- and drink-preparing personnel. Thus, more elaborate rules of procedure appear to arise from situations of interpersonal conflict.

Crisis and conflict arising from change We have discussed crisis and conflict as sources of change because they so often initiate it, but it is also true that change can promote or intensify crisis and conflict. Change often makes people uneasy; it uproots us from familiar surroundings, meanings, habits, and relationships, creating fear and anxiety. The psychologically disruptive potential of change is greatly influenced by the conditions under which change arises, the values shared in different societies, and the outlooks common to different groups. Even when members of society welcome change, when novelty is generally viewed as a blessing, change can bring about massive social upheaval. W. F. Cottrell's now classic study of Caliente, a railroad town located in the desert of the American Southwest, demonstrates the crisis potential of change.[7]

Caliente was a one-industry town that thrived on servicing steam locomotives. It was a stop on the railroad where railroad crews changed, engines were repaired, and trains took on fuel and water. With the development of the diesel engine, which required less frequent stops for fuel, water, and servicing, Caliente became superfluous. As the railroad closed its servicing facilities, there was less and less need for its hotel, clubhouse, and associated buildings. The town lost not only the bulk of its industry, but also the major source of its tax revenues. Many inhabitants were forced to leave and search for employment elsewhere. Merchants lost their clientele, churches their congregations; homeowners faced a continuing decline in property values. The more deeply rooted individuals were in Caliente, the heavier were their losses. The town's search for a new industrial base was not successful; without the railroad industry, Caliente was less desirable to would-be investors than it had been previously. Caliente, thus, joined the ranks of sociocultural dinosaurs.

The disruptive consequences of change are manifold. Introducing new elements into a culture— whether they be social, physical, or ideational (relating to ideas)—often may promote or intensify social conflict. If the large number of American Western films have any lesson about American history to convey, one of the themes is the ever-present conflict created by the westward migrations of European settlers across the continent. Conflict was generated between the settlers and the Native Americans, between the cattle-ranching interests and the would-be farmers, between the early migrant frontier types and the later-arriving homesteaders. As population continues to mount in the United States, there is a contemporary analogue to some of this earlier conflict. Nowadays, we find increasing discord on environmental matters between industrial interests, on the one hand, and the advocates of conservation, on the other.

As any technical innovation is introduced, it tends to arouse discord between those who stand to profit from it and those who are likely to sustain losses. The viewpoints people hold are not likely to be exclusively economic ones, however; they often embrace moral and other dimensions as well. Consider, for example, the development of a new mechanism for crowd control—a gas that more effectively quells collective behavior than other products. Its supporters are likely to be found among "law and order" advocates, the police and paramilitary interests; and its detractors are likely to be found among the proponents of participatory democracy and the youth movement.

Societies are often factionalized. The interests and actions of some subgroups often are seen as diametrically opposing those of others. In peasant societies, people advocating change often experience rejection and hostility after initially being accepted by certain members of the community. As George Foster puts it, "Establishing friendship with a person identifies the outsider with that person's group or faction, and by implication, he assumes the villagers' hostility to rival groups and factions."[8] In this sociocultural climate, change advocated by one group almost invariably produces

"Please don't be alarmed. We were wondering if you'd care to buy a pair of tickets for an ethnic dance festival."

New Yorker, January 13, 1973. Drawing by Opie; © 1973 The New Yorker Magazine, Inc.

Diffusion.

Caliente did not suffer the fate of this nineteenth century ghost town, but the cause of its decline (failure of a single technology) was the same.

opposition among the others; here change is likely to intensify conflict.

Factors Influencing the Response to Change

In different societies, the socially shared responses to novelty vary considerably. At some times change is readily accepted; on other occasions, it is greatly resisted. Below we will discuss some of the important factors that affect societal responses to change.

Beliefs, Attitudes, Values, Traditions, and Habits

Most urban-industrial societies view change positively. Most Americans, for instance, are enthusiastic about the latest ideas, fashions, and fads. One of the reasons industrialized societies welcome change is that their central values encourage and approve of innovation. Three basic values are particularly influential: emphasis on science and experimentation, preoccupation with progress, and the significance accorded to individual achievement. In the urban-industrial world, change not only is normal, it represents the fulfillment of the cultural ideal. Groups possessing these values and benefits not only enhance the acceptance of change, but are likely to be influential in spurring further novelty and revision.

In contrast, in most nonindustrialized parts of the world, novelty and change are far less appealing. In most nonindustrial societies, people venerate the past, worship their ancestors, conform to the expectations of their elders, and make every effort to preserve the status quo. In this context, the individual is conditioned to view new things with skepticism and not to deviate from past practice. It is clear that in societies where tradition is revered to this degree and where fear of criticism haunts the would-be innovator, change is likely to be strenuously resisted and, consequently, far less common than in industrial societies.

Aside from general attitudes toward change, members of different societies hold specific attitudes and beliefs that affect the acceptance of new patterns. Suppose, for example, that a new factory is set up in a traditional peasant community. De-

"Are there any new fads your mother and I should be picking up on, dear?"

Reprinted by permission of Newspaper Enterprise Association.

Most urban-industrial societies view change positively.

spite the fact that the employer offers considerably higher wages than those prevailing in the community, he finds it difficult to attract employees. Absenteeism is high, and many workers never return to work after their first payday. We might conclude that the peasants in this particular community are not especially ambitious and enterprising and that work is generally shunned. Yet, in conflict with this explanation, we might often observe the residents diligently working long hours on the many farms and other businesses in the community. What, then, might account for this seemingly erratic behavior?

Analysis of the problem could conceivably yield a number of explanations. Possibly, in this community we might find a very strong extended family orientation, where people are used to working with kin, and being paid not with money but with some kind of barter—food or help with tasks that require several people to perform. An impersonal, cash-based factory system would be at variance with the work attitudes of such a group, because in the factory people would not be employed in kin-structured work groups, and money pay does not have the traditional symbolic values of ritual recip-rocal obligation and status reinforcement.

Of course, peasants are not the only ones who hold specific attitudes and beliefs that resist change; members of developed societies often are fixed in their ways. We are frequently reminded that the worldwide food crisis affects the industrial world as well as underdeveloped nations. In the United States, many people, maybe even millions, either go hungry or suffer serious protein deficien-cies. Yet many nutritious food sources are totally ignored: horsemeat, insects, and so-called trash fish, like squid, shark, and sea robin. These foods are considered suitable only for consumption by pets, if at all. Yet, in other parts of the world many of them not only are acceptable but are considered delicacies.

Consider also the inefficient and immensely wasteful loss of protein that results from the Amer-ican penchant for eating meat, a habit most Ameri-cans do not want to change. Approximately half of the United States' total agricultural produce is used to feed livestock—as much grain as it would take to feed all the people of China *and* India for a year. The protein content taken from the average steer involves the conversion of about twenty-one pounds of crops into one pound of expensive steaks and roasts.[9] Despite the widely held view of the superior nutritional value of meat, most nutri-tionists find otherwise; their research shows that a higher consumption of agricultural produce would offer a healthier diet than the present one. A considerable part of the world's current food short-age could be reduced by changing American eating habits.

Value shifts may also have profound effects on a society. Figure 19-1 shows the change in the Amer-ican population in only ten years in the number of persons living as primary individuals, that is, living alone or with unrelated others. As you can see, the number of elderly people living alone has in-creased significantly, as has the number in the age group thirty-five to sixty-four. More younger people also lived as primary individuals in 1970. Although demographic factors have something to do with this pattern, changing American attitudes toward marriage and living together are unquestionably significant: it is less popular to be married—or

Figure 19-1

Increase in persons living as primary individuals, in the United States, 1960-1970

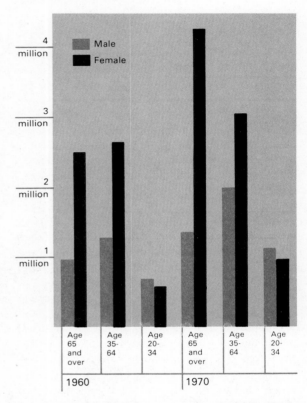

Value changes like the one shown here may radically alter a society. While these figures reflect mortality and health factors to some degree, they show alteration in values and habit patterns even more. In previous years, more older people were cared for in the homes of their children, and fewer younger people lived alone or with persons to whom they were not related.

living with your children—today than it was ten years ago, but it is more popular to live together without marriage.

Perceived Need and Demonstrability

When a need is widely perceived among a given group, innovations are more readily accepted. Inventions and discoveries that satisfy no need are often widely ignored until a need for them emerges. Leeuwenhoek invented an early microscope in 1674, but it was not until the germ theory of disease had been established—so that the need to identify microorganisms arose—that the value of the microscope to medicine and biology became established. Another example is the case of Teflon, a substance that refuses to let other material cling to it, which was accidentally discovered in 1938. It was not until 1964, however, when American gadget-consciousness had become widespread, that the DuPont Company could market a Teflon frying pan as a household "necessity."

Perceived needs provide a climate for the *acceptance* of innovation. But in and of themselves, they are insufficient to *generate* invention. At this time, people all over the world anxiously seek cures for cancer and heart diseases, new sources of energy that are nonpolluting, inexhaustible, and economical, and more simplified and effective birth control techniques. But the perceived desirability of these things is no guarantee that the needed invention or discovery will be made. Necessity, in other words, is the mother only of acceptability.

Before an innovation will be accepted and approved by a group, members must be convinced not only that they need this particular article or practice, but that its present form truly satisfies that need. Unless an invention yields visible proof of its utility, it will not be adopted. The typewriter and the automobile are good examples of the demonstrability of innovation. When the typewriter was first invented, many questioned the value of paying a great deal of money for a machine that would do the same work as the one-cent pen. There were also doubts as to whether women—who were then viewed as its potential users—could endure the strenuous course necessary to acquire typing proficiency. It was not until these stumbling blocks were surmounted that the typewriter was widely adopted in businesses and homes.

In the case of the automobile, early models of which ran erratically and required frequent mechanical attention, there emerged widespread public scorn and the derisive advice: "Get a horse." The first automobiles were viewed almost exclusively as "rich men's toys." Only after the cars had been mechanically improved, particularly by the development of the self-starter, and after the introduction of assembly-line techniques in building them, which greatly lowered costs, did the automobile begin to enjoy far-reaching acceptance among the consumer public.

The Cultural Base

The total accumulation of available knowledge and techniques has a great deal to do with both the quantity and the kind of innovations that are devised. This cultural repository limits the range of all inventions. In the late fifteenth century, Leonardo da Vinci sketched many machines—the airplane, helicopter, and submarine, among others—that were workable in principle, but the technology of his day was inadequate for building them. Without the necessary preliminary innovations in metallurgy, the internal combustion engine, advances in electricity, fuels, lubricants, and so on, inventive ideas had to be postponed until much later.

Or consider once more our indispensable automobile. Another of the obstacles that first impeded its acceptance was the lack of auxiliary services. There were few fuel and repair facilities, inadequate and insufficient highways, and overnight accommodations for travelers were not widely available. Sidney Aronson contends that the development of the bicycle inadvertently played a crucial role in increasing the use of the automobile.[10] The popularity of cycling was most instrumental for developing the kinds of facilities mentioned above, which later were readily adapted to servicing the automobile. (And recall that the Wright brothers were bicycle mechanics.) Thus, inventions tend to stimulate still more inventions.

As the culture base expands, there are likely to be increases in *rates* of change. The greater the number of elements in a given culture, the greater the number of possible combinations and recombinations. For example, glass gave birth to costume jewelry, drinking goblets, window panes, lenses, test tubes, X-ray tubes, electric light bulbs, radio and television tubes, and many other products. Lenses in turn gave birth to eyeglasses, magnifying glasses, telescopes, microscopes, cameras, rangefinders, searchlights, and the like. Thus, as cultures become more diverse and complex, rates of change are likely to accelerate.

Costs and Vested Interests

Costs are another important factor influencing the willingness to accept change. America's entry into the motoring age was postponed until the development of Henry Ford's assembly-line production system, which brought the automobile within the economic range of the majority of consumers. The early television receivers, aside from their technical imperfections, had a very limited appeal because of their high cost. In order for an innovation to gain wide public acceptance, it must be reasonably priced.

Costs are not exclusively economic, however; the liabilities of change also include social and cultural dislocations that may be taxing and unsettling. In 1932, August Dvorak developed a new keyboard for the typewriter, placing all the vowels and frequently used letters in closer proximity to one another. Dvorak's system has proven to be vastly superior to the conventional keyboard, called "qwerty" after the first six letters on the top row. Typists trained on Dvorak machines often double their typing speed and make fewer errors and report less fatigue than typists using "qwerty." Typewriter manufacturers have not been unwilling to produce Dvorak keyboards; most of them offer it for a slight additional charge. Yet this much more efficient system remains virtually unaccepted because users—typists, industries, and schools—are deeply committed to "qwerty" and agonize at the prospect of readjustment.[11]

Change affects people differently. Some individuals and groups are likely to lose more benefits and privileges from change than others. Those who benefit from the status quo often have a vested interest in maintaining it, and are likely to mount

Does a mere woman have the stamina to operate the machine? This and similar questions slowed the adoption of the typewriter for business.

considerable opposition to change when it threatens to diminish their power, rewards, and esteem. In traditional peasant societies, for example, native medical curers and midwives are likely to resent modern medical programs; large landlords are likely to oppose too much education for peasants for fear it may promote unrest and demands for land redistribution; and local moneylenders are likely to be opposed to low-interest government-managed credit programs. The more people benefit from maintaining the status quo, the more likely it is they will oppose change.

Despite the proven success of "socialized" medicine in many industrial societies, the American Medical Association (AMA) has consistently opposed its development in the United States. The AMA claims that under a "socialized" medicine system, the average citizen would lose his rights in selecting physicians, and that the quality of health care would decline if it is administered by a gigantic, impersonal, and inefficient bureaucracy. Yet the vested interests of the medical profession have failed to mention that physicians might lose income through socialized practice, that government agencies might exert more control over the practicing doctor, and that, as salaried employees, physicians might find their social status diminishing.

Usually, vested interests like the AMA are not entirely hypocritical; they hold strong convictions and earnestly believe that the society would be irreparably harmed by the innovations they oppose. They are deeply committed to the norms and social structures in which they participate. Often, such attachments may be effectively mobilized to retard change or to suppress it altogether. An example is the National Rifle Association's extensive propaganda campaign aimed at preventing the passage of legislation that would restrict the use of guns. The NRA's position is in part supported by arms manufacturers, but undoubtedly many NRA sympathizers genuinely fear the results of restrictive legislation.

Of course, when change is perceived as enhancing rewards, vested interests are likely to embrace it. American auto makers, for example, have resisted strenuously almost every federal requirement for increased safety features, which they perceive as increasing the price of cars without increasing the public's desire to buy them. But car manufacturers welcomed air conditioning, tape decks, mag wheels, and racing stripes, because buyers were eager to pay for these accessories.

Isolation and Contact

Because most cultural patterns are transmitted by diffusion, those societies in closest contact with others are most likely to change. Ecological factors may play a significant role in facilitating or retarding innovation. A society cut off from other cultural sources by a ring of impenetrable mountains, an impassable body of water, desert or jungle terrain, or a population that is dispersed in isolated settlements, is likely to be highly stable and quite resistant to change. For example, in research on American Anabaptist groups—the Amish and the Hutterites—William Pratt observes that the more isolated and widely scattered Hutterites, living in southwestern Canada, South Dakota, and Montana, have maintained close adherence to their Anabaptist ideal of unlimited procreation (the median number of children per Hutterite family is 10.4).[12] And there appear to be very few defectors from these groups to the mainstream culture. By contrast, the more highly concentrated Amish, living in more populous areas in Pennsylvania and Ohio, less closely approximate Anabaptist fertility ideals (the median number of children among the Amish is 6.7). And greater numbers of Amish defect to the dominant culture.

Groups that are adjacent to each other are more likely to share cultural traits. If their basic cultures are similar, the likelihood of mutual influence is increased even more. But if language barriers exist and cultural patterns sharply diverge, the tendency to accept innovation is diminished. It seems likely, for example, that the English-speaking provinces of Canada are more greatly "Americanized" than French-speaking Quebec.

Societies located at world crossroads are likely to be centers of change. Their accelerated change results from their greater exposure to new elements and the attempt to integrate these new patterns into their own sociocultural systems. We noted earlier that as the cultural base is enlarged, the combinations and possibilities for change increase dramatically. This fact might help account for the remarkably high volume of change found in capital cities and great seaports such as Paris, New York, London, Tokyo, Rio de Janeiro, Athens, and Cairo, which exhibit an interest in change often very different from the attitudes prevalent in their surrounding hinterlands.

During the twentieth century, isolation between cultures has been drastically reduced by spectacular innovations in transportation and communication. With modern transportation and mass communication, the transcultural flow of ideas has been vastly extended and intensified. Soon it will no longer be possible for cultures to enjoy the relative seclusion and isolation that existed throughout most of history. The reduction of isolation presents innumerable potentials for sharing knowledge among cultures. Yet, at the same time, it holds frightening prospects for destroying cultural diversity and promoting the dominance of some cultures over others.

Environment and Population

The environment is the underpinning of cultures. When environmental changes occur, they can have profound repercussions on culture. An earthquake, a volcanic eruption, or a hurricane can obviously have immensely destructive consequences for social life. And even minor changes can pose serious threats. For example, a few years ago several ocean currents changed direction, and as a result the Humboldt Current no longer brought the usual great quantities of anchovies to the Peruvian coast. Peruvian production of fish meal, used in making animal feed—one of the economy's fundamental industries—declined tremendously. The resulting losses in foreign exchange were drastic, precipitating an economic catastrophe.

Similarly, pollution, drought, soil erosion, and abnormally cold temperatures can produce far-reaching consequences on the economic and social life of the group affected. When a society depends heavily on one crop or industry, these consequences are likely to be compounded. The San Bernardino Valley of California, for instance, was once the heart of the American citrus industry, but air pollution has now made citrus trees there almost extinct.

Population changes, themselves social changes, are likely to produce still further changes in culture

Isolated societies are resistant to change. However, when they are located near other societies, as the Pennsylvania Amish are, they become vulnerable to intrusion. Ice cream on a stick is "fancy" (worldly) to many of the older Amish, but these youngsters obviously enjoy it.

and social structure. It is obvious that the influx of large numbers of a group bearing a divergent culture will influence those whose ranks they join. In turn, they are likely to be affected by their newly adopted culture. In addition, the culture they left is likely to undergo change as a result of their absence. Joseph Lopreato attributes the sharp surge of economic development in southern Italy since the end of World War II to the out-migration of large numbers of its inhabitants. For many years, southern Italian society was economically depressed, one of the last cultural backwaters of Europe. According to Lopreato, too many people attempted to provide for their existence in a fundamentally inhospitable environment characterized by low-grade soils, rocky terrain, and semi-arid climate. It was only after large-scale migrations took place that the economy could sustain the remaining population and absorb the innovative ideas and new capital that the emigrants sent back to their homeland.[13]

Internal population changes, such as fluctuations in birth and death rates, are also likely to produce social and cultural changes. As a consequence of fertility and mortality changes, some classes or kinship groups are likely to expand and others to contract. A population increase among a ruling elite could lead to political competition and conflict between people vying for leadership positions. By contrast, a decrease in population could create vacancies at the top, facilitating social mobility and serving to alleviate social discord and unrest. The declining birthrate among the Roman nobility in the last days of the empire—apparently caused, interestingly enough, by lead poisoning from cooking utensils, which were most definitely "in" at the time—may well have contributed to the political fluidity of the period.

As we saw in Chapter 11, demographic change inevitably results in altering the age composition of a group. A disproportionate increase of a particular age segment is likely to influence the values, beliefs, and attitudes held by the whole group. It is conceivable that a swelling of the ranks of youth could result in greater receptivity to some types of change. For example, many social analysts have noted that some profound changes and the social turbulence of the 1960s in the United States coin-

Soil erosion as a result of logging operations. Environment—and its deterioration—can have far-reaching effects on culture.

cided with the coming of age of the post–World War II "baby boom" population.

Increasing size also produces profound effects on a society, including the growth of impersonal relationships, the expansion of secondary groups, and greater institutional differentiation and specialization. Generally, social life is likely to become more complex in very large societies. Under these circumstances, the economy of the society is obliged to yield higher productivity if the expanded membership of the society is to be sustained. But when population growth is very high, as is true in many developing nations, the possibilities for increasing productivity and economic growth are diminished by the overwhelming growth of the population. As we saw in Chapter 11, rapidly expanding populations are more likely to have unusually large proportions of youthful members who can contribute very little to productivity and who are economically dependent. In both Costa Rica and Mexico, for example, approximately half of the population is under fifteen years of age. This fact imposes inescapable requirements on the economy.

In the developed world, by contrast, low population growth and advancing medical technology have created unprecedented possibilities for **gerontocratic** societies, those ruled or dominated by the elderly. Figure 19-2 permits us to estimate how soon the United States may become a gerontocratic society. Interpreted in terms of the late 1970s, it suggests a society of less-than-middle-aged people who are decreasingly inclined to have children, young "swingers" perhaps. But young swingers, inevitably, will become old. Add forty years to this chart and, assuming that the trend toward small families continues, we will see the portrait of a society dominated by old people with relatively few young people to replace them. How society's values, norms, and behavior patterns will be altered by this change remains to be seen.

Social Relations Networks

Another factor affecting the acceptance or rejection of change is the involvement in social relations networks of the individuals and organizations who introduce it. Research on the diffusion of medical technology, farming techniques, and political attitudes suggests a "two-step flow" in the adoption of many innovations.[14] First, the mass media serve as informing devices. They are most influential among early adopters of an innovation. In turn, these individuals serve as opinion leaders, influencing the adoption of new patterns among wider social segments. Early adopters provide the prestige, continuity, positive effect, and visible proof of the utility of new patterns that is often indispensable for widespread acceptance.

Other research on the acceptance of family planning in developing countries shows successful results obtained by paraprofessional field workers drawn from the ranks of former midwives.[15] Former midwives are not unlike their patient-clients and can readily communicate with those they serve. Most important from the standpoint of accepting family planning, they are recognized as the

gerontocratic: of or relating to gerontocracy, the rule or domination of the elderly. Gerontology is a subarea in sociology specializing in the study of the aged and the social characteristics of the aging process.

Figure 19-2
Children per family in the United States, 1945-1970

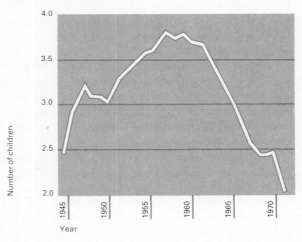

As the birth rate declines, the proportion of younger people in the population will also decline. By the year 2000, a significant segment of the American population will be elderly (the boom births of the 1950-1960 period), and will require very different social services than a population relatively young.

culturally appropriate contraceptive opinion leaders. Gaining the support and participation of local opinion leaders appears to be essential for those desiring to implement any social change.

Change Agents

Change is often proposed by individuals who deem it necessary or desirable. Such persons may be called **change agents**. They may be government officials—technical assistance workers, agricultural, industrial, or management specialists, public health officials, school administrators. Or they may represent religious interests (missionaries), social reform groups, political concerns, or commercial interests, among others. Usually, such change agents are strongly committed to the ideas they advocate; they are convinced that the adoption of their measures will improve life experiences. Of course, this is not always true. How much success such individuals have in promoting change has a great deal to do with how they conduct their activities, the social situation in which they attempt to introduce change, and their own positions in the social structure.

Generally, the greater the prestige of the change agent, the more likely the proposed innovation is to be accepted. Once innovations are adopted by those at the pinnacles of power and prestige, they tend to diffuse rapidly throughout the entire social structure. For example, after the mastectomy operations of the wives of two prominent politicians—President Ford and Vice President Rockefeller—American women became especially concerned about breast cancer, producing an unprecedented demand for breast cancer examinations.

Under some circumstances, the prestige of the change agent may retard acceptance. Ozzie Simmons reports a case in Chile where the high-status physicians in a health program tended to elicit terse and uncommunicative responses from their lower-status patients. These clients found it difficult to talk freely about their health and confide in the doctor, viewing such talk as bordering on impertinence. This failure of communication became a serious obstacle to medical treatment. Yet it was found that the patients would readily tell their problems to the nurses, whom they considered closer to them in status.[16]

Change agent. A Peace Corps volunteer teaches the women of a village in the British Honduras how to grind corn with a hand mill.

This leads us to a consideration of perhaps the most powerful factor in spreading change: change agents must be thoroughly familiar with the values, cultural patterns, and interpersonal relationships among those with whom they work. Allan Homberg observed that giving domestic fowl to the Stone Age Siriono tribe in Bolivia produced some unanticipated and undesirable consequences. Intrafamily relations were upset and interfamily patterns radically dislocated as those with the western fowl gained status over those without. Nomadic habits were also dislocated, as people had to adjust their movement patterns to the necessities of the birds. The same kinds of major dislocations also accompanied the introduction of the steel ax to the Siriono.[17] Along this same line, George Foster reports:

In village India, cooking is traditionally done over an open dung fire in the kitchen. There is no chimney and there are few windows, so the room fills with cooking smoke, which gradually filters through the thatch roof. Cooking is unpleasant under such conditions, and respiratory and eye ailments are common. The Community Development Programme has recognized this situation as a serious threat to health and has developed an inexpensive pottery stove, "a smokeless chula," which maximizes the efficiency of fuel and draws smoke off through a chimney. It is sold at very low cost to villagers. Yet, the smokeless chula has had limited success. In much of India woodboring white ants infest roofs; if they are not suppressed they ruin a roof in a very short time. The continual presence of smoke in the roof accomplishes this end. If smoke is eliminated roofs must be replaced far more often, and the expense is greater than farmers are able to support. So the problem of introducing the smokeless chula—at least in many areas—lies not in the villager's addiction to smoke irritated eyes, nor his love of tradition, nor his inability to understand the cooking advantages of the new stove, nor in the direct cost of the stove itself. He has considered the trade-off alternatives and decided that the disadvantages of the new stove outweigh the advantages.[18]

If change agents are to succeed in advancing their aims and in satisfying the needs of those they serve, they must be mindful of the manifold consequences that innovation may bring. They should exert every effort to anticipate all possible results of change. It is especially advisable to include the clientele in planning and implementing change, if possible. To take one example of planned change, consider the attempt to introduce a new farming technique to the Papago tribe of the American Southwest. The new technique, called the *bolsa* system, was supposed to increase the agricultural productivity of the Papago. The plan involved diverting flood waters into a specified area, the *bolsa*, or pocket, that subsequently was to be cultivated. The Bureau of Indian Affairs developed the plan and the Civilian Conservation Corps provided for the necessary construction.

Despite the sizable investment of energy and capital, the project was a dismal failure. Subsequent investigation revealed that the *bolsa* was poorly engineered and constructed, climatic conditions on the reservation were unsuitable, and the water supply was insufficient. Although the Papago were generally receptive to Anglo innovation, they recognized the weaknesses of the plan and reverted to their old agricultural practices. As Garth Jones commented, "The attempt failed because the administrators did not master the technique

> change agent: a person who initiates, causes, or introduces social or cultural change. Traders and missionaries are often change agents.

they borrowed before introducing it. . . . They did not bring the people into the planning . . . with the result that further technical difficulties developed which could have been avoided."[19] These mistakes were further compounded by unforeseen conditions and the fact that the agents of change did not share the clients' culture.

Technology and Cultural Lag

In this section, we will examine the leading role of technology in shaping the directions of change and consider also the cultural lags that often result from the imbalances produced when technology outstrips the nonmaterial components of culture. These cultural lags can cause conflict and strain for many, sometimes seriously impairing a society's cohesion and integrity.

Many social scientists have recognized that a society's economy and technology have a far-reaching impact on its social and cultural life, affecting how people organize their activities, how they coordinate their relationships, how they conceptualize and evaluate their experiences. The way people earn their living is likely to affect their family life, their religious beliefs, their political convictions, their ideas about education, and many other important social dimensions. Whether a group has large families or small ones, close or loose-knit ones, whether they revere rainfall and to what degree, even whether they personify the earth—which might mean they would not use a blade to cut it for plowing—and an unending range of other items, are all likely to be immensely affected by their technology.

Very often, technology exerts a dominating influence on shaping the direction and extent of change. Consider the revolutionary transformations that occurred when the automobile replaced horse-drawn transportation in the United States. The advent of the automobile contributed to an overwhelming number of changes in American social and cultural life: the demise of the blacksmith, the buggy maker, and the liveryman; the development of the massive car-producing industry, plus the birth of new industries connected with automobile use—motels, drive-in theaters and restaurants, filling stations, parking lots, and so on and on. The automobile brought with it industrial expansion and decentralization and greatly increased government functions and control: highway and bridge maintenance, automobile and fuel taxes, driving licenses, and motor vehicle regulations. It also increased some old health problems—emphysema and other lung diseases—and invented some new ones—automobile fatalities and injuries. Further, it led to the development of suburban living patterns, the diminution of extended family life, changing courtship patterns, and increasing premarital sexual activity—consider the effect the back seat of cars had on sexual practices.[20] (And we remarked in Chapter 12 the change wrought—or made possible—by the Pill.) When technology changes, it often brings with it changes in a variety of other realms.

In today's world, rapid advances in technology often far outstrip change in the nonmaterial parts of culture—customs, values, beliefs, and laws. This imbalance leads to the phenomenon of cultural lag we first discussed in Chapter 3. The development of nuclear weapons and the many other technical improvements in weaponry and warfare have far surpassed techniques in diplomacy and statesmanship, as is obvious from the lack of substantial progress in slowing down the "arms race." Our increasingly machine-dominated industry needs fewer and fewer workers with great physical strength and thus can easily accommodate many females in the work force, but these changes in technology have far outstripped society's conceptions of the rights and roles of women. (The women's liberation movement is, in part, a response to this condition.) Advances in medical science that have vastly extended life expectancy have resulted in a potentially catastrophic population explosion because of a lag in accepting and developing suitable birth control methods.

In a rapidly changing society, cultural lags are inevitable, and within varying lengths of time, they are ordinarily accommodated by the culture. But

Technology often exerts a dominating influence on change. A turn-of-the-century blacksmith and his nemesis, the automobile.

some cultural lags can have phenomenally disruptive consequences, which conceivably endanger the long-term survival of humankind, the Bomb being only one obvious example. It is conceivable that the Pill, with its possible effects on sexual behavior, childbearing, and the position of children in relation to parents, may prove even more disruptive.

Other obvious examples of cultural lag with potentially disastrous consequences include the effect of industrial pollution on the biosphere, the decimation of oceanic life—one of the great pillars of the life structure of the planet—the possible effect on the ozone layer of the use of spray cans, and so forth. Still others are the inability of human political systems to deal with the technological possibilities now in the hands of individuals and available for assassination, terrorism, and blackmail. No one has yet found a reliable way to prevent airplane hijacking. Or, for that matter, consider the individual's helplessness in the face of the technological assaults of government agencies through bugs, taps, long-distance recording equipment, sophisticated cameras, and listening devices.

Theories of Change

A fundamental and long-standing interest of sociologists has been to discern the regularities and uniformities of change. Here we will examine four influential theoretical perspectives on the process of change: *evolutionary*, *conflict*, *equilibrium*, and *cyclic* (or *rise-and-fall*) theories. Each perspective offers one kind of overview of change itself, and together they may yield fruitful insights for anticipating future changes in social relationships.

Evolutionary and Neo-Evolutionary Theory

Evolutionary theory   In the late nineteenth century, there was considerable interest in the **evolutionary theory of change**. Early evolutionary theorists tended to share a number of basic assumptions about change, including the following: (1) change tends to be cumulative; (2) it brings about increasing social and cultural differentiation and

evolutionary theory of change: the nineteenth-century view that sees change as cumulative, tends to equate it with "progress," and generally sees it as a one-way process leading to "civilization" and ever-increasing complexity in social organization.

History's first atomic artillery shell, fired from a 280-mm artillery gun. Will the lag in social-institutional reaction to nuclear weapons make humans obsolete?

complexity; and (3) it enhances adaptation, thereby promoting progress. Most contemporary sociologists probably would agree with the first two assumptions but would be somewhat doubtful about the third.

These early thinkers were convinced that change inevitably brought about improvement. For Lewis H. Morgan, change meant the passage from Savagery to Barbarism, and ultimately to Civilization. For Herbert Spencer, it meant the replacement of military-religious societies by industrial orders. For Auguste Comte, change meant the passage from what he called the theological stage of social organization to a scientific stage. Latter-day sociologists were less than satisfied with the unscientific ways these theories were propounded. Most of the early thinkers offered very limited, highly selective, and sometimes inaccurate information to substantiate their claims.

But two of them offered viewpoints that contemporary social scientists still find useful, as we saw in Chapter 7: Emile Durkheim and Ferdinand Tönnies. Not only have the latter-day social scientists found Durkheim's and Tönnies's procedures more consistent with contemporary scientific practice, but their viewpoints seem to describe rather well the trends observed in today's complex societies. Durkheim, you will recall, argued that change tends to transform the basis of social cohesion in society from a mechanical solidarity, characteristic of so-called primitive societies, to an organic solidarity, found in complex industrial societies. Durkheim held that as change brings increased technical progress, it also tends to weaken the relational bonds among members of society. This, of course, is exactly what we have seen in Part IV's discussions of the increasing specialization and diversification of social institutions.

Tönnies's theory, as we have seen, is consistent with Durkheim's view. The distinction between *Gemeinschaft* and *Gesellschaft* societies parallels Durkheim's distinction between mechanical and organic solidarity. Tönnies felt that the individualism and struggle for power characteristic of the urban world could result in cultural disintegration: as people become more socially fragmented, isolated, and independent of communal and institutional bonding, the integration and stability of traditional societies weakens. For both Durkheim

and Tönnies, change did not inevitably bring progress; it had varied consequences, some positive and some negative.

Notwithstanding Durkheim's and Tönnies's perceptive insights, during the early twentieth century evolutionary theories were subject to increasing criticism. Few new evolutionary theories were elaborated during this period. The armchair techniques and ethnocentric excesses of early exponents led others to shy away from this perspective. Since World War II however, there has been a resurgence of interest in evolutionary thought among sociologists and anthropologists, frequently called **neo-evolutionism**.

Neo-evolutionism Early evolutionary theorists looked upon progress as an all-pervasive phenomenon taking place throughout every facet of social and cultural life, including the moral realm. Most contemporary evolutionists have been reluctant to apply the notion of progress to all aspects of social and cultural affairs, confining the idea of increasing adaptation more or less exclusively to the technical sphere and to social-organizational complexity.

Leslie White was one of the first to revitalize evolutionary theory. White's general neo-evolutionary view holds that as culture evolves there is a progressive increase in the amount of energy placed under human control. In this conception, the idea of progress is confined to greater mastery of the environment.[21]

Elman Service, another neo-evolutionary theorist, sees progressive developments in social organization. According to Service, the earliest societies, usually hunting and gathering economies, are characterized by the band form. The band is a small group whose members live in nuclear or extended families in close proximity to each other, most often regarding each other as social equals.

With the domestication of plants and animals, the group is able to sustain a larger membership and consequently is likely to evolve into a tribal society. Tribes are composed of a variety of clans, embracing several groups of related families, who relate to each other on a more or less equal footing. Leadership in both tribes and bands is likely to be charismatic, based on the extraordinary talents or unique spiritual powers of the leader. The success of the tribe depends on the ability of its various clan components to act cooperatively and to defend themselves effectively against would-be invaders.

As agricultural economies become more proficient and capable of sustaining larger populations, differentiation and specialization of functions continue, and the tribe is likely to evolve into a chiefdom. The more differentiated chiefdom is characterized by the development of the (usually hereditary) position of chief. The chief coordinates the group's more highly specialized functions. In doing this, he is likely to develop a corps of specialized retainers, often kinsmen, thus creating an aristocratic hierarchy of authority. By its invention of such a hierarchy, the chiefdom is different from all previous social organizational forms.

The state is the last stage of social organizational development, characteristic of industrial societies. The distinguishing characteristic of the state is more effective control by the leadership over the members of the society. The state contains a police or military body, the only group legitimately empowered to exercise force. (A tribal chief might hold the *advantage* of force, but this differs from the *monopoly* of force available to leadership in the state.)[22]

Another variant of neo-evolutionary theory is found in Robert Redfield's work on "folk-urban drift." Redfield built his conceptual scheme on the pioneering work of Durkheim, Tönnies, and others. After conducting research among several communities in Yucatan, Mexico, Redfield concluded that social change tends to result in a gradual shift away from the "folk," or traditional, community to an urban society, where the values, the quality of life, and the social organizational features sharply diverge from traditional forms. Urban society represents a fundamental contrast with its folk antecedents.[23]

Conflict Theory

Another fundamental perspective on the process of social change is conflict theory, originally formulated by Karl Marx, as we saw in Chapter 1. In general, all conflict theorists maintain that the competition between groups for scarce resources inevitably produces divergence, opposition, and conflict. The enduring struggle of these social groups or forces

neo-evolutionism: the modern view that change is continuous and cumulative, but not necessarily "progressive" in all spheres. In general, neo-evolutionists restrict themselves to talking about increasing complexity, particularly in technology and social organization.

Welfare rights protesters take over HEW Secretary Finch's office in 1970 to demand higher welfare benefits. Conflict theorists see such confrontations as the means through which social structural relations are established.

makes for continuing change. Although much conflict is not necessarily turbulent, and may in fact be well organized, as is, for example, collective bargaining, occasional eruptions of violence do indeed flare up between various contending groups. As regimes succeed one another, those in power attempt to implement their ideas and impose their values on the rest of their society. Those subjected to their domination, in turn, inevitably rise up and oppose those in power. Once the formerly subordinated groups assume control, they are likely to be opposed by those among the vanquished, thus completing the cycle of conflict and change.

Many modern conflict theorists follow Marx in maintaining that conflict exhibits dialectical characteristics: that changes tend to generate increasing polarization between opposing forces, which finally clash, producing conflict and possibly warfare or revolution, out of which arises a new social order.

Marx, you will recall, thought that conflict stemmed from the clash between different economic interests, as represented by the proletariat and the bourgeoisie. Some recent theorists have attempted to refine Marxism in light of the changes taking place in post-capitalistic societies. Ralf Dahrendorf, for instance, points to authority relationships, rather than economic interests, as the fundamental point of cleavage in contemporary industrial society. Dahrendorf sees conflict arising as those who possess authority seek to maintain the status quo, while those who lack it attempt to expand their powers.[24] Other conflict theorists apply the dialectic in still a different way, conceiving of revolution as a rejuvenating response, promoting renovation and renewal of an otherwise decadent and perverted social order that has overextended its ideals and authority.[25]

Equilibrium Theory

The notion of equilibrium (balance) was borrowed originally from mechanics and the biological sciences. The fundamental assumption of **equilibrium theory** is that when change takes place in any one component in a system, it tends to spur further change in the other elements, which accommodate the new element and integrate it within the entire structure.

In general, systems strive toward equilibrium. For example, the perfection of jet airplanes during World War II revolutionized air transport and led to a number of further changes needed to accommodate it. New airports had to be built, both because jets needed longer runways than propeller planes and because more people were traveling on the new aircraft. These new airports had to be put at the outskirts of existing cities because they required large amounts of land. Thus, the city had to change to accommodate them. And the distances involved, in turn, spun off a host of other features: helicopter commuter flights, great airport complexes, almost minicities in themselves, and so forth. While each new development of this kind has tended to create problems of its own, equilibrium theorists might see in this history of events the kinds of adjustive responses that societies make to incorporate change and keep a social order "in balance."

Structural functionalism   Perhaps the best-known equilibrium theory is the *structural functionalist* viewpoint, which we first met in Chapter 1. Talcott Parsons, one of the major functionalist theorists, developed the perspective this way: Society is a system, composed of a set of interrelated parts or structures that are integrated with one another, functioning so as to promote overall social stability. Every society must provide for five basic needs if it is to endure: (1) member replacement; (2) member socialization; (3) production and distribution of goods and services; (4) preservation of order; and (5) provision and maintenance of a sense of purpose in order to assure committed participation in group activities. These needs tend to give rise to the development of a set of accommodating structures. The family provides for replacement, the educational system for socialization, and so on.

In primitive societies, these structures typically are fused together. For example, kinship institutions ordinarily provide for replacement, socialization, economic and religious needs, and may even sustain political ones. But as societies evolve—there is an evolutionary element to Parsons's view—structural elaboration and differentiation take place. Differentiation leads to further structural elaborations; institutions evolve to integrate the now more diverse structures. The institutional components of the social system are functionally interconnected with each other. When change occurs in any one part of the social system, it tends to have further reverberations among the others, whose overall thrust promotes adaptation, equilibrium, and social stability.[26]

During the 1940s and 1950s, equilibrium theories and structural functionalism in particular were popular in American sociology. In recent years, however, this perspective has been subjected to increasing criticism. Many charge that the structural functionalist model tends to minimize the importance of social change. Change is seen as an alien element, something that occurs outside the social system, unlikely to arise within the system itself. Others have claimed that structural functionalism has a conservative bias, tending to overestimate the amount of consensus in society and failing to take adequate account of social conflicts and their potential for change.

Cyclic (Rise-and-Fall) Theories

Another leading set of perspectives on social change are **cyclic (rise-and-fall) theories of change.** Cyclic theories do not envision long-run *trends* in change. Instead, they see societies as undergoing periods of growth and decline or as swinging back and forth between extremes along several important dimensions. A number of these theories compare societies to living organisms, viewing the pattern of change in society as following the stages of the life-cycle: birth, growth, maturity, and old age.

Oswald Spengler Oswald Spengler conceived of cultures as relatively autonomous and distinctive systems, each having its own style and possessing a unique destiny. Cultures pass through the same stages of growth and decline as individuals; each has its own childhood, youth, maturity, and old age (see Figure 19-3). Civilization is the final stage in the life of a culture. The usual life span of a culture is approximately a thousand years. In the generally gloomy mood that followed World War I, Spengler prophesied the end of Western civilization in his widely read work *The Decline of the West* (1926–1928).[27]

equilibrium theory: the view that when change takes place in one component of a social system, it inevitably produces a "ripple effect" of changes in other components as they adjust to the new element. The outstanding example of equilibrium theory is structural functionalism.

cyclic (rise-and-fall) theories of change: theories holding that societies either go through cycles of expansion and decline or follow a birth-growth-maturity-death pattern of change.

Figure 19-3
Spengler's model of cyclic change

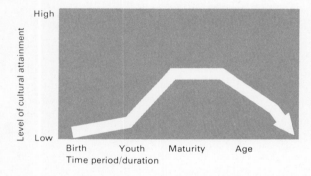

Arnold Toynbee   In *A Study of History* (1935–1961), Arnold Toynbee hypothesized that civilizations arise in response to some challenge from the social or physical environment (see Figure 19-4).[28] If the challenge is insufficient, or if it is too overwhelming, there will be a lack of effective drive toward attaining the cultural development known as civilization. For example, the frigid climate and scarce resources of the Arctic region have greatly limited the cultural response and development of Eskimo peoples. Conversely, the vast abundance of assets and good weather of the South Pacific islands have effectively reduced initiatives among the Polynesians. But when the challenge is powerful enough to stimulate without being overwhelming, as it was in the Nile River basin, the culture develops. The ancient Egyptians developed an elaborate and complex civilization.

Toynbee thought that there were twenty-one peoples who at one time or another in history attained civilization. Four or possibly five of these civilizations were original rather than derived from others. The original civilizations arose in Egypt, Sumer, China, among the Mayans, and possibly in India—all others are derivative.

The presence of a creative minority is necessary in order to launch a civilization, Toynbee thought. Through its leadership, ingeniousness, and inspiration, a society is able fully to realize its potential. Eventually, this creative minority fails to take the appropriate measures, thus bringing about their own downfall and the death of the civilization. In the terminal stages of the life of a civilization, internal discord prevails, and the ruling elite imposes itself by brute force, resulting in widespread opposition among the majority. The vitality of a civilization endures as long as its elite makes the correct adaptive responses to sustain it.

Pitirim Sorokin   Pitirim Sorokin (1941) contended that cultures tend to be characterized by one of two dominant themes: **Sensate cultures** stress values based on the importance of sensory experience, while **ideational cultures** give priority to spiritual and metaphysical values.[29] Once a culture tends to emphasize either extreme, it begins to revert back to its polar opposite. As a culture swings back and forth between these two themes, rather like a pendulum, there are periods when it reaches an

Figure 19-4
Toynbee's model of cyclic change

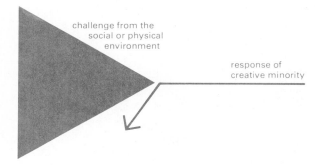

challenge from the
social or physical
environment

response of
creative minority

Case I: The challenge is too overwhelming and the culture fails or remains marginal, e.g. the Eskimo

Case II: The challenge is too easily overcome, the culture is not adequately stimulated, and it fails or remains marginal, e.g., Polynesia

Case III: The challenge is powerful enough to stimulate without being overwhelming, e.g. Egypt, and the culture becomes a true civilization

idealistic point, where a mixture of both sensate and ideational values prevail (see Figure 19-5).

Sorokin believed that one could identify which themes take precedence by surveying the artistic productions of a given culture. He contended that Ancient Greece was an ideational culture that became idealistic during the Golden Age. The development of Roman civilization marked a swing toward sensate life. During the Middle Ages, an ideational culture returned. Since then, there has been a shift back toward the sensate pole. The Renaissance was characterized by an idealistic synthesis, and from that point onward, art styles suggest we have been heading in the direction of a more sensate culture. If the revival of religious interest among many of those committed to communal life-styles reflects the latest trends, possibly we may anticipate a resurgence of the ideational theme.

Change and Societal Disorganization

One of the themes we have emphasized in this chapter is the disruptive potential of change. Change can usher in a host of social problems, and it may even cause social and cultural disorganization. Among the more impressive examples of the potentially devastating impact of change already mentioned is the disintegration of Caliente that resulted from the introduction of the diesel engine. And we have already seen how the introduction of steel axes destroyed the Yir Yorount and the adoption of domestic fowl tended to promote social conflict and disharmony among the Siriono. Nuclear weapons, of course, may yet destroy *us* and perhaps all life on earth as well.

Technological innovation, though often having the most obvious impact on societies, is not, of course, exclusively responsible for social and cultural dislocations. The historical record is filled with instances where the migration of groups or the diffusion of ideas and beliefs from one society to another resulted in increasing social problems and social disorganization. The contemporary plight of the Native American is ample testimony to the personal and social disorganizational consequences—pauperization, alcoholism, and suicide, among others—that have arisen as a result of their exposure to the new cultural elements introduced and imposed upon them by white Europeans.

Aboriginal peoples and peasants are not the only victims of the hardships and problems that change often brings. People in complex industrial societies have not gone unscathed by change. Among the many consequences of the automobile have been alarming increases in health problems and environmental pollution that seriously threaten human life, not to mention an appalling annual death toll from highway accidents. Sharp cleavages and

sensate culture: Pitirim Sorokin's term for cultures placing greatest value on sensory experience.

ideational culture: Sorokin's term for cultures placing greatest value on spiritual or metaphysical experience.

Figure 19-5
Sorokin's model of cyclic change

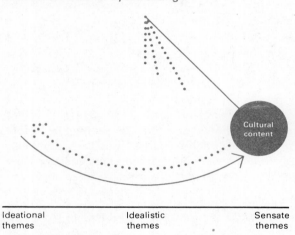

| Ideational themes | Idealistic themes | Sensate themes |

As a culture approaches either extreme, it begins to swing back toward the opposite extreme. In the intermediate period, which Sorokin called "idealistic," a mixture of ideational and sensate themes prevails.

conflicts have developed between the automobile interests and conservationists.

The foundation of the American economy is sustained by the automobile, with one out of every six workers directly or indirectly employed in its production and maintenance. Much of the U.S. economic recession of 1974-75 was attributable to the failure of the automobile industry. In order to run private cars and trucks, we spent over $24 billion in 1974 to pay for imported oil, a huge chunk of the nation's foreign exchange.

In addition to the dependence of the American economy on the automobile, Americans have begun to reconstruct their country to accommodate cars. In cities largely laid out since World War I—Los Angeles is the outstanding example—and in the urban and suburban areas developed since that time, builders and planners plainly *assumed* that the universal form of transportation would be the privately operated automobile. Cities abandoned or never built adequate public transportation systems; suburban streets wind for miles without a sidewalk; great parking plazas were paved for immense shopping centers miles from residential concentrations; freeways twine spaghettilike through the central cities to permit access to suburban population centers. It is interesting—and sobering—to speculate what would happen to the contemporary American city if gasoline became largely unavailable. (Los Angeles might have to be either demolished and rebuilt or else abandoned.)

Changes in ideas and other forms of nonmaterial culture also threaten the stability of modern societies. It was not long after *Brown* v. *Board of Education* in 1954 and similar rulings that a massive upsurge of racial conflict occurred in many American cities. In part, those outbreaks owe their origins to the rising expectations among blacks inspired by legal affirmations of equality that were not matched in black experience. Violent racial outbursts appear to have quieted in the mid-1970s, but could reoccur if black aspirations were again perceived as unachievable.

Is Planned Change Possible?

Today many people feel that the range and intensity of problems and the complexity of the forces

A black man on his way to pick up his daughter from school in South Boston is attacked by a white mob in 1974. Racial conflict in American cities is in part a response to rising expectations among blacks.

surrounding human action have assumed such immense scope that we can only blunder along, following the currents of change wherever they may take us. Yet others remain optimistic, believing that the course of change can be directed, that we can control our destiny. One of the guiding principles of science is that the systematic knowledge it develops can be applied to human experience to help direct the course of change. Admittedly, the results obtained thus far in social science have been much less impressive than those derived from physical science. Yet increasing numbers of social scientists remain confident that their work will contribute to social changes that will help sustain humanity and improve the quality of life on this planet.

A fundamental point social scientists have learned about attempting to plan change is that it is vitally important to involve those planned for *in the planning process*. If planned change is to be successful, it requires the support and participation of those who will be affected by it. Many studies have confirmed this principle.[30]

Elite direction of social planning is the prevailing mode in Communist societies. Yet throughout history, in all societies following Communist precepts, adherence to the authoritarian model has been far from complete. There has always been some measure of grass-roots involvement in planning in most Communist countries, and it seems to have been the Russian experience that plans involving the planned for work better than those created in Moscow.

Individuals reared in democratic capitalist societies sometimes find the idea of state management and control unappealing and contrary to the values of individual freedom and self-determination. It should be recognized, however, that the democratic approach is not necessarily the only or the most rapid way to effect change. In many developing nations, elite-led social and economic planning may be the only effective way of dealing with the massive problems these societies encounter, despite serious dislocations for individuals.

According to Robert Heilbroner's examination of economic underdevelopment, an uncoordinated free market system is unlikely to inspire the necessary postponements in consumption that will be required to generate investment capital for growth. Heilbroner holds that only in a planned economy is it possible to coordinate all the measures necessary to introduce and sustain economic development.[31] Only a planned economy is equipped to undertake the necessary massive land reforms, to move workers and capital in a coordinated way, to diversify the production process if need be, and to generate the sacrifices needed to spur development. Also, in some societies peasants may expect authoritarian leadership by government officials; they may find democratic efforts at change confusing and inappropriate.

Nuclear power plant. If planned change is to be successful, it requires the cooperation of those planned for; this is often ignored by proponents of nuclear power.

Commune members in the People's Republic of China are congratulated by a government official for improving agricultural production. Modern China is an outstanding example of the potential success of planned change. Americans, however, might find the price of this kind of planning too high.

Communist China offers a particularly impressive example of the success of planned change in peasant societies. One of the world's most populous societies, perennially plagued by the problems characteristic of underdeveloped areas, it has moved most significantly toward modernization in the last twenty-five years. Dramatic improvements have occurred in agricultural and industrial productivity, housing, health care, and family planning—indeed, the Chinese family planning program is the only really successful one so far mounted.[32] Economists estimate that economic growth in China in recent years has averaged approximately 8 percent, unmatched elsewhere in the developing world except perhaps among the major oil-producing nations, whose situations are unique. In most other developing nations, growth rates average around 3 percent, while population growth averages approximately 2 percent, resulting in very small economic gains, or none at all.[33] However much we may value the democratic approach to change, it is not necessarily the most effective for all cultures, in all situations.

Planning can be greatly facilitated by the assistance of modern computer technology. The advent of the computer has made it possible to perform calculations that would have taken many lifetimes to do by other methods. With the aid of computers, we can project far into the future the long-range

Home Cooking

Electronics technician Arthur Pearce used to spend his evenings relaxing in his Mountain View, Calif., apartment playing games with Henrietta. But Henrietta's capabilities were a bit limited, so Pearce got rid of her and acquired Priscilla, who's not only a whiz at blackjack and roulette but can also solve technical problems. That may sound a bit cavalier on Pearce's part, but Priscilla—like Henrietta before her—is no exploited woman. Priscilla's real name is IMSAI 8080—and she's a microcomputer Pearce keeps in his living room.

By whatever name, the desktop electronic brain is the product of a revolution in data-processing technology that has brought the price of small but sophisticated computers down to that of a good stereo system. And Pearce is one of a fast-growing legion of home-computer hobbyists who are buying and building their own systems in record numbers. In remarkably short order, more than 100 computer hobby shops have sprung up around the nation. Computer hobbyists have also formed more than 80 clubs—the largest has well over 8,000 members—and at least three new magazines cater to their special interest. "The hobby market started less than two years ago," says salesman Arnold Karush of IMS Associates, which makes the IMSAI 8080, "and it's growing exponentially." . . .

But home computers can be useful as well as entertaining. "Hobbyists use them for reckoning budgets, editing texts and as letter-writing or word-processing machines," says Dick Heiser, who owns The Computer Store, the first such shop to take advantage of the hobby boom. . . .

Newsweek, August 23, 1976, p. 71. Copyright 1976 by Newsweek, Inc. All rights reserved. Reprinted by permission.

We are only beginning to experience the impact of the computer.

consequences of our actions. Computers are now used throughout the world by both governments and private agencies in assisting almost every conceivable collective activity: agricultural and population policy making, industrial expansion and market practice, investment and construction.

The computer revolution marks a major technological change, whose total impact we have yet to experience. (It is not uncommonly believed, for example, that contemporary Americans may live to see money as such become obsolete, with all financial transactions taking place via credit card and computer. Such an idea was the stuff of science fiction only ten years ago.) But computers do not really *think* as human beings do, and they are utterly dependent for their (to many of us) miraculous abilities on the kind and quality of data fed them. ("Garbage in—garbage out," the programmers say.) Computers offer the possibility of facilitating planned change, but they cannot accomplish it for us. If modern society is to survive future shock, it remains for human beings to use computers well and to plan wisely and effectively, in ways no machine can do.

Summary

Social and cultural change is ever-present in all societies. *Rates* of change vary immensely in different societies and across time, but change itself is never entirely absent. *Social change* refers to alterations in patterns of social organization or activity; *cultural change* involves alterations in normative, cognitive, or material culture. One of the major social phenomena of the latter half of the twentieth century has been acceleration in the rate of change, a speeding up of the change process, so that, as some writers have put it, all of us are faced with living in the future, in the sense that radical alterations now occur within the span of a single lifetime. This means that the norms, values, and practices that we learned as children may be altered or become obsolescent in our own lifetimes, forcing us to make adaptations to changes of a kind unheard of in earlier centuries.

There are three basic sources of social and cultural change. *Innovations*—discoveries and inventions—are relatively rare. The most common source of change is *diffusion*, or the borrowing of things, practices, and ideas from other societies or cultures, although the thing borrowed is often altered or used differently in the process. *Crises and conflicts* may also be a major source of change, because they alter social structure and social relations and require new adaptations to the changed conditions.

Many factors play a part in determining whether change will be accepted or resisted. The degree of acceptance or resistance, in turn, affects the rate at which change occurs in a given situation. Among the influencing factors are *beliefs, attitudes, values, traditions, and habits*, which may relate either to the process of change itself or to the content of a particular change phenomenon. A society that places a high value on progress and novelty will change more rapidly than one that views change with suspicion. Or sometimes particular habits, values, attitudes, or traditions clash with specific new practices or artifacts, thus reducing the likelihood of their acceptance. In other cases, a new thing or idea may be interpreted simply as another example of something conventional or already positively valued, thus making adoption easier.

Perceived need and *demonstrability* is another factor that influences the acceptance or rejection of change. New ideas or things are more readily adopted if people see and acknowledge a need for them than if they do not. And items such as tools, which have a demonstrable utility, are more readily adopted than ideas, which have less, or less obvious, utility.

The nature and quality of the *cultural base* also influences change in that cultures must be ready for either ideas or things in order to adopt them. Many inventions have been thought of long before they could be manufactured or put to use, either because the technical capacity to make them did not exist (as with Leonardo's airplane) or because they appeared to have little utility at the time (the first microscope).

Similarly, the *cost* of adopting a change may retard its acceptance if it is high, or encourage it if it is low. And particular *vested interests* may either encourage or resist change, depending on *their* perceptions of its results for them.

Societal *isolation* from others reduces the rate and amount of change, while frequency of *contact* with other societies encourages both. In the same way, *environment* and *population* may either provide a ready base for change or discourage its adoption. Very mountainous terrain inhibits railroad construction, for example, and a climate that prohibits the accumulation of food reserves will probably not produce large urban concentrations. Similarly, a society with very high birth and death rates and a large proportion of children in its population will find it difficult to industrialize.

Finally, *social relations networks* and the presence or absence of *change agents* in strategic positions within them may also influence the acceptance or rejection of change.

Technology may have an immense influence on social change, often a dominating one reaching into every aspect of a society. The automobile, for example, has had far-reaching effects on American social structure and practices. Because technological changes are more readily adopted than new ideas, they sometimes create *cultural lags* when a new device is adopted some time before the norms and values of a society have a chance to "catch up." Cultural lag, in turn, sometimes leads to social disorganization of more or less severe kinds, occasionally so drastic as to destroy the society itself, as in the case of many preliterate groups who disappeared after contact with the West.

There have been four major varieties of theories relating to social change: (1) evolutionary, (2) conflict, (3) equilibrium, and (4) cyclic (rise-and-fall) theories. *Evolutionary* theories, which tended to equate change with progress, were popular during the last part of the nineteenth century and the early years of this one. They uncritically applied the concepts of biological evolution to social history and are discredited today. In recent times, however, a new variety of evolutionary theory called *neo-evolutionism* has developed. It concentrates on the continuous and cumulative nature of change, particularly complex changes in technical adaptation and complex changes in social organization. *Conflict* theories, based on Marx's ideas, view social change as the product of conflict between interest groups and social classes. *Equilibrium* theories see change in any one component of a social structure as initiating changes in all other components to restore "balance" throughout the social system. *Cyclic* theories view change either as following a pattern of swing or alternation between polar social types or else as following a growth-and-decay pattern based on an organic model.

Social change is related to *societal disorganization* in that change is likely to be profoundly disruptive to a social structure. Depending on the nature and flexibility of the social norms, and the content of the change itself, change may irreversibly alter a society's history or even destroy it. It is difficult to foresee the effects of a potential change, because it may produce a chain of reactions that cannot be envisioned when the change is instituted. (Probably no one in the United States in the year 1900 could have begun to visualize the compound effects the automobile and the airplane were to have.)

This makes *planned change* difficult, but it is not entirely impossible, although it may always be impossible to foresee all of the effects that a given change may generate. Planning, then, can never be complete, but serious planning with attention to all possible alternatives and with *involvement of those planned for* makes adaptation to change and directing change possible to some degree. Modernizing societies in particular, however, may feel they must plan centrally and impose change on their populations, whether willing or not. Although state planning may be distasteful to Americans, the example of China shows that it is possible.

Review Questions

1. Describe and contrast the four theories of social change: the evolutionary (and neo-evolutionary), the conflict, the equilibrium, and the cyclic (rise-and-fall) theories. Which seems best suited to the type of change occurring in your lifetime? Why? Which seems least applicable to modern change, if any? Why?

2. Explain the different phases of social organization discussed in this chapter. In what type of society is the band most characteristic? The chiefdom? The state? How do these three forms differ?

3. What circumstances bring about cultural lag? Which types of societies are more susceptible to this phenomenon? How is the problem of cultural lag finally resolved, if at all?

4. Contrast the different types of change discussed in this chapter. How does social change differ from cultural change? How does invention differ from discovery? Discuss the factors that make cultural diffusion take place. Which types of societies are most likely to exchange cultural traits?

5. Explain what is meant by the *two step flow* in the adoption of many innovations. What role is taken by the media? By opinion leaders? Who are the early adopters?

Suggestions for Research

1. Select twenty household items which you use frequently. Ask your parents and your grandparents or

someone in that general age group how many of these devices were used widely in their youth. How many were available two generations ago? One generation ago? What was used in the absence of modern devices that you selected? What can you conclude to be some of the more basic differences in these earlier life-styles as contrasted with your own? Explain your findings and assumptions in a paper.

2. Read and write a report on Alvin Toffler's *Future Shock*. Which innovations might you expect to see in your lifetime? Do you view this work as a realistic prediction of a world characterized by rapid change or as an attempt to frighten the reader?

3. Read and make a report on Aldous Huxley's *1984*. In which areas does he have success in his predictions? Which of his predictions appear totally unlikely in future society? What does Huxley think of the type of change he portrays? What do you think of it?

4. Conduct a small survey to determine what effect education has on people's general receptivity to change. Interview at least five persons with a high school education and another five with a college education. Are there any significant differences in the way these two groups see change in their lifetimes? Is one group more threatened than the other? How and why? What do the two groups believe they can do, if anything, to direct or control change?

5. Write an essay on change in your own lifetime. What material things do you employ which were not available during your childhood? What differences in your family's life-style, if any, can you attribute to change? If you do notice such changes, do you think they are generally beneficial or detrimental? Why? What is your feeling toward change in general?

EPILOGUE

This page concludes our introductory excursion in sociology. The vast majority of you who read it will have been assigned this book as a part of an introductory course in the field. Many, indeed most of you, will not take another soc course or, at best, will take only one or two in addition to the one for which the book was assigned. What, then, are you to make of all this now that it is nearly over for you?

Let us first make the point that it is not and will never be over for you so long as you live. You may never take another formal class called "sociology," but you will live as a social person in a society for the rest of your life. We promised in the letter to you that constituted the preface to the book that you might learn things from it that would be of value to you in your life. It is appropriate to take stock of that promise at this point.

One of the major aims of this book has been to explain what sociologists know and believe about the way in which your society works and the reasons it does so. We hope that in some instances you will have had an "ah-hah!" experience as you read it. ("Ah hah! So *that's* why . . .") We are also certain that in some cases you reacted to something you read by saying, "Well, I knew that all along," and that, in other cases, you may have reacted with outright disbelief. All of these responses are fine, of course. Indoctrinating you in something was not our purpose. The purpose was, however, to encourage you to *think about* society, and your life in it, in some ways that may have been new to you, and to offer you some tools for doing such thinking that you may not have known about before. If we have succeeded in doing that, and if you continue to use those tools as you go through life to better understand the world about you, your authors and I will feel we have served you well.

With best wishes,
The Editor

NOTES

Chapter 1

1. Modern editions of these works are: Emile Durkheim, *On the Division of Labor in Society* (New York: Free Press, 1964); Durkheim, *The Rules of Sociological Method* (New York: Free Press, 1964); Durkheim, *Suicide* (New York: Free Press, 1951); and Durkheim, *The Elementary Forms of the Religious Life* (New York: Humanities Press, 1964).

2. Modern editions of these works are: Karl Marx, *Capital* (2 vols.; New York: International Publishers, 1967); and Marx and Friedrich Engels, *The Communist Manifesto* (New York: Russell & Russell, 1963).

3. Karl Marx, *The Economic and Philosophic Manuscripts of 1844* (New York: International Publishers, 1964), pp. 106–119.

4. International Minerals and Chemical Corporation, "The Quiet Revolution" (Skokie, Ill., 1965), pp. 10–11, quoted in M. L. DeFleur, W. V. D'Antonio and L. B. DeFleur, *Sociology: Human Society* (Glenview, Ill.: Scott, Foresman, 1973), p. 255.

5. See Lewis A. Coser, *The Functions of Social Conflict* (New York: Free Press, 1956); Coser, *Continuities in the Study of Social Conflict* (New York: Free Press, 1967); and Ralf Dahrendorf, *Class and Class Conflict in Industrial Society* (Stanford, Calif.: Stanford University Press, 1959).

6. Jonathan H. Turner, *The Structure of Sociological Theory* (Homewood, Ill.: Dorsey Press, 1974), pp. 114–117.

7. These notes were collected after Mead's death and published in the form of posthumous books. The best-known is *Mind, Self, and Society* (Chicago: University of Chicago Press, 1934), which is the major statement of symbolic interactionism.

Chapter 2

1. Emile Durkheim, *Suicide: A Study in Sociology,* trans. John A. Spaulding and George Simpson (New York: Free Press, 1951).

2. Bonnie Bullough, "Poverty, Ethnic Identity, and Preventive Health Care," *Journal of Health and Social Behavior* 13 (December 1972), pp. 347–359; David Coburn and Clyde R. Pope, "Socioeconomic Status and Preventive Health Behaviour," *Journal of Health and Social Behavior* 15 (June 1974), pp. 67–78; and L. C. Deasy, "Socio-economic Status and Participation in the Poliomyelitis Vaccine Trial," *American Sociological Review* 21 (April 1956), pp. 185–191.

3. Bullough, "Poverty, Ethnic Identity, and Preventive Health Care."

4. Several reference books have been prepared to help researchers locate existing measures. See, for example, Charles M. Bonjean, Richard J. Hill, and S. Dale McLemore, *Sociological Measurement* (San Francisco: Chandler Publishing, 1967); Delbert Miller, *Handbook of Research Design and Social Measurement* (New York: David McKay, 1970); John Robinson, Jerrold G. Rusk, and Kendra B. Head, *Measurement of Political Attitudes* (Ann Arbor, Mich.: Institute for Social Research, University of Michigan, 1968); and Marvin E. Shaw and Jack M. Wright, *Scales for the Measurement of Attitudes* (New York: McGraw-Hill, 1967).

5. For a discussion of the broader uses of content analysis, see Bernard Berelson, *Content Analysis in Communication Research* (New York: Free Press, 1952).

6. Donald Auster, "A Content Analysis of Little Orphan Annie," *Social Problems* 2 (July 1954), pp. 26–33.

7. Walter Hirsch, "The Image of the Scientist in Science Fiction," in Bernard Barber and Walter Hirsch (eds.), *The Sociology of Science* (New York: Free Press, 1962).

8. For an excellent brief treatment of the scientific criteria for establishing causality, see Sanford Labovitz and Robert Hagedorn, *Introduction to Social Research* (New York: McGraw-Hill, 1971), pp. 3–12.

9. Darrell Huff, *How to Lie with Statistics* (New York: Norton, 1954).

10. Ibid., p. 24.

Chapter 3

1. Edward B. Tylor, *Primitive Culture* (London: Murray, 1871), p. 1.

2. Clyde Kluckhohn and William Kelly, "The Concept of Culture," in Ralph Linton (ed.), *The Science of Man in the World Crisis* (New York: Columbia University Press, 1945).

3. Alfred Kroeber and Clyde Kluckhohn, *Culture: A Critical Review of Concepts and Definitions* (New York: Vintage, 1963), p. 357.

4. W. G. Sumner, *Folkways* (New York: New American Library, 1907).

5. E. A. Hoebel, *Anthropology: The Study of Man* (New York: McGraw-Hill, 1972), p. 332.

6. O. Michael Watson, *Proxemic Behavior: A Cross-cultural Study* (The Hague: Mouton, 1970).

7. Robin Williams, Jr., *American Society: A Sociological Interpretation* (New York: Knopf, 1960).

8. Carlos Castaneda, *The Teachings of Don Juan: A Yaqui Way of Knowledge* (Berkeley and Los Angeles: University of California Press, 1968); Castaneda, *A Separate Reality: Further Conversations with Don Juan* (New York: Simon and Schuster, 1971); Castaneda, *Journey to Ixtlan* (New York: Simon and Schuster, 1972); and Castaneda, *Tales of Power* (New York: Simon and Schuster, 1974).

9. Philip L. Newman, *Knowing the Gururumba* (New York: Holt, Rinehart and Winston, 1965), p. 104.

10. P. Ekman and W. V. Friesen, "Constants across Cultures in the Face and Emotion," *Journal of Personality and Social Psychology* 17 (February 1971), pp. 124–129.

11. J. Itani, "The Society of Japanese Monkeys," *Japan Quarterly* 8 (October-December 1961), pp. 421–430.

12. See Harlan Lane, *The Wild Boy of Aveyron* (Cambridge, Mass.: Harvard University Press, 1976).

13. Clifford Geertz, "The Impact of the Concept of Culture on the Concept of Man," in Y. Cohen (ed.), *Man in Adaptation: The Cultural Present* (Chicago: Aldine Publishing, 1968).

14. Leslie White, with B. Dillingham, *The Concept of Culture* (Minneapolis: Burgess Publishing, 1973), p. 1.

15. W. N. Kellogg and L. Kellogg, *The Ape and the Child: A Study of Environmental Influence upon Early Behavior* (New York: McGraw-Hill, 1933).

16. K. J. Hayes and C. Hayes, "Imitation in a Home-Raised Chimpanzee," *Journal of Comparative Physiological Psychology* 45 (October 1952), pp. 450–459.

17. R. A. Gardner and B. T. Gardner, "Teaching Sign Language to a Chimpanzee," *Science* 165 (1969), pp. 664–672.

18. David Premack, "The Assessment of Language Competence in the Chimpanzee," in A. Schrier and F. Stollnitz (eds.), *Behavior of Nonhuman Primates* (New York: Academic Press, 1971).

19. Ralph Linton, *The Study of Man* (New York: Appleton-Century-Crofts, 1936), pp. 326–377.

20. Hoebel, *Anthropology: The Study of Man*, pp. 651–653.

21. James Mooney, *The Ghost Dance Religion and Sioux Outbreak of 1890* (Chicago: University of Chicago Press, 1895).

22. William F. Ogburn, *Social Change: With Respect to Culture and Original Nature* (New York: Huebsch, 1922).

23. Edward T. Hall, *The Silent Language* (Greenwich, Conn.: Fawcett, 1959).

Chapter 4

1. Theodosius Dobzhansky, "Differences Are Not Deficits," *Psychology Today*, December 1973, pp. 96–101.

2. Otto Klineberg, "What Psychological Tests Show," in Bernard J. Stern and Allain Locke (eds.), *When People Meet* (New York: Progressive Education Association, 1942).

3. Arthur R. Jensen, "How Much Can We Boost I.Q. and Scholastic Achievement?" *Harvard Educational Review* 39 (Winter 1969), pp. 1–123.

4. Margaret Mead, *Sex and Temperament in Three Primitive Societies* (New York: William Morrow, 1935).

5. Eleanor E. Maccoby and Carol N. Jacklin, *The Psychology of Sex Differences* (Stanford, Calif.: Stanford University Press, 1974).

6. George C. Homans, *Social Behavior: Its Elementary Forms*, 2d ed. (New York: Harcourt Brace Jovanovich, 1974).

7. William H. Sewell, "Infant Training and the Personality of the Child," *American Journal of Sociology* 58 (September 1952), pp. 150–159.

8. David Riesman, with Nathan Glaser and Reuel Denney, *The Lonely Crowd* (New Haven: Yale University Press, 1950).

9. James A. Schellenberg, *An Introduction to Social Psychology*, 2d ed. (New York: Random House, 1974).

10. The discussion of Mead's three stages is largely taken from Reece McGee, *Points of Departure*, 2d ed. (Hinsdale, Ill.: Dryden Press, 1975).

11. Albert Bandura, Dorothea Ross, and Sheila A. Ross, "A Comparative Test of the Status Envy, Social Power, and Secondary Reinforcement Theories of Identificatory Learning," *Journal of Abnormal and Social Psychology* 67 (December 1963), pp. 527–534.

12. Brian Sutton-Smith and B. G. Rosenberg, *The Sibling* (New York: Holt, Rinehart and Winston, 1970).

13. Surgeon General's Scientific Advisory Committee on Television and Social Behavior, *Television and Growing Up: The Impact of Televised Violence*, U.S. Department of Health, Education, and Welfare (Washington, D.C.: Government Printing Office, 1971).

14. Harry F. Harlow and M. K. Harlow, "Social Deprivation in Monkeys," *Scientific American*, November 1962, pp. 136–146.

15. Kingsley Davis, "Final Note on a Case of Extreme Isolation," *American Journal of Sociology* 52 (March 1947), pp. 432–437.

Chapter 5

1. Robert F. Bales, *Interaction Process Analysis* (Cambridge, Mass.: Addison-Wesley, 1950).

2. William I. Thomas, *The Unadjusted Girl* (Boston: Little, Brown, 1931), pp. 41–50.

3. Erving Goffman, *Asylums* (Garden City, N.Y.: Doubleday, 1961).

4. Gresham M. Sykes, *The Society of Captives* (Princeton: Princeton University Press, 1958).

5. Theodore Caplow, *Principles of Organization* (New York: Harcourt Brace Jovanovich, 1964), pp. 201–228.

6. J. Kenneth Benson and Edward W. Hassinger, "Organization Set and Resources as Determinants of Formalization in Religious Organizations," *Review of Religious Research* 14 (Fall 1972), pp. 30–36.

Chapter 6

1. Robert J. Kleiner and Seymour Parker, "Goal-Striving, Social Status, and Mental Disorder," *American Sociological Review* 28 (April 1963), pp. 189–203.

2. Ralf Dahrendorf, "Out of Utopia: Toward a Reorientation of Sociological Analysis," *American Journal of Sociology* 64 (September 1958), pp. 115–127.

3. See, for example, Richard Cloward and Lloyd Ohlin, *Delinquency and Opportunity: A Theory of Delinquent Gangs* (New York: Free Press, 1960).

4. Michel Crozier, *The Bureaucratic Phenomenon* (Chicago: University of Chicago Press, 1964).

5. William Foote Whyte, *Street Corner Society* (Chicago: University of Chicago Press, 1943).

6. See Robert F. Bales, *Interaction Process Analysis* (Cambridge, Mass.: Addison-Wesley, 1950).

7. Charles H. Cooley, *Social Organization* (New York: Scribner's, 1909).

8. See Georg Simmel, *The Sociology of Georg Simmel,* trans. Kurt H. Wolff (New York: Free Press, 1950).

9. Theodore Caplow, *Two against One* (Englewood Cliffs, N.J.: Prentice-Hall, 1968).

10. Muzafer Sherif, *Intergroup Conflict and Cooperation: The Robbers Cave Experiment* (Norman, Okla.: Institute of Group Relations, 1961).

11. Whyte, *Street Corner Society.*

12. Robert K. Merton, "Continuities in the Theory of Reference Groups and Social Structure," in Merton, *Social Theory and Social Structure* (New York: Free Press, 1968).

13. Samuel A. Stouffer et al., *The American Soldier* (Princeton: Princeton University Press, 1949).

14. Merton, "Continuities in the Theory of Reference Groups and Social Structure."

15. Solomon E. Asch, "Effects of Group Pressures upon the Modification and Distortion of Judgements," in H. Guetzhow (ed.), *Group, Leadership, and Men* (Pittsburgh: Carnegie Press, 1951).

16. Ibid.

17. J. S. Mouton, R. N. Blake, and J. A. Olmstead, "The Relationship between Frequency of Yielding and the Disclosure of Personal Identity," *Journal of Personality* 24 (March 1956), pp. 339–347.

Chapter 7

1. Peter M. Blau and W. Richard Scott, *Formal Organizations* (San Francisco: Chandler Publishing, 1962).

2. Amitai Etzioni, *A Comparative Analysis of Complex Organizations* (New York: Free Press, 1961).

3. Mayer Zald (ed.), *Social Welfare Institutions* (New York: Wiley, 1965).

4. David L. Sills, *The Volunteers* (New York: Free Press, 1958).

5. Phillip Selznick, *TVA and the Grass Roots* (Berkeley and Los Angeles: University of California Press, 1949).

6. Eliot Freidson, *Profession of Medicine* (New York: Dodd, Mead, 1970).

7. Gerhard Lenski and Joan Lenski, *Human Societies,* 2d ed. (New York: McGraw-Hill, 1974).

8. Karl von Clausewitz, *On War,* trans. O. J. Matthijs Jolles (New York: Random House, 1943).

9. Reinhard Bendix, *Work and Authority in Industry* (New York: Harper & Bros., 1956).

10. Ferdinand Tönnies, *Community and Society: Gemeinschaft and Gesellschaft,* trans. and ed. Charles P. Loomis (New York: Harper & Bros., 1957).

11. See, for example, Talcott Parsons, *Societies: Evolutionary and Comparative Perspectives* (Englewood Cliffs, N.J.: Prentice-Hall, 1966); Parsons, *The System of Modern Societies* (Englewood Cliffs, N.J.: Prentice-Hall, 1971); and S. N. Eisenstadt, *Social Differentiation and Stratification* (Glenview, Ill.: Scott, Foresman, 1971).

12. Lauriston Sharp, "Steel Axes for Stone Age Australians," in Edward H. Spicer (ed.), *Human Problems in Technological Change* (New York: Russell Sage Foundation, 1952).

13. Emile Durkheim, *The Division of Labor in Society,* trans. George Simpson (New York: Crowell–Collier and Macmillan, 1933).

14. Parsons, *Societies: Evolutionary and Comparative Perspectives,* and Parsons, *The System of Modern Societies.*

15. See Herbert Marcuse, *One Dimensional Man* (Boston: Beacon Press, 1964); and Jürgen Habermas, *Toward a Rational Society,* trans. Jeremy J. Shapiro (Boston: Beacon Press, 1970).

16. Max Weber, *The Protestant Ethic and the Spirit of Capitalism,* trans. Talcott Parsons (New York: Scribner's, 1930).

17. See Talcott Parsons, *The Social System* (New York: Free Press, 1951); and Seymour Martin Lipset, "The Value Patterns of Democracy: A Case Study in Comparative Analysis," *American Sociological Review* 28 (August 1963), pp. 515–531.

18. For varied treatments of these problems, see Henri Lefebvre, *Everyday Life in the Modern World,* trans. Sacha Rabinovitch (New York: Harper & Row, 1971); John Kenneth Galbraith, *The New Industrial State,* 2d ed. (New York: New American Library, 1971); Alain Touraine, *The Post-Industrial Society,* trans. Leonard F. X. Mayhew (New York: Random House, 1971); and Norman Birnbaum, *The Crisis of Industrial Society* (New York: Oxford University Press, 1969).

19. Amitai Etzioni, *The Active Society* (New York: Free Press, 1968).

20. Daniel Bell, *The Coming of Post-Industrial Society* (New York: Basic Books, 1973).

Chapter 8

1. The following discussion is based on Gerhard E. Lenski, *Power and Privilege: A Theory of Social Stratification* (New York: McGraw-Hill, 1966).

2. See Robert W. Hodge, Paul M. Siegel, and Peter H. Rossi, "Occupational Prestige in the United States, 1925–63," *American Journal of Sociology* 70 (November 1964), pp. 286–302.

3. Kingsley Davis and Wilbert T. Moore, "Some Principles of Stratification," *American Sociological Review* 10 (April 1945), pp. 242–249.

4. U.S. Bureau of the Census, *Census of Population: 1970, Subject Reports; Final Report PC(2)-8B: Earnings by Occupation and Education* (Washington, D.C.: Government Printing Office, 1973).

5. S. M. Miller and Pamela A. Roby, *The Future of Inequality* (New York: Basic Books, 1970), pp. 91–97.

6. Oscar Ornati, *Poverty amid Affluence* (New York: Twentieth Century Fund, 1966), pp. 73 and 184.

7. Miller and Roby, *The Future of Inequality,* pp. 92–93.

8. Richard Centers, *The Psychology of Social Classes* (Princeton: Princeton University Press, 1949).

9. Herman M. Case, "An Independent Test of the Interest-Group Theory of Social Class," *American Sociological Review* 17 (December 1952), pp. 751–755.

10. See, for example, Floyd Dotson, "Patterns of Voluntary Association among Urban Working Class Families," *American Sociological Review* 16 (October 1951), pp. 687–693; Lloyd W. Warner and Paul S. Lunt, *The Social Life of a Modern Community* (New Haven: Yale University Press, 1941); and Murray Hausknecht, *The Joiners* (New York: Bedminster Press, 1962).

11. Herbert H. Hyman and Charles R. Wright, "Trends in Voluntary Association Memberships of American Adults: Replication Based on Secondary Analysis of National Sample Surveys," *American Sociological Review* 36 (April 1971), pp. 191–206; and James Curtis, "Voluntary Association Joining: A Cross-National Comparative Note," *American Sociological Review* 36 (October 1971), pp. 872–880.

12. Herbert J. Gans, *The Urban Villagers* (New York: Free Press, 1962); and Albert K. Cohen and Harold M. Hodges, Jr., "Characteristics of the Lower-Blue-Collar-Class," *Social Problems* 10 (Spring 1963), pp. 303–334.

13. Cohen and Hodges, "Characteristics of the Lower-Blue-Collar-Class."

14. Gans, *The Urban Villagers;* Cohen and Hodges, "Characteristics of the Lower-Blue-Collar-Class"; and Elliot Liebow, *Tally's Corner* (Boston: Little, Brown, 1967).

15. Mirra Komarovsky, *Blue-Collar Marriage* (New York: Random House, 1962).

16. Melvin L. Kohn, *Class and Conformity: A Study in Values* (Homewood, Ill.: Dorsey Press, 1969), pp. 105–106.

17. Joseph A. Kahl, *The American Class Structure* (New York: Holt, Rinehart and Winston, 1957), pp. 187–220.

18. S. M. Miller and Frank Riessman, "The Working Class

Subculture: A New View," *Social Problems* 9 (Summer 1961), pp. 86–97.

19. Karl Marx and Friedrich Engels, *The Communist Manifesto*, trans. Samuel Moore and ed. Joseph Katz (New York: Washington Square Press, 1964).

20. See Holger Stub, *Status Communities in Modern Society* (Hinsdale, Ill.: Dryden Press, 1972).

21. G. William Domhoff, *Who Rules America?* (Englewood Cliffs, N.J.: Prentice-Hall, 1967), p. 5.

22. Donald R. Matthews, *U.S. Senators and Their World* (Chapel Hill: University of North Carolina Press, 1960).

23. Floyd Hunter, *Community Power Structure: A Study of Decision Makers* (Chapel Hill: University of North Carolina Press, 1960).

24. Robert A. Dahl, *Who Governs?* (New Haven: Yale University Press, 1961).

25. Arnold M. Rose, *The Power Structure: Political Process in American Society* (New York: Oxford University Press, 1967), p. 297.

26. C. Wright Mills, *The Power Elite* (New York: Oxford University Press, 1956).

27. Gerald D. Berreman, *Caste in the Modern World* (Morristown, N.J.: General Learning Press, 1973), pp. 2–11.

28. Valerie Kincade Oppenheimer, "Demographic Influence on Female Employment and the Status of Women," *American Journal of Sociology* 78 (January 1973), pp. 946–948.

29. Larry E. Suter and Herman P. Miller, "Income Differences between Men and Career Women," *American Journal of Sociology* 78 (January 1973), p. 962.

30. Eleanor E. Maccoby, "Sex Differences in Intellectual Functioning," in Maccoby (ed.), *The Development of Sex Differences* (Stanford, Calif.: Stanford University Press, 1966), pp. 26 and 48.

31. Eleanor E. Maccoby and Carl Nagy Jacklin, "What We Know and Don't Know about Sex Differences," *Psychology Today*, December 1974, p. 12.

32. Jeffrey Z. Rubin, Frank J. Provenzano, and Zella Luria, "The Eye of the Beholder: Parents' Views on Sex of Newborns," *American Journal of Orthopsychiatry* 44 (July 1974), pp. 512–519.

33. Jerrie Will, Patricia Self, and Nancy Datan, research reported in *Behavior Today*, October 7, 1974, p. 261.

34. The following discussion is based on Patricia Ruth Jette, "The Contemporary Status of Women in American Society," unpublished manuscript.

35. William H. Sewell and Vimal P. Shah, "Socioeconomic Status, Intelligence, and the Attainment of Higher Education," *Sociology of Education* 40 (Winter 1967), pp. 1–23.

36. Oscar Lewis, "The Culture of Poverty," *Scientific American*, October 1966, pp. 19–25.

37. Pitirim A. Sorokin, *Social and Cultural Mobility* (New York: Free Press, 1959).

38. Hodge, Siegel, and Rossi, "Occupational Prestige in the United States, 1925–63."

39. Jack P. Gibbs and Walter T. Martin, *Status Integration and Suicide: A Sociological Study* (Eugene: University of Oregon Books, 1964).

40. Seymour Martin Lipset and Reinhard Bendix, *Social Mobility in Industrial Society* (Berkeley and Los Angeles: University of California Press, 1959).

41. S. M. Miller, "Comparative Social Mobility: A Trend Report," *Current Sociology* 9 (1960), pp. 1–89.

42. Peter M. Blau and Otis Dudley Duncan, *The American Occupational Structure* (New York: Wiley, 1967), pp. 23–80.

43. See Lipset and Bendix, *Social Mobility in Industrial Society*, pp. 227–229; and Harry J. Crockett, Jr., "The Achievement Motive and Differential Occupational Mobility in the United States," *American Sociological Review* 27 (April 1962), pp. 191–204.

44. Joseph A. Kahl, "Educational and Occupational Aspirations of 'Common Man' Boys," *Harvard Educational Review* 23 (Summer 1953), pp. 186–203.

45. William H. Sewell, "Inequality of Opportunity for Higher Education," *American Sociological Review* 36 (October 1971), p. 800.

Chapter 9

1. Theodosius Dobzhansky, *Mankind Evolving: The Evolution of the Human Species* (New Haven: Yale University Press, 1962), p. 228.

2. Robert Blauner, *Racial Oppression in America* (New York: Harper & Row, 1972), pp. 51–81.

3. Gordon W. Allport, *The Nature of Prejudice* (Garden City, N.Y.: Doubleday, 1958), pp. 8–9.

4. Gunnar Myrdahl, *An American Dilemma* (New York: Harper & Bros., 1944).

5. See, for example, John Dollard, *Caste and Class in a Southern Town* (New Haven: Yale University Press, 1937).

6. Victoria F. Davison and Lyle W. Shannon, "Change in the Economic Absorption of Immigrant Mexican Americans and Negroes in Racine, Wisconsin, between 1960 and 1971" (mimeo), Iowa Urban Community Research Center, Iowa City, Iowa, 1975.

7. U.S. Bureau of the Census, *Statistical Abstract of the United States, 1972* (Washington, D.C.: Government Printing Office, 1972); and Alphonso Pinkney, *Black Americans*, 2d ed. (Englewood Cliffs, N.J.: Prentice-Hall, 1975).

8. U.S. Bureau of Census, *Statistical Abstract of the United States, 1972*, p. 61.

9. Bennett Harrison, "Education and Underemployment in the Urban Ghetto," in David Gordon (ed.), *Problems in Political Economy: An Urban Perspective* (Lexington, Mass.: D.C. Health, 1971).

10. Harold M. Baron and Bennett Hymer, "The Dynamics of the Dual Labor Market," in Gordon (ed.), *Problems in Political Economy: An Urban Perspective*.

11. Gary Becker, *The Economics of Discrimination* (Chicago: University of Chicago Press, 1957).

12. Michael Reich, "The Economics of Racism," in Gordon (ed.) *Problems in Political Economy: An Urban Perspective*.

13. Louis Wirth, "The Problem of Minority Groups," in Ralph Linton (ed.), *The Science of Man in the World Crisis* (New York: Columbia University Press, 1945).

14. John Hope Franklin, *From Slavery to Freedom* (New York: Knopf, 1948), p. 465.

15. Gilbert Osofsky, "Harlem: The Making of a Ghetto," Ph.D. thesis, Columbia University, 1963; and Allan Spear, *Black Chicago: The Making of a Negro Ghetto, 1890–1920* (Chicago: University of Chicago Press, 1967).

16. Pinkney, *Black Americans*, p. 330.

17. August Meier and Elliot Rudwick, *From Plantation to Ghetto* (New York: Hill and Wang, 1966), p. 213.

18. Sidney Wilhelm, *Who Needs the Negro?* (New York: Schenkman Publishing, 1970), p. 80.

19. Ibid.

20. Andrew Billingsley, *Black Families in White America* (Englewood Cliffs, N.J.: Prentice-Hall, 1968), p. 89.

21. U.S. Department of Labor, Bureau of Labor Statistics, *The Negroes in the United States: Their Economic and Social Situation* (Washington, D.C.: Government Printing Office, 1966), p. 211.

22. Pinkney, *Black Americans*, p. 75.

23. U.S. Bureau of the Census, *The Social and Economic Status of the Black Population in the United States, 1972* (Washington, D.C.: Government Printing Office, 1973), p. 49.

24. Pinkney, *Black Americans*, p. 83.

25. Paul M. Siegel, "On the Cost of Being Negro," *Sociological Inquiry* 35 (Winter 1965), pp. 41–57.

26. Rashi Fein, "An Economic and Social Profile of the Negro American," in Talcott Parsons and Kenneth Clark (eds.), *The Negro American* (Boston: Houghton Mifflin, 1966).

27. Stanford Lyman, *Chinese Americans* (New York: Random House, 1974), p. 63.

28. George E. Simpson and J. Milton Yinger, *Racial and Cultural Minorities*, 3rd ed. (New York: Harper & Row, 1965), p. 94.

29. Lyman, *Chinese Americans*, p. 151.

30. Calvin Schmid and Charles E. Nobbe, "Socio-economic Differentials among Nonwhite Races," *American Sociological Review* 30 (December 1965), pp. 909–922.

31. S. L. A. Marshall, *Crimsoned Prairie: The Indian Wars on the Great Plains* (New York: Scribner's, 1972).

32. Robert F. Spencer et al., *The Native Americans* (New York: Harper & Row, 1965), p. 500.

33. Harold E. Fey and D'Arcy McNickle, *Indians and Other Americans* (New York: Harper & Row, 1970), p. 63.

34. Spencer et al., *The Native Americans*.

35. Carey McWilliams, *North from Mexico* (New York: Greenwood Press, 1968), p. 267.

36. Joseph P. Fitzpatrick, *Puerto Rican Americans* (Englewood Cliffs, N.J.: Prentice-Hall, 1971), p. 17.

37. "Study Criticizes Migrant Camps," *New York Times,* August 27, 1972, p. 38.

38. "Spanish Origin Persons Found Lagging in Purchasing Power," *New York Times,* August 7, 1974, p. 14.

39. Michael Krause, *Immigration: The American Mosaic* (New York: Van Nostrand, 1966), p. 93.

40. See William Shannon, *The American Irish* (New York: Crowell-Collier and Macmillan, 1963); and John Higham, *Strangers in the Land* (New York: Atheneum, 1971).

41. H. M. Sachar, *The Course of Modern Jewish History* (New York: World Publishing, 1958).

42. W. I. Thomas and Florian Znaniecki, *The Polish Peasant in Europe and America*, 2d ed. (New York: Knopf, 1927).

43. Perry Weed, "The White Ethnic Movement and Ethnic Politics," in Joseph A. Ryan (ed.), *White Ethnics* (Englewood Cliffs, N.J.: Prentice-Hall, 1973).

44. Horace Kallen, *Americanism and Its Makers* (n.p.: Bureau of Jewish Education, 1944), pp. 13–14.

45. Harold Cruse, *Rebellion or Revolution* (New York: William Morrow, 1969), p. 106.

Chapter 10

1. Louis Wirth, "Urbanism as a Way of Life," *American Journal of Sociology* 40 (July 1938), pp. 1–24.

2. James Mellaart, "A Neolithic City in Turkey," *Scientific American,* April 1964, pp. 94–106.

3. Charles Glaab and Theodore A. Brown, *History of Urban America* (Madison: University of Wisconsin Press, 1967).

4. Gideon Sjoberg, *The Preindustrial City* (New York: Free Press, 1960).

5. Louis Wirth, *The Ghetto* (Chicago: University of Chicago Press, 1928); Herbert J. Gans, *The Urban Villagers* (New York: Free Press, 1962); and Jane Jacobs, *The Death and Life of Great American Cities* (New York: Random House, 1961).

6. Glaab and Brown, *History of Urban America.*

7. Donald J. Bogue, *The Structure of the Metropolitan Community* (Ann Arbor: University of Michigan Press, 1950).

8. Arthur Vidich and Joseph Bensman, *Small Town in Mass Society* (Princeton: Princeton University Press, 1968).

9. Glaab and Brown, *History of Urban America.*

10. Jean Gottman, *Megalopolis: The Urbanized Northeastern Seaboard of the United States* (Cambridge, Mass.: M.I.T. Press, 1964).

11. Robert Weller, "An Empirical Examination of Megalopolitan," in Kent P. Schwirian (ed.), *Comparative Urban Structure: Studies in the Ecology of Cities* (Lexington, Mass.: D. C. Heath, 1974).

12. Earl S. Johnson, "The Function of the Central Business District in the Metropolitan Community," in Paul K. Hapt and Albert J. Reiss, Jr. (eds.), *Cities and Society* (Glencoe, Ill.: Free Press, 1957).

13. Ernest Burgess, "The Growth of the City," in Robert Park, E. W. Burgess, and R. D. McKenzie (eds.), *The City* (Chicago: University of Chicago Press, 1925).

14. Homer Hoyt, *The Structure and Growth of Residential Neighborhoods in the United States* (Washington, D.C.: Federal Housing Administration, 1939).

15. Chauncy Harris and Edward L. Ullman, "The Nature of Cities," *Annals of the American Academy of Political and Social Science* 242 (November 1945), pp. 7–17.

16. Beverly Duncan, Georges Sobagh, and Maurice D. Van Arsdol, Jr., "Patterns of City Growth," *American Journal of Sociology* 68 (January 1962), pp. 418–429.

17. Wirth, *The Ghetto.*

18. Gilbert Osofsky, *Harlem: The Making of a Ghetto* (New York: Harper & Row, 1963); and Allan Spear, *Black Chicago: The Making of a Negro Ghetto, 1890–1920* (Chicago: University of Chicago Press, 1967).

19. Karl Taeuber, "Residential Segregation," *Scientific American,* August 1965, pp. 12–19.

Chapter 11

1. United Nations, *The Determinants and Consequences of Population Trends: New Summary of Findings on Interaction of Demographic, Economic, and Social Factors,* vol. 1, Department of Economic and Social Affairs, Population Studies No. 50 (New York: United Nations, 1973), p. 2.

2. Thomas Robert Malthus, *On Population,* ed. Gertrude Himmelfarb (New York: Modern Library, 1960).

3. See Roland Pressat, *Population* (Baltimore: Penguin Books, 1971), p. 112.

4. United Nations, *The Determinants and Consequences of Population Trends: New Summary of Findings on Interaction of Demographic, Economic, and Social Factors,* vol. 1, p. 31.

5. John D. Durand, "A Long-range View of World Population Growth," *Annals of the American Academy of Political and Social Science* 369 (January 1967), p. 7.

6. See Michael Micklin (ed.), *Population, Environment, and Social Organization: Current Issues in Human Ecology* (Hinsdale, Ill.: Dryden Press, 1973).

7. Shirley Foster Hartley, *Population: Quantity vs. Quality* (Englewood Cliffs, N.J.: Prentice-Hall, 1972), p. 87.

8. United Nations, *The Determinants and Consequences of Population Trends: New Summary of Findings on Interaction of Demographic, Economic, and Social Factors,* vol. 1, pp. 183 and 191.

9. Donald J. Bogue, *Principles of Demography* (New York: Wiley, 1969), p. 131; and U.S. Bureau of the Census, *Census of the Population,* vol. 1: *Characteristics of the Population* (Washington, D.C.: Government Printing Office, 1973), p. 42.

10. Philip M. Hauser, "The Chaotic Society: Product of the Social Morphological Revolution," *American Sociological Review* 34 (February 1969), pp. 1–19.

11. U.S. Bureau of the Census, *Population of the United States: Trends and Prospects, 1950–1990,* Current Population Reports, Series P-23, No. 49 (Washington, D.C.: Government Printing Office, 1974), p. 61.

12. Computed from data in ibid.

13. J. C. Elizaga, "Internal Migrations for Latin America," *Milbank Memorial Fund Quarterly* 43 (1965), pp. 144–161.

14. S. H. Ominde, *Land and Population Movements in Kenya* (Evanston: Northwestern University Press, 1968); and John C. Caldwell, *African Rural-Urban Migration: The Movement to Ghana's Towns* (New York: Columbia University Press, 1969).

15. United Nations, *The Determinants and Consequences of Population Trends: New Summary of Findings on Interaction of Demographic, Economic, and Social Factors,* vol. 1, p. 283.

16. Lester R. Brown, with Erik P. Eckholm, *By Bread Alone* (New York: Praeger, 1974), pp. 37–38.

17. Lester R. Brown, *Man, Land, and Food: Looking Ahead at World Food Needs,* Foreign Agricultural Economic Report No. 11 (Washington, D.C.: Government Printing Office, 1963), p. 31.

18. Brown and Eckholm, *By Bread Alone,* p. 60.

19. Ibid., p. 32.

20. See, for example, Robert F. Chandler, Jr., "The Scientific Basis for the Increased Yield Capacity of Rice and Wheat, and Its Present and Potential Impact on Food Production in the Developing Countries," in T. T. Poleman and D. K. Freebairn (eds.), *Food, Population, and Employment: The Impact of the Green Revolution* (New York: Praeger, 1973); Committee on Engineering Policy,

World Hunger: Approaches to Engineering Actions (Washington, D.C.: National Research Council, 1975); and S. H. Wittwer, "Food Production: Technology and the Resource Base," *Science* 188 (May 9, 1975), pp. 579–584.

21. See Clifton R. Wharton, Jr., "The Green Revolution: Cornucopia or Pandora's Box?" *Foreign Affairs* 47 (April 1969), pp. 464–476; Lester R. Brown, *In the Human Interest* (New York: Norton, 1974), pp. 50–53; Brown and Eckholm, *By Bread Alone,* pp. 133–146; and Pierre R. Crossen, "Institutional Obstacles to Expansion of World Food Production," *Science* 188 (May 9, 1975), pp. 519–524.

22. Brown and Eckholm, *By Bread Alone,* p. 11.

23. Joseph L. Fisher and Neal Potter, "Natural Resource Adequacy for the United States and the World," in P. M. Hauser (ed.), *The Population Dilemma,* 2d ed. (Englewood Cliffs, N.J.: Prentice-Hall, 1969).

24. United Nations, *The Determinants and Consequences of Population Trends: New Summary of Findings on Interaction of Demographic, Economic, and Social Factors,* vol. 1, p. 377.

25. Joel Darmstadter, "Energy Consumption: Trends and Patterns," in Sam H. Schurr (ed.), *Energy, Economic Growth, and the Environment* (Baltimore: Johns Hopkins University Press, 1972).

26. Donella H. Meadows, Dennis L. Meadows, Jorgen Randers, and William W. Behrens, III, *The Limits to Growth: A Report of the Club of Rome's Project on the Predicament of Mankind* (New York: Universe Books, 1972), pp. 64–68.

27. Paul R. Ehrlich, Ann H. Ehrlich, and John P. Holdren, *Human Ecology: Problems and Solutions* (San Francisco: W. H. Freeman, 1973), p. 115.

28. I. G. Simmons, *The Ecology of Natural Resources* (London: Edward Arnold, 1974), pp. 276–277.

29. Ibid., pp. 342–343.

30. Hartley, *Population: Quantity vs. Quality,* p. 181.

31. Lester R. Brown, *World without Borders* (New York: Random House, 1972), p. 42.

32. See Michael Micklin, "Demographic, Economic, and Social Change in Latin America: An Examination of Causes and Consequences," *Journal of Developing Areas* 4 (January 1970), pp. 173–197; and Brown, *In the Human Interest,* pp. 145–147.

33. Robert Heilbroner, *An Inquiry into the Human Prospect* (New York: Norton, 1974).

34. Dorothy Nortman, assisted by Ellen Hofstatter, "Population and Family Planning Programs: A Factbook," in *Reports on Population/Family Planning,* No. 2, 6th ed., December 1974.

35. Donald J. Bogue, "The End of the Population Explosion," *Public Interest* 7 (Spring 1967), p. 19.

36. Kingsley Davis, "Population Policy: Will Current Programs Succeed?" *Science* 158 (November 10, 1967), pp. 730–739.

37. Walter B. Watson and Robert J. Lapham (eds.), "Family Planning Programs: World Review, 1974," *Studies in Family Planning* 6 (August 1975), p. 219.

38. United Nations Economic and Social Council, Population Commission, *Report of the Ad Hoc Consultative Group of Experts on Population Policy* (C/CN, 9/267) (New York: United Nations, May 23, 1972), p. 6.

39. Nortman and Hofstatter, "Population and Family Planning Programs: A Factbook."

Chapter 12

1. Ernest L. Schusky, *Manual for Kinship Analysis* (New York: Holt, Rinehart and Winston, 1965).

2. George P. Murdock, *Social Structure* (New York: Crowell-Collier and Macmillan, 1949).

3. Ira Reiss, *The Family System in America* (New York: Holt, Rinehart and Winston, 1971).

4. Clyde Kluckhohn and Dorothea Leighton, *The Navaho,* rev. ed. (Garden City, N.Y.: Doubleday, 1962), p. 102.

5. Murdock, *Social Structure,* and Robert F. Winch, *Mate-Selection* (New York: Harper & Row, 1958).

6. J. Richard Udry, *The Social Context of Marriage* (Philadelphia: Lippincott, 1974).

7. William N. Kephart, *The Family, Society, and the Individual* (Boston: Houghton Mifflin, 1961).

8. David M. Heer, "Negro-White Marriage in the United States," *Journal of Marriage and the Family* 28 (August 1966), pp. 262–273.

9. J. Richard Udry, "Marital Instability by Race, Sex, and Income Based on 1960 Census Data," *American Journal of Sociology* 72 (1967), pp. 673–674.

10. Julius Roth and Robert F. Peck, "Social Class and Social Mobility Factors Related to Marital Adjustment," *American Sociological Review* 16 (1951), p. 481.

11. William J. Goode, *The Family* (Englewood Cliffs, N.J.: Prentice-Hall, 1969), p. 82.

12. Robert O. Blood, *Marriage* (New York: Free Press, 1962), p. 69.

13. Winch, *Mate-Selection.*

14. Bela Mittelmann, "Analysis of Reciprocal Neurotic Patterns in Family Relationships," in Victor W. Eisenstein (ed.), *Neurotic Interaction in Marriage* (New York: Basic Books, 1956).

15. Udry, *The Social Context of Marriage.*

16. Irving Berlin, "You're Just in Love," *Call Me Madam* (New York: Irving Berlin Music Corporation, n.d.).

17. Bernard Farber, *Family, Organization, and Interaction* (San Francisco: Chandler Publishing, 1964).

18. Clifford Kirkpatrick, *The Family as Process and Institution,* 2d ed. (New York: Ronald Press, 1963).

19. Joseph Ribal, unpublished case history.

20. Ibid.

21. Ibid.

22. George Levinger, "Sources of Marital Dissatisfaction among Applicants for Divorce," *American Journal of Orthopsychiatry* 36 (1966), pp. 803–807.

23. U.S. Bureau of the Census, *Statistical Abstract of the United States, 1970* (Washington, D.C.: Government Printing Office, 1970).

24. Udry, *The Social Context of Marriage.*

25. Ibid., p. 401.

26. Nena O'Neill and George O'Neill, *Open Marriage: A New Life Style for Couples* (New York: M. Evans, 1972).

Chapter 13

1. Robert M. Hutchins, "The Basis of Education," in John Martin Rich (ed.), *Readings in the Philosophy of Education* (Belmont, Calif.: Wadsworth Publishing, 1966).

2. Ibid., p. 19.

3. Theodore Brameld, "Education for the Emerging Age," in Thomas O. Buford (ed.), *Toward a Philosophy of Education* (New York: Holt, Rinehart and Winston, 1969).

4. Leo Kuper, "The Intellectuals," in Harry M. Lindquist (ed.), *Education: Readings in the Processes of Cultural Transmission* (Boston: Houghton Mifflin, 1970).

5. Rosalie H. Wax, "The Warrior Dropouts," in Lindquist (ed.), *Education: Readings in the Processes of Cultural Transmission.*

6. Jesse L. Jackson, "Give the People a Vision," *New York Times Magazine,* April 18, 1976, pp. 13, 71–73.

7. Philip J. Idenburg, "Europe—In Search of New Forms of Education," in George Z. F. Bereday (ed.), *Essays on World Education* (New York: Oxford University Press, 1969).

8. Edgar Z. Friedenberg, "Status and Role in Education," in Jerome H. Skolnick and Elliott Currie (eds.), *Crisis in American Institutions* (Boston: Little, Brown, 1970).

9. Christopher Jencks et al., *Inequality* (New York: Harper & Row, 1972).

10. Michael Novak, "White Ethnic," in Dushkin Publishing Group (ed.), *Readings in Sociology* (Guilford, Conn.: Dushkin Publishing Group, 1972).

11. Richard Hofstadter, *Anti-intellectualism in American Life* (New York: Knopf, 1964).

12. Robert Coles, *The Middle Americans* (Boston: Little, Brown, 1971), p. 47.
13. Christopher Jencks and Marsha Brown, "The Effects of Desegregation on Student Achievement," *Sociology of Education* 48 (Winter 1975), pp. 126–140.
14. Frederick Rudolph, *The American College and University* (New York: Random House, 1962), p. 486.
15. Jencks et al., *Inequality*, p. 7.
16. Charles E. Silberman, *Crisis in the Classroom* (New York: Random House, 1970), p. 19.

Chapter 14

1. Mark Twain, *Letters from the Earth* (Greenwich, Conn.: Fawcett, 1968), pp. 179–180.
2. See Max Weber, *The Religion of China* (New York: Free Press, 1951); and C. K. Yang, *Religion in Chinese Society* (Berkeley and Los Angeles: University of California Press, 1961).
3. Sir Edward B. Tylor, *Primitive Culture* (New York: Harper & Row, 1958).
4. Emile Durkheim, *The Elementary Forms of the Religious Life* (New York: Free Press, 1965).
5. Ibid., p. 62.
6. Rudolf Otto, *The Idea of the Holy* (New York: Oxford University Press, 1958).
7. See Andrew Dickson White, *A History of the Warfare of Science and Theology in Christendom* (New York: Free Press, 1965).
8. See Joachim Wach, *Sociology of Religion* (Chicago: University of Chicago Press, 1962), p. 35.
9. Ludwig Feuerbach, *The Essence of Christianity* (New York: Harper & Bros., 1957).
10. Karl Marx, *The Economic and Philosophic Manuscripts of 1844* (New York: International Publishers, 1964), pp. 170–174.
11. H. Richard Niebuhr, *The Social Sources of Denominationalism* (New York: Meridian Books, 1957).
12. N. J. Demerath, III, *Social Class in American Protestantism* (Chicago: Rand McNally, 1965).
13. Rodney Stark and Charles Y. Glock, *American Piety: The Nature of Religious Commitment* (Berkeley and Los Angeles: University of California Press, 1968).
14. W. Lloyd Warner, *The Family of God* (New Haven: Yale University Press, 1961).
15. Will Herberg, *Protestant-Catholic-Jew*, rev. ed. (Garden City, N.Y.: Doubleday, 1960).
16. Robert N. Bellah, "Civil Religion in America," *Daedalus* 96 (Winter 1967), pp. 1–21.
17. Max Weber, *The Protestant Ethic and the Spirit of Capitalism* (New York: Scribner's, 1958).
18. Robert K. Merton, *Social Theory and Social Structure* (New York: Free Press, 1968), pp. 628–660.
19. Gerhard Lenski, *The Religious Factor*, rev. ed. (Garden City, N.Y.: Doubleday, 1963).
20. Ernst Troeltsch, *The Social Teaching of the Christian Churches* (London: George Allen & Unwin, 1931).
21. Neibuhr, *The Social Sources of Denominationalism.*
22. Liston Pope, *Millhands and Preachers* (New Haven: Yale University Press, 1942).
23. J. Milton Yinger, *The Scientific Study of Religion* (New York: Crowell-Collier and Macmillan, 1970).
24. Peter L. Berger and Thomas Luckmann, *The Social Construction of Reality* (Garden City, N.Y.: Doubleday, 1966).
25. Sidney E. Mead, *The Lively Experiment* (New York: Harper & Row, 1963).
26. See Seymour Martin Lipset, *The First New Nation* (New York: Basic Books, 1963).
27. Perry Miller, *Errand into the Wilderness* (New York: Harper & Row, 1964), p. 150.
28. Lipset, *The First New Nation.*
29. Quoted in Richard F. Tomasson, *Sweden: Prototype of Modern Society* (New York: Random House, 1970), p. 78.
30. Ibid., pp. 74–77.
31. Jeffrey K. Hadden, *The Gathering Storm in the Churches* (Garden City, N.Y.: Doubleday, 1969), p. 25.
32. Stark and Glock, *American Piety: The Nature of Religious Commitment*, pp. 141–162.
33. Talcott Parsons, *Sociological Theory and Modern Society* (New York: Free Press, 1967), pp. 385–421.

Chapter 15

1. Betty Werther, "Jokes They Tell in Czechoslovakia," *International Herald Tribune* (Paris), December 9, 1964, p. 6.
2. John Kenneth Galbraith, *The New Industrial State* (Boston: Houghton Mifflin, 1967).
3. C. Wright Mills, *The Power Elite* (New York: Oxford University Press, 1950); and Suzanne Keller, "Elites," in vol. 7 of David Sills (ed.), *The International Encyclopedia of the Social Sciences* (New York: Crowell-Collier and Macmillan, 1968).
4. Robin M. Williams, Jr., *American Society: A Sociological Interpretation*, 3rd ed. (New York: Knopf, 1970), p. 217.
5. The following discussion is based on Mark J. Green, James M. Fallows, and David R. Zwick, *Who Runs Congress?* (New York: Bantam Books, 1972).
6. Max Weber, *The Theory of Social and Economic Organization* (New York: Free Press, 1964).
7. See *Newsweek*, November 19, 1973, p. 64, and June 24, 1974, p. 44.
8. *The Europa Year Book: A World Survey* (London: Europa Publications, 1974), pp. 405–415.
9. Bruce M. Russett, Hayward R. Alker, Karl W. Deutsch, and Harold D. Lasswell, *World Handbook of Political and Social Indicators* (New Haven: Yale University Press, 1964), p. 99.
10. Claude E. Welch, Jr., and Mavis Bunker Taintor (eds.), *Revolution and Political Change* (North Scituate, Mass., and Belmont, Calif.: Duxbury Press, 1972).
11. Samuel P. Huntington, *Political Order in Changing Societies* (New Haven: Yale University Press, 1968).
12. John Dunn, *Modern Revolutions* (Cambridge: Cambridge University Press, 1972).
13. The following discussion is based on Samuel P. Huntington, "Political Modernization: America vs. Europe," *World Politics* 18 (April 1966), pp. 378–414; reprinted in Welch and Taintor, *Revolution and Political Change*, pp. 22–30.
14. U.S. Bureau of the Census, "Government Units in 1972," quoted in a news release of March 1, 1973; as given in Milton C. Cummings, Jr., and David Wise, *Democracy under Pressure*, 2d ed. (New York: Harcourt Brace Jovanovich, 1974), p. 68.
15. See James A. Michener, *Report of the County Chairman* (New York: Random House, 1961), for one example of the way the Kennedy campaign worked at the grass-roots level.
16. Orde Coombs, "Blacks and Rednecks: The Holy Alliance of '76," *New York Magazine*, July 19, 1976, p. 57.
17. David R. Segal, *Society and Politics* (Glenview, Ill.: Scott, Foresman, 1974), pp. 184–187.
18. *New York Times*, August 15, 1976, p. 24.
19. Robert Michels, *Political Parties: A Sociological Study of the Oligarchical Tendencies of Modern Democracy* (New York: Free Press, 1962).
20. The discussion of the Cook County political machine is based on Mike Royko, *Boss: Richard J. Daley of Chicago* (New York: New American Library, 1971).
21. See Terrence E. Cook and Patrick M. Morgan, *Participatory Democracy* (San Francisco: Canfield Press, 1971); C. George Benello and Dimitrios Roussopoulos (eds.), *The Case for Participatory Democracy (New York: Viking Press, 1971); Benjamin S. Kleinberg, American Society in the Postindustrial Age: Technocracy, Power, and the End of Ideology* (Columbus: Charles E. Merrill Publishing, 1973); Richard Flacks, "The Uses of Participatory Democracy," *Dissent* 13 (November–December 1966), pp. 701–708; Staughton Lynd, "The New Radicals and 'Participatory

Democracy,'" *Dissent* 12 (Summer 1965), pp. 324–333; and Massimo Teodori (ed.), *The New Left: A Documentary History* (Indianapolis: Bobbs-Merrill, 1969).

Chapter 16

1. See Elman R. Service, *Profiles in Ethnology* (New York: Harper & Row, 1963), pp. 3–25.

2. Walter Goldschmidt, *Man's Way* (New York: Holt, Rinehart and Winston, 1959), pp. 193–194.

3. Ibid., p. 195.

4. Ibid., pp. 196–209 give an excellent brief summary of the central characteristics of advanced agricultural societies.

5. See S. M. Lipset, *Political Man* (Garden City, N.Y.: Doubleday, 1959), pp. 48–75, for an in-depth analysis of this issue.

6. See Joseph R. Strayer et al., *The Mainstream of Civilization* (New York: Harcourt Brace Jovanovich, 1969), pp. 577–591, for a good survey of some of the social effects of industrialization.

7. R. G. Lipsey and P. O. Steiner, *Economics* (New York: Harper & Row, 1975), p. 395.

8. Ralph Gray and John M. Peterson, *Economic Development of the United States* (Homewood, Ill.: Richard D. Irwin, 1974), pp. 505–506.

9. "Labor: Long Way from Pittsburgh," *Time,* May 16, 1955, p. 27.

10. Ibid.

11. J. M. Kreps and Joseph J. Spengler, "The Leisure Component of Economic Growth," in H. R. Bowen and Garth L. Mangum (eds.), *Automation and Economic Progress* (Englewood Cliffs, N.J.: Prentice-Hall, 1966).

12. U.S. Bureau of the Census, *Statistical Abstract of the United States, 1974* (Washington, D.C.: Government Printing Office, 1975), p. 345.

13. The data are from "Size Distribution of Income in 1963," *Survey of Current Business,* April 1964, Table 4. Figures for 1913 are very rough approximations. This table is in H. P. Miller, "The Distribution of Personal Income in the United States," in Dennis M. Wrong and Harry L. Gracey (eds.), *Readings in Introductory Sociology* (New York: Crowell-Collier and Macmillan, 1972).

14. Ibid., p. 406.

15. Lipset, *Political Man,* p. 66.

16. U.S. Bureau of the Census, *Statistical Abstract of the United States, 1972* (Washington, D.C.: Government Printing Office, 1972), Table 366.

17. See Edward Fried et al., *Setting National Priorities: The 1974 Budget* (Washington, D.C.: Brookings Institution, 1973), p. 42.

18. Elizabeth K. Nottingham, *Religion and Society* (New York: Random House, 1964), pp. 19–26.

19. Thomas F. O'Dea, *The Sociology of Religion* (Englewood Cliffs, N.J.: Prentice-Hall, 1966), pp. 72–97.

20. *Statistical Abstract of the United States, 1974,* Table 1040, p. 614.

21. *Manpower Report of the President* (Washington, D.C.: Government Printing Office, April 1974), p. 268.

22. A. A. Berle and G. C. Means, *The Modern Corporation and Private Property* (New York: Commerce Clearing House, 1932).

23. Paul A. Samuelson, *Economics,* 10th ed. (New York: McGraw-Hill, 1976), p. 113.

24. Ibid.

25. Ibid., p. 112.

26. Wilbert E. Moore, *The Conduct of the Corporation* (New York: Random House, 1966), p. 5.

27. See John Kenneth Galbraith, *The New Industrial State* (Boston: Houghton Mifflin, 1967), p. 320.

28. This percentage was calculated from *Statistical Abstract of the United States, 1974,* Table 567.

29. See Daniel R. Fusfeld, *Economics* (Lexington, Mass.: D. C. Heath, 1976), p. 608.

30. Ibid.

31. Samuelson, *Economics,* pp. 132–133.

32. Fusfeld, *Economics,* p. 576.

33. Samuelson, *Economics,* p. 152.

34. Ibid., p. 148.

35. See Lipset, *Political Man,* pp. 285–309.

36. Daniel Yankelovich, "The Meaning of Work," in Jerome M. Rosow (ed.), *The Worker and the Job* (Englewood Cliffs, N.J.: Prentice-Hall, 1974).

37. See Richard C. Wilcock and Walter H. Franke, *Unwanted Workers* (New York: Free Press, 1963).

38. Nancy C. Morse and Robert S. Weiss, "The Function and Meaning of Work and the Job," *American Sociological Review* 20 (April 1955).

39. H. C. Wilensky, "Work as a Social Problem," in Howard S. Becker (ed.), *Social Problems* (New York: Wiley, 1966), p. 143.

40. Ibid., p. 165.

41. Ibid., p. 148.

42. See, for example, Daniel Bell, *The Coming of Post-industrial Society* (New York: Basic Books, 1973); Bell (ed.), *Toward the Year 2000: Work in Progress* (Boston: Houghton Mifflin, 1968); Herman Kahn and Anthony J. Wiener, *The Year 2,000* (New York: Crowell-Collier and Macmillan, 1967); and Alvin Toffler, *Future Shock* (New York: Random House, 1970).

43. Kahn and Wiener, *The Year 2,000,* p. 195.

44. Kreps and Spengler, "The Leisure Component of Economic Growth," p. 128.

45. *Statistical Abstract of the United States, 1974,* p. 345.

46. Miller, "The Distribution of Personal Income in the United States," p. 407.

47. *Statistical Abstract of the United States, 1974,* p. 376.

48. See Daniel Bell, "Notes on the Post-industrial Society," *Public Interest* 1 (Winter 1967), and 2 (Spring 1967); and Bell, *The Coming of Post-industrial Society,* pp. 358–367.

49. Bell, *The Coming of Post-industrial Society,* p. 362.

50. Charles Reich, "The New Property," *Public Interest* 3 (Spring 1966), p. 57.

51. John Maynard Keynes, "Economic Possibilities for Our Grandchildren," in Paul A. Samuelson, *Readings in Economics,* 7th ed. (New York: McGraw-Hill, 1973).

Chapter 17

1. Howard S. Becker, *Outsiders: Studies in the Sociology of Deviance* (New York: Free Press, 1963), p. 26.

2. James S. Wallerstein and Clement J. Wylie, "Our Law-Abiding Law-Breakers," *Probation* 25 (April 1947), pp. 107–112.

3. Georg Simmel, *Conflict and the Web of Group Affiliation,* trans. Kurt Wolff (New York: Free Press, 1955).

4. Emile Durkheim, *The Division of Labor in Society* (New York: Free Press, 1960).

5. Lewis Coser, *The Functions of Social Conflict* (New York: Free Press, 1956); and Coser, *Continuities in the Study of Social Conflict* (New York: Free Press, 1967).

6. Edwin H. Sutherland, "Differential Association," in Marvin E. Wolfgang, Leonard Savity, and Norman Johnston (eds.), *The Sociology of Crime and Delinquency* (New York: Wiley, 1970).

7. President's Commission on Law Enforcement and the Administration of Justice, *The Challenge of Crime in a Free Society* (Washington, D.C.: Government Printing Office, 1967).

8. See, for example, Wallerstein and Wylie, "Our Law-Abiding Law-Breakers"; and Austin Porterfield, "Delinquency and Its Outcome in Court and College," *American Journal of Sociology* 49 (November 1943), pp. 199–208.

9. Jay R. Williams and Martin Gold, "From Delinquent Behavior to Official Delinquency," *Social Problems* 20 (Fall 1972), pp. 209–229.

10. Philip H. Ennis, "Crimes, Victims, and Police," *Transaction* 4 (1967), pp. 36–44.

11. "Wide Disparities in Crime Totals Found in Sampling of 8 Cities," *New York Times,* January 27, 1974, p. 34.

12. David Burnham, "New York Is Found Safest of 13 Cities in Crime Study," *New York Times,* April 15, 1974, p. 1.

13. For a thoroughgoing review of the system and philosophy of Anglo-American penology, see Sue Titus Reid, *Crime and Criminology* (Hinsdale, Ill.: Dryden Press, 1976).

14. President's Commission on Law Enforcement and the Administration of Justice, *The Challenge of Crime in a Free Society.*

15. See B. F. Skinner, *Beyond Freedom and Dignity* (New York: Knopf, 1971); and Anthony Burgess, *A Clockwork Orange* (New York: Norton, 1963).

16. Arthur A. Berger, *The Comic-Stripped American: What Dick Tracy, Blondie, Daddy Warbucks, and Charlie Brown Tell Us about Ourselves* (New York: Walker, 1973).

17. William H. Sheldon, *An Introduction to Constitutional Psychiatry* (New York: Harper & Bros., 1949).

18. Sheldon Glueck and Eleanor Glueck, *Unraveling Juvenile Delinquency* (New York: Harper & Bros., 1952).

19. George B. Vold, *Theoretical Criminology* (New York: Oxford University Press, 1958), p. 119.

20. National Commission on Law Observance and Enforcement, *Report on the Causes of Crime* (Washington, D.C.: Government Printing Office, 1931).

21. Robert K. Merton, "Social Structure and Anomie," *American Sociological Review* 3 (October 1938), pp. 672–682.

22. Albert K. Cohen, *Delinquent Boys* (New York: Free Press, 1955).

23. Gresham M. Sykes and David Matza, "Techniques of Neutralization," *American Sociological Review* 22 (December 1957), pp. 664–670.

24. Richard A. Cloward and Lloyd E. Ohlin, "Differential Opportunity Structure," in Wolfgang, Savitz, and Johnston (eds.), *The Sociology of Crime and Delinquency.*

25. Sutherland, "Differential Association."

26. Walter C. Reckless, *The Crime Problem* (New York: Appleton-Century-Crofts, 1961).

27. Becker, *Outsiders: Studies in the Sociology of Deviance.*

28. Erving Goffman, *Stigma: Notes on the Management of Spoiled Identity* (Englewood Cliffs, N.J.: Prentice-Hall, 1964).

29. Edwin M. Lemert, *Human Deviance, Social Problems, and Social Control* (Englewood Cliffs, N.J.: Prentice-Hall, 1967).

Chapter 18

1. See Roger Brown, *Social Psychology* (New York: Free Press, 1965), p. 709; Kurt Lang and Gladys Engel Lang, *Collective Dynamics* (New York: Crowell, 1961), p. 11; and Neil J. Smelser, *Theory of Collective Behavior* (New York: Free Press, 1962), p. 71.

2. Ralph H. Turner and Lewis M. Killian, *Collective Behavior* (Englewood Cliffs, N.J.: Prentice-Hall, 1972), p. 10.

3. See Hippolyte Taine, *Les origines de la France contemporaine: La revolution* (3 vols.; Paris, 1876); Edmund Burke, *Reflections on the Revolution in France* (New York: Liberal Arts Press, 1955); and Gustave LeBon, *The Crowd* (New York: Ballantine Books, 1969).

4. Robert E. Park and Ernest W. Burgess, *Introduction to the Science of Sociology* (Chicago: University of Chicago Press, 1969), p. 867.

5. Erich Fromm, *Escape from Freedom* (New York: Holt, Rinehart and Winston, 1941), p. 240.

6. T. H. Adorno, Else Frenkel-Brunswik, Daniel J. Levinson, and Sanford R. Nevitt, *The Authoritarian Personality* (New York: Harper & Bros., 1950).

7. Eric Hoffer, *The True Believer: Thoughts on the Nature of Mass Movements* (New York: Harper & Bros., 1951), p. 17.

8. Milton Rokeach, *The Open and Closed Mind* (New York: Basic Books, 1960).

9. See Katherine E. Gales, "A Campus Revolution," *British Journal of Sociology* 17 (March 1966), pp. 1–19; and Stanley Lieberson and Arnold R. Silverman, "The Precipitants and Underlying Conditions of Race Riots," *American Sociological Review* 30 (December 1965), pp. 887–898.

10. See Ted Robert Gurr, *Why Men Rebel* (Princeton: Princeton University Press, 1971).

11. John A. Buggs, "Report from Los Angeles," *Journal of Intergroup Relations* 5 (Fall 1966), pp. 27–40.

12. Irving L. Janis, Dwight W. Chapman, John P. Gillin, and John P. Siegel, "The Problem of Panic," in Duane P. Schultz (ed.), *Panic Behavior: Discussion and Readings* (New York: Random House, 1964), p. 120.

13. Alexander Mintz, "Non-adaptive Group Behavior," *Journal of Abnormal and Social Psychology* 46 (April 1951), p. 158.

14. Arthur F. Raper, *The Tragedy of Lynching* (Montclair, N.J.: Patterson Smith, 1969).

15. *New York Times* editors, *Report of the National Advisory Commission on Civil Disorders* (New York: E. P. Dutton, 1968), p. 102.

16. Don C. Gibbons, *Society, Crime, and Criminal Careers* (Englewood Cliffs, N.J.: Prentice-Hall, 1973), pp. 482–484.

17. George Rude, *The Crowd in the French Revolution* (New York: Oxford University Press, 1967).

18. *New York Times* editors, *Report of the National Advisory Commission on Civil Disorders.*

19. James Hundley, Jr., "The Dynamics of Recent Ghetto Riots," in Richard A. Chikota and Michael C. Moran (eds.), *Riot in the Cities* (Rutherford, N.J.: Fairleigh Dickinson University Press, 1968).

20. James C. Davies, "Toward a Theory of Revolution," *American Sociological Review* 27 (February 1962), pp. 5–19.

21. See Robert L. Heilbroner, *An Inquiry into the Human Prospect* (New York: Norton, 1974).

22. Smelser, *Theory of Collective Behavior.*

23. See Daniel Bell (ed.), *The Radical Right* (Garden City, N.Y.: Doubleday, 1964); Ira S. Rohter, "The Righteous Rightists," *Transaction/Society* 4 (May 1967), pp. 27–35; and Gerhard Lenski, "Status Inconsistency and the Vote," *American Sociological Review* 32 (April 1967), pp. 298–301.

24. See Walter J. Goodman, *The Committee* (New York: Farrar, Straus & Giroux, 1968).

25. Michael Lipsky, "Protest as a Political Resource," *American Political Science Review* 62 (December 1968), pp. 1144–1158.

26. See Katerina Breshkovskaia, *The Hidden Springs of the Russian Revolution* (Stanford, Calif.: Stanford University Press, 1931).

27. See Seymour Martin Lipset, *Political Man* (Garden City, N.Y.: Doubleday, 1960); Robert Dahl, *Who Governs?* (New Haven: Yale University Press, 1961); Arnold Rose, *The Power Structure* (New York: Oxford University Press, 1967); and William Kornhauser, *The Politics of Mass Culture* (New York: Free Press, 1959).

28. See Hannah Arendt, *The Origins of Totalitarianism* (New York: Harcourt, Brace and World, 1951); and Dwight MacDonald, *Memoirs of a Revolutionist* (New York: Farrar, Straus & Giroux, 1957).

29. See C. Wright Mills, *The Power Elite* (New York: Oxford University Press, 1956); and William Domhoff, *Who Rules America?* (Englewood Cliffs, N.J.: Prentice-Hall, 1967).

30. See Norval D. Glenn, "Massification versus Differentiation: Some Trend Data from National Surveys," *Social Forces* 46 (December 1967), pp. 172–180; Richard F. Hamilton, "Affluence and the Worker: The West German Case," *American Journal of Sociology* 71 (September 1965), pp. 144–152; and Charles M. Bonjean, "Mass, Class, and the Industrial Community: A Comparative Analysis of Managers, Businessmen, and Workers," *American Journal of Sociology* 72 (September 1966), pp. 149–162.

31. Nelson W. Polsby, *Community Power and Political Theory* (New Haven: Yale University Press, 1963).

32. Herbert Blumer, "Social Movements," in Robert E. Park (ed.), *An Outline of the Principles of Sociology* (New York: Barnes & Noble, 1939).

33. Turner and Killian, *Collective Behavior,* p. 246.

34. Ralph H. Turner, "Collective Behavior and Conflict: New Theoretical Frameworks," *Sociological Quarterly* 5 (Spring 1964), p. 126.

35. Roland Warren, "The Interorganizational Field as a Focus for Investigation," *Administrative Science Quarterly* 12 (December 1967), pp. 396–419.

36. Mayer N. Zald and Roberta Ash, "Social Movement Organi-

zations: Growth, Decay, and Change," *Social Forces* 44 (March 1966), pp. 327–341.

37. Jack Newfield, *A Prophetic Minority* (New York: New American Library, 1967), p. 157.

Chapter 19

1. Alvin Toffler, *Future Shock* (New York: Random House, 1970), pp. 15–16.

2. Bryce Ryan, *Social and Cultural Change* (New York: Ronald Press, 1969), pp. 99–100.

3. Marshall McLuhan, *Understanding Media* (New York: McGraw-Hill, 1965).

4. Ralph Linton, *The Study of Man* (New York: Appleton-Century-Crofts, 1936), pp. 326–327.

5. Homer Barnett, *Innovation: The Basis of Cultural Change* (New York: McGraw-Hill, 1953), pp. 375–377.

6. William F. Whyte, "The Social Structure of the Restaurant," *American Journal of Sociology* 54 (January 1949), pp. 302–308.

7. W. F. Cottrell, "Death by Dieselization," American Sociological Review 16 (June 1951), pp. 358–365.

8. George Foster, *Traditional Societies and Technological Change* (New York: Harper & Row, 1973), p. 116.

9. Frances Moore Lappe, "Fantasies of Famine," *Harper's Magazine*, February 1975, pp. 51–54, 87–90.

10. Sidney Aronson, "The Sociology of the Bicycle," *Social Forces* 30 (1952), pp. 305–312.

11. Charles Lekberg, "The Tyranny of Qwerty," *Saturday Review*, September 30, 1972, pp. 37–40.

12. William Pratt, "The Anabaptist Explosion," *Natural History Magazine*, February 1969, pp. 8–23.

13. Joseph Lopreato, *Peasants No More* (San Francisco: Chandler Publishing, 1967).

14. See James Coleman, Elihu Katz, and Herbert Menzel, "The Diffusion of an Innovation among Physicians," *Sociometry* 29 (1957), pp. 253–270; Everett Rogers, *Diffusion of Innovations* (New York: Free Press, 1962); and Elihu Katz and Paul Lazarsfeld, *Personal Influence* (New York: Free Press, 1955).

15. Everett Rogers, *Communication Strategies for Family Planning* (New York: Free Press, 1973).

16. Ozzie Simmons, "The Clinical Team in a Chilean Health Center," in Benjamin Paul (ed.), *Health, Culture, and Community: Case Studies in Public Reactions to Health Problems* (New York: Russell Sage Foundation, 1955).

17. Allen Homberg, *Nomads of the Long Bow: The Siriono of Eastern Bolivia* (Garden City, N.Y.: Doubleday, 1969); and Homberg, "Adventures in Culture Change," in Robert Spencer (ed.), *Method and Perspective in Anthropology* (Minneapolis: University of Minnesota Press, 1954).

18. Foster, *Traditional Societies and Technological Change*, p. 96.

19. Garth Jones, "Strategies and Tactics in Planned Organizational Change," *Human Organization* 24 (1965), pp. 192–200; see also Henry Dobyns, "Blunders with Bolsas," *Human Organization* 10 (Fall 1951), pp. 25–32.

20. See Francis Allen, "The Automobile," in Francis Allen, et al., *Technology and Social Change* (New York: Appleton-Century-Crofts, 1957).

21. Leslie White, *The Science of Culture* (New York: Grove Press, 1949).

22. Elman Service, *Primitive Social Organization* (New York: Random House, 1962).

23. Robert Redfield, *The Folk Culture of Yucatan* (Chicago: University of Chicago Press, 1941).

24. Ralf Dahrendorf, *Class and Class Conflict in Industrial Society* (Stanford, Calif.: Stanford University Press, 1959).

25. See, for example, Herbert Marcuse, *One Dimensional Man* (Boston: Beacon Press, 1964); and Frantz Fanon, *The Wretched of the Earth* (New York: Grove Press, 1968).

26. See Talcott Parsons, *The Social System* (New York: Free Press, 1951); and Parsons, *The System of Modern Societies* (Englewood Cliffs, N.J.: Prentice-Hall, 1971).

27. Oswald Spengler, *The Decline of the West,* trans. Charles F. Atkinson (New York: Knopf, 1926–1928).

28. Arnold Toynbee, *A Study of History* (New York: Oxford University Press, 1935–1961).

29. Pitirim Sorokin, *Social and Cultural Dynamics* (New York: American Book, 1941).

30. See, for example, L. Coch and J. French, "Overcoming Resistance to Change," *Human Relations* 1 (1948), pp. 512–532; and Kurt Lewin, "Group Decision and Social Change," in E. Maccoby, T. Newcomb, and E. Hartley (eds.), *Readings in Social Psychology*, 3rd ed. (New York: Holt, Rinehart and Winston, 1958).

31. Robert Heilbroner, *The Great Ascent* (New York: Harper & Row, 1963).

32. Rogers, *Communication Strategies for Family Planning*, pp. 20–23.

33. Heilbroner, *The Great Ascent,* p. 89.

CREDITS

Chapter 1

Chapter 2

Chapter 3

Chapter 4

Chapter 5

page 146, reprinted by permission of E. I. du Pont de Nemours & Co. Figure 5-5, page 148, based on Allan M. Cartter, *An Assessment of Quality in Graduate Education* (Washington, D.C.: American Council on Education, 1966). Reprinted by permission. Photo, page 151, courtesy of ACTION VISTA. Photo, page 152, by Sepp Seitz, Magnum.

Chapter 6

Print, page 158, from *Scribner's Magazine,* November 1891, courtesy of Jo-Anne Naples. Photo, page 167, by Elliott Erwitt, Magnum. Poster, page 169, reproduced from the collection of the Library of Congress. Photo, page 169, courtesy of Wide World Photos. Figure 6-1, page 170, from William F. Whyte, *Street Corner Society* (Chicago: University of Chicago Press, 1943), p. 13. © 1943 The University of Chicago Press. Reprinted by permission. Photos, page 171: top, by Steve Rapley; bottom, by Christopher Springman, Black Star. Photos, page 173, by Richard Stromberg/ Media House, Chicago. Photo, page 174, from *West Side Story.* © 1961 United Artists Corporation. Reprinted by permission of United Artists. Photo, page 176, from Solomon Asch, "Opinions and Social Pressure," *Scientific American,* November 1955. Reprinted by permission of Scientific American and the photographer, William Vandivert. Table 6-1, page 177, adapted, with permission, from J. S. Mouton, R. N. Blake, and J. A. Olmstead, "The Relationship between Frequency of Yielding and the Disclosure of Personal Identity," *Journal of Personality* 24: 339–347. Copyright 1956 by Duke University Press.

Chapter 7

Photo, page 182, courtesy of Wide World Photos. Photo, page 184, by Jo-Anne Naples. Photo, page 187, by Jon Randolph. Photos, page 190: left, by Richard Stromberg/Media House, Chicago; right, courtesy of UPI. Photo, page 193, Peace Corps photo by Phil Harsberger; courtesy of ACTION Peace Corps. Photos, page 197, courtesy of UPI. Print, page 200, courtesy of The Bettmann Archive. Photo, page 200, by Cary Wolinsky, Stock, Boston. Print, page 202, courtesy of The Bettmann Archive. Photo, page 202, by Hiroyuki Matsumoto, Black Star. Advertisement, page 207, reprinted by permission of Talman Federal Savings & Loan Association.

Photo, page 212, by Charles Gatewood, Magnum.

Chapter 8

Photo, page 219, courtesy of the American Museum of Natural History. Figure 8-2, page 222, adapted from U.S. Bureau of the Census, "Annual Mean Income, Lifetime Income, and Educational Attainment of Men in the United States, for Selected Years, 1956 to 1972," *Current Population Reports,* Series P-60, No. 92 (Washington, D.C.: Government Printing Office, 1974), p. 5. Figure 8-3, page 223, adapted from U.S. Bureau of the Census, "Annual Mean Income, Lifetime Income, and Educational Attainment of Men in the United States, for Selected Years, 1956 to 1972," *Current Population Reports,* Series P-60, No. 92 (Washington, D.C.: Government Printing Office, 1974), p. 4. Table 8-1, page 224, adapted from U.S. Bureau of the Census, Census of Population, *1970 Subject Reports,* Final Report PC (2)-8B, *Earnings by Occupation and Education* (Washington, D.C.: Government Printing Office, 1973), Table 1. Table 8-2, page 224, adapted from U.S. Bureau of the Census, Census of Population, *1970 Subject Reports,* Final Report PC (2)-7A, *Occupational Characteristics* (Washington, D.C.: Government Printing Office, 1973), Table 1. Photo, page 225, by Burt Glinn, Magnum. Table 8-3, page 226, based on data contained in U.S. Bureau of the Census, *Statistical Abstract of the United States, 1974* (Washington, D.C.: Government Printing

Office, 1974), Table 74. Figure 8-5, page 227, reprinted with permission of Macmillan Publishing Co., Inc. from *The Scientific Study of Religion* by J. Milton Yinger. Copyright © 1970 by J. Milton Yinger. Photo, page 227, by Michael Abramson, Black Star. Photos, page 230: left, by Leonard Freed, Magnum; right, by Cornell Capa, Magnum. Table 8-4, page 232, from Theodore Caplow, *The Sociology of Work,* University of Minnesota Press, Minneapolis. Copyright 1954. Reprinted by permission. Originally from Monsanto Chemical Company. Reprinted by permission. Photos, page 236: left, by Henri Cartier-Bresson, Magnum; right, courtesy of UPI. Figure 8-6, page 238, from the Women's Bureau, Employment Standards Administration, from April 1973 data published by the U.S. Department of Labor, Bureau of Labor Statistics. Table 8-5, page 243, adapted from William H. Sewell and Vimel P. Shah, "Socioeconomic Status, Intelligence, and the Attainment of Higher Education," *Sociology of Education* 40 (1967), 15. Reprinted by permission of the American Sociological Association. Photo, page 243, courtesy of UPI. Table 8-6, page 246, adapted from U.S. Bureau of the Census, *Statistical Abstract of the United States, 1974* (Washington, D.C.: Government Printing Office, 1974), p. 384.

Chapter 9

Photos, page 254, courtesy of Penny Weaver, Poverty Law Report, Southern Poverty Law Center. Photo, page 257, courtesy of The Bettmann Archive. Figure 9-1, page 265, from U.S. Bureau of the Census. Table 9-1, page 266, from Alphonse Pinckney, *Black Americans,* 2nd ed., © 1975, p. 92. Reprinted by permission of Prentice-Hall, Inc., Englewood Cliffs, New Jersey. Table 9-2, page 268, from Alphonse Pinckney, *Black Americans,* 2nd ed., © 1975, p. 75. Reprinted by permission of Prentice-Hall, Inc., Englewood Cliffs, New Jersey. Table 9-3, page 269, from Alphonse Pinckney, *Black Americans,* 2nd ed., © 1975, p. 86. Reprinted by permission of Prentice-Hall, Inc., Englewood Cliffs, New Jersey. Data for 1954–1959 from U.S. Bureau of Labor, Bureau of Labor Statistics, *The Negroes in the United States: Their Economic and Social Situation,* Bulletin No. 1511 (Washington, D.C.: Government Printing Office, 1966), p. 81; data for 1960–1972 from U.S. Bureau of the Census, *The Social and Economic Status of the Black Population in the United States* (Washington, D.C.: Government Printing Office, 1972), p. 38. Figure 9-2, page 269, from U.S. Bureau of the Census. Photo, page 270, courtesy of UPI. Print, page 271, courtesy of The Bettmann Archive. Figure 9-3, page 273, from Calvin F. Schmidt and Charles E. Nobbe, "Socioeconomic Differentials among Non-white Races," *American Sociological Review* 30 (1965), 919. Reprinted by permission of the American Sociological Association. Photo, page 273, courtesy of UPI. Photo, page 276, by Henri Cartier-Bresson, Magnum. Photo, page 279, courtesy of UPI. Photo, page 283, courtesy of the New York Convention and Visitors Bureau.

Chapter 10

Photo, page 288, by Erich Hartmann, Magnum. Figure 10-1, page 292, from U.S. Office of Management and Budget, Statistical Policy Division, *Standard Metropolitan Statistical Areas, 1975,* rev. ed. (Washington, D.C.: Government Printing Office, 1975). Table 10-1, page 294, data from U.S. Bureau of the Census, *1970 Census of Population,* vol. 1, *Characteristics of the Population, Part A, Section 1* (Washington, D.C.: Government Printing Office, May 1972), Tables 21, 29, 36. Table 10-2, page 295, from U.S. Bureau of the Census, *Census of Population, 1970: Number of Inhabitants,* United States Summary Final Report PC(1)-A1, p. 42. Photos, page 297, courtesy of the Jericho Excavation Fund. Photos, page 298: left, courtesy of the Chicago Historical Society; right, by Richard Stromberg/Media House, Chicago. Table 10-3, page 300, reprinted with permission of Macmillan Publishing Co., Inc. from *The Preindustrial City* by Gideon Sjoberg. Copyright © 1960 by The Free Press, a Corporation. Table 10-4, page 301, reprinted by permission from *The World Almanac and Book of Facts,* 1975 edition; copyright © Newspaper Enterprise Association, New York, 1974. Figure 10-2, page 302, from *The American City: An Urban Geography* by Raymond Murphy. Copyright © 1966 by McGraw-Hill, Inc. Used with permission of McGraw-Hill Book Company. After Edward L. Ullman, "Mobile: Industrial Seaport and Trade Center" (Ph.D. diss., University of Chicago, Department of Geography, 1943), figure 7. Figure 10-3, page 304, after Noel Pitts Gist and Sylvia Fleis Fava, *Urban Society,* 6th ed. (New York: Thomas Y. Crowell Co., 1974), p. 137. Reprinted by permission. Based on United Nations, *A Concise Summary of the World Population Situation in 1970* (New York: United Nations, 1971). Taken from *Population Bulletin,* April 1971, p. 12. Figure 10-4, page 305, after "Living Space: Troubled Cities Need More Green Space," *National Wildlife,* October/November 1971. Copyright 1971 by the National Wildlife Federation. Reprinted by permission from the October/November 1971 issue of *National Wildlife.* Figure 10-5, page 308, after James Johnson, *Urban Geography* (New York: Pergamon, 1967), p. 164. Reprinted by permission. Also after Robert E. Park, Ernest W. Burgess, and Roderick D. McKenzie, eds., *The City* (Chicago: University of Chicago Press, 1925), pp. 51–53. © 1925 The University of Chicago. Reprinted by permission. Figure 10-6, page 309, reprinted from "The Nature of Cities" by Chauncy D. Harris and Edward L. Ullman in vol. 242 (November 1945) of the *Annals of the American Academy of Political and Social Science.* © 1945 by the AAPSS. All rights reserved. Reprinted by permission. Figure 10-7, page 310, reprinted by permission from James Johnson, *Urban Geography* (New York: Pergamon, 1967), p. 167. Also reprinted by permission from P. J. Smith, "Calgary: A Study in Urban Pattern," *Economic Geography* 38 (1962), 318 and 328. Figure 10-8, page 311, reprinted from "The Nature of Cities" by Chauncy D. Harris and Edward L. Ullman in vol. 242 (November 1945) of the *Annals of the American Academy of Political and Social Science.* © 1945 by the AAPSS. All rights reserved. Reprinted by permission. Photo, page 313, by Tony Linck, Time Magazine, © Time Inc. Figure 10-9, page 314, from U.S. Bureau of the Census. Table 10-5, page 317, from U.S. Bureau of the Census, 1970 Census of Population and Housing, PHC(2), *General Demographic Trends for Metropolitan Areas, U.S. Summary* (Washington, D.C.: Government Printing Office, 1970). Photos, page 318: left, courtesy of UPI; right; by Danny Lyon, Magnum.

Chapter 11

Figure, page 324, computed from various sources. Table 11-1, page 325, from Donald J. Bogue, *Principles of Demography* (New York: Wiley, 1969), p. 102. Reprinted by permission. Photo, page 329, by Sepp Seitz, Magnum. Table 11-2, page 331, data prior to 1975 from United Nations, *The Determinants and Consequences of Population Trends: New Summary of Findings on Interaction of Demographic, Economic and Social Factors,* vol. 1, Population Studies No. 50 (New York: United Nations, 1973), p. 10, Table II-1; 1975 data from Population Reference Bureau, *1975 World Population Data Sheet* (Washington, D.C.: Government Printing Office, 1975). Figure 11-1, page 331, reprinted by permission from Ralph Thomlinson, *Population Dynamics* (New York: Random House, 1965), p. 23. Table 11-3, page 334, computed from various sources. Table 11-4, page 335, compiled from United Nations, *Demographic Yearbook, 1970* (New York: United Nations, 1970), p. 105, Table 1. Also from United Nations, *The Determinants and Consequences of Population Trends: New Summary of Findings on Interaction of Demographic Economic, and Social Factors,* vol 1, Population Studies No. 50 (New York: United Nations, 1973), p. 161, Table VI-1. Table 11-5, page 336, compiled from United Nations, *Growth of the World's Urban and Rural Population, 1920–2000,* Population Studies No. 44 (New York: United Nations, 1969), Tables 8 and 31. Also from United Nations, *The Determinants and Consequences of Population Trends: New Summary of Findings on Interaction of Demographic, Economic, and Social Factors,* vol. 1, Population Studies No. 50 (New York: United Nations, 1973), p. 188, Table VI.6. Table 11-6, page 337, figures for

1920 taken from United Nations, *Growth of the World's Urban and Rural Population, 1920–2000,* Population Studies No. 44 (New York: United Nations, 1969). Figures for later years compiled from United Nations Secretariat, "Demographic Trends in the World in Its Major Regions, 1950–1970," background paper for World Population Conference, 16 April 1974, E/CONF. 60/CBP/14, and Population Division, Department of Economic and Social Affairs of the United Nations Secretariat, "Trends and Prospects in the Populations of Urban Agglomerations, 1950–2000, as Assessed in 1973–1975," 21 November 1975, ESA/P/WP.58. Table 11-7, page 342, compiled from data in United Nations, *World Population Prospects as Assessed in 1968.* Also United Nations, *The Determinants and Consequences of Population Trends: New Summary of Findings on Interaction of Demographic, Economic, and Social Factors,* vol. 1, Population Studies No. 50 (New York: United Nations, 1973), p. 265, Table VIII.2. Figure 11-3, page 343, from United Nations, *The Determinants and Consequences of Population Trends: New Summary of Findings on Interaction of Demographic, Economic, and Social Factors,* vol. 1, Population Studies No. 50 (New York: United Nations, 1973), p. 267. Data compiled by the United Nations Population Division. Table 11-8, page 344, compiled from data in United Nations, *World Population Prospects as Assessed in 1968.* Also United Nations, *The Determinants and Consequences of Population Trends: New Summary of Findings on Interaction of Demographic, Economic, and Social Factors,* vol. 1, Population Studies No. 50 (New York: United Nations, 1973), p. 263, Table VIII.1. Photos, page 346, courtesy of U.S. Agency for International Development. Photo, page 347, courtesy of U.S. Environmental Protection Agency. Photos, page 349: top, courtesy of U.S. Environmental Protection Agency; bottom, by Eric Kroll. Photos, page 351: top, courtesy of U.S. Environmental Protection Agency; bottom, courtesy of U.S. Agency for International Development. Photo, page 352, courtesy of UPI. Photo, page 353, courtesy of U.S. Agency for International Development. Poster, page 354, courtesy of Zero Population Growth. Box, page 355, copyright 1971 by the National Wildlife Federation. Reprinted from the July/August 1971 issue of *International Wildlife* by permission.

Photo, page 360, by Tim Eagan.

Chapter 12

Photo, page 364, by Esther Bubley. Photo, page 367, by Constantine Manos, Magnum. Photo, page 369, by Richard Stromberg/Media House, Chicago. Photos, page 370: top, courtesy of The Bettmann Archive; bottom, by Bill Owens, Magnum. Figure 12-1, page 371, after page 151 of *The Study of Society,* second edition. Copyright © 1977 The Dushkin Publishing Group, Sluice Dock, Guilford, CT 06437. Advertisement, page 377, courtesy of Comdates. Table 12-1, page 379, from Robert F. Winch, *Mate Selection* (New York: Harper & Row, 1958), p. 129. Reprinted by permission. After Donald E. Roos, "Complementary Needs in Mate-Selection: A Study Based on R-Type Factor Analysis" (Ph.D. diss., Northwestern University, 1956), and Thomas Ktsanes, "Complementary Needs in Mate Selection: A Study Based upon an Empirical Typology of Personality" (Ph.D. diss., Northwestern University, 1953). The excerpts at page 380 are from "You're Just in Love" by Irving Berlin. © Copyright 1950 Irving Berlin. Reprinted by permission of Irving Berlin Music Corporation. Print, page 381, courtesy of The Bettmann Archive. Photo, page 383, by Alex Webb, Magnum. Box, page 385, reprinted from *Narrative of Sojourner Truth: A Bondswoman of Olden Time* (Battle Creek, Mich.: published for the author, 1878), part 2, "Book of Life," pp. 133–135. These words were spoken at the Woman's Rights Convention at Akron, Ohio, 1851. Photo, page 385, by Michael Abramson, Black Star. Figure 12-3, page 387, from U.S. Bureau of the Census, *Statistical Abstract of the United States, 1970* (Washington, D.C.: Government Printing Office, 1970). Figure appeared in Harold M. Hodges, Jr., *Conflict and Consensus: An Introduction to Sociology,* 1st ed. (New York: Harper & Row, 1971), p. 293.

Photo, page 389, by Sepp Seitz, Magnum. Figure 12-4, page 391, based on Paul C. Glick and Arthur J. Norton, U.S. Bureau of the Census; data from the National Center for Health Statistics. Figure appeared in the *New York Times Magazine*, August 10, 1975, p. 11. © 1975 by The New York Times Company. Reprinted by permission.

Chapter 13

Photo, page 396, courtesy of Wide World Photos. Photo, page 399, by Richard Stromberg/Media House, Chicago. Photo, page 402, by Henri Cartier-Bresson, Magnum. Photo, page 403, courtesy of the U.S. Bureau of Indian Affairs. Table 13-1, page 405, appeared in Wilbur B. Brookover and Edsel L. Erickson, *Sociology of Education* (Homewood, Ill.: Dorsey Press, 1975), p. 333. From an unpublished study of Wilbur B. Brookover, D. J. Leu, and R. Hugh Kariger, "Tracking," mimeographed (1965); and R. Hugh Kariger, "The Relationship of Lane Grouping to the Socioeconomic Status of the Parents of Seventh-Grade Pupils in Three Junior High Schools" (Ph.D. diss., Michigan State University, 1962). Reprinted by permission. Table 13-2, page 405, appeared in Wilbur B. Brookover and Edsel L. Erickson, *Sociology of Education* (Homewood, Ill.: Dorsey Press, 1975), p. 333. From an unpublished study of Wilbur B. Brookover, D. J. Leu, and R. Hugh Kariger, "Tracking," mimeographed (1965); and R. Hugh Kariger, "The Relationship of Lane Grouping to the Socioeconomic Status of the Parents of Seventh-Grade Pupils in Three Junior High Schools" (Ph.D. diss., Michigan State University, 1962). Reprinted by permission. Photo, page 407, by Charles Harbutt, Magnum. Table 13-3, page 409, from Herman C. Miller, *Income Distribution in the United States,* a monograph published in 1966 by the U.S. Census. Appeared in Donald J. Bogue, *Principles of Demography* (New York: Wiley, 1969), p. 408. Reprinted by permission. Photo, page 409, from Lafayette (Ind.) Journal & Courier, March 6, 1975. Reprinted by permission. Table 13-4, page 410, adapted from Peter M. Blau and Otis Dudley Duncan, *The American Occupational Structure* (New York: Wiley, 1967). Reprinted by permission. Also from Wilbur B. Brookover and Edsel L. Erickson, *Sociology of Education* (Homewood, Ill.: Dorsey Press, 1975), p. 116. Reprinted by permission. Photos, page 416: left, by Charles Harbutt, Magnum; right, by Leonard Freed, Magnum. Photo, page 423, courtesy of Wide World Photos. Photo, page 425, by Charles Gatewood, Magnum.

Chapter 14

Table 14-1, page 432, reprinted with permission from the 1974 Britannica Book of the Year, copyright 1974 by Encyclopaedia Britannica, Inc., Chicago, Ill. Photo, page 435, by Ian Berry, Magnum. Photo, page 437, by Karega Kofi Moyo. Photo, page 438, courtesy of The Bettmann Archive. Photo, page 439, by Dennis Stock, Magnum. Table 14-2, page 441, original data derived from National Council of Churches' survey; table from N. J. Demerath III, *Social Class in American Protestantism* (Chicago: Rand McNally, 1965), p. 2. Reprinted by permission. Photo, page 443, courtesy of Wide World Photos. Photo, page 445, by Martin Adler Levick, Black Star. Print, page 447, courtesy of Jo-Anne Naples. Photo, page 449, courtesy of UPI. Print, page 450, courtesy of The Bettmann Archive. Photo, page 451, by Richard Stromberg/Media House, Chicago. Photos, page 453: top left, by Eve Arnold, Magnum; bottom left, by Eve Arnold, Magnum; right, by T. Sheehan, Black Star. Table 14-3, page 455, from Yearbook of American and Canadian Churches, 1976, by Constant Jacquet, Jr. Copyright © 1976 by the National Council of the Churches of Christ in the United States of America. By permission. Figure 14-1, page 455, from Gallup Poll, *New York Times,* December 22, 1968. Reprinted by permission of The Gallup Poll (The American Institute of Public Opinion). © 1968 by The New York Times Company. Reprinted by permission. Photo, page 458, by Bruce Davidson, Magnum. Figure 14-2, page 459, from Gallup Poll, *New York Times,* December 22, 1968. Reprinted by permission of The Gallup

Poll, (The American Institute of Public Opinion). © 1968 by The New York Times Company. Reprinted by permission. Photo, page 460, by Robert Burroughs, Black Star.

Chapter 15

Photos, page 465, courtesy of UPI. Print, page 467, courtesy of The Bettmann Archive. Print, page 468, courtesy of The Bettmann Archive. Photo, page 468, courtesy of The Bettmann Archive. Photos, page 469: top, courtesy of Wide World Photos; bottom, courtesy of UPI. Cartoon, page 473, courtesy of The Bettmann Archive. Photo, page 474, courtesy of UPI. Print, page 475, courtesy of The Bettmann Archive. Photo, page 478, courtesy of Wide World Photos. Print, page 478, courtesy of The Bettmann Archive. Print, page 479, reproduced from the collection of the Library of Congress. Originally appeared in *Harper's Weekly,* November 16, 1867. Print, page 481, courtesy of The Bettmann Archive. Photo, page 481, courtesy of Wide World Photos. Photo, page 483, courtesy of Wide World Photos. Print, page 484, courtesy of The Bettmann Archeve. Photos, page 484, courtesy of UPI. Photo, page 486, by Richard Stromberg/Media House, Chicago. Photo, page 487, courtesy of Wide World Photos. Cartoon, page 489, courtesy of Jo-Anne Naples. Photo, page 489, courtesy of Wide World Photos. Table 15-1, page 490, based on Mike Royko, *Boss: Richard J. Daley of Chicago* (New York: E. P. Dutton, 1971). Reprinted by permission.

Chapter 16

Print, page 498, courtesy of The Bettmann Archive. Print, page 499, courtesy of The Bettmann Archive. Figure 16-1, page 501, data for 1950 and 1960 from U.S. Bureau of the Census, *Census of Population;* for 1965 from U.S. Bureau of the Census, *Statistical Abstract of the United States, 1966* (Washington, D.C.: Government Printing Office, 1966), Tables 307 and 314; for 1970 from U.S. Department of Labor, *Yearbook of Labor Statistics* (Washington, D.C.: Government Printing Office, 1970), p. 171. Appeared in Eshref Shevky and Marilyn Williams, *The Social Areas of Los Angeles* (Los Angeles and Berkeley: University of California Press, 1949), p. 4. Reprinted by permission. Also in Leonard Broom and Philip Selznick, *Sociology,* 5th ed. (New York: Harper & Row, 1973), p. 549. Reprinted by permission. Table 16-1, page 501, from U.S. Bureau of the Census, *Historical Statistics of the United States: Colonial Times to 1957* (Washington, D.C.: Government Printing Office, 1961); U.S. Bureau of the Census, *Statistical Abstract of the United States, 1950* (Washington, D.C.: Government Printing Office, 1950), p. 107; U.S. Bureau of the Census, *Current Population Reports,* Series P-25, No. 365, May 5, 1967, and Series P-20, No. 222, June 28, 1971. Figure 16-2, page 502, based on Seymour M. Lipset, "Political Sociology," in *Sociology,* ed. N. J. Smelser (New York: Wiley, 1973), p. 410. Reprinted by permission. Photos, page 503, reproduced from the collection of the Library of Congress. Photo, page 505, by Owen Franken, Stock, Boston. Table 16-2, page 506, from data in U.S. Bureau of the Census, *Historical Statistics of the United States: Colonial Times to 1957,* Series D72-122 (Washington, D.C.: Government Printing Office, 1961); and U.S. Bureau of the Census, *Statistical Abstract of the United States, 1972* (Washington, D.C.: Government Printing Office, 1972), Table 366. Table 16-3, page 507, from U.S. Bureau of the Census, *Census of Manufacturers, 1967,* vol. 1 (Washington, D.C.: Government Printing Office, 1971), Chapter 9, Table 5. Photo, page 507, by Charles Moore, Black Star. Photo, page 508, by Elliott Erwitt, Magnum. Table 16-4, page 509, from U.S. Department of Labor, 1970. Advertisement, page 510, from Sears Catalogue, 1897. Print, page 511, reproduced from the collection of the Library of Congress. Table 16-5, page 512, from the United Nations, with updating from *Economics* by Paul A. Samuelson. Copyright © 1976 by McGraw-Hill, Inc. Used with permission of McGraw-Hill Book Company. Table 16-6, page 513, from *The Common Cause Report from Washington* 7 (Spring

1976), pp. 7, 8. Reprinted by permission. Photo, page 513, courtesy of UPI. Table 16-7, page 514, from *The Common Cause Report from Washington* 7 (Spring 1976), pp. 7, 8. Reprinted by Permission. Table 16-8, page 516, from H. L. Wilensky, "Work as a Social Problem," in *Social Problems: A Modern Approach,* ed. Howard S. Becker (New York: Wiley, 1966), p. 134. Reprinted by permission. Data from H. L. Wilensky, "The Uneven Distribution of Leisure," *Social Problems* 9 (Summer 1961), pp. 32–56. Reprinted by permission. Table 16-9, page 517, reprinted by permission from Daniel Bell, *The Coming of Post-Industrial Society: A Venture in Social Forecasting* (New York: Basic Books, 1973), p. 359. Photo, page 518, by Henri Dauman, Time-Life Picture Agency, © Time, Inc.

Photo, page 522, courtesy of Wide World Photos.

Chapter 17

News Story, pages 526–527, copyright 1973 by Newsweek, Inc. All rights reserved. Reprinted by permission. Editorial cartoon, page 528, by Paul Conrad. Copyright © 1976 Los Angeles Times. Reprinted by permission. Photo, page 529, by Richard Stromberg/Media House, Chicago. Photos, page 531, by Karega Kofi Moyo. Advertisement, page 531, courtesy of NORML, the National Organization for the Reform of Marijuana Laws, 2317 M Street NW, Washington DC 20037. Photo, page 534, by Jon Randolph. Figure 17-1, page 536, after Leon Radzinowicz and Marvin E. Wolfgang, eds., *Crime and Justice,* vol. 1, *The Criminal in Society* (New York: Basic Books, 1971), p. 44. Reprinted by permission. Print, page 537, courtesy of Jo-Anne Naples. Tables 17-1 and 17-2, page 540, from Federal Bureau of Investigation, *Crime in the United States, Uniform Crime Reports* (Washington, D.C.: Government Printing Office, 1970). Photo, page 541, courtesy of UPI. Table 17-3, page 542, from Federal Bureau of Investigation, *Uniform Crime Reports* (Washington, D.C.: Government Printing Office, various years). Print, page 545, courtesy of Jo-Anne Naples. Cartoon, page 548, reprinted by permission of MAD Magazine. Photo, page 549, by Bruce Davidson, Magnum. Photo, page 550, by Dave Healey, Magnum. Photo, page 551, by Richard Stromberg/Media House, Chicago. Photo, page 555, by Leonard Freed, Magnum.

Chapter 18

Photo, page 560, courtesy of UPI. Print, page 563, courtesy of The Bettmann Archive. Photos, page 564: top, courtesy of Wide World Photos; bottom, courtesy of UPI. Photo, page 565, by Jo-Anne Naples. Photo, page 566, by Russell Lee, reproduced from the collection of the Library of Congress. Photo, page 567, courtesy of UPI. Photo, page 569, from *The Movement*/Magnum. Figure 18-1, page 571, after James C. Davies, "Toward a Theory of Revolution," *American Sociological Review* 27 (February 1962), pp. 5–19. Reprinted by permission. Photos, page 573, courtesy of UPI. Photo, page 574, courtesy of UPI. Figure 18-2, page 576, after Michael Lipsky, "Protest as a Political Resource," *American Political Science Review* 62 (December 1968), p. 1147. Reprinted by permission. Photo, page 577, courtesy of UPI. Photo, page 580, courtesy of UPI. Photos, page 581: top, courtesy of The Bettmann Archive; bottom, courtesy of UPI. Photos, page 583: left, courtesy of The Bettmann Archive; right, courtesy of UPI.

Chapter 19

Advertisement, page 588, from Sears Catalogue, 1902. Print, page 593, courtesy of The Bettmann Archive. Figure 19-1, page 595, based on data in U.S. Bureau of the Census, *Population Characteristics,* Series P-20, No. 233 (Washington, D.C.: Government Printing Office, 1972). Photo, page 597, courtesy of The Bettmann Archive. Photo, page 599, courtesy of Wide World Photos. Photo, page 600, courtesy of the U.S. Department of Agriculture. Figure 19-2, page 601, based on data from the U.S. Bureau of the Census, prepared by the New York Times Service, *San Francisco Chronicle,* March 3, 1973, p. 4. Reprinted by permission. Photo, page 602, by Jim Pickerell, courtesy of ACTION Peace Corps. Photos, page 604: top, reproduced from the collection of the Library of Congress; bottom, by Donald Dietz, Stock, Boston. Photo, page 605, courtesy of U.S. Army. Photo, page 607, courtesy of UPI. Photo, page 612, courtesy of UPI. Photo, page 613, courtesy of U.S. Environmental Protection Agency, EPA Documerica, Gene Daniels. Photo, page 614, courtesy of UPI.

Some data in Tables 11-2, 11-4, 11-5, and 11-8, copyright, United Nations, 1973. Reprinted by permission. Some data used in Figure 11-3, copyright, United Nations, 1973. Reprinted by permission. Table 15-1, page 490, based on *Boss: Richard J. Daley of Chicago,* by Mike Royko. Copyright © 1971 by Mike Royko. Reprinted by permission of the publishers, E. P. Dutton & Co., Inc. Figure 16-1, page 501, also reprinted by permission from Figure 16:2 "Working Population of the United States, 1820-1970" (page 549) from *Sociology,* 5th edition, by Leonard Broom and Philip Selznick, Harper & Row, 1973. Table 16-9, page 517, reprinted by permission, Table 6-1, "Stratification and Power," in *The Coming of Post-Industrial Society: A Venture in Social Forecasting,* by Daniel Bell, © 1973 by Daniel Bell, Basic Books, Inc., Publishers, New York. Figure 17-1, page 536, after Figure 4-1, "Contunuum of Good and Bad Acts, and the Cutting-Point for Various Types of Definitions," in *Crime and Justice,* vol. 1, *The Criminal in Society,* edited by Leon Radzinowicz and Marvin E. Wolfgang, © 1971 by Basic Books, Inc., Publishers, New York. Reprinted by permission. Figure 19-2, page 601, © 1973 by The New York Times Company. Reprinted by permission.

NAME INDEX

SUBJECT INDEX